Human Resource Management

A MANAGERIAL TOOL FOR COMPETITIVE ADVANTAGE

S0-CFQ-152

BOOK ACTIVATION KEY

159   EO7KPL

This key activates your online textbook.

- Scratch off gray area above to see your BOOK ACTIVATION KEY.
- If the key is already visible, then it has been used and is no longer valid. Contact us at www.atomicdog.com or 800-310-5661 x8 to purchase your Online Edition.
- Refer to the booklet, *How to Use Your Online Edition*, for further instructions.

Fourth Edition

Human Resource Management

A MANAGERIAL TOOL FOR COMPETITIVE ADVANTAGE

Lawrence S. Kleiman
Bloomsburg University of Pennsylvania

Cincinnati, Ohio
www.atomicdog.com

Book Team

Vice President/Publisher	Steve Scoble
Managing Editor	Kendra Leonard
Director of Interactive Media and Design	Joe Devine
Director of Quality Assurance	Tim Bair
Production Coordinator	Lori Bradshaw
Web Production Editor	Angela Makowski
Quality Assurance Editor	Dan Horton
Marketing Manager	Mikka Baker
Cover Design	Zack Hicks

Cover photo: Copyright © 2007 Atomic Dog Publishing and its licensors. All rights reserved.

When ordering this title, use ISBN 1-59260-268-1

Copyright © 2007 by Atomic Dog Publishing. All rights reserved.

ISBN 1-59260-267-3

Library of Congress Control Number: 2005936980

No part of this publication may be reproduced, stored in a retrieval system, or transmitted, in any form or by any means, electronic, mechanical, photocopying, recording, or otherwise, without the prior written permission of the publisher.

Printed in the United States of America by Atomic Dog Publishing, 35 East Seventh St., Suite 405, Cincinnati, OH 45202.

10 9 8 7 6 5 4 3 2 1

To Jared, Drew, Adam, and Mary Ellen

Brief Contents

Contents

Part Four
Human Resource Management Postselection Practices
171

Part **Five**   HRM Practices Affected by External Factors   305

Part **Six** Conclusion 419

Preface

Human Resource Management

This book addresses the educational needs of management students who are enrolled in an introductory human resource (HR) management class. The majority of these students will be seeking careers as either HR professionals or general managers. This book is appropriate for either or both audiences, depending on the areas of emphasis selected by the instructor. Students aspiring to be HR professionals will learn about such key HR practices as recruitment, selection, training, and performance appraisal, and they will come to understand how these practices can be successfully developed and implemented. Aspiring general managers will develop an understanding of HR's importance to an organization and learn about the manager's role in the HR process.

Theme of the Book

The theme of this book is that the effective management of human resources, like the effective management of all other organizational resources, leads to competitive advantage. The book visibly and continuously highlights the importance of HR and its potential contribution to a firm's competitive advantage.

Each chapter in Parts 2 through 5 is divided into three sections: (1) Gaining Competitive Advantage, (2) HRM Issues and Practices, and (3) The Manager's Guide.

Gaining Competitive Advantage

This section begins with a real-life case. The write-up describes the HR problem faced by a firm, presents the firm's solution, and explains how the solution enabled the firm to enhance its competitive advantage. The case serves as an attention-grabbing device designed to both sensitize the student to the information that follows and to increase the information's applicability in the student's mind.

This case is immediately followed by a discussion of how the HR practices addressed in the chapter can be used to enhance competitive advantage. For example, Chapter 8 discusses how an effective performance appraisal system can enhance competitive advantage by improving job performance, by helping employers make correct pay raise and promotion decisions, by ensuring legal compliance, and by minimizing job dissatisfaction and turnover.

HRM Issues and Practices

This section describes the various HR practices and how they can be developed and implemented to achieve competitive advantage. Premised on the idea that students need a conceptual understanding of the important HR issues and practices, the book avoids much of the technical details found in most other HR texts, details that can be covered in more advanced, specialized HR courses. For example, when discussing the topic of validity, statistical formulas are omitted. Rather, the emphasis is on what validity means in everyday terms, why it is important, and how a firm's HR professionals and managers can achieve it when selecting employees.

The Manager's Guide

This section is designed to help students understand the manager's role in the HR process and the relationship that exists between managers and HR professionals. The section consists of three parts. The first examines the manager's HR responsibilities. The second part, entitled "How the HRM Department Can Help," discusses the HR department's role and how HR professionals can help managers carry out their HR responsibilities. In the third part, the HR practices covered in the chapter are highlighted as part of a hands-on, how-to guide for managers. The purpose here is to teach students the skills necessary to implement the manager's HR responsibilities. Among the skills covered are these:

- Writing job descriptions
- Dealing with the EEOC during a discrimination investigation
- Giving applicants realistic job previews
- Interviewing job applicants
- Assessing employees' training needs
- Conducting performance appraisal conferences
- Complying with the overtime provisions of the Fair Labor Standards Act
- Conducting disciplinary conferences
- Handling employee grievances
- Performing safety audits
- Investigating accidents
- Managing employees within different cultures

Another distinguishing characteristic of this book is its length. Because they go into greater technical detail, most other HR texts are around 650–750 pages and consist of approximately 20 chapters. This text is less than 500 pages and consists of 15 chapters. As a result, this book can be more easily covered in a single semester—15 chapters in 15 weeks.

How the Book Is Organized

In Part 1, Chapter 1 introduces the notion of competitive advantage. The chapter defines the concept, presents evidence that links HR practices to competitive advantage, and proposes a model that demonstrates how such practices can lead to competitive advantage. Chapter 2 discusses the environmental context of HR, highlighting how factors in the outside environment (e.g., laws, cultural diversity, unions, business trends, safety issues, and globalization) profoundly affect the way in which a firm manages its employees.

Parts 2 through 4 cover basic HR practices that are used by all organizations. These three parts are organized according to the various phases of the employment cycle: preselection, selection, and postselection, as described next:

- Part 2 covers the preselection practices of HR planning and job analysis.
- Part 3 covers employee recruitment and selection.
- Part 4 describes the HR practices that "kick in" after employees are selected, practices that are designed to maintain or improve employee's job performance levels.

Part 5 covers the most important external factors that affect the management of human resources. These factors consist of workplace justice laws (Chapter 11), unions (Chapter 12), safety and health concerns (Chapter 13), and globalization of HR (Chapter 14). The concluding chapter describes what it is like to work in the HR field.

Online and in Print

Human Resource Management is available online as well as in print. The online version demonstrates how the interactive media components of the text enhance presentation and understanding. For example,

- Animated illustrations help to clarify concepts and bring them to life.
- QuickCheck interactive questions and chapter quizzes test students' knowledge of various topics and provide immediate feedback.
- Clickable glossary terms provide immediate definitions of key concepts.
- References and footnotes "pop up" with a click.
- Highlighting capabilities allow students to emphasize main ideas. They can also add personal notes in the margin.
- The search function allows students to quickly locate discussions of specific topics throughout the text.
- An interactive study guide at the end of each chapter provides tools for learning, such as interactive key-term matching and the ability to review customized content in one place.

Students may choose to use just the online version of the text, or both the online and print versions together. This gives them the flexibility to choose which combination of resources works best for them. To assist those who use the online and print versions together, the primary heads and subheads in each chapter are numbered the same. For example, the first primary head in Chapter 1 is labeled 1-1, the second primary head in this chapter is labeled 1-2, and so on. The subheads build from the designation of their corresponding primary head: 1-1a, 1-1b, etc. This numbering system is designed to make moving between the online and print versions as seamless as possible.

Finally, next to a number of figures and exhibits in the print version of the text, you will see an icon similar to those below. This icon indicates that this figure or exhibit in the Online Edition is interactive in a way that applies, illustrates, or reinforces the concept.

Changes in the Fourth Edition

In addition to updating each chapter to reflect current practices and research findings in the HRM field, the following topics have been added to the fourth edition:

- New or updated opening cases for most chapters
- Several new end-of-chapter experiential exercises
- Expanded discussion of the Pregnancy Discrimination Act
- More explicit instructions on writing job descriptions
- Suggestions for evaluating completed application forms
- Examples of the different types of employment interview questions
- Discussion of web-based training
- Expanded discussion of forced distribution rating systems
- Discussion of recent revisions in the Fair Labor Standards Act

Learning Aids

Many learning aids are included to help instructors create a flexible learning environment that best suits their needs as well as the needs of their students. A brief synopsis of the learning tools provided as part of the book follows.

Writing Style

As noted earlier, the book is written in a nontechnical, conversational tone. Many examples are used to illustrate key points.

Legal Emphasis

Because of the importance of legal issues in the HR area, students need to fully understand employment law and how it applies to both HR and management. Consequently, the book has a very strong legal orientation. The basics of equal employment opportunity and affirmative action are covered in Chapter 2. Workplace justice laws affecting employee rights (e.g., sexual harassment, wrongful discharge, employee privacy) are covered in Chapter 11. Each of the other chapters covers HR laws as they apply to the topic under consideration. For example, the legal ramifications of each selection technique are described in Chapter 6.

Chapter Outline and Objectives

Each chapter begins with an outline of the topics to be covered, followed by a list of chapter objectives. This gives the reader an overview of the chapter's content.

Chapter Objectives Revisited

The chapter objectives are restated at the end of the chapter with "bullets" indicating the main points concerning each objective.

Key Terms

In both the print and online versions of the text, key terms and concepts are highlighted and defined on first appearance. In the print version, key terms are also defined in the text margins and listed in alphabetical order at the beginning of each chapter. A glossary at the end of the print book presents all of the definitions alphabetically. The online version of the text has "pop-up" definitions of key terms, as well as a key-term matching quiz in each end-of-chapter study guide.

Boxed Features

Each chapter contains two types of boxed features. "On the Road to Competitive Advantage" boxes provide examples of how actual companies have used HR practices to gain a competitive advantage, while "Taking a Closer Look" boxes offer more detailed descriptions of certain topics without interrupting the flow of coverage in the text.

Review and Discussion Questions

Multiple-choice review questions and short-answer discussion questions at the end of each chapter test students' understanding of the chapter's main points.

Experiential Exercises and Cases

Each chapter (except Chapters 1 and 15) contains one or more experiential exercises and a case that relates to the topics covered in the chapter.

Supplements

Atomic Dog is pleased to offer a robust suite of supplemental materials for instructors using its textbooks. These ancillaries include a Test Bank, PowerPoint® slides, and Instructor's Manual.

The Test Bank for this book includes multiple-choice questions in a wide range of difficulty levels for each chapter. The Test Bank offers not only the correct answer for each question, but also a rationale or explanation for the correct answer and a reference—the location in the chapter where materials addressing the question content can be found. This Test Bank comes with ExamViewPro software for easily creating customized or multiple versions of a test, and includes the option of editing or adding to the existing question bank.

A full set of PowerPoint Slides is available for this text. These are designed to provide instructors with comprehensive visual aids for each chapter in the book. These slides include outlines of each chapter, highlighting important terms, concepts, and discussion points.

The Instructor's Manual for this book offers suggested syllabi; detailed lecture and outline; key terms; in-class and take-home assignments including review questions and answers, critical thinking exercises, discussion questions and answers, essay questions, and exercises; and other resources.

Acknowledgments

Writing a book is a formidable task. Luckily, I have had a lot of help. Many thanks go to my colleagues Marilyn Helms, Michael Gordon, and Mark Mendenhall for lending their vast expertise to Chapters 3, 12, and 14, respectively. I would also like to express my gratitude to my graduate assistants, Josh Kovitch and David Shur, for their valuable help in finding new case studies and updating facts and figures. Thanks also go to the following list of reviewers for their time and effort. Their suggestions significantly improved the manuscript.

Hrach Bedrosian
Stern School of Business
Gerald E. Calvasina
Southern Utah University
J. Philip Craiger
University of Nebraska–Omaha
Satish Deshpande
Western Michigan University
James Dick
Jamestown College
Dennis Dossett
University of Missouri
Allen D. Engle, Sr.
Eastern Kentucky University
Don Eskew
Otterbein College
Floyd Evans
Lamar University–Orange
Dale Feinauer
University of Wisconsin–Oshkosh
Hubert Field
Auburn University
Linda Gravett
Xavier University
David Harris
Rhode Island College
Robert Heneman
Ohio State University
Richard Jette
Northeastern University

Avis Johnson
University of Akron
Vickie Kaman
Colorado State University
Eileen Kaplan
Montclair State University
Gundars Kaupins
Boise State University
Timothy Keaveny
Marquette University
Russell Kent
Georgia Southern University
Dr. Kenyork
Oakland University
Albert King
Northern Illinois University
Brian Klaas
University of South Carolina
Ellen Kossek
Michigan State University
Elaine LeMay
Colorado State University
Mark Lengnick-Hall
Wichita State University
Lori Long
Kent State University
John Lust
Illinois State University
Patricia Madison-Manninen
Northshore Community College

Tom McFarland
Mt. San Antonio College
Jeff Miles
University of the Pacific
Jonathan Monat
California State University-Long Beach
Sharon Noone
Portland State University
Tamara Nordin
Southern Oregon University and Northwest Christian College
Pamela Perrewe
Florida State University
Alex Pomichowski
Ferris State University
Franklin Ramsoomair
Wilfrid Laurier University

Barbara Redman
Briar Cliff College
Joel Rudin
University of Central Oklahoma
William L. Smith
Emporia State University
Donald Spangler
S.U.N.Y. at Binghampton
Charles Vance
Loyola Marymount
Philip Weatherford
Glenwood, FL
Joel Weiss
University of Nebraska-Omaha
Ann Wendt
Wright State University
Kenneth York
Oakland University

Finally, I would like to thank the staff of Atomic Dog Publishing for giving me this opportunity. Specifically, thanks to Steve Scoble for quarterbacking this project and to Kendra Leonard for her invaluable help in preparing this manuscript.

About the Author

Lawrence S. Kleiman is a professor of management in the College of Business at Bloomsburg University. He received his Ph.D. in industrial/organizational psychology from the University of Tennessee at Knoxville in 1978. Prior to joining Bloomsburg University, he taught at the University of Tennessee at Chattanooga and worked for the Metropolitan Police Department of Washington, D.C., the U.S. Department of Agriculture, and the New Jersey Department of Civil Service. He has published over 40 articles appearing in such journals as *Personnel Psychology, American Psychologist, HRMagazine, Journal of Business and Psychology, Applied HRM Research, Public Personnel Management, Employee Relations Today,* and *The Journal of Individual Employment Rights.* Professor Kleiman has consulted for numerous organizations, including The Sathers Corporation, The Tennessee Valley Authority, McKee Foods, Union Carbide, Heinz, and AT&T.

Introduction

Human Resource Management and Competitive Advantage

Chapter One

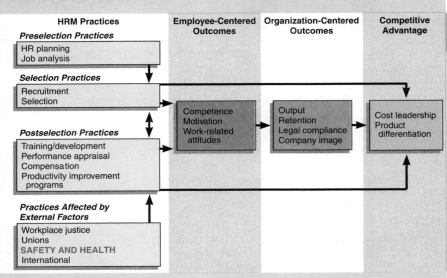

HRM Practices	Employee-Centered Outcomes	Organization-Centered Outcomes	Competitive Advantage
Preselection Practices HR planning Job analysis			
Selection Practices Recruitment Selection	Competence Motivation Work-related attitudes	Output Retention Legal compliance Company image	Cost leadership Product differentiation
Postselection Practices Training/development Performance appraisal Compensation Productivity improvement programs			
Practices Affected by External Factors Workplace justice Unions SAFETY AND HEALTH International			

Key Terms

benefits
compensation
competitive advantage
cost leadership strategy
development
human resource management
human resource planning
job analysis
job satisfaction
organizational citizenship

organizational commitment
pay
performance appraisal process
product differentiation
productivity improvement programs
recruitment
selection
training
unions
workplace justice

Chapter Objectives

Upon completion of this chapter, you will be able to:

- Understand the nature of a firm's human resource management practices.

- Understand the roles played by line managers and human resource professionals in the human resource management process.

- Understand what competitive advantage is and how companies can achieve it.

- Understand how a firm's human resource management practices can help it gain a competitive advantage.

- Understand why competitive advantage gained from human resource management practices is likely to be sustained over time.

Undoubtedly, any organization's success depends on how it manages its resources. A firm's resources propel it toward its goals, just as an engine propels an automobile toward its destination.

Many organizational resources are nonhuman, such as land, capital, and equipment. Although the management of these resources is very important, a business cannot succeed without also managing its human resources (i.e., its people) properly. Just as automobiles will not operate efficiently (or at all) if they are driven by incompetent people, organizations will not operate successfully unless they too are "driven" by competent people. People determine the organization's objectives, and people run the operations that allow the organization to reach its objectives.

1-1 Human Resource Management

An organization's **human resource management** (HRM) function focuses on the people aspect of management. It consists of practices that help the organization deal effectively with its people during the various phases of the employment cycle: preselection, selection, and postselection.

The preselection phase involves planning practices. The organization must decide what types of job openings will exist in the upcoming period and determine what qualifications are necessary to perform these jobs. During the selection phase, the organization selects its employees. Selection practices include recruiting applicants, assessing their qualifications, and ultimately selecting those who are deemed to be the most qualified.

In the postselection phase, the organization develops HRM practices for effectively managing people once they have "come through the door." These practices are designed to maximize the performance and satisfaction levels of a firm's employees by providing them with the necessary knowledge and skills to perform their jobs and by creating conditions that will energize, direct, and facilitate the employees' efforts toward meeting the organization's objectives.

We discuss these HRM practices throughout the remainder of this book. In the following paragraphs, we provide a preview of what is to come, as we briefly describe each practice and note the chapter in which it appears.

human resource management
The organizational function that consists of practices that help the organization deal effectively with its people during the various phases of the employment cycle.

1-1a HRM Preselection Practices

The HRM preselection practices, which are human resource planning and job analysis, lay the foundation for the other HRM practices. In other words, firms must analyze and plan for their treatment of workers before they can carry out the remaining HRM practices.

Uses of Job Analysis Information

Bob is the HR director of Spaniel Corp. Bob uses job analysis information to:

> Determine job qualifications for recruitment when he needs to make a hiring decision for the bookkeeping position he has open.

> Choose the best selection techniques for hiring that bookkeeper.

> Develop training programs for the employees of Spaniel Corp., including software training to keep the bookkeeping state-of-the-art.

> Develop performance appraisal rating forms, so everyone is evaluated fairly— from the bookkeeper to the boss.

> Help determine pay raises, so he can give the bookkeeper a salary boost that is appropriate.

> Set performance standards for productivity improvement programs, so that everyone—including the bookkeeper—can do things better.

Figure 1-1
Job Analysis

human resource planning
A process that helps companies identify their future HRM needs and how those needs can be met.

job analysis A systematic procedure for gathering, analyzing, and documenting information about particular jobs.

Human Resource Planning (Chapter 3)

Human resource planning helps managers anticipate and meet changing needs relating to the acquisition, deployment, and utilization of its employees.[1] The organization first maps out an overall plan (called a *strategic plan*). Then, through a process called *demand and supply forecasting,* it estimates the number and types of employees needed to carry out successfully its overall plan. Such information enables a firm to plan its recruitment, selection, and training strategies. For example, let's say that a firm's HR plan estimates that 15 additional engineers will be needed during the next year. The firm typically hires recent engineering graduates to fill such positions. Because these majors are in high demand, the firm decides to begin its campus recruiting early in the academic year, before other companies can "snatch away" the best candidates.

Job Analysis (Chapter 4)

Job analysis is a systematic procedure for gathering, analyzing, and documenting information about particular jobs. The analysis specifies what each worker does, the work conditions, and the worker qualifications necessary to perform the job successfully. Job analysis information is used to plan and coordinate nearly all HRM practices, including these (see Figure 1-1):

1. Determining job qualifications for recruitment purposes
2. Choosing the most appropriate selection techniques
3. Developing training programs
4. Developing performance appraisal rating forms
5. Helping to determine pay rates
6. Setting performance standards for productivity improvement programs

For example, an organization may decide to use a mechanical aptitude test to screen applicants because a job analysis indicated that mechanical aptitude is an important job skill. Or a firm may raise the pay of one of its employees because a job analysis indicated that the nature of the work had recently changed and was now more demanding.

1-1b HRM Selection Practices

By HRM selection practices, we mean policies and procedures used by organizations to staff their positions. We now briefly describe these practices.

Recruitment (Chapter 5)

Organizations use **recruitment** to locate and attract job applicants for particular positions. Organizations may recruit candidates internally (i.e., recruit current employees seeking to advance or change jobs) or externally. The aim of recruitment practices is to identify a suitable pool of applicants quickly, cost efficiently, and legally.

recruitment An HRM practice designed to locate and attract job applicants for particular positions.

Selection (Chapter 6)

Selection involves assessing and choosing job candidates. To be effective, selection processes must be technically sound (i.e., accurate) and legal.

selection An HRM practice in which companies assess and choose from among job candidates.

1-1c HRM Postselection Practices

Companies implement postselection practices to maintain or improve their workers' job performance levels.

Training and Development (Chapter 7)

Training and **development** are planned learning experiences that teach workers how to perform their current or future jobs effectively. Training focuses on current jobs, whereas development prepares employees for possible future jobs. Training and development practices are designed to improve organizational performance by enhancing the knowledge and skill levels of employees.

training Planned learning experiences that teach workers how to effectively perform their current jobs.

development Planned learning experiences that prepare workers to effectively perform possible future jobs.

Performance Appraisal (Chapter 8)

Through the **performance appraisal process,** organizations measure the adequacy of their employees' job performances and communicate these evaluations to them. One aim of appraisal systems is to motivate employees to continue appropriate behaviors and correct inappropriate ones. Management may also use performance appraisals as tools for making HRM-related decisions, such as promotions, demotions, discharges, and pay raises.

performance appraisal process A process used by companies to measure the adequacy of their employees' job performances and communicate these evaluations to them.

Compensation (Chapter 9)

Compensation entails pay and benefits. **Pay** refers to the wage or salary employees earn; **benefits** are a form of compensation provided to employees in addition to their pay, such as health insurance or employee discounts. The aim of compensation practices is to help the organization establish and maintain a competent and loyal workforce at an affordable cost.

compensation The pay and benefits that employees receive from the company.

pay The wage or salary that employees earn.

benefits A form of compensation provided to employees in addition to their pay, such as health insurance or employee discounts.

Productivity Improvement Programs (Chapter 10)

Productivity improvement programs tie job behavior to rewards. Rewards may be financial (e.g., bonuses, pay raises) or nonfinancial (i.e., improved job satisfaction). The aim of such programs is to motivate employees to engage in appropriate job behaviors.

productivity improvement programs Organizational interventions designed to improve productivity by increasing employee motivation.

1-1d HRM Practices Influenced by External Factors

HRM departments within organizations, like the organizations themselves, do not exist in vacuums. Events outside the work environment can have far-reaching effects on HRM practices. In the following paragraphs, we describe some of these events and indicate how they influence HRM practices.

Legal and Environmental Issues (Chapter 2)

During the past 40 years, the enactment of federal, state, and local laws that regulate workplace behavior has radically changed nearly all HRM practices. These laws, which are designed to guarantee employees' (and prospective employees') rights to fair and safe treatment, impact the manner in which many HRM practices are implemented.

Consider, for instance, the impact of antidiscrimination laws on firms' hiring practices. Prior to the passage of these laws, many firms hired people in somewhat arbitrary ways. Applicants were often hired because they had a firm handshake or because they graduated from the employer's alma mater. Today, such practices could result in charges of discrimination. For instance, a woman denied a job because of a weak handshake might end up suing the firm for sex discrimination.

To protect themselves from such charges, employers must conduct their selection practices "by the book." This means they should carefully determine needed job qualifications and choose selection methods that accurately measure those qualifications.

Social, economic, and technological events also strongly influence HRM practices. These events include:

- An expanding cultural diversity at the workplace
- The emergence of work and family issues
- The growing use of part-time, temporary employees
- An increased emphasis on quality and teamwork
- The occurrence of mergers and takeovers
- The occurrence of downsizing and layoffs
- Rapid advances in technology
- Emphasis on continuous quality improvement
- A high rate of illiteracy among the workforce

How do these events influence HRM practices? Let's look at some examples:

- Some firms are attempting to accommodate the needs of families by offering benefit options such as maternity leave, child care, flextime, and job sharing.
- Some firms are attempting to accommodate the needs of older workers through skill upgrading and training designed to facilitate acceptance of new techniques.[2]
- Some firms are educating their employees on basic reading, writing, and mathematical skills so that they can learn to keep up with rapidly advancing technologies.

Workplace Justice Laws (Chapter 11)

workplace justice
A concept that addresses the issue of treating employees in a fair, nondiscriminatory manner.

Workplace justice addresses the issue of employee rights. To have fair workplaces, organizations must comply with laws that give workers the right to be treated in a nondiscriminatory manner. Workplace justice laws constrain how employers may implement workplace rules, disciplinary and discharge procedures, and policies that infringe on employees' privacy, such as surveillance.

Union Influences (Chapter 12)

unions   Labor organizations in which employees, acting in concert, deal with employers on work issues.

Unions often influence a firm's HRM practices. Unionized companies must adhere to written contracts negotiated between each company and its union. Union contracts regulate many HRM practices, such as discipline, promotion, grievance procedures, and overtime allocations. HRM practices in nonunionized companies may be influenced by the threat of unions. For example, some companies have made their HRM practices more equitable (i.e., they treat their employees more fairly) simply to minimize the likelihood that employees will seek union representation.[3]

Safety and Health Concerns (Chapter 13)

Legal, social, and political pressures on organizations to ensure the health and safety of their employees have had a great impact on HRM practices. Organizations respond to these pressures by instituting accident prevention programs and programs such as wellness and employee assistance programs. These are designed to ensure the health and mental well-being of their employees.

International Influences (Chapter 14)

Today's global economy also influences some aspects of HRM. Many firms realize that they must enter foreign markets in order to compete as part of a globally interconnected set of business markets. From an HRM perspective, such organizations must foster the development of more globally oriented managers: individuals who understand foreign languages and cultures, as well as the dynamics of foreign marketplaces. These firms must also deal with issues related to expatriation, such as relocation costs, selection, compensation, and training.

1-2 Who Is Responsible for Developing and Implementing HRM Practices?

Most firms have an HRM department. However, this department does not have sole responsibility for a firm's HRM practices. This responsibility lies with both human resource (HR) professionals and line managers. The misconception that HR professionals have sole responsibility in this area can lead to serious problems. Consider the following example:

At Roy Rogers Restaurants, the annual turnover had been running between 80 to 90 percent across the corporation, costing the organization more than $3 million per year. The HRM department conducted a survey among field managers to get their views on the problem. The managers attributed the high turnover to several people-related problems, such as poor recruitment, pay, training, performance feedback, and promotional opportunities. Interestingly, restaurant managers who experienced the higher turnover within their own units were much more likely to hold the HRM department responsible for solving these problems; they did not see how these problems related to their own behavior. On the other hand, managers experiencing fewer turnovers held themselves accountable for solving these problems. Effective managers attempted to resolve them by:

- Providing input into selection decisions in the first place
- Trying to supervise people in a way that created a team feeling
- Providing training and coaching
- Creating opportunities for their employees' career advancement
- Providing flexible scheduling for students and other part-timers

This case illustrates the importance of the manager's role in the HRM process. It is the interplay between managers and HR professionals that leads to effective HRM practices. For example, consider performance appraisals. The success of a firm's performance appraisal systems depends on the ability of both parties to do their jobs correctly. HR professionals develop the system, and managers provide the actual performance evaluations.

Specific roles played by line managers and HR professionals in each HRM area are discussed throughout the text. Here, we provide a general overview of this topic by describing the roles that have traditionally been played by both parties. As we discuss in Chapter 15, "Working in the HRM Field," however, the distinction between the roles played by HR professionals and line managers is becoming less and less clear.

We must also acknowledge that the nature of these roles varies from company to company, depending primarily on the size of the organization. Our discussion assumes a large company with a sizable HR department. However, in smaller companies without large HRM departments, line managers must assume an even larger role in effective HRM practices.

1. Establish HRM procedures and methods.

Figure 1-2
The HR Professional's Role

2. Monitor/evaluate HRM practices.

3. Advise/assist managers on HRM-related matters.

1-2a HR Professional's Role

HR professionals typically assume the four areas of responsibility shown in Figure 1-2.

Establish HRM Procedures and Methods

HR professionals typically decide what procedures to follow when implementing an HRM practice. For example, an HR professional may decide that the company's selection process should consist of having all candidates (1) complete an application form, (2) take an employment test, and then (3) be interviewed by an HR professional and line manager. The HR professional may also develop or choose the actual methods to be used in this process. For example, he may construct the application form, purchase a selection test from a test publisher, or devise the actual interview questions that the managers should ask.

Monitor/Evaluate HR Practices

HR professionals must ensure that the firm's HRM practices are properly implemented. This responsibility involves evaluation and monitoring. For example, HR professionals may evaluate the usefulness of employment tests, the success of training programs, and the cost-effectiveness of HRM outcomes, such as selection, turnover, recruiting, and so forth. They may also monitor records to ensure that performance appraisals have been properly completed.

Advise/Assist Managers on HRM-Related Matters

Both managers and HR professionals view this role as the HRM department's most significant area of responsibility.[4] HR professionals consult on an array of HRM-related topics. They may assist by providing formal training programs on topics such as selection and the law, how to conduct an employment interview, how to appraise employee job performance, or how to discipline employees effectively. HR professionals also provide assistance by giving line managers advice about specific HRM-related concerns, such as how to deal with a "problem employee."

1-2b Line Manager's Role

Line managers direct employees' day-to-day tasks. From an HRM perspective, line managers are the main people responsible for implementing HRM practices and providing HR professionals with necessary input for developing effective practices.

Allison is a line manager at Spaniel Corp. Using the methods and procedures devised by Bob, the HR director, Allison does the following:

Interviews job applicants. For an open photography position, she interviews eight applicants and selects Claire.

Provides orientation, coaching, and on-the-job training. Allison introduces Claire to Spaniel's policies, and Claire is trained in the darkrooms.

Provides and communicates job performance ratings. After six months, Allison tells Claire that her work review is positive.

Recommends salary increases. Allison recommends that Claire get a 7 percent raise this year.

Carries out disciplinary procedures. When Paul continually mishandles Claire's negatives, Allison warns him and puts a letter in his file.

Investigates accidents. When Claire gets a chemical burn in the darkroom, Allison investigates and makes a report.

Settles grievance issues. Allison settles a dispute between Claire and Paul over darkroom access and scheduling.

Figure 1-3
The Line Manager's Role

Implementing HRM Practices

Managers carry out many procedures and methods devised by HR professionals. For instance, line managers might do these tasks (see Figure 1-3):

- Interview job applicants.
- Provide orientation, coaching, and on-the-job training.
- Provide and communicate job performance ratings.
- Recommend salary increases.
- Carry out disciplinary procedures.
- Investigate accidents.
- Settle grievance issues.

Providing HR Professionals with Needed Input

The development of HRM procedures and methods often requires input from line managers. For example, when conducting a job analysis, HR professionals often seek job information from managers and ask managers to review the final written product. When HR professionals determine an organization's training needs, managers often suggest what types of training are needed and who, in particular, needs the training.

1-3 Gaining a Competitive Advantage

Firms can gain a **competitive advantage** over competitors by effectively managing their human resources. Throughout this text, we discuss how each HRM practice can help a firm gain such an advantage. In this section, we introduce the notion of competitive advantage and then discuss how firms can achieve and sustain it through effective HRM practices.

competitive advantage
A status achieved by a company when gaining a superior marketplace position relative to its competition.

1-3a Competitive Advantage Defined

To succeed, an organization must gain and maintain an edge over its competitors—that is, a firm must develop a competitive advantage or superior marketplace position relative to its competition.[5] Firms can accomplish this aim in one of two ways: through cost leadership or product differentiation.[6]

1-3b Cost Leadership

cost leadership strategy
A strategy in which a company gains a competitive advantage by providing the same services or products as its competitors, but produces them at a lower cost.

Under a **cost leadership strategy,** a firm provides the same services or products as its competitors, but produces them at a lower cost. By doing so, the organization earns a better return on its investment in capital and human resources.[7] For example, Restaurants A and B sell the same number of hamburgers at the same price. Restaurant A can gain a competitive advantage over B (i.e., get a better return on its investment) if it is able to reduce its per unit cost, that is, produce each hamburger at a lower cost.

A per unit cost is the cost of producing one unit of product or service. It can be reduced by increasing the number of units produced relative to the total cost of producing them. A firm can reduce its per unit cost by increasing the value of the following ratio:

Number of units produced/Total cost of production

Increasing the numerator or decreasing the denominator can increase the value of this ratio. For instance, let's say that a manufacturer of buttons can produce 1,000 buttons at a cost of $100. The cost of producing one button is thus $.10. One way of lowering per unit costs would be to increase the numerator (i.e., produce more buttons) without increasing the overall cost. For example, the firm could lower its per unit cost to $.05 by producing 2,000 buttons at a cost of $100. Another way of lowering per unit costs would be to decrease the denominator (i.e., lower total production costs) without decreasing the number of units produced. For example, a per unit cost of $.05 could be achieved by producing 1,000 buttons at a cost of $50.

The key question is "How could a firm accomplish this aim?" There are a number of possible ways. For instance, using new technology or devising more efficient work methods could increase productivity. Cutting overhead costs could decrease production costs.

1-3c Product Differentiation

product differentiation
Gaining competitive advantage by producing a product or service that buyers prefer.

Product differentiation occurs when a firm produces a product or service that is preferred by buyers. A firm can accomplish this aim by:[8]

- Creating a better quality product or service than its competitors
- Providing innovative products or services that are not offered by its competitors
- Choosing a superior location—one that is more accessible to its customers
- Promoting and packaging its product to create the perception of higher quality

Product differentiation creates a competitive advantage if the firm's customers are willing to pay enough to cover any extra production costs.[9] For example, Restaurant A devises a way to make a better tasting hamburger by putting an extra ingredient into the recipe. This restaurant would gain a competitive advantage if sales increased as the result of this move and the additional revenues generated more than offset the additional costs of producing the better tasting hamburger.

On the Road to Competitive Advantage 1-1 provides an illustration of how one organization, Trader Joe's, has achieved a competitive advantage by using cost leadership and product differentiation strategies. A specialty grocer offering a varied assortment of bargain gourmet-style foods, wines, and health food supplements, Trader Joe's has achieved enormous success by offering unique products at relatively low prices.

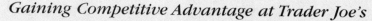

Gaining Competitive Advantage at Trader Joe's

Trader Joe's started out about 40 years ago as a specialty grocery store located in Southern California. From humble beginnings, it has grown into a $3-billion-a-year national chain with 217 stores, adding 8 to 25 stores per year. Sales at most stores average about $15 million per year, or $1,500 per square foot. Its closest competitor, Whole Foods, generates about $750 per square food, half the Trader's Joe's rate. Here's how Trader Joe's has done it:

Trader Joe's management team focuses on making money by saving money (cost leadership). They use private labels instead of name brands for nearly every

product in the store; they deal directly with producers to cut out the middleman; they keep their stores small, renting cheap real estate in existing neighborhood shopping centers. Trader Joe's success is also due to product differentiation; it differentiates itself from competitors by constantly changing its stock as its buyers travel the world looking for new and interesting products that can be packaged and sold profitably at a relatively low price.

Source: Speizer, I. (2004). Shopper's special. *Workforce Management,* September, 51-54.

1-4 Competitive Advantage and HRM

The HRM practices of an organization can be an important source of competitive advantage. As we shall see, effective HRM practices can enhance a firm's competitive advantage by creating both cost leadership and product differentiation. In the following paragraphs, we document this assertion with evidence derived from research and expert opinion. We then provide a model that attempts to explain why HRM practices can have such a dramatic impact on competitive advantage.

1-4a Evidence Linking HRM Practices to Competitive Advantage

A growing body of research-based evidence indicates that a firm's HRM practices can have a rather strong impact on competitive advantage. A growing number of studies have been published that link specific HR practices to profits. As noted by Shari Caudron, "Not only are executives beginning to understand that the human resource is the most valuable resource they have, but there's also proof available now to show that investment in human resources does pay off."[10] Studies linking specific HRM practices to competitive advantage are noted throughout this text. Here we report the results of three studies that examined the impact of the entire set of HRM practices used by various companies.

One study examined the HRM practices and productivity levels of 968 firms across 35 industries.[11] The effectiveness of each company's set of HRM practices was rated based on the presence of such things as incentive plans, employee grievance systems, formal performance appraisal systems, and worker participation in decision making. The study uncovered a strong link between HRM effectiveness and productivity: Specifically, companies with high HRM effectiveness ratings were 5 percent more productive than companies with average HRM ratings.

A similar study conducted among 293 publicly held U.S. firms yielded virtually the same results: Improving HRM practices from average to highly effective leads to a 5 percent productivity increase. The study went on to find that the net gain in annual productivity brought about by effective HRM practices equates to $44,380 per employee.[12]

The third study, conducted by Chris Ryan and his associates, evaluated the impact of a broad range of HRM practices on shareholder return. They concluded that 15-30

Sixteen HRM Practices That Enhance Competitive Advantage

1. *Employment security:* A guarantee of employment stating that no employee will be laid off for lack of work; provides a signal to the employees of long-term commitment by the organization to the work-force. This practice generates employee loyalty, commitment, and a willingness to expend extra effort for the organization's benefit.

2. *Selectivity in recruiting:* Carefully selecting the right employees in the right way. On average, a highly qualified employee produces twice as much as a poorly qualified one. Moreover, by being selective in its recruitment practices, the organization sends the message to applicants that they are joining an elite organization that has high expectations regarding employee performance.

3. *High wages:* Wages that are higher than that required by the market (i.e., higher than that paid by competitors). High wages tend to attract better-qualified applicants, make turnover less likely, and send a message that the firm values its employees.

4. *Incentive pay:* Allowing employees who are responsible for enhanced levels of performance and profitability to share in the benefits. Employees consider such a practice to be fair and just. If all the gains generated from the employees' ingenuity and effort go just to top management, people will view the situation as unfair, become discouraged, and abandon their efforts.

5. *Employee ownership:* Giving the employees owner-ship interests in the organization by providing them with such things as shares of company stock and profit-sharing programs. Employee ownership, if

properly implemented, can align the interests of employees with those of other shareholders. Such employees will likely take a long-term view of the organization, its strategy, and its investment policies.

6. *Information sharing:* Providing employees with information about operations, productivity, and profitability. Information sharing provides an informed basis for employees to appreciate how their own interests and those of the company are related, and thus provides them with the information they need in order to do what is required for success.

7. *Participation and empowerment:* Encouraging the decentralization of decision making and broader worker participation and empowerment in controlling their own work process. Organizations should move from a system of hierarchical control and coordination of activity to one in which lower-level employees are permitted to do things to enhance performance. Research has shown that participation increases both employee satisfaction and productivity.

8. *Teams and job redesign:* The use of interdisciplinary teams that coordinate and monitor their own work. Teams exert a powerful influence on individuals by setting norms regarding appropriate work quantity and quality. Positive results from group influences are more likely when there are rewards for group efforts, when groups have some autonomy and control over the work environment, and when groups are taken seriously by the organization.

9. *Training and skill development:* Providing workers with the skills necessary to do their jobs. Training

percent of the total value of a company could be attributed to the quality of its HRM practices. Those having the greatest impact were:[13]

- Providing employees with effective orientation training
- Letting employees know what is expected of them
- Discharging employees that are chronically poor performers

Stanford professor Jeffrey Pfeffer describes the potential impact of HRM practices on competitive advantage.[14] Pfeffer identified 16 HRM practices that, in his opinion, can enhance a firm's competitive advantage. These practices are listed in Taking a Closer Look 1-1; most of them are described in greater detail throughout this text.

1-4b A Model Linking HRM Practices to Competitive Advantage

Although the evidence just presented shows that effective HRM practices can strongly enhance a firm's competitive advantage, it fails to indicate why these practices have such an influence. In the following sections, we describe a model that attempts to explain this phenomenon. The model is illustrated in Figure 1-4, where

not only ensures that employees and managers can perform their jobs competently, but it also demonstrates the firm's commitment to its employees.

10. *Cross-utilization and cross-training:* Train people to perform several different tasks. Having people do several jobs can make work more interesting and provide management with greater flexibility in scheduling work. For instance, it can replace an absent worker with one who has been trained to perform those duties.

11. *Symbolic egalitarianism:* Equality of treatment among employees established by such actions as eliminating executive dining rooms and reserved parking spaces. The reduction in the number of social categories tends to diminish the "us" versus "them" thinking and provides a sense of everyone working toward a common goal.

12. *Wage compression:* Reducing the size of the pay differences among employees. When tasks are somewhat interdependent and cooperation is needed to accomplish the work, pay compression can lead to productivity gains by reducing interpersonal competition and enhancing cooperation.

13. *Promotion from within:* Filling job vacancies by promoting employees from jobs at a lower organizational level. Promotion increases training and skill development, offers employees an incentive for doing well, and can provide a sense of fairness and justice in the workplace.

14. *Long-term perspective:* The organization must realize that achieving competitive advantage through the workforce takes time to accomplish, and thus a long-term perspective is needed. In the short run, laying off people is probably more profitable than trying to maintain employment security, and cutting training is a quick way to maintain short-term profits. But once achieved, competitive advantage brought about by the use of these HRM practices (i.e., employment security and training) is likely to be substantially more enduring.

15. *Measurement of practices:* Organizations should measure such things as employee attitudes, the success of various programs and initiatives, and employee performance levels. Measurement can guide behavior by indicating "what counts," and it can provide the company and its employees with feedback as to how well they are performing relative to measurement standards.

16. *Overarching philosophy:* Having an underlying management philosophy that connects the various individual practices into a coherent whole. The success of the separate practices listed in items 1 through 15 is somewhat dependent on having a system of values and beliefs about the basis of success and how to manage people. For instance, the overarching philosophy at Advanced Micro Devices is "continuous rapid improvement; empowerment; seamless organizational boundaries; high expectations; and technical excellence."

Source: Pfeffer, J. (1994). *Competitive Advantage through People.* Boston: Harvard Business School Press.

the arrows indicate two paths from HRM practices to competitive advantage: direct and indirect. By direct path, we mean that the way an HRM practice is carried out can, by itself, have an immediate impact on competitive advantage. By indirect path, we mean that an HRM practice can impact competitive advantage by causing certain outcomes, which, in turn, create competitive advantage. We now take a closer look at this model.

The Direct Impact of HRM Practices on Competitive Advantage

In some instances, firms can achieve cost leadership through the use of effective HRM practices. HRM-related costs associated with recruitment, selection, training, compensation, and so forth comprise a significant portion of a firm's expenditures. These costs are especially high in service-related industries, where firms spend about 70 percent of their budgets on payroll costs alone. These HRM-related costs can vary significantly from competitor to competitor. Those doing the best job of containing them, therefore, stand to gain a financial advantage over their competitors.

Let's return to Restaurants A and B to illustrate how the containment of HRM costs can lower per unit cost. Assume that both restaurants produce 1,000 hamburgers per

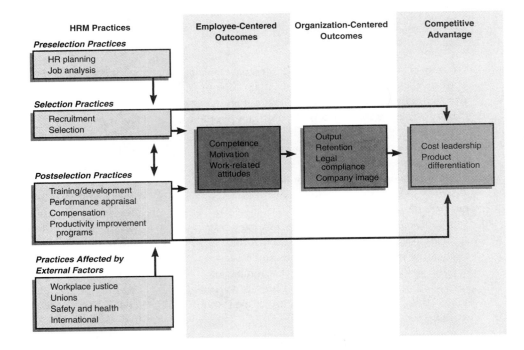

INTERACTIVE FIGURE

Figure 1-4
A Model Linking HRM Practices to Competitive Advantage

day at the same per unit cost. Restaurant A can gain a cost advantage over B if it can lower its HRM-related costs without decreasing its productivity. One way it could accomplish this aim would be to devise a less expensive means of recruitment. For instance, the restaurant may attempt to recruit new employees by asking its current employees to "spread the word" to their friends. This method of recruitment is certainly less expensive than the approach it had used in the past—placing a help-wanted ad in the local paper. If the applicants recruited by this method perform their jobs just as well as those recruited through help-wanted ads, the restaurant will have lowered its costs without sacrificing productivity.

The Indirect Impact of HRM Practices on Competitive Advantage

A firm's HRM practices can also impact competitive advantage in an indirect way. As the model illustrates, this path involves the following links:

HRM practices → Employee-centered outcomes
Employee-centered outcomes → Organization-centered outcomes
Organization-centered outcomes → Competitive advantage

We now examine each of these links. Specific examples illustrating each of them are given in Taking a Closer Look 1-2.

HRM Practices→Employee-Centered Outcomes

We first examine the nature of these employee-centered outcomes and then describe how effective HRM practices can lead to them.

Employee-centered outcomes refer to the competence, motivation, and work-related attitudes of a firm's employees, as defined in the following list:

- *Competence:* The extent to which employees possess the knowledge, skills, and abilities that their jobs require.

- *Motivation:* The extent to which employees are willing to exert the necessary effort to perform their jobs well.

- *Work-related attitudes:* The extent to which employees are satisfied with their jobs, committed to their organizations, and act as good organizational citizens.

Taking a Closer Look 1-2

Examples of HRM Practices—Competitive Advantage Linkages

HRM Practices→Employee-Centered Outcomes

- Because the firm's performance appraisal practices are too subjective and require no documentation, supervisors can give their "favorites" an unduly high evaluation and "nonfavorites" an unduly low one. A highly competent nonfavored employee loses a promotion because of an unfair rating, and thus becomes quite dissatisfied with his job.

- When the math department at a university screens applicants for the job of professor, it requires them to conduct a sample class, with faculty serving as "students." It then hires only those candidates who have demonstrated the ability to clearly explain abstract mathematical concepts. Because of this selection process, all those hired have excelled in the classroom.

- A firm uses an incentive system that rewards employees based on the quality and quantity of their output. The employees consequently work long and hard each day in order to maximize their pay.

Employee-Centered Outcomes→Organization-Centered Outcomes

- Because its agents are so knowledgeable and persuasive (worker competence), a long-distance telephone service increased its customer base (quantity of output) by 20 percent during the past year.

- Mary Smith, the firm's best manager, refuses a job offer from a competitor because of her commitment to her current employer.

Organization-Centered Outcomes→Cost Leadership

- A sizable number of its customers do business with a bank because they like dealing with Betty Smith, the bank's manager for the past five years. These customers believe this bank is the best one in town because Betty provides them with such outstanding service. If the bank were to lose Betty, business would surely suffer. Fortunately, because Betty loves her work and is committed to the bank, she has no intention of ever quitting. Thus, the bank is spared the cost of replacing Betty and the loss of business that would ensue if she ever left the bank.

Organization-Centered Outcomes→Product Differentiation

- A mousetrap manufacturer was able to increase its market share by inventing a "better mousetrap." It accomplished this aim by encouraging its work teams to be innovative, take risks, and assume a long-term perspective. Although it took many trials and errors, the team finally succeeded.

Let's take a closer look at the work-related attitudes. **Job satisfaction** concerns the favorableness of employee attitudes toward their jobs. Employees are likely to be satisfied with their jobs when they (1) enjoy their work, (2) have a realistic opportunity to advance within the company, (3) like the people they deal with, (4) like and respect their supervisors, and (5) believe their pay is fair.

Organizational commitment refers to "the psychological attachment to, identification with, and involvement in the organization.[15] Employees who are committed to their organizations are very loyal toward them. Such individuals stick with their company through "thick and thin."

Organizational citizenship refers to the willingness of employees to engage in behaviors that help the organization achieve its goals. Such behaviors include:[16]

- *Conscientiousness:* Performing tasks well beyond the minimum required levels
- *Altruism:* Giving help to others
- *Civic virtue:* Participating in the political life of the organization
- *Sportsmanship:* Doing things with a positive attitude; not complaining
- *Courtesy:* Treating others with respect

In essence, good organizational citizens go out of their way to help coworkers with job-related activities. They also accept orders willingly, tolerate temporary impositions without fussing, and make sacrifices for the good of the company, such as

job satisfaction The favorableness of employee attitudes toward their jobs.

organizational commitment The relative strength of an individual's identification and involvement in a particular organization.

organizational citizenship The willingness of employees to engage in behaviors that help the organization to achieve its goals.

being willing to work overtime when necessary.[17] Although these work behaviors contribute to an organization's goals, they are not usually specified in workers' job descriptions. Employees engage in these behaviors because they want to do so. They want to because the company has treated them well; that is, the company's HRM practices are effective.

Poor HRM practices can harm employee-centered outcomes by creating negative attitudes and destructive behaviors, such as low organizational commitment, distrust in management, job dissatisfaction, absenteeism, psychological stress, aggressive behavior, theft, and turnover.[18] Effective HRM practices, on the other hand, can lead to the opposite results. For instance, good selection practices can help identify applicants who are competent, motivated, and have good work attitudes. An effective training program can teach workers ways to improve their job performance, thus increasing their competence. Training can also teach managers how to better motivate their employees and to treat them in a way that will improve their job satisfaction. An effective productivity improvement program can motivate workers to try harder to help the company meet its goals.

Employee-Centered Outcomes →Organization-Centered Outcomes

As illustrated in the model, effective HRM practices can enhance competitive advantage when the employee-centered outcomes they produce lead to certain organization-centered outcomes. We first examine these organization-centered outcomes and then examine how they are affected by employee-centered outcomes. Organization-centered outcomes consist of output, employee retention, legal compliance, and company reputation or image. Output refers to the quantity, quality, and innovativeness of the product or service offered by a firm. Retention rates reflect the amount of employee turnover a firm experiences. Legal compliance concerns the issue of whether the firm's HRM practices conform to the requirements imposed by the various employment laws. Company reputation concerns how favorably "outsiders"—potential applicants and customers—view the organization.

Let's now discuss how the achievement of employee-centered outcomes can lead to favorable organization-centered outcomes. When employee-centered outcomes are favorable, employees have a positive job attitude and are both competent and motivated. Such people are usually very productive (with regard to both quality and quantity) because they have both the ability and the desire to perform well.

The results of a study conducted by Sears at 800 different stores illustrate the powerful impact that positive employee attitudes can have on service quality and, hence, customer satisfaction. When Sears improved its HRM practices, employee satisfaction rose, which, in turn, caused customer satisfaction to rise. Specifically, the study found that a 5 percent increase in employee satisfaction led to a 1.3 percent increase in customer satisfaction. The increase in customer satisfaction led to a ½ percent increase in total revenues for the chain.[19]

Satisfied employees are also less likely to quit. One study, for instance, found that workers' intentions to stay with their organizations are heavily dependent on their levels of organizational commitment and job satisfaction.[20] Another study, which surveyed 8,000 workers in 35 industries, found that the most important factors driving employee retention are such things as:[21]

- Career growth and learning opportunities
- Fair pay
- Company pride/organizational commitment
- Employee empowerment

In a similar vein, researcher Rosemary Batt found retention rates were higher for companies using "high involvement" HR systems. Such systems give employees the discretion to use their skills as they see fit and provide financial incentives to enhance employee motivation and commitment.[22]

Organizational citizenship behaviors can greatly enhance a firm's productivity. Specifically, a recent study found that when experienced employees helped less experienced ones solve work-related problems and taught them the "tricks of the trade," the quality/quantity of the recipient's performance improved. This behavior also increased group cohesiveness, making the company a better place to work, and thus reduced turnover.[23]

Organizational citizenship can also directly contribute to customer satisfaction. As noted by management expert Daniel Koys, employees exhibiting positive citizenship behaviors will exceed customer expectations, make suggestions aimed at improving quality and customer satisfaction, and create a positive climate among employees that spills over to customers.[24]

The occurrence of employee-centered outcomes can also reduce the likelihood of an HRM-related lawsuit. As we will note throughout this book, employers can generally comply with employment laws by instituting fair HRM practices. However, employees are more likely to legally challenge an HRM practice, even if fair, if they are dissatisfied with their jobs or lack organizational commitment. Once an employee's work attitude has soured, he or she is likely to perceive these practices as being unfair. For example, when a dissatisfied employee is rejected for a promotion, that individual is likely to cry "foul" even if the promotion decision was a just one. Unfortunately, employers sometimes lose such suits because they have not properly documented their decisions and thus cannot convince a court that they acted properly. On the other hand, employees who are satisfied and loyal are less likely to challenge the legality of their firm's HRM practices.

The achievement of employee-centered outcomes can also affect the image or reputation of a company. Employees who are satisfied and committed to their jobs are likely to "spread the word" that their company is a good place to work. Moreover, when employees are competent and deal with customers in a helpful and friendly manner, the customers will view the company in a favorable light.

Organization-Centered Outcomes → Competitive Advantage

When organization-centered outcomes are favorable, competitive advantage is usually achieved. We first examine the impact of these outcomes on cost leadership and then on product differentiation.

As noted earlier, cost leadership can be achieved by increasing the size of the ratio:

Number of units produced/Total cost of production

When firms can increase their quantity of output through effective HRM practices, their per unit costs are lowered. For example, let's say that, in a given year, a production worker earned $20,000 while producing 1,000 units. The labor cost would thus be $20 ($20,000/1,000) per unit. If the firm can motivate this worker to increase his or her productivity to 1,500 units, the per unit cost of production would be reduced from $20 to $13.33 ($20,000/1,500).

One of the most common ways of cutting HRM costs is to employ technology to replace some of the more expensive HR professional-delivered services. For instance, rather than conducting classroom-training sessions, companies are using e-learning to deliver programs. Expensive employee handbooks are now being put online. Baxter International, an Illinois firm, for example, slashed annual printing costs by $1.5 million by using a PC-based system to give employees online access to personnel information.[25]

The ability to minimize turnover rates can also enhance cost leadership by preventing unnecessary costs. When turnover occurs, not only does the organization lose a possibly productive member, but it must also face the costs of replacing this individual. Replacement costs include recruiting, selecting, and training new employees, and they can be quite high, typically ranging from $3,300 to $6,300.[26] In some cases, they can be much higher. For instance, it cost one company $418,000 to replace a single executive.[27]

Firms that do a good job of retaining employees can often reap an additional benefit—better customer retention. Customers prefer doing business with firms that have a stable workforce. This notion was confirmed in a study of 17 insurance companies that compared the customer retention rates of companies with low and high employee turnover. Firms with low turnover retained 10 percent more of their customers, a difference that has a financial value of $300 million for a typical insurance company![28]

Cost leadership can also be enhanced when an organization is able to avoid lawsuits resulting from noncompliance. Litigation costs can be enormous. These costs include attorney's fees, court costs, expert witness retainers, and the time spent by managers and support personnel to attend depositions and court hearings and to probe company records for documentation that supports company actions.[29] Of course, if the company loses the case, the settlement can be very expensive, costing as much as several million dollars. Between January 2000 and June 2001, 62 companies were forced to pay settlements exceeding $2 million in discrimination cases. Among them were Texaco ($176 million), Mitsubishi ($34 million), Coca-Cola ($192.5 million), and Voice of America ($508 million).[30]

The presence of organization-centered outcomes brought about through effective HRM practices can also serve to enhance competitive advantage through product differentiation. As noted previously, two ways of establishing product differentiation are to produce quality products or services that are superior to those offered by one's competitors or to produce products or services that are not offered by competitors.

The quality or uniqueness of a product or service depends on the actions of the people who produce it. To produce a quality service or product, individuals working for a company must perform their jobs well. The "secret" to Trader Joe's success that was cited in On the Road to Competitive Advantage 1-1 was its employees. The employees are the front line, the first customer contact. They are the soul of Trader Joe's that sets it apart from the competition, serving as a powerful marketing tool. Probably the most important thing that employees do is to create a very engaging experience for the customers. The upbeat and informal interactions they have with customers demonstrates how much they enjoy being at the stores, which, in turn, makes the customers enjoy being there. The bottom line is that cheerful and helpful clerks know how to move groceries![31] On the Road to Competitive Advantage 1-2 describes the HRM practices that Trader Joe's employs to create such a workforce.

When a company produces a better product or service, customers are satisfied and business improves. As noted by management expert Patrick Kiger, a company with strong customer satisfaction can prosper even when faced with a tough economy or an unforeseen disaster.[32] Southwest Airlines, for example, consistently ranks first among airlines in customer satisfaction. Following the September 11, 2001, terrorist attacks, which nearly bankrupted many airline companies, Southwest actually posted a profit in the last quarter of 2001.

On the other hand, low customer satisfaction can be devastating. Kmart, the once mighty retailer, went bankrupt in 2002 because it could not compete with customer-friendly Wal-Mart. In 2001, McDonald's lost $750 million because of customer dissatisfaction.[33]

Competitive advantage can also be enhanced when a company improves its image. Image affects competitive advantage by influencing customers' confidence in a company's products and services and thus affects their inclination to purchase from that company.[34]

1-4c HRM Practices and Sustained Competitive Advantage

It is one thing to create a competitive advantage, but another to sustain it over a prolonged period of time. Many of the strategies used to gain a competitive advantage are difficult to sustain because they can be easily imitated. For instance, Supermarket

The Trader Joe's Case Revisited

The creation a helpful and cheerful workforce begins with the hiring process. Trader Joe's seeks people who are ambitious and possess qualities that might apply equally to a cruise ship crew: out-going, engaging, upbeat, fun-loving, and adventurous. Applicants are immediately eliminated from consideration if they do not smile in the first 30 seconds of the interview.

Trader Joe's also strives to hire employees who understand and appreciate the company's products. Applicants for full-time positions must be Trader Joe's shoppers and be able to describe their favorite Trader Joe's products. Management imposes this requirement because it believes that the best sales associates are those who like the store and its products. The store keeps its employees' knowledge of its ever-changing stock up-to-date by offering them weekly tastings to sample the latest goods.

Trader Joe's uses performance appraisals to keep employees motivated. The store managers rate their employees' job performances every three months. To earn raises, employees must score well on such indicators as being friendly, creating a shopping experience that is fun for customers, providing customers with assistance in a helpful and friendly manner, and promoting high morale within store.

To ensure that the store attracts and retains the best employees, Trader Joe's offers a very generous compensation package. Full-time employees earn $16/hour, which is well above the industry average of $12. They also earn an average annual bonus of $950 and are provided with $6,300 in retirement plan contributions. Assistant managers earn $94,000 per year; managers, $132,000.

A can create a competitive advantage by offering special sales. However, if this policy is successful, competitors are likely to imitate it; the initial advantage is thus quickly lost. As management expert Larry Myler notes:[35]

> In today's business environment, traditional sources of competitive advantage—such as superior production capacity, excellent marketing research, quality manufacturing processes, careful inventory control and efficient product distribution systems—no longer offer the same advantage as they once did. Today, these strategies for competitive advantage have become prerequisites to simply remaining competitive in a national and international marketplace. Employers are learning they must now look instead to their employees for sustainable competitive advantage.

Because the management of human resources is less susceptible to imitation, the competitive advantage achieved through HRM practices is likely to be more sustainable than that achieved by other means. Jeffrey Pfeffer explains why this is so:[36]

1. Competitors rarely have access to a firm's HRM practices; that is, these practices are not very visible to outsiders and, thus, cannot be easily imitated.

2. Even when these practices are visible, their impact may not be as favorable when used by competitors. HRM practices represent an interrelated system. One particular HRM practice may be successful only when used in combination with other HRM practices.

These points are well illustrated by the unique success experienced by Trader Joe's. Its competitors can rather easily imitate their non-HRM initiatives, such as using private labels, cutting out the middleman, and finding inexpensive real estate. It would be more difficult for them to imitate their HRM practices, many of which are not known to the public. Moreover, these competitors would not be able to gain the type of competitive advantage enjoyed by Trader Joe's by simply imitating one of its HRM practices. For instance, matching Trader Joe's compensation rates would not enhance competitive advantage unless this action was taken in conjunction with Trader Joe's selection, appraisal, and training practices.

Chapter Objectives Revisited

1. Understand the nature of a firm's human resource management practices.

   - HRM preselection practices: HR planning and job analysis
   - HRM selection practices: Recruitment and selection
   - HRM postselection practices: Training, performance appraisal, compensation, and productivity improvement programs
   - HRM practices impacted by external factors: These factors include legal and environmental issues, workplace justice laws, union influences, safety and health concerns, and international influences.

2. Understand the roles played by line managers and human resource professionals in the human resource management process.

   - HR professionals: Establish HRM procedures and methods, monitor/evaluate HRM practices, and advise/assist managers on HRM-related matters.
   - Line managers: Implement HRM practices and provide input to HR professionals.

3. Understand what competitive advantage is and how companies can achieve it.

   - A firm gains a competitive advantage when it develops a superior marketplace position relative to its competition.
   - It is achieved through cost leadership (lowering production costs relative to output) and product differentiation (providing a service or product that is preferred by buyers).

4. Understand how a firm's human resource management practices can help it gain a competitive advantage.

   - Directly, by increasing the ratio of the number of units produced to the total cost of production
   - Indirectly, by causing employee-centered outcomes that trigger organization-centered outcomes, which, in turn, create a competitive advantage

5. Understand why competitive advantage gained from human resource management practices is likely to be sustained over time.

   - HRM practices are not visible to competitors.
   - Even when visible, the impact of an HRM practice may not be as favorable when used in a different organizational setting.

Review Questions

Note: You can find the correct answers to these questions by taking the quiz and then submitting your answers in the Online Edition. The program will automatically score your submission. If you miss a question, the program will provide the correct answer, a rationale for the answer, and the section number in the chapter where the topic is discussed.

1. The human resource management function

   a. is concerned with ensuring that a firm's human resources have the land, capital, and equipment needed to perform their jobs effectively.
   b. helps an organization deal effectively with its people during the various phases of the employment cycle—preselection, selection, and postselection.
   c. is necessary only in those organizations where labor-management relations are strained.
   d. is irrelevant in an age of rapidly changing work processes.

2. Human resource planning has as its primary goal

   a. gathering, analyzing, and documenting information about jobs.
   b. locating and attracting job applicants.
   c. helping managers anticipate and meet the changing need for human resources.
   d. measuring the adequacy of an employee's job performance.

3. Unions are most likely to influence company policies regarding

   a. human resource planning, job analysis, and recruitment.
   b. discipline, promotions, and grievances.
   c. international human resource management.
   d. strategic planning and resource allocation.

4. Which statement best describes the relationship between line management and HR professionals?

   a. HR professionals focus more on developing human resource programs; line managers are more involved in implementing those programs.

   b. HR professionals are solely responsible for evaluating programs designed to manage human resources.

   c. Line management requires the services of the HR professional only infrequently.

   d. Line management focuses more on developing human resource programs; the HR professional is more involved in implementing programs.

5. A competitive advantage is defined in the text as

   a. a demonstrated willingness to take on all competitors in the marketplace.

   b. hiring a workforce that has a high need for achievement.

   c. achieving a superior marketplace position relative to one's competition.

   d. organizational self-confidence.

6. Product differentiation can offer a firm a competitive advantage because

   a. it allows a firm to offer a unique product not being offered by competitors.

   b. it can reduce a product's cost per unit.

   c. it reduces a firm's dependence on one supplier for raw materials.

   d. imitating a competitor's strategy is the surest way to be competitive.

7. The use of HRM practices can promote a sustained competitive advantage because

   a. being the first to institute an innovative HR practice discourages a firm's competition.

   b. HR practices cannot be imitated.

   c. people are a firm's most valuable resource.

   d. the organizational environment in which innovative HR practices are implemented can rarely be duplicated.

8. Organizational citizenship concerns

   a. an employee's willingness to engage in work behaviors that are not usually specified in a job description.

   b. the relative strength of an employee's identification with and involvement in a particular organization.

   c. the favorableness of an employee's attitude toward his or her job.

   d. the tendency of an organization to be involved in the civic affairs of the community in which it resides.

9. Which of the following pairs of HRM practices is most likely to influence employee motivation?

   a. job analysis and HR planning

   b. selection and productivity improvement programs

   c. training and safety and health programs

   d. Motivation is one of the few variables that cannot be improved using HR practices.

10. An employee is overheard saying "I think the company is doing the right thing by introducing this new product line. I hope I get the chance to work on it." This statement most likely reflects the employee's

    a. organizational commitment.

    b. organizational citizenship.

    c. job satisfaction.

    d. self-efficacy.

Discussion Questions

1. Define human resource management.
2. Why are HR planning and job analysis considered preselection HRM practices?
3. What are the external factors that affect the practice of HRM? Choose one external factor and explain how it affects HRM practices.
4. Describe the roles played by a firm's HR professionals with respect to HRM.
5. What is the line manager's role in the area of HRM?
6. Define the following terms: competitive advantage, cost leadership, and product differentiation.
   Describe how cost leadership and product differentiation can create a competitive advantage.
7. Describe how effective HRM practices can ensure a competent workforce.
8. Choose two organization-centered outcomes included in the model and show how each is influenced by employee-centered outcomes.
9. The chapter states that the impact of HRM practices on competitive advantage is likely to be sustained. Explain.

Experiential Exercises

Do These Practices Enhance Competitive Advantage?

Overview

The class will evaluate the 16 HRM practices suggested by Pfeffer in the context of the model linking HRM practices to competitive advantage.

Steps

1. Divide the class into small groups.
2. Your instructor will assign one or more of the 16 HRM practices to each group.
3. Groups should prepare themselves to discuss the following issues: (a) What impact do you think this practice would have on competitive advantage? (b) Using the HRM-Competitive Advantage Model, explain how the HRM practice would affect the various components of the model (e.g., competence, motivation, etc.).

What HRM Practices Contribute to Competitive Advantage?

Overview

The class will be asked to discuss their own experiences as customers in order to gain an appreciation of how HRM practices can create or hinder product differentiation.

Steps

1. Choose an organization (e.g., restaurant, department store, auto repair) with which you have done business. Pick one that you either liked very much or disliked very much.
2. When called upon, give the name and type of organization and explain why you liked or disliked it.
3. In your estimation, how have the firm's HRM practices contributed to the positive or negative experience that you had? For example, if you chose a restaurant because of its friendly and efficient service, describe the possible role played by the restaurant's HRM practices in producing this service (e.g., good selection of servers; thorough training program; effective performance appraisal system).

The Manager's HRM Role

Overview

Each class member will interview a manager about one of his or her HRM experiences in order to gain a better understanding of the manager's HRM role.

Steps

1. Interview a person holding a management position. Questions should focus on one specific incident dealing with the process the manager followed when performing one of the following tasks:
   a. Dealing with a specific discrimination complaint filed by (or threatened to be filed by) an employee
   b. Filling a specific position opening in the department/unit
   c. Orienting/training/mentoring a newly hired employee
   d. Evaluating the job performance of an employee and giving that employee feedback
   e. Disciplining and/or discharging an employee for misbehavior
   f. Dealing with a safety violation
   g. Dealing with an employee grievance in a union environment

2. Ask the manager to describe the situation (e.g., if performance appraisal were the topic, the manager should briefly describe the appraisal system used by the company and give some background about the particular employee being evaluated).

3. Ask these specific questions during the interview:

   a. What major challenges did you face in this situation? Example: "The person being evaluated had very good technical skills, but poor interpersonal skills. I had to decide how low to rate him on the latter skills and find some nonthreatening way to make him aware of this weakness and help him overcome it."

   b. How did you handle the situation?

   c. What were the positive and/or negative consequences of your actions?

   d. In retrospect, would you handle the situation differently if you had to do it over again? If yes, how? If no, why not?

4. Summarize the manager's answers in an oral presentation. At the conclusion of your presentation, state your opinion about how well the manager handled the incident.

   a. If handled well, describe how competitive advantage was enhanced.

   b. If handled poorly, describe how competitive advantage was hindered.

References

1. Walker, J.W. (1980). *Human Resource Planning.* New York: McGraw-Hill.
2. Ibid.
3. Porter, A.A., and Murman, K.F. (1983). A survey of employer union-avoidance practices. *Personnel Administrator,* November, 66–71.
4. Martinez, M.N. (1997). Issues and trends in personnel. *HRMagazine,* August, 89–96.
5. Reed, R., and Defillippi, R.J. (1990). Causal ambiguity, barriers to imitation, and sustainable competitive advantage. *Academy of Management Review, 15* (1), 88–102.
6. Ibid.
7. Steffy, B.D., and Maurer, S.D. (1988). Conceptualizing and measuring the economic effectiveness of human resource activities. *Academy of Management Review, 13* (2), 271–286.
8. McConnell, C.R., and Brue, S.L. (1993). *Economics: Principles, Problems, and Policies* (12th ed.). New York: McGraw-Hill.
9. Porter, M.E. (1985). *Competitive Advantage: Creating and Sustaining Superior Performance.* New York: The Free Press.
10. Caudron, S. (2001). How HR drives profits. *Workforce,* December, 26–31.
11. Huselid, M.A. (1994). Documenting HR's effect on company performance. *HRMagazine,* January, 79–85.
12. Huselid, M.A., Jackson, S.E., and Schuler, R.S. (1997). Technical and strategic human resource management effectiveness as determinants of firm performance. *Academy of Management Journal, 40* (1), 171–188.
13. Caudron. How HR drives profits.
14. Pfeffer, J. (1994). *Competitive Advantage through People.* Boston: Harvard Business School Press.
15. Klein, H.J., and Weaver, N.A. (2000). The effectiveness of an organizational-level orientation training program in the socialization of new hires. *Personnel Psychology, 53* (1), 47–66.
16. Koys, D.J. (2001). The effects of employee satisfaction, organizational citizenship, and turnover on organizational effectiveness: A unit-level, longitudinal study. *Personnel Psychology, 54* (1), 101–114.
17. Gatewood, R.D., and Field, H.S. (2001). *Human Resource Selection* (5th ed.). Fort Worth: Harcourt.
18. Mollica, K. (2004). Perceptions of fairness. *HRMagazine,* June, 169–175.
19. Laabs, J. (1999). The HR side of Sears' comeback. *Workforce,* March, 24–29.
20. Iverson, R.D., and Roy, P. (1994). A causal model of behavioral commitment: Evidence from a study of Australian blue-collar employees. *Journal of Management, 20* (1), 15–41.
21. Kaye, B., and Joran-Evans, S. (2002). Retention in tough times. *Training and Development,* January, *56* (1), 32–37.
22. Batt, R. (2002). Managing customer services: Human resources practices, quit rates, and sales growth. *Academy of Management Journal, 45* (3), 587–597.
23. Podsakoff, P.M., Ahearne, M., and MacKenzie, S.B. (1997). Organizational citizenship and the quality of group work performance. *Journal of Applied Psychology, 82* (2), 262–270.
24. Koys. The effects of employee satisfaction.
25. Caudron. How HR drives profits.
26. Thaler-Carter, R.E. (1997). EMA model defines cost-per-hire as part of staffing performance. *HRMagazine,* December, 51–55.
27. Cascio, W.F. (1999). *Costing Human Resources: The Financial Impact of Behavior in Organizations* (4th ed.). Cincinnati: South-Western.
28. Micco, L. (1998). Effective HR management helps retain customers, grow business. Http://www.shrm.org/hrnews/articles/060898.htm (HR News Online).
29. Eyres, P.S. (1989). Legally defensible performance appraisal systems. *Personnel Journal, 68,* 58–62.
30. Speizer, I. (2004). Shopper's special. *Workforce Management,* September, 51–54.
31. Johnson, M.W. (2004). Harassment and discrimination prevention training: What the law requires. *Labor Law Journal, 55* (2), 119–130.
32. Kiger, P.J. (2002). Why customer satisfaction starts with HR. *Workforce,* May, 26–32.
33. Ibid.
34. Feinburg, R.A., Meoli-Stanton, J., and Gable, M. (1996). Employee rejection and acceptance letters and their unintended consequences on image, self-concept, and intentions. *Journal of Business and Psychology, 11* (1), 63–71.
35. Myler, L. (1997). New study will help you benchmark productivity. *Workforce,* November, 53–54.
36. Pfeffer. *Competitive Advantage.*

Understanding the Legal and Environmental Context of HRM

Chapter Two

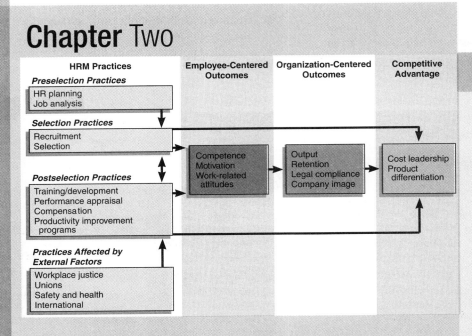

HRM Practices	Employee-Centered Outcomes	Organization-Centered Outcomes	Competitive Advantage
Preselection Practices			
HR planning / Job analysis			
Selection Practices			
Recruitment / Selection	Competence / Motivation / Work-related attitudes	Output / Retention / Legal compliance / Company image	Cost leadership / Product differentiation
Postselection Practices			
Training/development / Performance appraisal / Compensation / Productivity improvement programs			
Practices Affected by External Factors			
Workplace justice / Unions / Safety and health / International			

Key Terms

affirmative action
affirmative action plan (AAP)
Age Discrimination in Employment Act (ADEA)
Americans with Disabilities Act (ADA)
BFOQ defense
Civil Rights Act (CRA) of 1964
Civil Rights Act (CRA) of 1991
disparate impact
disparate treatment
downsizing
equal employment opportunity (EEO)
flextime
four-fifths rule

glass ceiling
Immigration Reform and Control Act (IRCA)
job sharing
McDonnell-Douglas test
mixed-motive cases
organizational restructuring
preferential treatment
Pregnancy Discrimination Act (PDA)
prima facie case
protected classifications
protected groups
telecommuting
utilization analysis

Chapter Objectives

Upon completion of this chapter, you will be able to:

- Understand the nature of the equal employment opportunity laws and how the courts interpret them.

- Understand the nature of affirmative action programs and how they should be implemented.

- Describe the impact of cultural diversity on organizations and how it may be successfully managed.

- Explain the changing nature of work and how this phenomenon impacts HRM practices.

- Describe the impact that the occurrence of mergers and takeovers has on HRM practices.

- Understand the causes of downsizing, its potential pitfalls, and how downsizing efforts should be managed.

As indicated in Chapter 1, "Human Resource Management and Competitive Advantage," legal and environmental issues significantly impact the practice of HRM. We now offer a more detailed account of these issues and discuss how they affect a firm's HRM practices.

2-1 Legal Issues in the Workplace

Legal issues permeate almost all aspects of HRM, from the initial recruitment and selection of applicants to their discharge, retirement, or layoff. HRM laws address a variety of issues. Some pertain to specific employment practices, such as the administration of polygraph tests or the need to offer medical or family-based leaves. Others deal with broader issues, such as employment discrimination, safety, privacy, and employees' rights to due process.

Throughout this text, these laws are discussed in conjunction with the HRM practices they affect. For instance, safety laws are discussed in Chapter 13 and privacy laws in Chapter 11. In this section, we focus on laws that deal with the issue of employment discrimination. This issue receives coverage throughout the book (e.g., discrimination in hiring is discussed in Chapter 6; discrimination in pay is discussed in Chapter 9; and discrimination in the day-to-day treatment of employees is discussed in Chapter 11). However, the topic of discrimination is so pervasive and the interpretation of antidiscrimination laws is so complex that we must first study and understand the "basics." What do the laws state, and how are they interpreted? Our discussion centers on two discrimination-related topics: equal employment opportunity and affirmative action.

2-1a Equal Employment Opportunity

As part of Lyndon Johnson's attempt in the 1960s to create the "Great Society," Congress passed an avalanche of legislation aimed at ensuring **equal employment opportunity (EEO)** in the workplace. These laws were specifically designed to eradicate certain types of employment discrimination that had been all too common—discrimination based on race, color, sex, religion, national origin, age, and disability. These categories are referred to as **protected classifications** because they are protected from discrimination by EEO laws. Subcategories of people within each protected classification are referred to as **protected groups.** For example, "male" and "female" are the protected groups within the protected classification of "sex."

EEO legislation affords protection to all protected groups within a protected classification, not just the minority groups. Thus, discrimination aimed at a man is just as

equal employment opportunity (EEO)
Providing equal treatment to all applicants and employees regardless of their race, color, sex, religion, national origin, age, or disability.

protected classifications
Categories of people (e.g., race, sex) who are legally protected from discrimination in the workplace.

protected groups
Subcategories of people within each protected classification (e.g., male, female).

25

> **EXHIBIT 2-1**   EEO Laws
>
> - *1964—Civil Rights Act (Title VII)*   Prohibits employment discrimination on the basis of race, color, religion, sex, and national origin. It covers most employers of 15 or more employees.
> - *1967—Age Discrimination in Employment Act*   Prohibits discrimination based on age. It protects workers 40 years of age and older, and applies to companies of 20 or more employees.
> - *1978—Pregnancy Discrimination Act*   An amendment to the 1964 Civil Rights Act, it prohibits discrimination because of a woman's pregnancy-related condition.
> - *1986—Immigration Reform and Control Act*   Prohibits employers from knowingly hiring aliens who are not authorized to work in the United States. It also prohibits discrimination based on national origin or citizenship.
> - *1990—Americans with Disabilities Act*   Prohibits discrimination based on an employee's disability and applies to most organizations employing at least 15 people.
> - *1991—Civil Rights Act of 1991*   An amendment to the Civil Rights Act of 1964, it extends the rights of claimants to receive punitive damages. It also provides a detailed description of the evidence needed to prove a discrimination claim.

unlawful as that aimed at a woman. The lone exception to this rule concerns the use of affirmative action programs, which, under certain circumstances, allow employers to treat members of certain protected groups preferentially. We discuss this issue later in the chapter.

EEO Laws

The major EEO laws are summarized in Exhibit 2-1. Each prohibits discrimination based on an individual's protected classification. These laws differ from one another primarily in terms of the specific protected classifications covered.

Civil Rights Act of 1964 (Title VII)

Civil Rights Act (CRA) of 1964   A law that prohibits employment based on race, color, sex, religion, and national origin.

Title VII of the **Civil Rights Act (CRA) of 1964** covers organizations that employ 15 or more workers for at least 20 weeks during the year. This law prohibits discrimination that is based on the protected classifications of race, color, religion, national origin, and sex. Specifically, the law states that:

> It shall be unlawful employment practice for an employer to fail or refuse to hire or discharge any individual, or otherwise to discriminate against any individual with respect to his compensation, terms, conditions, or privileges of employment, because of such individual's race, color, religion, sex, or national origin.

The CRA of 1964 is probably the most valuable tool that employees have for remedying workplace discrimination because it covers the greatest number of protected classifications. If a court determines that discrimination has occurred, the victim is entitled to relief in the form of legal costs and back pay (i.e., the salary the person would have been receiving had no discrimination occurred). For instance, let's say that a woman sues a company for rejecting her application for a $25,000 per year construction job because the company unlawfully excludes women from this job. The litigation process takes two years and, ultimately, the court rules in the applicant's favor. To remedy this discrimination, the court would require the company to pay her legal fees and grant her $50,000 in back pay (two years' salary).

The Civil Rights Act of 1964 has had an enormous impact on the HRM practices of many companies, forcing them to take a close look at the way they hire, promote, award pay raises, and discipline their employees. As a result of this self-scrutiny, many firms have changed their practices, making them more systematic and objective. For instance, most firms now require their supervisors to provide detailed documentation to justify the fairness of their disciplinary actions, and many firms are now more cautious with regard to their use of employment tests that restrict the employment opportunities for certain protected groups.

Civil Rights Act of 1991

As the 1990s approached, the impact of the CRA of 1964 began to fade. A number of Supreme Court decisions in the mid- to late 1980s made discrimination claims more difficult for employees to substantiate. To put more "teeth" into the law, Congress amended it by enacting the **Civil Rights Act (CRA) of 1991.** Its major provisions are summarized in Exhibit 2-2.

This 1991 amendment expands the list of remedies that may be awarded in a discrimination case; the employer now has more to lose if found guilty of discrimination. In addition to legal fees and back pay, an employer may now be charged with punitive and compensatory damages (for future financial losses, emotional pain, suffering, inconvenience, mental anguish, and loss of enjoyment of life). The "cap" for these damages ranges from $50,000 to $300,000, depending on the size of the company. Employees are entitled to such damages in cases where discrimination practices are "engaged in with malice or reckless indifference to the legal rights of the aggrieved individual" (e.g., the employer is aware that serious violations are occurring, but does nothing to rectify them).

Moreover, the CRA of 1991 adds additional bite to the 1964 law by providing a more detailed description of the evidence needed to prove a discrimination claim, making such claims easier to prove. This provision is discussed in more detail later in the chapter.

The CRA of 1991 also differs from the 1964 law by addressing the issue of **mixed-motive cases.** This type of case is one in which an employment decision, such as hiring or promotion, is based partly on a "legitimate" motive and partly on a discriminatory one. For instance, a company rejects the application of a woman because she behaves in an "unladylike manner": She is "too aggressive for a woman, wears no makeup, and swears like a man." The company is concerned that she would offend its customers. The employer's motives are thus mixed. Its concern about offending customers is a legitimate motive; its stereotyped view of how a "lady" should behave is a discriminatory one.

The CRA of 1991 states that mixed-motive decisions are unlawful. That is, a hiring practice is illegal when a candidate's protected group membership is a factor affecting an employment decision, even if other, more legitimate factors are also considered. Thus, if the "unladylike" applicant can prove to the court that her rejection was based, at least in part, on the employer's stereotyped view of how a woman should behave, she would win the case.

Pregnancy Discrimination Act of 1978

The **Pregnancy Discrimination Act (PDA)** of 1978 amends the CRA of 1964 by specifically including discrimination against women based on pregnancy, childbirth, or related medical conditions. It states that employees who are unable to perform their jobs because of a pregnancy-related condition must be treated in the same manner as employees who are temporarily disabled for other reasons.

A review of PDA court decisions published in 2003–2004 uncovered the following types of cases:[1]

- The employee was fired because her pregnancy caused excessive absences.

- The employee was fired, or the applicant was rejected, because her pregnancy was *expected* to cause excessive absences, especially during critical business periods.

- The employee was fired because she was expected to become less committed to her job once the baby was born.

- The employee was not reinstated to her old job following maternity leave because her replacement performed the job better.

- The employee was fired because her pregnancy prevented her from performing certain important duties.

Civil Rights Act (CRA) of 1991 An amendment to the Civil Rights Act of 1964. Its passage made discrimination claims less difficult for employees to substantiate.

mixed-motive cases A form of employment discrimination in which an employer bases an employment decision partly on a legitimate motive and partly on a discriminatory one.

Pregnancy Discrimination Act (PDA) A law stating that firms may not discriminate against employees on the basis of pregnancy, childbirth, or related medical conditions.

EXHIBIT 2-2	Summary of Main Provisions of the Civil Rights Act of 1991

I. **Purposes**

    A. To provide appropriate remedies for intentional discrimination and unlawful harassment in the workplace

    B. To codify the concepts of "business necessity" and "job related"

    C. To provide statutory guidelines for the adjudication of disparate impact suits under Title VII of the CRA

    D. To expand the scope of relevant civil rights statutes in order to provide adequate protection to victims of discrimination

II. **Damages in Cases of Intentional Discrimination**

    A. Right of Recovery

        1. In an action of intentional discrimination (disparate treatment) filed under the CRA of 1964, the Vocational Rehabilitation Act (VRA), or the Americans with Disabilities Act (ADA), the complaining party may recover punitive, as well as compensatory, damages.

        2. Punitive damages would be allowed if the discriminatory practices were engaged in with malice or reckless indifference to the legal rights of the aggrieved individual.

    B. Limitation

        1. Compensatory damages are awarded for future financial losses, emotional pain, suffering, inconvenience, mental anguish, and loss of enjoyment of life.

        2. Punitive damages are awarded for punishment.

        3. The total damages shall not exceed

            — $50,000 for firms employing 15–100 employees

            — $100,000 for 101–200 employees

            — $200,000 for 201–500 employees

            — $300,000 for 500+ employees

    C. Jury Trial—Either party may demand a trial by jury to determine the appropriate compensatory or punitive damages.

III. **Burden of Proof in Disparate Impact Cases**

    A. A disparate impact case of discrimination is established when either of the two following conditions is met:

        1. It is demonstrated that a company uses a particular employment practice that causes disparate impact and fails to demonstrate that the challenged practice is job related for the position in question and consistent with business necessity.

        2. The complaining party suggests an alternative employment practice (i.e., one that has less adverse impact than the challenged practice, but is equally job related) and the employer refuses to adopt it.

    B. A showing of job relatedness and business necessity is not required if the employer is able to demonstrate that the challenged practice does not cause adverse impact.

    C. The complaining party must be able to demonstrate that each particular challenged employment practice causes a disparate impact. The lone exception to this requirement is when the complaining party is able to demonstrate that the elements of the company's decision-making process are not capable of separation for analysis. In this case, the decision-making process may be analyzed as one employment process.

    D. The business necessity defense may not be used by an employer in a disparate treatment case.

    E. A rule barring the employment of individuals who are currently using or possessing illegal controlled substances is lawful unless such a rule is adopted or applied with the intent to discriminate because of color, race, religion, sex, or national origin.

IV. **Prohibition against Discriminatory Use of Test Scores**

It shall be unlawful for an employer to adjust the scores of, use different cutoff scores for, or otherwise alter the results of employment-related tests on the basis of race, color, religion, sex, or national origin.

V. **Mixed-Motive Cases of Disparate Treatment**

    A. A hiring practice is unlawful when the complaining party is able to demonstrate that race, color, sex, religion, or national origin was a motivating factor in the employment decision, even though other factors also motivated the practice.

    B. If the employer is able to demonstrate that it would have taken the same action in the absence of the impermissible motivating factor, the court will not award damages or issue an order requiring any admission, reinstatement, hiring, promotion, or payment. It may, however, grant attorney's fees and costs attributable to the suit.

In their decisions, the courts ruled that employers are not required to grant pregnant women preferential treatment. For instance, pregnant employees must meet the same attendance standards as the other employees. However, employers violate the PDA when they base employment decisions on stereotyped views regarding pregnancy, such as the view that pregnant women will become less committed to their jobs once their babies are born.

Immigration Reform and Control Act of 1986

The **Immigration Reform and Control Act (IRCA)** of 1986 prohibits discrimination based on national origin and citizenship. Specifically, the law states that employers of four or more employees cannot discriminate in the selection of any individual (other than an illegal alien) because of that person's national origin or citizenship status.

In addition to being an antidiscrimination law, this act makes it unlawful to knowingly hire an unauthorized alien. At the time of hiring, an employer must require proof that the person offered the job is not an illegal alien.

Immigration Reform and Control Act (IRCA) A law that prohibits discrimination based on national origin and citizenship.

Age Discrimination in Employment Act of 1967

The **Age Discrimination in Employment Act (ADEA)** of 1967 is intended to protect "older workers" (i.e., ages 40 and older) from age discrimination. The ADEA, which applies to nearly all employers of 20 or more employees, promotes the employment of older persons based on their ability, rather than age.[2]

Note that the ADEA protects only "older" individuals from discrimination; people under 40 are not protected. The act also prohibits employers from giving preference to individuals within the 40 or older group. For instance, an employer may not discriminate against a 50-year-old by giving preference to a 40-year-old.

Age Discrimination in Employment Act (ADEA) A law that protects "older workers" (i.e., ages 40 and over) from age discrimination in the workplace.

Americans with Disabilities Act of 1990 (Title I)

The **Americans with Disabilities Act (ADA)** of 1990 "provides a clear and comprehensive national mandate for the elimination of discrimination against individuals with disabilities." The employment implications of the act, which are delineated in Titles I (private section) and II (public sector) of the ADA, affect nearly all organizations employing 15 or more workers. According to the act, an individual is considered disabled if he or she has a physical or mental impairment that substantially limits one or more of the individual's major life activities, such as walking, seeing, hearing, breathing, and learning, as well as the ability to secure or retain employment.

To win a complaint, an individual who has been denied employment because of a disability must establish that, with accommodation (if necessary), he or she is qualified to perform the essential functions of the job in question. To defend successfully against such a suit, the employer must demonstrate that, even with reasonable accommodation, the candidate could not perform the job satisfactorily, or it must demonstrate that the accommodation would impose an undue hardship. The ADA defines "undue hardship" as those accommodations that require significant difficulty to implement or significant expense on the part of the employer.

An example of an ADA case would be one in which an employee is fired because of frequent absences caused by a particular disability. The employee may argue that the employer failed to offer a reasonable accommodation, such as a transfer to a part-time position. The employer, on the other hand, may argue that such an action would pose an undue hardship in that the creation of such a position would be too costly. ADA issues are discussed in greater detail in Chapter 6, "Selecting Applicants," and in Chapter 13, "Meeting Employee Safety and Health Needs."

Americans with Disabilities Act (ADA) A 1990 law that prohibits employment discrimination based on a person's disability.

Interpreting EEO Laws

It is clear from the preceding discussion that an employer may not discriminate on the basis of an individual's protected group membership. But exactly how does one determine whether a particular act is discriminatory? Consider the following examples:

Case 1: A woman was denied employment as a police officer because she failed a strength test. During the past year, that test had screened out 90 percent of all female applicants, but only 30 percent of all male applicants.

Case 2: A woman was denied employment as a construction worker because she failed to meet the company's requirement that all workers be at least 5'8" and weigh at least 160 pounds. During the past year, 70 percent of the female applicants, but only 20 percent of the male applicants, had been rejected because of this requirement.

Case 3: A female accountant was fired despite satisfactory performance ratings. The manager claims she violated company policy by moonlighting for another firm. However, the manager was heard making the comment, "Women don't belong in accounting, anyway."

Case 4: A male manager fired his female secretary because he thought she was too plain looking, replacing her with a woman who, in his opinion, is much prettier.

We know that the Civil Rights Acts of 1964 and 1991 prohibit sex discrimination. However, knowing that sex discrimination is unlawful provides very little guidance in these cases. For instance, how important are the intentions of the employer? How important are the outcomes of the employment decision? In the first two cases, the employers' intentions seem to be noble—the male and female applicants were judged according to the same standards. However, the outcomes of the employment decisions were clearly disadvantageous to the women. In the third case, the employer's intentions appear questionable, because the manager obviously has a bias against female accountants. However, the outcome seems fair. After all, she did violate the company policy. In the fourth case, the employer's intentions are clearly biased, but the outcome did not adversely affect women in the sense that another woman replaced the employee.

To determine whether an EEO law has been violated, one must know how the courts view the concept of *discrimination.* In actuality, the courts recognize two different types of discrimination: intentional and unintentional.

Intentional Discrimination

disparate treatment
A form of employment discrimination in which employers treat people unfairly because of their membership in a protected group.

Referred to as **disparate treatment** discrimination, this type of discrimination is defined as treating people unfairly based on their membership in a protected group.[3] For example, the firing of the female accountant in Case 3 is an example of disparate treatment because the discharge was allegedly triggered by the supervisor's bias toward female accountants. However, the employers' actions in Cases 1 and 2 would not be classified as disparate treatment because there was no apparent intent to discriminate. The employers judged all applicants according to the same criteria; it just so happened that fewer women than men met those criteria.

Although disparate treatment is often the result of an employer's bias or prejudice toward a particular group, it may also occur as the result of trying to "protect" the group members' interests. For instance, consider the employer who refuses to hire women for dangerous jobs in order to protect their safety. Although the intention might be noble, this employer would be just as guilty of discrimination as one with less noble intentions.

What about Case 4, where a secretary was fired for being "too plain"? Would this be a viable case of disparate treatment? The answer is "no" if the bias displayed by the manager was directed at appearance, not sex. Appearance is not a protected classification. The answer is "yes" if the appearance standard were being applied only to women; that is, the company fired women but not men on the basis of their looks.

Unintentional Discrimination

Called **disparate impact**, this type of discrimination is defined as any practice without business justification that has unequal consequences for people of different protected groups.[4] Disparate impact discrimination would occur, for instance, if an arbitrary selection practice (e.g., an irrelevant employment test) resulted in the selection of a disproportionately low number of females or African-Americans.

The key notion here is "arbitrary selection practice." If the selection practice were relevant or job related, rather than arbitrary, the employer's practice would be legal, regardless of its disproportionate outcome. For example, despite the fact that the female applicants were rejected at a higher rate than male applicants in Cases 1 and 2, the employer's actions would still be lawful if the selection criteria (e.g., the strength test and height and weight requirements) were deemed to be job related. Later in the chapter, we discuss how the courts make such a determination. As it turns out, strength tests are much more likely to be considered job related than height and weight requirements. Thus, the employer would probably win Case 1 and lose Case 2.

disparate impact A form of employment discrimination in which an employment practice that is not job related has unequal consequences for people of different protected groups.

Discrimination and the Courts

Ultimately, the courts decide whether a specific action of an employer is lawful. Employers must thus understand the decision-making process of the courts in order to be able to gauge the legality of their HRM practices.

When hearing a discrimination case, the courts first require that the plaintiff (i.e., the employee or applicant filing the discrimination complaint) establish a ***prima facie*** **case** of discrimination. *Prima facie* is a Latin phrase meaning "first appearance." To establish a *prima facie* case, the plaintiff must present evidence that makes the employer's actions appear discriminatory. For example, an African-American applicant who is denied a job could establish a *prima facie* case by proving that he or she is qualified for the job. At first appearance, this action seems discriminatory. Rejecting a qualified minority is exactly the kind of thing that a biased employer would do.

When a plaintiff establishes a *prima facie* case, the court does not automatically find the employer guilty. It simply means that the complainant has been able to establish the merits of his or her case sufficiently enough for the courts to agree to look into the matter further. The burden then shifts to the employer to rebut the case by presenting evidence that justifies the fairness of its actions. For instance, the employer could win its case by convincing the court that the qualified African-American was rejected because the person selected for the job was even more qualified.

prima facie **case** Established at trial when a complainant has been able to demonstrate the merits of his or her case sufficiently enough for the courts to agree to look into the matter further.

Establishing a Prima Facie *Case of Intentional Discrimination*

A *prima facie* case of disparate treatment may be established in a number of ways. The most commonly used approaches are described in the following paragraphs. The particular approach used depends on the nature of the case and the type of claim filed, that is, disparate treatment or disparate impact. A plaintiff's case can be strengthened by using more than one type of evidence.

Restricted Company Policy

A *prima facie* case of discrimination is automatically established when the plaintiff proves that the company has a formal policy that restricts the selection of an entire protected group. An example of such a policy would be one issued by a police department that states that no one over the age of 35 will be considered for the job

After rejection, the position remained open or was filled by someone who was not a member of the protected group.

Belongs to the protected group in question.

Has applied for and is qualified for the job for which the employer was seeking applicants.

Was rejected.

Meets the requirements for a *prima facie* case of discrimination.

Figure 2-1
The McDonnell-Douglas Test

of police officer. Thus, all people in the protected group of 40 and above would be barred from consideration.

Discriminatory Remarks

A plaintiff can also establish a *prima facie* case by producing evidence that certain biased remarks were made by an employer (orally or in writing) regarding the protected group in question. This type of evidence recently forced Texaco to settle a multimillion-dollar lawsuit when a group of its executives were "caught on tape" making derogatory statements about the company's African-American employees, plotting ways in which the company could prevent their promotions.

The McDonnell-Douglas Test

Plaintiffs do not always have such blatant evidence regarding an employer's intent to discriminate. For instance, suppose a 52-year-old male applicant is rejected for a job and believes that his advanced years triggered this rejection. However, there is no specific company policy banning older workers, nor have any derogatory comments been made about older workers. How would this individual establish a *prima facie* case?

The Supreme Court has developed a test (in the case of *McDonnell-Douglas v. Green*) that is used to infer the presence of discriminatory intent when more direct evidence of discrimination is lacking. Called the **McDonnell-Douglas test** (see Figure 2-1), it requires the plaintiff to show that he or she:

McDonnell-Douglas test
A test used by the courts to assess the merits of a *prima facie* case of disparate treatment when "smoking gun" evidence is lacking.

1. Belongs to the protected group in question.
2. Has applied for and is qualified for the job for which the employer was seeking applicants.
3. Was rejected.
4. After rejection, the position remained open or was filled by someone who was not a member of that protected group.

The courts modify this test when employees contest decisions that do not involve hiring. For instance, when contesting a discharge decision, steps 2–4 are modified in the following way:

2. Has performed the job satisfactorily.
3. Was discharged.
4. After the discharge, the position remained open or was filled by someone who was not a member of that protected group.

The McDonnell-Douglas test is further modified when applied to age discrimination cases by changing step 4 to read, ". . . the position remained open or was filled by someone who is substantially younger than the claimant." The 52-year-old male in question could thus establish a *prima facie* case by proving that he was qualified for the position and yet it was left open or filled by a person who was substantially younger than him, even in cases where the replacement is over 40.

Establishing a *Prima Facie Case—Unintentional Discrimination*

In the disparate treatment cases described in the previous paragraphs, the courts seek evidence of employer bias. In disparate impact cases, bias is not an issue. Therefore, the courts seek a different type of evidence. Specifically, the courts try to determine whether the HR decision being contested differentially impacts the various protected groups. The most common test of this effect is referred to as the **four-fifths rule.**

The Four-Fifths Rule

The four-fifths rule helps the courts determine whether between-group differences in hiring rates are large enough to be important. It is calculated by comparing the hiring rate of the "disadvantaged" protected group (i.e., the group claiming discrimination) with the rate of the "advantaged" group. (If there is more than one advantaged group, the group with the highest passing rate is used for comparison purposes.) A *prima facie* case of discrimination is established when the hiring rate of the former group is less than four-fifths of the latter group. To determine whether the hiring rate of a protected group satisfies the four-fifths rule, an employer should identify the protected group with the highest hiring rate and multiply that rate by .8. For instance, if 20 white males applied for a job and 10 were selected, the hiring rate would be 50 percent. Fifty percent multiplied by .8 is 40 percent. The four-fifths rule would be violated if any other protected group's hiring rate were less than 40 percent. For example, a *prima facie* case of sex discrimination would be established if the hiring rate for men were 80 percent, while the rate for women were 50 percent. In this instance, the needed hiring rate for women would be 80 × .8, or 64 percent, well above the actual rate of 50 percent.

four-fifths rule A test used by the courts to assess the merits of a *prima facie* case of disparate impact. It is calculated by comparing the passing rate of the "disadvantaged" protected group with the rate of the "advantaged" group.

Rebutting a *Prima Facie Case—Intentional Discrimination*

If the plaintiff succeeds in establishing a *prima facie* case of disparate treatment, the burden shifts to the employer to rebut that case. The type of evidence necessary to achieve this aim depends on the nature of the *prima facie* case.

Restricted Company Policy

When the employer has a policy that excludes an entire protected group, its only viable option is the use of a **BFOQ defense.** The term *BFOQ* refers to "bona fide occupational qualification." When using a BFOQ defense, the employer argues that it purposely discriminated against all members of a protected group for one of the following four reasons (see Figure 2-2):

BFOQ defense When using a BFOQ defense, the employer argues that it purposely discriminated against all members of a protected group because they lack the bona fide occupational qualifications for the position in question.

1. *All or nearly all:* All or nearly all of the members of that group are incapable of performing the job in question.
2. *Authenticity:* To be "authentic," the employer must limit its hiring to members of a particular protected group, thus excluding all others. For example, an "authentic" Japanese restaurant would use a BFOQ defense to justify its practice of hiring only Japanese servers. Victoria's Secret would use this defense to justify its exclusion of male models. (Men would not look "authentic" wearing women's undergarments.)
3. *Propriety:* It would be improper to hire members of one or the other sex for a particular job (e.g., hiring a woman to work as an attendant in a men's rest room).

All or nearly all: A man cannot work as a wet nurse.

Authenticity: Only women can model women's clothes.

Figure 2-2
The BFOQ Defense

Propriety: It is more fitting to hire only men to staff a men's restroom.

Safety: Hiring a pilot over 60 years of age might pose a safety risk to himself or herself and passengers because of diminishing skills.

4. *Safety:* The employment of an older worker would put the worker or others at risk. For example, commercial airlines will not employ pilots over the age of 60 because such pilots pose a greater risk of causing an accident than do younger pilots.

At one time, employers attempted to justify the exclusion of women from jobs traditionally held by men by using the all or nearly all rule. For example, women were often excluded from jobs that require above-average strength (e.g., police officer, firefighter, construction worker) because women are generally weaker than men. The courts, however, do not condone this type of BFOQ defense. They mandate that each applicant be evaluated according to his or her ability.

Employers' attempts to invoke the other BFOQ defenses (authenticity, propriety, and safety) have occasionally been successful. Hooter's restaurant, for instance, successfully used the "authenticity" defense to justify its policy of excluding male servers; the restaurant claimed that the use of scantily dressed female servers was essential for maintaining its image as a "sexy" restaurant. The "safety" defense has been successfully used in age-related cases where firms were able to prove that safety-related skills (e.g., vision or reaction time) diminish with age and that employing people over the maximum age would thus pose a safety risk to themselves or others.[5] We discuss this issue further in Chapter 6, "Selecting Applicants."

Discriminatory Remarks

Discriminatory remarks are considered strong evidence of bias. If a plaintiff can prove that such remarks have been made, the employer will lose the case unless it can successfully argue that the remarks were not very derogatory (e.g., calling a 62-year-old employee "Good *old* Charley"). The employer can also try to argue that the person who made the remarks had no influence on the hiring decision.

The McDonnell-Douglas Test

When a *prima facie* case has been established on the basis of the McDonnell-Douglas test, the employer's burden is to present evidence showing that its employment decision was based on legitimate, nondiscriminatory reasons. For instance, the employer could show that an applicant's rejection was due to the fact that the selected candidate was more qualified.

Once an employer has convinced a court that the reason for its employment decision was, indeed, legitimate, the plaintiff could still win the case. To do so, the plaintiff must prove that the reason offered by the employer was merely a pretext or an excuse; the "real" reason for the action was discrimination. For example, suppose an employer discharged a black employee for an unauthorized absence. Although such a reason would appear to be legitimate and nondiscriminatory, the plaintiff could prove that this reason is merely a pretext by demonstrating that several white employees had been guilty of the same infraction, and yet were not fired.

Rebutting a Prima Facie Case—Unintentional Discrimination

To defend itself against a violation of the four-fifths rule, a firm must demonstrate that the procedure in question is a business necessity. The issue of how to establish a business necessity defense is discussed in Chapter 6, "Selecting Applicants." For now, we quote the Supreme Court's decision in *Watson v. Fort Worth Bank:*[6]

> To be justified as a business necessity, employment criteria must bear more than an indirect or minimal relationship to job performance . . . the criteria must directly relate to the prospective employee's ability to perform the job effectively. *Evidence may include formal validation studies, expert testimony, and prior successful experience.* [emphasis added]

According to the CRA of 1991, when several selection devices are used, only those causing the disparate impact must be justified. For example, all applicants take a written test and are interviewed. Women do just as well as men on the test, but do more poorly on the interview. Women are thus hired at a lower rate than are men. In this instance, the employer must justify the business necessity of the interview, but not the test.

The lone exception to this rule occurs when the "elements of a respondent's decision-making process are not capable of separation for analysis, [then] the decision-making process may be analyzed as one employment practice." For example, an employer ranks each applicant by subjectively combining information derived from application blanks, interviews, and reference checks. Because the weight or importance of the separate elements cannot be specified, it is impossible to discern which selection instrument caused the disparate impact. In this instance, the employer must then justify the business necessity of each selection device.

2-1b Affirmative Action

The aim of **affirmative action** is to remedy past and current discrimination. Although the overall aim of affirmative action is thus identical to that of EEO (i.e., to advance the cause of protected groups by eliminating employment discrimination), the two approaches differ in the way they attempt to accomplish this aim. EEO initiatives are "color-blind," whereas affirmative action initiatives are "color-conscious." Affirmative action programs aim to redress past discrimination against protected classes and correct racial and gender imbalances in the workforce.[7]

affirmative action
An approach to eliminating employment discrimination by taking proactive initiatives to ensure proper minority group representation within an organization.

Affirmative action makes special provisions to recruit, train, retain, promote, or grant some other benefit to members of protected groups. To this end, an affirmative action program may actually countenance preference for an individual, based on the individual's race, sex, or other protected category. In fulfilling equal opportunity obligations, on the other hand, employers may not give preferential treatment to members of protected groups.[8]

Is Affirmative Action Legally Mandated?

In some cases, employers are legally required to institute affirmative action programs. For instance, Executive Order 11246, issued by former U.S. President Lyndon Johnson, makes such programs mandatory for all federal government contractors.

Affirmative action can also be court ordered as part of a settlement in a discrimination case. For example, the state of Alabama was ordered by the Supreme Court to select one black applicant for each white hired as a state trooper. The purpose of the decree was to rectify the effects of past discrimination that had been blatantly occurring for several years.

Most firms, however, are under no legal obligation to implement affirmative action programs. Those choosing to implement such programs do so voluntarily, believing that it makes good business sense. These firms believe that by implementing affirmative action they can (1) attract and retain a larger and better pool of applicants, (2) create a more diverse workforce, (3) avoid discrimination lawsuits, and (4) improve the firm's reputation within the community and its consumer base.

How Is Affirmative Action Implemented?

Affirmative action implementation consists of two primary steps. First, the organization conducts a utilization analysis to identify the "underutilized" protected groups within its various job categories (e.g., officials and managers, professionals, service workers, sales workers). It then develops a remedial plan that targets these underutilized groups.

Utilization Analysis

A **utilization analysis** is a statistical procedure that compares the percentage of each protected group for each job category within the organization to that in the available labor market. If the organizational percentage is less than the labor market percentage, the group is classified as being "underutilized."

For example, the percentage of professionals within the *organization* who are women would be compared to the percentage of professionals in the *available labor market* who are women. The organization would classify women as being underutilized if it discovered, for instance, that women constitute 5 percent of the firm's professionals and yet constitute 20 percent of the professionals in the available labor market.

Affirmative Action Plans

The second step is to develop an **affirmative action plan (AAP)** that targets the underutilized protected groups. An AAP is a written statement that specifies how the organization plans to increase the utilization of targeted groups. The AAP consists of three elements: goals, timetables, and action steps.

An AAP goal specifies the percentage of protected group representation it seeks to reach. The timetable specifies the time period within which it hopes to reach its goal. For example, an AAP may state: "The firm plans to increase its percentage of female professionals from 5 to 20 percent within the next five years."

The action steps specify how the organization plans to reach its goals and timetables. Action steps typically include such things as intensifying recruitment efforts, removing arbitrary selection standards, eliminating workplace prejudices, and offering employees better promotional and training opportunities. An example of a set of action steps follows:

- Meet with minority and female employees to request suggestions.
- Review current selection and promotion procedures to determine job relatedness.
- Design and implement a career counseling program for lower-level employees to encourage and assist in planning occupational and career goals.
- Install a new, less subjective, performance appraisal system.

---

utilization analysis
A statistical procedure used for setting affirmative action goals. It compares the percentage of each protected group for each job category within the organization to that in the available labor market.

affirmative action plan (AAP)   A written statement that specifies how the organization plans to increase the utilization of targeted groups.

| Taking a Closer Look 2-1 | *Forms of Preferential Treatment* |

1. Recruitment Efforts

The firm makes a special attempt to locate and attract members of underutilized groups. For example, it advertises job openings in sources that best reach these individuals, such as women's colleges and minority professional organizations.

This practice is legally acceptable.

2. One-for-One Hiring

The firm increases minority representation by hiring one minority for each nonminority hired.

This practice is legal under certain circumstances.

3. Preferential Layoffs

During layoffs, many companies use the policy "last hired, first fired." This policy often penalizes members of underutilized groups who, because of AA, are likely to be the most recently hired. When a firm uses preferential layoffs, it changes its layoff policy to protect these individuals. That is, it "leapfrogs" over them and begins laying off more tenured individuals from nonunderutilized groups.

This practice is illegal if it violates the provisions of a collective bargaining agreement. It may be unlawful under other circumstances, as well.

4. Extra Consideration in Hiring

Firms using this approach give hiring preference to members of underutilized groups. If "all else is equal," a member of such a group will be given preference in hiring. For example, if a man and a woman have equal qualifications, the woman would be hired.

This practice is considered, at present, to be legal. However, the employer must be able to prove that all else is equal.

5. Differential Standards

This practice involves the use of different hiring standards for members of different protected groups. For example, women may qualify for a physically demanding job by doing 10 push-ups, while men must do at least 20.

This practice is forbidden by the CRA of 1991 and is thus illegal.

6. Minority Positions

Firms using this practice consider only members from underutilized groups when filling a particular position. For example, a firm may state (usually privately) that another woman will fill the position recently vacated by Mary.

This practice is illegal.

Affirmative Action, Preferential Treatment, and the Law

When a company initiates an AAP as a remedy for underutilization, it attempts to bring qualified women or minorities into the workplace to make it more reflective of the population from which the employees are drawn. This practice sometimes involves the use of **preferential treatment** or giving members of underutilized groups some advantage over others in the employment process. Preferential treatment can take many forms, as noted in Taking a Closer Look 2-1.

The use of preferential treatment has triggered a storm of controversy, as detractors point to the seemingly inherent lack of fairness in giving preference to one individual over another based solely on that person's race or gender. AA supporters, however, believe that preferential treatment is sometimes needed to "level the playing field."

The debate on preferential treatment has reached several state legislatures, where referendums to ban affirmative action have been proposed. So far, only California has passed such legislation. (Proposition 209 prohibits preferential treatment in college admissions and government employment.) From a national perspective, the U.S. Supreme Court has ruled that preferential treatment is legal if engaged in as part of a bona fide affirmative action program that meets all of the criteria listed in Exhibit 2-3. In short, the affirmative action program must be designed to remedy underutilization and must be temporary, flexible, and reasonable.

Employers should proceed very carefully when granting someone preferential treatment. It should not be granted if there is no underutilization. When underutilization exits, an employer should select a strategy in which the degree of

preferential treatment
Giving members of underutilized groups some advantage over others in the employment process.

> **EXHIBIT 2-3**   Conditions under Which Preferential Treatment Is Legal

1. The AAP must serve a remedial purpose (i.e., it must be designed to correct for past employer discrimination or, in some instances, correct for past disparate impact).
2. The goals and timetables targeted by the AAP must not be achievable by using measures that are less extreme than preferential treatment (e.g., the use of unbiased selection methods).
3. One's protected group status must not be the only factor considered in the hiring decision.
4. The AAP must be temporary in nature, to be terminated when the goals have been reached.
5. The numerical hiring goals must be "reasonable" (as a general rule, they should not exceed 50 percent).
6. The AAP must not "unjustly burden" the rights of nonminorities. This means that the plan must not automatically exclude others from consideration simply because they do not belong to the underutilized group.
7. The applicant hired must meet the minimum qualifications for the job.

Source: Kleiman, L.S., and Faley, R.H. (1988). Voluntary affirmative action and preferential treatment: Legal and research implications. *Personnel Psychology, 41* (3), 481–496.

---

preferential treatment is commensurate with the severity of the problem that necessitates it.[9] For instance, a one-for-one hiring strategy (see item 2, Taking a Closer Look 2-1) could be used for resolving severe cases of underutilization, extra consideration in hiring (see item 4) for moderate cases, and redirecting recruitment efforts (see item 1) for mild cases.

2-2 Environmental Issues in the Workplace

As noted in Chapter 1, "Human Resource Management and Competitive Advantage," the environment within which an organization exists can have profound effects on the way it manages its human resources. The environmental influences having the greatest impact on HRM (i.e., workplace justice laws, unions, safety and health requirements, and the internationalization of business) are covered in Part 5 of this text. Here, we discuss some of the other environmental trends that have an important bearing on HRM practices.

2-2a Cultural Diversity in the Workplace

The advent of EEO laws and affirmative action programs created new employment opportunities for members of protected groups that had previously been victimized by employment discrimination. The demographic mix within the workplace has consequently become much more diverse because many workers now entering the workforce are not white, male, or English speaking.

Current Trends in Cultural Diversity

The increased cultural diversity witnessed thus far, however, merely represents the "tip of the iceberg." The ethnic minority share of the workforce is expected to increase rapidly during the next few years. By the year 2025, the African-American population is expected to increase from 11.7 to 12.7 percent of the total population; the Hispanic population from 10 to 17 percent; and the Asian and Pacific Islander population from 3.4 to 8 percent.[10] The workforce is also becoming older. In 2000, the fastest growing segment of the working population was workers in the 55–64-year-old age group. By 2030, the number of people who are at least 65 years old will grow from 35 to 70 million.[11] The workplace is also experiencing a dramatic increase in the number of dual-income families (many of whom have young children), single-parent families, and families facing the demands of elder care.[12]

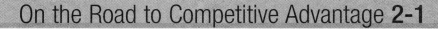

Components of Denny's Diversity Management Program

Denny's is the nation's largest family-style full-service restaurant chain. Comprised of more than 1,600 restaurants, its annual revenue is $2.2 billion. In the early 1990s, Denny's was hit with a series of discrimination lawsuits. The ensuing publicity generated such bad press that the chain was tagged as one of the most racist companies in America. At that time, Denny's had no diversity training and almost no minorities held management positions, franchises, or supply contracts. During the past decade, Denny's turned things around by taking several diversity initiatives. It is now ranked by *Fortune* as the best company in America for minorities. Here's how they did it:

1. Denny's held diversity training sessions for all of its employees and managers. Line workers are required to attend classes that cover the basics of equality and respect for heritage. All managers must attend a 2-day workshop that covers diversity in hiring and the basics of antidiscrimination law. Since 1995, over 1 million employees have completed this training.

2. Each department and division of the company sets goals to boost minority representation in franchises, supply contractors, and management.

3. Denny's revised its management bonus system, tying 25 percent of the bonus to meeting these diversity goals. Today, 48 percent of its workforce and 29 percent of its management team are minorities; 12 to 18 percent of its annual contracts go to minority-owned firms; and its franchises are 45 percent minority-owned.

Source: Speizer, I. (2004). Diversity on the menu. *Workforce Management, 83* (12), 41–45.

Managing Cultural Diversity

When properly managed, cultural diversity can represent a key strategic advantage. By opening its doors to a wider diversity of individuals, an organization can attract a larger and better pool of applicants.[13] These new entrants can bring original ideas and approaches to the workplace that can help a firm target products and services to a marketplace that is itself becoming more and more diverse.[14] For instance, a group of Reebok's female employees once bemoaned the fact they could not find a good aerobics shoe. Reebok latched onto that concern and began marketing aerobic shoes. Within two years, the company became a leader in the athletic shoe industry, transforming itself from a $12 million a year company to a $3 billion powerhouse.[15] When poorly managed, however, the transition to a more culturally diverse workforce can lead to a host of problems, such as high turnover among newly hired women and minorities, low morale, and instances of intergroup conflict.[16]

To manage diversity effectively, an organization must be sensitive to the needs of these new workers and seek to identify and eliminate barriers standing in their way. The approach taken by Denny's, described in On the Road to Competitive Advantage 2-1, illustrates this point.

We now take a closer look at these and other initiatives designed to promote effective diversity management.

Diversity Training

Diversity training attempts first to make employees aware of their biases or stereotyped views regarding various minority groups and then teaches them ways to overcome these biases in their day-to-day dealings with such individuals. According to management experts Lee Gardenswartz and Anita Rowe, such programs aim to raise the awareness and sensitivity levels of employees and managers about cultural differences and how they impact interactions, teamwork, and productivity.[17] Trainees are taught to understand how culture influences behavior and how to manage their

---

Taking a Closer Look 2-2   *An Example of a Diversity Training Exercise*

Name of Exercise

Asset Recognition Training

Aim of Exercise

Using a diverse group of people to solve a problem can be beneficial because the individual group members view the problem from different perspectives and, thus, can suggest a variety of problem-solving approaches. However, the process can be thwarted when a person's ideas are devalued by other group members because that individual's cultural background is different from their own. Asset recognition training is designed to expose prejudice and hostility toward people who are different and help them recognize that such differences can actually become assets.

How Asset Recognition Training Is Conducted

The training program consists of the following steps:

1. The participants list background experiences regarding such things as unusual work assignments, games they played as children, hobbies, special interests, and personal goals.

2. Participants then share this information with the group.

3. Group members then develop a list of special contributions that person can make when the opportunity arises.

Example of How This Training Can Help

One group member, an African-American female secretary, revealed that she sang in her church choir. The ensuing group discussion of this activity revealed that this experience improved her breathing, voice control, resonance, clarity of diction, and dramatic expression. The group suggested that these skills could be used on the job to make sales presentations to clients—a totally new activity for her. Within a year, she was making such presentations regularly.

Source: Shea, G.F. (1992). Learn how to treasure differences. *HRMagazine,* December, 34–37.

---

own stereotypical views and prejudices. Taking a Closer Look 2-2 provides an example of a diversity training exercise used in such programs. Taking a Closer Look 2-3 displays some steps a company can take to create a greater tolerance for diversity issues.

Breaking the "Glass Ceiling"

Although women and minorities have been entering the workforce in record numbers, their quest to reach the top of the corporate ladder has been thwarted. Many have "topped-out" at entry- or mid-level management positions. Consider the following statistics:

Taking a Closer Look 2-3   *Steps for Creating a Diversity-Friendly Workplace*

- Make diversity a corporate goal and secure high commitment from all employees.
- Hold a "brown bag lunch" series to talk about cultural diversity issues.
- Provide employees with opportunities to attend local cultural events and exhibits.
- Avoid singling out employees of a particular race or ethnicity to handle diversity issues on behalf of everyone else.

- Start a mentoring program that pairs employees of diverse backgrounds.
- Foster an open, friendly work environment.
- Establish an internal procedure for employees to report incidents of harassment or discrimination.

Source: Adapted from Gardenswartz, L., and Rowe, A. (2002). Important steps for implementing diversity training. *Mosaics, 8* (3), 3–5.

EXHIBIT 2-4 | Factors Creating a Glass Ceiling for Women

The stereotyped views held by male executives toward women, such as:

- Women lack organizational commitment, being more concerned with the demands of family and parenthood.
- Women do not have the traits necessary for managerial success, such as aggressiveness and competitiveness.

The women's lack of opportunity to "bond" with other managers and executives. For example:

- Women are often denied the opportunity to join their male counterparts on golf courses or at bars after hours.

The subjectiveness of a firm's promotional procedures. Rather than selecting candidates on the basis of the qualities identified as necessary for the promoted position, the choice is subjective, and is often biased.

- Too often, selections are made by male executives who choose other males who are most similar to them.

Because women are more likely than men to assume primary responsibility for child care, many of them are:

- Less willing to put in long hours, travel, and relocate.
- More likely to leave the workforce for extended periods of time. For instance, women are eight times more likely than men to spend four years or more out of the labor force.

Sources: Horgan, D.D. (1989). A cognitive learning perspective on women becoming expert managers. *Journal of Business and Psychology, 3* (3), 299–313; Stuart, P. (1992). What does the glass ceiling cost you? *Personnel Journal,* November, 70–80; and Jones, D. (2005, February 16), *USA Today.* Retrieved from http://www.usatoday.com/money/industries/2005-02-09-women-carly_x.htm.

- Women represent only about 2 percent of the executive workforce.[18]
- A survey of *Fortune* 500 companies found that nearly half have no female directors.[19]
- During the past decade or so, the percentage of minorities and women in top executive positions in America's 1,000 largest companies has risen by only 2 percent, despite EEO and affirmative action programs.[20]

Women and minorities have failed to reach the highest levels of management partly because many have only recently entered the managerial ranks; it takes time to climb the corporate ladder. However, this explanation does not account for the magnitude of the problem. An invisible, yet very real barrier found in the structure of many organizations has often stymied the advancement of these individuals. This barrier has been termed the **glass ceiling.** Exhibit 2-4 describes some of the factors contributing to the glass ceiling that females face. See also Figure 2-3.

How can the glass ceiling be broken? Effective diversity training that helps decision makers overcome their biases would certainly help. But diversity training, by itself, is not enough. An organization must also take steps to help minorities and women reach their career goals, such as providing them with training, career counseling, and mentoring. The organization must also implement promotion procedures that are less subject to bias—procedures that ensure that candidates are chosen solely

glass ceiling An invisible, yet very real, barrier found in the structure of many organizations that has stymied the advancement of women and other protected groups.

Women have trouble breaking through the glass ceiling because they are seen as being more interested in their families than in their careers and as being uncompetitive. Women lack the opportunities to bond with male colleagues at traditional bastions of male camaraderie, such as clubs and bars. Females are often overlooked in the hiring process because some men feel more comfortable with hiring males than with hiring females.

Figure 2-3
The Glass Ceiling

on the basis of their qualifications. We discuss how this aim can be achieved in Chapter 3 (in our discussion of management succession planning), Chapter 7 (in our discussion of management training), and Chapter 8 (in our discussion of performance appraisal systems).

Meeting the Needs of Older Employees

As noted earlier, the workforce is rapidly aging. In 2004, the youngest "baby boomers" turned 40; older workers now comprise about half the workforce.[21] The employment of a larger number of older workers can be advantageous. Older individuals are generally more stable and experienced than younger ones and can thus be a great asset to an organization.[22]

The management of older workers can pose some unique problems, however. For instance, younger managers often feel uncomfortable directing the work of people who are old enough to be their parents and grandparents.[23] Moreover, the capabilities of older workers may decline in certain types of jobs as some of their skills begin to diminish with age. The skills most affected by the aging process are speed and accuracy of movement, the process of translation between perception and action, problem solving, perception, hearing, and vision.[24]

An organization can take steps to ease these problems. Its diversity training program, for instance, could include the topic of ageism in order to help younger managers recognize and deal with their "uncomfortable" feelings.[25] Additionally, organizations can help older workers compensate for their diminishing skills. For instance, companies can provide increased sound amplification or lighting to accommodate those who have begun to experience hearing and vision problems.[26] They can also place workers in jobs that rely less on physical prowess and more on maturity and experience.

Implementing Work and Family Programs

Many of today's workers are experiencing great difficulty trying to juggle both work and family responsibilities. Because so many employees are single parents or members of dual-income families, often there is no one available at home during working hours to care for the family.[27] In addition to attending to the needs of children (e.g., caring for a sick child, attending parent-teacher conferences), many employees must also care for aging parents.[28]

A number of companies have thus begun to institute work and family programs in an effort to help employees cope with these problems. Examples of such programs are given in Exhibit 2-5. Many of these companies report an increase in both productivity and job satisfaction among their workers. They have also found that family-friendly programs can serve as useful recruiting and retention tools.[29] In addition to the programs listed in Exhibit 2-5, many organizations now offer nontraditional work arrangements, such as telecommuting, flextime, and job sharing, to help workers cope with their personal and family-related responsibilities.

telecommuting
A nontraditional work arrangement in which employees work at home.

In **telecommuting**, a nontraditional work-at-home arrangement, employees typically have an office set up in their home similar to that at the office, with a computer, photocopier, fax machine, and phone line. Telecommuting can enhance recruitment and retention because many employees find they can save time and money by not having to commute to work, can better balance their work and personal lives, and can reduce or eliminate child-care expenses.[30] On the negative side, when an employee is working at home, there is no supervisor present to monitor the employee's job behavior. Success thus depends on the amount of self-discipline that employees can demonstrate. Another potential drawback is that telecommuting employees are not always available to attend meetings, meet clients, and so forth. Finally, telecommuting is inappropriate for certain jobs, such as those requiring the use of heavy equipment or work on the assembly line. Supervisory jobs are also poor candidates for telecommuting because the management of employees requires some face-to-face interaction.[31]

EXHIBIT 2-5   Examples of Work and Family Programs

Los Angeles Department of Water and Power[a]
- Reduced-cost child care
- Care for mildly ill children
- Parenting classes and counseling
- Expectant parent program
- Parenting support groups
- A "Beeper-Alert" program (in which employees are loaned beepers when they have an imminent family emergency)

The St. Petersburg Times[b]
- Subsidized child care and care for sick children
- Flexible work schedules
- Family leave
- Job sharing
- Resource and referral services

Eli Lilly[c]
- On-site day-care center
- Summer camp for children who are too old for day care

New Age Transportation[d]
- Bring your baby to work program that enables moms to return to work four weeks after giving birth

Sun Microsystems[e]
- Created iWork program, which is a combination of a virtual office and flextime. Employees can use this program to log onto the company's computer network from home to view files. They can also use portal technology, collaboration tools, and videoconferencing.
- The program has saved the company $255 million by boosting job satisfaction and reducing turnover.

Lost Arrow[f]
- Created on-site day-care center that cares for 83 children
- Flexible work schedules
- Extended parental leave
- These programs cost $530,000 per year. In return, the company gets a tax break of $190,000 and saves an estimated $350,000 in costs associated with reduced turnover.

Sources:
[a]Solomon, C.M. (1992). Work/family ideas that break boundaries. *Personnel Journal,* October, 112–117.

[b]Martinez, M.N. (1993). Family support makes business sense. *HRMagazine,* January, 38–43.

[c]Poe, A.C. (1999). Parenting programs take off. *HRMagazine,* November, 42–50.

[d]Marchetti, M. (2005). In good company. *Working Mother, 28* (2), 38–43.

[e]Greengard, S. (2005). Sun's shining example. *Workforce Management, 84* (3), 48–49.

[f]Demby, E.R. (2004). Do your family-friendly programs make cents? *HRMagazine, 49* (1), 74–78.

Flextime refers to setting up a flexible work schedule in which workers must put in their eight hours each day, but can choose their starting and ending times. For instance, they may come in at 6 A.M. and work until 2 P.M. or they may come in at 10 A.M. and work until 6 P.M. The use of flextime gives employees the flexibility to control their own work schedules. For instance, a mother can be free to pick up her child from school at 3 P.M. if she reports to work early enough in the day. Some employees may schedule their work hours simply to avoid rush hour traffic.

About 20 percent of federal employers and 13 percent of private-sector employers allow flextime.[32] When using flextime, employers must ensure that the office is covered; that is, a sufficient number of people must be available at the work site when needed.

Job sharing is another form of alternative work scheduling in which a full-time job is shared by two people. It can be implemented in several ways:[33]

- Each working a half-day, five days a week
- Each working two or three full days a week
- Each working every other week
- Each working alternate months or seasons

One advantage of job sharing is that it enables a company to retain valued employees who, for personal reasons, no longer want to work full-time. Its use can also decrease maternity leave time and provide better coverage during vacation and sick days. (The individual's sharing partner can be brought in as a substitute on those days.)[34] In most cases, each worker receives half the pay and benefits of a full-time worker. When implementing such a program, the firm must ensure that job sharing is appropriate for the given position; that is, the work can be effectively completed under this work arrangement without causing a lot of chaos. The employer must also ensure that the two people sharing the job are compatible.

Such work and family programs often make good business sense. By helping employees balance work and family responsibilities, companies can increase their

flextime   A nontraditional work arrangement in which work hours are flexible in that workers must put in their eight hours, but can choose their starting and ending times.

job sharing   A form of alternate work scheduling in which a full-time job is shared by two people.

overall productivity, reduce absenteeism, and better retain valued employees.[35] For instance, the Los Angeles Department of Water and Power (see Exhibit 2-5) found that its work and family program reduced turnover and improved recruitment; it estimates that the program yields a return of $10 for each dollar invested.

2-2b The Changing Nature of Work

Another trend affecting the management of human resources is the changing nature of work now occurring within many organizations. This change has been spurred by changes in technology and by the movement of jobs from the manufacturing to the service sector of the economy. We first describe these trends and then discuss their impact on a firm's HRM practices.

How Work Has Changed

Some segments of industry are being severely affected by the technological advances that have taken place during the past 20 years. The advent of computer-driven technologies has changed the way most companies conduct their business and transformed the skill set needed at just about every employee level. For example, secretaries must now learn how to use word processing, spreadsheet, and database software applications, rather than rely on a typewriter, calculator, and Rolodex to do his or her job.

In addition to technological changes, today's workplaces are experiencing a major shift in the type of work being performed—from manufacturing to service. Millions of blue-collar jobs have recently disappeared in such industries as steel, heavy construction, railroads, machinery, and metalwork, and robots have replaced many assembly-line workers. At the same time, some additional white-collar jobs were created in such industries as restaurants, personnel agencies, computers, hospitals, legal services, accounting, and communications equipment.[36] The Bureau of Labor Statistics estimates that the number of service-providing jobs will increase by 21 million from 2002 to 2012, while manufacturing jobs are expected to increase by only 700,000 during that same period.[37]

How the Changing Nature of Work Impacts HRM Practices

These workplace changes signal the need for training programs to provide employees with the skills needed to move into these more technical and/or service-oriented jobs. For instance, programs are needed to teach workers such things as how to operate new equipment, how to use a computer, and how to communicate more effectively.[38] When replacing assembly-line workers, for example, many firms offer these individuals the opportunity to train for more technically advanced jobs, such as machine repair.

Unfortunately, more workers experience difficulty learning these more advanced skills because of deficiencies in their more basic skills. It has been estimated, for instance, that nearly 30 million adults in the United States are illiterate; that is, they have serious deficiencies in such basic skills as reading, writing, and mathematics.[39] Such individuals must overcome these deficiencies before they can master the more advanced skills. This problem surfaced recently in one company when it built a new plant with computer-integrated manufacturing and statistical process controls and discovered that many of its employees were unable to figure out how to operate the equipment.[40]

To deal with this problem, many firms are now offering literacy training programs.[41] RJR Nabisco, for instance, offers its employees literacy training to help fulfill its pledge that no employee will be denied a promotion or transfer because of a lack of basic skills. Its literacy training course covers mathematical skills, reading comprehension, basic computer skills, and communication skills (both verbal and written).[42]

> **EXHIBIT 2-6**   The Potential Impact of Mergers and Takeovers on Organizations

- The achievement of company financial and operating goals may be thwarted.
- Schedules may be thrown off-target.
- Morale may be hurt.
- Productivity and/or quality may be lowered.
- Managers may not have the necessary information to facilitate the merger; they may not be able to give employees a clear picture of how the change will occur.
- Job assignment and reporting relationships may be unclear.
- Employees may not understand new policies and procedures.
- Employees may not have the resources or equipment they need.
- Employees may not know how to get the information they need.
- Intergroup relationships may be damaged.

Source: Marks, M.L., and Mirvis, P.H. (1992). Track the impact of mergers and acquisitions. *Personnel Journal*, April, 70–79.

2-2c Mergers and Takeovers

The occurrence of mergers and takeovers is another environmental factor impacting organizations and their HRM practices. "Merger mania" began to sweep through American businesses in the early 1980s. Many of these were not mergers of choice, but were actually hostile takeovers based on pure speculation—undervalued firms were bought by "takeover artists" solely for the purpose of dismembering the companies and selling off assets to make a quick profit. For example, Irwin Jacobs (nicknamed "Irv the Liquidator") did this when he bought and quickly liquidated W.T. Grant & Co., a large retailer.

The occurrence of a merger or takeover can create a variety of problems for an organization, as illustrated in Exhibit 2-6. In the case of one manufacturer, for instance, the secrecy of preacquisition negotiations created an air of distrust between employees and management. Morale dropped and employees began clamoring for union representation.[43]

In many of the firms in which mergers and takeovers have occurred, individuals who had been loyal, longtime employees learned (the hard way) that their jobs were no longer safe. As a result, this merger mania has substantially changed the way many employees think of their employers and, subsequently, the loyalty that bonded the two parties.

One consequence of this trend is increased voluntary turnover among employees who once would have been more inclined to spend their future working careers with a single employer. Another consequence is a rise in organizational conflict as employees seek to protect their own jobs at the expense of others. HRM practices that help restore employee loyalty and organizational commitment are thus becoming increasingly important.

2-2d Corporate Downsizing

During the past decade, many organizations have taken steps to reduce the size of their workforce. This process, called **downsizing**, usually takes the form of massive layoffs, actions in which 50 or more employees lose their jobs. From 1996 to 2004, the yearly number of massive layoff events ranged from 14,000 to 21,000, costing the jobs of at least 1.4 million employees each year.[44]

downsizing   A management action taken to drastically reduce the size of a company's workforce.

Why So Many Companies Are Downsizing
The recent trend toward downsizing has been triggered by three factors. First, many organizations have found it necessary to cut the size of their workforce due to a decline or crisis in the firm. For instance, many firms experience a decreased demand

for their products or services due to a recessionary business climate, increased international competition, and/or competition from inexpensive store brands.[45]

A second factor accounting for the rash of recent downsizing is the advent of technological advances, which has enabled many companies to produce more with fewer people. For instance, because today's computers have fewer parts, they are assembled with less labor than was needed just a few years ago. If computer manufacturers fail to cut their workforce, they will produce too much, and they will be stuck with an oversupply of products that quickly become obsolete.[46]

A third factor accounting for the recent wave of corporate downsizing is **organizational restructuring,** in which the structure of a firm is modified to become less hierarchical by cutting out the "layer" of middle management. Middle managers have become expendable in these firms because information and communications technologies make it easier for top managers to monitor and control operations directly. Moreover, the style of management in these restructured companies is participative, so decision making is decentralized. Employee teams, task forces, and committees now make many of the decisions typically reserved for middle managers. Consequently, many middle management jobs have been abolished. In fact, roughly 20 percent of all layoffs from 1988 to 1993 came from middle management positions.[47]

organizational restructuring
When a firm modifies its structure to become less hierarchical by cutting out the "layer" of middle management.

Problems Associated with Downsizing Efforts

Although massive layoffs can save a company money in the short term, downsizing often creates as many problems as it solves.[48] One of the biggest problems is poor employee morale. Morale within an organization can take a drastic drop as employees begin to worry about job security after seeing their colleagues leave the organization. Moreover, the economic benefits expected by the organization often fail to materialize. For instance, based on a 15-year study of 537 companies, management professor Wayne Cascio and his colleagues concluded that:[49]

> What is striking about the results of the downsizings is their negligible impact on firm profitability relative to the size of the layoffs. . . . They not only failed to increase their return on assets, but also actually experienced very slight declines. . . . We conclude that downsizing may not necessarily generate the benefits sought by management. Managers must be very cautious in implementing a strategy that can impose such traumatic costs on employees, both those who leave and those who stay.

Deciding When and How to Downsize

Downsizing does not have to mean massive layoffs. Numerous alternatives to layoffs should be considered before drastic cuts are made. Some of these alternatives are listed in Exhibit 2-7. For instance, Hewlett-Packard implemented a plan in which workers were given a choice of taking a 10 percent pay cut and losing eight days of paid vacation, or taking a 5 percent pay cut and losing four days of paid vacation.[50]

EXHIBIT 2-7	Alternatives to Layoffs

- Delay any pay increases.
- Shift some health costs to employees.
- Freeze hiring.
- Restrict overtime.
- Retrain or redeploy employees.
- Switch to part-time employees.
- Switch to job sharing.
- Switch to consultants.
- Require workers to use unpaid vacations, sabbaticals, and days off.
- Use a shorter workweek.
- Use across-the-board pay reductions.
- Implement early retirement programs.

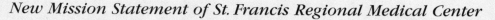

New Mission Statement of St. Francis Regional Medical Center

1. To live the core values of service, human dignity, vision, and wisdom
2. To work and live in a compassionate manner
3. To meet and exceed the service expectations of our patients, their families, our physicians, and other employees
4. To create an environment of accountability, ownership, and recognition
5. To address internal and external customers' needs through interdisciplinary collaboration
6. To achieve excellence through continuing education
7. To address dedication and training of our vital human resources
8. To realize our mission of excellence through the quality improvement process

Source: Egan, M.S. (1995). Reorganization as rebirth. *HRMagazine,* January, 84–88.

When a massive layoff is the only viable option, the firm must manage this workforce reduction very carefully. One of management's most difficult tasks is to reestablish morale and motivation following layoffs. The management team should draft a new corporate mission statement that conveys the organization's new vision and goals in an optimistic way—one that encourages employees to recommit to the company.[51] An example of such a mission statement is illustrated in On the Road to Competitive Advantage 2-2.

To help employees who have lost their jobs, employers can provide services such as outplacement, relocation assistance, and personal and family counseling.[52] The layoff-related initiatives taken by Sky Chef, an in-service flight corporation, are described in On the Road to Competitive Advantage 2-3.

On the Road to Competitive Advantage **2-3**

The Components of the Downsizing Program at Sky Chef

1. Generous separation package (given to individuals who voluntarily left the organization, as well as those who were laid off)
2. Transition services, including financial counseling, psychological counseling, job training, and consumer credit counseling
3. Career center offering career transition counseling, workshops on networking, assistance with resume preparation, training on interviewing, and a resource center to further assist transitioning employees in finding new jobs

Source: Schreitmueller, J.P. (1993). Employees drive reorganization at Sky Chef. *Personnel Journal,* September, 144–150.

Chapter Objectives Revisited

1. Understand the nature of the equal employment opportunity laws and how the courts interpret them.

   - EEO laws include the Civil Rights Acts of 1964 and 1991, the Pregnancy Discrimination Act of 1978, the Immigration Reform and Control Act of 1986, the Age Discrimination in Employment Act of 1967, and the Americans with Disabilities Act of 1990.
   - These laws differ from one another primarily in terms of the specific protected classifications covered. In all, the following classifications are protected from discrimination: race, color, sex, religion, national origin, age (40 and above), and disability.
   - The legal definition of discrimination takes two forms: disparate treatment (intentional discrimination) and disparate impact (unintentional discrimination).
   - The courts require that the plaintiff must first establish a prima facie case; the defendant must then rebut that case.

2. Understand the nature of affirmative action programs and how they should be implemented.

   - AA programs seek to eliminate discrimination by setting "color-conscious" initiatives. AA programs are sometimes legally required, but they are usually implemented on a voluntary basis.
   - AA programs consist of two steps: utilization analysis and action planning.
   - AA programs sometimes grant individuals preferential treatment. This practice is legal if engaged in as part of a bona fide affirmative action program.

3. Describe the impact of cultural diversity on organizations and how it may be successfully managed.

   - The workforce is becoming older and more culturally diverse.
   - Management initiatives include diversity training, steps taken to break the glass ceiling and meet the needs of older workers, and implementation of work and family programs.

4. Explain the changing nature of work and how this phenomenon impacts HRM practices.

   - Technological advances and a shift in the type of work being performed have created a need for a new set of worker skills.
   - These trends signal a need for training programs (including literacy training).

5. Describe the impact that the occurrence of mergers and takeovers has on HRM practices.

   - The occurrence of mergers and takeovers can lower employee loyalty and morale and increase voluntary turnover rates and the number of organizational conflicts.

6. Understand the causes of downsizing, its potential pitfalls, and how downsizing efforts should be managed.

   - Organizational decline, technological advances, and organizational restructuring cause downsizing.
   - Downsizing efforts often fail to achieve economic goals and may weaken employee morale.
   - Firms should consider alternatives to layoffs.
   - When implementing layoffs, firms should attempt to reestablish employee morale and try to help employees who have lost their jobs.

Review Questions

Note: You can find the correct answers to these questions by taking the quiz and then submitting your answers in the Online Edition. The program will automatically score your submission. If you miss a question, the program will provide the correct answer, a rationale for the answer, and the section number in the chapter where the topic is discussed.

1. Which of the following statements regarding the Civil Rights Act of 1991 is true?

   a. Employers may be charged with punitive and compensatory damages.
   b. Compared to the Civil Rights Act of 1964, the 1991 act makes discrimination claims more difficult to prove.
   c. It states that mixed-motive decisions are lawful.
   d. All of the above.

2. An employer refuses to hire any women for the job of construction worker. Mary Jones' application is automatically rejected. If Mary were to sue this company for sex discrimination, which approach should she use in order to establish a *prima facie* case?

   a. restricted company policy
   b. discriminatory remarks
   c. McDonnell-Douglas Test
   d. four-fifths rule

3. An employer must demonstrate a legitimate, nondiscriminatory reason for its employment decision in order to rebut a *prima facie* case of discrimination established under the _____ approach.

   a. company policy
   b. discriminatory remarks
   c. McDonnell-Douglas test
   d. four-fifths rule

4. An employer must demonstrate the business necessity of job-relatedness of its employment decision in order to rebut a *prima facie* case of discrimination established under the _____ approach.

   a. company policy
   b. discriminatory remarks
   c. McDonnell-Douglas test
   d. four-fifths rule

5. The implementation of affirmative action consists of two steps: _____ and _____.

   a. EEO review/EEO implementation
   b. affirmative action analysis/affirmative action implementation
   c. discriminatory cause/antidiscriminatory steps
   d. utilization analysis/affirmative action plans

6. _____ training attempts to make employees aware of their biases or stereotyped views regarding various minority groups and then to teach them ways to overcome these biases in their day-to-day dealings with such individuals.

   a. Sensitivity
   b. Affirmative action
   c. Diversity
   d. Race relations

7. Which of the following statements about older workers is true?

   a. Young managers often feel uncomfortable directing their work.
   b. One of the skills most affected by the aging process is speed/accuracy of movement.
   c. Companies can sometimes solve age-related performance problems by placing older workers in jobs that rely less on physical prowess and more on maturity and experience.
   d. All of the above.

8. "Merger mania" is leading to

   a. increased voluntary turnover.
   b. increased employee commitment.
   c. decreased union representation.
   d. all of the above.

9. Which of the following practices does the chapter recommend in order to reestablish morale following a massive layoff?

   a. The management team should draft a new corporate mission statement that conveys the organization's new vision and goals in an optimistic way.
   b. Management should give the surviving workers a large pay raise, as a show of good faith.
   c. Management should give the surviving workers more vacation time during the first year following the layoff.
   d. All of the above.

10. The preferential treatment of a protected group is

    a. legal under any circumstances.
    b. legal under any circumstances, but only if given to minorities.
    c. legal, but only if engaged in as part of a bona fide AA program.
    d. never legal.

Discussion Questions

1. Define the terms protected classification and protected group.

2. In what ways does the CRA of 1991 differ from the CRA of 1964?

3. Summarize the major provisions of the following laws: Pregnancy Discrimination Act, Age Discrimination in Employment Act, and Americans with Disabilities Act.

4. Describe the four approaches a plaintiff can take in order to establish a *prima facie* case of discrimination.

5. For each of the following situations, state the type of *prima facie* case (i.e., disparate treatment or disparate impact) the plaintiff would try to establish. If a *prima facie* case were established, how would the employer try to defend itself in each situation?

   a. The Metropolitan Police Department uses a written test for selecting new officers. The test is professionally developed. Eighty percent of the green applicants pass, but only 10 percent of the orange applicants pass.

   b. A boss looks at his female secretary and states: "You're fired because you make lousy coffee." He then hires another woman to replace her.

   c. An employee of foreign origin has been passed over for promotion to management because of a poor recommendation from his boss. His performance appraisal ratings have been excellent. In the past 5 years, 15 management positions have been filled; none of the 27 employees of foreign origin eligible for such a promotion has received one.

6. Describe the two steps involved in implementing an affirmative action program.

7. What is meant by the term *glass ceiling?* What steps must an organization take to break this ceiling?

8. In what ways is the nature of work changing? How does this trend affect the practice of HRM?

9. What types of problems have been created as a result of the rash of recent mergers and takeovers?

10. Describe three reasons why so many companies have begun downsizing.

11. How should an organization manage its downsizing efforts?

Experiential Exercise

Affirmative Action Debate

Overview

The class will engage in a debate of the following proposition:

Affirmative action is a fair method of achieving equal employment opportunity for minority groups and women.

Steps

1. Every student sitting on the left side of the room will take the "pro" position; those sitting on the right side will take the "con" position.

2. Break into groups of four or five students and develop a list of arguments supporting your position.

3. Both the pro and con sides should then develop a master list of arguments supporting their position. Develop the master list by having a representative from each subgroup meet with one another and compare lists. There will thus be two master lists: pro and con.

4. The subgroup representatives from each side will become the debate teams.

5. The debate should be conducted according to the following procedure:

Round 1

Each team gets 10 minutes to present its case. All debaters should participate. The pro side goes first.

Round 2

Each team gets 5 minutes to rebut the arguments given by the other side and reconstruct or rebuild its own arguments, as needed. The rebuttal should directly address the arguments made by the other side. Its purpose is to cast doubt on those arguments. The con side goes first. (*Note:* Give your arguments in round 1; do not rebut until round 2.)

Round 3

The other class members (i.e., the audience) are given 10 minutes to cross-examine members of either team. The class then votes on which position they hold.

Cases

Jackson v. Happy-Time

Doris Jackson, a 32-year-old African-American, was fired from her job as a teacher at Happy-Time Daycare. She files a race discrimination complaint with the EEOC.

Facts

1. Doris had been a teacher with Happy-Time for nine years. There are eight other teachers at the site where she works. Happy-Time has eight other locations in the county, employing a total of 85 teachers.

2. One of Doris' students, a 4-year-old named Mary, came to class very upset one day. When the other children started teasing her, Mary began to cry. Doris took her to the rest room, wiped her face, and talked until she calmed down. When Doris took her back to class, she became upset again and tried to leave. Doris took her into the hallway and let her cry it out. Ms. Jones, the program director, came by and saw Mary standing alone in the hall. She took the child back to the classroom and told Doris to pack her things—she was fired. Happy-Time replaced Ms. Jackson with a white female.

Doris' Arguments

1. I left Mary in the hall for about 5 minutes to cry it out. I knew she was still there because I could hear her crying. My plan was to send one of my older children down the hall to get Ms. Jones, but Ms. Jones came by just before I did that.

2. In my nine years at Happy-Time, my performance has been satisfactory. There have only been two complaints about me, both of which were quite minor.

3. The company's policy states that for noncritical misconduct, the center will follow a progressive discipline system of warning and suspension prior to discharge. I never received either of these.

4. Another teacher, Betty, who is white, did something worse and was not fired. Betty took kids on a field trip and dropped a child off without checking to see if the parents were home. As it turned out, they were not home and the child had to find a neighbor to take care of him.

The Center's Argument

1. Doris was fired for "improper isolation of a child," which was in violation of job rules.

2. Although we normally give employees warnings before discharge, our employee handbook states that we reserve the right to immediately discharge an employee for serious instances of misconduct. We believe that improper isolation of a child is very serious.

3. The "Betty situation" occurred seven years ago when the center had a different director and had no formal discharge policies. I (Ms. Jones) would have fired Betty if I had been in charge. In the three years I have been director, one other teacher, Joanie, who is white, was fired for improper isolation. She left a child outside on the playground.

Discussion Questions

1. How would Ms. Jackson establish a *prima facie* case of discrimination?

2. If a *prima facie* case were established, what defense would the employer use?

3. If you were the judge, how would you rule? Explain.

Is Preferential Treatment Warranted?

Review the following two situations. Set short-term (i.e., 1-year) affirmative action goals and suggest ways these organizations can meet these goals. Is some form of preferential treatment warranted in either case?

Situation 1

To promote someone to the ranks of management, the ABC Company convenes a panel of upper managers to review the work records of employees who have been nominated by their supervisors. This panel has been encouraged to consider female candidates in a fair manner. Despite this encouragement, only 5 of its 50 managers are women. The company's utilization analysis reveals that the company "should" have 10 female managers. The turnover rate for managers is about one per year. What steps would you take to remedy this underutilization?

Situation 2

The Metropolitan Police Department has had a history of employment discrimination when hiring officers—it had long refused to hire any African-Americans. It was taken to court on race discrimination charges and lost the case. The judge ordered it to cease its discriminatory practices and institute a bona fide affirmative action program. Currently, none of the 250 troopers are African-American. The number "should" be 100. The state hires about 20 troopers per year. What steps would you take to remedy this underutilization?

References

1. Kleiman, L.S., and Kass, D.S. (In press). Justifying pregnancy-related employment decisions under the Pregnancy Discrimination Act. *Journal of Individual Employment Rights.*

2. *Final Interpretations: Age Discrimination in Employment Act* (1981). Code of Federal Regulations, Part 1625.

3. Ledvinka, J., and Scarpello, V.G. (1991). *Federal Regulation of Personnel and Human Resource Management* (2nd ed.). Boston: PWS-Kent.

4. Ibid.

5. Faley, R.H., Kleiman, L.S., and Lengnick-Hall, M.L. (1984). Age discrimination and personnel psychology: A review and synthesis of the legal literature with implications for future research. *Personnel Psychology, 37,* 327–350.

6. *Watson v. Fort Worth Bank* (1988). 487 U.S. 977.

7. Allen, R.Y. (2003). Examining the implementation of affirmative action in law enforcement. *Public Personnel Management, 32* (3), 411–415.

8. Panaro, G.P. (1990). *Employment Law Manual.* Boston: Warren, Gorham & Lamont.

9. Kleiman, L.S., and Faley, R.H. (1988). Voluntary affirmative action and preferential treatment: Legal and research implications. *Personnel Psychology, 41* (3), 481–496.

10. Minehan, M. (1997). The fastest-growing U.S. ethnic groups. *HRMagazine,* May, 160.

11. Bolch, M. (2000). The changing face of the workforce. *Training,* December, 73–78.

12. Front, M.R., Russell, M., and Cooper, M.L. (1992). Antecedents and outcomes of work–family conflict: Testing a model of the work–family interface. *Journal of Applied Psychology, 77* (1), 65–78.

13. Parry, L.E. (1993). Workforce America! Managing employee diversity as a vital resource. In J.L. Pierce and J.W. Newstrom (eds.). *The Manager's Bookshelf* (194–200). New York: HarperCollins.

14. Staff. (1993, Spring/Summer). Managing diversity helps employers attain top performance. *BNAC Communicator,* 14.

15. Http://www.equalopportunity.on.ca/enggraf/gandz/castu.html.

16. Parry. Workforce America!

17. Gardenswartz, L., and Rowe, A. (2002). Important steps for implementing diversity training. *Mosaics, 8* (3), 3–5.

18. Ragins, B.R., Townsend, B., and Mattis, M. (1998). Gender gap in the executive suite: CEOs and female executives report on breaking the glass ceiling. *Academy of Management Executive, 12* (1), 28–42.

19. Staff. (1992, May 31). The workplace. *Dallas Morning News,* 11.

20. Dominguez, C.M. (1990). A crack in the glass ceiling. *HRMagazine,* December, 65–66.

21. Bible, J.D. (2004). *Grosjean v. First Energy Corp.*: The relevance of age differentials in a *prima facie* case ADEA case. *Labor Law Journal, 55* (2), 112–119.

22. Winning with diversity. *Nation's Business, 80* (9), U.S. Chamber of Commerce, 1615 H. Street NW, Washington, DC 20062.

23. Fyock, C.D. (1994). Finding the gold in the graying of America. *HRMagazine,* February, 74–76.

24. Rhodes, S.R. (1983). Age-related differences in work attitudes and behaviors: A review and conceptual analysis. *Psychological Bulletin, 93* (2), 328–367.

25. Fyock. Finding the gold.

26. Faley et al. Age discrimination.

27. Morrison, P.A. (1990). HRM: Its growing scope and future direction. *The Futurist,* March/April, 9–15.

28. Sit, M. (1989). Family and work collide. *Boston Globe,* 25–26.

29. Poe, A.C. (1999). Parenting programs take off. *HRMagazine,* November, 42–50.

30. McGee, L.F. (1988). Setting up work at home. *Personnel Administrator,* December, 58–62.

31. Segal, J.A. (1998). Home sweet office? *HRMagazine,* April, 119–129.

32. Buckley, M.R., Fedor, D.B., and Dicza, D.C. (1988). Work patterns altered by new lifestyles. *Personnel Administrator,* December, 40–43.

33. Cacti, W.G. (1988). Part-year vs. part-time employment. *Personnel Administrator,* May, 60–63.

34. Solomon, C.M. (1994). Job sharing: One job, double headache? *Personnel Journal,* September, 88–96.

35. Morrison. HRM: Its growing scope.

36. Kravetz, D.J. (1991). Increase finances through progressive management. *HRMagazine,* February, 57–62.

37. Http:www.bls.gov/opub/ooq/2003/winter/art03.pdf.

38. Hines, A. (1993). Transferable skills land future jobs. *HRMagazine,* April, 55–56.

39. Zalman, R.G. (1991). The "basics" of in-house skills training. *HRMagazine,* February, 74–78.

40. Hitt, M.A., Hoskisson, R.E., and Harrison, J.S. (1991). Strategic competitiveness in the 1990s: Challenges and opportunities for U.S. executives. *Academy of Management Executive, 5* (2), 7–22.

41. Ibid.

42. Santora, J.E. (1992). Nabisco tackles tomorrow's skills gap. *Personnel Journal,* September, 47–50.

43. Marks, M.L., and Murvis, P.H. (1992). Track the impact of mergers and acquisitions. *Personnel Journal,* April, 70–79.

44. Http://www.bls.gov/mls.

45. Http://stats.bls.gov/newrels.htm.

46. Vollman T., and Brazas, M. (1993). Downsizing. *European Management Journal, 11* (1), 18–29.

47. Floyd, S.W., and Wooldridge, B. (1994). Dinosaurs or dynamos? Recognizing middle management's strategic role. *Academy of Management Executive, 8* (4), 47–57.

48. Fuchsberg, G. (1993, October 1). Why shake-ups work for some, not for others. *The Wall Street Journal,* B1–2.

49. Cascio, W.F., Young, C.E., and Morris, J.R. (1997). Financial consequences of employment-change decisions in major U.S. corporations. *Academy of Management Journal, 40* (5), 1175–1189.

50. Todd, R. (2001). Hold the line on salaries and benefits. *Workforce, 80* (9), 38–42.

51. Weinstein, H., and Leibman, M. (1991). Corporate scale down, what comes next? *HRMagazine, 36* (8), 33–37.

52. Vollman and Brazas. Downsizing.

Human Resource Management Preselection Practices

Planning for Human Resources

Chapter Three

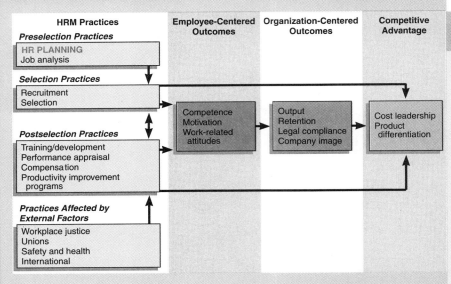

Key Terms

business factors
corporate culture
demand forecasting
extranet
group brainstorming
human resource information system (HRIS)
intranet
mission statement

ratio analysis
regression analysis
sales force estimates
strategic goals
strategic plan
strategic planning
supply forecasting
trend analysis

Chapter Objectives

Upon completion of this chapter, you will be able to:

- Understand how human resource planning contributes to a firm's competitive advantage.

- Explain why and how firms engage in strategic planning.

- Explain why and how human resource planning activities are conducted.

- Describe how HRM practices are developed in response to an HR plan.

- Understand the role of human resource information systems in planning and other HRM practices.

3-1 Gaining Competitive Advantage

3-1a Opening Case: Gaining Competitive Advantage at General Motors[1]

The Problem: Time Spent Completing HR Transactions Hurts Employee and HR Productivity

General Motors (GM) is the world's largest manufacturer of automobiles. Its vast number of employees must spend an enormous amount of time filling out paperwork and meeting with HR professionals to complete the various HR transactions, such as enrolling in benefit plans, changing their pension plans, registering for training classes, and learning about career development opportunities. GM believed that this time expenditure was hurting the workers' productivity. Members of the HR Department, serving as the middlemen in these transactions, also spent enormous amounts of time providing information and forms to the employees, time that could be better used on more value-added activities and services.

The Solution: Developing an Employee Services Center Website

GM addressed this problem by putting as many HR-related activities as possible online, creating what it calls the "Employee Services Center." The center, which employees can access on the Internet, provides a large menu of HR-related information and interactive tools that allow employees to do such things as change their addresses, see their pay stubs, read the employee handbook, review job postings, and complete various HR enrollment forms, such as pension transaction forms, flexible benefit enrollment forms, and requests for direct pay deposits. The site also provides employees with the opportunity to enroll in online classes at GM University, examine records of their training history, and build personal development plans that the workers and their supervisor can review and maintain.

How the Career Services Center Enhanced Competitive Advantage

The use of this website has saved GM a significant amount of money and time. It costs GM about $2 per minute to conduct business the "old-fashioned" way; i.e., by forcing employees to deal directly with the HR staff in order to obtain services. Identical services conducted over the Internet cost less than a nickel a minute. Moreover, completing their HR transactions online frees up the employees' time, allowing them to improve the speed and quality of their work. Employee self-service through the web also improves the productivity of the HR Department, which now spends less time filing and maintaining employee records and more time in business units solving problems.

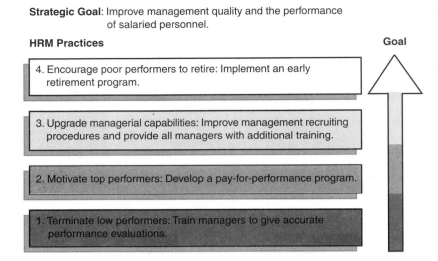

Figure 3-1

*Tying HRM Practices
to Organizational Goals:
An Example*

3-1b Linking Human Resource Planning to Competitive Advantage

As we discussed in Chapter 2, "Understanding the Legal and Environmental Context of HRM," American companies must now operate in a rapidly changing business environment. These changes have important implications for HRM practices. To ensure that management practices support business needs, organizations must continually monitor changing environmental conditions and devise HRM strategies for dealing with them. The procedure used to tie human resource issues to the organization's business needs is called *human resource planning* (or HR planning).

HR planning is defined as the "process of identifying and responding to [organizational needs] . . . and charting new policies, systems, and programs that will assure effective human resource management under changing conditions."[2] The purposes of HR planning, then, are (1) to enable organizations to anticipate their future HRM needs and (2) to identify practices that will help them meet those needs.

The fact that effective HR planning can enhance competitive advantage has been supported by a body of research showing that firms that engage in HR planning consistently outperform those that do not.[3] We now discuss how HR planning activities enhance competitive advantage.

Linking HRM Practices to Organizational Goals

As management experts Susan Jackson and Randall Schuler note, HR planning is "the thread that ties together all other human resource activities and integrates these with the rest of the organization."[4] Figure 3-1 illustrates an example of how a firm's HRM practices can be integrated with the goals of an organization.

Serving as a Building Block for Future HRM Practices

As noted in Chapter 1, "Human Resource Management and Competitive Advantage," HR planning is a major building block of HRM. That is, the successful implementation of many of the HRM practices described throughout this book depends on careful HR planning. Through the HR planning process, an organization can identify the mix of skills it will need in the future. It can then use this information to plan for its recruitment, selection, and training and development practices. The important role that HR planning plays in the training and development process, for example, is described by management consultant L. James Harvey in the following passage:[5]

> One thing is certain: unless the corporation is doing effective strategic planning and the human resource development planning is tied to it . . . the human resource development effort cannot fulfill its maximum potential.

EXHIBIT 3-1	Benefits Stemming from HR Forecasting

- Aids in the planning of job assignments
- Helps cope with fluctuations in staffing requirements
- Identifies recruiting needs
- Provides information regarding:
  - How corporate goals affect the need to hire, train, and keep employees
  - Whether shortages or surpluses of personnel are expected in certain areas
  - How well employees are being developed to fill future needs
  - How business changes are likely to affect human resource needs

Source: Walker, J.W. (1980). *Human Resource Planning.* New York: McGraw-Hill.

Consequences Associated with the Failure to Plan for Human Resources

Some of the benefits derived from HR planning are listed in Exhibit 3-1. As one can see from this exhibit, the use of HR planning enables companies to gain control of their future by preparing for events that are likely to occur. That is, they can anticipate change and devise appropriate courses of action. When companies learn how to capitalize on future events, their own future improves.

As valuable as HR planning is, many companies ignore this opportunity. Some see it as too difficult and frustrating. Others simply do not see the need for it. As one writer notes:[6]

Although the current trend is to integrate human resource planning with strategic planning, many organizations only pay "lip service" to the idea. Rarely is as much detailed, thoughtful analysis given to the acquisition and utilization of human resources as is typically given to acquiring and using economic resources. Executives seem confident that they can always recruit whatever employees are needed from the marketplace. Much evidence exists that points to the folly and potential consequences of such thinking.

For instance, when failing to plan properly for human resources, employers are forced to respond to events after they occur, rather than before; that is, they become *reactive*, rather than *proactive*. When this outcome occurs, an organization may be unable to correctly anticipate an increase in its future demand for employees. At best, such a company would be forced to recruit employees at the last minute and may thus fail to find the best candidate. At worst, the company may become seriously understaffed.

If a company remains understaffed for a prolonged period, it may ultimately suffer a variety of consequences. For instance, the understaffing could cause existing employees to experience a great deal of stress as they attempt to meet the additional demand without adequate resources and assistance. If the needed work is not getting done, the firm may ultimately experience an increase in back orders, which could cause a decrease in customer goodwill, an increase in competition, and a loss of market share.

3-2 HRM Issues and Practices

3-2a Strategic Planning

If you do not know where you are going, how will you ever get there? It is through the **strategic planning** process that organizations determine where they are going. When developing a strategic plan, an organization specifies its overall purpose and objectives and indicates how these are to be achieved. The strategic planning process typically consists of the following activities:[7]

strategic planning
A process in which a company specifies its overall purposes and objectives, and indicates how these are to be achieved.

Ben and Jerry's Mission Statement

To make, distribute, and sell the finest quality all natural ice cream and euphoric concoctions with a continued commitment to incorporating wholesome, natural ingredients and promoting business practices that respect the earth and the environment.

Source: Http://www.benjerry.com/our_mission/index.cfm.

1. Determine the organizational mission.
2. Scan the organizational environment.
3. Set strategic goals.
4. Formulate a strategic plan, part of which addresses human resource needs.

Step 1: Determine the Organizational Mission

mission statement
A declaration of the organization's overall purpose.

The first step in the strategic planning process is the development of a **mission statement,** which is a declaration of the organization's overall purpose. The mission statement defines the basic business scope and operations that distinguish the organization from others of a similar nature.[8] It answers these questions: "Why does our organization exist?" and "What unique contributions can it make?"[9] An example of a mission statement appears in On the Road to Competitive Advantage 3-1.

Step 2: Scan the Organizational Environment

Organizational planners must next scan both the firm's external and internal environments in order to identify the threats and opportunities each poses. The external environment is scanned to identify challenges posed by political, legal, economic, social, and technological issues, such as those described in Chapter 2, "Understanding the Legal and Environmental Context of HRM," (e.g., increasing legal demands, rapidly changing technology). Planners must also scan their industry environment to identify what their competitors are doing, what new firms may be entering the market, and what substitute products and services may be on the horizon.

When scanning the internal environment, planners assess the firm's strengths and weaknesses, because the firm's strategic goals should be designed to take advantage of its strengths and minimize its weaknesses. Key internal factors to consider include an organization's culture, structure, current mission, past history, number of layers of management, span of control of management, skills of the human resources, leadership and power, and the number of functional areas. As noted in Chapter 2, for instance, many firms are now attempting to correct weaknesses stemming from their hierarchical structure by cutting out layers of management and empowering their lower-level employees.

How to Get the Necessary Environmental Information

Although most strategic decisions are approved by the chief executive officer (CEO) of an organization, the task of gathering information for strategy formulation rests with all managers and employees. Vice presidents of the functional areas, for instance, usually provide input into decisions regarding new strategic directions for the firm. As one moves further down the managerial hierarchy, individuals have a more specialized, or narrow, focus.

Exhibit 3-2 illustrates the various functional areas that supply information to the overall strategic plan. Because of the plan's importance, a firm should encourage all of its managers and employees to provide input. To help ensure participation, a firm can empower a committee of employees and managers that represents the various functional areas to gather data.

EXHIBIT 3-2	Managerial Inputs to the Strategic Plan (by Functional Area)

Area	Planning Inputs
Marketing	Product forecasts
	Economic conditions
	Competitor behavior
	New product acceptance
	Advertising and promotional activities
	Consumer behavior issues
	Buying/usage habits
Manufacturing	Machine capacities
	Process improvements
	Overall product quality data
	Workforce productivity
	New equipment plans
Finance	Cost data
	Debt levels
	Financial condition of the firm
	Financial performance data
Human resources	Labor market conditions
	Training programs
	Staffing capacity
	Human resources capabilities
	Government laws and hiring regulations
Engineering	New product development
	Labor and machine standards
	Project and product changes
	Design modifications
Purchasing	Raw materials availability
	Inventory levels
	Storage and warehouse capacity
	Supplier and vendor capabilities

Step 3: Set Strategic Goals

The third step of the strategic planning process is to set **strategic goals,** which specify the desired outcomes that must be reached if the firm is to accomplish its mission. Strategic goals should be specific, challenging, and measurable. The goals should address such areas as:[10]

- Arenas: Where will we be active?
- Vehicles: How will we get there?
- Differentiators: How will we win the marketplace?
- Staging: What will be our speed and sequence of moves?
- Economic logic: How will we obtain our returns?

strategic goals The desired outcomes that must be reached for the firm to accomplish its mission.

Step 4: Formulate a Strategic Plan

Once external and internal environments have been scanned, and goals set, an organization should formulate its **strategic plan.** A strategic plan specifies the courses of action a firm must take in order to meet its strategic goals. It is formulated by translating organizational goals into more narrow functional or departmental goals and then devising strategies for meeting these goals. Strategic plans are typically set for finance, marketing, management, production and operations, accounting, information systems, and human resources. In the following sections, we discuss how a firm's strategic plan can be formulated and implemented in the human resource area.

strategic plan A plan that specifies the courses of action a firm must take in order to meets its strategic goals.

3-2b Human Resource Planning

As noted earlier, HR planning involves linking a firm's HRM practices to its strategic business needs, which have been identified by the strategic planning process.[11] HR planning may be done on both a short- and long-term (three or more years) basis. Its aim is to ensure that people will be available with the appropriate characteristics and skills when and where the organization needs them.[12] Through the HR planning process, an organization is able to generate (1) a list of future human resource needs (i.e., future job vacancies and the types of people needed to fill them) and (2) a plan for meeting them.

To derive its human resource needs, the organization first forecasts its *demand* for human resources (i.e., the number and types of people needed to carry out the work of the organization at some future point in time). It then forecasts its *supply* (i.e., the positions that are expected to be already filled). The difference between the two forecasts signifies the firm's HR *needs*. For example, if a firm estimates that it will "demand" 12 accountants during the next fiscal year and expects to have a "supply" of 9 onboard at that time, its HR need would be to hire 3 additional accountants.

We now take a closer look at how a company can determine its human resource needs and devise plans to meet these needs.

Demand Forecasting

demand forecasting
A process used in HR planning that entails predicting the number and types of people the organization will need at some future point in time.

Demand forecasting involves predicting the number and types of people the organization will need at some future point in time. There are two general approaches to demand forecasting: statistical and judgmental.

Statistical Approaches

business factors   Attributes of a business, such as sales volume or market share, that closely relate to the size of the needed workforce.

Using a statistical approach, an organization predicts needed workforce size on the basis of certain **business factors.** A business factor is an attribute of the business, such as sales volume or market share, that closely relates to the size of the needed workforce. For example, a hospital could use the business factor of projected patient load to predict the number of nurses it would need at some point in time.

A statistical approach to demand forecasting is typically used when an organization operates in a stable environment, where an appropriate business factor can be predicted with some degree of certainty. For example, a statistical approach may be appropriate for a hospital located in an area with little population growth. Organizations operating in less stable environments (e.g., a hospital in an area experiencing explosive growth and change) are more likely to rely on a judgmental approach.

trend analysis   A process used in HR planning in which the future demand for human resources is projected on the basis of past business trends regarding a business factor.

The most commonly used statistical methods of demand forecasting are trend, ratio, and regression analysis. In **trend analysis,** the future demand for human resources is projected on the basis of past business trends regarding a business factor. An example of a trend analysis is illustrated in Exhibit 3-3, which depicts the relationship between a business factor (namely, sales volume) and workforce size. As one can see from the exhibit, if the company expects its 2007 sales to be $10 million, it will need to increase its workforce to a size of nearly 240, which is the number of employees it had in 2003 when sales were $10.2 million.

ratio analysis   A process used in HR planning to determine future HR demand by computing an exact ratio between the specific business factor and the number of employees needed.

Ratio analysis is the process of determining future HR demand by computing an exact ratio between the specific business factor and the number of employees

EXHIBIT 3-3	HR Trend Analysis for a Manufacturing Firm				
	2003	2004	2005	2006	2007*
Sales (thousands of dollars)	$10,200	$8,700	$7,800	$9,500	$10,000
Number of employees	240	200	165	215	239
* Projected sales.					

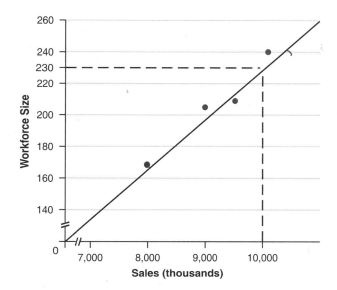

Figure 3-2
Regression Line Depicting Relationship between Sales Volume and Workforce Size

needed. It thus provides a more precise estimate than trend analysis. For instance, the demand for professors at a university could be forecast on the basis of the student-faculty ratio. Let's suppose, for example, that a university has 10,000 students and 500 professors; the student-faculty ratio is thus 10,000:500 or 20:1. This ratio means that for every 20 students, the university needs 1 professor. If the university anticipates an increase in student enrollment for next year of 1,000 students, it would need to hire 50 (1,000/20) additional professors (assuming that none of the 500 current professors leaves prior to next year).

Regression analysis is similar to both trend and ratio analyses in that forecasts are based on the relationship between a business factor and workforce size. This method is more statistically sophisticated, however. An organization first draws a scatter diagram depicting the relationship between the business factor and workforce size. It then calculates a regression line—a line that cuts right through the center of the points on the scatter diagram. (The regression line is mathematically determined using a formula found in most statistical texts). By inspecting the regression line, one can see how many employees are needed at each value of the business factor.

An example of how regression analysis can be used to project HR demand is shown in Figure 3-2. In this example, the figures used in the trend analysis are now depicted in the form of a scatter diagram. The line running through the center of the points plotted on the scatter diagram is the regression line.

To determine the number of employees needed when the sales volume is $10 million, one would follow the path indicated by the dashed line. One would start at the point on the *x*-axis reading "10,000" and then move up vertically until reaching the regression line. The value on the *y*-axis corresponding to that point (i.e., 230) reflects the needed workforce size.

regression analysis
A statistical tool used in HR planning to determine the number of employees needed by a company at some future point in time.

Precaution Regarding the Use of Statistical Methods

Statistical methods of demand forecasting assume that the relationship between workforce size and the business factor remains constant over time. If this relationship were to change unexpectedly, the forecast would become inaccurate. For example, the forecast of needed professors based on the student-faculty ratio would be inaccurate if the university decided to change its teaching approach and institute "distance learning" classes. This approach to teaching involves the use of video equipment, which can beam the professor's lectures to many different locations, thus allowing many more students to enroll in the class. Consequently, the 20:1 ratio would no longer apply; the university would now be able to function with fewer professors.

Judgmental Methods of Demand Forecasting

As the name implies, judgmental approaches to demand forecasting involve the use of human judgment, rather than a manipulation of numbers. Two of the most commonly used judgmental techniques are group brainstorming and sales force estimates.

The **group brainstorming** technique of demand forecasting uses a panel of "experts"—people within the organization who, collectively, understand the market, the industry, and the technological developments bearing on HRM needs and who are asked to "put their heads together" to generate a forecast. A variety of group brainstorming techniques exist. Most involve a face-to-face discussion among group members, who are asked to reach a consensus.

When using a group brainstorming technique to forecast demand for human resources, participants must make certain assumptions regarding the future. That is, they must examine the firm's strategic plans for developing new products or services, expanding to new markets, and so forth, and then try to predict such things as:[13]

- Future demands from the marketplace for the organization's products and services
- The percentage of the market that the organization will serve
- The availability and nature of new technologies that may affect the amounts and types of products or services that can be offered

The accuracy of the forecasts depends on the correctness of these assumptions. Of course, the future is very difficult to predict, because it can be subject to many uncertainties. The organization must therefore continually monitor its demand forecasts in light of any unexpected changes.

The use of **sales force estimates** represents another judgmental approach for forecasting HR demand. This approach is most appropriately used when the need for additional employees arises from the introduction of new products. When a new product is launched, salespeople are asked to estimate the demand for the product (i.e., expected sales volume) based on their knowledge of customer needs and interests. The organization then uses this information to estimate how many employees will be needed to meet this demand. A drawback of this approach concerns the possibility of bias. That is, some salespeople may purposely underestimate product demands so they will look good when their own sales exceed the forecasts. Others may overestimate demand because they are overly optimistic about what they can sell.

Supply Forecasting

Once its demand forecast has been made, the organization has a pretty good idea of the number and nature of positions it will need to carry out its work at a particular point in time. It then estimates which of these positions will be filled at that time. The process used to make this estimation is called **supply forecasting.**

Steps to Supply Forecasting

Supply forecasting is a two-step process. In the first step, the organization groups its positions by title, function, and level of responsibility. The groupings should reflect levels of positions across which employees may be expected to advance. For instance, the HRM group might include the job titles of HR assistant, HR manager, and HR director. The secretarial group might include secretarial clerk, principal secretary, senior secretary, and administrative assistant.

The second step of supply forecasting is to estimate, within each job group, how many of its current employees will remain in their positions during the planning period, how many will move to another position (e.g., through transfer, promotion, demotion), and how many will leave the organization. These predictions are based, in part, on past mobility trends (e.g., turnover and promotion rates). The organization

---

group brainstorming
A technique of demand forecasting in which a panel of "experts" generates a forecast in collaboration.

sales force estimates
A technique of demand forecasting in which sales personnel are asked to estimate the demand for a new product based on their knowledge of customer needs and interests.

supply forecasting
A process used to estimate which organizational positions will be filled at some future point in time.

should also take into account any plans for mergers, acquisitions, divestitures of units or divisions, layoffs, retrenchments and downsizings, and even hostile takeovers.

When making its supply forecast, the organization should also look at specific individuals. Some may have already announced, for instance, that they are retiring at the end of the year, returning to school in the fall, or getting married and plan on moving to a different part of the country in June.

Computerized statistical packages are available to help estimate the flow of employees through an organization.[14] The estimates generated by these packages can be fairly accurate in stable environments. When the environment is unstable, of course, these estimates are suspect. For instance, an organization may base its estimates on past turnover rates, which have been about 10 percent during each of the past five years. If the turnover rate were to change drastically (because of job dissatisfaction, downsizing, etc.), the organization would severely underestimate its future staffing needs.

Estimating Future Human Resource Needs

A firm derives its specific staffing needs by combining the results of the supply and demand forecasts within each job group. For example, let's say that a firm currently employs 25 secretaries. As the result of its supply forecast, it predicts that 5 of these secretarial positions will become vacant by the end of the planning period (because of retirements, promotions, and so forth). Its demand forecast predicts that 3 new secretarial positions will be needed during the coming period (because of an increased demand for the company's product). By combining these two estimates, the firm now realizes that it must hire 8 new secretaries (5 to replace those expected to vacate their positions, plus 3 to fill the newly created positions).

3-2c Outcomes of the HR Planning Process

When the HR planning process is completed, a firm must establish and implement HRM practices to help it meet its human resource needs. Actually, we will discuss the implementation of specific HRM practices within the context of strategic and HR planning throughout the remainder of this text. In the following paragraphs, however, we provide a brief overview of this topic, focusing on HRM practices designed to help organizations deal with anticipated oversupplies and undersupplies of employees.

Dealing with an Oversupply of Employees

As we noted in Chapter 2, the current trend toward organizational restructuring usually results in a smaller workforce. Therefore, when an organization's strategic plan calls for restructuring, the HRM response is usually one of downsizing. As we also noted in Chapter 2, downsizing usually means layoffs. Because of the negative outcomes that are often associated with layoffs, employers are encouraged to seek alternatives, such as hiring freezes, early retirements, restricted overtime, job sharing, pay reductions, and the like.

Dealing with an Undersupply of Employees

When the results of the demand and supply forecasting project an undersupply of employees at some future point in time, the organization must decide how to resolve this problem. The solution may involve hiring additional staff, but there are other options, as well, which we now discuss.

Hiring Additional Workers

When HR plans indicate an undersupply of employees, firms can recruit applicants to staff jobs with anticipated vacancies. The first step is to conduct a job analysis to determine the qualifications needed for each vacant job. The topic of job analysis is addressed in Chapter 4, "Analyzing Jobs."

Barden's Approach to Resolving a Recruitment Problem

The Barden Corporation confronted the need to increase its hourly workforce by 125 people. Despite the fact that the local unemployment rate was only 2.5 percent, the company was able to recruit a sufficient number of people. It accomplished this by focusing recruiting efforts on a group whose unemployment rate was high—foreign immigrants. Because of their lack of fluency in English, however, they needed to be taught the language. Barden thus provided them with an intensive 15-day English course.

Source: Jackson, S.E., and Schuler, R.S. (1990). Human resource planning: Challenges for industrial/organizational psychologists. *American Psychologist, 45* (2), 223–239.

The next step is to determine where and how to recruit the needed individuals. For instance, a company must decide whether to fill its vacancies externally (i.e., from the external labor market) or internally (i.e., from its own current workforce). The factors to consider when making this choice are discussed in Chapter 5, "Recruiting Applicants."

When recruiting externally, an organization should first assess its attractiveness in the eyes of potential applicants; "unattractive" employers may have trouble generating a sufficiently large applicant pool. Such employers should attempt to increase the number of people who are attracted to the organization and thus interested in applying for a job there. It could accomplish this aim by increasing starting pay levels and/or improving benefit packages. Another option is to target certain protected groups whose members may be underemployed in the local labor market, such as older, disabled, or foreign-origin individuals. On the Road to Competitive Advantage 3-2 illustrates how one company benefited from choosing this option.

Internal recruitment efforts can be improved by the use of career development programs. When designing such a program, the organization should collect information regarding the work history and skill levels of each of its employees. Such information would include age, education level, training, special skills (e.g., foreign language spoken), and promotion record. This information could be stored on a computer just as it was at GM in the opening case. We discuss the role of the computer in Section 3-2d, "Human Resource Information Systems."

This employee information allows the organization to determine which current employees are qualified to assume jobs with greater levels of responsibility. For instance, in departments where skilled managers are in short supply, a management replacement chart can be prepared that lists current managers, proposes likely future replacements, and gives an estimate of when the replacement candidate will be trained and available to fill an open position. This topic, called *management succession planning,* is discussed further in Chapter 7, "Training and Developing Employees."

Alternatives to Additional Hiring

Instead of hiring new workers to meet increasing demands, an organization may decide to improve the productivity of the existing workforce through additional training. Other options would be the use of overtime, additional shifts, job reassignments, or temporary workers (as discussed in Chapter 5).

Another option is to improve retention rates. When this aim is met, firms will have fewer job vacancies to fill. Many of the HRM practices described throughout the remainder of this text can be implemented in ways that enhance employee retention rates. What follows is a "sampling" of those activities.

Retention rates can be improved at the outset of the employer/employee relationship, when applicants are first recruited. As we discuss in Chapter 5, for example, retention rates are likely to improve when applicants are given a realistic preview of what their jobs would actually be like (warts and all), rather than an overly glowing one.

Workers want to feel valued and needed by their organization. As we noted in Chapter 2, the current climate of mergers, acquisitions, and layoffs has made many workers feel very insecure about their jobs. Employees with such feelings often begin shopping around for other jobs. These fears could be eased by implementing HR plans for training and cross-training of workers to perform a variety of functions, thus ensuring that they have the necessary skills to continue to make ongoing contributions to the firm.

Management training is also crucial in this regard. The organization must train managers to be good supervisors. Poor "people management" is a primary cause of voluntary turnover. Managers at all levels should know what is expected of them in terms of managing people instead of just managing budgets.[15]

Companies can also improve retention rates by creating a work environment that encourages employees to participate actively in the company's total welfare.[16] Workers want recognition for their contributions to organizational progress, but this recognition must be tailored to the individual needs of workers. Whereas some workers may be motivated by monetary rewards, others seek different rewards, such as recognition by peers and managers, a feeling of accomplishment, or job satisfaction. We discuss how an organization can best structure reward/recognition programs in Chapter 10, "Implementing Productivity Improvement Programs."

As we discussed in Chapter 2, workers are now demanding more flexible schedules to best fit their lifestyles. Organizations can improve their retention rates by implementing programs to accommodate these needs, such as job sharing, shortened workweeks, and telecommuting via computer and modem.

Companies can also improve their retention rates by offering attractive benefit packages, such as generous retirement plans, stock ownership, health and dental insurance, employee discount programs, and the like.[17] As we note in Chapter 9, "Determining Pay and Benefits," many firms are now offering "cafeteria plan" benefit packages, which are tailored to the specific needs of each of their employees.

3-2d Human Resource Information Systems

As indicated earlier, the HR planning activities of most organizations rely on a computer to store and process necessary information. This HR planning function is usually part of a larger computerized system called a **human resource information system or HRIS.** An HRIS is a computerized information package that provides management with increasing capacity to record, store, manipulate, and communicate information across wide geographic boundaries, with access to many users.[18] Some organizations store their data in a mainframe linked to personal computers; others use a decentralized network system with smaller computers in workstations in various functional areas.[19]

Such systems are used for a variety of purposes, in addition to HR planning. In the following paragraphs, we discuss the types of data stored by an HRIS and the uses for this information. We conclude by discussing the confidentiality of sensitive data and describing procedures to secure the data.

Types of Data Contained in an HRIS

An HRIS contains information about a company's jobs and employees. The job file typically lists the number and types of jobs needed to achieve the organization's strategic goals, the number of people needed in each job, and the qualifications needed to perform each job (based on job analysis information; see Chapter 4).

The employee file lists such information as an individual's equal employment opportunity classification, date of hire, salary history, performance ratings, and so on.

human resource information system (HRIS) A computerized information package that provides management with increasing capacity to record, store, manipulate, and communicate information to users.

EXHIBIT 3-4	Information Typically Included in an HRIS

Job Information	**Employee Information**
Position title	Biographical data
Number of current vacancies	EEO classification
Qualifications needed	Education
Place in career ladder	Date of hire
Salary range	Position held with company
Replacement candidates	Salary history
Turnover rate	Performance ratings
	Training received
	Prior work experience
	Developmental needs
	Career interests/objectives
	Specialized skills
	Honors and awards
	Benefits received
	Licenses and certifications held
	Payroll information
	Attendance data
	Tax deduction information
	Pension contributions
	Turnover

A more complete list of information typically included in an HRIS database is shown in Exhibit 3-4.

A firm's HR professionals are usually responsible for gathering and inputting information into the HRIS and for maintaining the system as employee records change. Many companies, however, allow others outside the HRM department to add data.

Purposes Served by an HRIS

Information contained in an HRIS can serve many purposes. An HRIS can handle most of the record keeping done by HR professionals, making it easier for these individuals to track compensation, payroll, benefits, insurance policies, career paths, and employee history. Seagate, a California-based computer disk drive maker, uses its HRIS to:[20]

- Provide a central repository for information on benefits, HR policies, and processes
- Allow users to compare different benefit packages
- Provide managers with instructions on how to implement 15 different HR practices
- Serve as a basis for the firm's succession planning program, in which employees submit a personal profile over the web and keep it updated

By automating tasks previously done by hand, an HRIS can reduce paperwork and cut administrative costs. At National Cash Register, for example, the computerization of its pension record keeping eliminated several paper-and-pencil entries and manual calculations, and helped cut administrative costs. It also increased the accuracy of pension payout estimates by nearly 90 percent.[21]

Additionally, organizational members outside the HRM department can more easily access the information. By providing such access, the administrative function of the HRM department can become more decentralized. For instance, Thomas W. Ruff Company, an office furniture supplier, uses an HRIS to track payroll and employee information from its three store locations. By merging the functions of human resources and payroll, the program reduces labor costs and allows for improved com-

---

EXHIBIT 3-5 | Purposes Served by an HRIS in Addition to HR Planning

Make Budget-Related Calculations

An HRIS can be used to calculate overtime pay and employee pension benefits at different retirement ages. It could also be used to compare current payroll levels against budgets.

Report Turnover Rates by Department

Many systems allow users to list reasons for voluntary and involuntary terminations. The HRIS can thus create monthly reports showing how many employees left the organization and why they left.

Track External Candidates

The HRIS can retrieve a range of highly detailed information about applicants and their employment needs.

Track Employee Participation in Each Benefit Option

The HRIS enables a company to calculate employer-paid and employee-contribution values.

Track Accruals of Vacation Days and Sick Leave

The HRIS can track vacation and sick days taken by each employee and the number of eligible days remaining.

Sources: Andrews, J. (1989). Proving that HRIS equals success. *Personnel,* October, 56–59; Broderick, R., and Boudreau, J.W. (1992). Human resource management, information technology, and competitive edge. *Academy of Management Executive, 6* (2), 7–17.

---

munication with employees because information regarding salary, performance reviews, years of service, and skills is more efficiently tracked.[22]

From an HR planning perspective, the information contained in HRIS files can be essential for filling vacant positions. As we saw in the opening case, an HRIS can serve a career progression system by having the computer search through employee records to identify those having the requisite skills, experience, training, and interest in an open position.

Some other purposes served by an HRIS are described in Exhibit 3-5 and Figure 3-3.

HRIS on the "Net"

Many companies have begun expanding their HR information systems by adding a couple of Internet-related features—the **intranet** and **extranet.** Intranets are Internet networks that are accessible only to employees within the company; intranets can store a great deal of HR information, such as employee handbooks, benefits information, phone directories, and job postings. Intranet usage allows companies to

intranet Internet networks that are accessible to people within a company.

extranet Technology that links a company's intranet to outside organizations and vendors.

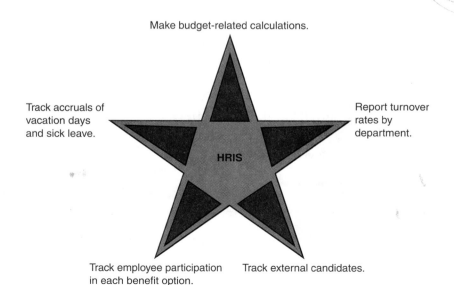

Make budget-related calculations.

Track accruals of vacation days and sick leave.

Report turnover rates by department.

HRIS

Track employee participation in each benefit option.

Track external candidates.

Figure 3-3
Five Purposes Served by an HRIS

> **EXHIBIT 3-6** | Security Measures for Protecting the Confidentiality of Sensitive HRIS Data

- Ensure that all users log off before they leave the PC, even if they plan to be away only for a short time.
- Warn users not to give their password to anyone.
- Change passwords on a regular basis.
- Ensure that current and backup copies, data files, software, and printouts are properly controlled so that only authorized users can obtain them.
- Monitor procedures to ensure that PC users are maintaining an effective level of security.
- Encrypt the raw data so that it makes no sense to an unauthorized user.
- Keep a detailed audit trail. Make sure that any operation performed on the data is captured in a detailed transaction file.

Sources: Adams, L.D. (1992). Securing your HRIS in a microcomputer environment. *HRMagazine,* February, 56–61; Leonard, B. (1991). Open and shut HRIS. *Personnel Journal,* July, 59–62.

---

save money by eliminating printing and distribution costs. Employees like it because it allows them to quickly and privately access HR information. Because of these advantages, the use of intranets is increasing rapidly. By late 1996, more than 90 percent of *Fortune* 500 companies were using them.[23]

Companies are now taking this technology to the next level by creating extranets, which link a firm's intranet to a variety of outside organizations and vendors. The extranet gives employees secure access to information and services from outside parties. For instance, employees can log onto their company's intranet and access its insurance provider. They can then review the needed information and take action—enroll in a plan, select a physician, and so forth. Or they can access their pension plans. At The Compaq Computer Corporation, for example, employees can view charts and graphs showing how their pension savings will build over the next 10 or 20 years. They can review their fund allocations and the past performances of funds, learn about investment options, and view their mutual portfolio in real time. Moreover, they can conduct online transactions, including relocation of funds.[24]

Ensuring the Confidentiality of HRIS Information

Because many of the directories included in an HRIS contain highly sensitive data, the organization must ensure that user access is limited to relevant information. As a general rule, sensitive and confidential records should only be accessible by the HRM department or specified individuals. (The legal issues regarding an employee's privacy rights are discussed in Chapter 11, "Complying with Workplace Justice Laws.")

One way to protect the integrity and confidentiality of sensitive information is to institute strong written policies that stipulate the organization's intention to protect employee privacy rights. The policy should specify the consequences for gaining unauthorized access to the data or for using the data for any purpose other than that for which it is intended. The penalties for violating this policy should be stiff.[25]

Other possible security measures are listed in Exhibit 3-6.

3-3 The Manager's Guide

3-3a HR Planning and the Manager's Job

HR planning is an essential function for all line managers—they must thus ensure that work conducted within their units is aligned with the strategic goals of the organization. To accomplish this aim, they formulate goals for their units, develop strategies for meeting those goals, and formulate individual performance goals (usually in collaboration with each of their employees, as discussed in Chapter 8, "Appraising Employee Job Performance").

Staffing

One of a line manager's most important responsibilities is to ensure that his or her work unit is properly staffed at all times. To meet this responsibility, the manager must be able to accurately forecast the volume of work to be completed during the upcoming period and then devise a work schedule that assures the work can be completed competently and on schedule. During this process, the manager must schedule overtime, vacations, and so forth, and adjust work schedules in "emergency" situations. If projections show that work volume will be too great for current staff to handle, the manager may need to request authorization to create new positions.

Employee Retention

Line managers also play an important role in the area of employee retention, because their style of management can have a major impact on a subordinate's decision to remain with the company. Managers must be able to establish good working relationships with their employees by treating them in a fair and consistent manner, while exhibiting concern for their well-being. Managers must also be effective teachers, motivators, and communicators. These "people skills" are especially important in today's environment in which managers face the challenge of having to manage a diverse and newly empowered workforce.

3-3b How the HR Department Can Help

Obviously, a major role played by the HRM department is the development and implementation of the firm's HR plans. However, the HRM department can also help in the HR planning process in other ways as well. In fact, HR professionals are now often included in all aspects of planning.

The Role of the HR Professional in Strategic Planning

Until recently, organizations did not normally include HR professionals in the strategic planning process. Strategic planners tended to be high-level executives who regarded employees as organizational expenses, rather than assets or resources that could enable a firm to achieve its mission. These planners often failed to realize that in order for a firm to pursue the best opportunities, it must be able to utilize its human resources efficiently.[26]

Because they did not always understand the human dimensions of their decisions, organizations found themselves planning their futures without first understanding the HR implications of these decisions. Organizations have now come to realize that many of their corporate business objectives have HR ramifications, and achieving competitive advantage through better human resource management requires that HR professionals help shape, not just implement, overall business strategy. For instance, it is the HR professional who best understands the shifting nature of the labor force and is more aware of skill shortages in some labor markets and the oversupply of other kinds of skills. This information could be crucial. Suppose, for example, that a hospital was considering the option of adding a new cancer wing. The HR professional could provide input into determining the feasibility of this action. For instance, if there was an acute nursing shortage in the local labor market, the HR professional could tell the other planners of the difficulties the hospital would face when trying to staff the new wing.

HR professionals are now being increasingly utilized as key players in the strategic planning process. A recent survey of hospitals, for instance, found a majority of them had HR professionals on their strategic planning teams.[27] This means that the HR professional, like those in finance, operations, and marketing, are now often considered a full partner in the strategic planning process.

Developing and Implementing HR Plans

HR professionals' plans must be aligned with changes spurred by the organization's strategic plan. The plan may call for such interventions as:

- Greater flexibility in the workplace
- Greater rigor in training
- Increased responsibilities for management
- Increased worker participation
- The use of performance incentives[28]

To address these needs, HR professionals must devise plans for implementing new management initiatives, such as work teams and worker participation, changing reward systems, modifying benefit packages, and assisting with organizational redesign.

As they implement these kinds of programs, HR professionals must consider the corporate culture. **Corporate culture** is the pattern of shared values, mores, and behaviors that separates one organization from others operating in the same industry. New strategies and HR plans must fit the corporate culture if they are to work. Accordingly, HR professionals must sometimes work with management to change the corporate culture prior to implementing HRM programs. For instance, the corporation may need to create a more open and trusting environment before implementing worker participation programs. We discuss this topic further in Chapter 10.

> **corporate culture** The pattern of shared values, mores, and behaviors that separates one organization from others who are operating in the same industry.

Evaluation of HR Plans

Only when the operational plans of the HRM department are evaluated can the organization know if the HR strategies were effective. Analysis and measurement of the work of the HRM department should be ongoing. The department's policies, rules, and standards must be worked into the overall organizational control system, including activities related to target setting, measuring, and monitoring performance. Exhibit 3-7 presents a series of questions the HRM department can use to assess its overall contribution to successful implementation of the HR planning process.

Specific HRM practices should also be evaluated. For instance, do the company's selection practices identify the best candidates? Are employees getting the training they need? Is the performance appraisal system having its desired effect on employee motivation? The evaluation of these specific HRM practices is discussed throughout this book when such practices are addressed. For instance, the evaluation of selection procedures is discussed in Chapter 6, "Selecting Applicants."

EXHIBIT 3-7	Key Questions for Assessing the Planning Process of the Human Resource Department

1. Does the firm use strategic planning concepts?
2. Is the HR department involved in overall strategic planning for the organization?
3. Are company objectives and goals measurable and well communicated to everyone in the organization?
4. Do managers delegate authority to departments following strategic plans?
5. Do managers at all hierarchical levels plan effectively and continually?
6. Is the organization's structure shaped so that all departments are involved in the strategic planning process?
7. Is employee morale acceptable?
8. Are job duties, specifications, and descriptions clear?
9. Are employee turnover and absenteeism low?
10. Are organizational reward and control mechanisms effective and tied to overall strategic goals and objectives?
11. Are all units, departments, employees, managers, etc., working toward the same, congruent goals?

3-3c HRM Skill-Building for Managers

Gauging Future Human Resource Needs

You should view a human resource plan as a necessary and important document that requires the continual input of all functional area managers. Information regarding the future needs and workforce demands of your unit will better enable the HRM department to help identify, select, and train current and future workers as needed. Because not all departments have the same needs for human resources, the functional managers must work together to develop a comprehensive plan.

The most direct approach to getting this information is to meet with an HR professional, top managers, and other line managers on a regular basis, certainly at least semiannually. The format of these meetings should be as follows:

1. Ask top management to clarify the organization's strategic plan and explain how this plan is expected to impact each department.

2. Specify the number of people you will need to fill future positions. Discuss if current employees can be trained or prepared to assume new job responsibilities.

3. Examine external industry trends to determine how these changes will translate into employee needs.

4. Brainstorm several scenarios for the future position of the company, both long term and short term, and discuss how these will change staffing needs. Be sure to report any significant changes affecting your own unit.

5. Discuss plans for encouraging employees to attend professional meetings and seminars so as to stay current on changes and trends developing in their particular areas of expertise.

6. List any training your employees will need, describing in detail how much training and what kinds are needed. For example, many individuals now need sexual harassment training, instruction in business ethics, instruction on how to respond to the Americans with Disabilities Act, and training on how to work more effectively in a culturally diverse environment.

7. As a team, prepare this plan to distribute to top management, as well as the HRM department. Try to assign an accurate time frame to the needs and separate them into immediate, short-term, and long-term categories. The more accurate the information, the better the HRM department can support these business plans.

8. Discuss how the functional departments can and should work with HRM. What ways can HRM benefit the other functional areas? What information must the functions provide to HRM? How can communication between the functions and HRM be facilitated?

Be realistic about industry and company growth projections and bring to light any problems in your unit that can be resolved through an HR plan. The key to planning future needs is active, frequent, and open communications between all areas. If conditions are extremely volatile, more frequent meetings and opportunities for input into the HRM plan will be needed.

Chapter Objectives Revisited

1. Understand how human resource planning contributes to a firm's competitive advantage.

   - By linking HRM practices to organizational goals
   - By helping a firm plan its future recruitment, selection, and training and development practices
   - By helping a firm avoid problems by operating proactively, rather than reactively

2. Explain why and how firms engage in strategic planning.

   - The aim of strategic planning is to formulate an overall business plan and specify how the plan will be achieved.
   - A strategic plan is implemented in four stages:
     - Determine the organizational mission.
     - Scan the organizational environment.
     - Set strategic goals.
     - Formulate a strategic plan.

3. Explain why and how human resource planning activities are conducted.

   - The aim of human resource planning is to ensure that people are available with the appropriate characteristics and skills when and where the organization needs them.
   - HR planning consists of the following activities:
     - Demand forecasting, which involves making predictions about the number and types of people that the organization will need at some future point in time
     - Supply forecasting, which provides an estimate of the number of future positions that the company expects to fill during the planning period

   - An HR plan is derived by combining the results of supply and demand forecasts made for each organizational job group.

4. Describe how HRM practices are developed in response to an HR plan.

   - If an oversupply of employees is projected, the organization must downsize or implement an alternative to downsizing, such as hiring freezes or early retirements.
   - If an undersupply of employees is projected, the organization must recruit and hire additional workers or seek an alternative, such as overtime, temporary workers, or an improvement of retention rates.

5. Understand the role of human resource information systems in planning and other HRM practices.

   - An HRIS is a computerized information package that provides management with increasing capability to record, store, manipulate, and communicate information across wide geographic boundaries, with access to many users.
   - An HRIS carries information about a company's jobs and employees and serves these purposes:
     - Serves the company's career progression system
     - Reduces paperwork and cuts administrative costs
     - Provides organizational members outside the HRM department with easy access to employee records

Review Questions

Note: You can find the correct answers to these questions by taking the quiz and then submitting your answers in the Online Edition. The program will automatically score your submission. If you miss a question, the program will provide the correct answer, a rationale for the answer, and the section number in the chapter where the topic is discussed.

1. HR planning is defined as

   a. a reactive method of dealing with human resource problems.

   b. a self-contained process that seeks to identify the strengths and weaknesses of human resource systems apart from general strategic planning.

   c. a process and a set of activities that attempts to respond to an organization's need for human resources under changing conditions.

   d. the process by which resources (e.g., equipment, raw materials) are allocated to specific individuals (i.e., humans) in the work organization.

2. Which of the following steps is not a part of the strategic planning process?

   a. scanning the organizational environment

   b. setting strategic goals

   c. conducting a utility analysis

   d. determining the organizational mission

3. Name one factor that organizational planners are attempting to assess when scanning the external environment for strategic planning purposes.

   a. the opportunities and threats posed by the competition
   b. the strengths and weaknesses of their own organization
   c. the supply of and demand for resources
   d. organizational culture and climate

4. A human resource need is defined as

   a. labor market conditions minus workforce skills.
   b. workforce demands minus labor market supply.
   c. management needs minus employees needs.
   d. the percentage of minority employees to the total labor force.

5. Supply and demand forecasting are

   a. routine HR planning tools used by almost all organizations.
   b. dependent on government employment statistics to be completed accurately.
   c. combined to identify a firm's specific staffing needs.
   d. more difficult to complete in times of business stability.

6. Which of the following techniques would not be used to minimize the problems associated with oversupply of personnel?

   a. pay reductions
   b. job sharing
   c. layoffs
   d. training

7. Organizations can improve employee retention by using all of the following *except*

   a. realistic job previews.
   b. training.
   c. quality of work life programs.
   d. scientific management.

8. A human resource information system is

   a. a computerized system that contains job and employee information including the work history, skills, and demographic characteristics of employees.
   b. a database containing standard operating procedures for performing work activities.
   c. a computerized system for tracking organizational indicators of productivity including downtime, profits, scrap, rework, and sales.
   d. a referral system that enables new employees to identify current employees who are most likely to have answers to their questions about the company.

9. To avoid violations of employee privacy when using human resource information systems, an organization should

   a. require new hires, as a condition of employment, to complete a form that allows free access to their records.
   b. limit access to sensitive and confidential records to those who have a "need to know."
   c. allow each employee to decide which parts of his or her file may be reviewed by others in the organization.
   d. avoid storing information about a person's strengths and development needs.

10. Which of the following factors is *not* considered when using the group brainstorming approach to forecasting demand?

    a. future demands from the marketplace for the organization's products and services
    b. the percentage of the market that the organization will serve
    c. the availability of employees with the skills needed to implement the strategic plan
    d. the availability and nature of new technologies that may affect the amounts and types of products or services that can be offered

Discussion Questions

1. Describe three ways in which effective HR planning can enhance a firm's competitive advantage.

2. Why do some companies avoid HR planning? What are the likely consequences when HR planning is omitted?

3. Describe the way in which an organization scans its environment. Why is this an important process?

4. Define the following terms: *mission statement*, *strategic goal*, and *strategic plan*.

5. What is the aim of demand forecasting? Briefly describe each of the methods of demand forecasting.

6. What is meant by "past mobility trends"? What bearing do they have on supply forecasting?

7. What options does an organization have for dealing with predicted job vacancies?

8. Describe three ways in which an organization can enhance its retention rates.

9. Describe the two types of data contained in an HRIS.

10. What are the advantages of using an HRIS as opposed to using a manual system?

11. Describe three uses for an HRIS.

12. Describe the manager's role with regard to HR planning.

13. Describe the role of the HR professional with regard to HR planning.

Experiential Exercise

Forecasting HR Demand for Installers

A large kitchen cabinet and appliance distributor in the Southeast expects an increase in annual sales during the next 10 years from $1,500,000 to $2,250,000. In scanning its external environment, it notes that the local environment is changing:

- Many new employees have entered the market area.

- The population is aging; many are now "empty-nest" couples whose children have moved away. These individuals are remodeling their homes and seek larger, more expensive kitchens.

- Many new families have entered the area who are budget conscious and want a kitchen to fit into their price range.

- Building costs are steady.

The HR planner for the kitchen distributor wants to forecast the requirements for installers for the next 10-year period. Because installers require 8 months of on-the-job training in addition to classroom instruction, an accurate forecast is needed. The CEO wants to use their own installers in the future rather than relying on the more expensive outside subcontractors. Mr. Rodriguez, the HR planner, decides to forecast HR demand by determining the relationship between the sales of the distributor and the number of installers required. He contacts several distributors of various sizes in the United States and obtains the following information:

Sales in Millions ($)	Number of Installers
1.0	4
1.5	7
2.0	9
2.5	15
3.0	17

1. Plot these figures on a piece of graph paper. Estimate a regression line. That is, draw a line that cuts straight through the center of the points (one that minimizes the distance between the lines and the plotted points).

2. Using your plot, estimate the number of installers needed for forecasted sales of $2.25 million.

3. Given the trends and the nature of the industry, what other advice can you give the HR planner? Why might using the plotted information alone be risky? What other factors should Mr. Rodriguez consider? Why?

Case

Succession Planning for Federal Express Corporation[29]

In a June 3, 1993, article in *The Memphis Commercial Appeal,* Federal Express Corporation, the leader of the air package delivery industry, announced the sudden resignation of two top executives. Thomas R. Oliver, vice president for worldwide customer operations at Federal Express, resigned effective June 21, 1993, to accept a position as president and chief executive officer of VoiceCom Systems Inc.

Carole A. Presley, a senior vice president for marketing and corporate communications, announced her resignation effective September 1, 1993. Her plans were to move to Florida, write, and start a consulting business. Her decision to resign was sudden and voluntary.

The company named William Razzouk to succeed Oliver. He was the former senior vice president of sales and customer service. No replacements for Ms. Presley or for the position vacated by the promotion of Mr. Razzouk were announced.

Both key resignations came at a time when the company had reported international losses and a drop in corporate earnings. Oliver was said to have improved international operations, although they still were not profitable.

Following these resignations, Federal Express Corporation's stock price fell. One brokerage firm removed the stock from its recommended list and another changed the rating to "moderately attractive" from "buy" as the market reacted to the resignations of these two top executives. The company's stock closed on Thursday, June 3, at $45.50 a share, down $4.37 a share. There were 764,100 shares traded on the New York Stock Exchange during the day, compared with an average daily trading volume of 165,000 shares. Trading in the stock was even delayed at the opening of the market due to an order imbalance caused by having more sellers than buyers of shares. An analyst at Lehman Brothers admitted that she was concerned with the company's continued loss of management talent. Turnover is not a good sign, according to another analyst at Morgan Stanley.

Questions

1. Why do you think these individuals resigned?
2. Outline a plan the organization can take to avoid future problems of this nature.
3. How will overall strategic planning for the short-term and long-term future of the firm be influenced by these resignations?

References

1. Jossi, F. (2001). Taking the E-HR plunge. *HRMagazine, 46* (9), 96–103.
2. Walker, J.W. (1980). *Human Resource Planning.* New York: McGraw-Hill.
3. Bommer, M., and DeLaPorte, R. (1992). A context for envisioning the future. *National Productivity Review, 11* (4), 549–552.
4. Jackson, S.E., and Schuler, R.S. (1990). Human resource planning: Challenges for industrial/organizational psychologists. *American Psychologist, 45* (2), 223–239.
5. Harvey, L.J. (1983). Effective planning for human resource development. *Personnel Administrator, 28* (10), 45–54.
6. EEI/INPO Task Force. (1978). *A human resource management system for the nuclear power industry: System implementation manual.* Unpublished manuscript.
7. Wilson, I. (1986). The strategic management technology: Corporate fad or strategic necessity. *Long-Range Planning, 19* (2), 21–22.
8. David, F. (1987). Corporate mission statements: The bottom line. *Academy of Management Executive, 1* (2), 109–116.
9. Walker. *Human Resource Planning.*
10. Hambrick, D.C., and Fredrickson, J.W. (2001). Are you sure you have a strategy? *Academy of Management Executive, 15* (4), 48–59.
11. Schuler, R.S., Fulkerson, J.R., and Dowling, P.J. (1991). Strategic performance measurement and management in multinational corporations. *Human Resource Management, 30* (3), 365–392.
12. Jackson and Schuler. Human resource planning.
13. Ibid.
14. Ibid.
15. Sheehan, W. (1992). A CEO's strategic plan for training. *Training, 29* (11), 86.
16. Charof, E. (1991). Staffing during a recession. *HRMagazine, 36* (8), 86–88.
17. Ahrens, R. (1992). Financial planning for growing your business. *Inc.,* September, 61–65.
18. Broderick, R., and Boudreau, J.W. (1992). Human resource management, information technology, and competitive edge. *Academy of Management Executive, 6* (2), 7–17.
19. Grensing, L. (1992). Computers revolutionize human resources industry. *Office Systems, 9* (3), 12–14.
20. Roberts, B. (2002). Content to order. *HRMagazine,* July, 79–83.
21. Broderick and Boudreau. Human resource management.
22. Fox, M. (1992). Furniture dealer links payroll with human resources. *Office Technology Management,* January, 56–58.
23. Greengard, S. (1997). Increase the value of your intranet. *Workforce,* March, 88–94.
24. Greengard, S. (1997). Extranets: Linking employees with your vendors. *Workforce,* November, 28–34.
25. Leonard, B. (1991). Open and shut HRIS. *Personnel Journal,* July, 59–62.
26. Oswald, S., Scott, C., and Woerner, W. (1991). Strategic management of human resources: The American Steel and Wire Company. *Business Horizons,* May–June, 77–81.
27. Scott, L. (1992). The personnel touch in mapping strategies. *Modern Healthcare, 22* (45), 28–32.
28. Saborido, I., Florez, R., and Castro, M. (1992). Human resource management in Spain. *Employee Relations, 14* (5), 39–61.
29. McKenzie, K. (1993). Distribution: Two Fed Ex executives resign. *The Memphis Commercial Appeal,* June 3, B4–5; and McKenzie, K. (1993). Air Express: Fed Ex stock drops after resignations, rating shift. *The Memphis Commercial Appeal,* June 5, B3.

Analyzing Jobs

Chapter Four

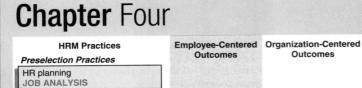

HRM Practices	Employee-Centered Outcomes	Organization-Centered Outcomes	Competitive Advantage

Preselection Practices
- HR planning
- JOB ANALYSIS

Selection Practices
- Recruitment
- Selection

Postselection Practices
- Training/development
- Performance appraisal
- Compensation
- Productivity improvement programs

Practices Affected by External Factors
- Workplace justice
- Unions
- Safety and health
- International

- Competence
- Motivation
- Work-related attitudes

- Output
- Retention
- Legal compliance
- Company image

- Cost leadership
- Product differentiation

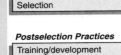

Chapter Outline

Key Terms

ability inventory
Ability Requirements Approach (ARA)
Critical Incident Technique (CIT)
job analysis inventory
job content

job context
job description
Position Analysis Questionnaire (PAQ)
task inventory
worker requirements

Chapter Objectives

Upon completion of this chapter, you will be able to:

- Discuss how job analysis lays the foundation for HRM practices that lead to competitive advantage.

- Explain how an organization conducts a job analysis.

- Describe how an organization records the final results of a job analysis.

4-1 Gaining Competitive Advantage

4-1a Opening Case: Gaining Competitive Advantage at Armco Inc.[1]

The Problem: Not Knowing Whether New Workers Were Qualified for Their First Job Assignment

When Armco hires new steelworkers, it initially places them in a general labor pool in temporary assignments until permanent positions open. The temporary assignment may be quite different from their permanent assignment. Because newly hired steelworkers could be placed anywhere in the general labor pool, each applicant must be qualified to perform all the jobs when hired.

This situation posed a major problem for Armco because it did not know the specific qualifications needed for each job in the general pool and thus had no way to gauge whether applicants would be fully qualified to perform their initial temporary assignments. If an unqualified worker filled a position, Armco could experience a drop in productivity and an increased risk of accident. If an ensuing injury were to occur, Armco would be faced with increasing costs from possible lawsuits, medical payments, workers' compensation claims, and staffing costs to replace injured workers.

The Solution: Developing Job Analysis–Based Employment Tests

To solve this problem, Armco first determined the necessary qualifications for each job in the general labor pool. It then administered tests to all applicants to measure these qualifications. Only those applicants passing each test would be considered fully qualified and thus eligible for hire.

Job analysis played a key role in this process. The firm's HR professionals analyzed each job in the general labor pool for the purposes of identifying lists of activities or tasks associated with the various jobs and determining the skills needed to perform them (e.g., strength, balance, flexibility). HR professionals obtained this information by observing workers as they performed their jobs and by interviewing their supervisors. Tests were then chosen to measure these skills.

How the Use of Job Analysis–Based Employment Tests Enhanced Competitive Advantage

To determine the value or payoff associated with the use of these tests, Armco administered them to current employees and then compared the job performance of high versus low test scorers. Armco discovered that individuals who did well on the tests performed their jobs much better than those who did poorly. The high scorers could do twice as much work as the low scorers.

This finding allowed Armco to estimate the productivity gain resulting from the testing procedures. That gain turned out to be $4,900 per employee per year. That is, a person selected by these tests would be expected to out-produce someone selected without the tests by $4,900 per year. Because the company hires nearly 2,000 entry-level steelworkers each year, the overall yearly productivity gain attributed to the use of these tests was nearly $10 million.

The success of the testing program was due to the fact that the tests measured important job skills. The job analysis laid the foundation for this program by identifying those skills.

4-1b Linking Job Analysis to Competitive Advantage

As any gardener knows, poor spadework results in a poor garden. This bit of wisdom has relevance to HRM practices, as well: The "spadework" is the job analysis; the "garden" is the HRM practices. Just as a seed cannot blossom into a flower unless the ground is properly prepared, many HRM practices cannot "blossom" into competitive advantage unless grounded on an adequate job analysis. As noted in Chapter 1, "Human Resource Management and Competitive Advantage," successful HRM practices can lead to outcomes that create competitive advantage. Job analyses, properly done, enhance the success of these HRM practices.

Taking a Closer Look 4-1 shows how job analysis information can be applied to a variety of HRM practices. Although each of these applications is described in more detail throughout the text, we next take a brief look at some of them so that the reader may begin to appreciate the HRM role played by job analysis.

Laying the Foundation for Recruitment and Selection Practices

An employer's recruitment and selection practices seek to identify and hire the most suitable applicants. Job analysis information helps employers achieve this aim by identifying selection criteria (i.e., the knowledge, skills, and abilities needed to perform a job successfully). A firm's managers and HR professionals can then use this information to choose or develop the appropriate selection devices (e.g., interview questions, tests). The opening case, for example, shows how job analysis information can be used as the basis for preparing employment tests.

An additional reason for basing recruitment and selection practices on job analysis information is a legal one. As we discussed in Chapter 2, "Understanding the Legal and Environmental Context of HRM," an employer facing discrimination charges would be required to demonstrate to the courts that its selection criteria are job-related. To support a claim of job-relatedness, a firm must demonstrate that the challenged selection practice was developed on the basis of job analysis information. As one judge noted during a discrimination hearing, without a job analysis on which to base selection practices, an employer "is aiming in the dark and can only hope to achieve job-relatedness by blind luck."[2]

The need for firms to base selection criteria on job analysis information has recently become even more important due to the passage of the Americans with Disabilities Act. As noted in Chapter 2, this law states that employment decisions concerning disabled candidates must be based on their ability to perform the essential functions of the job. For instance, if "report reading" were an essential job function, then applicants whose disabilities prevented them from reading could be lawfully denied employment (assuming there was no reasonable way to accommodate them). If, however, "report reading" were not an essential function, the inability to read could not lawfully serve as a basis for denial. The determination of which job functions are essential is made during a job analysis.

Laying the Foundation for Training and Development Programs

Firms use job analysis information to assess training needs and to develop and evaluate training programs. Job analyses can identify tasks a worker must perform. Then,

| Taking a Closer Look 4-1 | *How Companies Use Job Analyses* |

Recruitment/Selection

- Selection criteria
- Selection methods

Training and Development

- Training needs for new and current employees
- Training program content
- Training evaluation

Performance Appraisal

- Criteria for judging job performance
- Appraisal forms
- Communicate performance expectations to employees

Compensation

- Judging worth of job
- Pay adjustments

Performance Improvement Programs

- Performance standards

Employee Discipline

- Delineates job responsibilities and limits of authority
- Prevent/resolve grievances

Safety and Health

- Physical and medical qualifications
- Sources of potential job hazards

through the performance appraisal process, supervisors can identify which tasks are being performed properly and which are being performed improperly. The supervisor can then determine whether improperly performed work can be corrected through training, as we shall see in Chapter 7, "Training and Developing Employees."

HR professionals also use job analysis information to develop relevant training programs. The job analysis specifies how each job is performed, step by step. HR professionals then develop training materials to teach trainees how to perform each step.

To evaluate the effectiveness of a training program, the organization must first specify training objectives or the level of performance expected of trainees when they finish the program. The success of a training program is judged on the basis of the extent to which those performance levels have been reached. Expected performance levels are often specified during a job analysis.

Laying the Foundation for Performance Appraisal Forms

Information obtained from a job analysis can be used to develop performance appraisal forms. An example of a job analysis–based form would be one that lists the job's tasks or behaviors and specifies the expected performance level for each.

The role of job analysis is crucial here. Without job analysis information, organizations typically use a single, generalized form in which all workers are appraised on the basis of a common set of characteristics or traits that are presumed to be needed for all jobs (e.g., personal appearance, cooperation, dependability, leadership). As we demonstrate in Chapter 8, "Appraising Employee Job Performance," job analysis–based appraisal forms are superior to the generalized forms because they do a better job of communicating performance expectations and because they provide a better basis for giving feedback and for making HRM decisions.

Laying the Foundation for Compensation Decisions

Most companies base pay rates, in part, on the relative worth or importance of each job to the organization. As we note in Chapter 9, "Determining Pay and Benefits," job worth is typically determined by evaluating or rating jobs based on important factors such as skill level, effort, responsibility, and working conditions. The information provided by a job analysis serves as the basis for job worth evaluations.

Laying the Foundation for Productivity Improvement Programs

Job analysis also plays an important role in the development of productivity improvement programs. As we discuss in Chapter 10, "Implementing Productivity Improvement Programs," various pay-for-performance programs provide rewards to employees who perform their jobs at or above some desired level. Job analysis is used to identify that level of performance.

Laying the Foundation for Employee Discipline Decisions

As we discuss in Chapters 11, "Complying with Workplace Justice Laws," and 12, "Understanding Unions and Their Impact on HRM," managers must sometimes discipline employees for their failure to properly carry out their job responsibilities. For instance, workers may be disciplined for refusing to perform tasks they believe are not part of their jobs. If the responsibilities and limits of authority of a job are delineated in a job analysis, this information may be used to help resolve such problems.

Laying the Foundation for Safety and Health Programs

Job analysis information can also be useful from a safety and health point of view. While conducting a job analysis, an employer may uncover potential dangers or hazards of a job. It may also identify unsafe practices—tasks that are performed in a way that could cause injury.[3]

4-2 HRM Issues and Practices

We now discuss the actual practice of job analysis. When conducting a job analysis, the organization must determine (1) the type of information to be collected, (2) how it will be collected, and (3) how it will be recorded or documented.

4-2a Determining the Type of Information to Be Collected

A wealth of information may be gathered during a job analysis. We first describe the nature of this information and then discuss how an employer decides which information to collect.

A Menu of Job Analysis Information

Job analysis information may be divided into three categories: job content, job context, and worker requirements. **Job content** refers to workers' job activities—what workers actually do on the job. **Job context** refers to the conditions under which the work is performed and the demands such jobs impose on the worker. **Worker requirements** refer to the worker qualifications needed to perform the job successfully. The specific information falling within each category is described in Taking a Closer Look 4-2 and Figure 4-1.

Job Content

Job content can be described in a number of ways, depending on how specific one wants (or needs) to be. The different types of job content information are described in Taking a Closer Look 4-2.

When gathering information about tasks, the job analyst seeks to determine what the worker does, the purpose of the action, and the tools, equipment, or machinery used in the process. The analyst may also gather additional information about tasks, such as their relative importance, the expected performance levels, and the type of training, if any, needed by a new worker in order to perform the tasks satisfactorily.

Job Context

Job context refers to the conditions under which work is performed and the demands such work imposes on workers. Specific types of job context information typically identified during a job analysis appear in Taking a Closer Look 4-3 and Figure 4-2.

job content What workers actually do on their jobs.

job context The conditions under which a person's job is performed and the demands such jobs impose upon the individual.

worker requirements The qualifications a worker needs to successfully perform a particular job.

| **Taking a Closer Look 4-2** | *The Different Types of Job Content Information* |

Broad Level

Function or Duty

- Definition: The major areas of the jobholder's responsibility.
- Example: A professor's functions are teaching, research, and service to the university/community.

Intermediate Level

Task

- Definition: What a worker does when carrying out a function of the job; it is an activity that results in a specific product or service.
- Example: The function of teaching requires a professor to perform several tasks like lecturing, giving/grading exams, and meeting with students.

Work Behavior

- Definition: An important activity that is not task specific; such behavior is engaged in when performing a variety of tasks.

- Example: "Communicating"—a professor engages in this behavior when performing several tasks, such as lecturing and meeting with students.

Specific Level

Subtasks

- Definition: The steps carried out in the completion of a task.
- Example: The task of providing lectures consists of several subtasks, such as reading the text and other relevant materials, deciding on what information to convey, and determining how this information can be communicated in a clear and interesting manner.

Critical Incidents

- Definition: Specific activities that distinguish effective from ineffective job performance.
- Example: "The professor uses several examples when explaining difficult concepts."

Worker Requirements

Worker requirements refer to the knowledge, skill, ability, personal characteristics, and credentials needed for effective job performance. These terms are defined as follows:

- *Knowledge:* The body of information one needs to perform the job
- *Skill:* The capability to perform a learned motor task, such as forklift operating skills and word-processing skills
- *Ability:* The capability needed to perform a nonmotor task, such as communication ability, mathematical ability, reasoning or problem-solving ability
- *Personal characteristics:* An individual's traits (e.g., tact, assertiveness, concern for others, objectivity, work ethic) or their willingness/ability to adapt to the

CREDENTIALS →

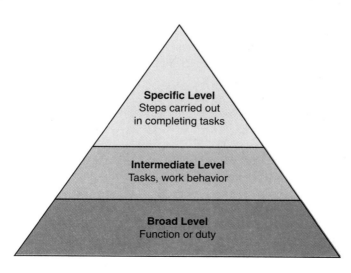

Specific Level
Steps carried out
in completing tasks

Intermediate Level
Tasks, work behavior

Broad Level
Function or duty

Figure 4-1
Types of Job Content Information

Taking a Closer Look 4-3 — The Different Types of Job Context Information

Reporting Relationships

Where the job fits in the organizational hierarchy.

Supervision Received

How closely the job is supervised.

Judgment

How much discretion the worker has in determining how the job will be carried out.

Authority

How much authority the worker has with respect to such things as hiring, firing, disciplining, budgeting, and making capital expenditures.

Personal Contacts

The type of people with whom the worker comes in contact and the nature of the contact.

Working Conditions

Factors within the work environment that cause discomfort or danger. Discomfort factors include such things as the presence of extreme temperatures, poor ventilation, and excessive noise. Dangers include such things as working in high places and exposure to toxic chemicals.

Physical Demands

Aspects of the job that are physically taxing, such as the need to run, climb, crawl, stand for long periods, reach, lift, and visually monitor a process over a prolonged period.

Personal Demands

Aspects of the job causing possible stress, such as competing demands, constant interruptions, difficult customers, boredom, conflicting or ambiguous job responsibilities, and required overtime.

circumstances in the environment (e.g., ability to withstand boredom, willingness to work overtime, willingness to treat others cordially)

- *Credentials:* Proof or documentation that an individual possesses certain competencies, such as diplomas, certifications, and licenses

Figure 4-2
Types of Job Context Information

Choosing Job Analysis Information from the Menu

The sheer amount of information that can be uncovered during a job analysis may be overwhelming, but it is usually unnecessary to gather all possible data. The purpose or intended use of the job analysis dictates the particular information to be gathered. Therefore, the analyst must decide how the job analysis will be used before deciding what information to seek.

For instance, if a job analysis were to be used to develop a technical training program for new employees, the analyst should focus on information about subtasks (a step-by-step description of how the job is carried out) and the specific knowledge, skills, and abilities (KSAs) one would need to do well on that job. If the purpose were to develop a written employment test to assess applicants' knowledge of the job, the analyst should target information about the specific tasks of the job and the knowledge required to perform each task (i.e., the facts, theories, and principles one must know to be able to perform each task satisfactorily).

4-2b Determining How to Collect the Information

HR professionals often gather job analysis information. However, because these individuals lack sufficient expertise in the jobs being analyzed, they must enlist the actual job incumbents and their supervisors to gather and interpret the pertinent information.

HR professionals gather job analysis information by interviewing the workers, observing them at work, and/or having them complete job analysis questionnaires. The appropriateness of each approach depends, in part, on the type of information sought. The information most readily obtainable from each of the different methods is shown in Exhibit 4-1.

EXHIBIT 4-1	HR Information Obtainable from Different Job Analysis Methods		
	Job Analysis Methods		
HR Information	Interview	Observation	Questionnaire
Job Content			
Function	X	X	
Tasks	X	X	X
Importance	X		X
Standard	X		
Training	X		
Work behaviors	X	X	X
Subtasks	X	X	
Critical incidents	X		X
Job Context			
Reporting relationships	X		
Supervision received	X		
Judgment	X		
Authority	X		
Working conditions	X	X	
Physical demands	X	X	
Personal demands	X		
Worker Requirements			
Knowledge	X		X
Skill	X	X	X
Ability	X		X
Personal characteristics	X		X
Credentials	X		

Job Analysis Interviews

Job analysis interviews are structured conversations between the job analyst and one or more subject-matter experts. Interviews are typically held with both job incumbents and their supervisors. Interviews with incumbents tend to focus on job content and job context information. That is, incumbents are asked to describe what they do, how they do it, and the conditions under which they perform their jobs. The typical role of the supervisor is to review and verify the accuracy of the workers' responses and to provide the job analyst with additional information concerning task importance, expected performance levels, training needs of new workers, and worker requirements. Specific instructions for completing a job analysis interview can be found in Section 4-3, "The Manager's Guide."

❋ The most frequently used job analysis method—interviews—provides a potential wealth of information. As illustrated in Exhibit 4-1, interviews can be used to collect all types of job analysis information and are the only way to collect some types. However, one-on-one interviews can be quite time-consuming. An interview usually takes between one and eight hours, depending on the amount and depth of information sought. Thus, the interview can eat up a lot of time, especially when the analyst must interview several people. When time constraints pose a problem, the best alternative is to conduct a group interview, where several subject-matter experts are interviewed simultaneously.

Job Analysis Observation

Sometimes, a job analyst will supplement interviews with job analysis observations. As the name suggests, observation means watching the incumbent perform the job. Observation is most useful when jobs are complex and difficult to accurately describe. When analyzing such jobs, the analyst observes or videotapes the job and then interviews the worker for clarification or explanation. The observation allows the analyst to gain a better understanding of how the work is done and the KSAs needed to perform it—"A picture is worth a thousand words."

Although observation is usually used as a supplement to the interview, HR professionals sometimes base job analysis solely on observation. Whether or not observation yields sufficient data for the analysis depends on the type of information being collected. For instance, it is an excellent method for identifying subtasks performed in routine/repetitive types of jobs, such as assembly-line work. When using this approach, however, analysts should be alert to the possibility that some workers may behave atypically when being observed. For instance, they may increase their speed to impress the observer or slow down in an effort to demonstrate how difficult their jobs are.

Job Analysis Questionnaires

Job analysis questionnaires ask subject-matter experts—workers and/or supervisors—to record job information in writing. Job analysis questionnaires contain either open-ended or close-ended questions. Open-ended questions ask respondents to provide their own answers to the questions. Close-ended questions ask respondents to select an answer from a list provided on the questionnaire. Close-ended questions are more commonly used because they provide greater uniformity of responses and are more easily scored.[4]

A job analysis questionnaire containing only close-ended questions is called a **job analysis inventory.** An inventory containing a listing of task statements is called a **task inventory;** one containing a listing of worker ability requirements is called an **ability inventory.** Job analysis inventories ask respondents to rate each item in terms of its importance to the job. Task inventories also request information regarding the frequency or time spent performing each task. An illustration of a task inventory is shown in Exhibit 4-2.

Companies use job analysis inventories when information is needed from several people (e.g., when many people hold the same job title). Compared to interviews,

job analysis inventory
A job analysis questionnaire that contains only close-ended questions.

task inventory   A job analysis inventory that contains a listing of task statements.

ability inventory   A job analysis inventory that contains a listing of ability requirements.

EXHIBIT 4-2	A Section of a Task Inventory for the Job of Police Sergeant

Task	Importance	Time Spent
1. Inspects personnel for appearance.	_____	_____
2. Inspects equipment and vehicles.	_____	_____
3. Observes officers in field.	_____	_____
4. Investigates police vehicle accidents.	_____	_____
5. Writes disciplinary reports.	_____	_____
6. Counsels subordinates on work problems.	_____	_____
7. Writes letters of commendation.	_____	_____
8. Evaluates performance of subordinates.	_____	_____
9. Advises subordinates on handling problems.	_____	_____
10. Reviews written reports.	_____	_____
11. Supervises team operations.	_____	_____
12. Disciplines subordinates.	_____	_____
13. Supervises at crime scene.	_____	_____

information can be collected much more quickly using this approach. They also use inventories as a means of grouping jobs. Grouping refers to categorizing jobs based on the similarity of tasks performed or skills needed; a group would consist of jobs in which all workers performed similar tasks or needed similar skills. Once groups are established, the organization can determine selection criteria, training needs, and evaluation criteria applicable to all jobs within a group.[5] Job analysis inventories are also used to determine workers' training needs. Workers are presented with a list of tasks or abilities and are asked to indicate those for which they need training. A five-point rating scale, ranging from "great need" to "no need," is typically used.

4-2c Determining How Job Analysis Information Will Be Recorded

Once HR professionals have collected job analysis information, it must be recorded in some systematic way to produce a job description (i.e., a summary of job analysis findings). The format of job descriptions may be general purpose or special purpose.

Job Descriptions: General Purpose

A general-purpose **job description** is one that contains a variety of information that can be used for several purposes, such as communicating job responsibilities to employees and specifying minimum job requirements. For instance, a manager would pull out a job description to review essential functions and worker requirements prior to developing interview questions for a job applicant. The particular information contained in the job description varies depending on company preference and the intended use of the instrument. A typical general-purpose job description contains the following sections: job identification, job summary, essential functions, job context, worker requirements, and minimum qualifications. An example of a general-purpose job description is presented in Exhibit 4-3. Section 4-3, "The Manager's Guide," provides step-by-step instructions for writing descriptions.

job description A short (one- or two-page) written summary of job analysis findings.

General-purpose job descriptions that are used by most companies provide only a brief summary of job analysis information and thus lack sufficient detail for some HRM applications. For instance, the job description presented in Exhibit 4-3 fails to indicate subtasks and performance standards. Subtask information may serve as a basis for developing training programs; performance standards may serve as a basis for developing certain types of performance appraisal forms.

Job Descriptions: Special Purpose

A number of special-purpose job description formats have been developed by a variety of HRM experts during the past 20–25 years. A key difference between general- and special-purpose formats lies in the amount of detail they include. Special-purpose

> **EXHIBIT 4-3**   An Example of a Job Description for Servers

Job Identification
Title: Server
Department: Not Applicable
Supervisor: Restaurant Manager
Date: June 1, 2006

Job Summary
Serves food in an efficient, timely, and friendly manner to ensure that patrons have a pleasurable dining experience.

Essential Functions
- Greets patrons in a friendly manner when they are first seated in order to make them feel welcome.
- Presents menus to patrons and answers questions regarding item selections in order to help patrons select their meals.
- Suggests alternative menu selections in order to increase sales.
- Writes down patrons' beverage and food orders and enters that information into the computer in order to inform the kitchen staff of the meals they must prepare.
- Picks up food from the kitchen and examines it in order to ensure that the food is served with the correct accompaniments and garnishes.
- Delivers food expeditiously in order to provide patrons with their meals in a timely manner.
- Reports any patron complaints or product deficiencies to the manager in order to make the manager aware of any problems.
- Observes the patrons and periodically asks them how they are enjoying their meals in order to determine their needs for services, such as condiments, beverage refills, or check.
- Changes ashtrays and removes clutter throughout the patrons' meals in order to maintain a good table appearance.
- Calculates patrons' check totals on the computer in order to inform them of the payment that they must make.
- Takes cash or credit card from the patrons and returns change/receipts in order to collect payment for the patrons' meals.
- Gives patrons a warm and friendly farewell and invites them to return in order to make them feel that their patronage is valued.

Job Context
A. Supervision Received
    The host/hostess assigns the server to tables. The manager periodically assesses the server's performance by means of observation, reviewing comment cards, and listening to customer complaints or compliments. The manager completes a formal performance appraisal annually.
B. Available Guidelines
    Policies and procedures for waiting tables are specified in the Employee's Training Manual. There is very little judgment needed to apply them.

C. Research and Analysis
    Not applicable
D. Accountability/Consequence of Error
    The employee handles cash and the customer's credit cards and is responsible for any breakage of glasses or plates.
E. Personal Contacts
    The server interacts with patrons, coworkers, host/hostess, and the manager.
F. Supervision Exercised
    Not applicable
G. Physical Demands
    The job requires continual standing and walking. The worker is required to carry trays weighing as much as 25 pounds.
H. Work Hazards
    Not applicable
I. Personal Demands
    The work is performed in an indoor, environmentally controlled setting. The server must occasionally deal with unpleasant or angry patrons. The job may be quite stressful during peak periods.

Knowledge, Skills, Abilities, and Personal Characteristics
- Knowledge of meal and beverage menu sufficient to answer customer questions.
- Willingness to be service oriented, as demonstrated by being friendly and actively looking for ways to help customers.
- Ability to actively listen, as demonstrated by giving full attention to what patrons are saying, asking appropriate questions, and not interrupting at inappropriate times.
- Ability to communicate information clearly and effectively sufficient to be understood by patrons.
- Ability to carry heavy objects, sufficient to transport trays weighing as much as 25 lbs.
- Ability to keep composure, as demonstrated by remaining friendly with patrons who are rude or angry, especially during busy periods.
- Ability to operate effectively as part of a team, as demonstrated by developing and maintaining constructive and cooperative relationships with managers and other servers, helping them when the need arises.
- Ability to use computer sufficient to enter orders and calculate checks.
- Ability to withstand 8-hour periods of continual standing and walking.

Minimum Qualifications
- Education: High school diploma or equivalent (Required)
- Experience: One year of previous server experience (Preferred)
- Licenses/Certifications: None

---

formats cover fewer topics, but the topics covered are analyzed in more depth. Some of the more commonly used special-purpose approaches are described next.

Ability Requirements Approach (ARA)
A systematic method of recording job analysis information in which a job analyst specifies needed abilities from a list of all the possible abilities needed for any job.

The **Ability Requirements Approach (ARA)** assumes that the skills needed to perform a job can be described in terms of abilities that are more basic. For example, the skill of hitting a baseball can be described in terms of such basic abilities as reaction time, wrist strength, and eye–hand coordination.

The ARA presents the job analyst with a list of all the possible abilities needed for any job.[6] This list, shown in Taking a Closer Look 4-4, is derived from research studies spanning several years. It contains 52 abilities divided into five categories.

The job analyst presents the abilities list to subject-matter experts and asks them to specify the level of each ability needed to perform the job adequately. They record their judgments on a rating scale. The points on the scale are defined by concrete

Taking a Closer Look 4-4	*ARA Categories of All Known Abilities*

Mental Abilities

Oral comprehension, written comprehension, oral expression, written expression, fluency of ideas, originality, memorization, problem sensitivity, mathematical reasoning, number facility, deductive reasoning, inductive reasoning, information ordering, and category flexibility

Perception Abilities

Speed of closure, flexibility of closure, spatial orientation, visualization, and perceptual speed

Psychomotor Abilities

Control precision, multilimb coordination, response orientation, rate control, reaction time, arm–hand steadiness, manual dexterity, finger dexterity, wrist–finger speed, speed of limb movement, selective attention, and time sharing

Physical Abilities

Static strength, explosive strength, dynamic strength, trunk strength, extent flexibility, dynamic flexibility, gross body coordination, gross body equilibrium, and stamina

Sensory Abilities

Near vision, far vision, visual color discrimination, night vision, peripheral vision, depth perception, glare sensitivity, general hearing, auditory attention, sound localization, speech hearing, and speech clarity

Source: Fleishman, E.A. (1975). *Development of Ability Requirements Scales for the Analysis of Bell System Jobs.* Bethesda, MD: Management Research Institute.

examples of tasks representing different amounts of that ability. An example of a rating scale for the ability "verbal comprehension" is shown in Figure 4-3. A job would receive a high rating on this ability if it required a worker to understand difficult material such as a mortgage contract.

The ARA is often used for employee selection, especially in those instances where applicants are not expected to possess particular skills upon entry into the job. For example, applicants for an entry-level position as a police officer would not be expected to be skilled at firing a revolver. Rather than testing applicants on this skill, they could be tested on the abilities needed to acquire the skill, as identified by the ARA.[7]

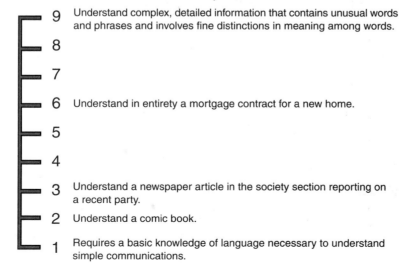

Verbal Comprehension

9 — Understand complex, detailed information that contains unusual words and phrases and involves fine distinctions in meaning among words.

8 —

7 —

6 — Understand in entirety a mortgage contract for a new home.

5 —

4 —

3 — Understand a newspaper article in the society section reporting on a recent party.

2 — Understand a comic book.

1 — Requires a basic knowledge of language necessary to understand simple communications.

Figure 4-3
Example of Ability Requirement Scale

Source: Fleishman, E.A., and Mumford, M.D. (1991). Evaluating classifications of job behavior: A construct validation of the ability requirement scales. *Personnel Psychology, 44* (3), 523–575.

Taking a Closer Look 4-5	*Overall Job Dimensions on the PAQ*

1. Having decision, communicating, and general responsibilities
2. Operating machines and equipment
3. Performing clerical and/or related activities
4. Performing technical and/or related activities
5. Performing service and/or related activities
6. Working regular day versus other work schedules
7. Performing routine and/or repetitive activities
8. Being aware of work environment
9. Engaging in physical activities
10. Supervising/directing/estimating
11. Public, customer, and/or related contacts
12. Working in an unpleasant/ hazardous/demanding environment
13. Miscellaneous

The ARA can also be used to set medical standards for jobs, which can help physicians decide what medical conditions should qualify or disqualify applicants for jobs. For example, if the ARA revealed that a job required a great deal of stamina, then cardiovascular diseases such as anemia and severe hypertension could serve as a disqualifier.[8] Thus, the ARA serves as a useful technique for ensuring compliance with the Americans with Disabilities Act.

Position Analysis Questionnaire (PAQ)
A systematic method of recording job analysis information in which the behavioral dimensions of a job are specified.

The **Position Analysis Questionnaire (PAQ)** is premised on the notion that "there is some underlying behavioral structure or order to the domain of human work,"[9] and there is a limited set of job characteristics that describe this domain.[10] Jobs differ from one another in terms of the extent to which each of these characteristics is present. The characteristics or dimensions measured by the PAQ are shown in Taking a Closer Look 4-5. Analysts assess these characteristics by interviewing several incumbents and then rating the job on 194 items contained on a standardized questionnaire. A job is then given a set of 13 scores (one for each dimension) based on these ratings.

The PAQ is particularly useful for establishing compensation rates. A statistical formula has been established for combining the 13 dimension scores of a job to arrive at an appropriate rate (i.e., a rate similar to jobs in other companies that have the same profile).[11] PAQ scores can also be used to group jobs into "families." That is, jobs having a similar profile of dimension scores can be grouped and treated alike for various HRM applications.

Critical Incident Technique (CIT) A systematic method of recording job analysis information that identifies specific work behavior that determines success or failure in executing an assigned task.

The **Critical Incident Technique (CIT)** was developed in the military during World War II as a means of identifying critical factors in human performance in a variety of military situations. The rationale for this technique, according to its originator, John Flanagan, is described in the following passage:[12]

The principal objective of job analysis procedures should be the determination of critical requirements. These requirements include those that have been demonstrated to make the difference between success and failure in carrying out an important part of the job assigned in a significant number of instances. Too often, statements regarding job requirements are merely lists of all the desirable traits of human beings. These are practically no help in selecting, classifying, or training individuals for specific jobs.

As noted earlier, a critical incident is a specific work behavior that may determine success or failure in executing an assigned task. The Critical Incident Technique requires the job analyst to collect critical incidents from people familiar with the job. The incidents are usually collected in the form of stories or anecdotes that depict successful and unsuccessful job behaviors. The stories are then condensed to a single statement that "captures the essence" of the story. Examples of critical incident statements are presented in On the Road to Competitive Advantage 4-1. They are derived from stories regarding unreliable behaviors of nuclear power operators.

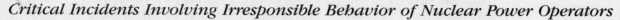

Critical Incidents Involving Irresponsible Behavior of Nuclear Power Operators

A nuclear power agency was experiencing difficulty because many of its workers were "unreliable," that is, behaving in ways that could lead to operation failures or, worse, serious accidents. The organization attempted to resolve the problem, in part, by identifying these irresponsible behaviors and then taking management actions to stop or prevent them from occurring. The Critical Incident Technique was used to identify these employee behaviors. The findings are as follows:

Definition of Irresponsible Behavior

Irresponsible behavior involves horseplay on the job and failure to take the job seriously, refusal to comply with regulations, and impulsive actions taken with an apparent lack of concern for the consequences.

Examples

- Takes action without thinking
- Shows questionable judgment on the spur of the moment

- Plays frequent pranks
- Shows little concern for disciplinary threats; laughs off errors or reprimands
- Is often tardy or absent
- Denies mistakes
- Operates equipment carelessly
- Is frequently sloppy or fails to complete work
- Ignores time limits or procedures
- Creates excitement when bored on the job
- Engages in theft or sabotage; lies or cheats; commits acts of vandalism
- Provides incorrect or inaccurate information when questioned

Source: Davis, S.L. (1986). *Categories of unreliable job behavior in nuclear facilities.* Paper presented at the meeting of the American Psychological Association (Division 14), Washington, DC.

The CIT has a number of useful HRM applications. For instance, it is a good tool for identifying selection criteria and training needs and for developing performance appraisal forms. Some of the HRM techniques discussed later in the text are developed from information derived from the CIT. For example, Chapter 6, "Selecting Applicants," discusses behavior description interviews, and Chapter 8, "Appraising Employee Job Performance," discusses behaviorally anchored rating scales and behavior observation scales.

Recording Job Analysis Information: Selecting the Best Approach
With so many job analysis approaches to choose from, how does an HR professional decide which to use? As noted earlier, the purpose or intended use of the job analysis dictates the particular information to be gathered. The analyst should select a method that provides the information needed. One study concluded that the job analyst should:[13]

> [C]hoose the method that yields [the best] results in the context in which the study is being conducted . . . there is nothing sacrosanct about any of these methods. Each has its advantages and its limitations, and none is foolproof.

4-3 The Manager's Guide

4-3a Job Analysis and the Manager's Job

Managers have two primary job analysis roles. First, they help HR professionals complete the analysis. Second, managers implement job analysis results in their day-to-day activities.

Completing the Job Analysis

Managers nearly always have input in the completion of the final job analysis product. The nature and extent of their input vary, however, from company to company. At one extreme, a manager may be responsible for the whole thing. For instance, some managers are required to write a job description for each of the jobs they supervise. In other instances, an HR professional conducts the job analysis. Here the manager provides the HR professional with additional information. For example, managers might be asked to specify performance standards and/or worker requirements needed for each job; or they might be asked to provide critical incidents.

Managers may also review and maintain the accuracy of job descriptions. When the content, context, or worker requirements of a job change significantly, managers must notify the HRM department and request a reanalysis of the job.

Implementing Job Analysis Results

We have already discussed the variety of ways in which job analysis information may be used by an organization. Managers most commonly use job analysis to help them determine selection criteria and to help them communicate job responsibilities to their employees.

Selecting Applicants

As they assess applicants for a job, managers should carefully review the content, context, and worker requirement information to form a clear picture of the type of applicant best suited for the job. As we note in Chapter 6, this information provides the basis for developing appropriate interview questions, as well as questions to ask of references.

Communicating Job Responsibilities

From a communication perspective, the job analysis results should drive the orientation process for new employees. Managers should review job descriptions with new employees in order to convey job responsibilities. Once employees are trained, managers should frequently communicate the performance standards so their employees will continue to know what is expected of them.

4-3b How the HRM Department Can Help

The HRM department serves two primary roles with regard to job analysis: (1) Gain the support of upper management and (2) plan and implement a job analysis project.

Gaining Upper-Management Support

Unfortunately, not all upper managers appreciate the importance of job analysis in achieving competitive advantage. Some believe that job analysis is simply not worth the effort; others believe that conducting a job analysis is actually counterproductive. Employers espousing the latter view apparently believe that putting job information in writing somehow ties their hands and robs them of their managerial discretion.[14]

Because job analysis is not fully appreciated by some employers, it is often conducted in a perfunctory manner, if at all. Employers who take such a lackadaisical approach end up basing their HRM practices on intuition and guesswork. The resulting job descriptions are neither very useful nor legally defensible.

To avoid the negative consequences associated with this approach, HR professionals must solicit support for job analysis from upper-level managers. They can accomplish this by forcibly and continually emphasizing the importance of conducting job analyses that are sufficiently thorough and accurate. They must also stress the need to update job analysis information on a regular basis.

Planning and Implementing a Job Analysis Project

In most companies, the primary responsibility for planning and conducting a job analysis is placed in the hands of the HR professionals, who must complete these tasks:[15]

- Determine goals and objectives.
- Choose methods for collecting and recording job analysis information.
- Select subject-matter experts.
- Gather data.
- Establish a project schedule.
- Document the data.
- Disseminate the information.
- Manage the study.

4-3c HRM Skill-Building for Managers

In some organizations, managers, rather than the HR professionals, conduct job analyses. This is actually a more efficient approach when many jobs need to be analyzed, because job analyses can be completed much more quickly if conducted by each line manager rather than a single HR professional.

The following material is presented as a guide for situations in which you are asked to analyze the positions you supervise. First, we discuss how to collect the necessary information; we then discuss how this information may be documented.

Collecting Job Analysis Information

Managers responsible for conducting job analyses for the positions they supervise generally use an interview approach to data collection. When interviewing your workers for this purpose, adhere to the following guidelines:[16]

1. *State the purpose of the interview.* The workers must fully understand the reason for the interviews so that they will not interpret them as efficiency evaluations or as pay audits. Most employees are not interested in all the details concerning how the information is to be used. The purpose can thus be stated succinctly: "I am going to interview you about your job so that we may write a job description."

2. *Structure the interview.* An interview can be structured in a number of ways, but all of them focus first on job content, then on job context, and, last, on worker requirements. Information regarding worker requirements is collected last because it is inferred from the job content and context information. The various ways of structuring the interviews to determine job content are described in the following list:

   - Ask the employee to describe the major functions of the job. After the job has been broken down into functions, ask the worker to state the tasks associated with each function.
   - If the job is performed at various duty stations, you may structure the interview according to job location. For example, you may ask the worker to describe his or her tasks on Machine 1, then Machine 2, and so forth.
   - If functions vary on a seasonal basis, structure the interview in terms of seasons. For example, you may ask, "What are your tasks during the Christmas season? During the summer?"
   - If the job is project oriented, structure the interview by developing a list of projects and discussing the tasks involved in each.

3. *Steer the interview.* Ask the worker to describe the job in his or her own words; insist on a thorough description of each activity. Ask questions about terms you

do not understand. Ask to see forms or equipment with which you are unfamiliar. You should adhere to the following guidelines:

- Control the interview with respect to time and subject matter. If workers stray from the subject, redirect them by summarizing the information collected to that point.
- Show sincere interest in what is being said. Make eye contact.
- Frequently restate and summarize the main points you think the worker has made.
- Do not take issue with statements made by the worker.
- Do not be critical or attempt to suggest any changes or improvements in work methods.

4. *Record the interview.* You should record the information as you obtain it. Note-taking represents one approach. Follow these guidelines when taking notes:

- Take notes while listening to what is being said.
- Use some type of shorthand.
- Rewrite your notes immediately after the interview.

A tape recorder may be used to replace or supplement note-taking. The use of a tape recorder relieves you of the pressure of having to get it all down during the interview. If your notes are incomplete, you can retrieve needed information from the tape. This allows you to focus your attention during the interview on listening, asking questions, and making eye contact to strengthen lines of communication.

5. *Close the interview.* Summarize the information obtained from the worker, indicating the major activities performed and the details concerning each task. End the interview on a friendly note.

Documenting Job Analysis Information

I. Job Identification
- Job title
- Department in which job is located
- Name of supervisor
- Date of job description

II. Job Summary

This section requires a brief, specific statement of why this position exists. It orients the reader to the job's primary purpose for being included in the organization.

Examples

- Airport Public Safety Supervisor

  Aids Airport Public Safety Director in ensuring the public safety and security at the airport.

- Maintenance Supervisor

  Supervises personnel in the upkeep, repair, and renovation of corporate facilities in 10 buildings.

III. Essential Functions

Important job activities that a worker performs to create a product or a service.

- Level of specificity
  1. Must be neither too broad nor too specific.
  2. Example (college professor):

Too broad—Teaches classes

Too specific—Writes first draft of lecture

Correct level—Prepares lecture material for classes

   3. Most job descriptions include 8–12 essential functions.

- Writing essential functions

   1. State what action is performed using an action verb, which is a verb that clearly specifies what the person is actually doing.

      a. Poor verbs—assists, coordinates, interfaces, assures.

      b. Good verbs—removes, fills, clears, places, reads, types, writes.

   2. Use compound verbs, if necessary, by using the "ing" form of the verb.

      a. Role-plays sales presentation demonstrating product and answering questions in order to provide on-the-job training to sales staff using promotional materials.

   3. Specify the object of the action—What is acted upon?

      a. When specifying what is acted upon, use single (types letters) or compound objects (types letters, memos, and reports).

   4. Specify the purpose/expected outcome, preface this with "in order to" or "for the purpose of."

IV. Job Context

Questions to answer:

1. Supervision received

   a. How are assignments given?

   b. At what point is work reviewed?

   c. Is the employee physically separated from the supervisor?

   d. What is the frequency of contact between the worker and supervisor?

2. Available guidelines

   a. What manuals, policies, procedures, and forms are available to the worker?

   b. How much judgment is needed to apply them?

3. Research and analysis

   a. What reports are prepared and who receives them?

   b. To what extent is complex interpretation required?

4. Accountability/consequence of error

   a. Is the employee responsible for the security of, or maintaining records on, money or other valuables?

   b. Is the employee responsible for the operation of expensive equipment?

   c. To what extent is the employee responsible for the accomplishment of a goal or profit?

   d. Could others be threatened by injury, loss of life, loss of time and/or loss of money as the result of an error made by the employee?

5. Personal contacts

   a. With whom in the organization does the employee make contact?—coworkers, other departments, upper levels of management

   b. What external contacts are required?—customers, representatives of regulatory agencies, job applicants

6. Supervision exercised

   a. How many employees does the person supervise?

   b. What type(s) of employees are supervised?—skilled, semiskilled, or unskilled; clerical, technical, professional

   c. What is the nature of the employee's supervisory responsibility?—train, hire/fire, review work, evaluate performance

7. Physical demands

   a. What are the job requirements with respect to standing, walking, sitting, stooping, kneeling, crouching, crawling, and climbing?

   b. Are there any lifting requirements? If so, is the working required to lift objects that are light, medium, heavy, or very heavy? Explain.

   c. Is any kind of reaching required? Explain.

8. Work hazards

   a. What, if any, work hazards are present? Hazards include mechanical, electrical, fire, chemical, explosive or radiation.

   b. Is the work done at heights or underground? Explain.

   c. Are there bad atmosphere conditions, such as fumes, odors, dusts, mists, gases, stagnant air?

9. Personal demands

   a. Does the job involve work in heat, cold, dampness, confined space, or around noise and vibration?

   b. Does the job involve shift work, availability for callout during nonworking periods, or mandatory overtime during emergency situations?

   c. Are there stress factors built into the job, such as interruptions, demanding customers, competing demands?

V. Worker Requirements

The knowledge, skills, abilities and personal characteristics (KSAPs) that workers need to succeed on the job.

- Identifying KSAPs

   1. Review each essential function, asking what particular KSAP a worker would need to perform it at a satisfactory level.

      a. Do not list KSAPs that all applicants would be expected to be proficient at (e.g., ability to speak English; ability to add single-digit numbers).

   2. Go through the job context factors, one at a time, and ask the same question.

- Writing KSAPs

Some companies incorrectly write KSAPs very succinctly, indicating just the name of the competency, such as an "ability to communicate." KSAPs should be defined in a way that their application to the performance of the job is clear. Although the former approach is simpler, the latter yields more useful information.

   1. Start with a descriptive phrase, such as:

      knowledge of
      skill to
      ability to
      willingness to

   2. Next, state the actual KSAP, followed by the level of competency. Level is indicated by adding "sufficient to" or "as demonstrated by" after the general competency.

VI. Minimum Qualifications

- Education and experience: Set at the employer's discretion. Points to keep in mind:

   1. The more education and experience that the employer seeks, the greater the salary that must be paid.

   2. When set high, the employer must consider the possibility of disparate impact. In such a case, the employer must prove to a court that the requirements are job-related.

      a. As a general rule, a college degree is job-related for professional or exempt jobs.

      b. The courts are usually lenient when the employer imposes a high experience requirement.

      c. Legal red flag: Requiring a high school diploma for unskilled positions.

      d. Can use "preferred" instead of "required."

- Licenses and other credentials

   1. May be required by law in some instances (e.g., an RN must be licensed by the state).

   2. If not legally mandated, they may be imposed at the employer's discretion, if job-related (e.g., an applicant for an HR job must be certified in HR).

Chapter Objectives Revisited

1. Discuss how job analysis lays the foundation for HRM practices that lead to competitive advantage.

   - Lays the foundation for recruiting, selection, training, performance appraisal, compensation, productivity improvement programs, employee discipline, and safety and health programs

2. Explain how an organization conducts a job analysis.

   - Information that may be collected:
     - Job content: Refers to the workers' job activities
     - Job context: Refers to the conditions under which the work is performed and the demands that are imposed upon the worker
     - Worker requirements: Refer to the competencies a worker needs to successfully perform the job

   - Methods of information collection:
     - Interview workers and supervisors about the job.
     - Observe workers as they perform their jobs.
     - Have workers and/or supervisors complete a job analysis inventory.

3. Describe how an organization records the final results of a job analysis.

   - General-purpose job descriptions
   - Special-purpose job descriptions (Ability Requirements Approach, Position Analysis Questionnaire, Critical Incident Technique)

Review Questions

Note: You can find the correct answers to these questions by taking the quiz and then submitting your answers in the Online Edition. The program will automatically score your submission. If you miss a question, the program will provide the correct answer, a rationale for the answer, and the section number in the chapter where the topic is discussed.

1. Information regarding what a worker does, the purpose of the action, and the tools, equipment, or machinery used is gathered when analyzing
   a. job context.
   b. worker requirements.
   c. job specifications.
   d. job content.

2. Which type of job analysis information would be most useful for communicating job tasks to a new worker?
   a. job content
   b. job context
   c. worker requirements
   d. performance standards

3. Which of the following statements best expresses the relationship between HR professionals and line managers when it comes to gathering job analysis information?
   a. Line managers are responsible for determining the type of information that is gathered; HR professionals actually gather and interpret the pertinent information.
   b. HR professionals are responsible for determining the type of information that is gathered; line managers actually gather and interpret the pertinent information.
   c. HR professionals are responsible both for determining the type of information that is gathered and actually collecting it; line managers interpret the pertinent information.
   d. Although HR professionals may determine what type of information is to be collected, both line managers and HR professionals assist in collecting and interpreting the data.

4. A job description is a
   a. summary of job analysis findings.
   b. term that is used interchangeably with the term job analysis.
   c. pictorial representation of the work environment.
   d. written agreement between workers and management specifying performance standards.

5. Which of the following pieces of information deals with job content?
   a. Greet visitors as they enter the store
   b. Works in cramped quarters with poor ventilation
   c. Able to type at least 40 words per minute
   d. Must possess a CPA (accounting)

6. One of the advantages of the Ability Requirements Approach (ARA) is that it
   a. provides a very thorough description of job content.
   b. focuses on job context.
   c. generates information that enables an organization to comply with the American's with Disabilities Act.
   d. focuses on specific job tasks rather than on more generic job performance dimensions.

7. The Position Analysis Questionnaire (PAQ) is particularly well suited for
   a. establishing compensation rates.
   b. defending a claim of employment discrimination.
   c. identifying critical work behaviors.
   d. linking people, data, and things ratings to the human resource information system.

8. A Critical Incident Technique (CIT) is defined as
   a. an event that has had a major impact on defining the mission and vision of the organization.
   b. a story that depicts either successful or unsuccessful work behaviors.
   c. criticism directed at an employee for improper handling of a work-related situation.
   d. a workplace safety violation that endangers more than 50 percent of the workforce.

9. In which method of job analysis does the job analyst specify needed abilities from a list of all possible abilities needed for any job?
   a. ARA
   b. PAQ
   c. CIT
   d. General purpose job description

10. Regarding the choice of job analysis methods, research suggests that
    a. the Versatile Job Analysis system should be used whenever possible.
    b. multiple job analysis methods should be used.
    c. the Critical Incident Technique is the most useful.
    d. the Position Analysis Questionnaire is the most useful.

Discussion Questions

1. Describe how job analysis results can contribute to the effectiveness of three HRM practices.

2. Define job content, job context, and worker requirements. Give an example of each for a job you have held.

3. Define the terms *function, task, subtask, work behavior,* and *critical incident.*

4. Why is it necessary to determine the purpose to be served by the job analysis before choosing the job analysis method to be used?

5. What are the advantages and disadvantages associated with the use of job analysis interviews?

6. What are the drawbacks associated with the use of job descriptions as the sole means of recording job analysis information?

7. Give an original example of how the ARA can be used to develop selection criteria for a job.

8. Write two critical incidents describing a professor's classroom behavior. One should be an effective behavior; the other, an ineffective one. Summarize the incidents into critical incident statements.

9. Why should a line manager be knowledgeable about the topic of job analysis?

10. Why is it difficult to get upper-level management to accept the notion that job analyses should be conducted in a thorough manner? What can the HR professional do to gain upper-management support?

Experiential Exercise

Conducting a Job Analysis for the Job of U.S. President

Divide into groups of five. Each group must review the following problem and propose a solution. Select a representative to present the group's solution to the class. After all the solutions have been presented, the class, as a whole, will attempt to arrive at a consensus.

Problem

Congress has commissioned you to analyze the job of U.S. president in order to identify the worker requirements needed for the job. This information will be communicated to the voters, who will then have a sound basis for comparing candidates. Assume you have unlimited time and resources for this project. What method of job analysis would you use? Why?

Writing a Job Description

Divide into groups of three. Each group should have a jobholder, i.e., someone who is currently employed (or someone who has recently been employed). The other two members must interview the jobholder about his or her job following the instructions for collecting job analysis information contained in "The Manager's Guide." Write a job description based on the information gleaned from the interview, using the servers' job description (Exhibit 4-3) as a model.

Case

Was This Job Analysis Properly Conducted?[17]

Black applicants who had failed the written exam for the position of firefighter brought a race discrimination lawsuit against the Jacksonville Fire Department. The failure prevented them from taking further steps to become firefighters. The applicants argued that they failed the test solely because it was racially discriminatory and that it was not related to the skills and duties necessary to perform the job.

One of the key issues before the court was whether the examination was based on an adequately performed job analysis. That is, did the job analysis identify the appropriate worker requirements on which to base the test?

Here is how the job analysis was conducted:

1. A committee of incumbent fire department personnel was appointed by the chief to serve as subject-matter experts. The committee was composed of four firefighters, two fire lieutenants, and one fire captain. One of the firefighters and one of the lieutenants were black; all others were white.

2. The committee first defined all essential work behaviors performed by firefighters using a group brainstorming technique.

3. The criticality of each job behavior was rated on the basis of time spent performing the behavior, the frequency of its occurrence, and the importance of the work behavior in overall job performance.

4. If a work behavior was one that was learned on the job or was not performed at job entry, it was disregarded.

5. Four work behaviors were determined to have weight:

    • Studies manuals and procedures to become familiar with basic fire-fighting procedures. Weight: 40%

    • Studies procedures and/or manuals to become familiar with tools and equipment. Weight: 30%

    • Studies manuals and procedures to become familiar with first aid. Weight: 20%

    • Studies manuals to become familiar with standard operating procedures. Weight: 10%

6. These work behaviors were then analyzed to determine their task components. Each essential work behavior consisted of one essential task. Number 1, for example, would be "studies fire-fighting manuals and procedures to become familiar with the use of these procedures at an emergency scene."

7. Each task was then analyzed to determine which knowledge, skills, and abilities (KSAs) were required for successful performance of the task.

8. Each KSA was carefully defined and assessed for relative weight based on its importance to job performance.

9. The final weight of each KSA was obtained by multiplying the KSA weight by the behavior weight.

Questions

1. If you were the judge, would you conclude that the job analysis had been properly done? Explain.

2. Which of the job analysis recording methods discussed in this chapter would be the most appropriate for this situation? Explain.

References

1. Arnold, J.D., Rauschenberger, J.M., Soubel, W.G., and Guion, R.M. (1982). Validation and utility of a strength test for selecting steelworkers. *Journal of Applied Psychology, 67* (5), 588–604.

2. *Kirkland v. Department of Correctional Services,* 7 FEP 694.

3. Bemis, S.E., Belenky, A.H., and Soder, D.A. (1983). *Job Analysis: An Effective Management Tool.* Washington, DC: Bureau of National Affairs.

4. Babbie, E. (1983). *The Practice of Social Research* (3rd ed.). Belmont, CA: Wadsworth.

5. Bemis et al. *Job analysis.*

6. Fleishman, E.A., and Mumford, M.D. (1991). Evaluating classifications of job behavior: A construct validation of the ability requirement scales. *Personnel Psychology, 44* (3), 523–575.

7. Fleishman, E.A. (1982). Evaluating physical abilities required by jobs. In H.G. Heneman III and D.P. Schwab (eds.). *Perspectives on Personnel/Human Resource Management* (49–62). Homewood, IL: Richard D. Irwin.

8. Fleishman E.A. (1988). Some new frontiers in personnel selection research. *Personnel Psychology, 41* (4), 679–701.

9. McCormick, E.J., Jeanneret, P.R., and Mecham, R.C. (1972). A study of job characteristics and job dimensions as based on the Position Analysis Questionnaire (PAQ). *Journal of Applied Psychology, 56,* 347–368.

10. Harvey, R.J., Friedman, L., Hakel, M.D., and Cornelius, E.T. (1988). Dimensionality of the job element inventory: A simplified worker-oriented job analysis questionnaire. *Journal of Applied Psychology, 73* (4), 639–646.

11. Ibid.

12. Flanagan, J.C. (1954). The critical incident technique. *Psychological Bulletin, 51,* 327–358.

13. Ghorpade, J., and Atchison, T.J. (1980). The concept of job analysis: A review and some suggestions. *Public Personnel Management, 9* (3), 134–144.

14. Mathis, R.L., and Jackson, J.H. (1991). *Personnel/Human Resource Management* (6th ed.). St. Paul, MN: West.

15. Bemis et al. *Job analysis.*

16. Adapted from Bemis et al. *Job analysis.*

17. Adapted from *Corley v. City of Jacksonville* (1981), 28 FEP Cases 110.

Human Resource Management Selection Practices

Recruiting Applicants

Chapter Five

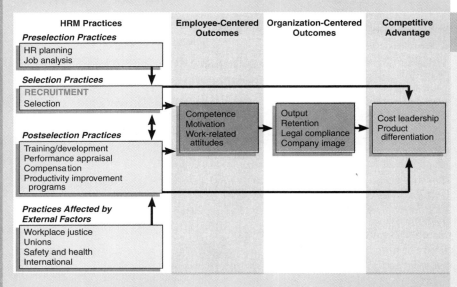

HRM Practices	Employee-Centered Outcomes	Organization-Centered Outcomes	Competitive Advantage
Preselection Practices			
HR planning			
Job analysis			
Selection Practices	Competence	Output	Cost leadership
RECRUITMENT	Motivation	Retention	Product
Selection	Work-related attitudes	Legal compliance	differentiation
		Company image	
Postselection Practices			
Training/development			
Performance appraisal			
Compensation			
Productivity improvement programs			
Practices Affected by External Factors			
Workplace justice			
Unions			
Safety and health			
International			

Key Terms

applicant-initiated recruitment

campus recruiting

career development systems

contingency personnel

core personnel

employee referrals

executive search firms

help-wanted advertisements

independent contractors

job posting

labor leasors

online recruiting

private employment agencies

public employment agencies

realistic job previews (RJPs)

temporary employment agencies

Chapter Objectives

Upon completion of this chapter, you will be able to:

- Understand how a firm's recruiting practices can lead to competitive advantage.
- Explain the choices involved in planning a recruitment strategy.
- Discuss the various recruitment methods.

5-1 Gaining Competitive Advantage

5-1a Opening Case: Gaining Competitive Advantage at the Los Angeles United School District[1]

The Problem: A Poor Recruiting System Resulting in Low-Quality Hires

When Deborah Hirsh was hired to head the HR Department at the Los Angeles United School District, the district had less than a stellar reputation among prospective recruits. Its recruitment process was cumbersome, as applicants faced long lines, surly attendants, misplaced records, endless shuttling back and forth between two locations, and a jungle of red tape. The district received about 35,000 applications each year. Applicants typically waited months for a response; some never received one because their applications were lost. By the time an offer was made, many of the best applicants had already accepted other positions. The most serious consequence of this user-unfriendly system was the quality of the teachers that were ultimately hired. The No Child Left Behind Act requires that all teachers be designated as "highly qualified" (i.e., have a bachelor's degree with subject-matter expertise, as demonstrated by passing a subject-matter test). When Hirsh took the helm, only 83 percent of the teachers were so designated. In the year prior to her arrival, only 67 percent of the new hires were highly qualified.

The Solution: Using an Online System and Rolling Out the Red Carpet

Ms. Hirsh took immediate steps to upgrade the recruitment process. Her first action was to invest $65,000 in an online application system that made it possible for applicants to receive responses within 24 hours, allowing the district to quickly identify the best and brightest applicants and promptly invite them for an interview. She also switched the hiring process from seasonal to year-round, offering contracts to high-potential teachers in advance of their actual employment. The recruiters called these individuals immediately to arrange an interview, at which time they "laid out the red carpet." This "royal treatment" made the recruits feel highly coveted. According to Ms. Hirsh, when you ask these individuals why they accepted their job offers, the first thing they'll tell you is "Because I could tell that you really wanted me."

How the New Recruitment Process Enhanced Competitive Advantage

The recruitment process has led to dramatic changes. The district, which previously had the reputation as an employer of last resort, is now able to attract top candidates. Ninety-five percent of all new hires during the past year were highly qualified. Moreover, by improving efficiency through the use of automated procedures, the new recruiting system saves the district about $10 million per year!

5-1b Linking Recruitment to Competitive Advantage

Recruitment was defined in Chapter 1, "Human Resource Management and Competitive Advantage," as a process used by an organization to locate and attract job applicants in order to fill a position. As illustrated in the opening case, an effective approach to recruitment can help a company successfully compete for limited human resources. To maximize competitive advantage, a company must choose the recruiting method that produces the best pool of candidates quickly and cost efficiently. A recruiting program thus has five goals:[2]

1. Achieve cost efficiency.
2. Attract highly qualified candidates.
3. Help ensure that individuals who are hired will stay with the company.
4. Assist a company's efforts to comply with nondiscrimination laws.
5. Help a company create a more culturally diverse workforce.

We now take a closer look at each of these goals and discuss their link to competitive advantage.

Achieving Cost Efficiency

As a central function of virtually all HRM departments, recruitment represents a major expense. Recruitment costs per hire typically equal one-third of a new hire's annual salary.[3] Expenses incurred during recruitment include the cost of advertising, recruiter and candidate travel, possible referral or sign-on bonuses, agency or search firm fees, recruiters' salaries and benefits, and managers' time. Total recruitment costs can be quite high. A sample of 614 companies, for instance, reported spending $3.4 billion on recruitment services during a recent 3-year period.[4]

As we noted in Chapter 1, competitive advantage can be gained by holding down costs, while keeping productivity levels constant. If a company can find a way to limit recruitment costs, without lowering productivity, competitive advantage is enhanced. As we saw in the opening case, Los Angeles United School District accomplished this aim by automating the computer process. The cost of the automation was more than offset by the $10 million savings that ensued. The strategy used by Dime Savings Bank of New York, described in On the Road to Competitive Advantage 5-1, provides an additional illustration of how this aim can be achieved.

Attracting Highly Qualified Candidates

To attain (or maintain) competitive advantage, an organization must successfully compete with other organizations in its recruitment efforts. Specifically, the HRM department must ensure that its recruitment efforts reach a sufficient number of qualified applicants, and it must take action to enhance the likelihood that the best applicants will accept their job offers. The Los Angeles United School District accomplished the latter aim by making the process user-friendly and royally treating the top candidates.

Qualified individuals cannot join an organization if they do not know about existing job openings. One way to ensure a sufficient number of qualified candidates, then, is to locate these individuals and notify them of available opportunities. Notifications should capture candidates' attention and stimulate their interest in applying for positions. The achievement of this aim may, at times, require innovation on the part of an employer, as illustrated in On the Road to Competitive Advantage 5-2 on page 104.

Attracting qualified applicants also requires that an organization take steps to increase the likelihood that the best candidate will *accept* a job offer. Admittedly, one's decision to accept an offer is influenced by many factors not directly related to recruitment. These factors, shown in Exhibit 5-1, include such things as the attractiveness of the company and the job.[5]

Recruiting Strategy Used by Dime Savings Bank of New York

The Jobline is a voice-mail system that allows an applicant to learn about job openings by calling the appropriate phone number. Callers who appear to be qualified for a vacant position are scheduled for an interview. The telephone system cost $1,500 to install. No further recruitment costs were incurred (except for the time spent retrieving messages, recording new weekly job listings, and interviewing viable candidates).

The return on investment has been in excess of 2,400 percent!

Source: Micolo, A.M. (1991). High-tech recruiting at low cost. *HRMagazine,* August, 49-52.

02667831306 Lizabeth Lukasic

Although other factors do influence the candidate, the manner in which the company recruits its applicants is still very important. The firm's approach to recruitment is especially important when the actual attributes of the job in question are neither clearly positive nor negative. Under these conditions, a candidate's perception of job attractiveness is heavily influenced by the nature of the information given by the firm, how it is given, and how well the applicants are treated.[6] As we saw in the opening case, working for the district had not been a particularly attractive alternative. The district succeeded in hiring top-notch applicants by treating them well—rolling out the red carpet.

The recruiter thus plays a major role in attracting applicants. The recruiter's behavior is often viewed as an extension of the organization's "personality." Consequently, applicants perceive the recruiter's behavior as a model of such things as the quality of interpersonal relationships and the nature of supervision existing within the company.[7] For example, rude treatment during an interview may be perceived as an indication of rudeness throughout the organization. Disrespect shown to a female candidate may be seen as a sign of a male chauvinistic environment.[8]

Improving Retention Rates through the Use of Realistic Job Previews

In most organizations, turnover occurs most frequently among newly hired employees—those in their first six months of the job.[9] Much of this turnover is caused by overzealous recruiters who "oversell" the job by creating unrealistically high expectations. Oversold applicants quickly become disenchanted with their jobs when their high expectations are not met, and they may leave the organization.[10] The author fondly recalls his days as a recruit in marine corps boot camp and the resounding cry of "Wait 'til I get my hands on that recruiter." To their chagrin, however, these recruits were not permitted to leave the organization until they finished their commitment.

EXHIBIT 5-1	Factors Influencing An Applicant's Decision to Accept a Job Offer

Alternative Job Opportunities	**Attractiveness of Job**
Number of opportunities	Nature of work
Attractiveness of opportunities	Work schedule
	Friendliness of coworkers
Attractiveness of Company	Nature of supervision
Pay	
Benefits	**Recruitment Activities**
Advancement opportunities	Information conveyed to the candidate
Desirability of geographic location	Manner in which the candidate is recruited
Organization's reputation as a good place to work	

INTERACTIVE EXHIBIT

Innovative Recruitment Strategy Used at IOMEGA

IOMEGA, a disk drive manufacturer located in Ogden, Utah, was having difficulty filling engineering and other high-tech positions. Its aim was to attract candidates located in San Jose, California. The problem was that many of these individuals felt that a move to Ogden would be "worse than an assignment in Siberia." IOMEGA adopted a recruitment strategy that focused on elements intended to appeal to those fed up with San Jose's hectic lifestyle. Its ad touted the high quality of life in Ogden, listing 24 specific attributes that made Ogden a good place to live (e.g., friendly neighborhoods, safe streets, affordable housing, concerts, golf courses). The result? More than 250 qualified applicants replied to the ad.

Source: Stevens, L. (1993). Resume scanning simplifies tracking. *Personnel Journal,* April, 77–79.

realistic job previews (RJPs) Conveying to applicants what organizational life will actually be like on the job, warts and all.

Providing applicants with **realistic job previews (RJPs)** can reduce turnover by giving applicants more realistic information (unfavorable, as well as favorable) about the job and the organization. When applicants are told about the unpleasant aspects of the job, they are able to make a more informed choice about whether or not to accept the job offer.[11]

After they are given a realistic view of the job, some applicants will withdraw from the selection process because their needs are not compatible with the demands of the job.[12] For instance, when applicants for a loading dock position are told how strenuous the job is, some may withdraw their applications because they do not want such a difficult job. Those who remain interested in the job, however, are likely to stay with the company, if hired, because they knew how tough it would be right from the start. Some may erect defenses that enable them to better cope with these aspects.[13] For instance, when accepting the job on a loading dock, an applicant might think, "This job is tough, but it will help me get into shape."

Reducing turnover rates can result in substantial savings, especially in companies experiencing high turnover rates among their new employees. One study, for instance, demonstrated that RJPs in such companies can be expected to reduce turnover rates by 24 percent, resulting in annual savings averaging $271,600.[14] Section 5-3, "The Manager's Guide," at the end of this chapter provides guidelines on when and how to provide applicants with realistic job previews.

Achieving Legal Compliance

An organization's recruitment practices also influence the company's success in complying with the various antidiscrimination laws and affirmative action requirements described in Chapter 2, "Understanding the Legal and Environmental Context of HRM." Organizations can help prevent discrimination charges by targeting recruitment efforts toward underutilized groups; that is, by reaching out to members of protected groups that have been disadvantaged by past workplace hiring practices (e.g., blacks, females, Hispanics, elderly, disabled). For instance, a company could target blacks, Hispanics, or disabled individuals by placing ads in the publications listed in Exhibit 5-2.

Creating a More Culturally Diverse Workforce

Extending recruitment practices to disadvantaged groups can create benefits beyond compliance; it can also create a more culturally diverse workforce. Realizing that the achievement of this aim can contribute to competitive advantage (as discussed in Chapter 2), many companies have begun targeting these groups,[15] reaching out to seniors, minorities, welfare-to-work candidates, and people leaving the armed forces.[16]

> **EXHIBIT 5-2**   Recruiting Sources for Certain Protected Groups

African-American Recruitment Sources

Dawn Magazine
Black Enterprise
Black Employment and Education Magazine
Black Collegian
Black Americans Information Directory

Hispanic Recruitment Sources

Vista
Hispanic Business
Hispanic Times Magazine
Hispanic Americans Information/Directory
SER/Jobs for Progress

Disability Recruitment Sources

Paraplegia News
Independent Living
Accent on Living
Careers and the Disabled

Source: Guide to Recruitment Markets. (1992). Supplement to the December 1992 issue of *Personnel Journal.*

For example, approximately 200 companies nationwide are now targeting their recruitment efforts toward older workers.[17] Among the companies with formal programs to attract older workers are The Travelers, Banker's Life and Casualty, Honeywell, Motorola, and some fast-food organizations such as KFC and McDonald's. As noted by one manager, "Fast foods have found older workers to be productive and cost-effective. Older workers provide a stabilizing effect and bring a good work ethic with them."[18]

Other employers have begun to target their recruitment efforts toward qualified workers with disabilities. One such company is Kreonite, a film manufacturer. After increasing the number of employees with disabilities, Kreonite's annual turnover rate dropped from 32 percent to 10 to 12 percent.[19]

A company's success at attracting members of underutilized groups is heavily dependent on the manner in which they treat these candidates during the recruitment process. Unfortunately, many organizations lose these (and other) candidates because the recruiters act in a way that could be described as "rude, boring, obnoxious, full of themselves, incompetent, barely literate, and jerks."[20] For example, one study found that female applicants often withdraw their candidacy during the recruiting process because they receive inappropriate comments about their personal appearance, are asked to interview in a man's hotel room, or are given the impression that the company is run according to an "old boys' network."[21]

5-2 HRM Issues and Practices

5-2a Recruitment Planning

Effective recruitment requires a great deal of careful planning. Figure 5-1 shows that the path to an effective planning process consists of many steps, with several important decision points along the way. We now examine these steps and discuss the issues that arise at each decision point.

Step 1: Identify the Job Opening

This step would appear to be an easy one—just wait until an employee turns in a notice of resignation. Many job openings are, in fact, identified in this way. A major

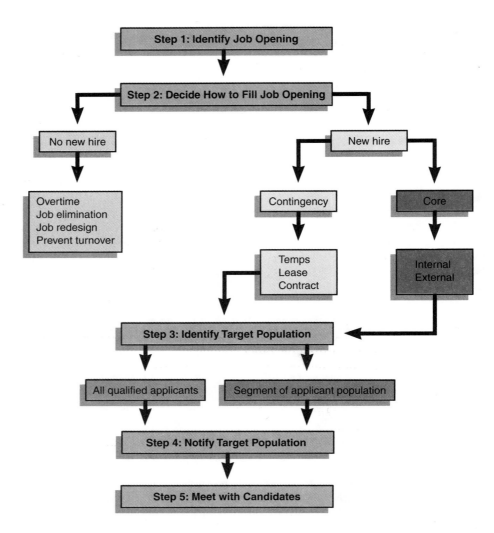

Figure 5-1
*Steps in the Recruitment
Planning Process*

problem with this approach is that it may take the company a long time to fill the opening. For instance, it usually takes six to eight weeks to notify and screen applicants, and a week or more to make a decision regarding a job offer. After the decision is made, the selected candidate must give notice (usually about two weeks) to his or her previous employer. Thus, the job in question is likely to remain vacant for many weeks, even if the process runs smoothly.

Ideally, organizations should attempt to identify job openings well in advance of an announced resignation. As discussed in Chapter 3, "Planning for Human Resources," the HRM department should plan for future openings in both the short and long term. The projection of future openings provides organizations with the time needed to plan and implement recruitment strategies so that they do not fall prey to the "must-hire-by-last-week" syndrome.[22] As noted in Chapter 3, the HR plan should answer at least the following questions:[23]

- Are any newly budgeted positions opening soon?

- Is a contract under negotiation that may result in the need for additional hires?

- What is the amount of expected turnover in the next several months?

Step 2: Decide How to Fill the Job Opening

The first question to ask after determining that an opening exists is "Do we need to find a new person to fill the vacant position?" Sometimes it is unnecessary to staff a vacant position because the firm can rely on other alternatives. For instance, it may

[handwritten margin notes:] + No overhead costs + No true commitment + flexibility + Cntrct 2 hire

be more prudent to provide overtime opportunities to current workers to complete the needed work. Other alternatives include job elimination and job redesign (i.e., incorporating the tasks of the vacant position into currently existing positions).

If the firm chooses to fill the vacancy, it must address two issues: (1) whether to fill it with **core** or with **contingency personnel** and (2) if core personnel are to be used, whether to recruit them internally or externally.

Core versus Contingency Personnel

Many companies have begun to adopt the strategy of staffing their positions with both core personnel and contingency personnel. Core personnel consist of employees who are hired in the "traditional" manner; that is, they are placed on the organization's payroll and are considered "permanent employees." Contingency personnel perform work for the company, but they are not included on the organization's payroll. Rather, they are employed by a supplier agency and are "loaned" to the firm on a temporary basis for a fixed fee. The supplier pays the workers' salaries and benefits.

Supplier agencies fall into three categories: **labor leasors, temporary employment agencies, and independent contractors.** Leased and temporary employees work side by side with core employees, often in the same jobs. Leased employees differ from temporary ones mainly in terms of their length of employment; contracts run longer for leased employees. Individuals secured through independent contractors, on the other hand, differ from the other contingency personnel in that they are selected to perform an entire function. For example, companies frequently contract all their maintenance work through a skilled-trades contractor.[24]

The use of contingency personnel is rapidly escalating. According to a 2001 Department of Labor survey, there are now 8.6 million independent contractors in this country and 1.2 million temps, together constituting over 7 percent of the U.S. workforce.[25] There are now over 7,000 temporary staffing firms, and these firms are being used at an increasing rate by nearly all companies.[26] Seventy-two percent of employers are now employing at least one contingent worker.[27] As one team of experts notes:[28]

If the current trend continues, typical large corporations of the future may consist

of a relatively small core of permanent employees, with the remainder of the workforce composed of individuals hired for specific, temporary assignments.

Four advantages result from the use of contingency personnel. One is that this practice provides management with the flexibility to control fixed employee costs.[29] Unlike core workers, the number of contingency workers can be easily increased or decreased according to the rise and fall of business conditions.[30]

Another advantage is that the use of such personnel relieves a company of many of its HRM burdens. The supplier handles the administrative work associated with payroll, insurance administration, and benefits. The supplier also screens and hires the workers.

A third advantage is cost savings. Contingency workers cost less than core personnel because the supplier pays certain overhead costs, such as payroll and insurance. Noel Ice Company, for instance, was able to reduce its monthly health coverage costs from $112 to $87 per employee through the use of employee leasing.[31] The fourth advantage is that the contingency workers who excel at their jobs can be offered core positions. Companies can minimize their risk of making a poor hiring decision by giving contingency workers a trial period before hiring where they can "show their stuff." The use of contingency personnel is not without its disadvantages, however. When beginning their job assignments with a company, contingency employees may need a considerable amount of orientation and training regarding company procedures and policies. This raises questions regarding the cost-effectiveness of this approach.[32]

contingency personnel Workers who are employed by a supplier agency and are "loaned" to the firm on a temporary basis for a fixed fee.

core personnel Employees who are hired in the "traditional" manner; that is, they are placed on the organization's payroll and are considered "permanent employees."

labor leasors Supplier agencies that provide companies with contingency workers on a lease basis.

temporary employment agencies Supplier agencies that provide companies with contingency workers on a short-term, temporary basis.

independent contractors Supplier agencies that provide companies with contingency workers to perform an entire work function.

Another problem is the possibility that, compared to core employees, contingency workers might be less loyal or committed to the "host organization." The use of contingency personnel could also lead to problems stemming from the fact that these individuals often receive better wages than core personnel for performing the same work. This inequity could cause resentment among the core workers.

In general, firms should use contingency workers in these types of situations:[33]

- Certain types of hard-to-find expertise are required.
- Companies are trying to staff new offices in geographic areas far from main headquarters.
- Companies are trying to staff positions to work on projects in which unusually high risk factors may jeopardize a company's existing workers' compensation rates. *time frames, culturally shocking*

Internal versus External Recruiting

As it hires core personnel, an organization must decide whether to recruit them internally or externally. That is, the company must decide whether to fill its vacant jobs with current employees or with applicants from outside the organization.

In most firms, external recruitment is limited primarily to entry-level jobs. Jobs above the entry level are usually filled with current employees through promotions. Promotion possibilities often enhance morale and motivation because they give employees a chance to advance their careers within the company. One study, for example, found that promotional opportunities led to reduced turnover, increased job satisfaction, and better job performance.[34]

Other advantages of internal recruitment over external are as follows:[35]

- The qualifications of internal candidates are already well known to the employer.
- Internal recruitment is less expensive.
- Job openings can be filled more quickly through internal recruitment.
- Internal candidates are more familiar with organizational policies and practices, and thus require less orientation and training.

Internal recruitment can lead to problems, however. When a position becomes vacant, many employees may be considered for that slot. Most, of course, will be rejected, and some of the rejected candidates may become resentful. One study, for instance, found that employees who were denied promotions reported greater feelings of inequity and had higher rates of absenteeism than their promoted counterparts.[36]

Another potential problem associated with internal recruitment occurs when workers are promoted into supervisory positions in the units in which they were already working. These individuals must now assume a new role with their past coworkers, and difficulties often arise as past friends become subordinates.

Despite potential hazards associated with internal recruitment, most jobs are filled in this manner. External recruitment for jobs above the entry level is usually restricted to situations such as these:[37]

- An outsider is needed to expose the organization to new ideas and innovations.
- No qualified internal candidates apply.
- The organization needs to increase its percentage of employees within a particular underutilized group.

According to management expert Ken Jordan, ensuring fairness is the key to implementing a successful internal recruitment system. His specific recommendations are presented in Taking a Closer Look 5-1.

Step 3: Identify the Target Population

Now the organization must answer the question "What type of individuals are we looking for to fill the vacant positions?" To address this question, an organization must

Taking a Closer Look 5-1	*Principles of Procedure Fairness for Internal Recruiting Systems*

1. *Use Objective Selection Tools*

   Avoid subjective selection methods such as unstructured interviews, employee reputation, and letters of recommendation. In their place, use interviews and/or tests that objectively measure the needed worker competencies specified in the job description. The use of objective selection methods sends the employees the message that the selection procedure is fair and the probability of being offered a position is directly related to ability, rather than favoritism and politics.

2. *Communicate Openly with Applicants*

   Inform applicants about the way the selection process works and what standards the successful applicant must meet. Be open about how the decision will be made. For instance, if interpersonal skills are crucial for the job, state this up front.

3. *Provide Helpful Feedback to Unsuccessful Applicants*

   Inform the unsuccessful applicants of the selection decision and the reasons for it. Counsel them regarding their strengths and weakness, and identify areas they need to improve upon in order to be viable candidates for future openings.

Source: Jordan, K. (1997). Play fair and square when hiring from within. *HRMagazine,* January, 49–51.

define its target population. Two issues arise here: (1) specifying worker requirements and (2) deciding whether to target a certain segment of the applicant population.

Specifying Worker Requirements

An organization must identify specific requirements of the job: the duties, reporting relationships, salary range for hiring, and competencies needed by a new worker (e.g., education, experience, knowledge, skills, and abilities).[38] Ideally, much of this information will have been gathered during a job analysis (see Chapter 4, "Analyzing Jobs") and thus be contained in the job description. If not, the recruiter should gather it from the hiring manager.

Deciding Whether to Target Certain Segments of the Applicant Population

An organization must also decide at this point whether to target all qualified applicants or to focus its recruitment efforts on certain segments of the qualified applicant population.

When recruiting internally, the issue is this: Should the company post the job so that all qualified employees can be considered? Or should the company select certain "high-potential" employees and groom them for the position?

When recruiting externally, the company must decide whether to inform all potential applicants or target certain types. As we noted previously, companies may reap advantages when they target members of certain underutilized groups. Another strategy is to target graduates of specific schools that have exceptionally strong programs in the functional areas of concern.[39] Additionally, some companies target top performing employees working for another company.[40] Recruitment of such individuals poses some unique problems, however. These individuals may be difficult to reach because they are not actively seeking a new job. Moreover, the practice of "pirating" employees from other firms raises some serious ethical questions.

Step 4: Notify the Target Population

Once an applicant population has been targeted, the company must determine how to notify these individuals of the vacant position. A variety of recruitment methods may be used for communicating vacancies, such as job postings, newspaper ads, campus interviews, and so forth, which are described later in the chapter. In this section, we discuss what companies can do during the notification process to limit the applicant pool to a manageable size.

Because of economic conditions (described in Chapter 2), the job market often fluctuates. When unemployment rates are high, there will be a glut of applicants, especially for certain job categories that have experienced heavy layoffs. Under this condition, firms may need to devise plans to limit the size of the applicant pool by attracting only the most qualified applicants. To avoid spending an inordinate amount of time weeding through applications, firms must discourage all but the best applicants from applying.

A good way to discourage unqualified applicants is to clearly state the job qualifications in the vacancy notification. Texas Instruments' approach takes it one step further. Its Internet recruiting page (http://www.ti.com/recruit) features a "Career Mapper," which offers a series of questions designed to measure an applicant's work style (e.g., "I prefer work that involves a certain amount of ambiguity"; "I can usually distinguish important from unimportant details"). Applicants are encouraged to apply only if told that their work styles are compatible with the job.[41]

Step 5: Meet with the Candidates

Finally, the most qualified candidates are brought in for interviews and other assessment procedures. These procedures serve both selection and recruitment purposes. From a selection perspective, they give the firm a chance to further assess the candidates' qualifications. (We discuss this perspective in Chapter 6 "Selecting Applicants.") From a recruitment perspective, they provide the candidates with an opportunity to learn more about the employment opportunity.

Candidates should be provided with information about the company and the job (see Section 5-3, "The Manager's Guide," for a description of this information). Failure to provide a sufficient amount of information could be detrimental to the recruiting process. For example, it may be interpreted by the candidates as an attempt to evade discussion of unattractive job attributes, or it may be viewed as an indication of the recruiter's disinterest in them.[42] Without specific information, applicants might accept a job offer without knowing about aspects of it that might affect their long-term job satisfaction, or they may refuse an offer without knowing about some of the job's attractive attributes.[43]

5-2b Methods of Internal Recruitment

The most common approaches to internal recruitment are discussed in the following subsections.

Computerized Career Progression Systems

Computerized career progression systems are used primarily by very large multisite organizations. Employees are asked to complete a questionnaire, listing their career interests, skills and other qualifications. This information is stored in an HRIS. When a job becomes vacant, the computer searches its files in order to identify employees having the requisite skills for the vacant job.

Strengths

Candidates can be found quickly using this method. The firm can also identify a broad spectrum of candidates using this approach and thus are not limited to candidates working in the department where the vacancy exists.

Weaknesses

The skills inventory contained in the computer database is limited only to objective or factual information, such as educational degrees, certifications, training courses taken, and languages spoken. Information of a more subjective nature (e.g., interpersonal skills, judgment, integrity) is excluded. However, for many jobs, this type of information is crucial.

Supervisor Selection

In this method of internal recruiting, hiring supervisors are asked to select an employee for the position. Supervisors will typically choose an individual whose work capabilities are well known to them.

Strengths

As one might expect, this method is very popular among supervisors. They like it because it gives them total discretion in selecting the individual who will report to them. Moreover, the supervisor is generally in a good position to know the capabilities of potential candidates, especially ones who already work for them and are seeking a promotion.

Weaknesses

The supervisor's choice of which employee(s) to select is usually very subjective and is thus susceptible to bias and possible discrimination. Moreover, some qualified employees may be overlooked. That is, supervisors may bypass good candidates in order to get their "favorites" promoted, or they may simply be unaware of the capabilities possessed by some individuals.

The courts have frowned on this method of internal recruitment, concluding that it is susceptible to bias and thus provides a ready mechanism for discrimination.[44] The courts prefer the use of a system in which all potentially qualified internal candidates are notified of promotional opportunities and are given a fair chance to apply.[45]

Job Posting

Job posting is the most commonly used approach to internal recruitment, at least at the nonmanagerial level. In the typical job posting system, a job vacancy notice is posted for all employees to see. The notice describes the job, salary, work schedule, and necessary worker qualifications. All employees possessing these qualifications may apply or "bid" for the job. The HRM department and/or the hiring manager then screens the bids. The most qualified applicants are chosen for interviews.

It is not easy to develop an effective job posting system. The HR professional must decide many issues about how to best implement the system, as indicated in the Taking a Closer Look 5-2. From the employees' point of view, the most important features of the posting system concern how well they are treated during the job interview and the amount of helpful career counseling they receive.[46]

job posting A method of internal recruitment in which a job vacancy notice is posted and all qualified employees may bid.

Strengths

Job posting systems have many pluses. The method successfully addresses the courts' concern that all eligible candidates be notified of vacant positions. Moreover, job postings have these advantages:

- Enhances the probability that the firm's most qualified employees will be considered for the job.

- Gives employees an opportunity to become more responsible for their own career development. Many may attempt to improve their job skills and performance because they perceive that such an effort can lead to greater promotional opportunities.

- Enables employees to leave a "bad" work situation. In the same vein, it encourages their current supervisors to manage more effectively in order to discourage employees from "jumping ship."

| **Taking a Closer Look 5-2** | *Issues to Address When Developing a Job Posting System* |

Plan for Success

1. Determine feasibility.
2. Ensure employee acceptance.
3. Consider legal standards.

Determine Eligibility Requirements

1. Minimum time with company (usually one year)
2. Minimum time at current job (usually six months to one year)
3. Allowable number of yearly bids (usually two or three)
4. Allowable number of simultaneous bids (usually two)
5. Permissibility of lateral moves (usually discouraged)
6. Standing with company (usually requires satisfactory rating on most recent performance appraisal, good attendance record, and no probationary sanction)

Determine Types of Jobs to Be Posted

1. About 80 percent of firms post blue-collar jobs.
2. About 50 percent of firms post professional jobs.

Determine Information to Be Included in the Posting

1. Job title and department
2. Listing of specific duties
3. Necessary qualifications
4. Salary range
5. Information on how to apply for the job
6. Work schedule
7. Affirmative action statement

Determine Where to Place Job Postings

1. Bulletin boards located in easily accessible and highly visible locations
2. Designated listing centers
3. Employee newsletter
4. "Position Alert" handouts

Determine Time Restraints

1. Length of time for posting (usually jobs are posted for a week)

2. Time limit for notifying applicants of employment decision (usually three weeks)
3. Time to allow between accepting an offer and leaving one's current job (varies from 30 days to six weeks)

Determine When to Notify the Current Supervisor of Bid

1. Inform supervisor prior to bid.
2. Inform supervisor if bidder becomes serious candidate.
3. Inform supervisor after the employee has accepted an offer.

Establish a Procedure for Reviewing Applications

1. Screening of applicants by HR department
2. Interview with hiring supervisor
3. Hiring decision (usually based on such factors as past performance appraisal ratings, attendance, length of company service, supervisor's recommendation, and interview results)

Provide Applicant Feedback

1. Document decisions; complete a form for each unsuccessful candidate, stating the reason for rejection.
2. Notify all applicants of decision in writing as soon as possible.
3. Offer career counseling, which provides
   a. Reasons for nonacceptance
   b. Remedial measures, such as training needed to qualify for better positions
   c. Information regarding the job-seeking process (e.g., how to bid, how to conduct oneself during an interview)

Establish an Appeals Procedure

1. Improves employee trust in the system
2. Helps counteract charges of bias in the selection process

Source: Kleiman, L.S., and Clark, K.J. (1984). Recruitment: An effective job posting system. *Personnel Journal,* February, 20–25.

Weaknesses

These are some of the weaknesses associated with job posting:

- The position may remain open for an extended period because it takes a long time to fill an opening this way.

- The system may prevent supervisors from hiring the individuals of their choice. This circumstance can lead to gamesmanship—supervisory maneuvers intended to "beat the system."
- Some employees may hop from job to job without any clear direction.
- Employees whose bids are rejected may become alienated from the organization.

Career Development Systems

Career development systems represent an alternative approach to filling job openings from within. Rather than encouraging all qualified employees to bid for a job, a firm may place some "fast-track" or high-potential employees on a career path where they are groomed or trained for certain targeted jobs. An approach to career development for managers is described in Chapter 7, "Training and Developing Employees." A critical issue in the implementation of a career development system is how to identify the most suitable candidates. The selection procedures must meet the professional and legal guidelines described in Chapters 2 and 6. Subjective supervisor nominations should be avoided.

career development systems   A method of internal recruiting in which a firm places "fast-track" or high-potential employees on a career path where they are groomed for certain targeted jobs.

Strengths

Career development systems are often effective for these reasons:

- The firm's top performers (i.e., those selected for the program) are more likely to remain with the organization.
- Such systems help ensure that someone is always ready to fill a position when it becomes open.

Weaknesses

The primary weaknesses associated with career development systems are as follows:

- An employee who is not selected for grooming may become disenchanted with the organization and leave, even though he or she may be a good, solid employee—just not top tier.
- The selected employee may become frustrated if the expected promotion does not materialize because the targeted position never becomes vacant.

5-2c Methods of External Recruitment

A variety of methods can be used to recruit candidates externally, some of which are discussed next.

Employee Referrals

When a position becomes vacant, firms often use **employee referrals** to fill them. That is, HR professionals or line managers ask employees to solicit applications from qualified friends and associates. In some instances, companies will offer an incentive, such as a bonus or prize, for each referral actually hired.

employee referrals A method of external recruitment in which firms ask their employees to solicit applications from qualified friends and associates.

Strengths

Because many companies have found this approach to be effective, it is quite popular. The typical firm recruits about 15 percent of its workforce through referrals.[47] Applicants referred by employees tend to perform better and remain with the company longer than applicants recruited by other means.[48] Employees tend to be good recruiters because they know a lot about both the job being filled and the individual, and can therefore accurately judge the "fit" between the two. Additionally, employees make good recruiters because, believing their reputation is on the line, they are encouraged to refer only the highest quality applicants.[49]

MCI's Computerized System for Tracking Unsolicited Resumes

The system used by telecommunications company MCI consists of the following steps:

1. When a resume arrives in the mail, a clerk scans it into the computer.
2. When the hiring manager needs to fill a position, he or she informs the recruiter of the qualifications needed for the job.
3. The recruiter searches the database, using keywords.

4. The computer displays the number of resumes that meet the required criteria. If the number is too large or small, the recruiter can broaden or narrow the list of keywords to generate a more appropriately sized list of candidates.
5. The recruiter can then view the resumes on screen and eliminate inappropriate candidates.
6. Hard copies of the best resumes are then sent to the hiring manager through email or by fax.

The use of employee referrals can be very cost efficient. Extensity, a San Francisco–based company, realized large savings from its employee referral program. Here, the company established a program that entered employees with successful referrals into a lottery to compete for a 2-year lease on a Porsche. The number of referrals quickly doubled, leading to the hire of 46 new employees within six months. The program savings outweighed its costs by $130,000.[50]

Weaknesses

Employee referrals may serve as a barrier to equal employment opportunity. An EEO problem may surface because employees are most likely to refer those most similar to themselves with respect to race, sex, and so forth. Consequently, if an organization's workforce is predominantly while males, then females and minorities may be inadvertently barred from consideration.

Applicant-Initiated Recruitment

applicant-initiated recruitment A method of external recruitment in which a company accepts unsolicited applications or resumes from individuals interested in working for the company.

Organizations often receive unsolicited applications or resumes from individuals interested in working for the company, so "active" recruiting is not always necessary. **Applicant-initiated recruitment** is most prevalent in firms that enjoy a reputation for being a good place to work in terms of compensation policies, working conditions, employee relations, and/or participation in community activities.

Many firms now track such unsolicited resumes on their HRIS. An example of such a firm is given in On the Road to Competitive Advantage 5-3.

Strengths

The applicant-initiated approach to recruitment is both efficient and low cost. In addition, the candidates are likely to be highly motivated, because they have taken the time to learn about the company.[51]

Weaknesses

help-wanted advertisements A method of external recruitment in which a company places an advertisement of the position in the appropriate media (e.g., newspaper, magazine).

Drawing on self-initiated applicants presents a timing problem. Applications and resumes may remain "on file" for some time. By the time a job becomes vacant, many of these individuals may have already found other jobs.

Help-Wanted Advertisements

Probably the best-known way to notify potential applicants of job openings is **help-wanted advertisements.** The appropriate medium for placing an ad depends primarily on the geographic recruitment area. When applicants in the local geographic

Taking a Closer Look 5-3	*Tips for Writing Effective Help-Wanted Ads*

1. Design the ad so that it will grab the readers' attention and motivate them to read further. Use a headline that will help sell the job to the candidate. Do not merely list the job title. However, the ad should not be overly clever or creative.
2. Do not misrepresent the job by making promises you cannot keep. Be honest about advancement opportunities, challenge, responsibility, and so forth.
3. Be specific about the job requirements and the needed qualifications (i.e., education, experience, and personal characteristics).
4. Describe the advantages of working for the company.
5. Use advertising space economically. The size of the ad should be proportional to the importance of the position and the number of candidates sought.
6. Make sure the ad is easy to read and grammatically correct. The typeface should be attractive and legible.
7. Provide the readers with a source (i.e., address or phone number) for further information.

Source: Adapted from Kuzmits, F.E. (1986). *Experiential Exercises in Personnel* (2nd ed.). Columbus, OH: Merrill.

area are being sought, a firm may place an ad in the local newspaper, advertise on TV or radio, or place notices on billboards. To reach a broader geographic area, ads may be placed in nationally distributed newspapers (e.g., *The Wall Street Journal, USA Today*), magazines, professional/trade journals, or on the Internet.

Strengths

Help-wanted advertisements allow an employer to reach a large audience in a relatively short period of time. In fact, such ads are used by nearly all companies.[52] Not only does this method help ensure a large applicant pool, but it also helps ensure that members of all protected groups get an opportunity to apply for the opening.

Weaknesses

Somewhat surprisingly, help-wanted advertisements are often ineffective. For example, studies have found that people hired through newspaper advertisements, compared to those hired through other recruiting methods, do not perform their jobs as well and are absent from work more often.[53] Perhaps ads are ineffective because they fail to reach the most viable candidates—successful individuals who are not currently looking for a new job. Further, other recruitment methods, such as employee referrals, may do a better job of *enticing* the most qualified applicants—a friend can be more persuasive than a written ad.[54]

Help-wanted advertising reaches a large audience, which can quickly turn into a disadvantage if too many people respond to an ad. As noted earlier in the chapter, the process of screening vast numbers of applications often becomes an administrative nightmare.

To be effective, help-wanted advertising must dissuade unqualified individuals from applying. At the same time, ads must capture the attention of qualified applicants and attract them to the job. Tips for writing effective help-wanted ads appear in Taking a Closer Look 5-3.

Employment Agencies and Executive Search Firms

Employment agencies and **executive search firms** represent another option for recruiting external job applicants. Here, an employer initiates the recruitment process by contacting the appropriate agency/firm and telling it of the qualifications needed for the job in question. The agency/firm assumes the task of soliciting and screening applications, and then refers top applicants to the employer for further screening. Three types of employment agencies/firms—public agencies,

executive search firms Employment agencies used to recruit mid- and senior-level managers with salaries generally above $60,000.

private agencies, and executive search firms—have experienced remarkable growth in the past decade. We now discuss each one.

Public Employment Agencies

public employment agencies Run by each state under the auspices of the U.S. Employment Service, these agencies place workers in jobs that are primarily clerical and blue-collar positions.

Public employment agencies are run by each state under the auspices of the U.S. Employment Service (USES). Under federal law, individuals who receive unemployment compensation must register for work with the public agency in their state.

Public agencies provide personnel most frequently for clerical and blue-collar jobs. Using public agencies to fill these types of jobs is cost- and time-efficient. Cost is low because the agency does not charge employers a fee. The method is efficient because jobs can be filled fairly quickly—potential applicants are already registered with the state agency and, because they are unemployed, are available for work immediately. On the negative side, some employers are concerned about the motivational level of the applicants—they may be applying for work simply to keep their eligibility for unemployment compensation and may not actually be interested in a job offer.

Private Employment Agencies

private employment agencies Privately run agencies that, for a fee, provide companies with clerical, blue-collar, technical, and lower-level managerial personnel.

Private employment agencies differ from public ones in three important ways:

1. Private agencies have the resources to fill a wider variety of jobs. In addition to providing clerical and blue-collar personnel, private agencies may be used to fill technical and lower-level managerial jobs.
2. Candidates register with the agency voluntarily and thus may be more committed than public agency candidates to accepting a job offer.
3. The agency charges a fee for its services, usually paid by the company when higher-level positions are being filled. Clerical and blue-collar candidates pay the fees themselves.

Because private employment agencies relieve a firm of the administrative burden of finding, contacting, and prescreening applicants, they are especially useful when many individuals are expected to apply for a job or when qualified candidates are hard to find.

Executive Search Firms

Executive search firms (popularly known as "headhunters") specialize in the recruitment of mid- and senior-level managers with salaries generally above $60,000. Search firms charge an employer a rather large fee for their services. In fact, fee payment is usually required even if none of the firm's candidates is actually hired. The steps involved in the executive search process are shown in Figure 5-2.

Executive search firms are widely used. These firms contact more than 4 million prospective candidates per year, about 80,000 of whom are hired.[55] Executive search firms can locate successful executives working elsewhere—people who are not actively seeking a new job.

Executive searches, however, can be unsuccessful. Only 50 to 60 percent of all executive searches result in the selection of the type of individual initially specified.[56] To maximize the chances of an effective search, employers should follow the guidelines listed in Taking a Closer Look 5-4.

campus recruiting A recruiting method in which the firm's recruiters visit various college and university campuses to recruit individuals for positions requiring a college degree.

Campus Recruiting

Campus recruiting involves the firm's recruiters visiting various college and university campuses to recruit individuals for positions requiring a college degree. The campus recruitment process is described in Exhibit 5-3.

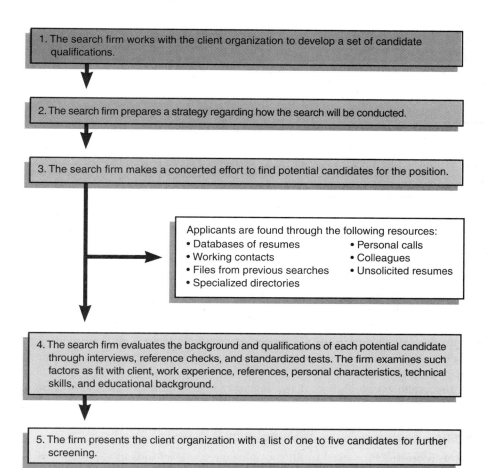

1. The search firm works with the client organization to develop a set of candidate qualifications.

2. The search firm prepares a strategy regarding how the search will be conducted.

3. The search firm makes a concerted effort to find potential candidates for the position.

Applicants are found through the following resources:
- Databases of resumes
- Working contacts
- Files from previous searches
- Specialized directories
- Personal calls
- Colleagues
- Unsolicited resumes

4. The search firm evaluates the background and qualifications of each potential candidate through interviews, reference checks, and standardized tests. The firm examines such factors as fit with client, work experience, references, personal characteristics, technical skills, and educational background.

5. The firm presents the client organization with a list of one to five candidates for further screening.

Figure 5-2
Steps in the Recruitment Process When Using an Executive Search Firm

Source: Brown, L.A., and Martin, D.C. (1991). What to expect from an executive search firm. *HRMagazine,* December, 56–58.

Taking a Closer Look 5-4 *How to Deal Effectively with Executive Search Firms*

1. *Pick the right firm:* What specific experience should the firm have had? Why is this firm motivated to accept the assignment?

2. *Know what you want at the start of the search:* You have every right to expect the firm to help you formulate your needs before the recruiting process begins. By the time you sign off on the job specification, you should know what type of individual you expect to interview.

3. *Don't make the position specification a moving target:* If the original needs change, cancel the search and pay the fee. Do not expect two searches for the price of one fee. Start the search again from scratch.

4. *Be honest:* Tell the search consultant everything you would need to know if you were in his or her position. Be honest with yourself in terms of whether the candidate you want really exists, whether you can afford the salary expected by such a candidate,

and whether the ideal candidate would be interested in the offered position.

5. *Communicate:* Maintain an active dialogue with the consultant. Allow him or her to meet with all members of the selection process.

6. *Make the hiring decision as rapidly as possible:* When you take too long to evaluate a candidate, you place a burden on the consultant who cannot be expected to keep a candidate waiting indefinitely.

7. *Don't expect an endless search:* Once the search firm has contacted between 50 to 100 potential candidates and presented its list of three to five finalists, those finalists should be interviewed as soon as possible. In most cases, if the search firm has done its job, one of those finalists should be given an offer.

Source: Hutton, T.J. (1987). Increasing the odds for successful searches, *Personnel Journal,* September, 140-152.

> **EXHIBIT 5-3** | Steps in the Campus Recruitment Process

1. *Conduct a recruitment analysis:* The firm performs a recruitment analysis to estimate the specific new talent requirements needed in the long and short term.
2. *Prepare a position requisition:* Each new position request is formalized into a requisition that describes the job responsibilities and the skills and abilities needed for the job.
3. *Select schools:* The recruiting schools are chosen, and the recruiting schedule is set in the summer.
4. *Conduct campus interviews:* Recruiters conduct campus interviews during the fall and spring semesters.
5. *Screen candidates:* Recruiters invite the best candidates to attend on-site interviews.
6. *Evaluate recruitment:* The recruiting effort is evaluated by the HRM department to determine whether job vacancies still exist, the quality of the new hires, and the cost efficiency of the program.

Source: Adapted from Kolenko, T.A. (1988). College recruiting: Models, myths, and management. In Gerald R. Ferris and Kendrith M. Rowland (eds.). *Human Resources Management: Perspectives and Issues.* Boston: Allyn & Bacon.

During on-campus interviews, which typically last 20 to 30 minutes, recruiters and students make decisions about one another. The recruiter makes a preliminary assessment of the student's fitness for the job, and the student makes a preliminary assessment of the attractiveness of the firm.

A student's interest in working for a particular firm depends largely on the actions and attitudes of the recruiter during the interview.[57] If recruiters are perceived as being poorly informed (because they have not read the student's resume or have little specific knowledge of the job), the student may quickly become disenchanted with the organization.[58] Also, if the recruiter is cold and distant, the student may assume that the firm is likewise cold and distant.

Strengths

Campus recruitment is used to fill specialized entry-level jobs in such fields as engineering, finance, accounting, computer science, law, and supervisory management.[59] In fact, approximately 50 percent of all managers and professionals with less than three years of work experience were recruited on campus.[60] A survey of *Fortune* 1,000 firms revealed that, on the average, college recruitment activities comprise 16 percent of a firm's total human resource management budget.[61]

Weaknesses

Campus recruitment is costly and time-consuming. Costs range from $1,500 to $6,000 per hire.[62] Moreover, the recruitment process can be a rather slow one: Organizations must determine their recruitment needs at least 9 to 11 months in advance, and they must normally wait until graduation to hire.

Online Recruiting

online recruiting
Advertising job openings
on the Internet.

The newest approach to external recruiting, **online recruiting,** is using the Internet to advertise jobs and find resumes of job seekers. There are a number of websites offering these services (see Taking a Closer Look 5-5). For example, Career Builder is an online collection of Sunday help-wanted ads from 50 major newspapers throughout the United States. America's Job Bank, run by the federal government, contains employment listings from over 2,000 employment offices. The most popular site is probably Monster. In June 2001, it posted over one million jobs.

Strengths

Online recruiting is becoming quite popular. The online recruiting business is a $26 billion dollar industry, with 2,5000 websites that offer recruiting services, not counting internal corporate sites. At any given time, the web holds 110 million job listings

Taking a Closer Look 5-5	*Websites for Online Recruiting*

America's Job Bank
http://www.ajb.dni.us
Career Builder
http://www.careerbuilder.com
College Central
http://www.collegecentral.com
Federal Jobs
http://fedjobs.com
Flip Dog
http://www.flipdog.monster.com
Hot Jobs
http://www.hotjobs.com

Monster
http://www.monster.com
Monstertrak (college-oriented Monster)
http://www.monstertrak.com
NationJob
http://www.nationjob.com
Society for Human Resource Management
http://www.shrm.org

Source: Crispin, G., and Mehler, M. (1997). Recruiting rockets through cyberspace. *HRMagazine,* December, 72–77.

and 20 million applicant resumes.[63] Compared to newspaper advertising, online recruiting is much faster and reaches a much larger audience; within minutes of posting, the job vacancy can be viewed by millions of people.

Weaknesses

Online recruiting is not always the best approach for recruiting external candidates. It can be quite expensive compared to other recruiting methods. For example, the Monster.com website specifies a charge of $365 to post one job; it charges $4,740 to post 30 jobs within a 12-month period. Online recruiting is mostly used for regional/national searches to fill jobs paying between $25,000 and $60,000.[64]

The number of applications generated can create an administrative burden. Charles Schwab & Company, for instance, typically receives about 15,000 resumes per month.[65] Many of these resumes are from unqualified people who send resumes in the hopes of getting a recruiter's attention. This situation makes the recruiter's job very difficult because of all the time it takes to screen these applications.

Choosing the Right Method

The choice of an external recruitment method depends largely on the circumstances surrounding the hiring situation. The following factors are the most relevant:

• The type of job being filled
• How quickly the job needs to be filled
• The geographic region of recruitment
• The cost of implementing the recruitment method
• Whether the method will attract the right mix of candidates from an EEO perspective

Exhibit 5-4 compares the various external recruitment methods on the basis of these factors.

Legally, employers must ensure that their recruitment efforts extend to females and other minority groups, especially when certain groups within the organization are underutilized. Overreliance on employee referrals and applicant-initiated recruitment methods may put an employer at risk of EEO violations because these methods offer no assurances that a proper mix of individuals will apply. Help-wanted ads, on the other hand, have a much greater potential for successfully reaching these individuals.

EXHIBIT 5-4	Comparison of External Recruitment Methods				
Recruitment Method	**Types of Job(s)**	**Speed**	**Geographic Location**	**Cost**	**EEO Compliance**
Employee referrals	All	Fast	All	Low	Potentially poor
Applicant initiated	All	Fast	All	Low	Potentially poor
Help-wanted advertisements	All	Fast/moderate	All	Moderate	Good
Public agencies	Clerical Blue-collar	Moderate	Local	Low	Good
Private agencies	Sales Clerical Technical Lower management	Moderate	Local	Moderate	Fair
Executive search firms	Executives Management	Slow	Regional/national	High	Fair
Campus recruiting	College grads	Slow	Regional/national	Moderate/High	Good
Online recruiting	$25,000–60,000	Fast	Regional/national	Moderate	Good

5-3 The Manager's Guide

5-3a HR Recruitment and the Manager's Job

The line manager plays three key roles in the recruitment process.

Identifying Recruitment Needs

Line managers usually identify recruitment needs for their own units. The need to recruit may be triggered by any of the following conditions:

- An outgoing incumbent must be replaced.
- Additional positions are added in response to increased workload.
- A newly created job is established.

Communicating Recruitment Needs to the HRM Department

Second, line managers must convey certain information to the HR professional (i.e., the recruiter):

- The needed skills/qualifications for the job
- The attractive features of the job
- The unattractive features of the job
- How the recruiter should discuss these unattractive job features with the candidates[66]

Interacting with Applicants

Third, line managers interact with applicants. This role is especially important because, as we mentioned earlier, the actions of managers can have a significant bearing on the perceptions of applicants. The manager's behavior sends applicants strong signals about what work would really be like if one were to accept a job offer.[67] To ensure the signal is a positive one, a manager should do the following:[68]

- Keep applicants informed of their status during the recruiting process. If delays occur, let candidates know when they can expect further information or action.
- Schedule interviews at the candidate's convenience.
- Allow candidates to speak to their future coworkers. This gives them a chance to ask questions they might not ask the manager and also gives them a feel for what it would be like to work for the company.

5-3b How the HR Department Can Help

Although line managers play an important part in the recruitment process, most of the work is actually done by the HR professionals.

Planning the Recruitment Process

HR professionals' tasks begin when they receive a requisition from the line managers. After conferring with the managers to identify their specific needs, HR professionals must plan the recruitment process. That is, they determine where to find the applicants and how to attract them.

Implementing the Recruitment Process

The HR professional must then implement the recruitment process (e.g., write an ad, choose the employment agency, conduct campus interviews). When candidates are invited for on-site visits, the HR professional generally coordinates these visits. This activity involves these tasks:[69]

- Make travel arrangements.
- Schedule candidate interviews.
- Monitor the status of candidates throughout the recruitment process.
- Expedite the final disposition of candidates (e.g., writing rejection/acceptance letters).

Evaluating the Recruitment Process

The final role played by HR professionals is that of evaluation. Evaluation involves the following activities:[70]

- Calculating the number of applicants generated from each recruitment method, the number hired, and the job success of each hire
- Determining the cost-effectiveness of each recruitment method
- Monitoring EEO statistics to ensure compliance

5-3c HRM Skill-Building for Managers

We now discuss the specific skills needed by managers to carry out successfully their recruitment responsibilities.

What Information to Give Candidates

You should spend about 20 minutes telling applicants about the job and the organization. As we explain in Chapter 6, you should provide this information at the end of the employment interview. This part of the interview should be structured along the following lines:[71]

1. Describe what the company does. Provide enough information so that the applicant will understand the nature of the business, what products or services the company offers, and how its products or services are differentiated from that of its competitors.
2. Present relevant facts and figures. State how many people are employed by the company, how many divisions it has, and how profitable the company has been.
3. Describe the company's history. When was it founded? What made it successful? What is the corporate philosophy?
4. Describe the department in which the opening exists. What type of work does it do? How many people work in it? What special projects are ongoing? What is the work climate?

5. Describe the job itself. What are the duties? What are the positive and negative aspects of the job?

6. Describe yourself as a manager. What is your management and leadership style? What type of worker impresses you? What type of worker do you find troublesome?

7. Describe the work setting. Will the employee have a private office? A personal secretary? Give the applicant a tour of the work site.

8. Discuss salary. If the salary is nonnegotiable, communicate this to the applicant. Otherwise, indicate the range of salary associated with the job.

9. Describe the workweek and the payroll period. Indicate the length of the lunch period, the working hours, the necessity for overtime, and when the first paycheck will be received. Also, describe time-off options (sick days, personal days, vacation days, etc.) and whether the amount of time off increases with increasing tenure.

10. Describe career opportunities. Does the company promote from within? Is there a formalized procedure for requesting promotions, such as job postings? Discuss performance evaluation and salary increase timetables. When can the worker expect a first raise and how often thereafter?

11. Describe what employees like best about the company. Do employees socialize after work? Are there company-sponsored athletic teams? Is the work challenging? Is top management accessible and down to earth?

12. Encourage the applicant to ask questions. Are there any points the applicant would like clarified? Only when the applicant has asked all of his or her questions should the interview be terminated.

How to Provide the Information

During the interview, you need to make a favorable impression on the candidate. In addition to being informative, you should appear competent and personable.[72] To be viewed as competent, avoid acting defensively and being self-conscious, avoid discussing irrelevant topics, be easy to get along with, and answer the candidate's questions satisfactorily.[73] To be viewed as personable, you should display warmth, show an interest in the applicant's outside activities, and be enthusiastic about the organization.[74]

Providing Realistic Job Previews

Traditional recruiting methods sometimes "sell" the organization by emphasizing only the positive aspects of the job; managers purposely withhold information regarding the problems and difficulties faced on the job. The expectation is that the more positive approach will attract a larger pool of applicants.

As noted earlier, when employers communicate what organizational life will actually be like on the job (referred to as realistic job previews), job retention rates often improve.[75] However, given the fact that RJPs will tend to dissuade some people from an interest in the job, they may not be appropriate in all situations. The use of RJPs would appear to be most suitable when the following conditions exist:

• Turnover and associated separation costs are high.

• There are negative facets of the job that applicants do not know about, and these facets may strongly influence their subsequent intentions to quit.

• Qualified applicants are plentiful.

The RJP should be given to applicants before they accept a job offer. It should provide a balanced picture of the job and should include the important facets of the job that most employees view as either particularly satisfying or dissatisfying. When providing an RJP, you should:[76]

- Include descriptive information (starting salaries, average length of time to promotion, hours of work) and judgmental information (aspects that satisfy and dissatisfy employees). For example, you might tell candidates that you monitor employee behavior very closely.

- Avoid giving candidates all possible information. Limit your discussion of negatives to issues that have created turnover problems in the past, like dangers of the job, sexism at the workplace, games people play at work, necessary overtime required, lack of praise, lack of challenge, and the need to deal with such problems as irate customers, rapidly changing departmental priorities, and boredom. As you decide what negative information to specify, the two basic questions to ask are "Do candidates have inaccurate expectations about this issue?" and "Is this issue important enough to affect an employee's decision to quit or stay?"

- The relative emphasis you give to positive and negative information should reflect the actual balance of positive–negative factors found in the environment. In other words, if the positive aspects equal the negative ones, then 50 percent of the interview time should be spent discussing each.

Chapter Objectives Revisited

1. Understand how a firm's recruiting practices can lead to competitive advantage.
   - Enhance cost efficiency
   - Attract highly qualified/productive applicants
   - Improve retention rates through realistic job previews
   - Rectify legal compliance problems
   - Help create a more culturally diverse workplace

2. Explain the choices involved in planning a recruitment strategy.
   - Identify job opening. Choices:
     - Wait for resignation.
     - Human resource planning.
   - Decide how to fill opening. Choices:
     - Fill or not fill.
     - Use core or contingency workers.
     - Recruit internally or externally.
   - Identify target population. Choices:
     - Internal: Identify all or a preselected group of employees.
     - External: Identify all or target certain groups of applicants.
   - Notify target population.
     - Limit size of applicant pool, if necessary.
   - Meet with candidates.
     - Provide information.
     - Make good impression.

3. Discuss the various recruitment methods.
   - Internal recruitment:
     - Supervisory recommendations: Candidates chosen by hiring supervisor
     - Job posting: A job vacancy notice is posted, and all qualified employees may bid.
   - Computerized career progression systems: "Fast-track" or high-potential employees are placed on a career path where they are groomed for certain targeted jobs.
   - External recruitment:
     - Employee referrals: Firms ask their employees to solicit applications from qualified friends and associates.
     - Applicant-initiated recruitment: A company accepts unsolicited applications or resumes from individuals interested in working for the company.
     - Help-wanted advertisements: A company places an advertisement of the position in the appropriate media.
     - Public employment agencies: Run by each state under the auspices of the U.S. Employment Service, these agencies place workers in jobs that are primarily clerical and blue-collar jobs.
     - Private employment agencies: Privately run agencies that, for a fee, provide companies with clerical, blue-collar, technical, and lower-level managerial personnel.
     - Executive search firms: Employment agencies used to recruit mid- and senior-level managers with salaries generally above $60,000.
     - Campus recruiting: The firm's recruiters visit various college and university campuses to recruit individuals for positions requiring a college degree.
     - Online recruiting: Posting job vacancies on the Internet

Review Questions

Note: You can find the correct answers to these questions by taking the quiz and then submitting your answers in the Online Edition. The program will automatically score your submission. If you miss a question, the program will provide the correct answer, a rationale for the answer, and the section number in the chapter where the topic is discussed.

1. The main difference between core personnel and contingent personnel is

   a. contingent workers are considered to be "permanent employees"; core employees are considered to be temporary workers.
   b. core workers are paid by the employing organization; contingent workers are "loaned" employees who are paid by the supplier organization.
   c. contingent employees are variable fee workers; core employees are fixed fee workers.
   d. contingent employees receive a salary from the employing organization and benefits from the supplier; core employees receive both salary and benefits from the employing organization.

2. Which of the following is *not* an advantage of using contingency personnel?

   a. It provides management with the flexibility to control fixed employee costs.
   b. It relieves the organization of many of the administrative burdens of hiring a new employee (e.g., payroll, benefits).
   c. It saves companies overhead costs (e.g., insurance premiums).
   d. It promotes greater commitment to the employing organization.

3. Using an internal recruiting strategy can

   a. lead to feelings of resentment among current employees if an individual is promoted into a supervisory role over his or her former coworkers.
   b. lead to feelings of resentment among current employees because they are not considered for job vacancies.
   c. limit an organization's ability to develop a cohesive team spirit.
   d. be much more expensive than external recruiting.

4. Deciding whether or not to use a job posting system as part of internal recruiting is mentioned in the text in connection with which step in the recruitment planning process?

   a. Step 1: Identify job opening.
   b. Step 2: Decide how to fill job opening.
   c. Step 4: Notify the target population.
   d. Step 5: Meet the candidates.

5. Computerized career progression systems are an effective tool for internal recruitment because

   a. the firm can identify a broad spectrum of candidates.
   b. the system consists of the kind of subjective information that is often used to determine the best "fit" between applicant and job.
   c. the system is invariably easier to use than paper-based systems.
   d. employees can take control of their careers.

6. Which method of internal recruitment is most preferred by management?

   a. job posting
   b. employee referral
   c. supervisor recommendations
   d. computerized career progressions systems

7. The major difference between a private and public employment agency is that

   a. candidates register with private agencies voluntarily and thus are more committed to accepting a job offer.
   b. public agencies have the resources to fill a wider array of jobs than do private agencies.
   c. public agencies charge a fee for their services directly to the job seeker; private agencies always bill companies for their services.
   d. public agencies are most useful for screening executive-level applicants; private agencies handle primarily clerical employees.

8. Choosing the most appropriate recruiting method should depend on all of the following except

   a. the type of job being filled.
   b. the cost of implementing the method.
   c. how quickly the job needs to be filled.
   d. the amount of experience that a firm has with using a particular recruiting method.

9. Employee referral systems tend to be effective because
   a. they can often ward off potential EEO problems.
   b. managers are usually not able to assess an applicant's qualifications adequately.
   c. employees refer only the highest quality applicants because their reputation is on the line.
   d. it gives employees an opportunity to be more responsible for their own career development.

10. According to the text, which of the following is among the most important considerations for employees when participating in the job posting system?
    a. the formatting of the job information
    b. the amount of helpful career counseling they receive
    c. the quantity of information provided about posted jobs
    d. the timeliness of feedback about jobs to which they have posted

Discussion Questions

1. Describe three ways in which effective recruitment activities can help an organization gain competitive advantage.
2. What explanations have been presented to account for the fact that the use of RJPs improves retention rates?
3. Explain the impact of a recruiter's behavior on the success of the recruitment effort.
4. It is not always necessary to staff a position when it becomes vacant. List three alternatives to staffing.
5. Distinguish between core and contingency personnel. Discuss the strengths and weaknesses associated with each.
6. Why do most organizations usually fill positions higher than entry-level jobs by means of internal recruitment?
7. Under what set of conditions is external recruitment recommended?
8. When notifying the target applicant population of a job opening, what can an organization do to limit the number of unqualified applicants?
9. The text recommends that organizations avoid the use of supervisor recommendations when recruiting internally. What are the potential problems with supervisor recommendations?
10. Compare and contrast the three types of employment agencies.
11. Describe the manager's roles in the recruitment process.
12. How can a manager make a favorable impression on the candidate during an interview?
13. Under what circumstances is it best to use an RJP? Explain.

Experiential Exercises

What Attributes Does a Campus Recruiter Seek?

1. Divide into groups of five.
2. Each group should construct a list of what applicant attributes or qualities a campus recruiter looks for when interviewing a student for an entry-level management position.
3. For each attribute on the list, state the recruiter's basis for judgment. For example, if your list includes "leadership skills," state how this attribute would be judged (e.g., offices held in campus organizations, students' answers to certain interview questions, and so forth).
4. A spokesperson for each group should present the group's responses.
5. The class as a whole should discuss how one can impress a campus recruiter during the campus interview.

Conducting an RJP

1. Divide into groups of five.
2. Assume your group has been asked to provide an RJP to possible incoming freshmen interested in a management major.
3. Using the information in Section 5-3, "The Manager's Guide," construct an RJP that should be given to these students.
4. Each group should present its RJP in front of the class.

5. Class discussion should focus on the usefulness of these RJPs. That is, would the consequences of using RJPs be beneficial to the school? What type of student would be dissuaded from majoring in management? Would those still interested become more committed to the program because of the RJP? Do you think your school should implement this approach?

Case

The Geographical Area of Recruitment

Where to Draw the Line

Bristle Inc., a manufacturer of over-the-counter pharmaceuticals and cosmetics, is located about 25 miles outside Atlanta. A *Fortune* 500 company, Bristle employs 420 individuals on a full-time basis and grosses more than $100 million annually.

Jim Green, a human resource manager, is responsible for the recruiting function of the company. When recruiting for clerical jobs at the entry level, Jim uses a local private employment agency. The agency is under strict orders to recruit people from within a 15-mile radius of the company. Individuals living in Atlanta are excluded because Jim prefers people with a rural work ethic. He believes that the use of this strategy greatly lessens the likelihood of high turnover, absenteeism, and tardiness. He also believes that those hired from local neighborhoods would enhance the cohesiveness of the work groups in which they are placed.

Questions

1. Do you agree with Jim's recruitment strategy?
2. What possible legal problems may arise from the use of this strategy?
3. If you were in Jim's place, what approach would you take? That is, would you extend the recruiting area to include Atlanta? (Remember, you want to keep group cohesiveness up and absenteeism, turnover, and tardiness down.)

References

1. Booe, M. (2004). Full speed ahead. *Workforce Management,* November, 54–58.
2. Herring, J.J. (1986). Establishing an integrated employee recruiting system. *Personnel,* July, 47–56.
3. Ibid.
4. Grossman, M.E., and Magnus, M. (1989). Hire spending. *Personnel Journal,* February, 73–76.
5. Taylor, M.S., and Bergmann, T.J. (1987). Organizational recruitment activities and applicant's reactions at different stages of the recruitment process. *Personnel Psychology, 40,* 261–285; Macan, T.H., and Dipboye, R.L. (1990). The relationship of interviewers' preinterview impressions to selection and recruitment outcomes. *Personnel Psychology, 43* (4), 745–768.
6. Rynes, S.L., and Miller, H.E. (1983). Recruiter and job influences on candidates for employment. *Journal of Applied Psychology, 68* (1), 147–154.
7. Ibid.
8. Taylor and Bergmann. Organizational recruitment activities.
9. Wanous, J.P. (1980). Tell it like it is at realistic job previews. In Kendrith M. Roland, Manual London, Gerald R. Ferris, and Jay L. Sherman (eds.). *Current Issues in Personnel Management.* Boston: Allyn & Bacon.
10. Ibid.
11. Ibid.
12. Meglino, B.M., Denisi, A.S., and Ravlin, E.C. (1993). Effects of previous job exposure and subsequent job status on the functioning of a realistic job preview. *Personnel Psychology, 46* (4), 803–822.
13. Ibid.
14. Premack, S.L., and Wanous, J.P. (1985). A meta-analysis of realistic job preview experiments. *Journal of Applied Psychology, 70* (4), 706–719.
15. Goya, D. (1990). How should we view affirmative action? *HRMagazine,* May, 160.
16. Sunoo, B.P. (1999). Temp firms turn up the heat on hiring. *Workforce,* April, 50–54.
17. Lewis, D.V. (1990). Make way for the older worker. *HRMagazine,* May, 75–77.
18. Ibid.
19. Schmitt, N. (1993). *Personnel Selection in Organizations.* San Francisco: Jossey-Bass.
20. Rynes, S.L., Bretz, R.D., and Gerhart, B. (1991). The importance of recruitment in job choice: A different way of looking. *Personnel Psychology, 44* (3), 487–521.
21. Ibid.
22. Edwards, C. (1986). Aggressive recruitment: The lessons of high tech hiring. *Personnel Journal,* January, 40–48.
23. Ibid.
24. Ross, J. (1991). Effective ways to hire contingency personnel. *HRMagazine,* February, 52–54.
25. Http://www.offsiteworks.com/trends.htm (2001).
26. Sunoo. Temp firms turn up the heat.
27. Http://www.shrm.org/trends (2002).
28. Sunoo, B.P., and Laabs, J.J. (1994). Winning strategies for outsourcing contracts. *Personnel Journal,* March, 69–78.
29. Maniscalco, R. (1992). High-tech temps in supply and demand. *HRMagazine,* March, 66–67.
30. Ross. Effective ways to hire.
31. Bargerstock, A.S., and Swanson, G. (1991). Four ways to build cooperative recruitment alliances. *HRMagazine,* March, 49–51, 79.
32. Sturve, J.E. (1991). Making the most of temporary workers. *Personnel Journal,* November, 43–46.

33. Driskell, P.C. (1986). Recruitment: A manager's checklist for labor leasing. *Personnel Journal,* October, 108–112.

34. Noe, R.A., Steffy, B.D., and Barber, A.E. (1988). An investigation of the factors influencing employees' willingness to accept mobility opportunities. *Personnel Psychology, 41,* (3), 559–580.

35. Breaugh, J.A. (1992). *Recruitment: Science and Practice.* Boston: PWS-Kent.

36. Schwarzwald, J., Koslowsky, M., and Shalit, B. (1992). A field study of employees' attitudes and behaviors after promotion decisions. *Journal of Applied Psychology, 77* (4), 511–514.

37. Breaugh. *Recruitment.*

38. Edwards. Aggressive recruitment.

39. Herring. Establishing an integrated employee recruiting cycle.

40. Bargerstock, A.S. (1989). Establish a direct mail recruitment program. *Recruitment Today,* Summer, 52–56.

41. Flynn, G. (1998). Texas Instruments engineers a holistic HR. *Workforce,* February, 30–35.

42. Rynes and Miller. Recruiter and job influences.

43. Berger, L. (1989). What applicants should be told. *Recruitment Today,* Summer, 14–19.

44. *Rowe v. General Motors* (1984). 457 F.2d 348.

45. *Baxter v. Savannah Sugar Refining Corp.* (1984). 350 F. Supp. 139.

46. Kleiman, L.S., and Clark, K. (1984). User's satisfaction with job posting: Some hard data. *Personnel Administrator, 29* (9), 104–110.

47. Robin, L.B. (1988). Troubleshoot recruitment problems. *Personnel Journal,* September, 94–96.

48. Kirnan, J.P., Farley, J.A., and Geisinger, K.F. (1989). The relationship between recruiting source, applicant quality, and hire performance: An analysis by sex, ethnicity, and age. *Personnel Psychology, 42* (2), 293–308.

49. Ibid.

50. Frase-Blunt, M. (2001). Driving home your awards program. *HRMagazine,* February, 109–115.

51. Kirnan. The relationship between recruiting source.

52. Grossman and Magnus. Hire spending.

53. Breaugh. *Recruitment.*

54. Swaroff, P.G., Barclay, L.A., and Bass, A.R. (1985). Recruiting sources: Another look. *Journal of Applied Psychology, 70* (4), 720–728.

55. Ibid.

56. Hutton, T.J. (1987). Increasing the odds for successful searches. *Personnel Journal,* September, 140–152.

57. Turban, D.B., and Dougherty, T. W. (1992). Influence of campus recruiting on applicant attraction to firms. *Academy of Management Journal, 35* (4), 739–765.

58. Gilmore, D.C., and Ferris, G.R. (1983). The recruitment interview. In Kendrith M. Rowland, Gerald R. Ferris, and Jay L. Sherman (eds.). *Current Issues in Personnel Management.* Boston: Allyn & Bacon.

59. Kolenko, T.A. (1988). College recruiting: Models, myths, and management. In Gerald R. Ferris and Kendrith M. Rowland (eds.). *Human Resource Management: Perspectives and Issues.* Boston: Allyn & Bacon.

60. Rynes, S.L., and Boudreau, J.W. (1986). College recruiting in large organizations: Practice, evaluation, and research implications. *Personnel Psychology, 39* (4) 729–758.

61. Kolenko. College recruiting.

62. Ibid.

63. Corsini, S. (2001). Wired to hire. *Training, 38* (6), 50–55.

64. Martinez, M.N. (1997). How top recruiters snag new grads. *HRMagazine,* August, 61–65

65. Corsini. Wired to hire.

66. Robin. Troubleshoot recruitment problems.

67. Rynes et al. The importance of recruitment.

68. Robin. Troubleshoot recruitment problems.

69. Algar, B.S. (1986). How to hire in a hurry: Meet increased demands for personnel. *Personnel Journal,* September, 86–94.

70. Anthony, P. (1990). Track applicants, track costs. *Personnel Journal,* April, 75–81.

71. Rynes, S.L. (1989). The employment interview as a recruitment device. In R.W. Eder and G.R. Ferris (eds.). *The Employment Interview: Theory, Research, and Practice* (127–141). Newbury Park, CA: Sage Publications.

72. Linden, R.C., and Parsons, C.K. (1986). A field study of job applicant interview perceptions, alternative opportunities, and demographic characteristics. *Personnel Psychology, 39* (1), 109–122.

73. Ibid.

74. Ibid.

75. Meglino, B.M., DeNisi, A.S., Youngblood, S.A., and Williams, K.J. (1988). Effects of realistic job previews: A comparison using an enhancement and a reduction preview. *Journal of Applied Psychology, 73* (2), 259–266.

76. Wanous, J.P. (1989). Installing a realistic job preview. *Personnel Psychology, 42* (1), 117–134.

Selecting Applicants

Chapter Six

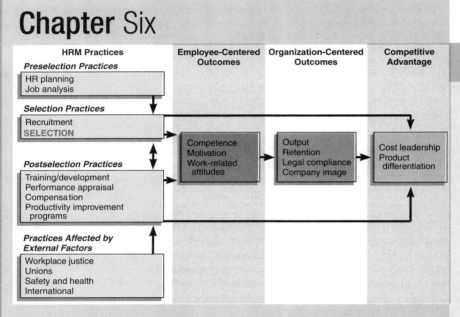

HRM Practices	Employee-Centered Outcomes	Organization-Centered Outcomes	Competitive Advantage
Preselection Practices			
HR planning / Job analysis			
Selection Practices			
Recruitment / SELECTION	Competence / Motivation / Work-related attitudes	Output / Retention / Legal compliance / Company image	Cost leadership / Product differentiation
Postselection Practices			
Training/development / Performance appraisal / Compensation / Productivity improvement programs			
Practices Affected by External Factors			
Workplace justice / Unions / Safety and health / International			

Key Terms

assessment center
background investigation
behavior consistency model
biodata inventories
biographical information blank
concurrent validation study
content-oriented strategy
criterion-related strategy
defamation
drug tests
Employee Polygraph Protection Act (EPPA)
Equal Employment Opportunity Commission (EEOC)
Fair Credit Reporting Act
Fifth Amendment
Fourteenth Amendment
Fourth Amendment

mental ability tests
negligent hiring
paper-and-pencil honesty tests
personality tests
polygraph tests
predictive validation study
reasonable accommodation
reference checking
reliability
tort law
undue hardship
validity
validity coefficient
validity generalization strategy
weighted application blank
work sample tests

Chapter Objectives

Upon completion of this chapter, you will be able to:

- Describe what the term *validity* means with regard to employee selection and how a company can achieve and document it.

- Understand the legal constraints imposed by EEOC guidelines, constitutional law, and tort law that companies face when selecting employees.

- Explain the various selection methods used by firms.

6-1 Gaining Competitive Advantage

6-1a Opening Case: Gaining Competitive Advantage at Southwest Airlines[1]

The Problem: Selecting the Best Employees from Thousands of Applicants
Selecting the best candidates to hire is not an easy task under any circumstances. It is especially difficult when a company must screen many applicants for a single position. Southwest Airlines (SWA) frequently encounters this situation, as it sorts through thousands of job applications each year. For instance, in 1994, SWA received more than 126,000 applications for 4,500 position openings as flight attendants, pilots, reservation agents, and mechanics. Twelve hundred applicants were hired in the first two months alone.

The Solution: Implementing Targeted Selection
Fortunately, SWA has found a systematic way to accurately evaluate all of its applicants. It uses a selection system, developed by Developmental Dimensions International, called *targeted selection*. The system is based on the following principles:

- Identify the critical job requirements for the position.
- Organize selection elements into a comprehensive system.
- Use past behavior to predict future behavior.
- Apply effective interviewing skills and techniques.
- Involve several interviewers in organized data-exchange discussions.
- Augment the interview with observations from behavior simulations.

SWA begins it selection process by conducting a job analysis to identify the specific "behaviors, knowledge, and motivations" needed to be successful in the job. The managers then devise interview questions to measure those qualities. The questions are based on the assumption that past behavior is a good predictor of future behavior—if someone has handled various situations well in the past, odds are that he or she will continue to do so. The interview questions are thus designed to discover how well applicants have demonstrated the needed capabilities in previous situations.

Here are some examples of the qualities SWA looks for in certain jobs and the questions they ask to assess these qualities:

- *Judgment:* "What was the toughest decision you had to make in your last job? Describe the circumstances surrounding that decision, the decision itself, and the outcome of that decision."

- *Teamwork:* "Tell me about a time in one of your prior jobs where you went above and beyond to assist a coworker." Or, "Tell me about a time you had a conflict with a coworker."

SWA believes this approach to selection is much more objective than the traditional approach, where people are evaluated based on their responses to theoretical questions about what the applicant *would* or *should* do. SWA focuses on what the applicants have *actually* done, which provides a much better, less subjective, view of the applicants' abilities.

How the Use of Targeted Selection Enhanced Competitive Advantage

According to Sherry Phelps, director of employment at Southwest Airlines, hiring the best applicants is a key to competitive advantage:

> Our fares can be matched; our airplanes and routes can be copied. But we pride ourselves on our customer service. That's why SWA looks for candidates who generate enthusiasm and lean toward extroverted personalities. By hiring effectively, we can save the company money and achieve greater levels of productivity and customer service.

SWA has been quite successful in achieving a competitive advantage, due, in part, to its selection practices. For instance, in an industry that is losing money, SWA produced a net income of $313 million in 2004. Each year, from 1992 to 1996, SWA won the U.S. Department of Transportation's "Triple Crown" award for its on-time performance, baggage handling, and fewest customer complaints. In 2003, Air Transport World selected it as the "Airline of the Year," and *InsideFlyer* magazine awarded it the "Freddie Award" for providing the best customer service among all airlines.

6-1b Linking Selection Practices to Competitive Advantage

During the hiring or *selection* process, a firm decides which of the recruited candidates will be offered the position. The effectiveness of a firm's selection practices can impact an organization's competitive advantage in a number of ways. Let's take a look at them.

Improving Productivity

When a firm is able to identify and hire the most suitable candidates, productivity increases because such candidates usually become very productive employees. The potential impact of sound selection practices on organizational productivity is illustrated in the following hypothetical example:

Suppose a car dealership needs to hire a salesperson to sell new cars. Assume that among its current workforce, the best salesperson grosses $200,000 per month, and the worst grosses $120,000. The difference in sales between an excellent salesperson and a poor salesperson is thus $80,000 per month. If the dealership can hire a candidate who turns out to be an excellent salesperson, as opposed to one who turns out to be a poor one, its monthly productivity would be $80,000 higher, which adds up to $960,000 per year. If the dealership were to hire 10 excellent salespeople during the year, the increase in annual gross sales attributable to effective selection practices would be 10 times $960,000 or nearly 10 million dollars!

As this example illustrates, sound selection practices can greatly affect the bottom line. Several research studies support this notion by demonstrating that companies that have improved their selection practices have increased their annual profits by as much as several million dollars.[2] For example, the federal government, unhappy with the capabilities of some of its computer programmers, decided to change its selection strategy. It had previously hired computer programmers solely on the basis of interviews. However, the interviewers were unable to accurately gauge the applicants' aptitude for learning programming. So the organization added a test to the selection process that measured this aptitude. The programmers selected by this test performed much better than their predecessors. Within their first year with the government, these new programmers managed to increase productivity levels by $5 million.[3]

Achieving Legal Compliance

Companies run a great risk of litigation due to their selection practices; rejected individuals often feel cheated and become bitter—even when the selection process is fair. When applicants perceive the process as unfair, these feelings intensify. Applicants' negative feelings are greatest when these individuals believe they have not been fairly evaluated during the selection process (e.g., the employer asked irrelevant personal questions or gave a test that had nothing to do with the job). This situation can result in a potentially costly and time-consuming lawsuit.

On the other hand, when applicants are rejected on the basis of assessments they perceive as thorough and accurate, bitterness is less likely to surface, and the likelihood of a lawsuit is reduced. Moreover, if a suit were lodged, firms could demonstrate effective or job-related selection practices as a defense. As we noted in Chapter 2, "Understanding the Legal and Environmental Context of HRM," firms need to provide evidence that a selection procedure is job related or "legitimate and nondiscriminatory" to rebut *prima facie* cases of discrimination.

Reducing Training Costs

When companies base selections on ineffective procedures, newly hired applicants will often lack some of the knowledge or skills needed for the job. To remedy such deficiencies, these individuals will need some sort of training. Thus, accurate selection procedures can help organizations minimize or even eliminate the need for some training (and thus reduce training costs) if the selection procedures help to identify applicants who possess all the qualifications required for entry into the position.

For example, it is not unusual for organizations to select first-line supervisors solely on the basis of technical expertise. When promoting engineers to supervision, for instance, the most productive engineer is typically chosen. Unfortunately, these individuals may lack some of the nontechnical attributes (e.g., interpersonal, leadership, and communication skills) needed by a good supervisor. The firm must then train these individuals. This need for training may have been avoided had the firm assessed these nontechnical skills during the selection process.

6-2 HRM Issues and Practices

6-2a Technical Standards for Selection Practices

Up to this point, we have discussed the notion of "effectiveness" of selection practices in rather general terms. In the following sections, we get more specific as we define what we mean by effectiveness and discuss how it can be achieved and documented.

Validity Defined

As managers assess job applicants, they infer how well each applicant would perform the job, if hired. **Validity** refers to the appropriateness, meaningfulness, and usefulness of these inferences.[4] Validity is thus the technical term for effectiveness. It is concerned with the issue of whether applicants would actually perform the job as well as expected, based on the inferences made during the selection process. The closer applicants' actual job performances match their expected performances, the greater the validity of the selection process.

validity An index of selection effectiveness, reflecting the extent to which applicants would perform the job as well as expected, based on the inferences made during the selection process.

Achieving Validity

How can managers best ensure that their inferences regarding applicants' job capabilities will be valid and, hence, lead to a correct employment decision? The manager

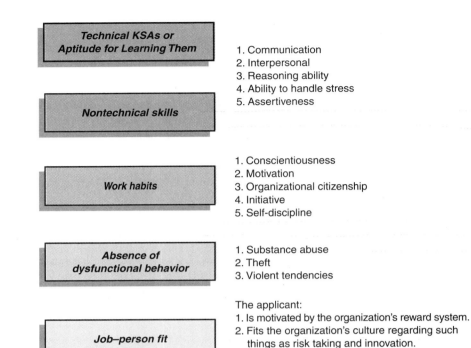

INTERACTIVE FIGURE

Figure 6-1
A Menu of Possible Qualities Needed for Job Success

must have a clear notion of the needed job qualifications and use selection methods that reliably and accurately measure these qualifications.

Determining Job Qualifications

Job qualifications refer to the personal qualities an employer seeks when filling a position. A "master list" of such qualities is presented in Figure 6-1. Some qualifications, such as technical KSAs (knowledge, skills, and abilities) and nontechnical skills, are job specific—each job has a unique set. The other qualifications are universal in that nearly all employers consider these qualities important, regardless of the job. That is, employers want all their employees to be motivated and have good work habits.

Managers should rely on job analysis information when specifying the qualifications that are unique to the particular job in question. As we discussed in Chapter 4, "Analyzing Jobs," the job analysis should describe the KSAs needed to perform each important task. By basing qualifications on job analysis information, a company ensures that the qualities being assessed are important for the job.

Job analyses are also needed for legal reasons. In discrimination suits, courts often judge the job-relatedness of a selection practice on whether the selection criteria are based on job analysis information. For instance, when someone lodges a complaint that a particular test discriminated against a protected group, the court would (1) determine whether the qualities measured by the test were selected on the basis of job analysis findings and (2) scrutinize the job analysis study, itself, to determine whether it had been properly conducted.[5]

Choosing Selection Methods

The attainment of validity depends heavily on the appropriateness of the particular selection technique used. A firm should use selection methods that reliably and accurately measure the needed qualifications.

The **reliability** of a measure refers to its consistency. It is defined as "the degree of self-consistency among the scores earned by an individual."[6] Reliable evaluations are consistent across both people and time. That is, reliability is maximized when

reliability An index reflecting the degree of self-consistency among the selection scores earned by an individual.

| Taking a Closer Look 6-1 | *Factors Affecting the Reliability of Selection Methods* |

Administrative Factors

- *Emotional and physical states of candidates:* Reliability would suffer if candidates were particularly nervous during the assessment process.
- *Lack of rapport with the administrator of the measure:* Reliability would suffer if candidates were "turned off" by the interviewer and, thus, did not "show their stuff" during the interview.
- *Inadequate knowledge of how to respond to a measure:* Reliability would suffer if candidates were asked questions that were vague or confusing.

Technical Factors

- *Individual differences among respondents:* If the range or differences in scores on the attribute measured by a selection device is large, the device can more reliably distinguish among people.

- *Question difficulty:* Questions of moderate difficulty produce the most reliable measures. If questions are too easy, many applicants will give the correct answer, and individual differences will be lessened; if questions are too difficult, few applicants will give the correct answer, and again, individual differences will be lessened.
- *Length of measure:* As the length of a measure increases, its reliability will also increase. For example, an interviewer can better gauge an applicant's level of interpersonal skill by asking several questions, rather than just one or two.

Source: Gatewood, R.D., and Field, H.S. (1994). *Human Resource Selection* (3rd ed.). Fort Worth, TX: Dryden.

two people evaluating the same candidate provide the same ratings and when the ratings of a candidate taken at two different times are the same. When selection scores are unreliable, their validity is diminished. Some of the factors affecting the reliability of selection measures are described in Taking a Closer Look 6-1.

The information in Taking a Closer Look 6-1 suggests a number of things a manager can do to increase the reliability of selection practices:

- Establish a good rapport with candidates. Make them feel at ease.
- Ask questions that are clear.
- Ask questions that are moderately difficult.
- Administer several measures to assess each important KSA (e.g., ask several interview questions for each quality assessed).

In addition to providing reliable assessments, the firm's assessments should accurately measure the needed worker requirements. As we will see later in the chapter, many selection techniques are available for assessing candidates. How does a company decide which ones to use?

A particularly effective approach or model to follow when making this decision is known as the **behavior consistency model.**[7] This model specifies that the best predictor of future job behavior is past behavior performed under similar circumstances. The model implies that the most effective selection procedures are those that focus on the candidates' past or present behaviors in situations that closely match those they will encounter on the job. The closer the selection procedure simulates actual work behaviors, the greater its validity. Recall how Southwest Airlines followed this approach in the opening case.

To implement the behavior consistency model, employers should follow this process:[8]

1. Thoroughly assess each applicant's previous work experience to determine if the candidate has exhibited relevant behaviors in the past.
2. If such behaviors are found, the manager should evaluate the applicant's past success on each behavior based on carefully developed rating scales.

behavior consistency model This model specifies that the best predictor of future job behavior is past behavior performed under similar circumstances.

Taking a Closer Look 6-2 | *How to Apply the Behavior Consistency Model: An Example*

The ABC Company employs 50 maintenance engineers (janitors). The job consists mainly of cleaning offices and other areas of a building. It is not very difficult; almost anyone can do it. The problem is that many of the workers hired are not dependable. These workers commit the following transgressions, even though they "know better":

- They do not show up for work consistently.
- They do not do a thorough job of cleaning offices.
- They take long breaks and often leave early.

ABC anticipates that it will be hiring 20 maintenance engineers during the next year. The company is intent on doing a better hiring job so that the undependable applicants are screened out.

Following the behavior consistency model, the company would assess the applicants' dependability by determining how dependable they have been in the past, in similar situations. This information could be gleaned, for example, from the applicants (during an interview) or from previous employers (during a reference check) where the employer asks questions regarding the applicants' past behavior. For instance, the previous employer could be asked whether the applicant took frequent breaks, lacked thoroughness, and failed to report to work on a regular basis.

---

3. If the applicant has not had an opportunity to exhibit such behaviors, the employer should estimate the future likelihood of these behaviors by administering various types of assessments. The more closely an assessment simulates actual job behaviors, the better the prediction.

An example of how a manager would apply the behavior consistency model is presented in Taking a Closer Look 6-2.

Assessing and Documenting Validity

How can an organization assess and document the validity of its selection practices? Three strategies can be used:

1. *Content-oriented strategy:* Demonstrate that it followed "proper" procedures in the development and use of its selection devices.

2. *Criterion-related strategy:* Provide statistical evidence showing a relationship between applicant selection scores and subsequent job performance levels.

3. *Validity generalization strategy:* Demonstrate that other companies have already demonstrated the validity of the selection instruments.

We now take a closer look at these strategies.

Content-Oriented Strategy

content-oriented strategy
A method of collecting validity evidence that focuses on expert judgment regarding the extent to which selection devices are properly designed and provide an accurate assessment of the needed worker requirements.

When using a **content-oriented strategy** to document validity, a firm gathers evidence that it followed appropriate procedures in developing its selection program. The evidence would show that the selection devices were properly designed and were accurate measures of the needed worker requirements. A listing of content-oriented evidence that the courts require to justify validity in a discrimination suit is presented in Taking a Closer Look 6-3.

Most importantly, the employer must demonstrate that the selection devices were chosen on the basis of an acceptable job analysis and that they measured a representative sample of the KSAs identified. For example, a firm's job analysis for an HR professional position states that a candidate must possess a working knowledge of all the concepts covered in this book. When assessing a candidate's knowledge of HRM, the firm should attempt to measure the applicants' knowledge of a *representative sample* of these concepts.

| Taking a Closer Look 6-3 | *A List of Content-Oriented Evidence Required by the Courts* |

1. The instrument must be based on a proper job analysis.
2. When jobs are grouped for selection purposes, there must be a sound basis for the grouping. For instance, all the jobs within a group should require similar skills.
3. The components of the selection process should be properly weighted. That is, when several skills are assessed, they should be weighted in a way that reflects their relative importance to the job.
4. The items (e.g., test items, interview questions) should be properly constructed so that they accu-

rately measure the attributes they have been designed to measure.
5. The difficulty level of the items should be appropriate for the job in question.
6. The items must appropriately sample the domain of all possible items that could have been asked.
7. The cutoff or passing score should be set in an appropriate manner.

Source: Kleiman, L.S., and Faley, R.H. (1978). Assessing content validity: Standards set by the court. *Personnel Psychology, 31,* 701–713.

Criterion-Related Strategy

The sole use of a content-oriented strategy for demonstrating validity is most appropriate for selection devices that directly assess job behavior. For example, one could safely infer that a candidate who performs well on a properly developed typing test would type well on the job because the test is directly measuring the actual behavior required on the job.

However, when the connection between the selection device and job behavior is less direct, content-oriented evidence alone is insufficient. Consider, for example, an item found on a civil service exam for police officer positions. The item stated: "In the Northern Hemisphere, what direction does water circulate when going down the drain?" The aim of the question was to measure "mental alertness," which is an important trait for good police officers. However, can one really be sure that the ability to answer this question correctly really measures mental alertness? Perhaps, but the "inferential leap" is a rather large one.

When employers must make such large inferential leaps, a content-oriented strategy, by itself, is insufficient to document validity; some other strategy is needed. This is where a **criterion-related strategy** comes into play. When a firm uses this strategy, it attempts to demonstrate statistically that someone who does well on a selection instrument is more likely to be a good job performer than someone who does poorly.

To gather criterion-related evidence, the HR professional needs to collect two pieces of information on each person: a predictor score and a criterion score:

- Predictor scores represent how well the individual fared during the selection process (as indicated by a test score, an interview rating, etc., or an overall selection score).

- Criterion scores represent the job performance level achieved by the individual, usually based on supervisor evaluations.

Validity is calculated by statistically correlating predictor scores with criterion scores. (Statistical formulas for computing correlation can be found in most introductory statistical texts.) This correlation coefficient is called a **validity coefficient.** To be considered valid, the coefficient must be statistically significant, and its magnitude must be sufficiently large to be of practical value. As a rule of thumb, a validity coefficient should be at least $r = .3$. When such a validity coefficient is attained, a firm can conclude that the inferences made during the selection process have been confirmed. In other words, it can conclude that, in general, applicants scoring well dur-

criterion-related strategy
A method of collecting validity evidence that demonstrates statistically that someone who does well on a selection instrument is more likely to be a good job performer than someone who does poorly.

validity coefficient
An index of criterion-related validity reflecting the correlation between selection and criterion scores.

Taking a Closer Look 6-4 — Steps in the Predictive and Concurrent Validation Processes

Predictive Validation

1. Perform a job analysis to identify needed competencies.
2. Develop/choose a selection procedure(s) designed to assess needed competencies.
3. Administer the selection procedure(s) to a group of applicants.
4. Randomly select applicants or select all applicants. Disregard selection scores.
5. Obtain measures of the job performance for the applicants after they have been employed for a sufficient amount of time. For most jobs, this would be six months to a year.

6. Correlate job performance scores of this group with the scores they received on the selection procedure(s).

Concurrent Validation

1. and 2. These steps are identical to those taken in a predictive validation study.
3. Administer the selection procedure(s) to a "representative" group of job incumbents.
4. Obtain measures of the current job performance level of the job incumbents who have been assessed in step 3.
5. Identical to step 6 in a predictive study.

---

predictive validation study
A criterion-related strategy in which applicants' selection scores are correlated with measures of their subsequent job performance.

concurrent validation study
A criterion-related strategy in which current employees' selection scores are correlated with measures of their current job performance.

ing selection turned out to be good performers, while those who did not do as well became poor performers.

A criterion-related validation study may be conducted in one of two ways: a **predictive validation study** or a **concurrent validation study.** The two approaches differ primarily in terms of the individuals assessed. In a predictive validation study, information is gathered on actual job applicants; in a concurrent study, current employees are used. The steps to each approach are shown in Taking a Closer Look 6-4.

Concurrent studies are more commonly used than predictive ones because they can be conducted more quickly—the assessed individuals are already on the job, and performance measures can thus be more quickly obtained. (In a predictive study, the criterion scores cannot be gathered until the applicants have been hired and have been on the job for several months.) Although concurrent validity studies have certain disadvantages compared to predictive ones, available research indicates that the two types of studies seem to yield approximately the same results.[9]

Validity Generalization Strategy

Up to this point, our discussion has assumed that an employer needs to validate each of its selection practices. But what if it is using a selection device that has been used and properly validated by other companies? Could it rely on that validity evidence and thus avoid having to conduct its own study?

validity generalization strategy A method of documenting the validity of a selection device by demonstrating that the same (or similar) device has been consistently found to be valid in many other similar settings.

The answer is "yes." It can do so by using a **validity generalization strategy.** Validity generalization is established by demonstrating that a selection device has been consistently found to be valid in many other similar settings. An impressive amount of evidence points to the validity generalization of many specific devices.[10] For example, some mental aptitude tests have been found to be valid predictors for nearly all jobs and thus can be justified without performing a new validation study to demonstrate job-relatedness.[11]

To use validity generalization evidence, an organization must present the following data:[12]

• Studies summarizing a selection measure's validity for similar jobs in other settings

• Data showing the similarity between jobs for which the validity evidence is reported and the job in the new employment setting

- Data showing the similarity between the selection measures in the other studies composing the validity evidence and those measures to be used in the new employment setting

6-2b Legal Constraints on Employee Selection

In addition to being technically sound or valid, a company's selection procedures must comply with the law. The following scenarios depict a typical day in the life of line manager Jane Smith and illustrate the types of "legal situations" line managers often face during the selection process:

> After reviewing several applications, Jane decides that Mary Jones appears to be the best-qualified applicant. However, during the interview, she learns that Mary is seven months pregnant. Jane fears that Mary would miss a lot of work due to her "condition" and that she may choose not to return to work after the baby is born. She wonders whether she may legally reject her application.

> Jane must fill a position that requires Saturday work. Bill Cooper is the most qualified applicant. However, during the interview, Bill states that his religion prohibits him from working on Saturdays. Although Jane could hire a part-timer to fill in for him on Saturdays, she would prefer not to do so. Jane wonders what legal ramifications would ensue if she rejected Bill's application.

> Bill George, an HR professional at a nearby company, calls Jane to ask about Kate Johnson, who is applying for a job at his company. Kate worked for Jane during the past two years. Bill wants to know if Kate was a good worker. Although Jane feels that Kate had an "attitude problem," always talking back and often ignoring orders, she is hesitant about expressing this concern to Bill. Jane is afraid that Kate could successfully sue her if she were to do so.

Before making decisions of this nature, a manager must know the law and its interpretations. To interpret the law, one must be familiar with the appropriate government guidelines, which are written documents that suggest, or in some instances *dictate,* how management practices should be implemented in accordance with the law. We now examine some of the government guidelines pertaining to employment discrimination law.

The Equal Employment Opportunity Commission and Its Guidelines on Employment Discrimination

When Congress passes a law, a government agency is assigned (or created) to administer the law. The agency assigned to administer employment discrimination laws is the **Equal Employment Opportunity Commission (EEOC),** which serves two functions: enforcement and interpretation. When someone alleges that the law has been violated, the EEOC's role is to enforce the law by investigating the complaint. "The Manager's Guide" (Section 6-3) describes how such investigations are conducted.

The EEOC's other function is interpretation of the law. Discrimination laws are written in a fairly general way and thus do not address many of the specific circumstances that may arise at the workplace. In an effort to resolve this problem, the EEOC has developed several sets of written guidelines to serve as its interpretation of these laws. We now discuss what these guidelines have to say about employee selection.

Equal Employment Opportunity Commission (EEOC) A government agency responsible for enforcing and interpreting federal antidiscrimination laws.

The Uniform Guidelines

The *Uniform Guidelines on Employee Selection Procedures,*[13] issued in 1978, apply to nearly all organizations employing 15 or more people. They are designed to assist organizations in understanding the compliance requirements imposed by Title VII of the Civil Rights Act, primarily with regard to disparate impact claims.

Taking a Closer Look 6-5

Job Analysis Requirements Imposed by the Uniform Guidelines

1. The knowledge, skills, and abilities (KSAs) should be clearly defined in terms of observable work behaviors.

   Mere labels (e.g., conscientiousness) should not be used because they are open to various interpretations and thus cannot be adequately assessed.

2. The KSAs should be prerequisites for important work behaviors, and the relationship between each KSA and work behavior should be properly noted.

By noting the relationship between the two, it becomes clear why the KSA is needed for the job, and thus the KSA's job-relatedness is documented.

3. The list of KSAs should be restricted to those that the applicant should possess at entry into the position.

   KSAs that can be readily learned on the job should be excluded.

The *Uniform Guidelines* specify that if an employment decision (e.g., selection, promotion, transfer, retention) results in disparate impact, the organization must take one of two actions: (1) eliminate the selection device(s) causing the disparate impact or (2) demonstrate the validity of the selection device(s). Although no absolute preference is given to the type of validation strategy needed, the guidelines do state that it is inappropriate to justify validity solely on the basis of content-oriented evidence when the selection device measures attributes requiring a large inferential leap, as we noted earlier.

A content-oriented strategy is not appropriate for demonstrating the validity of selection procedures that purport to measure traits or constructs, such as intelligence, aptitude, personality, common sense, judgment, leadership, and spatial ability.

Demonstration of a proper job analysis is crucial for proving validity. Though not advocating any specific job analysis method, the *Uniform Guidelines* list the features that a job analysis should have, as shown in Taking a Closer Look 6-5.

National Origin Discrimination Guidelines

According to the EEOC's national origin guidelines,[14] individuals rejected for employment have just cause for legal redress if their rejection was based on any of the following factors:

- Place of origin
- Ancestor's place of origin
- Marriage to a person of a foreign origin
- Membership in an association seeking to promote the interests of a national origin group

National origin discrimination can take many forms. For instance, foreign-origin applicants may be unfairly rejected because of their foreign accents, their physical appearance and dress, or because they were educated in a foreign country. The guidelines state that when claims of this nature are lodged, the EEOC will closely scrutinize the firm's behavior. For example, if a firm rejects an applicant because of a heavy accent, the EEOC would require it to produce evidence that the applicant's accent prohibited him or her from adequately performing an important job function.

Additionally, the guidelines prohibit employers from harassing applicants because of their national origin. Examples of harassment are ethnic slurs or other verbal or physical conduct relating to an individual's national origin.

Sexual Harassment Guidelines

Most of the litigation surrounding sexual harassment centers on the harassment of current employees and, thus, is discussed in Chapter 11, "Complying with Workplace Justice Laws," along with other workplace issues of a legal nature. With regard to the sexual harassment of *applicants,* the guidelines state the following:

> The employer is liable for unlawful sex discrimination if (1) an employment opportunity is granted because of a candidate's submission to an employer's request for sexual favors, or (2) an employment opportunity is withheld because of the candidate's refusal to grant such favors.[15]

Pregnancy Discrimination Guidelines

According to the EEOC's pregnancy discrimination guidelines,[16] a female applicant who is temporarily unable to perform some job function due to her pregnancy-related condition must be treated in the same manner as any other applicant with a temporary disability. Thus, if she is the most qualified candidate, she should be hired with the provision that she be given modified tasks, alternate assignments (e.g., light duty), disability leave, etc., if other applicants with a temporary disability are so treated.

Moreover, the preferences of coworkers, clients, or customers would not serve as a legitimate, nondiscriminatory reason for rejecting such a candidate. For example, a manager should not reject a pregnant woman for a receptionist's job simply because it may be a "turn-off" to some customers.

Managers should avoid asking any questions regarding pregnancy during an employment interview. For instance, they should avoid the topic of whether the applicant is pregnant or plans to become pregnant. If the applicant's pregnancy is readily apparent, managers should ignore the condition unless her due date coincides with a critical business period. As noted in *Maldono v. U.S. Bank and Manufacturer's Bank,*[17] the Pregnancy Discrimination Act was not designed to handcuff employers by forcing them to wait until an employee's pregnancy causes them economic hardship. An employer may take anticipatory adverse action against a pregnant applicant or employee when "it has a good faith basis, supported by sufficiently strong evidence, that the normal inconveniences of an employee's pregnancy will require special treatment" (p. 6).

Age Discrimination Guidelines

The EEOC guidelines on age discrimination prohibit *disparate treatment* directed toward applicants age 40 and above. That is, an employer may not treat applicants below 40 any better than those 40 and above. For instance, a company may not publish help-wanted ads that indicate a preference for younger workers. Nor may an employer justify its rejection of an older applicant on the grounds that it costs more to employ such workers.[18]

If charged with age-based disparate treatment, a firm must demonstrate that the hiring decision was not based on age, but on some "reasonable factor other than age," such as lack of skill. When an employer imposes a policy that bars all individuals above a certain age from a particular job, it must prove that age is a BFOQ (bona fide occupational qualification) for the position. As indicated in Chapter 2, this defense is most appropriately used for jobs that involve public safety considerations, such as police officers, firefighters, airline pilots, and bus drivers. BFOQs based on age are easier to establish than those based on other protected classifications. As noted by one judge:[19]

> Employers who attempt to establish BFOQ where safety of third parties is at risk must be afforded substantial discretion in selecting specific age-related standards which, if they err at all, should be on the side of preservation of life and limb.

To establish age as a BFOQ, the employer must prove the following:[20]

1. The BFOQ is reasonably necessary to the essence of the company's business, *AND*

2. The company has a reasonable cause for believing that all or substantially all persons within the protected age group would be unable to perform the job safely or effectively, *AND*

3. It would be impossible or impractical for the company to accurately assess the job capabilities of applicants on an individual basis; that is, no foolproof measures exist to predict whether a person could safely perform the job.

For example, a bus line has a policy that bars all bus driver applicants over the age of 55. If challenged, the firm would defend itself by stating:

1. Safe driving is reasonably necessary to the essence of its business.

2. People over 55 are a greater accident risk. (The firm must show evidence supporting this assertion.)

3. There is no foolproof test to determine whether a person over 55 has the necessary skills to drive a bus safely; that is, age is the best predictor.

The age discrimination guidelines also state that an employment practice that has a *disparate impact* on individuals protected under the Age Discrimination in Employment Act is unlawful unless it can be justified by a business necessity. For instance, if downsizing resulted in the layoff of a disproportionate number of older workers, the company must demonstrate that it had a sound basis for making the layoffs. For instance, it could claim that people were laid off based on past job performance ratings. Or it could claim that layoff decisions were based on the importance of the job to the company.

Religious Discrimination Guidelines

undue hardship A legal argument stating that an accommodation is not reasonable because it would unduly burden the employer.

As interpreted by the Supreme Court in its 1978 decision in *TWA vs. Hardison,* the Civil Rights Act of 1964 requires employers to accommodate a reasonable request for religious accommodation, as long as the accommodation does not pose an **undue hardship** on their business operations. Government guidelines define religious practices as those pertaining to one's moral or ethical beliefs about what is right or wrong and which are sincerely held with the strength of traditionally held religious views.[21] Religion is thus not restricted to traditional denominations; people not belonging to a formal religion are also protected. Religious protection is also extended to people's "freedom not to believe," so discrimination against atheists is also prohibited.

As the result of such factors as immigration, globalization, and a new political and religious climate, today's employers face a wide variety of accommodation requests, making the goal of legal compliance a difficult one to achieve. The following real-life examples illustrate this point:

- A counselor requested to be excused from counseling homosexuals because this lifestyle conflicted with the counselor's religious beliefs.[22]

- A job applicant refused to provide her Social Security number because of her belief that Social Security numbers represent the "mark of the beast" as described in the Bible's Book of Revelation.[23]

reasonable accommodation A legal concept that applies to situations where individuals are unable to successfully perform a job because of their religion or disability. The employer must consider viable strategies for helping these people overcome such inabilities.

Before rejecting candidates or disciplining employees because their religious views or practices would interfere with management aims, a manager must first consider whether a **reasonable accommodation** can be made, like restructuring the job or allowing a voluntary exchange of work schedules.[24]

An accommodation is *reasonable* if it does not pose an undue hardship on an employer's business operation. When judging a claim of undue hardship, the courts apply a standard called the *de minimis* principle. Basically, this principle states that to be declared an undue hardship, the cost of accommodation must be more than minimal. The determination of "more than minimal" depends on a number of factors, such as the size and nature of the business, the type of accommodation required, whether the employee gives reasonable notice to the employer, and the amount of expense involved.[25] For instance, financially troubled organizations could claim fairly minor expenses as an undue hardship, such as those incurred by paying another worker overtime to fill in for the absent worker.

The guidelines further state that employers must first inform candidates of the working hours and then ask if they are available to work those hours. Questions bearing on religion may be asked only if candidates are unable to work during those hours due to religious reasons.

Disability Discrimination Guidelines

As we noted in Chapter 2, the Americans with Disabilities Act (ADA) aims to protect disabled persons from job discrimination. The act defines "disability" as a physical or mental impairment that substantially limits one or more of an individual's major life activities. This definition is quite broad and thus includes many types of disorders, such as:[26]

- Illnesses (e.g., AIDS, cancer, diabetes)

- Losses (e.g., loss of limbs, sight, hearing, as well as learning disabilities and mental retardation)

- Emotional and mental illnesses (e.g., manic depression, epilepsy, and schizophrenia)

- Recovery (e.g., recovering alcoholics and drug addicts)

A summary of the ADA guidelines appears in the appendix to this chapter. These guidelines give a detailed account of what an organization may (or must) do and what it may not do when it considers employing a disabled applicant. The notions of accommodation and undue hardship, initially formulated for use in religious discrimination cases, also apply here. However, as the information in the appendix indicates, the employer's burden to provide accommodation is much greater in ADA cases than in religious discrimination cases.

An organization can make a number of accommodations for various disabilities, such as installing talking computers, computers that respond to voice command, software that displays extra large type, and programmable wheelchairs.[27] Other accommodations include putting wood blocks under the legs of a table or desk so that an individual in a wheelchair could work there and rearranging shelves or drawers that contain office supplies so that individuals in wheelchairs or those with one arm can reach them.[28] For example, Hughes Aircraft purchased a new hearing aid as a low vision assistant device that allowed the individual to hear and see better. It also purchased a voice-activated system for a quadriplegic, a talking terminal for a blind employee, and an electric wheelchair for an employee who lost the use of his legs.[29]

Constitutional Constraints on Selection

The selection of candidates is also governed by the U.S. Constitution, specifically the Fourth, Fifth, and Fourteenth Amendments. Because the intent of these amendments was to place constraints on government behavior when dealing with U.S. citizens, only governmental units or the public sector must adhere to these amendments.

The Fourth Amendment of the U.S. Constitution

The **Fourth Amendment** pertains to an individual's privacy rights—it protects job candidates and employees from unreasonable intrusions by the employer (i.e., the government).

This amendment has been the basis of a number of workplace-related lawsuits dealing with the use of certain physiological screening devices, such as urinalysis and blood testing (used to detect such conditions as drug addiction and AIDS). This

Fourth Amendment
Constitutional amendment granting privacy rights to public sector employees.

amendment also imposes constraints on the type of information that employers may lawfully collect about an applicant. For instance, applicant inquiries that are overly intrusive or offensive, such as those dealing with marriage, family, and sexual activities, are legally suspect.

The Fifth and Fourteenth Amendments of the U.S. Constitution

Fifth Amendment
An amendment to the U.S. Constitution that provides all federal employees with equal protection under the law.

Fourteenth Amendment
An amendment to the U.S. Constitution that provides all state employees with equal protection under the law.

tort law   Civil laws designed to discourage individuals from subjecting others to unreasonable risks and to compensate those who have been injured by unreasonably risky behavior.

negligent hiring   Occurs when an employer negligently hires an applicant who is somehow unfit for the job and, because of this unfitness, commits an act that causes harm to another.

The **Fifth** and **Fourteenth Amendments** provide all citizens with *equal protection under the law*. The Fifth Amendment applies to federal employees; the Fourteenth, to state employees. The constraints imposed by these amendments are similar to those imposed by the various EEO laws. A key difference between these amendments and the EEO laws is that the former are not restricted to protected classifications. These amendments deem any form of unjustifiable discrimination unlawful. For example, gay rights are not protected by Title VII, but these rights are protected under the Fifth and Fourteenth Amendments.

Tort Law Constraints on Selection

Tort law refers to civil laws designed to discourage individuals from subjecting others to unreasonable risks and to compensate those who have been injured by unreasonably risky behavior. The two areas of tort law that bear the most influence on employee selection are negligent hiring and defamation.

Negligent Hiring

Negligent hiring refers to situations in which employers hire an applicant who is somehow unfit for the job and, because of this unfitness, commits an act that causes harm to another. An individual would be considered unfit in a negligent hiring case if he or she lacked the necessary training and experience, had a physical or mental infirmity, was frequently intoxicated, experienced constant forgetfulness, liked to engage in horseplay, or was reckless or malicious.[30]

An employer could be found guilty of negligent hiring if it failed to conduct a background investigation of the applicant, when such an investigation would have uncovered the problem that led to a harmful act. For example, Avis was found guilty of negligent hiring when a coworker raped a female employee; the coworker had a conviction record involving violent acts, but Avis made no attempt to uncover this information.[31] The female employee was awarded $750,000.

> An employer's obligation to inquire into someone's fitness varies, depending on the nature of the job in question. The obligation is heaviest for jobs classified as "special duty of care," which are jobs that involve access to the homes of others (e.g., an apartment manager, bellhop); access to equipment, merchandise, and cash of third parties (e.g., bank teller); and jobs involving public safety (e.g., police). For these types of positions, the employer should thoroughly investigate an applicant's background, including any criminal history.[32]

An employer's burden to search an applicant's background for signs of unfitness is less for jobs not classified as special duty of care. However, some burden remains. Remember that the Avis case did not involve a special duty of care job. At a minimum, employers should inquire about an applicant's past during the interview and reference checking process. This burden requires that employers walk a "legal tightrope" when making preemployment inquiries. That is, when seeking background information on candidates, they must avoid inquiries that are discriminatory or an invasion of privacy. We discuss the legal dos and don'ts of such inquiries later in the chapter.

defamation
The unprivileged publication of a false oral or written statement that harms the reputation of another person.

Defamation

Defamation, also a tort, is defined as "the unprivileged publication of a false oral or written statement that harms the reputation of another person." Defamation claims often arise when giving reference information. The communication of negative information about an applicant could be unlawful if untrue or if its truth could not be verified. It would also be unlawful if given with malicious intentions or conveyed to someone who was not considered to be an "interested party" (i.e., someone with a right to know). Coworkers or subordinates who were not a part of the selection process would be considered disinterested parties and, thus, should not be privy to such information. We discuss this topic further later in the chapter when we talk about reference checking.

6-2c Selection Methods

Thus far in the chapter, we have described the technical and legal standards a firm must meet when selecting employees. We now turn our discussion to actual selection methods.

Application Blanks

Nearly all companies require outside candidates to complete application blanks as the first step in the selection process. The typical application blank asks candidates for background information, such as name, address, position desired, date available for work, education, work and salary history, reasons for leaving previous jobs, and the names of personal references.

*appl.
on ex. 3*

Uses of the Application Blank

A completed application blank serves three primary purposes. One is to determine whether candidates meet the minimum qualifications for the job (e.g., whether they have the requisite education and experience).

Second, applications help employers judge the presence (or absence) of certain job-related attributes. For instance, an employer may infer that a candidate has the needed job knowledge by noting that the individual has had several years of previous work experience that directly relates to the position in question.

Third, information contained on the application blank can be used to "red flag" any potential problem areas concerning the applicant. For example, frequent job-hopping may be indicative of instability; unanswered or vaguely answered questions may signal that the applicant is hiding some important information; unexplained gaps in employment may indicate a prison record or the fact that the applicant held a job during that period, but does not want the employer to check any references there. Employers should refrain from drawing final conclusions from red flags. Their presence should merely signal the need to seek further information. For instance, the employer could ask the applicant during an interview to explain why certain questions were not answered on the application blank.

Some further suggestions for evaluating information contained on application blanks are provided in Exhibit 6-1.

Application Blanks and the Law

A popular misconception suggests that federal law prohibits employers from including a host of different types of questions on an application blank. In reality, the only federal law that expressly forbids particular questions is the ADA (see the chapter appendix), which prohibits all questions regarding an applicant's health.

This lack of federal regulation does not mean that an employer should feel free to ask anything. Certain questions are ill advised, because their presence on an application blank could be used as evidence of discrimination. There are three categories of questions that should be avoided in addition to health-related questions. Topics falling within each category are listed in Figure 6-2.

As a general rule, an employer should refrain from asking the following types of questions:

EXHIBIT 6-1   Suggestions for Evaluating Application Forms

Educational History

Level of education
- Does the applicant meet the minimum qualifications?
- Is the person overqualified?

Educational institution
- What is the academic quality of the school from which the applicant graduated?
- Did the applicant engage in "school hopping"?

College major
- Is the applicant's major closely related to the job being applied for?
- Has the applicant studied subjects that will contribute to performance on the job being applied for?

Accomplishments in school
- Does the applicant mention any leadership activities?
- Is the applicant's grade-point average listed?
- Does the applicant list any awards or scholarships on the application?
- Did the applicant work while in school?

Employment History

Dates of employment
- Are there any time gaps?
- Is there a history of job-hopping?

Nature of employment
- What job titles has this person held and for how long?
- How closely related is the applicant's past job experience to the job being applied for?

Salary history
- What were the starting and ending salaries for each job?
- Will the applicant's salary expectations be realistic?

Reason for leaving
- What reasons did the applicant give for leaving each job?
- Has the applicant made job changes that enhance his or her career?

Other
- How well did the person follow instructions when completing the application?
- Was the application neatly filled out?

---

1. *Questions that allow the employer to identify an applicant's protected group membership, such as date of birth, sex, or religious preferences.* The reason such questions should be avoided is that when an employer asks about an applicant's protected group membership, it is assumed that this information is needed to make a hiring decision. A court would thus question the motives of the employer for making such an inquiry, reasoning that "if the individual's protected group membership were not a factor, why was the question asked?"

2. *Questions that are not directly job related yet have a disproportionate impact on one or more protected groups.* For example, the question "What is your height and weight?" would have a disproportionate impact on women, who are generally smaller than men. If not job related, it would be judged discriminatory under the disparate impact theory. To be job related, the courts require that the questions have a direct bearing on job performance (e.g., one needs to be at least 5'10" to reach a control panel). Often, height and weight are used as a measure of strength (small people are usually weaker than large people). The employer

Figure 6-2

Examples of Potentially Unlawful Questions

Questions that allow an employer to identify an applicant's protected group membership	Questions that are not directly job related, yet have a disproportionate impact on one or more protected groups	Questions that seek information that has traditionally been used to screen out members of certain protected groups
• Date of birth • Sex • Race • Religious preference • Maiden name • Physical/health condition • Birthplace • Pregnancy • Organization membership	• Height and weight • Arrest record • Ownership (e.g., home, car) • Parents' occupations	• Marital status • Number of children • Child-care provisions • Spouse's occupation • Intention to have children

would be much better off giving a strength test, which is a more direct measure of strength than height and weight.

3. *Questions that seek information that traditionally has been used to screen out members of certain protected groups.* For instance, the question "How many children do you have?" should not be asked because such information has traditionally been used to screen out women, but not men. If a female candidate with children were to be rejected, that question would serve as evidence of discriminatory intent.

Biodata Inventories

Biodata inventories are similar to application blanks in that they ask applicants to provide background information about themselves. However, the two selection devices differ in terms of how the firm interprets applicant responses: Application blank responses are evaluated *subjectively;* biodata inventory responses are *objectively* evaluated, just as they would be on a written test. That is, applicants can earn a certain number of points for each question on the biodata inventory based in the correlation between the item and a criterion, such as job performance. HR professionals score the completed inventory by adding the points earned on each question.

The item-criterion correlations are usually determined from available data on the company's current workforce. Employees' responses to biodata inventory items at the time of hire are correlated with their subsequent level of job success. For example, the item "number of clubs joined in high school" would be heavily weighted if "successful" employees had joined significantly more clubs than "unsuccessful" employees. When this question is used on a biodata inventory, applicants stating that they had joined many high school clubs would earn more points than those stating "few" or "none."

There are two types of biodata inventories: **weighted application blanks** and **biographical information blanks.** When the questions included on the biodata inventory are identical to those included on the application blank, the instrument is called a weighted application blank. When the instrument consists of a set of questions designed to cover a broader array of background information, such as school suspension, drug use, quitting school, employment experiences, grades and school clubs, legal system contacts, and socioeconomic status, it is called a biographical information blank.[33] Both types of instruments are weighted and scored in the same manner.

Uses of Biodata Inventories

HR professionals typically use biodata inventories as a prescreening device to predict tenure. Such an inventory would contain questions that have been identified through the statistical weighting process as being good predictors of tenure (e.g., "How far from this office do you live?" and "How many jobs have you held in the past five years?"). Applicants who provide the "wrong" answers and thus fail to earn many points are classified as "short-termers" and are dropped from further consideration early in the selection process. Such prescreening can save an organization a great deal of money. For instance, one company was able to save $25,000 by using a biodata inventory to prescreen applicants for clerical positions on the basis of their predicted tenure.[34]

Research studies have found that biodata instruments are excellent predictors of job success.[35] Surprisingly, however, few companies use this method.[36] According to one study, some companies shy away from using biodata inventories because they are not familiar with them, lack the resources needed to develop such instruments, or have concerns regarding the legality of the method.[37]

Biodata Inventories and the Law

Some legal concerns may be justified. There are no legal precedents for deciding whether an item with disparate impact could be legally justified by the mere

biodata inventories
A selection technique in which an applicant's responses to background information questions are objectively scored.

weighted application blank
A biodata inventory containing the same questions as an application blank.

biographical information blank   A biodata inventory consisting of a set of questions designed to cover a broad array of background information.

presence of a statistical relationship between the item and job success. The courts may also demand that the relationship be justified on logical grounds.

For instance, the question "How far from this firm do you live?" could have a disparate impact against a protected group, if most members of that group live in an area of town that is far removed from the firm. However, this question would probably be legal because it makes sense: People who live far from work would tend to quit when an opening closer to home becomes available. An illogical item-criterion correlation, like one between "number of siblings" and tenure, may not pass court scrutiny. Until the courts decide this issue, an employer would be well advised to exclude any items having disparate impact if they do not bear a logical relationship with job success.

Background Investigations

background investigation
An in-depth probe of an applicant's background usually conducted by an investigative agency.

Companies sometimes hire investigative agencies to conduct **background investigations.** Such agencies gather information through applicant interviews and written or verbal communication with past employers, neighbors, relatives, and references. Additional information is gathered from law enforcement agencies and credit bureaus.[38]

Uses of Background Investigations

These investigations have traditionally been used for two purposes: (1) to screen applicants for positions of trust in such occupations as law enforcement, private security, and nuclear power and (2) to screen candidates for "special duty of care" positions in order to satisfy requirements imposed by negligent hiring law. Under the nation's heightened security concerns following the September 11, 2001, terrorist attacks, many firms are now conducting international background investigations.[39] The information gleaned from background investigations may yield important insights into the character or trustworthiness of an applicant.

Background Investigations and the Law

Fair Credit Reporting Act
A law designed to protect applicants' rights in the event of a background investigation conducted by an investigative agency.

When employing an investigative agency to run a background investigation, an employer must avoid violating the legal rights of applicants. The primary law in this area is the **Fair Credit Reporting Act.** Although dealing mainly with consumer credit rights, this law also covers background investigations, stipulating that applicants be notified of the background investigation when an investigative agency is used. Applicants must also be notified if employment is denied because of information obtained during such an investigation.

Reference Checks

reference checking
Collecting selection information from an applicant's previous employers (or associates).

Reference checking, which involves collecting information from applicants' previous employers (usually by phone), provides another potentially useful means of assessment. Most employers check applicant references in the final stages of the hiring process (i.e., to evaluate candidates on their "short-list," the list of job finalists).[40]

Uses of Reference Checks

Reference checks serve two important purposes. One is to verify information provided by applicants to ensure that they have not fabricated their qualifications and past work histories.

Reference checks also provide additional information about applicants, which may be predictive of job performance. For instance, an employer may ask references to discuss an applicant's previous job behaviors in order to better assess their technical competence, honesty, reliability, conscientiousness, and ability to get along with others. The topics addressed during a typical reference check are listed in Exhibit 6-2.

As noted earlier in the chapter, using past job behavior to predict future job behavior is an effective selection strategy. Reference checking serves this strategy by

EXHIBIT 6-2	Topics Typically Addressed during a Reference Check

- Dates of employment
- Job titles held
- Rate of pay
- Attendance
- Performance evaluations
- Discipline problems

- Character traits
- Ability to get along with others
- Strengths and weaknesses
- Overall opinion of candidate
- Person's reason for leaving
- Willingness to rehire that person

obtaining such information from parties who had witnessed the applicant's past behavior firsthand.

Reference Checks and the Law

Although reference checks may potentially provide relevant background information, companies employing this technique often have reason to question the accuracy and completeness of the information obtained. People who are asked for references are often reluctant to disclose truthfully all the needed information about applicants. Many former employers provide only job title and dates of employment; others "sugar-coat" the information, giving only favorable recommendations, even if unwarranted.

Former employers are reluctant to fully disclose relevant information because they fear that unfavorable responses may lead to defamation lawsuits.[41] Such suits may be lodged by applicants who believe that the information given by the reference is untrue and has prevented them from obtaining employment.

As noted earlier in the chapter, those giving references can defend against defamation claims by providing information that is:

- Truthful and its truth can be proven

- Not conveyed with malicious intent

- Communicated only to individuals who are "interested parties"

- Job related; that is, the information pertains to issues about which the reference-seeker has a legitimate need to know

A more complete list of legal guidelines for giving references is shown in Exhibit 6-3.

Employment Interviews

Nearly all companies consider the employment interview to be a vital selection tool. Rarely would an applicant be hired without having first been interviewed. In fact, several members of an organization usually interview viable candidates: HR professionals, the manager of the vacant position, and one or more upper-level managers.

EXHIBIT 6-3	Guidelines for Giving Reference Information

- Become familiar with all applicable laws pertaining to defamation within your state.
- Appoint a "reference czar" to handle all requests for information.
- Obtain written consent from the employee prior to giving any information.
- Use a "call-back" procedure to verify the legitimacy of the caller's credentials. Is he or she an interested party with a need to know?
- Provide only the information requested.

- Be truthful.
- Report only fully documented and provable facts.
- Avoid subjective statements.
- When giving negative information, specify the reasons or specific incidents that led you to that conclusion.
- Avoid giving your overall opinion or stating whether you would rehire the individual.
- Make a written record of all released information.

Selection is then based on the consensus of these individuals. Unfortunately, these individuals often "fumble the ball" when it comes to properly conducting an interview, focusing on style, rather than substance. A recent study, for instance, found that interviewers are more influenced by the applicant's demeanor during an interview than the applicant's actual qualifications.[42] Candidates are much more likely to be offered a job when they act in a pleasant and agreeable way during the interview and go out of their way to compliment the interviewer.

Uses of the Interview

A properly conducted interview provides an opportunity for applicants to describe their previous work experience, educational history, career interests, likes and dislikes, etc. This information, which may be difficult or impossible to obtain by other means, is usually critical to the selection process. Pointers on effective interviewing are offered in "The Manager's Guide" (Section 6-3) later in this chapter. Here, we focus on the types of information that can be obtained from interviews.

Interviewers may seek four types of valuable information during an interview, as described in the following paragraphs.[43] Taking a Closer Look 6-6 provides examples of questions used to gather each type of information.

Technical Knowledge An applicant's technical knowledge about the position is often quite important. One approach to assessing technical knowledge is to inquire about the applicant's educational history and work experience. In doing so, the interviewer attempts to determine whether applicants have acquired the necessary knowledge while in school or while working in previous jobs.

- One potential hazard with this approach is that interviewers often misinterpret the information by assuming incorrectly that a candidate who has done something has done it well, or a person who has studied something has learned it well.[44]

- An interviewer can form a better picture of the applicants' technical knowledge by asking specific technical questions. For instance, an individual applying for the job of bartender could be asked, "What ingredients go into a Bloody Mary?"

Self-Evaluative Information This type of information examines the applicants' likes and dislikes, strengths and weaknesses, goals, attitudes, and philosophies. Such information can be quite valuable in helping an employer determine whether an applicant would "fit" in the particular context of the job. Applicant responses can indicate, for instance, whether the individual's career goals are in line with the opportunities provided by the organization or whether the applicant would enjoy the job. For example, a poor fit would be indicated if an applicant stated that she loves to work independently, while, in actuality, the job entails much teamwork.

Situational Information Situational information examines how an applicant would react in certain hypothetical job-related situations. For example, an applicant might be asked "What would you do if you saw one of your subordinates act rudely toward a customer?" Applicants' answers to such questions are evaluated based on how well they correspond to predetermined preferred answers. That is, the interviewer compares the applicant's answer to those on a list of possible good, average, and poor answers. Gathering situational information can aid an employer in determining whether an applicant can make effective decisions in various job-related circumstances. The validity of "situational interviews" is usually quite high.[45]

Behavior Description Information Behavior description information examines how applicants have behaved in past situations that are similar to those that would be

Taking a Closer Look 6-6

Interview Question Examples for the Job of Compensation Manager

Job Knowledge Questions (Assesses the knowledge needed to perform the job)

1. Describe the steps you go through when you perform a job evaluation study.
2. I see you took an EEO course at school. What topics did the course cover? How would this information apply to our company?
3. What criteria are used to determine whether a job is exempt or nonexempt?
4. What kinds of problems are associated with the use of merit pay plans? If we asked you to institute such a plan, what steps would you take to overcome these problems?

Self-Evaluative Questions (Assesses the job–person fit)

1. What is your view of the compensation manager's role in an organization?
2. What did you like most about your last job? Least? Why?
3. What kinds of things motivate you to work hard? What things demotivate you?
4. Describe your ideal job.
5. What kind of people do you get along with best? Worst?
6. What kinds of things most stress you out? How do you deal with the stress in such instances?
7. What is your greatest weakness? Are you taking any action to overcome it? Please explain.

Situational Questions (Assesses ability to make job-related decisions)

1. An employee is very sick and needs an expensive operation. The firm's insurance carrier refuses to pay for it. The employee comes to you, as compensation manager, for help. You think the insurance carrier may have erred in its decision. What steps would you take to help the employee?

2. All 500 employees in your firm must switch insurance carriers. They have 2 months to complete the paperwork indicating which of the two new carriers they desire. Employees who fail to return the paperwork within this timeframe will be uninsured for the following 12 months. As the firm's compensation manager, what steps would you take to ensure that all employees remain covered?

Behavior Description Questions (Assesses how well the candidate has previously handled the type of situations that will occur on the job)

1. As a compensation manager, it is often necessary to work with a group of managers to accomplish a task. Can you tell me about the most recent experience that you have had working as part of a group?
   a. What was the task?
   b. How many people were in the group?
   c. What difficulties arose?
   d. What role did you play in resolving these difficulties?
   e. How successful was the group in completing its task?
   f. If you had to do it over again would you change your behavior in that group?
2. As a compensation manager, you will be asked to give formal presentations to upper-management. Describe for me the last time you gave a formal presentation.
   a. What was the presentation?
   b. How did you gather the necessary information to prepare?
   c. What steps did you go through in organizing the task?
   d. Describe any visual aids you used.
   e. What sort of feedback did you receive from those who attended the presentation?

faced on the new job. For example, an interviewer could ask "Tell me about the last time you faced the situation in which one of your subordinates wasn't performing well. What was the situation, how did you deal with it, and how did the employee respond?"[46] This type of question was successfully employed by Southwest Airlines in the opening case. On the Road to Competitive Advantage 6-1 provides an additional example of its use.

The "behavior description interview" has been found to be extremely valid because it is patterned along the lines of the behavior consistency model—applicants

The Use of Behavior Description Interviewing at S.C. Johnson and Sons

John T. Phillips is an HR professional at S.C. Johnson and Sons, which produces Johnson Wax. During an employment interview, Mr. Phillips used to ask applicants questions about their opinions and philosophies (e.g., "How should a supervisor reprimand an employee?"). After a while, Mr. Phillips began to realize that these traditional types of questions resulted in canned answers; that is, candidates were simply telling him what he wanted to hear.

Mr. Phillips thus changed his approach to conducting interviews. He now uses behavior description questions, which focus on what the candidates *have done*, rather than on what they *should do*. Specifically, he asks applicants to describe how they have behaved in actual situations (e.g., "Give me a specific example of a time you had to reprimand an employee. What action did you take? What was the result of your actions?").

He believes this type of question helps interviewers avoid canned answers and thus obtain a more accurate picture of an applicant's qualifications.

The use of behavior description questions has helped Mr. Phillips identify strong candidates who may have otherwise been overlooked. In one case, a woman with only theatrical experience competed against several experienced applicants for a sales position. Phillips was looking for an experienced salesperson and was skeptical. But the woman interviewed extremely well. Although she had no past sales experience to discuss, her past behavior in related settings (e.g., convincing a producer to give her a part) convinced Phillips that she possessed the characteristics needed for successfully performing a sales job. She was thus given the job and ultimately broke all sales records!

are being assessed based on their previous behavior in situations that closely match those they would encounter on the new job.

Interviewing and the Law

Interviews raise the same legal concerns as application blanks; the recommendations given earlier regarding application blank questions would thus also apply to interview questions.

Employment Tests

Employment testing is another tool in the HR professional's "bag of selection devices." A number of different types of tests exist. We will discuss three types here: **mental ability tests, personality tests,** and **work sample tests.**

Mental Ability Tests

Mental ability tests are designed to measure intelligence or aptitude. Aptitude is a very general mental capability that involves the ability to reason, plan, solve problems, think abstractly, comprehend complex ideas, learn quickly, and learn from experience.[47] Research has consistently found general aptitude to be a good predictor of job performance in nearly all jobs, especially complex ones like biologist, retail food manager, fish and game warden, and city circulation manager.[48] General mental ability tests have an average validity coefficient of .51, making them the most powerful single predictor of overall job performance.[49] This is why Bill Gates, CEO of Microsoft Corp., requires Microsoft recruiters to seek high-aptitude candidates; he believes that the company can teach them job-specific skills after they are hired.[50]

Companies use mental ability tests primarily for assessing entry-level applicants for jobs that do not require specific job-related skills at the time of hire; the tests determine whether the applicants have the capacity to learn these skills successfully. Some employers, however, are reluctant to use mental ability tests despite their validity, because these tests often have a disparate impact on certain protected groups. Their use may thus be at cross-purposes with the firm's affirmative action efforts.

mental ability tests
Employment tests designed to measure an applicant's aptitude.

personality tests
Employment tests designed to assess a variety of personality characteristics that are important for applicants when hired for certain jobs.

work sample tests
Employment tests that require applicants to perform some of the actual (or simulated) duties of the vacant position.

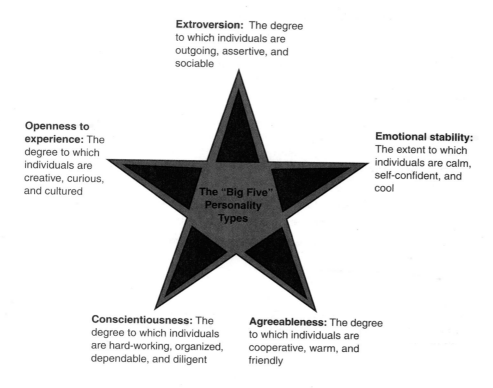

Figure 6-3
The "Big Five"
Personality Types

Personality Tests

An individual's personality characteristics can have an important bearing on job success. For instance, a salesperson may need to be assertive, extroverted, and have strong social skills in order to succeed; a manager may need to be self-confident and decisive; a social worker may need to be tolerant and open-minded.

Most employers recognize the importance of personality and try to assess it during the interview process. Unfortunately, their assessments are often inaccurate. Researcher Murray Barrick and his associates, for instance, found that an interviewer's assessments of a candidate's personality traits are often not much better than those made by a total stranger. They attribute this finding to the fact that applicants "self-manage" their behavior during the interview. That is, they pretend to be conscientious, outgoing, etc., in order to impress the interviewer.[51]

Many companies are now using personality tests to supplement the interviews because they believe that such tests provide a more objective way to gauge personality. A variety of personality tests are commercially available. The five personality characteristics most often measured by these tests, called "The Big Five," are shown in Figure 6-3.[52]

Research evidence on the validity of personality tests for employee selection has been mixed. Although many studies have failed to uncover validity, some have. Apparently, the validity of a personality test is situation specific. That is, a well-designed test can be a valid predictor of job performance for some jobs, but not for others.

Among the Big Five, conscientiousness seems to be the best predictor of performance. One study, for instance, found that tests measuring "conscientiousness" have been predictive of job success in nearly all occupational groups.[53] Tests measuring this trait have validity coefficients typically around .31.[54] Researchers have also found the trait "agreeableness" to be valid for predicting performance in many jobs.[55] The validity record of the other Big Five traits has been much less impressive.

Employers must be cautious when considering the use of personality tests. In addition to their uncertain validity, there may be a legal problem associated with their use. For example, some personality tests ask very personal questions that could be considered an invasion of privacy in some states. For instance, a California privacy law forbids businesses from collecting unnecessary information from applicants. The information collected must specifically, directly, and narrowly relate to performance on the job. Personality tests that ask "Does your soul sometimes leave your body?" and "Do you sometimes hate your mother?" violate that law.

Work Sample Tests

Work sample tests require applicants to perform some of the actual (or simulated) duties of the vacant position. For example, an applicant for the position of forklift operator might be asked to actually operate one, or an applicant for a teaching position might be asked to give a lecture. An HR professional develops these tests in this manner:

1. Conduct a job analysis to identify the important tasks of the position.

2. Choose a representative sample of tasks to be included on the test.

3. Develop a scoring procedure for assessing how effectively an applicant performs each task.

4. Administer the test to applicants under standardized conditions.

Work sample tests may be used to assess manual skills (e.g., handling various pieces of equipment), clerical skills (e.g., typing ability), and managerial skills (e.g., leadership, administrative, and diagnostic skills). They are appropriate for situations in which an applicant is expected to be skilled at the time of hire.

When companies properly construct and implement work sample tests, they are usually quite valid because they provide direct measures of job performance. Moviemakers use this method when selecting actors for a part (they "read" for the part). When basketball coaches have "tryouts," they too are using the work sample method. Although some of these individuals have probably never heard of "behavioral consistency theory," they know the principle that past behavior is the best predictor of future behavior when performed under similar circumstances. Because work samples simulate actual job duties, one would expect such tests to be predictive of job performance.

Two primary disadvantages are associated with work sample tests. One, they are quite expensive. Two, there could be a safety problem. For instance, it may not be wise to use a work sample test for a telephone pole climber's job; unqualified candidates could fall and break their necks!

Assessment Centers

When used to select managerial candidates, work sample tests are often administered as part of an **assessment center,** "a comprehensive, standardized procedure in which multiple assessment techniques such as situational exercises and job simulations (i.e., business games, discussion groups, reports, and presentations) are used to evaluate individual employees for various purposes."[56]

An assessment center may last from two to five days, during which time a group of candidates (usually 6 to 12) takes a battery of work sample tests and other selection devices, such as interviews and various written tests. The most commonly used work sample tests are:

1. *The leaderless group discussion:* Participants are given a problem to solve and are instructed to discuss it among themselves and arrive at a group decision within a specified period of time. Their behavior is rated by trained observers who evaluate such characteristics as communication skills, leadership, persuasiveness, and sensitivity.

2. *Management games:* These involve some activity such as buying and selling supplies, where individuals (or subgroups) compete in trying to maximize gains (e.g., profits, market share). This type of test often measures risk taking, initiative, analytical skills, and leadership.

assessment center
A selection technique that consists of work samples and other assessment techniques. It is primarily used to select managers.

3. *In-basket:* In this exercise, participants are provided with a set of memos, typical of those found in a manager's in-basket. The participants are required to prioritize and respond to the information. The test attempts to measure planning and organizing skills, judgment, and work standards.

Assessment centers have been found to be quite valid when appropriately developed and used.[57] Because they are comprised primarily of work sample tests, the advantages and disadvantages discussed in the previous section apply here, as well.

Screening for Dysfunctional Behavior

As noted in Figure 6-1, employers do not want to hire applicants with dysfunctional tendencies, such as drug addiction and dishonesty. In the following sections, we discuss how companies assess these tendencies.

Drug Abuse

Triggered by concern about drug abuse in the workplace, many organizations have begun to administer **drug tests** to applicants in order to eliminate drug users from further consideration. By doing so, organizations hope to reduce the costs associated with workplace drug abuse, such as absenteeism, poor performance, increased accidents, and health insurance costs.

drug tests Assessing individuals to detect possible drug use.

One needs to be aware of one caveat regarding the use of drug tests: Test results are not always accurate. Urinalysis testing, the most frequently used testing procedure, often incorrectly identifies people as drug users. Such individuals are referred to as false positives. The rejection of such "innocent" persons would have serious ethical consequences.

From a legal perspective, few restrictions apply to drug testing in the private sector. Applicants for public sector jobs, however, may bring lawsuits based on the Fourth Amendment. This amendment prohibits the government from *unreasonably invading the physiological being* of its applicants by taking urine or blood samples. To justify such a privacy invasion, the public sector employer must prove that its reason for administering these tests is "compelling."

For example, in *National Treasury Employees Union v. Von Raab*,[58] the Supreme Court sanctioned the drug testing program for U.S. Customs Service applicants for jobs involved with drug interdiction and those requiring employees to carry firearms. The government's interest was compelling, according to the Court, because "the public interest demands effective measures to bar drug users from positions directly involved in the interdiction of illegal drugs."

Assessing Applicant Honesty

Many organizations, especially banks and large retailers, assess applicant honesty in an effort to reduce instances of employee theft at the workplace. The two primary methods for predicting dishonesty are polygraph tests and paper-and-pencil honesty tests.

Polygraph tests (i.e., lie detector tests) purport to ascertain truthfulness of the information given by the examinee. The tests' interpretation assumes that lying can be detected by observing changes in the examinee's physiological response (galvanic skin response, cardiac cycle, and respiration pattern) during a polygraph-monitored interview. Applicants are rejected if the polygraph results indicate they gave untruthful answers or if applicants confess to past indiscretions or crimes during the exam.

polygraph tests Physiological tests designed to ascertain truthfulness of the information given by the examinee.

The **Employee Polygraph Protection Act (EPPA)** of 1988 bans most private-sector (but not public-sector) employers from using polygraph tests in the selection of candidates. EPPA restrictions do not apply in all circumstances: Pharmaceutical companies that test applicants for jobs that would allow access to controlled substances are exempt, as are employers who provide security services when they assess

Employee Polygraph Protection Act (EPPA) A law that bans most private-sector (but not public-sector) employers from using polygraph tests in the selection of candidates.

EXHIBIT 6-4	Examples of the Type of Items Found on Personality-Based Honesty Tests

- I often engage in barroom fights.
- I am easily bored.
- I don't like to be told what to do.
- I feel very uncomfortable in cramped spaces.

- I am easily annoyed.
- I feel restless most of the time.
- I have no difficulty talking to strangers.
- I often have trouble holding my temper

paper-and-pencil honesty tests Written tests that employers use to estimate an applicant's propensity to steal from an employer.

prospective guards. When used under these circumstances, the EPPA states that the exam must be "properly" administered by licensed polygraph examiners.

Paper-and-pencil honesty tests represent an alternative to polygraph testing for predicting theft. The tests may either be overt or personality-based measures. Overt tests inquire directly about attitudes toward theft and about prior dishonest behavior, such as "Have you ever stolen property valued at more than five dollars from a previous employer?" Because the purpose of these questions is often transparent to applicants, answers can be easily faked.

Personality-based measures do not contain any obvious references toward theft and thus are less prone to faking. Personality-based measures assume that certain personality characteristics predispose people to engage in theft.[59] These tests use items from personality tests that have been found to correlate with other indices of dishonesty or theft.[60] Examples of such items are shown in Exhibit 6-4.

Paper-and-pencil honesty tests are being used with increasing frequency now that polygraph testing has been largely banned. Such tests are used by more than 5,000 companies.[61] Research on their validity has been generally supportive, indicating that individuals who pass these tests are less likely to steal than those who fail.[62] Their average validity for predicting theft is a very respectable .47.[63] However, critics of these tests point out that although many people failing the test are potential thieves, a significant portion are "innocent victims."[64] Before using these tests, employers must wrestle with this ethical concern.

6-3 The Manager's Guide

6-3a Employee Selection and the Manager's Job

Managers play a principal role in the selection of employees. They help determine the needed competencies for the job, participate in the assessment of job candidates, give input into selection decisions, and, in many cases, make the actual job offer. The manager also plays an important role with regard to validation and complaint investigations.

Determining Needed Competencies

We covered job analysis in Chapter 4. In this chapter, we discussed how to base candidate assessments on information uncovered by a job analysis. Before beginning the selection process, the manager must ensure that job analysis information is thorough and up-to-date, given ever-changing technologies.

Assessing Job Candidates

In most organizations, managers conduct employment interviews. Effectively conducted interviews are vital to valid selection procedures. Section 6-3c, "HRM Skill-Building for Managers" discusses the how-tos of effective interviewing.

Providing Input into Selection Decisions

When candidate assessments are finished, the manager is usually faced with the task of making a selection decision—choosing the best candidate. To make a valid choice, a line manager must effectively combine all the available information on each applicant. Unfortunately, most line managers do not use effective strategies to do this; their strategies vary unpredictably from time to time.[65] "Proper" strategies for assessing applicant information are described in Section 6-3c, "HRM Skill-Building for Managers."

Making Job Offers
Managers usually extend job offers to candidates. As they do so, managers should be aware of two important principles:[66]

1. The offer should not be perceived as a gift; it must be sold to the candidate.
2. The offer should not remain open awaiting response for too long, which would preclude making an offer to another candidate.

However, if the selectee has serious reservations about the job, he or she should not be oversold. As noted in Chapter 5, "Recruiting Applicants," candidates should be given realistic information about the job so that they can decide for themselves whether they are properly matched to the position.[67]

The Manager's Role in Validation
Managers do not bear responsibility for validating selection procedures, but they do play two very important parts in the process. First, the actions they take in the selection process (e.g., interviewing applicants, evaluating information) affect the validity of the process. Without line managers' effective input, selection processes may be invalid, and even the most technically sound validation study may come up short.

Second, when the validity of the selection process is challenged, as it may be in a discrimination suit, courts will scrutinize the manager's actions. When content-oriented evidence is challenged, managers would be asked such questions as:

"Were the interview questions job related?"

"Was the selection decision based on relevant criteria?"

"Was the job description (which the manager may have written) accurate?"

When criterion-related evidence is challenged, performance evaluations the managers completed would be carefully scrutinized because they would serve as the criterion measure. If those evaluations were inaccurate, the validity of the selection instruments would come into question.

The Manager's Role in Complaint Investigations
When a disgruntled applicant files a discrimination charge with the EEOC, all organizational members involved in the selection process will be questioned about the selection decision. Section 6-3c, "HRM Skill-Building for Managers," describes how such investigations are conducted and the role played by the manager.

6-3b How the HRM Department Can Help

HR professionals play two primary roles in the selection process: providing technical support and helping managers conform to legal and technical standards throughout the selection process.

Providing Technical Support
HR professionals usually perform the following technical functions:

1. Conduct job analyses and write job descriptions.
2. Set minimum qualifications for jobs.
3. Determine which selection methods to use.
4. Develop application blanks.

5. Select/develop and administer employment tests.

6. Conduct initial screening of applicants (e.g., review application blanks, conduct initial interviews).

7. Conduct (or commission) background or reference checks.

8. Approve selection decisions made by line managers.

9. Monitor the firm's hiring practices for EEO compliance and validity.

Assisting the Manager

HR professionals are also called on to assist the manager in various ways: answering EEO-related questions, offering interviewer training programs, or helping the manager choose a selection device that would be most appropriate for a given situation. For example, the HR professional may be asked to recommend an appropriate employment test to be used to identify applicants who possess the necessary mechanical aptitude for a job.

HR professionals can provide managers with valuable assistance by offering legal/EEO training, which should be part of any program designed to orient new managers to their jobs. Veteran managers need periodic updating in order to keep abreast of the continually changing legal requirements.

6-3c HRM Skill-Building for Managers

We now discuss some specific skills that managers need when engaging in selection practices.

Avoiding Interviewer Mistakes[68]

What follows is a listing of the steps a manager goes through during an applicant interview, the mistakes managers commonly make during each step, and recommendations for avoiding or minimizing these mistakes.[69]

Step 1: The interviewer forms an initial impression of the applicant based on job requirements and information already collected from the application blank or resume.

Mistakes:

a. The interviewer is ignorant of the job requirements and of the needed worker qualifications.

- The interviewer must have a clear notion of the type of person needed to fill the job. Review/revise the job description.

b. The interviewer enters into the interview with a biased view of the candidate. Bias reduces interview validity by inappropriately influencing the interviewer's final assessment of the candidate.[70]

- Correctly interpret the available information contained on the application blank. Remember that the completed application blank merely provides a basis for *tentative* inferences about an applicant's capabilities; these inferences need to be verified during the interview. The interviewer must keep an open mind throughout the process.

Step 2: The interviewer questions the applicant in a face-to-face interview.

Mistake:

a. Interviewers often err during this step by asking the "wrong" questions (i.e., questions that are not job related).

- The manager should prepare a set of job-related questions prior to the interview and ensure that each is covered during the interview. (This type of interview, called a "structured interview," has been found to be more valid than unstructured interviews, in which interviewers make up questions as they go along.)[71] Questions designed to gather various types of information are described in an earlier part of this chapter.

Step 3: The interviewee responds to the questions.

Mistake:

a. Because of the way the questions are asked, the interviewee's responses are generally favorable; unfavorable information is not revealed. (After all, because applicants want the job, they often attempt to provide the "right answers" to the questions asked.)

- Do not "telegraph" the right answer prior to asking the question. For example, do not state that the job requires tact in dealing with customers and then ask, "Do you have tact?" How many applicants do you know who would answer "no" to that question?

- Withhold information regarding the job and worker requirements until the end of the interview, which makes it more difficult for the applicant to guess the right answers. For instance, applicants could be asked what type of people they work best with before being informed about the personalities of their coworkers.

- Ask questions that make it difficult for applicants to always present themselves favorably. Self-evaluative questions such as "What are your greatest weaknesses?" or "What did you most dislike about your previous job?" would be effective in this regard. Questions seeking behavior description information (i.e., asking candidates to describe a mistake they had made in their previous jobs) would also be effective.

Step 4: The interviewer interprets and processes the information obtained. (Actually, this is not a separate step, but occurs simultaneously with the interview process.) Each response tells the interviewer something about the applicant, and these responses must be correctly interpreted.

Mistake:

a. The primary mistake interviewers make here is jumping to conclusions. For example, an applicant states that he did not get along with his previous supervisor, and the interviewer quickly concludes that the applicant is insubordinate or unruly.

- The key to overcoming this error lies in the interviewer's ability to probe in order to get applicants to elaborate and clarify previous responses. For example, when applicants state that they have experienced difficulty in getting along with their previous supervisor, follow up with these questions: What were the circumstances? What was done about it? What role did you play in causing the problem?

- Managers should also note any inconsistencies among the responses given by an applicant. For example, the applicant may have expressed an interest in working as part of a team, yet may have always been a loner in the past. The applicant should be asked to explain this apparent inconsistency.

Step 5: The interviewer forms a postinterview impression of the interviewee's job qualifications.

Mistakes:

a. In forming a postinterview impression of the applicant's qualifications, managers often commit judgmental errors. Several types of errors have been identified, perhaps the most prevalent of which is snap judgments. Many interviewers make their selection decision within the first five minutes of the interview, after which the interview becomes a case of "Don't confuse me with the facts; I've already made up my mind."[72] The remainder of the interview becomes a biased search for information to support the manager's snap judgment.

- To avoid making snap judgments, managers should prepare rating forms prior to the interview, listing relevant attributes. At the conclusion of the interview, the applicant's standing on each separate attribute should be rated. The manager should avoid forming an overall impression of the applicant until it is time to make a final hiring decision.

  b. Another judgmental error is the "candidate order effect." When interviewing several candidates for a position, an interviewer is often inadvertently influenced by the order in which candidates were interviewed. Usually the first and last interviews are best remembered and thus may be given preference.

  - Because it is difficult for an interviewer to remember responses made by each applicant, you should evaluate each candidate immediately after the interview. Also, you should take careful notes during the interview. In addition to serving as a recall aid, interview notes may provide documentation needed to defend against discrimination suits.

Conducting a Structured Interview

We now put it all together and discuss how you should conduct an interview from start to finish.

Step 1: Preparing for the Interview

a. Review the job description to determine relevant attributes.

b. Prepare an attribute rating form listing the attributes needed for the job, the rating scale, and a space for documentation.

c. Review completed application blanks. Identify areas that need clarification or raise questions in your mind (e.g., unanswered questions, gaps in employment, unclear job titles).

d. Prepare a list of questions to ask. Questions should be specifically aimed at assessing job-related qualifications.

e. Schedule the interview so that it can be conducted in a private setting, without interruptions.

Step 2: Beginning the Interview

a. Give the applicant a warm and friendly greeting.

b. Conduct the interview in a friendly but businesslike manner.

c. Put the applicant at ease by beginning the interview with a minimum amount of "small talk." Get the applicant to speak by asking a nonthreatening question such as "Did you have any trouble finding this place?"

d. Discuss the purpose of the interview, and then ask "What interests you about this position?"

Step 3: Soliciting Information

a. As you ask questions, be nonjudgmental and accepting of the applicant's answers. Periodically give signs that you are interested in what the applicant is saying by nodding your head, smiling, and saying "that's very interesting."

b. Keep control of the interview, ensuring that all questions will be answered within a reasonable time frame. If the applicant goes off track, redirect the interview to the original question.

c. Probe. Ask applicants to elaborate if necessary. For instance, if an applicant states that she did not get along well with her previous supervisor, ask her to describe the nature of the problem.

d. Take notes. Put the notebook on your lap. Record the information in your own shorthand. Try to maintain eye contact with the applicant as you take notes. Do not take notes concerning a particularly positive or negative statement made by the applicant immediately after the statement is made. Doing so would cue the applicant on the preferred or nonpreferred answers being sought.

Step 4: Giving Information

a. Give pertinent information about the job and the organization. Include both positive and negative aspects. This should be done after all necessary information about the applicant has been collected.

b. Honestly answer any questions the applicant might have concerning the job/organization, such as advancement opportunities, benefits, salary range, etc.

Step 5: Terminating the Interview

a. Ask if the applicant has anything to add that would be pertinent to the hiring decision.

b. Express appreciation for the applicant's time and interest.

c. Inform the applicant of the procedure by which the company will arrive at its selection decision.

d. Give the time frame within which the selection decision will be made and how and when the applicant will be notified. Make sure you follow through on any promises made.

e. Give a cordial parting.

Identifying the Best Candidate

One viable strategy for arriving at a sound selection decision is to first evaluate the applicants on each individual attribute needed for the job. That is, at the conclusion of the selection process, each applicant could be rated on a scale (say, from one to five) on each important attribute based on all the information collected during the selection process. For example, you could arrive at an overall rating of a candidate's "dependability" by combining information derived from references, interviews, and tests that relate to this attribute.

After applicants are rated on each attribute, the ratings could be statistically combined to form a composite score—the composite being a weighted average, reflecting the relative importance of each attribute (as specified in the job analysis). The applicant with the highest score would then be selected.

This approach is appropriate when a compensatory model is operating, that is, when it is correct to assume that a high score on one attribute can compensate for a low score on another. For example, a baseball player may compensate for a lack of power in hitting by being a fast base runner. In some selection situations, however, proficiency in one area cannot compensate for deficiencies in another. When a noncompensatory model is operating, deficiencies in any one area would eliminate the candidate from future consideration. Lack of honesty or an inability to get along with people, for example, may serve to eliminate candidates for some jobs, regardless of their other abilities.

When a noncompensatory model is operating, the "successive hurdles" approach might be most appropriate. Under this approach, a subset of candidates may be eliminated during various stages of the selection process if you learn that a candidate possesses a noncompensable deficiency. For example, some applicants may be eliminated during the first stage if they do not meet the minimum education and experience qualifications. Additional candidates may be eliminated at later points, e.g., after failing a drug or honesty test or after demonstrating poor interpersonal skills during an interview. The use of successive hurdles lowers selection costs by requiring fewer assessments to be made, as the list of viable candidates continues to shrink.

Dealing with EEOC Investigations

Any time a hiring decision is made, an employer faces the possibility of discrimination charges. A disgruntled applicant may file charges with the EEOC, which would then investigate the complaint. As a line manager, you need to know what happens during these investigations and what role you will be asked to play.

The process starts when an applicant files a discrimination complaint with the EEOC, indicating the nature and type of discrimination (e.g., sex discrimination, race discrimination, etc.) that has allegedly occurred. For example, the charge may specify that the employer discriminated on the basis of sex as indicated by several derogatory comments about women that were made during the employment interview.

The EEOC will notify the employer of the charge in writing within 10 days. At this point, the company should launch its own investigation of the charges. Witness statements should be carefully prepared to preserve evidence and to aid witnesses in preparing for a possible full-scale EEOC investigation and subsequent litigation.[73] If serving as a witness, remember these guidelines:[74]

1. Give the attorney all known facts. Do not condense them, and do not be reluctant to disclose all information, even if it is damaging.

2. When giving facts, be prepared to provide supporting documents such as memos, letters, or other written support.

3. Separate facts from assumptions.

Upon completion of its own thorough investigation, the company must decide whether to fight the charges or to settle. If no settlement is reached, the EEOC requires the employer and the complaining party to attend a "no-fault" conference. During this conference, the EEOC official hears both sides of the story. Each party is expected to bring any witnesses who may shed light on the charge. About 40 percent of all cases are settled at this stage.[75]

If the matter is not resolved during this conference, the EEOC will conduct a full-scale investigation. The company may be asked to respond, in writing, to interrogatories (i.e., requests for information that would have a bearing on the validity of the charge). For example, a company may be asked to describe its selection process and to supply statistics bearing on possible disparate impact.

As part of its investigation, the EEOC officials are likely to examine records and conduct interviews with company officials, witnesses, and other "interested" parties. You must bear two things in mind if you should become involved in this investigation. First, be courteous and cooperative with the investigators. After all, investigators' recommendations often sway the EEOC's decision. Second, limit the information you supply to these EEOC investigators to only those issues raised as part of the charge itself. For instance, if the charge is sex discrimination, do not volunteer any information concerning the way in which the company deals with members of other protected groups. Doing so may lead investigators to expand the scope of the investigation.

The EEOC will ultimately make a determination of "cause" or "no cause." A finding of "cause" would indicate that there is reason to believe that discrimination has taken place. Companies should seriously consider making a settlement if this occurs, especially if its own internal investigation supports some or all of the charges. However, they are not legally required to do so. A company's ultimate decision should be based on the merits of the case and possible litigation costs.

A finding of "no cause" indicates that there is insufficient evidence to support the discrimination claim. The complaining party is nevertheless issued a "right to sue" letter and has 90 days to file a lawsuit.

Chapter Objectives Revisited

1. Describe what the term *validity* means with regard to employee selection and how a company can achieve and document it.

   - Validity is concerned with the issue of whether applicants would actually perform the job as well as expected, based on the inferences made during the selection process.
   - To achieve validity, the manager must:
     - Have a clear notion of the needed job qualifications.
     - Use selection methods that reliably and accurately measure these qualifications.
   - There are three strategies that a company can use to document validity.
     - Content-oriented: Demonstrate that it followed "proper" procedures in the development and use of its selection devices.
     - Criterion-related: Provide statistical evidence showing a relationship between selection scores and job performance levels.
     - Validity generalization: Demonstrate that other companies have already established the validity of its selection practices.

2. Understand the legal constraints imposed by EEOC guidelines, constitutional law, and tort law that companies face when selecting employees.

   - EEOC Guidelines
     - *Uniform Guidelines on Employee Selection Procedures:* State that a company must demonstrate the job-relatedness of its selection procedures when they have a disparate impact on a protected group.
     - National origin discrimination guidelines: Describe employers' legal constraints when hiring people of various national origin groups.
     - Sexual harassment guidelines: State that a hiring decision may not be based on an applicant's acceptance or rejection of an employer's request for sexual favors.
     - Pregnancy discrimination guidelines: State that applicants with pregnancy-related conditions must be treated in the same manner as those with temporary disabilities.
     - Age discrimination guidelines: Describe employers' legal constraints when hiring people age 40 and above.
     - Religious discrimination guidelines: State that employers must accommodate the religious-based needs of applicants unless the accommodation is an undue hardship.
     - Disability discrimination guidelines: State that employers must accommodate the disability-related needs of applicants unless the accommodation is an undue hardship.
   - Constitutional Law (Public Sector Only)
     - Fourth Amendment (privacy)
     - Fifth and Fourteenth Amendments (equal protection)
   - Tort Law
     - Negligent hiring: Occurs when an employer negligently hires an applicant who is somehow unfit for the job and, because of this unfitness, commits an act that causes harm to another
     - Defamation: The unprivileged publication of a false oral or written statement that harms the reputation of another person

3. Explain the various selection methods used by firms.

   - Application blanks: Forms completed by applicants asking for background information, such as educational and work histories and reason for leaving previous jobs
   - Biodata inventories: A selection technique in which an applicant's responses to background information questions are objectively scored
   - Background investigations: An in-depth probe of an applicant's background usually conducted by an investigative agency
   - Reference checks: Selection information collected from an applicant's previous employers (or associates)
   - Employment interviews: Structured conversations between employers and applicants designed to assess the applicants' qualifications
   - Employment tests: Used primarily to assess mental ability, personality, and job skills
   - Assessment center: Consists of work sample tests and other assessment techniques. It is primarily used to select managers.
   - Screening for dysfunctional behavior: Screening devices, including drug, polygraph, and paper-and-pencil honesty tests

Review Questions

Note: You can find the correct answers to these questions by taking the quiz and then submitting your answers in the Online Edition. The program will automatically score your submission. If you miss a question, the program will provide the correct answer, a rationale for the answer, and the section number in the chapter where the topic is discussed.

1. Behavior consistency theory states that
   a. people who behave consistently are better performers than those who behave inconsistently.
   b. an applicant's past behavior is a good predictor of future behavior.
   c. employers should assess applicants in a consistent manner.
   d. consistency is a sign of mediocrity.

2. *The Uniform Guidelines on Employee Selection Procedures* are designed to assist organizations in understanding Title VII compliance requirements with regard to
   a. disparate treatment claims.
   b. disparate impact claims.
   c. record keeping.
   d. organizational dressing/uniform policies.

3. If a firm rejects an applicant because of a heavy foreign accent, the EEOC would
   a. overturn that decision under any circumstances.
   b. support that decision under any circumstances.
   c. support that decision only if the accent would prohibit the applicant from performing an important job function.
   d. support that decision only if the applicant is a U.S. citizen.

4. When judging a claim of undue hardship in a religious discrimination case, the courts apply a standard called the _____ principle.
   a. reasonable accommodation
   b. hardship
   c. *de minimus*
   d. good faith

5. The constitutional amendment pertaining to employee privacy is the _____ Amendment.
   a. First
   b. Fourth
   c. Fifth
   d. Fourteenth

6. What law specifies that applicants must be notified if their employment is being denied because of information uncovered in a background investigation?
   a. The Civil Rights Act
   b. The Fair Credit Reporting Act
   c. The Background Investigation Limitation Act
   d. The Fair Employment Act

7. "Tell me about the last time you had a conflict with another employee. What was the nature of the conflict, and how did you deal with it?" This is a _____ question.
   a. job knowledge
   b. self-evaluative
   c. situational
   d. behavior description

8. In its decision in *National Treasury Union v. Von Raab,* the Supreme Court
   a. sanctioned the drug-testing program because the government has a compelling reason to test for drugs.
   b. sanctioned the drug-testing program because the government has absolute discretion to test for drug use at any time.
   c. ruled that the drug testing violated the workers' privacy rights.
   d. ruled that the drug testing violated the workers' civil rights.

9. _____ tests are paper-and-pencil honesty tests that inquire directly about attitudes toward theft and about prior dishonest behavior.
   a. Overt
   b. Covert
   c. Personality-based
   d. Direct

10. When used in the context of drug testing, the term *false positive* refers to a person who
    a. uses drugs and passed the test.
    b. uses drugs and failed the test.
    c. does not use drugs and passed the test.
    d. does not use drugs and failed the test.

Discussion Questions

1. Describe how the practices your university uses to select professors can impact its competitive advantage.

2. Define the term *validity*. Describe the two keys to ensuring validity.

3. Compare and contrast the content-oriented strategy of documenting validity with the criterion-related strategy. When is the criterion-related strategy preferred?

4. What are the main provisions of the *Uniform Guidelines?*

5. Define the legal requirements for establishing undue hardship for (a) religious discrimination cases and (b) disability discrimination cases.

6. What are an employer's obligations with regard to the issue of negligent hiring?

7. Describe the uses of and precautions regarding application blanks.

8. Explain how the items on a biodata inventory are weighted.

9. What are the major legal issues associated with reference checking?

10. Under what conditions may a public-sector employer administer a drug test?

11. Describe the two types of paper-and-pencil honesty tests.

12. What is the manager's role regarding validation?

13. In what ways may an HR professional assist a manager with regard to employee selection?

14. Describe three mistakes that are often made by managers during the interview process. How can these mistakes be avoided?

Experiential Exercises

What Information Will the EEOC Seek?

Carl Jackson, a black man, filed a race discrimination charge against the ABC Police Department. The charge reads as follows:

1. I was not hired for the position of patrol officer, in spite of the fact that I was qualified and applied for the job.

2. Lieutenant Smith told me there were no openings at present, but he would keep me in mind.

3. I have a B.S. degree in criminal justice from Metropolitan University and served an internship with the Metropolitan Police Department. I received a good recommendation from Lieutenant Horton, the officer to whom I was assigned.

4. I applied for the position in July 1990 following my graduation. I kept in touch with Lieutenant Smith regarding my continued desire to work for the department.

5. There is currently one black working in the department as a patrol officer. I found out in September that a Caucasian, Jim Spencer, was hired during the time I was told there was no opening. I believe I am more qualified for the position. Mr. Spencer does not even have a degree in criminal justice.

Assignment

Please answer the following questions:

1. What information/records would the EEOC request in its investigation of this claim?

2. How could this information be used in its determination of "cause" or "no cause?"

3. Give examples of the type of information that would lead the EEOC to a finding of "cause."

What Should Jane Smith Do?

Refer to the scenarios described earlier in the chapter depicting a day in the life of line manager Jane Smith.

Assignment

Please answer the following questions:

1. What would you tell Jane regarding her decision to reject the application of Mary Jones because of her pregnancy?

2. What arguments could Jane use to support her decision to reject the candidacy of Bill Cooper because Bill could not work on Saturdays?

3. What are the legal ramifications of giving Kate Johnson an unfavorable reference? What advice would you give Jane?

Planning How to Assess Worker Qualifications

Methods of Selection

1. Application blank
2. Biodata inventory
3. Background investigation
4. Reference check
5. Employment interview
6. Mental ability test
7. Personality test
8. Work sample test
9. Assessment center
10. Honesty testing

Instructions

Indicate what selection method or methods from the preceding list should be used to assess each of the characteristics shown in the following list for the job of HR professional. Be prepared to explain your choices.

Method(s)	Characteristics to Assess
_____	1. Would the applicant enjoy the job?
_____	2. Would the applicant fit well with the people/culture?
_____	3. Are the applicant's career aspirations congruent with those offered by the job?
_____	4. Will the applicant be highly motivated?
_____	5. Will the applicant be a good organizational citizen?
_____	6. Does the applicant have the ability to communicate clearly?
_____	7. Does the applicant have the ability to deal with people tactfully?
_____	8. Would the applicant deal assertively with members of upper management?
_____	9. Would the applicant be able to handle the stress of the job (e.g., short deadlines, constantly changing priorities)?
_____	10. Would the applicant be a good employee advocate (e.g., show concern for other employees' well-being)?
_____	11. Does the applicant possess the technical knowledge and skills required by the job (e.g., job analysis, employment, training, incentive systems, safety and health)?

Developing a Selection Plan and Interview Questions

Overview

You will be working with the job description that was assembled in the experiential exercise in Chapter 4. Your task is to develop a selection plan and interview questions for selecting applicants for that job. You will then be asked to conduct an actual interview with one of your class members.

Steps

1. Reconvene into the groups of three that were used in the job description exercise.

2. Each group should prepare a selection plan that would be used in the assessment of applicants for the position. The plan should be expressed as a matrix. On the left-hand side, list each basic and special competency. Across the top of the matrix, list each type of selection device that would be used in the selection process (e.g., application blank, biodata inventory, interview, etc.).

3. Put an "X" in each matrix cell, indicating which selection device(s) would be used to measure each competency.

4. Prepare a list of the interview questions you would ask an applicant in order to assess the competencies that can be measured by means of the interview (as indicated in the matrix developed in step 2).

5. The instructor will select one group to conduct an interview for the job it had analyzed. The instructor will then select a class member in another group to serve as the interviewee. The group conducting the interview will distribute a list of the competencies to be assessed to the other groups. The candidate will be interviewed using the questions developed in step 3, as well as follow-up or probing questions. The interview may be conducted by one individual within the group or by the entire group (i.e., alternate questioning among group members).

6. Upon completion of the interview, all groups should rate the candidate on each KSA.

7. Hold a class discussion for the purpose of comparing the ratings made by the various groups. Did each group rate the candidate identically on each competency? If not, discuss the possible reasons for the disagreements.

Case

Is This Hiring Process Sound?

Harlin's Department Store has 36 locations throughout the United States. The human resource function is carried out by a staff of nine HR professionals located at company headquarters in Akron, Ohio. The HR staff is responsible for hiring managers for each store. When a new store opens, an HR professional travels to the location to hire a manager for the store. The new store manager is then given the responsibility of hiring all the needed personnel for that store.

Mike Barker, an HR professional, recently selected Lou Johnson as manager for a recently opened store in Macon, Georgia. Within the first six months of operation, the turnover rate among store personnel was 120 percent. The assistant manager position had already turned over three times. The average salesperson lasted only two months. Mike was sent to Macon to investigate the problem.

Mike asked Lou to describe the hiring practices he used in selecting personnel. Lou responded as follows:

I base all my selections on personal interviews I conduct with each candidate. I ask all candidates certain basic questions, such as their willingness to work weekends and to work overtime. Beyond that, I do not follow a predetermined sequence of questions but, rather, I try to tailor my questions to each applicant. Prior to the interview, I review the applicants' resumes and application forms to become familiar with their background and past experience. From this information, I determine whether they meet the minimum qualifications for the job. I then interview all applicants who are at least minimally qualified. During the interview, I try to determine whether the applicant is an extrovert who likes working with people. When interviewing an assistant manager, I also look for leadership skills.

Mike then asked Lou how he decides which candidate to hire. Lou responded by stating:

My first impression of the applicant is very important. How a person presents himself, his opening remarks, and his attire are all very important and do have some impact on my final decision. However, it is an applicant's eye contact that is probably the most influential factor. When someone gives eye contact, it is a sign that he is listening and that he is sincere. Smiling, a firm handshake, and sitting in a straight position with both feet flat on the floor are also important factors in my decision. Finally, if a candidate is to be hired, he must be interested in working for Harlin's and not just interested in a job. My first question is "Why do you want to work for Harlin's?" I am very impressed with applicants who already know a great deal about Harlin's.

Mike must now make an assessment of Lou's hiring practices to determine if they might be a contributing factor to the turnover problem.

Questions

1. If you were Mike, what conclusions would you draw regarding the soundness of Lou's hiring practices?

2. What recommendations would you make to Lou regarding how he could improve his selection procedure?

References

1. Sunoo, B.P. (1995). How fun flies at Southwest Airlines. *Personnel Journal,* June, 62-73.

2. See, for example, Cascio, W.F., and Sibley, V. (1979). Utility of the assessment center as a selection device. *Journal of Applied Psychology, 64,* 107-118; Schmidt, F.L., Hunter, J.E., McKensie, R.C., and Muldrow, T.W. (1979). Impact of valid selection procedures on work-force productivity. *Journal of Applied Psychology, 64,* 609-626.

3. Schmidt et al. Impact of valid selection procedures.

4. American Psychological Association. (1985). *Standards for Educational and Psychological Testing* (4th ed.). Washington, DC.

5. Kleiman, L.S., and Faley, R.H. (1978). Assessing content validity: Standards set by the court. *Personnel Psychology, 31,* 701-713.

6. Ghiselli, E.E., Campbell, J.P., and Zeldeck, S. (1981). *Measurement Theory for the Behavioral Sciences.* San Francisco: Freeman.

7. Wernimont, P.F., and Campbell, J.P. (1968). Signs, samples, and criteria. *Journal of Applied Psychology, 52,* 372-376.

8. Ibid.

9. Barrett, G.V., Phillips, J.S., and Alexander, R.A. (1981). Concurrent and predictive validity designs: A critical reanalysis. *Journal of Applied Psychology, 66,* 1-6.

10. Baker, D.D., and Terpstra, D.E. (1982). Employee selection: Must every job test be validated? *Personnel Journal, 61,* 602-605.

11. See, for example, Hunter, J.E. (1986). Cognitive ability, cognitive aptitudes, job knowledge, and job performance. *Journal of Vocational Behavior, 29,* 340-362.

12. Gatewood, R.D., and Field, H.S. (2000). *Human Resource Selection* (5th ed.). Fort Worth, TX: Dryden Press.

13. *Uniform Guidelines on Employee Selection Procedures* (1978). 29 Code of Federal Regulations, Part 1607.

14. *Guidelines on Discrimination Because of National Origin* (1987). 29 Code of Federal Regulations, Part 1606.

15. *Final Guidelines on Sexual Harassment* (1980). Code of Federal Regulations, Part 1604.

16. *Questions and Answers on the Pregnancy Discrimination Act* (1992). Equal Employment Opportunity Commission, 29 CFR Ch. XIV (7-1-92 ed.).

17. *Maldano v. U.S. Bank and Manufacturer's Bank* (1999). U.S. App 7th Cir. LEXIS 15118.

18. *Final Interpretations: The Age Discrimination in Employment Act* (1981). Federal Register, 29 CFR Part 1625.

19. *Usery v. Tamiami Trail Tours, Inc.* (1976). 12 FEP 1233.

20. Faley, R.H., and Kleiman, L.S. (1984). Age discrimination and personnel psychology: A review and synthesis of the legal literature with implications for future research. *Personnel Psychology, 37* (2), 327-350

21. *Guidelines on Discrimination Because of Religion* (1985). 29 Code of Federal Regulations, Part 1605.

22. *Bruff v. North Mississippi Health Services* (2001). U.S. App. LEXIS 4977.

23. *Baltgalvis v. Newport News Shipbuilding* (2001). U.S. Dist. LEXIS 1864.

24. Overman, S. (1994). Good faith is the answer. *HRMagazine,* January, 74-76.

25. Ibid.

26. Hall, F.S., and Halle, E.L. (1994). The ADA: Going beyond the law. *Academy of Management Executive, 8* (1), 17-26.

27. Williams, J.M. (1988). Technology and the disabled. *Personnel Administrator,* July, 81-83.

28. Verespej, M.A. (1992), Time to focus on the disabilities. *Industry Week,* April 6, 15-26.

29. Williams. Technology and the disabled.

30. Ryan, A.M., and Lasek, M. (1991). Negligent hiring and defamation: Areas of liability related to pre-employment inquiries. *Personnel Psychology, 44* (20), 293-319.

31. Stanton, E.S. (1988). Fast and easy reference checking by telephone. *Personnel Journal, 66* (8), 135-138.

32. Ryan and Lasek. Negligent hiring and defamation.

33. McDaniel, M.A. (1989). Biographical constructs for predicting employee suitability. *Journal of Applied Psychology, 74,* 964-977.

34. Lee, R., and Booth, J.M. (1974). A utility analysis of weighted application blanks designed to predict turnover for clerical employees. *Journal of Applied Psychology, 59,* 516-518.

35. Reilly, R.R., and Chao, G.E. (1982). Validity and fairness of some alternative selection procedures. *Personnel Psychology, 35,* 1-62.

36. Terpstra, D.E., and Rozell, E.J. (1993). The relationship of staffing practices to organizational level measures of performance. *Personnel Psychology, 46* (1), 27-48.

37. Hammer, E.G., and Kleiman, L.S. (1988). Getting to know you. *Personnel Administrator,* May, 86-92.

38. McDaniel. Biographical constructs.

39. Mayer, M. (2002). Background checks in focus. *HRMagazine,* January, 59-62.

40. Pyron, H.C. (1970). The use and misuse of previous employer references in hiring. *Management of Personnel Quarterly,* Summer, 15-22.

41. Dube, L.E. (1986). Employment references and the law. *Personnel Journal,* February, 87-91.

42. Higgins, C.A., and Judge, T.A. (2004). The effect of applicant influence tactics on recruiter perceptions of fit and hiring recommendations: A field study. *Journal of Applied Psychology, 89* (4), 622-632.

43. Janz, T., Hellervik, L., and Gilmore, D.C. (1986). *Behavior Descriptive Interviewing.* Boston: Allyn and Bacon.

44. Ibid.

45. Harris. Reconsidering the employment interview.

46. Janz et al. *Behavior Descriptive Interviewing.*

47. Gottfredson, L.S. (1997). Mainstream science on intelligence: An editorial with 52 signatures, history, and bibliography. *Intelligence: A Multidimensional Journal, 24* (1), 13-23.

48. Gottfredson, L.S. (1997). Why g matters: The complexity of everyday life. *Intelligence: A Multidimensional Journal, 24* (1), 79-132.

49. Rynes, S.L., Brown, K.G., and Colbert, A.E. (2002). Seven common misconceptions about human resource practices: Research findings versus practitioner beliefs. *Academy of Management Executive, 16* (3), 92-102.

50. Behling, O. (1998). Employee selection. Will intelligence and conscientiousness do the job? *Academy and Management Executive, 12* (1), 77-86.

51. Barrick, M.R., Patton, G.K., and Haugland, S.N. (2000). Accuracy of interviewer judgments of job applicant personality traits. *Personnel Psychology, 53* (4), 925-947.

52. Salgado, J.F. (1997). The five factor model of personality and job performance in the European community. *Journal of Applied Psychology, 82* (1), 30-43.

53. Barrick, M.R., and Mount, M.K. (1991). The big five personality dimensions and job performance: A meta-analysis. *Personnel Psychology, 44* (1), 1-26.

54. Rynes et. al. Seven common misperceptions.

55. Tett, R.P., Jackson, D.N., and Rothstein, M. (1991). Personality measures as predictors of job performance: A meta-analytic review. *Personnel Psychology, 44* (4), 703-742.

56. Thornton, G.C., and Byham, W.C. (1982). *Assessment Centers and Managerial Performance*. New York: Academic Press.

57. Reilly and Chao. Validity and fairness.

58. *National Treasury Employee's Union v. Von Raab* (1989) 489 U.S. 656, 4 IER Cases 246.

59. Hogan, J., and Hogan, R. (1989). How to measure employee reliability. *Journal of Applied Psychology, 74,* 273-279.

60. Sackett, P.R., Burns, L.R., and Callahan, C. (1989). Integrity testing for personnel selection: An update. *Personnel Psychology, 42,* 491-530.

61. Sackett, P.H. (1985). Honesty testing for personnel selection. *Personnel Administrator, 30,* 67-76, 121.

62. Sackett et al. Integrity testing.

63. Rynes et. al. Seven common misperceptions.

64. Sackett et al. Integrity testing.

65. Landy, F.J. (1985). *Psychology of Work Behavior*. Homewood, IL: Dorsey.

66. Goddard, R., Fox, J., and Patton, W.E. (1969). The job hire sale. *Personnel Administrator,* June, 120-124.

67. Ibid.

68. Alvis, J.M., and Kleiman, L.S. (1994). Don't blunder when interviewing job candidates. *Today's CPA,* January/February, 26-31.

69. Phillips, A.P., and Dipboye, R.L. (1989). Correlation tests of predictions from a process model of the interview. *Journal of Applied Psychology, 74,* 41-52.

70. Ibid.

71. Harris. Reconsidering the employment interview.

72. Buckley, M.R., and Eder, R.W. (1989). The first impression. *Personnel Administrator,* Spring, 76-81.

73. Sheahan, R.H. (1981). Responding to employment discrimination charges. *Personnel Journal,* March, 217-220.

74. Sovereign, K.L. (1984). *Personnel Law*. Reston, VA: Reston.

75. McCulloch, K.J. (1981). *Selecting Employees Safely under the Law*. Englewood Cliffs, NJ: Prentice Hall.

Summary of the Government's ADA Regulations

1. Aim of the ADA

   Prevent discrimination against someone with a disability regarding job application procedures, hiring, advancement, discharge, compensation, training, and other terms, conditions, and privileges of employment. Moreover, an employer may not discriminate against someone because of the known disability of an individual with whom the applicant is related or associated (e.g., the applicant has a disabled child or spouse and the employer discriminates because it feels that the association will cause that person to miss work).

2. Definition of "Disability"

   a. The person has a physical or mental impairment that substantially limits one or more of his or her major life activities; or

   b. has a record of such an impairment; or

   c. is regarded as having such an impairment.

3. Rules Governing the Hiring Process

   a. Determine if the person meets the minimum qualifications for the job (e.g., meets the education, experience, licensure requirements).

   b. If the person meets the minimum qualifications, determine if he or she can perform the essential functions of the job *without* accommodation.
      - If no, consider accommodation.
      - If yes, hire if most qualified.

   c. If accommodation is necessary, determine if, with accommodation, the person can perform the essential functions of the job.
      - If no, need not hire.
      - If yes, determine whether the accommodation would pose an undue hardship for the employer.
      - If yes, need not hire.
      - If no, hire if most qualified.

4. Determining the Essential Functions of the Job

   a. An essential function is a fundamental job duty that must be performed by the jobholder.

   b. Methods of establishing which duties are essential functions:
      - The use of the employer's judgment
      - The essential nature of the duty is so stated in the job description based on such considerations as time spent, consequence of poorly performing that duty, etc.
      - The collective bargaining agreement refers to the duty as essential.
      - The work experience of past/current incumbents indicates that the duty is essential.

5. Determining Whether a Disabled Applicant Can Perform the Essential Functions of a Job, with or without Accommodation

a. *Qualification standards:* It is illegal to use a qualification standard that tends to screen out disproportionately individuals with disabilities unless the standard is job related and is consistent with business necessity.

b. *Employment interviews:* The employer may not inquire about an applicant's disabilities or history of workers' compensation claims prior to making a job offer. The employer should take the applicant on a tour of the work site and/or explain the essential functions of the job. The applicant should then be asked whether there are any essential functions he or she cannot perform. Some dos and don'ts:
   - *Don't* list possible disabilities on an application form and have the applicants check those that apply to them.
   - *Don't* ask applicants how they became disabled or what their prognosis is.
   - *Don't* ask how often the applicant will be required to take sick leave.
   - *Do* inform applicants of the company's attendance policy and ask if they can meet the requirements.

c. *Preemployment testing:* The tests used must provide a valid assessment of the skills needed for the job. That is, the test results should accurately reflect the skills the test purports to measure, rather than reflecting impaired sensory, manual, or speaking skills (if these latter skills are not themselves job related).
   - An employer is required to accommodate a disabled applicant during testing if it is known beforehand that the individual has a disability that impairs sensory, manual, or speaking skills.

d. *Medical exams:* A medical exam may be given, but only *after* a job offer has been made. The employment offer may then be rescinded if the applicant "fails" the examination. The following guidelines apply to medical examinations:
   - All selectees, not just disabled ones, must be subject to examination.
   - The employer must physically separate the employee's medical file from the personnel file to help ensure that the medical information remains confidential.
   - The medical information given to the employee's manager is restricted. The manager may only be informed of the work restrictions necessitated by the disability and the accommodation needed.
   - The employer may inform first-aid and safety personnel of the disability if that disability may require emergency treatment.

e. *Drug tests:* These tests are not considered a medical exam and therefore may be given prior to the employment offer.

6. Accommodation

a. Types of accommodation:
   - That required to ensure equal opportunity in the application process
   - That which enables a disabled person to perform an essential function of the job
   - That which enables a disabled person to enjoy equal benefits and privileges enjoyed by nondisabled workers (e.g., providing an attendant to assist a blind employee on a business trip)

b. Examples of accommodation:
   - Make facilities accessible to a wheelchair-bound applicant.
   - Restructure the job.
   - Modify equipment.
   - Provide readers or interpreters.

7. Undue Hardship

    a. There are no ironclad limits set regarding cost limitations for the accommodation. The cutoff point for determining undue hardship must be determined on a case-by-case basis. Whether a particular cost is considered to pose an undue hardship on the employer depends on:

- The financial realities of the employer
- The extent to which the accommodation would be unduly costly or disruptive. The employer must consider whether the accommodation would fundamentally alter the nature or operation of the business. For example, a restaurant, which uses dim lighting to create a romantic atmosphere, is asked to accommodate a visually impaired applicant by increasing the lighting. This accommodation would pose an undue hardship because it would cause an employer to change the fundamental nature of the business; it would no longer be a romantic restaurant.

    b. When considering financial hardship:

- Consider the financial resources that would be available to the facility responsible for making the accommodation, rather than the financial resources of the company as a whole.
- If the accommodation is to be a great financial burden, the employer has the responsibility of looking for outside funding, such as that from a state vocational rehabilitation agency.
- If the employer cannot afford the accommodation, it should provide the disabled person with the option of paying for it, in whole or in part.

8. Other Important Provisions of the ADA

    a. *Communicable diseases transmitted through food handling:* The Department of Health and Human Services has prepared a list of diseases that may be transmitted through food handling. When encountering an employee or applicant who has such a disease, it is the employer's responsibility to find an accommodation that will eliminate the risk. If it cannot, the applicant/ employee may be rejected/discharged if he or she cannot be placed in a vacant job where no such risk exists.

    b. *Employee benefits:* Health insurance, life insurance, and other benefits must be made available to disabled persons on an equal basis with other employees.

Human Resource Management Postselection Practices

Training and Developing Employees

Chapter Seven

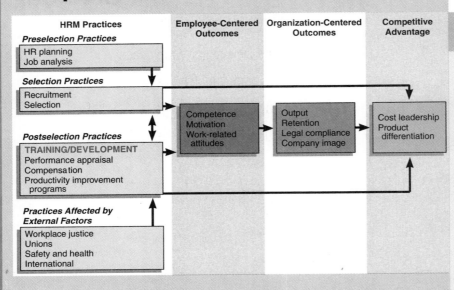

Key Terms

action learning
action plan
behavior modeling
career resource centers
case method
change-related training
computer-based instruction (CBI)
distributed practice
feedback
interactive video training (IVT)
job instruction training (JIT)
job rotation
lecture
massed practice
mentors

multiphase training program
on-the-job training (OJT)
orientation training
overlearning
performance aids
performance analysis
remedial training
replacement charts
role-playing
succession planning
task force
training evaluation
training need
training objectives
web-based training

Chapter Objectives

Upon completion of this chapter, you will be able to:

- Understand why effective training and development programs enhance competitive advantage.
- Describe how companies assess their training needs.
- Explain how companies can present training programs to maximize learning.
- Describe the various methods of training.

- Explain how companies can ensure that training is transferred to the job.
- Describe how training evaluations should be conducted.
- Describe the steps involved in management succession planning.
- Describe the type of training provided in management development programs.

7-1 Gaining Competitive Advantage

7-1a Opening Case: Gaining Competitive Advantage at Tesco[1]

The Problem: Getting New Employees Properly Oriented to their Jobs

Tesco is the U.K.'s Number 1 food retailer, with more than 970 stores worldwide. It hires more than 40,000 new employees each year. Because these employees are an ultimate reflection of Tesco to its customers, they play a very important role in ensuring continued customer satisfaction on a daily basis. A major Tesco challenge is to ensure that all of these employees recognize their roles and how their actions affect the company's success. To do so, they must understand what customers expect from Tesco and why they need to project positive, customer-friendly attitudes.

The Solution: Providing an Effective Employee Orientation Training Program

All new Tesco employees are required to participate in an orientation training program. Taught by their new line managers, the program's content is presented in an informal, fun, and visual way that allows employees to "discover" the information for themselves and assimilate it to their own life experiences, making it more relevant to them and therefore more likely to be retained. The program covers the following subjects:

- The history of Tesco, its core purpose, values, goals, financial aims, marketing strategies, and customer commitment
- Information on market share and how Tesco's supply chain operates
- Customer development strategies and their importance to developing customer loyalty
- How employees can demonstrate Tesco values to customers in their everyday actions

How the Orientation Program Enhanced Competitive Advantage

According to its HR director, Judith Nelson, program feedback from the trainers and the participants has been excellent. By seeing what is important and why, the new employees are able to understand their role in keeping customers satisfied and thus help the organization meet its goals. The participants feel involved from day one and experience a sense of ownership of Tesco's core values, thus raising their motivation levels. The program also helps forge good relationships between the new staff and their managers. It makes managers seem more approachable and gives managers an insight into the new employee's personality and commitment to the job.

7-1b Linking Training and Development to Competitive Advantage

Chapter, 5, "Recruiting Applicants," and Chapter 6, "Selecting Applicants," focused on organizational efforts to recruit and select the most qualified applicants. Even if the organization hires only very qualified individuals, it cannot ensure that fully competent people will fill all jobs. In fact, such an outcome is quite unlikely. Nearly all employees, even those who were highly qualified at the time of hire, require some additional training in order to perform their jobs optimally. An organization's training and development practices ensure that the employees receive the necessary instruction.

In Chapter 1, "Human Resource Management and Competitive Advantage," we defined training and development as planned learning experiences designed to provide workers with the competencies needed to perform their current or future jobs. *Training* focuses on current jobs, whereas *development* prepares employees for future jobs. A firm's training and development practices can contribute to competitive advantage by enhancing recruitment, building worker competence, and reducing the likelihood of unwanted turnover. Firms must bear in mind, however, that training and development programs should also be cost-efficient. We first discuss these potential contributions and then discuss the issue of cost efficiency.

Enhancing Recruitment

Companies with excellent training programs stand the best chances of landing top candidates. As Motorola training specialist Judy Weins points out, job candidates are becoming increasingly interested in the type of training a company offers. With technology changing so fast, they want to know that their company will provide training to help them keep up with these changes.[2] According to management professor Bill Pomerenke, "Students are very focused on choosing the right career. . . . They know that part of their happiness in a career is to keep building on their skills. So they're interested in what type of training companies offer."[3]

Increasing Worker Competence

Training and development programs are designed to make workers better employees by bringing about permanent changes in their knowledge base, attitudes, and skills.[4] Workers who lack the needed competencies can create problems that undermine efficient operations. For example, such employees may make mistakes that require costly rework, cause the entire system to break down, or cause serious accidents.[5]

In the following paragraphs, we discuss how a firm's training and development practices can serve to increase worker competence. Because newly hired workers need different instruction than more experienced employees, we discuss these two groups separately.

Increasing the Competence of New Employees

To meet the needs of new workers, HRM departments typically offer three types of training: technical, orientation, and literacy training.

Individuals hired to fill entry-level jobs are not always expected to possess needed technical knowledge and skills because the employer assumes training responsibilities. A fire department, for example, would not expect entry-level applicants to know how to perform specific firefighter duties, such as responding to alarms, performing ladder truck operations, using a fire extinguisher, or maintaining apparatus and equipment. This expertise would be acquired during "recruit training." Selection processes in this type of situation try to identify people who are capable of successfully completing the training program. As we stated in Chapter 6, mental ability tests are often used for this purpose.

All new employees, even those with appropriate technical skills, need some sort of **orientation training** to learn about their jobs, the company, and its policies and procedures.[6] We discuss the specific content of an orientation program in Section 7-3, "The Manager's Guide."

New employees may also need literacy training. As we noted in Chapter 2, "Understanding the Legal and Environmental Context of HRM," many individuals now being hired for entry-level jobs lack basic skills in such areas as writing, basic arithmetic, listening/following oral instructions, speaking, and understanding manuals, graphs, and schedules.[7] In addition to improving job performance, literacy training often provides individuals with abilities they will need to benefit from more advanced training, such as learning how to operate a new piece of technical equipment.

Increasing the Competence of Current Workers

Current workers may also require certain types of training or retraining, classified as remedial, change-related, and developmental instruction.

Companies must face the fact that no selection process is perfect; a company may soon discover that even its seemingly most qualified applicants are deficient in some skills and may thus need **remedial training.** It may turn out, for example, that a supervisor selected on the basis of technical skills may have trouble communicating effectively with subordinates; or a professor, hired because of an excellent publication record, may lack certain teaching skills.

Workers may need **change-related training** to keep up to date with various types of changes dealing with technological advances, new laws or procedures, or a change in the organization's strategic plan. Companies also need instructional programs for developmental purposes. Developmental programs provide employees with the appropriate skills needed for higher level positions to which they may eventually be promoted. Developmental programs for managers are discussed in Section 7-2b, "Management Development."

Reducing the Likelihood of Unwanted Turnover

Some employees, often the best ones, choose to leave an organization because they are unhappy with the way the company manages its employees. A company's training and development practices can help alleviate this problem, changing poor management practices through instructional programs designed to modify the behavior of those who practice ineffective managerial styles.

Poor job performance also causes turnover: Workers may be discharged because they lack requisite job skills. Although in some instances such individuals should be terminated, training can prevent unnecessary terminations by:

- Building employee job skills, thereby improving job performance
- Improving supervisors' capabilities for managing "underperforming" workers
- Reeducating people whose skills have become obsolete, allowing the organization to assign them to new job responsibilities

Moreover, effective training programs can reduce turnover by strengthening employee loyalty. Management consultant Thomas Mahan drew this conclusion from interviews with 60,000 employees who had recently quit their jobs. He learned that turnover rates were heavily influenced by employee loyalty, which in turn was influenced by the firms' training and mentoring programs. Employees who were dissatisfied with their growth opportunities were three times more likely than satisfied employees to quit their jobs. Based on this finding, Mahan estimated that effective training programs can save a company with 1,000 employees $14.5 million per year by reducing turnover costs.[8]

orientation training Training designed to inform new employees about their jobs, the company, and its policies and procedures.

remedial training Training designed to correct deficiencies in employee skill or knowledge levels or to improve employee attitudes.

change-related training Training that enables employees to keep up-to-date with various types of changes dealing with technological advances, new laws or procedures, or a change in the organization's strategic plan.

The Cost Efficiency of Training and Development Practices

Most organizations spend a great deal of time and money on training and development because these practices can have such an important bearing on competitive advantage. Consider the following facts:

- The average employee receives 15 hours of training per year; the total amount of hours spent in training in the United States is 15 billion per year.[9]
- The average large company spends $527,000 per year on training and development; the average small company spends $218,000.[10]
- Nationwide, $51 billion is spent annually on formal training programs.[11]
- On average, 20 million employees receive employer-sponsored education each year.[12]

Employers expect (or at least hope) that these investments of time and money will return sizable dividends. Unfortunately, however, the training and development practices of many organizations fail to result in any real benefit to employees or to the company itself. The success rate of training and development practices in many U.S. organizations has been quite dismal. For instance, about half the cost of training in the typical company is wasted,[13] and only 10 percent of the material learned in training is actually applied to the job.[14]

Training and development programs have failed so miserably that they have been cited as a chief contributor to the low productivity growth in the United States:[15]

The long-term neglect to human capital in the U.S. is undermining the nation's economic future. Current industry training programs are inadequate and these inadequacies are strongly contributing to low productivity growth in the U.S.

7-2 HRM Issues and Practices

7-2a The Instructional Process

Why have the training and development practices of so many organizations failed to contribute to competitive advantage? Simply put, the way companies carry out instructional programs is ineffective. Exhibit 7-1 lists each of the steps involved in an effective instructional process, along with typical barriers to its success. We now discuss these steps and indicate how they should be carried out (i.e., how the barriers can be avoided or overcome).

Step 1: Deciding What to Teach

Obviously, training material and content must be relevant. Training programs must contain material and exercises that help participants learn the knowledge, skills, and abilities necessary for effective job performance.[16] When training programs are not job relevant, trainees will fail to acquire the skills or knowledge needed for the job. Or, possibly worse, they may wind up learning skills that are *inappropriate* for effective job performance.[17]

To ensure job relevance, an organization must carefully and systematically assess its training needs and then set training objectives designed to meet those needs.

Assessing Training Needs

training need   A problem, such as poor job performance or inadequate skill level, that can be rectified through training.

A **training need** exists when (1) employees' job behavior is somehow inappropriate, or (2) their level of knowledge or skill is less than that required by the job, and (3) such problems can be corrected through training.

Although assessing training needs seems obviously necessary, companies often skip this step as they develop training programs. Trainers often seem more interested in *conducting* training programs than in *assessing the needs* of their organizations.

> **EXHIBIT 7-1**   Steps and Barriers in the Instructional Process

Step 1: Deciding What to Teach

The program should contain material that instills knowledge, abilities, and/or skills necessary for effective job performance.

Barriers:

- Failure to perform an adequate needs analysis
- Failure to set instructional objectives
- Failure to seek input of line managers
- Overreliance on "packaged programs"

Step 2: Deciding How to Maximize Participant Learning

The material should be presented in a way that maximizes learning.

Barriers:

- Inadequate training of instructors
- Failure to incorporate principles of learning

Step 3: Choosing the Appropriate Training Method

Training method(s) must be appropriate for achieving the instructional objectives of the program.

Barriers:

- Inappropriate methods used (e.g., overreliance on lecture)

Step 4: Ensuring That Training Is Used on the Job

Trainees must correctly apply the learned material to the job.

Barriers:

- Lack of on-the-job reinforcement of new skills
- Training materials not relevant to the job
- Failure to remember material learned in training upon returning to the job
- Lack of willingness to make the extra effort to integrate learned behaviors into existing behavior repertoires

Step 5: Determining Whether Training Programs Are Effective

The training program must be evaluated to determine whether the instructional objectives have been met in a cost-efficient manner.

Barriers:

- Failure to apply the appropriate measures of training success (e.g., overreliance on trainees' self-reports)
- Failure to apply the appropriate methodology to gauge the impact of training on any changes in employee behavior

Sources: Hitt, M.A., Hoskisson, R.E., and Harrison, J.S. (1991). Strategic competitiveness in the 1990s: Challenges and opportunities for U.S. executives. *Academy of Management Executive, 5* (20), 7–22; Meals, D.W. (1986). Five efficient ways to waste money on training. *Personnel,* May, 56–58; Baldwin, T.T., and Ford, J.K. (1988). Transfer of training: A review and directions for future research. *Personnel Psychology, 41* (1), 63–105; Spitzer, D.R. (1982). But will they use training on the job? *Training,* September, 48, 105; Walton, J.M. (1989). Training: Self-reinforcing behavioral change. *Personnel Journal,* October, 64–68.

When this occurs, the programs are doomed to failure.[18] For instance, many companies assign their employees to training programs simply because such programs are "hot" (i.e., many other companies are using them), not because the programs cover topics that address important company needs.

How are training needs assessed? The particular approach chosen depends on the circumstances. In some instances, training needs are rather obvious and require very little analysis on the part of the organization. For example, when a new piece of equipment is purchased or a change in procedure implemented, employees will obviously need training on how to use the equipment properly or comply with the procedural change. When a new worker is hired, an organization will typically conduct a job analysis that identifies the job tasks. The company then develops a training program to teach the worker how each task should be performed.

In some instances, however, training needs are more difficult to identify, requiring firms to conduct rather in-depth analyses. The most difficult needs to identify are the remedial training needs of current employees. As noted earlier, employees require remedial training when they are deficient in some area (i.e., they lack information, knowledge, or skills, or they need to improve their behavior or attitudes). For example, some employees may need to improve their customer relations skills or some managers may need to learn how to better delegate responsibility.

A firm can use a number of methods to identify remedial training needs. In some cases, managers are asked to identify the remedial training needs of their subordinates. An effective method for doing this is **performance analysis,** which requires managers to identify their employees' performance deficiencies and determine which of these deficiencies can be effectively remedied through training. The how-tos of this method are described later in Section 7-3, "The Manager's Guide."

In some cases, the firm asks its employees to identify their own, job-specific training needs. Anheuser-Busch, for instance, recently implemented an online needs analysis system, called "Wholesaler Integrated Learning (WIL)." An employee can access the WIL website anytime from anywhere and take a test that measures his proficiency in

performance analysis
A method of training needs analysis in which managers identify their employees' performance deficiencies and determine which of these deficiencies can be effectively remedied through training.

job-related competencies. The test is scored instantly, at which time a screen appears indicating his weak competency areas. The system then offers suggestions on how to enhance those competencies, such as classroom training, online courses, books, and on-the-job activities. The employee is then given an opportunity to enroll online in the appropriate program.[19]

When assessing the remedial needs of individual employees through management or self-assessment, firms miss out on seeing the "big picture," that is, the training needs of all organizational employees. The big picture tells firms where the greatest training needs are. This information enables them to determine priorities. Training needs are usually prioritized base on these criteria:

- The number of employees experiencing a deficiency in a particular skill and the severity of the deficiency
- The importance of the skill for meeting organizational goals
- The extent to which skill improvement can be achieved through training

HR professionals, using any of several methods, collect the information regarding organization-wide training needs. One method consists of distributing ability inventories (see Chapter 4, "Analyzing Jobs") to employees that ask them to indicate the abilities for which they need training. Abilities identified by the greatest number of employees would go to the top of the priority list. The company then offers the employees training programs based on those needed abilities that are highest on the list.

Although the use of ability inventories can yield valuable information, the results are sometimes flawed because some employees are unwilling to admit to having training needs, and others are unaware of their needs. For instance, people with poor interpersonal skills are often unaware of this fault and would thus be unlikely to specify a need for such training.

HR professionals should thus collect additional information to supplement that obtained from ability inventories. This information can be collected by examining company records for problems that can be remedied by training, such as customer complaints, EEO charges, employee grievances, and the like. It can also be collected by interviewing a cross-section of managers (individually or in groups), conducting customer satisfaction surveys, or simply observing employees as they perform their jobs. It is best to use a combination of these methods.

Determining Training Objectives

training objectives
Statements describing what the trainees should be able to do as the result of training.

Once a firm has identified training needs, training program designers must specify **training objectives.** Objectives describe what the trainee should be able to do as the result of training. A set of training objectives used by Provident Accident and Insurance for a training program teaching telephone skills is presented in On the Road to Competitive Advantage 7-1.

Objectives provide input for the design of the training program; without clearly established criteria, trainers would be hard-pressed to achieve them. Objectives also help identify the measures of success that will be used to judge the effectiveness of the training program. For instance, Provident can evaluate its telephone effectiveness program by monitoring the participants' calls for a period of time to determine the extent to which the training objectives are being met.

Step 2: Deciding How to Maximize Participant Learning

Once the firm identifies appropriate training needs and objectives, trainers must prepare instructional materials. Before discussing the specific training methods that can be used to teach this material (which we will do in the next section), we first examine the principles that program developers should follow to ensure that learning takes place.

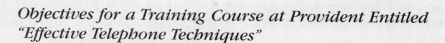

Objectives for a Training Course at Provident Entitled "Effective Telephone Techniques"

Upon your return to work following this course, you should:

1. Answer the phone promptly, by the second ring, if possible.
2. Keep a list of frequently called numbers.
3. Identify yourself at the beginning of the conversation.
4. Keep telephone message forms and a pen by your phone at all times.
5. Be informative and helpful when taking calls from others. Personalize the conversation by using the caller's name.
6. Indicate the date, time, caller's correct name, caller's number, the message, and your name when leaving a written message.
7. Inform the caller about what you intend to do prior to transferring a call.
8. Treat all calls as important and thank the party for calling.
9. Use polite terms such as "May I," "Please," and "Thank you."

When preparing training materials, one must keep the following adage in mind: "Adults can be ordered into a classroom and prodded into a seat, but they cannot be forced to learn."[20] Trainers must ensure that learning takes place. To maximize learning, the program should be presented in a way that (1) gains and maintains the trainees' attention, (2) provides the trainees with an opportunity to practice the skills being taught, and (3) provides the trainees with feedback on their performance. Exhibit 7-2 provides a more complete listing of things an instructor can do to increase participant learning.

Learner Attention

Learners must be attentive to the program. The trainer must thus design and present the program in a way that gains and maintains their attention.

> **EXHIBIT 7-2** | Applying Principles of Learning to Classroom Training

Gain the Trainees' Attention by:
1. Getting each participant involved very early in program (warm up)
2. Stressing the importance of the training program
3. Letting them know how they will benefit from training—Why is this experience important?
4. Reviewing program objectives and content

Maintain the Trainees' Attention by:
1. Varying pace and kind of material presented.
   - Avoid long lectures and periods of passivity.
   - There should be lots of participation.
   - Use a variety of methods, like cases, role-plays, and other experiential techniques.
2. Presenting material in an interesting way.
   - Use learner experience as the basis for examples and applications.
   - Make the content immediately applicable.
   - Give examples.
   - Use voice inflection.
   - Vary instructor movement.
   - Display a sense of humor.

Structure the Learning Experience by:
1. Allowing plenty of opportunity for practice (overlearning).
   - Practice should be as realistic as possible.
2. Giving feedback. Feedback should be specific and timely.
   - Videotape is helpful.
3. Providing visual images.
   - PowerPoint
   - Videos
   - Handouts
4. Emphasizing the important concepts—make key points stand out.
5. Relating new information to previously learned information.
6. Linking material to current jobs/experience.
7. Using realistic examples. Relate to their jobs. Do not use jargon.
8. Modeling desired behavior. (People learn by observing and imitating.)
9. Allowing trainees to learn from each other—group discussions/exercises.
10. Trying to make learning fun.

To *gain* their attention, trainees must realize the importance and relevance of the training. Trainers must demonstrate how the content of the program relates to their jobs and how their attendance will benefit them. For example, when offering an EEO training program for managers, the trainer could state:

> Employees who lodge discrimination complaints can cost companies thousands, or millions, of dollars. But many of these complaints can be avoided by following the advice that will be given to you in this session. So listen carefully and you can save your company lots of money and remain in good standing with your boss, as well.

Trainers can *maintain* the attention of the trainees by varying the pace and kind of material presented. They should avoid using prolonged lectures and other passive learning methods. Training programs should be presented in short segments and involve frequent opportunities for audience participation.[21] For instance, trainers can ask the group questions, give them cases to analyze, or have them role-play different situations. Trainees will also be attentive if the material is presented in an interesting way—using frequent examples, voice inflection, videos, and a sense of humor (where appropriate).

Practice

An individual cannot become proficient at a skill without practice. Consider athletes, for example. Even the most highly skilled professional athletes practice regularly. In the same way, trainees learn better when given the opportunity to practice, as evidenced by the finding that people remember about 25 percent of what they hear, 45 percent of what they hear and see, and 70 percent of what they hear, see, and *do.*[22]

Practice is essential to effective learning because it strengthens the stimulus–response bond; that is, the necessary response to a situation becomes more automatic with practice. For example, learning how to drive a car can be quite difficult. The new driver must remember so many different responses (e.g., putting on the directional signal before a turn, checking the rearview mirror before changing lanes). With practice, however, these responses become so routine that drivers begin making them automatically, without thinking.

Trainers must address two practice-related issues when designing an instructional program. One is whether the practice sessions should be distributed or massed. **Distributed practice** refers to dividing the practice into segments or sessions; **massed practice** means providing all the practice in one longer session. Distributed practice is akin to preparing for a college exam by keeping up with material on a daily basis—distributing the studying time over the course of the semester. Massed practice is akin to cramming for an exam the night before it is given. Distributed practice is usually preferred because it leads to better long-term retention.[23]

The second practice-related issue concerns the relative effectiveness of practicing the whole task or practicing one part at a time. When the material to be learned is simple, the "whole method" is generally preferable; as the material becomes more complex, it is better to divide the material into parts.[24] For instance, the whole method should be used to teach someone how to enter data into a computer because it is a relatively simple process. The "part method" should be used to teach someone how to use a word processing software program. This training should be done in parts because the trainee must learn and "absorb" the basics before learning more advanced applications.

Feedback

We often hear that "practice makes perfect," but this axiom is only partially true. Learners also need **feedback** to let them know whether their behavior is correct. Trainers should give positive feedback to trainees whenever they perform the task correctly; such feedback can be very encouraging to the trainee and thus serve as a motivator. When trainees perform incorrectly, they need corrective feedback. Such

distributed practice A training procedure in which trainees practice a skill over several sessions.

massed practice A training procedure in which trainees practice a skill in one session.

feedback Information given to trainees that lets them know whether their behavior is correct.

feedback should provide information regarding what the trainee is doing wrong and how this behavior can be corrected.

Step 3: Choosing the Appropriate Training Method

A variety of instructional methods may be used to train employees. Some of the more commonly used methods are discussed in the following paragraphs. In most training situations, these methods are used in combination. Exhibit 7-3 summarizes the various training methods and their advantages and disadvantages.

On-the-Job Training

Almost all new employees receive some form of **on-the-job training (OJT).** Unfortunately, OJT is often conducted haphazardly; in the typical OJT program, a trainee is expected to learn the job by watching an experienced worker and by asking questions. Although trainees may be exposed to some useful things, this type of OJT leaves serious gaps in employee learning.[25]

For example, a department store hires a man as a cashier and trains him by having him watch an experienced cashier for one day. The trainee is told to ask questions, if necessary. The trainee may be ill prepared for his job at the program's conclusion because he was afraid to ask questions and thus did not fully understand the whys and hows of each task. Moreover, he may not have had the opportunity to observe all the different types of transactions he may face on the job (e.g., what to do when the computer rejects someone's check). Moreover, his learning is impeded because he is just observing and not doing the tasks (no practice or feedback). Of course, learning is further impeded if the worker providing the training performs the job incorrectly or inefficiently.

A successful OJT program should be designed as follows:

1. List all the information/skills the trainees need to learn.

2. Set learning objectives.

3. Devise an OJT experience that ensures the trainee has an opportunity to observe a competent worker perform each important task of the job.

4. When demonstrating a task, the worker should explain the "hows" and "whys" to the trainee.

5. Give the trainee an opportunity to perform each of the important tasks of the job. He or she should be provided with sufficient opportunity to practice the task, accompanied with necessary feedback.

> **on-the-job training (OJT)** A training method in which trainees are taught how to perform their jobs in the actual job setting.

Job Instruction Training

A particularly effective method of OJT is **job instruction training or JIT.** JIT is a method of training developed during World War II. Because of the rapidly expanding war-related industries, organizations needed a way to quickly and efficiently train thousands of new employees, many of whom had never worked before.[26]

The development of a JIT program starts with a job breakdown, which is a step-by-step listing of how the job should be performed. Accompanying the job breakdown is a description of key points, if any, for each step. Key points, which are suggestions that will help workers perform the task effectively and safely, should address the following questions:

- Is there anything in the step that will make or break the job?

- Are there any potential dangers in the step?

- Are there any pointers for making the task easier to perform?

An example of a job breakdown and key points for changing oil in a car is presented in Exhibit 7-4 on page 184.

> **job instruction training (JIT)** A training method in which trainers demonstrate each step of a task, discuss its key points, and then provide the trainees with guided practice.

EXHIBIT 7-3	Training Methods		
Training Method	**Description**	**Pros**	**Cons**
OJT (on-the-job training)	On-the-job training involves one employee showing a newer one the skills and tasks that are needed for the job. Usually, a short amount of time is set aside for OJT.	OJT allows trainees to watch more experienced workers and ask them questions as they perform the job.	OJT is often conducted haphazardly, and new employees may feel unprepared to go out on their own. Trainees are shown tasks but do not actually do them, impeding learning.
JIT (job instruction training)	Job instruction training involves trainers showing trainees each step of a job, talking over the key points at each juncture, and guiding the trainee's practice.	JIT is a good method for teaching tasks that can be broken down into step-by-step procedures. Learners practice under the watchful eye of more experienced workers and gain confidence.	JIT is not the best method for intuitive tasks or those in which case-by-case decisions and alterations need to be made.
Lecture	A lecture is just that—a speaker presenting material, usually to a large group of workers.	Lectures are ideal for giving simple knowledge—the history of a company, for example, or a company's new vacation policy.	The downside to lectures is that the communication flows in just one way, and listeners may become bored or impatient, resulting in not paying attention and not acquiring the knowledge presented.
Cases	Cases ask trainees to read sample scenarios of events and situations they may encounter on the job and then analyze the circumstances.	Cases allow trainees to learn through guided discovery and teach them to think critically about problems.	Because trainers who use the case method to train shy away from insisting on right and wrong answers, trainees may not always receive the best guidance. In addition, case study does not provide direct practice.
Role-playing	In role-playing, trainees act out a situation and its resolution and receive feedback from the trainer and other trainees.	Role-playing is a good method for teaching better communication and interaction skills.	Role-players may make mistakes without being able to correct them, causing embarrassment and loss of self-confidence. Shy or quiet trainees may feel uncomfortable acting in a group situation.

When using the JIT method, the trainer first explains and demonstrates the task, and then allows the trainee to perform it, one step at a time. Corrective feedback is given, when necessary. The training is complete when the trainee is able to perform the task, without feedback, two consecutive times.

JIT is very effective for teaching trainees how to perform relatively simple tasks that can be performed in a step-by-step manner. Its effectiveness can be attributed to the ample opportunity trainees have to practice the task and receive helpful feedback.

Lecture

lecture A training method in which the trainer teaches a topic by verbally communicating the information.

The reader is most assuredly familiar with the **lecture** method, having endured long lectures in many classes! Most training experts criticize lectures because they are passive learning devices, focusing on one-way communication to learners who do not have the opportunity to clarify material. Lectures generally fail to gain and maintain learner attention unless they are given by someone able to make the material meaningful and promote questions and discussions.

Lectures are most appropriate for situations where simple acquisition of knowledge is the goal (e.g., describing company history during an orientation training session for new employees). However, it is not well suited to serve as the sole training method for teaching motor skills because it provides neither feedback nor the oppor-

Training Method	Description	Pros	Cons
Behavior modeling	Behavior modeling is based on the idea that workers should observe a task, practice it, and receive constant feedback until they are competent. Trainees learn the "right way" to do something the first time.	Behavior modeling captures the attention of the learner; provides clear, correct instruction; and monitors progress toward competency.	Critics of behavior modeling cite the amount of time it takes to train workers using this method.
CBI (computer-based instruction)	Computer-based instruction uses a computer to take students through tutorials, drills, games, and simulations.	The high level of interactivity in CBI results in higher levels of trainees' acquisition and retention of the materials taught, offers self-paced learning, and can be cost-saving, especially in terms of simulations.	CBI can be very expensive, and some workers may be frustrated by working with a computer instead of a live person.
Video	Video training uses video to demonstrate tasks or to present material.	With video training, users can skip over material they already know or watch a procedure several times in order to better grasp it.	Some users will find the lack of personal contact in a video training session boring, leading to a lack of paying attention and thus a lack of knowledge acquisition.
IVT (interactive video training)	Interactive video training combines video and computer technology. Trainees watch a video segment and respond via the computer.	IVT allows trainees to repeat sections until they respond to training questions correctly. Learners can replay situations that end badly until they are able to succeed. Learners can be at remote locations, and large numbers of workers can be trained at once.	IVT can be somewhat expensive and requires setup in training locations.
Web-based	Through the web, using computer software such as WebCT or Blackboard, the instructor can provide information in a number of ways, such as audio, interactive video, typed notes, and PowerPoint slides. Moreover, students can interact with the instructor and other students via the use of chat rooms.	Companies cite convenience and lower cost as their primary reasons for implementing web-based programs.	Certain subject matter, such as contract negotiations, customer service, sales, and interpersonal skills training, does not lend itself to web-based methods. Moreover, web-based training makes some participants feel isolated and out of touch.

tunity for practice.[27] For example, one could not effectively teach someone how to drive a car solely on the basis of a lecture.

Case Method

As the name suggests, the **case method** requires trainees to analyze cases depicting realistic job situations. Cases are often structured like a play that opens in the middle of a story and uses flashbacks to describe the action that led up to the opening scene, where an employee has just made a key decision. The rest of the case lays out the documentation and data available to the decision maker at the time of the decision. Questions are posed at the end of the case that ask the trainees to analyze the situation and recommend a solution. For instance, they may be asked to state the nature of the problem, identify the events that led to the problem, and indicate what the individual should do to resolve the problem. The end-of-chapter cases in this text serve as an illustration of this technique. Taking a Closer Look 7-1 provides a more detailed explanation and rationale for the case method.

The case method rests on the assumption that people are most likely to retain and use what they learn if they reach an understanding through "guided discovery." Trainers act as guides or facilitators. Cases do not typically have right or wrong answers. The aim of the method, therefore, is not to teach trainees the "right" answer, but

case method A training method in which trainees analyze realistic job situations.

> **EXHIBIT 7-4** JIT Job Breakdown for the Job "Changing the Oil in a Car"

Breakdown	Key Point
1. Determine the amount and type of oil your car requires.	Check the owner's manual for this information.
2. Raise the hood of your vehicle.	Make sure you "latch" the hood so it will remain open.
3. Locate the oil plug on your car's oil pan.	The oil pan is located on the bottom of the engine just behind the radiator. The plug has a small square protrusion on it.
4. Place a container directly under the oil plug.	The container must be large enough to catch the amount of oil your car holds.
5. Unscrew the oil plug with a pair of pliers and let the oil drain into the containers.	Use medium-sized pliers.
6. Carefully remove the container from under the car.	Make sure all the oil is drained out.
7. Replace the oil plug.	Make sure it is tight.
8. Remove the oil filter.	The cap is located on the engine valve cover. Check the owner's manual for the exact location.
9. Place a funnel in the hole where the cap has been.	Make sure the funnel is secure.
10. Pour the appropriate amount of oil into the funnel.	Check the owner's manual to determine the appropriate amount.
11. Replace the oil filter.	Make sure it is on tight.
12. Wipe any spilled oil off the engine.	Do this quickly before the oil dries.
13. Dispose of the used oil.	Most garages will accept used oil for disposal.

rather, to teach them how to identify potential problems and recommend realistic actions.[28]

Critics of this method balk at the lack of direction trainees receive when analyzing a case. What if they arrive at a poor decision? Moreover, trainees do not get the oppor-

---

> **Taking a Closer Look 7-1** *The Case Method*

Aim of Method

The aim of the case method is to teach critical thinking/problem-solving skills. The case discussion process requires students to become actively involved in their own learning, to discover for themselves rather than accept verbal or written pronouncements. That is, students discover and develop their own unique framework for approaching, understanding, and dealing with business problems by combining past experiences with present experiences in order to better understand future experiences. To grow, the individual must continually reorganize and reformulate past experiences in light of new experiences.

Teacher's Role

The teachers function as facilitators or catalysts. Their role is to provide a permissive environment for group discussion. They help students to discover for themselves the facts and ideas that are most significant to them. Students should be made to feel free to:

- Try out ideas "for size"
- Cite firsthand experiences
- Speak their mind
- Disagree with one another

Questions to Promote Case Discussion

- *Open-Ended:* What do you think is going on here?
- *Diagnostic:* Why do you think the employee became less motivated?
- *Challenge:* If the company followed your suggestion, do you think that would solve the problem? Or do you think there is more to the problem?
- Your answer is just the opposite of what Student B said. Can you persuade him/her that you're right?
- *Priority:* Which issue do you consider most important? What would you do first?
- *Action:* How would you solve this problem? How would you do that? (Keep asking "how?")
- *Generalizing:* What inferences about effective management can we make from this discussion? What were the most important points brought out in this discussion?

Taking a Closer Look 7-2 — *Role-Playing*

1. What Is Role-Playing?

A. Trainees are presented with a problem involving some sort of human interaction.
 1. Grievance handling
 2. Sales
 3. Performance review
 4. Handling difficult employees/customers
B. Problem is acted out.
C. Role-play is followed by a discussion of how well the problem was handled.

2. Types of Role-Playing

A. Single
 1. Description:
  • Two or three people role-play in front of class. Class serves as observers.
 2. Advantages:
  • Class gets to see a demonstration.
  • All parties benefit from ensuing discussion.
 3. Disadvantages:
  • Can be embarrassing for role-players if they make mistakes.
  • Class may be uncomfortable giving negative feedback.
  • Only one person actually gets practice.
B. Multiple
 1. Description:
  • Class is divided into groups.
  • Each group includes role-players and observers.
  • Observers provide feedback.
  • Then whole class discusses issue.
 2. Advantages:
  • No embarrassment of players.
  • No discomfort of observers.
  • Half the class gets practice. (Reverse roles in next role-play, so that all get practice.)
  • Whole class discussion demonstrates a broad variety of approaches that may be taken.
 3. Disadvantages:
  • Loss of trainer control.
  • Some may not take it seriously because no one outside their group is watching them.

3. Feedback—The Postenactment Discussion

A. Single role-play
 1. Get reaction of key player.
  • How did he/she think things went?
  • What problems did they encounter? How did they handle them?
 2. Get reaction of nonkey role-player.
  • How did he/she feel about the way the situation was handled?
  • Would a different approach have worked better?
 3. Get reactions from audience.
  • What are the characteristics of good problem handling in this type of situation?
B. Multiple role-play
 1. Ask observers in each group to state the outcome and the reasons for it.
 2. Have class discuss the various outcomes.

---

tunity to practice their skills. For instance, after analyzing a case involving a subordinate who has repeatedly arrived at work late, the trainees may conclude that the manager should have said something sooner and must now counsel him. However, the case method does not afford trainees the opportunity to practice their counseling skills.

Role-Playing

Role-playing as an instructional technique presents some problem involving human interaction. A detailed description of the role-playing technique and how it is implemented is provided in Taking a Closer Look 7-2. In brief, role-playing requires participants to spontaneously act out some situation, face to face.[29] The role-players are then given feedback by the trainer and the rest of the group on their performance so they may gain insight regarding the impact of their behavior on others. The issues addressed during feedback typically revolve around these types of questions:

role-playing A training method in which trainees spontaneously act out some problem involving human interaction.

• What was correct about the participant's behavior?

• What was incorrect about the participant's behavior?

• How did the participant's behavior make the other participants feel?

• How could the trainee have handled the situation more effectively?

Role-playing may be used to develop skill in any area that involves interaction between people. The method is most often used for teaching human relations skills and sales techniques.[30] Role-playing provides trainees with an opportunity to practice the skill being taught. It thus goes beyond the case method, which merely requires the trainee to make a decision regarding how to handle a situation. These two methods are often used in conjunction with one another. That is, after analyzing a case and recommending a solution, trainees are asked to act out the solution in the form of a role-play. For instance, the case regarding the tardy subordinate mentioned earlier could be followed with a role-play, where one trainee plays the subordinate and the other, the manager, who would be getting counseling practice.

Critics of the role-playing method point out that role-players are given little guidance beforehand on how to handle the transaction and thus may make mistakes, causing embarrassment and a loss of self-confidence. When their mistake-ridden role-play is finished, they sit, never getting the opportunity to do it correctly.

Behavior Modeling

behavior modeling
A training method in which trainees are shown how a task should be performed and then practice the task with feedback until they are competent.

Behavior modeling is based on the idea that workers learn best when they see how a task should be performed and then practice the task with feedback until they are competent.[31] This method is similar to role-playing in that trainees act out situations playing certain roles. The methods differ in two important ways, however. First, behavior modeling teaches trainees the "right way" to perform a task. Second, the interactions occurring during behavior modeling are practice sessions, not role-plays. The trainees practice only the right way. If they make a mistake, the trainer immediately corrects them and asks them to repeat the step correctly.

A behavior modeling program typically consists of the following steps:[32]

1. *Present an overview of the material:* This usually consists of a brief lecture that describes the objectives of the training and the importance of the skill to be learned.

2. *Describe the procedural steps:* The trainee learns the *one best* way (or at least an effective way) to handle a situation. Case and role-playing methods, on the other hand, stress the variety of effective ways to handle a situation and do not emphasize any one particular approach.

3. *Model or demonstrate the procedural steps:* The trainee is shown a "model" of how the task is to be performed correctly. The model is usually presented in the form of a videotape or live demonstration.

4. *Allow guided practice:* The trainees then practice the modeled behaviors. As we stated earlier, these sessions are similar to role-plays, except that trainees are given feedback by the instructor (or classmates) *during* the skill practice session, rather than *after.* This procedure forces the trainees to correct mistakes as soon as they are made, assuring them an opportunity to practice the *correct* way of performing the task. Practice sessions start with simple problems similar to those depicted in the model. Later practice sessions are made more realistic by adding complexity to the situation.

Behavior modeling has become very popular in recent years. Research examining its effectiveness has been quite favorable.[33] Behavior modeling works because it successfully incorporates each of the learning principles described earlier: It captures and maintains the attention of the trainees and provides ample opportunity for practice and feedback.

Computer-Based Instruction

computer-based instruction (CBI) A training method that uses a computer to instruct students through drills/tutorials, games, and simulations.

Computer-based instruction (CBI) uses a computer to instruct students through drills/tutorials, games, and simulations.[34]

- *Drills* are question-and-answer exercises where basic facts/procedures are practiced. For instance, when used to teach math, the computer provides an explanation of how problems should be solved and then presents a series of such problems. If the student answers incorrectly, the computer screen shows a *tutorial* (i.e., a written lecture) that explains the procedure more thoroughly.

- *Games* consist of a description of a situation similar to that faced on the job. The trainees are asked questions about how the situation should be handled. The computer screen then offers feedback regarding the possible consequences of their decision. For instance, trainees may be presented with a sales situation where they are asked what product features should be emphasized to the customer. The computer then explains why that choice was or was not a good one.

- *Computer simulations* train students how to operate or maintain a particular piece of equipment (e.g., airplane, missile launcher). The computer generates displays, students respond to the displays, and the computer determines if the students have performed the correct operation.

CBI has several positive features.[35] One is interactivity: The trainees' responses to questions cause different screen sequences to appear. Each move to the next level depends on the student's proficiency in preceding steps. For example, if students answer incorrectly, they may be presented with previous screens for review, or they may be given tutorial exercises.

CBI also offers self-paced learning. Because the CBI program is individualized, trainees proceed at their own pace. Thus, faster learners do not become bored, and slower learners get to spend all the time they need to master skills or procedures.

Computer simulations are advantageous because they provide a step-by-step walk-through of procedures without the cost and risks associated with training done on actual equipment. Simulators have been used heavily in the aviation and aerospace industries to train pilots, navigators, and air traffic controllers.[36]

On the negative side, CBI is quite expensive; some computer simulations cost hundreds of thousands of dollars. Student attitudes toward computers can pose an additional problem. Some suffer from "computer phobia," and some find working with a computer frustrating because there is no "live" person present to answer their questions. To illustrate this point, IBM replaced a 5-day classroom training program for managers with a 50-hour online class. Although IBM is a technology company, its managers overwhelmingly preferred the classroom to online programs for learning behavior skills.[37]

CBI can now be given on the Internet. Employees can view course descriptions, make selections, and obtain materials online. By using certain software, they can then read articles, take tests, collaborate on assignments, and engage in online discussions with one another and the instructor using email and bulletin boards. Days Inn, for instance, uses CBI Internet training to teach reservation operations, housekeeping duties, supervision, and specific skills like dealing with surly guests.[38] Graybar Electric Co., a manufacturer and distributor of telecommunications equipment, has constructed a virtual campus on the Net. The company offers more than 250 courses online to 6,800 employees in 240 locations. When workers decide to enroll in one of the firm's courses, they can view the course syllabus online, click to specific lessons to learn what the course entails, and sign up electronically. They then receive lessons and coursework online and take tests, which if passed, allows them to advance to the next level.[39]

The primary advantages of online training are cost savings (although there are significant up-front costs) and convenience, as employees do not have to be simultaneously herded into a classroom from several locations—they can complete the course at their desks at convenient times.

A primary disadvantage of Internet training is that the use of certain training methods, such as role-playing and behavior modeling, is difficult, at best. Moreover, a visible instructor is not present. As management expert James Farrell points out, the advantage of using a "live" instructor is that the instructor can:[40]

- Give participants personalized attention where they have a chance to communicate a lack of understanding and get immediate feedback
- More accurately communicate by using multiple cues, such as body language and voice inflection
- Introduce personal meaning to the situation by expressing emotion, discussing personal experiences, and eliciting personal examples from participants

Video Training

Videotapes or videodiscs have two training uses. First, they may be used to present prerecorded content to demonstrate a point. For instance, a salesperson can be shown how one would apply a particular sales approach; a surgeon can be shown a tape of a new operating procedure. We noted earlier how videotapes are used in behavior modeling as a "model" of the correct behavior. Videodiscs have interactive capabilities: Viewers can skip some segments and repeat others, and thus they are well suited for self-study instruction.[41]

Second, the video may be used to record and play back trainees' performance during the program. For instance, trainees can view their role-playing experiences and self-critique their performances.

Interactive Video Training

interactive video training (IVT)   A training method in which a TV screen and a videodisc (or videotape) player are hooked to a microcomputer, and trainees interact with the screen through a keyboard or voice command system.

Interactive video training (IVT) combines computer and video technology. IVT systems hook a TV screen and a videodisc (or videotape) player to a microcomputer. Trainees interact with the screen through a keyboard or voice command system. The trainee watches a video segment and responds to questions on the screen. Depending on the trainee's response, the program will either move on to one of several different segments or repeat the same segment until the user makes the correct response.[42] For example, Bank of America's loan officer training program uses a streaming video and audio that enables a loan officer to interact with a prospective client. The student is asked a series of questions to ascertain loan eligibility and is then given online feedback. If she asks an illegal question, for instance, a lawyer appears on screen to "scold" her.[43]

IVT works especially well when human error has grave consequences. A medical school, for instance, has used IVT for teaching diagnostic skills. Students are able to use the computer to speak to a patient on the video screen. Only by asking correct questions are students able to elicit information about a patient's marital difficulties, which may be related to her medical problem. If the patient dies because the student made the wrong diagnosis, she can easily be "brought back to life" to be worked on by other students.[44]

Many companies have begun using IVT.[45] Ford Motor Company, for instance, uses IVT with more than 4,000 dealers to teach sales, service, and product knowledge. Ninety percent of the dealers said the IVT training has improved the overall quality of their sales program.[46] Federal Express implemented several IVT programs to allow employees to learn more about their jobs, company policy and procedures, and to brush up on customer service issues.[47] Federal Express evaluated the success of its IVT program and found the following:

- Training time was reduced, compared to traditional classroom instruction.
- Large numbers of employees could be trained at remote locations.
- Travel expenses were reduced.
- Greater learning took place, compared to traditional classroom training, because the instruction was individualized.

Web-Based Training

With **web-based training,** students can download courses with a web browser or run the courses interactively while connected to the Internet using computer software such as WebCT or Blackboard. Through the web, the instructor can provide information in a number of ways, such as audio, interactive video, typed notes, and PowerPoint slides. Moreover, students can interact with the instructor and other students via the use of chat rooms.[48]

web-based training   A type of training for which students can download courses with a Web browser or run the courses interactively while connected to the Internet using computer software.

Recent surveys have found that 60 to 70 percent of all companies in the United States have adopted some form of web-based training, making it a booming, $6 billion business. Companies cite convenience and lower cost as their primary reasons for implementing these programs. It is not always feasible for a worker to leave the office and spend a day or two in the classroom. By offering web-based courses, employees can get training when they have free time during the day, without worrying about scheduling issues. The use of web-based training also lowers training costs, as companies can save a significant amount of money by cutting out travel costs, such as transportation, lodging, and meals.[49]

Web-based training does present some limitations, however. Certain subjects, such as contract negotiations, customer service, sales transactions, and interpersonal skills, do not readily lend themselves to web-based methods.[50] Moreover, web-based training makes some participants feel isolated and out of touch. Such individuals require a great deal of face-to-face dialogue with their instructors and may become frustrated when not able to do so.[51] Finally, web-based training is not as effective as classroom training in capturing the students' attention and providing needed feedback.[52] Because of these limitations, web-based instruction was rated by training experts as only the eleventh best training method (out of 20) for imparting knowledge and teaching problem-solving skills.[53] According to researcher Stephen Crow and his associates, web-based training is most effective when it uses reliable technology, teaches quantitative subjects, and when the students and instructors are computer savvy.[54]

Step 4: Ensuring That Training Is Used on the Job

Even when a company effectively develops and presents its training program, it has no guarantee that trainees will apply their new knowledge or skills to the job setting. As we noted earlier, typically only 10 percent of the training information transfers to the job. Because improved job performance is the very reason for giving training, such a lack of transfer renders a program virtually worthless. Certainly, a company gains no competitive advantage if 90 percent of the learned skills go unused.

For transfer to occur, the trainees must generalize the learned behavior from the classroom to the job context and maintain those behaviors over time on the job.[55] Trainees' failure to apply learned material once they are back on the job is partly a function of the work environment, such as productivity pressures, lack of supervisory support, and pressures to do the job just like everyone else.[56]

For example, say a manager has just been trained to conduct an employment interview by following the procedure described in "The Manager's Guide," Section 6-3 in Chapter 6. Although the manager acknowledges that the procedure is a good one, she also realizes that it takes a great deal of time (e.g., identifying KSAs, constructing a rating scale, devising questions in advance). With all her other duties, she may not have the time to do it the way she was taught and instead relies on her old approach—winging it!

Some additional reasons for the trainees' failures to transfer their training follow:

- Failure to learn the material in the first place
- Inability to understand how to apply the training information to "real-life" situations
- Lack of confidence in one's ability to perform the newly learned skill correctly

- Forgetting the material
- A temptation to regress to old, more familiar behaviors due to the trainees' unwillingness to take the time and effort necessary to integrate the new learned behaviors into existing behavior repertoires.[57]

A discussion follows of what companies can do to help ensure transfer of training to the job setting.

Overlearning

overlearning   Learning training material so well that it will be long remembered, even without frequent practice.

For transfer to occur, training material must be learned and remembered. One way to ensure this outcome is to provide the trainees with continued practice far beyond the point when the task has been performed successfully. This process is called **over-learning.** The greater the overlearning, the greater the subsequent retention and transfer. Overlearning is especially appropriate when trainees are learning skills that will not be used very often on the job, such as how to handle an emergency situation.

Matching Course Content to the Job

Another strategy for enhancing transfer is to ensure a close link between the training and job settings so that the trainees will understand how the learned material can be applied to the job setting. The use of realistic examples, role-playing, and computer simulations can help establish this linkage.

Action Plans

action plan   A plan developed by trainees at the end of a session that indicates the steps they will take on the job to apply the new skills.

The likelihood that trainees will apply newly learned skill increases when trainees develop an **action plan** at the conclusion of the training program. Such a plan should indicate the steps employees plan to take to apply the new skills when they return to the job. For instance, at the completion of a communications training program, a manager's action plan might state "Give Tom (my subordinate) feedback on his weekly report the day I receive it."[58] To help ensure trainees' commitment to their plans, they should write plans as contracts, verbally communicate their plans to the other trainees, and communicate their plans to their managers on their return to the job.[59]

Multiphase Programming

multiphase training program   A training program administered in several sessions in which trainees are given "homework" that requires them to apply that lesson back on the job and to discuss this experience during the next training session.

A **multiphase training program** is administered in several sessions. After each session, trainees are given "homework," which requires them to apply that lesson back on the job. Then they share their successes and problems with the other trainees in the next session to try to find better ways to apply what they have learned.

This approach might be used to teach managers how to give performance appraisals. In phase 1, they could be taught how to complete the appraisal forms. They would then return to the job, complete the forms on their "real" employees, and come back to the training program to discuss any difficulties they may have experienced. In phase 2, they could be taught how to provide performance feedback to their employees. They would again apply their learning to the job and return to the training program to discuss their experiences.

Performance Aids

performance aids   Devices given to trainees to help them remember training material when they return to their jobs.

Performance aids include checklists, decision tables, charts, and diagrams that trainees use for guidance back on the job. These devices trigger trainees' responses when they attempt to apply their newly learned behaviors on the job.

For example, at the conclusion of an employee discipline training program for managers, trainees may receive a card listing the eight steps to follow when disciplining an employee. The manager may then review this card just prior to disciplining an employee in order to recall the steps.

Taking a Closer Look 7-3	*Issues to Be Addressed by a Training Evaluation*

Program Content

- Did the content of the program adequately cover all the needed areas?

Program Presentation

- Was the program taught efficiently and effectively?
- Have trainees learned what they were supposed to learn?
- Do any aspects of the program need to be improved/revised?

Transfer of Training

- Did the trainees' job behavior change favorably because of the training?

Cost Efficiencies

- Did organization performance improve (e.g., improved rejection rate, decreased scrappage, reduced turnover)?
- Did the improvements offset the cost of the program?

Posttraining Follow-Up Resources

Follow-up resources include a hot-line number and instructor visits. A hot-line number is one on which the instructor can be reached in case the trainees need advice about how to apply the training material on the job. Instructors may also visit the work site to observe and assist workers as they apply learned behaviors.

Building a Supportive Work Environment

Trainees' intentions to change their job behavior cannot succeed without the support of their peers and superiors. Peer support can be gained by using a "buddy system," in which trainers pair participants and ask them to reinforce each other back on the job. Buddies provide advice and support and watch for signs of relapse.

Trainers should also encourage the trainees' managers to create a supportive environment where trainees are encouraged to apply what they have learned to their jobs. When such application takes place, trainees are more likely to retain and possibly improve proficiency on trained skills.[60]

Step 5: Determining Whether Training Programs Are Effective

When HR professionals assess the effectiveness of their companies' training programs, they engage in **training evaluation.** A company that fails to properly evaluate its training programs would not know whether the programs have met their objectives. Such a company may continue to use an ineffective program or may wrongly terminate an effective one. On the other hand, if an HR professional can present strong evidence (from an evaluation) that a training program is accomplishing its objectives, he or she may be able to continue to secure funding for it.[61]

Of the vast number of training programs offered by U.S. companies, relatively few are evaluated properly, if at all. For instance, one study reported that only 12 percent of 285 companies surveyed properly evaluated the results of their supervisory training programs.[62]

training evaluation
An assessment of the effectiveness of a company's training program.

What to Evaluate

Evaluations should determine whether training programs have met their objectives. The particular questions an evaluation should address are shown in Taking a Closer Look 7-3. Organizations must design measures to assess each of the issues mentioned here. Some measuring instruments that may be used for evaluation purposes are briefly described in the following list:

1. *Trainee reactions:* Trainees may be asked to express their opinions (either verbally or in writing) regarding the effectiveness of training at the conclusion of the program and/or when back on the job. Trainees may be asked to evaluate how relevant the program was to their jobs, how effective they found the instruction, and how much they learned.

This procedure is akin to the course evaluations provided by students at the conclusion of a college course. Although this information can be useful, its accuracy may be questionable. In many cases, the trainees paint an unduly favorable picture of the quality of the program, which is why evaluation forms are sometimes called "happy sheets."

2. *Testing:* Testing often provides a good measure of learning. The content of the tests should reflect the training objectives. Recall the objectives Provident used in its effective telephone techniques course. The firm could determine if appropriate learning occurred by giving a test based on those objectives. Questions might include these:

   - Before what ring should the telephone be answered?
   - What information should be included on a written message?
   - What should you do just prior to transferring a call?

3. *Performance appraisal:* Performance appraisal ratings (to be discussed in Chapter 8, "Appraising Employee Job Performance") can measure posttraining job behavior and thus help an organization determine whether trainees have applied what they learn when performing their jobs.

4. *Records of organizational performance:* Such measures include turnover, productivity, sales volume, and the number of grievances/EEO complaints filed. Such records may be used to determine whether the training program has had a favorable impact on the operation of the company. Records of organizational performance should be selected on the basis of their relevance to the course objectives. For example, grievance records may be an appropriate measure for determining the success of a supervisory training program on employee relations.

Evaluation Design

Training evaluations seek to determine whether participation in a training program has led to desirable outcomes, such as learning and improved job performance. Evaluations must therefore be able to detect whether the desirable outcomes have been achieved and, if so, whether they can be attributed to the training. Let's take a look at one company's efforts to design a training evaluation study.[63]

American Acme, a construction equipment firm, recently discovered that its share of the market was dwindling. A needs assessment revealed that its salespeople needed training to improve their basic selling skills—specifically, how to sell against competitors. Its entire sales force was thus put through a $200,000 training program.

To evaluate the effectiveness of the program, the company compared its sales revenues for the years preceding and following the training. Its revenues increased by $0.5 million during that period.

Was the training program effective? Not necessarily. While the training took place, American Acme also initiated a new advertising campaign and a sales bonus plan. Perhaps these initiatives were partially, or even fully, responsible for the increased revenues.[64]

To properly evaluate its training program, Acme must choose a better experimental design. A variety of designs can be used to evaluate the effects of a training program. The best designs typically include the following features:

- *Pretest:* To show the trainees' base or pretraining level of knowledge, skill, or performance
- *Posttest:* To show the trainees' posttraining level of knowledge, skill, or performance
- *Control group:* Identical in makeup to the group trained, except that these people have not received the training

A Training Program Evaluation Conducted at General Motors

General Motor's Service Parts Operations Division (SPO) was not meeting its customers' needs as evidenced by customer survey results that ranked the GM unit last out of 10 companies. To address this problem, SPO hired a consulting firm that put all SPO managers through a two-day assessment center (see Chapter 6) to identify each of their strengths and weaknesses. An individualized training program was offered to each manager, who had to enroll in one or more of the following classes (based on their diagnosed weaknesses): coaching, developing accountability, promoting teamwork, quality, safety, communications, and customer relations. SPO used the following indices to evaluate the program: (1) organizational culture (e.g., continuous improvement, interdepartmental cooperation, support from management), (2) job satisfaction among employees and managers, and (3) firm performance (e.g., schedule attainment, quality, productivity, health and safety, employee absenteeism).

Success of the training program was measured by comparing the trained and untrained units on these measures, both before (1994) and after (1996) the training. The untrained units were four plants that were similar to the one receiving the training. In other words, the company used a pretest, posttest control group design. The company found that the control group was superior on nearly all of the indices in 1994. By 1996, however, the trained group had improved dramatically, while the control group actually declined on most measures. The firm concluded that the training was successful, and further analysis revealed that the training improved overall productivity by 21 percent, resulting in savings of more than $4 million.

The use of pretests and posttests is important because they allow an evaluator to gauge whether expected improvements have occurred. For example, these measures can be used to assess whether job performance after training (posttest) is better than it was before training (pretest).

The American Acme case illustrates the importance of using a control group when evaluating a training program. Had the company used a control group, it could have determined the extent to which the increased sales were *due to training.* For instance, the company could have chosen half of the employees at random for training and used the remaining half as a control group. It could then have gauged the success of the training program by comparing the revenue totals of the two groups. If, for instance, the control group's revenues had increased as much as those of the trained groups, then one could conclude that training *did not* cause the improvement. An example of a training evaluation study conducted at General Motors is illustrated in On the Road to Competitive Advantage 7-2.

7-2b Management Development

Manager effectiveness has an enormous impact on competitive advantage. As a company grows and matures, high-quality management talent is crucial to its success. Companies must therefore provide instruction for their managers and their high-potential management candidates to help these individuals perform their current or future jobs with the utmost proficiency.[65]

Management development has long been an important component of the strategic plans in many companies. A 1981 survey of *Fortune* 500 and *Fortune* 50 companies found that identifying and developing the next generation of managers was their top human resource challenge.[66] Since 1981, this challenge has intensified, as illustrated in On the Road to Competitive Advantage 7-3.

Management development is important for new managers because these individuals really need instruction on how to perform their new supervisory jobs. Yet, companies often allow these individuals to make the transition to management with little or no training, leaving them with feelings of frustration, inadequacy, and dismay.[67]

The U.S. Postal Service

In 2001, the U.S. Postal Service was facing a crisis. Seventy percent of its 1,000 senior executives would become eligible for retirement in the next decade, and no one was being groomed to take their place. This problem was so grave that the General Accounting Office placed the postal service on its "high risk" list. In June of that year, Senator Joseph Lieberman, chair of the Senate's Committee for Government Affairs, requested that the Postmaster General develop a suitable plan to resolve this problem by the end of 2001. The postal service developed a strategic initiative called the Advanced Leadership Program (ALP), in which high-potential managers were to be identified and trained to replace the retiring executives.

In developing the ALP, the postal service identified 31 competencies that all effective leaders must possess. It then built a curriculum to teach these competencies to its high-potential candidates during a four-week residential program. Week one focuses on personal awareness. The remaining weeks cover business foundations, business decisions, and business leadership.

Participants have been very impressed with the quality of the program, voicing such accolades as "This is the best training I've ever had." The real success of the program, of course, will not be known until the graduates assume their leadership positions.

Source: Delahoussaye, M. (2002). Licking the leadership crisis. *Training*, January, 24–29.

More experienced managers also benefit from management development. Nearly 75 percent of first-line managers have their sights set on their bosses' jobs or on higher level management jobs.[68] Given these ambitions, companies need to provide lower-level and midlevel managers with formal development programs to help them in their quest to climb the corporate ladder.

Developing a Succession Planning Program

succession planning
A systematic process of defining future management requirements and identifying candidates who best meet these requirements.

As we noted in Chapter 3, " Planning for Human Resources," most organizations base their management development and training efforts on **succession planning,** a systematic process of defining future management requirements and identifying candidates who best meet these requirements.[69]

Unfortunately, many companies take a very informal approach to succession planning. Identification of high-potential candidates is largely subjective, based on the opinions of the nominating managers, who choose "fast-track" or "superstar" employees with little consideration of the actual requirements of future positions.[70]

A study conducted by Fred Luthans underscored this failure to base managerial promotion decisions on relevant criteria. Luthans found that promotions within the management ranks are often based on employee behaviors that have no bearing on managerial effectiveness.[71] Specifically, networking (i.e., socializing, politicking, and interacting with outsiders) had the greatest influence on managerial promotions. Networking, however, made no contribution to effective performance. This same study reported that effective management depended on the ability to communicate with employees and the ability to successfully engage in *HRM activities!*

Ill-conceived succession planning activities can have disastrous consequences. For example, one survey found that because many companies have done such a poor job of grooming managers for executive positions, nearly 30 percent of all newly placed executives are unprepared for their jobs and ultimately fail to meet company expectations.[72]

Elements of an effective succession planning program are described in the following subsections.

Tying Management Development to HR Planning

The first step in succession planning is human resource planning. As discussed in Chapter 3, such plans forecast human resource requirements in order to answer the question "What are the projected staffing needs for the next several years?" Based on these needs, management succession plans should specify key management positions for which staffing should be targeted.

Defining Managerial Requirements

Succession plans should next define pertinent individual qualifications needed for each targeted position. These qualifications should be based on information derived from a job analysis.

Assessing Management Potential

The next step in succession planning is to identify individuals with high potential for promotion into or through the management ranks, i.e., individuals who possess the pertinent qualifications. At this point, the organization must assess the abilities and career interests of its employees.

Companies assess employees in much the same way as they assess external candidates, using such selection devices as mental ability and personality tests, biodata inventories, and assessment centers. A key difference does exist, however, when selecting internal, rather than external, candidates—the company has much more data on each candidate. These data include records of an employee's career progress, experience, past performance, and self-reported interests regarding future career steps.

Identifying Career Paths

Next, the organization identifies a career path for each high-potential candidate (i.e., those who have the interest and ability to move upward in the organization). A career path typically appears as a flowchart, indicating the sequencing of specific jobs that may lead one up the organizational ladder to a targeted job.

Developing Replacement Charts

Replacement charts indicate the availability of candidates and their readiness to step into the various management positions. Such charts are usually depicted as diagrams superimposed on the organizational chart, showing the possible replacement candidates, in rank order, for each management position. Rank orders are often based on the candidates' "overall potential scores," derived on the basis of their past performance, experience, test scores, and so on. An example of a replacement chart for a specific management position is shown in Exhibit 7-5. The exhibit indicates that H. Johnson is the top candidate based on a job performance rating of 5 ("outstanding") and the fact that Johnson is ready for promotion right now; the other candidates need two more years of "grooming."

replacement charts Charts indicating the availability of candidates and their readiness to step into the various management positions.

EXHIBIT 7-5	Replacement Chart for the Position of District Manager

Position: District Manager

Criteria	S. Jones	B. Smith	H. Johnson
Performance in current job	4	3	5
When qualified to advance	2 years	2 years	Now
Advancement potential score	85	78	87
Rank	2	3	1

Designing the Instructional Program: Timing and Content

After the succession plan has been completed, the organization must specify the timing and content of training and development activities needed to prepare trainees for future managerial jobs.

Timing

Instruction may be given before or after the candidate has been selected and placed on the job. Both strategies have their advantages and disadvantages.

The main advantage of giving instruction prior to placement is that new managers will feel well prepared to perform their new jobs from the start. However, some problems are associated with this approach, such as the following:[73]

- *Inefficiency:* Some trainees may never be promoted.
- *Time lapse:* The value of the instruction may be lost if the length of time passing between the instruction and the job assignment is a long one.
- *Inability to relate the training to the targeted job:* Trainees may not be able to relate the instructional material to the future job setting because they have not yet occupied the job.

Because of these problems, most organizations provide instruction *after* candidates have been assigned to new jobs. With this approach, new managers have an opportunity to appreciate how the skills, examples, and situations covered in the instructional program apply to the problems they now face. The disadvantage of this approach, of course, is that the new managers will be unprepared when they assume their new jobs and may thus make many mistakes, leading to frustration and a loss of confidence.

Content

Management instruction programs should bridge gaps in what individuals already know and what they need to know for their new positions.[74] Managers need different skills at each managerial level. The instructional programs needed to produce those skills are shown in Figure 7-1.

Designing the Instructional Program: Instructional Methods

A variety of approaches are used to develop managers, including classroom instruction, career resource centers, job rotation, mentoring, and the assignment of special projects.

Figure 7-1

Instructional Needs for People at Different Managerial Levels

Source: Kraut, A.I., Pedigo, R.R., McKenna, D.D., and Dunnette, M.D. (1989). The role of the manager: What's really important in different management jobs. *Academy of Management Executive, 3* (4), 286–293.

First-Line Managers	Middle Managers	Executives
• Basic supervision • Motivation • Career planning • Performance feedback	• Designing and implementing effective group and intergroup work and information systems • Defining and monitoring group-level performance indicators • Diagnosing and resolving problems within and among work groups • Designing and implementing reward systems that support cooperative behavior	• Broadening one's understanding of how the following factors influence the effectiveness of the organization: competition, world economies, politics, and social trends

| **EXHIBIT 7-6** | Content Areas of Classroom Instruction |

- *Job duties and responsibilities:* Trainees learn what they must do to fulfill the company's expectations of them.
- *Policies and procedures:* Trainees learn company policy and procedures.
- *Employee familiarization:* Trainees become familiar with the job functions of their employees. The training provides specific instructions on how to review job descriptions, performance standards, personnel files, and so forth.
- *Attitudes and confidence:* The training attempts to establish new attitudes toward the job, employees, and the manager, and to build the confidence necessary for managers to be effective on the job.
- *Handling employee interactions:* Trainees are taught how to handle interpersonal problems effectively through such techniques as behavior modeling.
- *Career development:* Trainees learn about career opportunities in higher levels of management and how they may advance in the future.
- *General management training:* These courses typically cover labor relations, management theory and practice, labor economics, and general management functions.

- *Human relations/leadership programs:* These topics are narrower than general management programs. They focus on the human relations problems of leadership, supervision, attitude toward employees, and communication.
- *Self-awareness programs:* The content of these programs is understanding one's own behavior and how that behavior is viewed by others, identifying the so-called games people play, and learning about one's strengths and weaknesses.
- *Problem-solving/decision-making programs:* The emphasis is on teaching generalized problem-solving and decision-making skills that would be applicable to the wide range of work problems that managers encounter.

Sources: Phillips, J.J. (1986). Corporate boot camp for newly appointed supervisors. *Personnel Journal*, January, 70–74; Burke, M.J., and Day, R.R. (1986). A cumulative study of the effectiveness of managerial training. *Journal of Applied Psychology, 71*, 232–245.

Classroom Instruction

Classroom training takes place within the organization or outside, at seminars and universities. The subjects typically covered in these programs are briefly described in Exhibit 7-6.

Career Resource Centers

Some organizations make learning opportunities available to interested candidates by establishing **career resource centers.** These centers usually include an in-house library with relevant reading material. In some companies, candidates are simply given recommended readings lists; other companies provide their management candidates with comprehensive career planning guides that contain company-related information about resources available, career options, and contacts for counseling.[75] These individuals may also be provided with workbooks, where they must complete written assignments.[76]

career resource centers A location in which companies make learning opportunities available to interested managerial candidates.

Job Rotation

Job rotation exposes candidates to various organizational settings by rotating them through a number of departments. Thus, candidates have an opportunity to gain an overall perspective of the organization and learn how various parts interrelate. Additionally, candidates face new challenges during these assignments that may foster the development of new skills.

Candidates usually have full management responsibility during these assignments. For example, in one hospital, new department supervisors rotate through all major departments on a monthly basis, serving in a managerial capacity during their "tours." Although candidates learn a lot from such OJT, they may also make harmful mistakes during their learning period because they lack knowledge of the functional area they are supervising.

job rotation A method of management development in which companies rotate trainees through a number of departments to serve managers.

(Key bank mang.) program

Mentoring

Mentors are experienced supervisors who establish relationships with new managers. A mentor is usually someone two or three levels higher in the organization than the trainee who sponsors the trainee by teaching, guiding, advising, counseling,

mentors Experienced supervisors who are assigned to new managers to teach, guide, advise, counsel, and serve as role models.

and serving as a role model. Mentoring "provides members with a common value base, and with implicit knowledge of what is expected of them and what they in turn can expect from the organization."[77]

Special Projects

action learning
A management development activity in which management gives candidates real problems to solve.

Sometimes companies assign special, nonroutine job duties to candidates to prepare them for future job assignments. One such special project is called **action learning,** which derives its name from the fact that the trainees learn by doing. Candidates are given real problems generated by management.[78] Trainees might be given a written assignment that specifies objectives, action plans, target dates, and the name of the person responsible for monitoring the completion of the assignment. For instance, trainees might be asked to study the company's budgeting procedures and submit a written critique.[79]

task force   A management development activity in which a team of trainees tries to resolve an actual organizational problem.

Another type of special project is the **task force.** Trainees are grouped into a task force and asked to tackle an actual organizational problem. For example, the task force may be asked to develop a new performance appraisal form, solve a quality problem, or design a program to train new employees.[80] Trainees not only gain valuable experience serving on a task force, but also have the opportunity to "show their stuff" to others in the organization.

7-3 The Manager's Guide

7-3a Training and Development and the Manager's Job

Many line managers tend to view training and development as outside of their domain. Their function, as they see it, is solely to oversee the production of a product or the provision of a service.[81]

This view, however, is misguided. Line managers play a critical role in the training and development of their employees, as noted in the following passage:[82]

> But who is really in a better position to function as a teacher, coach, or helper than the first-line supervisor? After all, it's this individual who interacts with employees on a daily basis, who is the first to notice employees' job-related training needs, and who often possesses the skills necessary to help employees improve facets of their job performance.

Line managers' specific roles in the training and development process are described in the following section.

Providing Employee Orientation Training

As we saw in the opening case, orientation programs provide workers with information to acclimate successfully to their new jobs. During orientation, workers receive information about the company, their work units, and their specific jobs. The goals of orientation include:[83]

- Fostering pride in belonging to a quality company
- Creating an awareness of the scope of the company's business
- Decreasing new employee concerns associated with their new jobs

Line managers play key roles in orienting new employees. Specifically, it is the line manager's responsibility to:

- Provide the employee with a tour of company facilities and introduce them to key organizational members working in other departments.
- Introduce the new worker to coworkers within the department.
- Discuss the employee's job responsibilities and the manager's performance expectations of the employee.

- Explain the nitty-gritty aspects of the job of immediate concern to the employee, such as meals, breaks, parking, job procedures, and so on.

Assessing Training Needs and Planning Developmental Strategies

Managers, more than anyone, are in a position to identify their employees' training needs and suggest ways in which these needs can be met. An effective method for determining training needs is discussed in Section 7-3c, "HRM Skill-Building for Managers."

Once needs have been determined, the manager may recommend appropriate developmental activities. They may suggest, for instance, that an employee attend certain training programs. Or they may provide the employee with developmental job assignments.

Providing On-the-Job Training

In some instances, managers provide OJT for new employees. Unfortunately, many managers are negligent in this regard. The viewpoint reflected in the following passage is all too typical:[84]

> Our store managers are caught in the middle. They're afraid their customers are being neglected when they take time to train. But they also know that customers can't be properly served unless they instruct their people. It's like renewing your driver's license or getting your car fixed. There's a natural tendency to put it off.

Managers who put off training because of insufficient time or motivation usually end up spending even more time correcting the mistakes caused by untrained workers. The JIT method of training, described earlier, is especially well suited for OJT.

Ensuring Transfer of Training

A manager can help ensure that material learned in training is applied to the job by these means:[85]

- Discuss with employees what the program covered and how it can be applied to the job.
- Assign employees tasks that require them to apply the knowledge learned in training.
- Give employees coaching and feedback regarding their performance of assigned tasks.

7-3b How the HRM Department Can Help

HRM departments usually direct training and development functions. To meet the demands of this role successfully, many larger organizations create special departments, human resource development (HRD) departments, which deal exclusively with the training and development function. HRDs serve the roles discussed in the following sections.

Providing Employee Orientation Training

Orientation training provided by HR professionals focuses on organizational, rather than departmental, concerns. Topics typically covered during this HRM phase of orientation training include the following:

- Corporate history
- Corporate products and services
- The role and importance of each employee to the corporation
- Corporate policy and procedures, such as those related to pay, benefits, work schedules, overtime, career advancement, and equal employment opportunity

Most companies present this information to employees in formal group sessions during their initial employment period. HRD departments may also provide new employees with employee handbooks, which fully describe each of the preceding topics.

Contributing to Management Development Programs

HR professionals conduct a variety of assessments as part of a management development program. Assessments include job analyses (to determine career paths and needed worker competencies), tests, performance appraisal forms, and career interest inventories. HR professionals may also be responsible for developing and choosing a human resource information system (HRIS, see Chapter 3) to computerize this information.

Providing Training and Development

HR professionals often develop and present in-house classroom training programs. In some cases, it is necessary to outsource the training. When this need occurs, the HR professional must locate training programs offered by consulting firms, universities, and so forth.

Evaluating Training

Training program evaluations are usually designed and implemented by HR professionals. Evaluation efforts should be planned in advance of training so that control groups can be selected and given pretests. HR professionals also communicate evaluation results to upper-level management and recommend future program uses based on evaluation results.

7-3c HRM Skill-Building for Managers

As we stated earlier, managers are often asked to specify the training needs of their employees. We now discuss an effective way to do this.

Conducting a Performance Analysis

Performance analysis is premised on the idea that a variety of factors may cause individuals to perform their jobs unsatisfactorily. To determine the training needs of their employees, managers must identify specific causes of employees' performance problems and decide whether training or some other intervention can provide a solution.

Performance analysis often takes place in conjunction with employee performance appraisals. When conducting a performance analysis, you should follow these steps:[86]

Step 1: Examine the job requirements to determine what is expected or desired of the individual.

Step 2: Assess the individual's performance in relation to expectations.

Step 3: Analyze any discrepancy between the two and determine whether it is caused by *knowledge deficiency* or *execution deficiency*.

    a. Knowledge deficiency occurs when an employee does not know what to do or when to do it.

    b. Execution deficiency occurs when an employee fails to perform well despite knowing how to do the job. Specifically, execution deficiencies may result from any of the following factors:

- Poor feedback about employee performance and what can be done to correct the performance
- Punishment or insufficient positive consequences for doing as expected
- Task interference resulting from a factor outside the employee's control

Step 4: Implement changes for improving performance. Changes might include training, modifying consequences for various performances, changing information flow to provide better feedback on performance, and/or changing the design of certain jobs or functions.

The following example illustrates how performance analysis could be applied to examine the causes and solutions of poor teaching in the college classroom:

Dr. Mary Smith, the head of the Management Department at State University, has received several complaints about the teaching methods of Dr. Bill Pearson from students in his Management 101 class. It seems that Dr. Pearson goes over the material much too quickly and refuses to answer any student questions.

How should Dr. Smith analyze this performance problem?

Step 1: Examine the job requirements to determine what is expected or desired of the individual.

Step 2: Assess the individual's performance in relation to expectations.

We assume steps 1 and 2 have already been completed, that is, the students' complaints are valid, and thus Dr. Pearson is not meeting his performance expectations.

Step 3: Analyze any discrepancy between the two and determine whether it is caused by *knowledge deficiency* or *execution deficiency.*

Dr. Smith should analyze the cause of the problem:

The poor teaching may be the result of a knowledge deficiency; it may be that Dr. Pearson does not know how to lecture properly, or perhaps he does not possess an adequate understanding of the content of the course.

A good way to determine whether his problem is caused by knowledge deficiency is to answer the question "Could he teach effectively if his life depended on it?" If the answer were "no," then a knowledge deficiency is indicated.

If the answer to the question were "yes" (he could do it if his life depended on it), then the problem is probably an execution deficiency.

Perhaps it is due to task interference. Dr. Pearson may have so many classes to teach that he does not have the time to prepare properly for his management course.

Perhaps the problem is due to insufficient positive consequences. Dr. Smith should examine the organizational reward structure. Are rewards given for effective teaching? It may be that awards of tenure, promotion, and pay raises are given on the basis of research productivity, rather than teaching. The problem may be that Dr. Pearson is not motivated to teach well because he has chosen to devote most of his time to the performance of "rewarded" activities.

Step 4: Implement changes for improving performance.

   a. If a knowledge deficiency is indicated, training may provide a viable solution. Dr. Pearson may need to attend a seminar on effective teaching methods or he may need to take some management courses in order to become more familiar with the subject matter.

   b. If an execution deficiency were indicated, employee training would not be an appropriate solution. Instead, the university could reduce his teaching load if that were the problem. If, however, the problem were caused by the reward system, the university could introduce punishments for continued poor performance and/or rewards for improved performance.

Chapter Objectives Revisited

1. Understand why effective training and development programs enhance competitive advantage.
   - Increase the competence levels of new and experienced employees.
   - Reduce the likelihood of unwanted turnover.
   - Enhance cost leadership, ensuring training and development programs are cost-efficient.
2. Describe how companies assess their training needs.
   - Inform employees of changes.
   - Skill training for new workers: Identify subtasks.
   - Remedial training: Performance analysis, ability inventories, examining company records for problems
3. Explain how companies can present training programs to maximize learning.
   - Gain and maintain learner attention.
   - Provide trainees with opportunity for practice.
   - Provide feedback to trainees.
4. Describe the various methods of training.
   - On-the-job training (OJT): A training method in which trainees are taught how to perform their jobs in the actual job setting.
   - Job instruction training: A training method in which trainers demonstrate each step of a task, discuss its key points, and then provide the trainees with guided practice.
   - Lecture: A training method in which the trainer teaches a topic by verbally communicating the information.
   - Case method: A training method in which trainees analyze realistic job situations.
   - Role-playing: A training method in which trainees spontaneously act out some problem involving human interaction.
   - Behavior modeling: A training method in which trainees are shown how a task should be performed and then practice the task with feedback until they are competent.
   - Computer-based instruction: A training method that uses a computer to instruct students through drills/tutorials, games, and simulations.
   - Interactive video training: A training method in which a TV screen and a videodisc (or videotape) player are hooked to a microcomputer, and trainees interact with the screen through a keyboard or voice command system.
   - Web-based training: A training method in which students can download courses with a web browser or run the courses interactively using computer software, such as WebCT or Black-

board, while connected to the Internet. Through the web, the instructor can provide information in a number of ways, such as audio, interactive video, typed notes, and PowerPoint slides. Moreover, students can interact with the instructor and other students via the use of chat rooms.
5. Explain how companies can ensure that training is transferred to the job.
   - Overlearning: Learning training materials so well that it will be long remembered, even without frequent practice
   - Matching course content to job: For example, using cases, simulation, role-plays, and examples
   - Using action plans: A plan developed by trainees at the end of a session that indicates the steps they will take on the job to apply the new skills
   - Multiphase programming: A training program administered in several sessions in which trainees are given "homework" that requires them to apply that lesson back on the job. They discuss this experience during the next training session.
   - Using performance aids back on the job: For example, decision tables, charts, and diagrams
   - Using posttraining follow-up resources: Hot-line and instructor visits
6. Describe how training evaluations should be conducted.
   - Measures
     - Trainee reactions
     - Testing
     - Performance appraisal
     - Records of organizational performance
   - Evaluation Design
     - Pretests
     - Posttests
     - Control groups
7. Describe the steps involved in management succession planning.
   - HR planning: To identify targeted management positions
   - Defining managerial requirements: The qualifications needed to perform targeted positions
   - Assessing managerial potential: Using selection devices and career interest inventories
   - Identifying career paths: Indicates sequencing of specific jobs that lead to a targeted job
   - Developing replacement charts: Indicates the availability of candidates and their readiness to step into targeted positions

8. Describe the type of training provided in management development programs.

- Classroom instruction
- Career resource center: A location in which companies make learning opportunities available to interested managerial candidates
- Job rotation: A method of management development in which companies rotate trainees through a number of departments to serve as managers

- Mentoring: Using experienced upp
agers to teach, guide, advise, counsel,
role models for new managers
- Special projects: Action learning and ᵁᵉ use of task forces, for example

Review Questions

Note: You can find the correct answers to these questions by taking the quiz and then submitting your answers in the Online Edition. The program will automatically score your submission. If you miss a question, the program will provide the correct answer, a rationale for the answer, and the section number in the chapter where the topic is discussed.

1. Training needs analysis takes place during which phase of the training process?
   a. deciding what to teach
   b. deciding how to maximize participant learning
   c. choosing appropriate instructional methods
   d. determining whether training programs are effective

2. A method of training needs analysis often used to identify organization-wide training needs is
   a. performance analysis. —
   b. task analysis.
   c. ability inventory.
   d. none of the above.

3. Which of the following training program attributes is *least* effective at maintaining the trainees' attention?
   a. long lectures
   b. audience participation
   c. role-playing
   d. sense of humor

4. The method of practice that is akin to cramming for an exam is called
   a. massed practice.
   b. distributed practice.
   c. the whole method of practice.
   d. the part method of practice.

5. On-the-job training is often ineffective because
   a. employers are not willing to devote sufficient resources to it.
   b. rapid technological changes make the learned skills obsolete.

   c. it is conducted haphazardly.
   d. it fails to maintain learner attention.

6. In the typical training program, _____ percent of the training information transfers to the job.
   a. 10
   b. 25
   c. 50
   d. 75

7. Which of the following is *not* a measuring instrument used for evaluating training programs?
   a. trainee reactions
   b. control groups
   c. testing
   d. records of organizational performance

8. A systematic process of defining future management requirements and identifying candidates who best meet these requirements is called
   a. managerial planning.
   b. succession planning.
   c. executive planning.
   d. career pathing.

9. A management development trainee is asked to study the company's budgeting procedures and prepare a written technique. This type of learning technique is called
   a. job rotation.
   b. mentoring.
   c. action learning.
   d. budget analysis.

10. Overlearning is most appropriately used when teaching
    a. motor skills.
    b. verbal skills.
    c. tasks that are frequently performed on the job.
    d. tasks that are infrequently performed on the job.

Discussion Questions

1. Describe the ways in which effective training and development practices can increase worker competence.

2. What is a training need? Describe how HR professionals assess organization-wide training needs.

3. Describe three things a training instructor can do to ensure that a trainee's attention is gained and maintained.

4. Describe the method of behavior modeling. How does this method differ from role-playing?

5. What is interactive video training? Give an original example of how such a program could be used in industry.

6. What is meant by "transfer of training"? What can be done to help ensure transfer?

7. Why are pretests, posttests, and control groups important components of a training evaluation study?

8. Briefly describe the steps involved in succession planning.

9. Describe three methods of management training done outside the classroom. Describe the roles of the manager and the HR professional regarding orientation training.

10. What is a performance analysis? Describe the steps involved.

Experiential Exercises

Developing and Implementing a JIT Program

1. Divide into groups of five.

2. Each group should choose a training topic. Pick one that would take about 15 minutes to teach; make it one that most other people would not know how to do. Some examples are shooting a free throw, putting, serving in tennis, changing a diaper, tying a tie, or giving CPR.

3. Develop a job breakdown of the task, that is, a step-by-step JIT training guide.

4. List the key points associated with each step.

5. Deliver the training program in class. Choose a trainee from another group. It should be someone who does not know how to do this task. Train that person following the five-step process described in the text.

Developing an Orientation Program for Freshmen

1. Divide into groups of five.

2. Pretend that your group has been asked to develop an orientation session for freshmen business majors at your school. This orientation program will be given to them the week before classes start.

3. Your group must perform the following tasks:
   - List the topics that should be covered during the program.
   - Indicate how these topics will be taught (e.g., lecture, walking tour, PowerPoint, etc.).

4. The instructor will lead a class discussion of the value of orientation training. Be prepared to discuss the advantages of providing freshmen with orientation training. Do you think that orientation programs hold the same advantages at the workplace?

Case

Delivering Bread at the Helton Baking Company

Three brothers founded the Helton Baking Company more than 50 years ago. Since then, Helton has become a very large, diversified company, manufacturing over 1,000 different food products. Helton employs more than 10,000 people and covers about 23 states, nationwide.

One of the key jobs at Helton is that of bread deliverer. When hired, deliverers are assigned a territory and given a list of customers within that territory. It is their job to deliver bread products and take new orders.

All new employees receive skills training upon entering the job. The training, which lasts one week, is given one on one with the district manager. The trainee accompanies the manager on what will become his or her route. The trainee is expected to observe and remember the activities performed by the district manager at the various stops along the route. During the stops, the trainee's main responsibilities are to observe and to help the manager complete the necessary tasks.

There is considerable driving time between stops, giving the manager an opportunity to answer all the questions asked and to quiz the trainee on details that must be remembered regarding such things as paperwork and the order of stops. The manager also uses this time to review with the trainee various situations that might arise and state how they may be handled correctly.

In the second week, trainees are on their own. They are told to phone the manager if any questions arise on their routes.

Questions

1. Analyze the effectiveness of this training program. In what ways does it successfully follow the steps in the instructional process? In what ways does it fall short?

2. How would you redesign the program to make it more effective? Be specific in your recommendations. Include a rationale for each of your suggestions.

References

1. Whitelock, N. (2003). Tesco's new recruits see the big picture. *Training & Management Development Methods, 17* (1), 801–805.
2. Olesen, L. (1999). What makes employees stay? *Training and Development, 53* (10), 48–52.
3. Ibid.
4. Noe, R.A. (1986). Trainees' attributes and attitudes: Neglected influences on training effectiveness. *Academy of Management Review, 11* (4), 736–749.
5. Helfgott, R.B. (1988). Can training catch up with technology? *Personnel Journal*, February, 67–71.
6. Ostroff, C., and Kozlowski, S.W. (1992). Organizational socialization as a learning process: The role of information acquisition. *Personnel Psychology, 45* (4), 849–874.
7. Kelly, D. (1992, May 19). New hires lacking in basic job skills. *USA Today*, 6D.
8. Olesen. What makes employees stay?
9. Noe. Trainees' attributes and attitudes.
10. Calvert, R. (1985). Training America: The numbers add up. *Training and Development Journal*, November, 35–37.
11. Glavin, T. (2003). 2003 industry report. *Training, 40* (9), 21–38.
12. Mayadas, A.F. (1997). Online networks build time savings into employee education. *HRMagazine*, October, 31–35.
13. Meals, D.W. (1986). Five efficient ways to waste money on training. *Personnel*, May, 56–58.
14. Baldwin, T.T., and Ford, J.K. (1988). Transfer of training: A review and directions for future research. *Personnel Psychology, 41* (1), 63–105.
15. Hitt, M.A., Hoskisson, R.E., and Harrison, J.S. (1991). Strategic competitiveness in the 1990s: Challenges and opportunities for U.S. executives. *Academy of Management Executive, 5* (20), 7–22.
16. Ford, K.J., and Wroten, S.P. (1984). Introducing new methods for conducting training evaluation and for linking training evaluation for program redesign. *Personnel Psychology, 37*, 651–663.
17. Baldwin and Ford. Transfer of training.
18. Goldstein, I.L. (1986). *Training in Organizations* (2nd ed.). Monterey, CA: Brooks/Cole.
19. Tyler, K. (2002). Taking e-learning to the next step. *HRMagazine*, February, 57–61.
20. Zemke, R., and Zemke, S. (1981). 30 things we know for sure about adult learning. *Training*, June, 45–52.
21. Cartwright, SR. (1992). Produce award-winning training videos. *HRMagazine*, January, 58–62.
22. Donahue, T.J., and Donahue, M.A. (1983). Understanding interactive video. *Training and Development Journal*, December, 26–31.
23. Baldwin and Ford. Transfer of training.
24. Ibid.
25. Kello, J.E. (1986). Developing training step-by-step. *Training and Development Journal*, January, 50–52.
26. Gold, L. (1981). Job instruction: Four steps to success. *Training and Development Journal*, September, 28–32.
27. Goldstein. *Training in Organizations*.
28. Kelly, H. (1983). Case method training: What it is, how it works. *Training*, February, 46–49.
29. Wohlking, W. (1976). Role-playing. In R.L. Craig (ed.). *Training and Development Handbook* (2nd ed.). New York: McGraw-Hill.
30. Ibid.
31. Goldstein, A.P., and Sorcher, M. (1974). *Changing Supervisory Behavior.* New York: Pergamon Press.
32. Zemke, R. (1982). Building behavior models that work—the way you want them to. *Training*, January, 22–27.

33. Burke, M.J., and Day, R.R. (1986). A cumulative study of the effectiveness of managerial training. *Journal of Applied Psychology, 71*, 232–245.

34. Kearsly, G. (1984). *Training and Technology.* Reading, MA: Addison-Wesley.

35. Granger, R.E. (1989). Computer-based training improves job performance. *Personnel Journal*, June, 116–123.

36. Kearsly. *Training and Technology.*

37. Lewis, N.J., and Orton, P. (2000). The five attributes of innovative e-learning. *Training and Development, 54* (6), 47–51.

38. Roberts, B. (1998). Training via the desktop. *HRMagazine*, August, 99–104.

39. Greengard, S. (1998). Going for distance. *Industry Week*, May 4, 22–29.

40. Farrell, J.N. (2000). Long live c-learning. *Training and Development, 54* (9), 43–46.

41. Kearsly. *Training and Technology.*

42. Broderick, R. (1982). Interactive video: Why trainers are tuning in. *Training*, November, 46–53.

43. Dobbs, K. (2000). What the online world needs now: Quality. *Training, 37* (9), 84–90.

44. Ruhl, M.J., and Atkinson, K. (1986). Interactive video training: One step beyond. *Personnel Administrator*, October, 66–76.

45. Donahue and Donahue. Understanding interactive video.

46. Ibid.

47. Wilson, W. (1994). Video training and testing supports customer service goals. *Personnel Journal*, June, 47–50.

48. Kaupins, G. (2002). Trainer opinions of selected computer-based training methods. *Journal of Education for Business, 77* (6), 319–323.

49. Ouellette, T. (1999). Training: Pros and cons. *Computerworld, 33* (17), 61–62.

50. Meyers, C. (1998). Catch the e-train. *Successful Meeting, 47* (9), 11.

51. Crow, S.M., Cheek, R.G., and Hartman, S.J. (2003). Anatomy of a train wreck: A case study in the distance learning of strategic management. *International Journal of Management, 20* (3), 335–339.

52. Ouellette. Training.

53. Kaupins. Trainer opinions.

54. Crow et. al. Anatomy of a train wreck.

55. Wilson. Video training.

56. Spitzer, D.R. (1982). But will they use training on the job? *Training*, September.

57. Ibid.

58. Walton, J.M. (1989). Self-reinforcing behavior change. *Personnel Journal, 68* (10), 64–68.

59. Spitzer. But will they use training.

60. Ford, J.K., Quinones, M.A., Sego, D.J. and Sorra, J.S. (1992). Factors affecting the opportunity to perform trained tasks on the job. *Personnel Psychology, 45* (3), 511–527.

61. Ibid.

62. Bell, J.D., and Kerr, D. L. (1987). Measuring training results. *Training and Development Journal*, January, 70–73.

63. Adapted from Kearsly. *Training and Technology.*

64. Ibid.

65. Kleiman, L.S., and Faley, R.H. (1992). Identifying the training needs of managers in high technology firms: A case study. In L.R. Gomez-Mejia and M.W. Lawless (eds.). *Advances in Global High-Technology Management* (Vol. 1). Greenwich, CT: JAI Press.

66. Lee, C. (1981). Identifying and developing the next generation of managers. *Training*, October, 36–39.

67. Phillips, J.J. (1986). Corporate boot camp for newly appointed supervisors. *Personnel Journal*, January, 70–74.

68. Phillips, J.J. (1986b). Four practical approaches to supervisors' career development. *Personnel, 63*, March, 13–15.

69. Walker, J.W. (1980). *Human Resource Planning.* New York: McGraw-Hill.

70. Ibid.

71. Luthans, F. (1988). Successful vs. effective real managers. *The Academy of Management Executive, 11* (2), 127–132.

72. Duda, H. (1992). The honeymoon is over for corporate America. *HRMagazine*, February, 66–72.

73. Phillips, J.J. Corporate boot camp.

74. Walker, J.W. (1980). *Human Resource Planning.*

75. Phillips, J.J. Four practical approaches.

76. Phillips, J.J. (1986c). Training supervisors outside the classroom. *Training and Development Journal*, February, 46–49.

77. Wilson, J.A., and Elman, N.S. (1990). Organizational benefits of mentoring. *Academy of Management Executive, 4* (4), 88–102.

78. Raelin, J.A., and LeBien, M. (1993). Learn by doing. *HRMagazine*, February, 61–70.

79. Adapted from Fraser, R.F. (1977). *Executive Work Assignments.* Hyattsville, MD: United States Department of Agriculture.

80. Phillips. Training supervisors.

81. Day, D. (1988). A new look at orientation. *Training and Development Journal*, January, 18–23.

82. Ibid.

83. Berger, S., and Huchendorf, K. (1989). Ongoing orientation at Metropolitan Life. *Personnel Journal*, December, 28–35.

84. Gold, L. Job instruction.

85. Zorn, T.E. (1984). A roadmap for managers as developers. *Training and Development Journal*, July, 71–73.

86. Rummler, G.A. (1976). The performance audit. In R.L. Craig (ed.). *Training and Development Handbook.* New York: McGraw-Hill.

Appraising Employee Job Performance

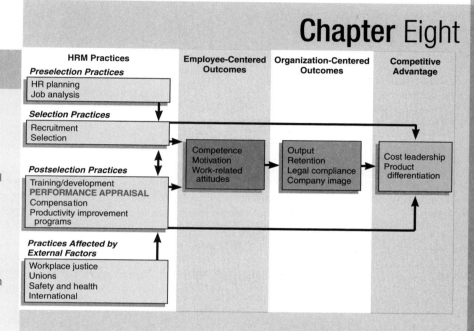

Key Terms

360-degree feedback	implicit personality theory
behavior observation scale (BOS)	leniency error
behaviorally anchored rating scale (BARS)	management by objectives (MBO)
central tendency error	paired comparison
criterion contamination	performance appraisals
criterion deficiency	performance standards
employee comparison systems	recency error
forced distribution	relevance
graphic rating scale (GRS)	severity error
halo effect	simple rankings

Chapter Objectives

Upon completion of this chapter, you will be able to:

- Understand how effective performance appraisal systems enhance competitive advantage.
- Specify the standards an effective performance appraisal system must meet.
- Describe the different types of appraisal rating instruments.
- Explain how a firm should develop its performance appraisal system.

8-1 Gaining Competitive Advantage

8-1a Opening Case: Gaining Competitive Advantage at McKesson Information Solutions[1]

The Problem: An Inadequate Performance Appraisal System

McKesson Information Solutions, a healthcare software company, was experiencing severe HR-related problems—a 23 percent turnover rate, low employee satisfaction and morale, and a multitude of customer service problems. As noted by its vice president of HR, Terry Geraghty, "From an HR perspective, we were in crisis mode." The company's problem was attributable to the fact that it had just completed 20 acquisitions to become the largest healthcare IT company in the industry. As a result, there were at least 17 different formal performance appraisal systems floating around. Geraghty's goal was to build a single system that would form the glue to hold the company together.

The Solution: Develop an Effective Performance Appraisal System

The company developed a performance appraisal system that requires each employee to have six to 10 objectives that relate to their individual jobs. The employee and manager agree on the top three or four objectives that will have the greatest impact on the employee's success during the year. Managers measure and track those objectives using a web-based system and provide their employees with coaching throughout the year. At year's end, managers rate their employees on a one-to-five scale.

The system did not work smoothly in its first year of operation, as managers rated over 70 percent of their employees as exceeding their job expectations. Unfortunately, the firm's business results did not suggest that level of employee success. In an attempt to hold down the number of inflated ratings, Geraghty modified the system so that managers were now required to place the following percentage of their employees in each rating category.

1 = Significantly exceeds expectations	(7 percent)
2 = Exceeds expectations	(23 percent)
3 = Expectations fully met	(55 percent)
4 = Met some, but not all expectations	(10 percent)
5 = Did not meet expectations	(5 percent)

Managers were permitted to exceed these guidelines if such ratings were justified by business results. But, as Geraghty notes, managers would be hard pressed to justify "generous" ratings if their departments were struggling. The success of the new appraisal was also hindered by the fact that managers were not effectively giving their

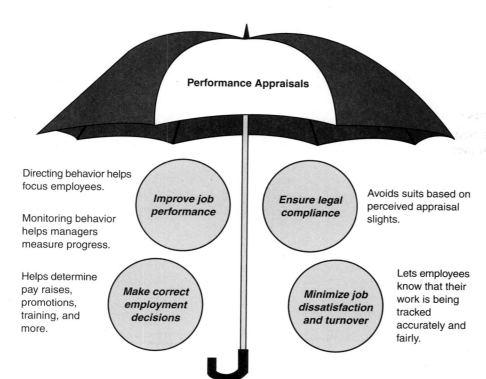

Directing behavior helps focus employees.

Monitoring behavior helps managers measure progress.

Helps determine pay raises, promotions, training, and more.

Avoids suits based on perceived appraisal slights.

Lets employees know that their work is being tracked accurately and fairly.

Figure 8-1
Performance Appraisals Can Help Assess the Quality of Employee Performance

employees constructive feedback that would improve their job performance. According to Geraghty, "Our managers must have the guts to sit down with someone and tell them that they do not meet all their expectations and here's what they need to do." To achieve this aim, the company now requires its managers to attend annual training where they are taught how to provide effective performance feedback to their employees.

How the New Performance Appraisal System Enhanced Competitive Advantage

Since fine-tuning its new performance appraisal system, the company has gone from "crisis to celebration." The workforce has become much more motivated as employees now understand what is expected of them and receive feedback on how they can more effectively meet those expectations. The new system has also enhanced the employees' job satisfaction levels, resulting in improved retention rates. Turnover has dropped in each of the 31 months that the system has been in place. Because of the high levels of employee motivation and job satisfaction, the company now ranks #52 nationwide in *Computerworld's* top 100 places to work in IT. The *Atlanta Chronicle* ranks the company as the second best place to work in Atlanta.

8-1b Linking Performance Appraisal to Competitive Advantage

Performance appraisals should accurately assess the quality of employee job performance. The opening case illustrates some of the possible ways in which an effective appraisal system can lead to competitive advantage. We now take a closer look at the connection between effective performance appraisals and a firm's overall competitive position (see Figure 8-1).

performance appraisals
Assessments of employees' job performance levels.

Improving Job Performance

An effective performance appraisal system can create competitive advantage by improving employee job performance in two ways: by directing employee behavior

A Performance Appraisal's Powerful Effect on Steering Managers' Behavior toward Organizational Goals

A company decided to stress EEO considerations as one of its strategic goals. The HRM department set up goals and timetables for achieving EEO aims for each department. Yet, these goals were not being met. Then, in a "stroke of genius," an HR professional made the suggestion to include EEO compliance as an item on each manager's performance appraisal form (good appraisals could lead to a variety of perks, such as promotion and salary increases). This simple change in the appraisal system had a dramatic effect—within a year, the company experienced a "miraculous" turnaround and started moving closer to meeting its EEO goals.

toward organizational goals and by monitoring that behavior to ensure that goals are met.

Directing Behavior

A good performance appraisal system reinforces an organization's strategic business plan by focusing attention on employees' progress toward meeting their portion of the plan. In effect, the appraisal system lets employees know what is expected of them and thus channels their behavior in proper directions, as illustrated in On the Road to Competitive Advantage 8-1.[2] Another illustration can be seen in the opening case, where the new appraisal system is helping the employees focus their behavior on their most important performance objectives.

Monitoring Behavior

Second, a good performance appraisal system gives managers a way to monitor their subordinates' job performances systematically and, hence, measure adherence to the strategic business plan. Such monitoring enables managers to motivate workers whose performance is "on target" by recognizing and rewarding their good job performance. Further, managers can use performance appraisals to improve employee performance, if unsatisfactory, by identifying and correcting any performance problems. In the opening case, for instance, the company uses a web-based system to track employees' performance on each goal.

Making the Correct Employment Decisions

Performance appraisal systems often yield information for making employment decisions, like pay raises, promotions, discharges, demotions, transfers, training, and the completion of probationary periods. The use of performance appraisal for determining pay raises is discussed in Chapter 10, "Implementing Productivity Improvement Programs." As we shall see, pay decisions based on accurate appraisals can enhance competitive advantage by improving employee morale and motivation.

The use of an effective performance appraisal system for making promotion decisions can enhance competitive advantage by ensuring that promoted employees are competent to assume the duties of the new position, and thus will do a good job.

Ensuring Legal Compliance

As we stressed in Chapter 6, "Selecting Applicants," basing selection decisions on invalid criteria can trigger costly EEO lawsuits. "Selection" decisions based on performance appraisals that may trigger such suits are demotions, failure to promote, layoffs, and discharges.

If such a suit is lodged, the employer must convince the court that the decision made regarding the individual's employment status was a fair one; i.e., it was based on an accurate assessment of job performance. For example, in *U.S. v. City of Chicago*, a judge ruled against the employer because he believed that the appraisals in question were not a fair measure of the employee's suitability for promotion.[3]

Organizations can minimize costly performance appraisal-related litigation by using performance appraisal systems that result in accurate and fair ratings. The legal criteria for judging accuracy and fairness relate to our discussion from Chapter 2, "Understanding the Legal and Environmental Context of HRM," and are spelled out later in this chapter.

Minimizing Job Dissatisfaction and Turnover

Employees can get quite emotional and discouraged if they receive ratings that they perceive as being inaccurate and unfair. For example, on receiving such a rating, an employee of a California-based company stormed out of his supervisor's office in a rage. He later returned with a pistol and fatally wounded his supervisor.

Although employee reactions are rarely this extreme (fortunately), poorly conceived appraisal systems cause morale and turnover problems. Most employees believe that rewards such as pay raises and promotions should be given on the basis of merit or past performance. Individuals may become quite upset when some other basis (e.g., favoritism) is used, and they may begin to look elsewhere for employment.

On the other hand, an effective appraisal system can help employers retain their employees, especially the best ones. Why? Because such employees desire to work in an atmosphere they perceive as being fair, progressive, and dynamic, and an effective performance appraisal system fosters this perception.[4]

8-2 HRM Issues and Practices

8-2a Standards for Effective Performance Appraisal Systems

It should now be clear that a good performance appraisal system can greatly benefit an organization. Developing and implementing such a system is no easy task, however. The McKesson Information Solutions system took much time to develop and required the joint cooperation of company managers and employees to implement.

In actual practice, most appraisal systems fail to achieve the success realized by McKesson Information Solutions. For instance, one study found that a majority of companies (65 percent) are dissatisfied with their performance appraisal systems.[5] Another study found that 90 percent of the HR professionals and business executives interviewed believed that their firms' performance appraisal systems needed reform.[6]

A third study found that only 20 percent of employees surveyed believed that their firms' performance appraisal systems actually helped poorly performing employees improve their job performance.[7] Why are effective performance appraisal systems so rare? Exhibit 8-1 lists problems with performance appraisal systems identified by a variety of experts. We discuss these problems, and how they can be avoided, throughout the chapter. First, we examine the technical and legal standards for performance appraisal systems and the problems associated with achieving these standards.

The Quality of the Rating Form

In the vast majority of organizations, managers rate employee job performance on a standardized form. As we shall see later in the chapter, a variety of forms exist, but not all of them work equally well. To be effective, the form must be relevant, and the rating standards must be clear.

EXHIBIT 8-1	Problems Plaguing Existing Appraisal Systems

Findings from Study 1
- Use of only one rater
- No opportunity for employees to review their ratings
- No appeals system
- No rater training
- No written instructions on how to complete rating forms
- Failure to base appraisal instrument on job analysis

Findings from Study 2
- Lack of management commitment to appraisal system
- Poor communication between superiors and subordinates
- Poor feedback skills of appraisers
- Poor observational skills of appraisers

Findings from Study 3
- Managers unwilling to devote sufficient time for ratings
- Managers rewarding seniority and loyalty, not performance
- Managers defining success differently from one another
- Failure to isolate a worker's role in success

Sources: Findings from Study 1: Bernardin, H.J., and Klatt, L.A. (1985). Managerial appraisal systems: Has practice caught up to state of the art? *Personnel Administrator, 30,* 79–86. Findings from Study 2: Banks, C.G., and Murphy, K.R. (1985). Toward narrowing the research practice gap in performance appraisal. *Personnel Psychology, 38,* 335–346. Findings from Study 3: Schneier, C.E., Beatty, R.W., and Baird, L.S. (1986). How to construct a successful performance appraisal system. *Training and Development Journal,* April, 38–42.

Relevance

relevance The degree to which the rating form includes necessary information.

Relevance refers to the degree to which the rating form includes necessary information, that is, information that indicates the level or merit of a person's job performance. To be relevant, the form must:

- Include all the pertinent criteria for evaluating performance.
- Exclude criteria that are irrelevant to job performance.

criterion deficiency The omission of pertinent performance criteria on a rating form.

The omission of pertinent performance criteria is referred to as **criterion deficiency.** An example would be an appraisal form that rated the performance of police officers solely on the basis of the number of arrests made. This criterion is deficient because it fails to include other aspects of the job performance, such as conviction record, court performance, number of commendations, and so on. Such a "deficient" form may steer employee behavior away from organizational goals.[8] For instance, the police officer may focus on arrests and neglect other important duties.

criterion contamination The inclusion of irrelevant performance criteria on a rating form.

When irrelevant criteria are included on the rating form, **criterion contamination** occurs, causing employees to be unfairly evaluated on factors that are irrelevant to the job. For example, criterion contamination would occur if an auto mechanic were evaluated on the basis of personal cleanliness, despite the fact that this characteristic has nothing to do with effective job performance.

Clear Performance Standards

performance standards The level of performance that an employee is expected to achieve.

Performance standards indicate the level of performance an employee is expected to achieve. Such standards should be clearly defined so that employees know exactly what the company expects of them. For instance, the standard "load a truck within one hour" is much clearer than "work quickly." Not only does the use of clear performance standards help direct employee behavior, but it also helps supervisors provide more accurate ratings; for instance, two supervisors may disagree on what the term "quickly" means, but both attribute the same meaning to "one hour."

EXHIBIT 8-2	Rating Errors and the Likely Causes

	Causes					
Errors	**A**	**B**	**C**	**D**	**E**	**F**
Leniency		X		X		X
Severity		X		X		
Central tendency	X	X				
Halo		X				X
Implicit personality theory					X	
Recency			X			

A = Administrative procedures
B = Poorly defined rating standards
C = Memory decay
D = Political considerations
E = Incomplete information
F = Rater's lack of conscientiousness

Accuracy of the Ratings

Accurate ratings reflect the employees' actual job performance levels. Employment decisions that are based on inaccurate ratings are not valid and would thus be difficult to justify if legally challenged. Moreover, employees tend to lose their trust in the system when ratings do not accurately reflect their performance levels, causing morale and turnover problems.[9]

Unfortunately, accurate ratings seem to be rare. Inaccuracy is most often attributable to the presence of rater errors. These errors and their causes are illustrated in Exhibit 8-2 and discussed in the following subsections.

Leniency and Severity Errors

Leniency error occurs when raters provide ratings that are unduly high; **severity error** occurs when ratings are unduly low. When raters make these errors, a firm is unable to provide its employees with useful feedback regarding their performance. An employee who receives a lenient rating, for instance, may be lulled into thinking that performance improvement is unnecessary. Severity errors, on the other hand, can create morale/motivation problems and possibly lead to discrimination lawsuits.

Why do appraisers distort their ratings in an upward or downward direction? Some do it for political reasons; that is, they manipulate the ratings to enhance or protect their self-interests.[10] For instance, a recent study examining the performance appraisal practices of 60 executives found that nearly all appraisals were influenced by political considerations.[11] The reasons given for purposely assigning lenient and severe ratings are shown in Exhibit 8-3.

In other instances, leniency and severity come about from raters' lack of conscientiousness. Raters may allow personal feelings to affect their judgments. For example, a lenient rating may be given simply because the rater likes the employee.[12] Conversely, severe ratings may be given out of a dislike for an individual, perhaps due to personal bias. For example, a male appraiser may underrate a highly performing female employee because she threatens his self-esteem; a disabled employee may receive an unduly low rating because the employee's presence makes the appraiser feel embarrassed and tense; or an appraiser may provide harsh ratings to minorities out of a fear and distrust of people with different nationalities or skin color.[13]

Central Tendency Error

Central tendency error occurs when appraisers purposely avoid giving extreme ratings even when such ratings are warranted. For example, when rating subordinates on a five-point scale, an appraiser would avoid giving any ones or fives. When this error occurs, all employees end up being rated as average or near average, and the employer is thus unable to discern who its best and worst performers are.

leniency error　Ratings that are unduly favorable.

severity error　Ratings that are unduly unfavorable.

central tendency error　Rating employees in the middle of the rating scale when more extreme ratings are warranted.

> **EXHIBIT 8-3** Reasons Given for Politically Motivated Ratings

Appraisers stated that they gave *lenient ratings* in order to:

- Maximize a subordinate's merit pay raise.
- Encourage a subordinate whose performance suffered because of personal problems.
- Protect an employee whose appraisal would be seen by others outside the organization.
- Prevent a written record of poor performance from becoming part of the employee's permanent record.
- Avoid possible confrontations with subordinates who would be displeased if given low ratings.
- Encourage employees who have only recently begun to perform well.
- Rid the manager's staff of a poor performer by helping him or her get promoted.

Appraisers stated they gave *severe ratings* in order to:

- Motivate the employee to perform even better.
- Show rebellious employees who is in charge.
- Encourage a subordinate to leave the organization.
- Serve as documentation of poor performance for a planned termination.

Source: Longenecker, C.O., Sims, H.P., and Gioia, D.A. (1987). Behind the mask: The politics of employee appraisal. *The Academy of Management Executive, 1,* 183–193.

Central tendency error is likely to occur as the result of administrative procedures. That is, it frequently occurs when an organization requires appraisers to provide extensive documentation to support extreme ratings. The extra paperwork often discourages appraisers from assigning high or low ratings. Central tendency errors also occur when the end points of the rating scale are unrealistically defined (e.g., a "five" means "the employee can walk on water"; a "one" means "the employee would drown in a puddle").

Halo Effect

halo effect Ratings on each scale are influenced by the appraiser's overall impression of an employee.

Appraisals are also subject to the **halo effect,** which occurs when an appraiser's overall impression of an employee is based on a particular characteristic, such as intelligence or appearance. When rating each aspect of employees' work, raters may be unduly influenced by their overall impression. For example, a rater impressed by an employee's intelligence may overlook some deficiencies and give that employee all fives on a five-point scale; an employee perceived to be of average intelligence may be given all threes.

The halo effect acts as a barrier to accurate appraisals because those guilty of it fail to identify specific strengths and weaknesses of their employees. As indicated in Exhibit 8-2, the halo effect occurs most often when the rating standards are vague and the rater fails to conscientiously complete the rating form. For instance, the rater may simply go down the form checking all fives or all threes.

The Rater's Use of Implicit Personality Theory

Sometimes raters cannot observe all aspects of a worker's performance and thus must "fill in the blanks" when completing the rating form. When this situation arises, a rater may first classify the employee according to perceived personality type (e.g., a conscientious person, a lazy person, a devious person). The rater then estimates how well that "type of person" would perform the unobserved behavior being rated.

implicit personality theory A rater's personal theory of how different types of people behave in certain situations.

The rater's estimation, based on a personal "theory" of how different types of people behave in certain situations, is called an **implicit personality theory.**[14] Consider the following example:

Let's assume that a rater has observed that the employee always comes to work early. Based on that observation, the appraiser classifies this individual as a conscientious person. When rating a specific aspect of this individual's performance that the rater has not observed, such as "attention to detail," the rater relies on his or her implicit personality theory of what a "conscientious person" is like. If the rater believes that conscientious people pay close attention to detail, he or she would give the worker a high rating on that aspect of performance.

This rating error causes problems similar to those caused by the halo effect. When raters make assumptions based on their implicit personality theories, the organization is unable to identify employees' specific strengths and weaknesses. For instance, in the preceding example, if attention to detail had been a weakness of the employee, it would have gone undetected.

Recency Error

Most organizations require that employee performance be assessed once a year. When rating an employee on a particular characteristic, a rater may be unable to recall all of the employee's pertinent job behaviors that have taken place during that rating period. The failure to recall such information is called memory decay.[15] The usual consequence of memory decay is the occurrence of **recency error;** that is, that ratings are heavily influenced by recent events that are more easily remembered.[16]

Ratings that unduly reflect recent events can present a false picture of the individual's job performance during the entire rating period. For instance, the employee may have received a poor rating because he or she performed poorly during the most recent month, despite an excellent performance record during the preceding 11 months.

recency error An error that occurs when ratings are heavily influenced by recent events.

Legal Standards

As we noted earlier, when an employee challenges an appraisal-based employment decision (e.g., promotion, demotion, discharge) in a discrimination suit, the employer must be prepared to defend its appraisal system. To do so successfully, the employer must demonstrate that the appraisal system meets all the criteria imposed by EEO laws. Specifically, the court would examine the nature of the appraisal instrument and the fairness and accuracy of the ratings. Many of the issues that the court would address appear in Taking a Closer Look 8-1.

Taking a Closer Look 8-1 | *Legality of Appraisal Systems: Possible Court Inquiries*

The Appraisal Instrument

- Is there a formal, structured rating instrument?
- Have the factors necessary for successful job performance been isolated and included on the form?
- If serving as a basis for promotion, how relevant is performance on the current job to that on the new job?
- Are the rating factors well defined or are they vague and ambiguous?
- Have the rating factors been properly weighted based on importance?
- Are there more objective indicators available, other than ratings? Can they be used to corroborate the ratings?

Accuracy and Fairness Issues

- Is the appraiser knowledgeable about the job to be rated?

- Is the appraiser familiar with the employee's performance?
- Have the appraisers been provided with instructions and training?
- Does the appraisal rest on the evaluations made by a single rater? Are other knowledgeable raters available?
- Does the employee have the opportunity to review and appeal the appraisals?
- If a panel-evaluation process is used, does the panel include representatives of the employee's protected group?
- Is there a formal mechanism by which employees are made aware of job/promotional opportunities?

Source: Kleiman, L.S., and Durham, R.L. (1981). Performance appraisal, promotion, and the courts: A critical review. *Personnel Psychology*, 34, 103–121.

Particular questions addressed in a given case are dictated by the type of charges being lodged.[17] For example, if employees brought charges of disparate impact in promotions (e.g., where proportionately fewer members of a certain protected group are being promoted), a court would scrutinize the job-relatedness of the appraisal form and accuracy of the ratings. When faced with a disparate treatment case related to promotion (i.e., someone claiming to be denied a promotion because of a biased appraisal), a court would be more interested in the issue of fairness. The judge would assess whether appropriate safeguards have been taken to ensure that the rater did not give biased ratings. Such safeguards would include an upper-management review of ratings and a formal system that allows employees to appeal their ratings if perceived as unfair.

8-2b Types of Rating Instruments

To meet the standards described in the previous section, a firm must use an effective rating form. The form provides the basis for the appraisal, indicating aspects or dimensions of performance that are to be evaluated and the rating scale for judging that performance. HR experts have developed a variety of instruments for appraising performance. A description of the most commonly used instruments, along with their strengths and weaknesses, is given in the following paragraphs.

Employee Comparison Systems

employee comparison systems Appraisal instruments that require raters to evaluate employees in relation to other employees.

Most appraisal instruments require raters to evaluate employees in relation to some standard of excellence. With **employee comparison systems,** however, employee performance is evaluated relative to other employees' performances. In other words, employee comparison systems use *rankings,* rather than *ratings.*

Ranking Formats

simple rankings Appraisal instruments that require raters to rank-order their employees from best to worst, according to their job performance.

Any of a number of formats can be used to rank employees, such as simple rankings, paired comparisons, or forced distributions. **Simple rankings** require raters to rank-order their employees from best to worst, according to their job performance. When using the **paired comparison** approach, a rater compares each possible pair of employees. For example, Employee 1 is compared to Employees 2 and 3, and Employee 2 is compared to Employee 3. The employee winning the most "contests" receives the highest ranking. A **forced distribution** approach requires a rater to assign a certain percentage of employees to each category of excellence, such as "best," "average," or "worst." McKesson Information Solutions used this type of system in the opening case. It is also used by a number of other companies, such as General Electric, PepsiCo, and Conoco. General Electric, for instance, requires that managers be ranked on a bell-shaped curve, in which 10 percent are placed in the bottom grade. If they don't improve by the next year, they are fired.[18]

paired comparison Appraisal instrument that requires raters to compare each possible pair of employees in terms of their job performance.

forced distribution Appraisal instrument that requires raters to assign a certain percentage of employees to each category of excellence.

Strengths

Employee comparison systems are low cost and practical; the ratings take very little time and effort. Moreover, this approach to performance appraisal effectively eliminates *some* of the rating errors discussed earlier. Leniency is eliminated, for instance, because the rater cannot give every employee an outstanding rating. In the opening case, McKesson's new performance appraisal system was plagued with leniency error, compelling it to switch to a forced distribution format. As you may recall, only 30 percent of its employees may now be rated in the top two categories. By forcing raters to specify their best and worst performers, employment decisions, such as pay raises and promotions, become much easier to make.

| EXHIBIT 8-4 | An Illustration of a Graphic Rating Scale |

Instructions

Evaluate the worker on each quality, using the following rating scale:

5 = Outstanding; one of the best workers you have known
4 = Good; meets all job standards; exceeds some
3 = Adequate; meets job standards
2 = Needs improvement in some way
1 = Unsatisfactory; not acceptable

a. Dress and appearance	1_____	2_____	3_____	4_____	5_____
b. Self-confidence	1_____	2_____	3_____	4_____	5_____
c. Dependability	1_____	2_____	3_____	4_____	5_____
d. Tact and diplomacy	1_____	2_____	3_____	4_____	5_____
e. Attitude	1_____	2_____	3_____	4_____	5_____
f. Cooperation	1_____	2_____	3_____	4_____	5_____
g. Enthusiasm	1_____	2_____	3_____	4_____	5_____
h. Knowledge	1_____	2_____	3_____	4_____	5_____

Weaknesses

Employee comparison systems are plagued with several weaknesses. Forcing raters to rank-order their employees creates an environment where employees are encouraged to compete with their colleagues in order to earn a higher ranking. According to management consultant Bob Rogers, such appraisal systems send negative signals to employees and thus disrupt teamwork.[19] Moreover, employees who are designated as the worst performers in their units understandably become alienated and resentful.[20] Another problem with employee comparison systems is that they rarely specify ranking criteria, as the rating standards for judging performance are vague or nonexistent. The accuracy and fairness of ratings made under these circumstances can be seriously questioned. An additional problem is that these raking systems do not specify what a worker must do to receive a good rating and, thus, they fail to adequately direct employee behavior. Finally, companies using such systems cannot compare the performance of people from different departments fairly. For example, the sixth-ranked employee in Department A may be a better performer than the top-ranked employee in Department B.

Graphic Rating Scales

A **graphic rating scale (GRS)** presents appraisers with a list of traits assumed to be necessary to successful job performance (e.g., cooperativeness, adaptability, maturity, motivation). A five- or seven-point rating scale accompanies each trait. Numbers and/or descriptive words or phrases that indicate the level of performance define the points along the scale. The midpoint of the scale is usually anchored by such words as "average," "adequate," "satisfactory," or "meets standards." An example of a graphic rating scale is shown in Exhibit 8-4.

graphic rating scale (GRS)
A rating instrument comprised of traits anchored by adjectives descriptive of job performance levels.

Strengths

Many organizations use graphic rating scales because they are practical and cost little to develop. HR professionals can develop such forms quickly, and because the traits and anchors are written at a general level, a single form is applicable to all or most jobs within an organization.

Weaknesses

Graphic rating scales do present a number of problems, especially when raters are given vaguely defined traits to evaluate, such as those listed in Exhibit 8-4. Such instruments do not effectively direct behavior because employees do not know what to do to achieve a favorable rating. For example, an employee given a rating of "2" on "attitude" may have a difficult time figuring out how to improve.

Graphic rating scales also fail to provide a good mechanism for providing specific, nonthreatening feedback. As we discuss later, negative feedback should focus on specific behaviors, rather than on the vaguely defined traits the GRSs describe. For example, if told that they are not dependable, most employees would become angered and defensive; they would become less angry and defensive if such feedback were given in behavioral terms: "Six customers complained to me last week that you did not return their phone calls."

Another problem with GRSs concerns rating accuracy. Accurate ratings are not likely to be achieved because the points on the rating scale are not clearly defined. For instance, two raters may interpret the standard "average" in very different ways. The failure to clearly define performance standards can lead to a multitude of rating errors (as noted earlier) and provides a ready mechanism for the occurrence of bias. The courts consequently frown on the use of GRSs. One court noted that ratings made on a graphic rating scale amounted to no more than a "subjective judgment call" and ruled that such rating scales should not be used for promotion decisions because of the potential bias inherent in such a subjective process.[21]

Behaviorally Anchored Rating Scales

A **behaviorally anchored rating scale (BARS),** like a graphic rating scale, requires appraisers to rate employees on their traits. The typical BARS includes seven or eight traits, referred to as "dimensions," each anchored by a seven- or nine-point scale.

But the rating scales used on BARS are constructed differently from those used on graphic rating scales. Rather than using numbers or adjectives, a BARS anchors each trait with examples of specific job behaviors that reflect varying levels of performance. An example of a BARS is shown in Figure 8-2.

The process for developing a BARS, which is rather complex, is described in Taking a Closer Look 8-2. Briefly summarized: It starts with a job analysis, using the critical incident technique. The incidents or behaviors are then categorized by dimension. A rating scale is then developed for each dimension, using these behaviors as "anchors" to define points along the scale.

behaviorally anchored rating scale (BARS) A rating instrument comprised of traits anchored by job behaviors. Raters select the behavior that best describes the worker's performance level.

Figure 8-2
An Illustration of a BARS for Job of College Professor

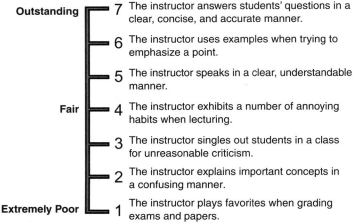

Dimension: Classroom Teaching Skills

Outstanding

7 — The instructor answers students' questions in a clear, concise, and accurate manner.

6 — The instructor uses examples when trying to emphasize a point.

5 — The instructor speaks in a clear, understandable manner.

Fair

4 — The instructor exhibits a number of annoying habits when lecturing.

3 — The instructor singles out students in a class for unreasonable criticism.

2 — The instructor explains important concepts in a confusing manner.

Extremely Poor

1 — The instructor plays favorites when grading exams and papers.

> **Taking a Closer Look 8-2** *How to Develop a BARS*
>
> 1. The critical incident technique of job analysis is used to derive a list of effective and ineffective job behavior (see Chapter 4, "Analyzing Jobs").
> 2. The job analyst sorts these behaviors into job dimensions or worker traits that the individual behaviors appear to characterize. These traits are then labeled and defined by the analyst.
> 3. Subject-matter experts (managers and/or employees) review the list of behaviors without knowing their assigned dimensions. That is, these individuals are given the names and definitions of each dimension and are asked to classify all behaviors into the appropriate dimensions. This step is called "retranslation" and serves as a check on the analyst's original classification of behaviors. A behavior is retained if most of the experts (usually 80 percent or more) assign it to the same dimension to which the job analyst assigned it.
> 4. "Surviving" behaviors are reviewed by a second group of subject-matter experts. These individuals
>
> rate each behavior's effectiveness in the performance of a job. For example, if a seven-point scale were used, a "7" would indicate that the behavior represents an extremely effective level of performance; a "1" would be indicative of extremely ineffective performance.
> 5. The analysts compute the standard deviation of the effectiveness ratings given to each behavior. If the standard deviation reflects a wide variability of ratings (experts do not agree on how effective the behavior is), the behavior is discarded. The mean effectiveness rating is then calculated for each of the remaining behaviors.
> 6. Analysts construct a rating scale for each trait, listing the name and definition of the trait along with the rating scale. Behavioral statements are placed on the scale at a point corresponding to their mean effectiveness ratings.

Strengths

When initially formulated, BARS was expected to be vastly superior to graphic rating scales. HRM experts thought that the behavioral anchors would lead to more accurate ratings because they enabled appraisers to better interpret the meaning of the various points along the rating scale. As we shall see, however, this expectation has not been met.

Perhaps the greatest strength of BARS is its ability to direct and monitor behavior. The behavioral anchors let employees know what types of behaviors are expected of them and gives appraisers the opportunity to provide behaviorally based feedback. For example, if rated on the BARS shown in Figure 8-2, a professor knows that she must give clear, concise, and accurate answers to students' questions in order to get the highest rating on that dimension.

Weaknesses

The superiority of BARS over graphic rating scales has not been substantiated by research. In fact, the great majority of the studies have failed to "offer evidence that the tremendous amount of time and effort . . . involved in constructing and using BARS is worth the outcome."[22]

The failure of BARS may lie in the difficulty raters experience when trying to select the *one* behavior on the scale that is most indicative of the employee's performance level.[23] Sometimes an employee may exhibit behaviors at both ends of the scale, so the rater would not know which rating to assign. For example, an instructor rated on the BARS shown in Figure 8-2 may answer questions clearly *and* single out students for unreasonable criticism.

> **EXHIBIT 8-5**   A Portion of a BOS for Rating Managers on Their Leadership Performance

Instructions

Evaluate performance by indicating how frequently the employee engages in each of the following behaviors. Place your rating in the space indicated using the following rating scale:

5 = Always   4 = Usually   3 = Sometimes   2 = Occasionally   1 = Rarely or never

Leadership

_____   Keeps employees abreast of information they need to do their jobs.
_____   Gives feedback in a constructive and timely manner.
_____   Allocates decision making at the appropriate level
_____   Acts in a way to build team trust and commitment.
_____   Supports team activities and decisions.
_____   Structures work assignments to appropriate level to effectively use resources.
_____   Motivates team members to seek development opportunities, when appropriate.
_____   Adheres to the team performance management process
_____   Seeks feedback and input from team members.
_____   Provides timely follow-up and resolution to team issues.
_____   Supports company's efforts to create and manage a diverse workforce.
_____   Constructively resolves conflicts among team members.
_____   Recognizes team members for their accomplishments.

---

behavior observation scale (BOS)   A rating instrument comprised of traits anchored by behaviors. Raters evaluate worker performance on each behavior.

Behavior Observation Scales

A **behavior observation scale (BOS)** contains a list of desired behaviors required for the successful performance of specific jobs. BOSs are developed like BARS—critical incidents are collected and categorized into dimensions. The key difference between the two methods is that with BOS, *each* behavior is rated by the appraiser.[24]

When using BOS, an appraiser rates job performance by indicating the frequency with which the employee engages in each behavior. A five-point scale is used ranging from "almost never" (1) to "almost always" (5). Companies calculate an overall rating for each dimension by adding employees' score on each behavioral item. A high score means that an individual frequently engages in desired behaviors. A portion of a BOS instrument appears in Exhibit 8-5.

Strengths

Because it was more recently developed, the research on BOS has been far less extensive than that on BARS. The available evidence, however, is favorable. One study found that both managers and subordinates preferred appraisals based on BOS to both BARS and graphic rating scales. The same study found that EEO attorneys believed BOS is more legally defensible than the other two approaches.[25]

Because raters do not have to choose one behavior most descriptive of an employee's performance level, the problem noted earlier regarding BARS does not arise. Moreover, like BARS, BOS is effective in directing employees' behavior because it specifies what they need to do in order to receive high performance ratings. Managers can also effectively use BOS to monitor behavior and give feedback in specific behavioral terms so that the employees know what they are doing right and what behavior needs to be corrected. For example, using the BOS described earlier, a supervisor informs the manager, "I like the way you always motivate your team members to pursue developmental opportunities." Or, "You need to seek more feedback and input from your team members."

Weaknesses

The use of a BOS is not always practical because, like BARS, a BOS instrument takes a great deal of time to develop. This difficulty stems from the fact that a separate instrument is needed for each job because different jobs call for different behaviors.

| EXHIBIT 8-6 | Illustration of a Segment of an MBO Form for a Secretarial Position |

Objective	Measurement of Results	Performance Standard	Target Date
1. Transcribe correspondence correctly.	Error count by supervisor	98 percent accurate	Weekly
2. Reduce frequency of retyping.	Number of rewrites requested by supervisor	Decrease by 2 percent	Weekly
3. Handle phone calls tactfully.	Random monitoring of calls by supervisor	95 percent of calls handled appropriately	Monthly

Developing a BOS for a particular job would not be cost-efficient unless the job had many incumbents.

Management by Objectives

Management by objectives (MBO) is a management system designed to achieve organizational effectiveness by steering each employee's behavior toward the organization's mission.[26] The MBO process includes goal setting, planning, and evaluation.

Goal Setting

As we noted in Chapter 3, "Planning for Human Resources," goal setting starts at the top of the organization with the establishment of the organization's mission statement and strategic goals. The goal-setting process then cascades down through the organizational hierarchy to the level of the individual employee. An individual's goals should represent outcomes that, if achieved, would most contribute to the attainment of the organization's strategic goals.

In most instances, individual goals are mutually set by employees and their supervisors, at which time they also set specific performance standards and determine how goal attainment will be measured. An illustration of an MBO form is shown in Exhibit 8-6.

Planning

As they plan, employees and supervisors work together to identify potential obstacles to reaching goals and devise strategies to overcome these obstacles. The two parties periodically meet to discuss the employee's progress to date and to identify any changes in goals necessitated by organizational circumstances.

Evaluation

In the final phase, the employee's success at meeting goals is evaluated against the agreed-on performance standards. The final evaluation, occurring annually in most cases, serves as a measure of the employee's performance effectiveness.

Strengths

MBO systems are outcome-focused, defining and rigorously measuring success at every level of the organization. The use of such measures ensures that each person, team, and business unit focuses its efforts on the task of meeting performance goals.[27] Because of this feature, MBO is widely practiced throughout the United States. The research evaluating its effectiveness as a performance appraisal tool has been quite favorable.[28] These findings suggest that MBO improves job performance by directing behavior. For example, a secretary who is rated on the form shown in Exhibit 8-6 knows how important it is for him to handle phone calls accurately. By performing well on this task, he is helping the company to reach an important organizational objective (e.g., fewer customer complaints). Note how the goals in this

management by objectives (MBO) A rating instrument comprised of objectives and performance standards for meeting them.

exhibit are specific and challenging. Research points out that employees perform best when goals are written in this way.[29]

From a fairness viewpoint, MBO fares well because the performance standards are stated in relatively objective terms. Hence, the ratings should be relatively free from bias. For instance, if the secretary reduces the need for retyping, he will get a good rating regardless of any personal animosity on the part of his supervisor.

Another strength of an MBO system is practicality and cost. The development of objectives does not require as much effort as does the development of a BARS or BOS. With each employee working on his or her own rating scale (in conjunction with the supervisor), an MBO can typically be constructed in less than two weeks. It can take several months to construct a BOS.

Another plus is that allowing employees to have a say in how their performance will be measured gives them a greater stake in achieving their goals and more perceived control over their work environment. The mutual collaboration inherent in the goal-setting process also fosters better communication between employees and supervisors.

Weaknesses

MBO presents several potential problems, four of which we discuss here. First, although it focuses an employee's attention on goals, it does not specify the behaviors required to reach them—What must secretaries do to become more tactful in handling phone calls? This may be a problem for some employees, especially new ones, who may require more guidance. Such employees should be provided with "action steps," specifying what they need to do to successfully reach their goals.

Second, the successful achievement of MBO goals may be partly a function of factors outside the worker's control. For instance, an auto dealer manager may fail to increase sales volume because the competitors offer better cars or better prices. Most people believe that a manager should not be penalized if, for no fault of her own, she fails to reach a performance objective.

Third, performance standards vary from employee to employee and, thus, MBO provides no common basis for comparison. For instance, the goals set for an "average" employee may be less challenging than those set for a "superior" employee. How can the two be compared? Because of this problem, the instrument's usefulness as a decision-making tool is limited. For instance, who should get the bigger raise this year—the average employee who exceeded his performance standards, or the excellent employee who merely met his performance standards?

Last, some employees dislike MBO because of the performance pressures it places on them and the stress that it creates.[30] For instance, a car sales associate must sell 15 cars per month. It is now the 28th of the month, and Joe has only sold 12 cars. Needless to say, he will be under great pressure for the next couple of days. Some employees dislike working under such conditions.

A summary of the commonly used rating instruments appears in Exhibit 8-7. It should be noted, however, that companies could create additional types of instruments. For instance, they could rate employees on job task performance, using graphic or behavior rating scales.

EXHIBIT 8-7	Comparison of Rating Instruments					
	Cost	Practical Behavior	Direct Behavior	Monitor Decisions	Employment	Legal
Employee comparisons	+	+	−	−	+/−	−
GRS	+	+	−	−	−	−
BARS	−	−	+	+	−	−
BOS	−	−	+	+	+	+
MBO	+/−	+/−	+	+	+/−	+/−

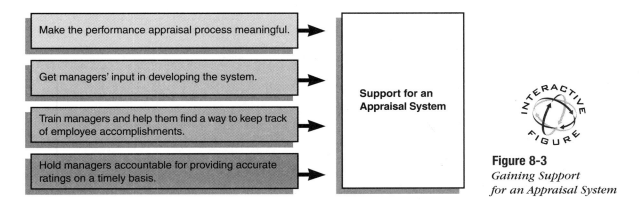

INTERACTIVE FIGURE

Figure 8-3
*Gaining Support
for an Appraisal System*

8-2c Designing an Appraisal System

Appraisal system development requires more than merely choosing an appropriate rating instrument. The designers of the system must also determine how it will be developed and administered. We now discuss the steps an HR professional should take to develop an effective performance appraisal system.

Step 1: Gaining Support for the System

An appraisal system cannot be fully successful unless it has the support of the entire workforce; it must be acceptable to appraisers, employees, and upper management. If appraisers do not approve of the system, they may respond with direct resistance or sabotage. For instance, if supervisors are not convinced that the system is practical, and think it is just another time-consuming, personnel paperwork requirement having no "real-world" significance, they may not properly complete the forms (or may not complete them at all).[31] If employees do not trust the system or feel it is invalid, morale and motivation will drop, and the possibility of a lawsuit will increase.[32]

What must HR professionals do to ensure that those using the system will accept and support it?

Gain the Support of Upper-Level Managers

HR professionals must get upper-level managers to support the system or it is doomed to failure. High-level managers must agree to endorse the system publicly, devote sufficient resources to it, and model appropriate behavior by complying with the procedures that everyone else must follow.[33] Additional suggestions for gaining management support include (see Figure 8-3):[34]

- Make the performance appraisal process meaningful. Demonstrate how the appraisal can be an effective tool in helping employees improve their job performance.
- Get managers' input in developing the system. Most managers complain about the complexity and length of the form. Get their insights and suggestions on how the company's form could be improved.
- Train managers and help them find a way to keep track of all the things their employees have done during the review period. This way, managers will not view the process as such a chore.
- Hold managers accountable for providing accurate ratings on a timely basis. Put a specific line item in the managers' performance evaluations to rate their effectiveness in providing employee evaluations.

Gain the Support of Employees

Encouraging users (both managers and workers) to participate in the planning and development of the system will enhance support for it. Management experts John

Bernardin and Richard Beatty suggest the use of a task force comprised of organizational members representing the various groups affected by the proposed system. The task force would be empowered to devise a step-by-step approach for developing, implementing, and administering the system.[35]

Step 2: Choosing the Appropriate Rating Instrument

As we saw earlier, HR professionals may choose from a variety of appraisal instruments. On what bases should the choice be made? The organization must consider many factors. Three of the most important factors—practicality, cost, and nature of job—are discussed next.

Practicality

The performance appraisal instrument must be practical if it is to meet the needs of the organization. It would not be practical, for instance, to require immediate implementation of a proposed instrument that would take several years to develop. Nor would it be practical if the instrument measured behaviors that the appraisers could not observe, or required more time and effort than the appraisers were able to give.

Cost

The costs of an appraisal system include development costs (e.g., constructing an appraisal instrument), implementation costs (e.g., training appraisers, developing written guidelines), and utilization costs (e.g., appraiser's time observing, rating, and giving performance feedback).

All things being equal, the lower the cost, the more useful the system. However, as wise consumers are aware—"you get what you pay for." Although simple employee comparisons and graphic rating scales cost companies very little to develop and administer, they may well contain hidden costs. As we noted earlier, for instance, such instruments may cause morale problems or lead to successful discrimination lawsuits.

Nature of Job

The choice of rating instrument depends, in part, on the type of data that can be realistically collected about a particular job. For example, some rating scales, such as BARS and BOS, require appraisers to rate employee job behaviors. Some jobs, however, offer raters little or no opportunity to make such observations. School principals, for instance, cannot accurately rate teachers' classroom behavior (unless they sit in on several classes); police sergeants cannot rate patrol officers' "field behavior" (unless they frequently accompany their officers while on patrol). In such cases, a results or trait-based evaluation form would be preferable.

MBO systems focus on end results. Although results provide a meaningful index of performance, they are sometimes difficult to accurately measure. For instance, a doctor's office receptionist does not produce measurable results, rendering an MBO useless. It would make more sense to rate receptionists' job performances on a BOS where they can be judged based on such behaviors as being polite, friendly, and helpful to patients.

Therefore, when trying to choose between a behaviorally based method, such as BARS or BOS, and a results-oriented method, such as MBO, a firm should use the following criteria:[36]

- If the appraiser is aware of the behavior required for the job and has the opportunity to observe that behavior, use a behaviorally based method.
- If valid output measures are available, use a results-oriented method.
- If both circumstances exist, use either or both approaches.
- If neither circumstance exists, use a graphic rating scale.

As a general rule, executive, managerial, and professional employees are usually rated based on results; employees occupying lower-level jobs are most often rated on behavioral or trait-oriented criteria.[37]

Step 3: Choosing the Rater(s)

Supervisors, peers, and the employees themselves may provide performance ratings, as discussed in the following paragraphs.

Supervisory Ratings

Performance appraisals are the responsibility of the immediate supervisor about 98 percent of the time.[38] Supervisors make the appraisals because they are usually the ones most familiar with the employee's work. Additionally, appraisals serve as management tools for supervisors, giving them a means to direct and monitor employee behavior. Indeed, if supervisors were not allowed to make the appraisals, their authority or control over their subordinates could be diminished.[39]

Peer Ratings

Although supervisory ratings can be quite valuable, some companies have added peer appraisals to replace or supplement those given by the supervisor.[40] Peers and supervisors view an individual's performance from different perspectives. Supervisors usually possess greater information about job requirements and performance outcomes. On the other hand, peers often see a different, more realistic view of the employee's job performance because people often behave differently when the boss is present.

Using peer ratings to supplement supervisory ratings may thus help to develop a consensus about an individual's performance. It may also help eliminate biases and lead to greater employee acceptance of appraisal systems.[41]

Potential problems may limit the usefulness of peer ratings, especially if they are used in lieu of supervisory ratings:[42]

- *The competitive nature of the organization's reward system:* Peers may perceive a conflict of interest. High ratings given to a peer may be perceived as harming the individual's own chances for advancement.

- *Friendships:* A peer may fear that low ratings given to a colleague will harm their friendship or hurt the cohesiveness of the work group. On the other hand, some peer ratings may be influenced by dislike for the employee being rated.

Self-Ratings

Some organizations use self-ratings to supplement supervisory ratings. As one might expect, self-ratings are generally more favorable than those made by supervisors and peers, and therefore may not be effective as an evaluative tool.[43]

However, self-ratings may be used for employee development.[44] Their use, for instance, may uncover areas of subordinate–supervisor disagreement, encourage employees to reflect on their strengths and weaknesses, lead to more constructive appraisal interviews, and make employees more receptive to suggestions.[45] We further discuss the developmental use of self-ratings in Section 8-3, "The Manager's Guide."

Using Multiple Raters: 360-Degree Feedback Systems

Some companies evaluate their managers' performance using several raters. This approach is called **360-degree feedback** because the ratings are made by a "circle" of people who frequently interact with the manager, such as subordinates, superiors, peers, and customers. Self-rating can also be used. The raters limit their evaluations to job behaviors that they have directly observed. For example, subordinates might be asked whether the manager[46]

360-degree feedback
An appraisal system for managers, who are rated by subordinates, peers, superiors, customers, and themselves.

- Follows up on problems, decisions, and requests in a timely manner
- Shares information when appropriate
- Provides subordinates with coaching when needed
- Evaluates subordinates fairly

The number of firms using 360-degree feedback systems is growing rapidly.[47] In 1998, the usage rate was 40 percent; it had jumped to 65 percent by 2000.[48] Companies use these systems primarily as feedback devices. Managers gain insight into their strengths and weaknesses when they discover how their "circle" of raters views them, enabling them to improve their performance. The ratings are usually collected anonymously so that the raters will feel more comfortable about giving frank evaluations. The information is then communicated to managers in the aggregate, where only the manager being rated sees the feedback. The downside to this approach, of course, is a lack of accountability. That is, if a manager who receives poor ratings chooses to ignore the feedback, no one would know.

Some companies use 360-degree feedback systems for evaluative, as well as feedback, purposes. That is, the managers' ratings are revealed to their superiors, who can use them as the basis for employment decisions, such as promotions or dismissals. When used for evaluative purposes, managers are held accountable for their ratings and should thus be more motivated to make improvements. However, as management expert David Waldman and his colleagues note,[49] the use of 360-degree ratings for evaluative purposes could lead to the following consequences:

- Managers try to sabotage the program by striking a deal with employees to give high ratings in exchange for high ratings.
- Anonymous ratings cannot be used to legally document adverse personnel actions. However, if anonymity is discarded, raters may be hesitant to give unfavorable ratings.
- The 360-degree ratings may encourage the wrong type of behavior. To earn high ratings from customers, for instance, managers might give overly generous discounts; to win their employees' favor, managers might become too lax in disciplinary matters.

Companies that are considering the use of 360-degree ratings for evaluative purposes should proceed cautiously. The ratings should be introduced solely for developmental purposes and be revealed only to the managers who are rated. This approach would give both raters and managers time to adjust to the system. Raters should feel less apprehensive about rating managers once they see that negative repercussions are unlikely. Managers should feel less apprehensive because the confidential nature of the feedback would give them an opportunity to make changes without revealing their weaknesses to others.

A firm should then assess its readiness to use the 360-degree feedback system for evaluative purposes. To determine readiness, firms should be able to give affirmative answers to all or most of the questions contained in Taking a Closer Look 8-3.

Step 4: Determining the Appropriate Timing of Appraisals

Most firms appraise employee performance annually. Some evaluate all employees at about the same time of year; others evaluate employees on a staggered schedule based on their anniversary date of hire.

Many companies avoid more frequent appraisals because they are considered too time-consuming.[50] The presence of a one-year interval between appraisals may cause a problem, however: Appraisers may have a difficult time remembering all relevant events transpiring during that period. To minimize this problem, appraisers must maintain records of employee performance. Such record keeping also serves as documentation for EEO suits. Suggestions for documenting behavior are given in Taking a Closer Look 8-4.

Taking a Closer Look 8-3

Questions to Assess a Firm's Readiness for Using 360-Degree Feedback for Evaluative Purposes

Must be able to answer the following questions in the affirmative:

1. Is participative decision making valued in this company?
2. Is there good cooperation among employees in different departments?
3. Do employees feel free to speak up?
4. Do employees have a positive attitude about working for the company?
5. Do most employees at all levels have high ethical standards?

6. Are promotion and reward systems free from favoritism?
7. Do employees hold valuable information about the performance of their peers and superiors?
8. Do customers hold valuable information about the performance of the managers?
9. Are decisions within the company rarely based on hearsay?
10. Can employees be trusted to give unbiased ratings?

Source: Atwater, L., and Waldman, D. (1998). Accountability in 360-degree feedback. *HRMagazine,* May, 96–105.

Step 5: Ensuring Appraisal Fairness

Biased appraisals (or the perception of bias) may foster feelings of ill will toward supervisors and the organization. They may also lead to successful EEO suits. An organization must therefore take steps to ensure that the appraisal process is a fair one.

Upper-Level Management Review

To help ensure fairness, most organizations require an upper-level management review of the completed appraisals. Typically, the supervisor's boss checks for rating errors. For instance, upper-level managers can spot whether some evaluators appear more lenient or severe than others. They can also determine if halo or central tendency errors may be occurring. Halo is evidenced when an employee receives the same rating on each factor; central tendency is evidenced by the absence of any extreme ratings. When these "symptoms" are spotted, the upper-level manager should ask for justification, and perhaps ask the evaluator to do another evaluation.

In addition to spotting rating inaccuracies, the use of a review process may serve to keep appraisers "honest." Knowing that their boss is going to carefully review their ratings, managers will think twice about making purposeful errors, like leniency or severity. The value of the review process will be lost, however, if upper-level managers do not carefully scrutinize the ratings; that is, they merely "rubber-stamp" them.

Appeals System

An appeals system provides a means for employees to obtain a fair hearing if they are dissatisfied with their appraisals. Such a system is beneficial because it:

Taking a Closer Look 8-4

Suggestions for Documenting Behavior

1. Document all relevant job behaviors, both favorable and unfavorable, as soon as possible.
2. Note whether the observation is firsthand (observed by you) or secondhand (observed by another manager, coworker, or customer).
3. Record the time, date, and location of occurrence, and the time and date that the notation was made.

4. Describe the observed behavior by noting what occurred, the circumstances surrounding the behavior, and the results of the behavior.
5. The documented behavior should be available and open to employee review.

Source: Henderson, R. (1980). *Performance Appraisal: Theory to Practice.* Reston, VA: Dryden.

Taking a Closer Look 8-5 *Steps in a Performance Appraisal Appeals System*

1. The employee discusses the complaint with his or her immediate supervisor.
2. If unresolved, a written record of disagreement is placed in the employee's personnel file.
3. The next level of management hears the disagreement.

4. A peer review committee and representatives of management hear an unresolved complaint.

Source: Statton, K. (1988). Performance appraisal and the need for an organizational grievance procedure: A review of the literature and recommendations for future research. *Employee Responsibilities and Rights Journal, 1,* 167–179.

- Allows employees to voice their concerns
- Fosters more accurate ratings—the fear of a possible challenge may discourage raters from assigning arbitrary or biased ratings
- Often prevents the involvement of outside third parties (e.g., unions, courts)

When such a system is absent, management power may be exercised arbitrarily and unfairly. When this occurs, morale suffers because it makes employees feel powerless, dependent, and without rights. The downside of using an appeals system is that it tends to undermine the authority of the supervisor and may encourage leniency error. For example, a supervisor may give lenient ratings to avoid going through the hassle of an appeal.

An appeals system typically includes the steps listed in Taking a Closer Look 8-5.

8-3 The Manager's Guide

8-3a Performance Appraisal and the Manager's Job

No matter how well an appraisal system is designed, it will not be effective if improperly implemented. Managers are chiefly responsible for implementation; they must complete the ratings and provide feedback to employees. Furthermore, when MBO is used, managers must collaborate with employees to set performance goals and standards.

Completing the Ratings

In all likelihood, a performance appraisal system's success is most heavily influenced by the accuracy and fairness of the ratings a manager supplies. Unfortunately, managers are often the weak spot in the system: As noted earlier, they often commit a host of errors when evaluating their employees, some of which are intentional or politically motivated.

How can managers avoid making these errors? Managers must become aware of the importance of accurate ratings and how rating errors can impede the success of an appraisal system. Certainly, any political gains associated with lenient and severe ratings shown in Exhibit 8-3 are illusionary. Consider the assignment of class grades as an analogy. Would any of these political reasons justify the assignment of a lenient or severe grade for this course? For example, should a student receive an undeserved "A" simply because the professor wants to avoid a confrontation? Conversely, should the professor grade students lower than they deserve because that will motivate them to work even harder? Would it, in fact, motivate them to work harder?

In addition to enhancing their awareness, managers must develop their observational and evaluation skills. The HRM department can help by providing training, as we note later.

Providing Performance Feedback

One of the key objectives of feedback is to improve employee performance by giving them constructive criticism, when necessary, to make them aware of their shortcomings. Even the best managers find it difficult to give such criticism effectively. Criticism causes most people to feel threatened and become defensive. When criticized, employees begin searching mentally for information to defend themselves and thus do not listen to subsequent feedback.[51]

To make matters worse, managers all too often provide negative feedback in inappropriate ways; they criticize subordinates when they are upset, angry, and cannot hold their tempers in check. Such criticism may be sarcastic or include threats.[52]

Managers' failure to provide effective feedback is often the death knell of an effective appraisal system. When employees perceive corrective feedback as unjust criticism, they feel hurt and angry and consequently become less motivated and committed to the firm.[53]

Setting Performance Goals

When an MBO system is used, a manager jointly sets goals with subordinates and evaluates their subsequent performance. Section 8-3c, "HRM Skill-Building for Managers," discusses how such goals should be set.

8-3b How the HRM Department Can Help

HRM departments serve three main functions in performance appraisal: (1) Develop the performance appraisal system, (2) provide appraiser training, and (3) monitor and evaluate the implementation of the system.

Developing the Appraisal System

Without an effective performance appraisal system, managers would be hard pressed to provide meaningful ratings. For example, a manager would have great difficulty giving accurate ratings and useful feedback if required to provide them on a graphic rating scale because the performance criteria are so poorly defined on these instruments.

Providing Rater Training

HR professionals also provide raters with appropriate training. Raters need to understand why accurate ratings and effective feedback are important and how these outcomes can be achieved. Rater training usually focuses on:[54]

- Establishing work expectations.
- Observing and documenting behavior.
- Conducting day-to-day performance feedback and coaching.
- Appraising performance and avoiding rating errors.
- Providing written justifications for ratings.
- Conducting formal performance appraisal feedback conferences.
- Identifying training needs and formulating a development plan for employees.

Monitoring and Evaluating the Appraisal System

HR professionals also monitor and evaluate appraisal systems to ensure that they have been properly implemented. Monitoring means taking steps to ensure that each appraisal has been completed on time and that instructions have been followed. Evaluation consists of gauging the users' satisfaction with the appraisal system. If employees are displeased with the system, there is probably something wrong with it.[55] User satisfaction can be gleaned from organizational records (e.g., number of grievances or EEO charges filed against the system) or from attitude surveys in which appraisers and appraisees are asked whether they think the system has been appropriately designed and used.

8-3c HRM Skill-Building for Managers

In this section, we discuss the issues of feedback conferences and goal setting, two important management duties.

Conducting Periodic Performance Review Sessions

You should hold periodic meetings with your employees to discuss their performance. These meetings should be brief, informal, and employee-centered. Their objective is to identify problems the employee is facing and to discuss solutions to these problems. Without such sessions:

- You may fail to gain an accurate picture of the subordinate's progress toward meeting performance expectations.
- You may be unaware of any performance problems subordinates are having.
- Your employees may be unaware of what is expected of them or how well they are doing. They might then approach annual review sessions with great anxiety.

These informal meetings should last about 10 to 30 minutes. The atmosphere should be as relaxed as possible; your attitude should be constructive and supportive. You should seek information without judging the employee and should take a positive approach toward correcting any problems or errors; do not accuse or criticize. Your aim is to discover whether there is anything you could do to help the employee improve his or her performance.

Encourage the workers to do most of the talking, describing their progress, problems, and concerns. For instance, a worker might reveal how coworkers often interrupt her or that she feels her accomplishments are not appreciated. When problems are uncovered, you should attempt to identify their cause and discuss possible solutions with the employee. Avoid discussions of promotions, adverse actions, merit pay raises, and performance ratings during this conference.

Conducting the Annual Performance Review Conference

The objectives of annual conferences should be to (1) inform employees of their ratings and how the information will be used (e.g., pay raises, promotions), (2) keep effective workers "on target," and (3) improve ineffective workers' performance.

Conferences should be conducted in the following sequence:

1. *Inform employees:* Inform employees of the conference a few days in advance. Ask them to think about how well they have done and the problems they have faced. Many managers find it helpful at this point to have the subordinates complete a self-appraisal, as we discuss in step 5.

2. *Arrange a time and place:* Hold the conference in a private place. Make sure there are no interruptions. A good time for holding the conference is immediately after lunch.

3. *Review information:* Start off by reviewing the job requirements listed in your subordinate's job description. Then review the ratings you gave to the employee. Be prepared to state the reasons for rating the subordinate as you did. Use documented illustrations where possible.

4. *Starting the interview:* Create the impression that you consider this conference to be very important. Do not kid around or make statements like, "This is no big deal, but. . . ." Take a constructive attitude. Do not argue or become defensive. Assure confidentiality by noting that nothing said by the worker "will leave this room"—and keep your word.

5. *Discuss the worker's performance:* Discuss performance in specific areas. A good principle to follow here is that it is best to help employees discover things for themselves. Thus, rather than starting out by stating the employee's scores, begin by asking for the employee's own perceptions. Self-ratings, if made, should be discussed here.[56]

   - If employee perceptions are on target, you should simply agree and communicate each rating and the reasons for it.

   - If the employee is unaware of some of the issues you plan to raise, first discuss areas of agreement, starting with the positive ratings. Then discuss the other areas.

   When you must give negative feedback, do so in non-emotional terms. The feedback should focus on specific behavior. For instance, if the employee gossips about other employees do not say, "You don't respect your coworkers." Rather, describe the specific behavior you have observed, such as "I frequently hear you talking about other workers when they are not present."

6. *Discuss implications:* Indicate how the employee's performance ratings will affect employment decisions, such as pay and promotion.

7. *Set goals for improvement:* Get the worker to set improvement goals; i.e., the steps he or she needs to take to improve performance. Set a follow-up date for the purpose of determining the employee's progress in meeting these goals.

Setting Goals for MBO

If your company employs an MBO system, the performance goals of each employee must be set. The success of an MBO system greatly depends on the relevance and clarity of these goal statements.

Goal setting is usually a collaborative effort between you and each of your employees. Ultimately, however, you are responsible for ensuring that the goals have been properly set. To be effective, an individual's goals must be:

- Consistent with goals set at the higher organizational levels
- Specific and challenging
- Realistic and achievable
- Measurable

Goals Must Be Consistent with Goals Set at the Higher Organizational Levels

As noted earlier, the goal-setting process begins at the organizational level. Goals set at each succeeding level down the hierarchy should be in line with those set at higher levels. An individual's goals should indicate what that person must accomplish in order to best help his or her work unit meet its goals.

Goals Must Be Specific and Challenging

Specific and challenging goals produce the best results. A challenging goal is one that can be achieved only if employees put forward their best efforts. A common error made by managers is allowing goals to be set that are too easily accomplished.

Goals Must Be Realistic and Achievable

Although goals should be challenging, they must also be realistic and achievable.[57] The assignment of unrealistically challenging goals leads to stress, burnout, and in some cases unethical behavior, as some employees will violate rules or ethical codes when attempting to achieve their goals.[58] Accomplishment of a goal should be within the control of the employee. You must ensure that employees have the resources and authority necessary to accomplish the goal. If a goal subsequently proves unattainable or becomes irrelevant, it should be scrapped.

Goals Must Be Measurable

Goal statements should specify performance standards and proposed measurement of those standards. Performance standards should specify the desired level of performance in terms of both quality and quantity of results, and should indicate the time frame in which the results are expected to occur. The following is an example of a goal statement and the accompanying performance standard for a nurse:

- *Goal:* The nurse's care plan will accurately reflect current problems, patient needs, expected outcome, and nursing intervention leading to problem resolution.
- *Performance standard:* The performance standard is 95 percent accuracy as measured by an audit of care plans completed during the previous year.

Chapter Objectives Revisited

1. Understand how effective performance appraisal systems enhance competitive advantage.

    - Improving job performance by directing employee behavior toward organizational goals and by monitoring that behavior to ensure that goals are met
    - Providing a basis for making employment decisions, such as pay raises, promotions, discharges, demotions, transfers, training, and the completion of probationary periods
    - Preventing successful discrimination lawsuits associated with demotions, failure to promote, layoffs, and discharges
    - Minimizing job dissatisfaction and turnover by creating the perception that a firm treats its people fairly

2. Specify the standards an effective performance appraisal system must meet.

    - Quality of the rating form:
        - Relevance
        - Clear performance standards
    - Accuracy of ratings, avoiding the following rater errors:
        - Leniency and severity: Unduly favorable or unfavorable ratings
        - Central tendency: Failure to provide extreme ratings, when warranted
        - Halo effect: Ratings on each rating scale influenced by rater's opinion of a single ratee characteristic
        - Implicit personality theory: Rater has own theory about the ratee's personality and rates unobserved behavior based on that theory
        - Recency: Ratings unduly swayed by recent events

    - Legal compliance:
        - Disparate impact—Need to demonstrate job-related forms and accurate ratings
        - Disparate treatment—Need to demonstrate fairness of the ratings

3. Describe the different types of appraisal rating instruments.

    - Employee comparison systems: Rank-order employees
    - Graphic rating scales (GRS): Rate traits on a 5- or 7-point scale
    - Behaviorally anchored rating scales (BARS): Rate traits or dimensions on a scale anchored by behavioral examples
    - Behavior observation scales (BOS): Like BARS, except that employees are rated on each behavior
    - Management by objectives (MBO): Evaluates employees based on the attainment of goals set jointly by managers and employees

4. Explain how a firm should develop its performance appraisal system.

    - Gain support for system: Gain support of upper management and seek employee input when developing the system.
    - Develop rating instruments: Instrument of choice depends on practicality, cost, and the nature of jobs being evaluated.
    - Choose raters: Choices include supervisors, peers, self, and 360-degree feedback.
    - Determine when appraisals will be given: Usually once a year. Ensure documentation.
    - Include safeguards to ensure fairness: Should include an upper-management review and an appeals system.

Review Questions

Note: You can find the correct answers to these questions by taking the quiz and then submitting your answers in the Online Edition. The program will automatically score your submission. If you miss a question, the program will provide the correct answer, a rationale for the answer, and the section number in the chapter where the topic is discussed.

1. An employee, Joe Smith, performed at the "2" level (needs improvement) during the past year. His boss gave him a "3," however, on his performance evaluation because he wanted to avoid a big confrontation. This rating error is called

   a. recency.
   b. halo.
   c. central tendency.
   d. leniency.

2. Jill Jones is an extremely intelligent employee. Her boss is so impressed by her intelligence that he rated her high on all aspects of her job performance (even those that she was weak on). This error is called

   a. recency.
   b. halo.
   c. central tendency.
   d. leniency.

3. Which of the following rating instruments is *not* an employee comparison system?

   a. simple ranking
   b. paired comparisons
   c. graphic rating scale
   d. forced distribution

4. An advantage of using employee comparison systems to evaluate performance is that such systems

   a. are usually approved by the courts in a discrimination case.
   b. do a good job of directing and monitoring employee behavior.
   c. minimize leniency errors.
   d. all of the above.

5. Which of the following conclusions was drawn from the research study that compared BARS, BOS, and graphic rating scales?

   a. Employees and managers prefer graphic rating scales; EEO attorneys prefer BARS.
   b. Employees and managers prefer BARS; EEO attorneys prefer BOS.
   c. Employees and managers prefer BOS; EEO attorneys prefer graphic rating scales.
   d. All groups prefer BOS.

6. The main difference between BOS and BARS is that

   a. BOS is trait-based; BARS is behaviorally based.
   b. the appraiser rates *each behavior* on BOS, but rates *one behavior per dimension* on BARS.
   c. the appraiser rates *each behavior* on BARS, but rates *one behavior per dimension* on BOS.
   d. BOS requires peer ratings; BARS requires supervisory ratings.

7. Most firms evaluate employee performance _____ time(s) per year.

   a. one
   b. two
   c. three
   d. four

8. A favorable characteristic of peer ratings, compared to supervisory ratings, is that

   a. peer ratings are usually less biased.
   b. peer ratings are usually more valid.
   c. peer ratings often reflect a more realistic view of the employee's job performance.
   d. all of the above.

9. When choosing an appraisal form, the organization should consider the following three factors:

   a. validity, reliability, and precision.
   b. practicality, cost, and nature of job.
   c. validity, precision, and cost.
   d. validity, practicality, and nature of job.

10. As a general rule, executive, managerial, and professional employees are usually rated on the basis of

    a. employee comparisons.
    b. traits.
    c. behaviors.
    d. results.

Discussion Questions

1. How can the use of an effective performance appraisal system improve employee job performance?

2. Discuss the impact of a performance appraisal system on employee satisfaction and retention.

3. What is meant by the term relevance in the context of performance appraisal? What can an organization do to ensure its rating instruments are relevant?

4. What are some of the causes of inaccurate ratings? How can ratings be made more accurate?

5. Why are graphic rating scales so frequently used? What are the major problems associated with their use?

6. Summarize the steps involved in the development of a BOS. What are the advantages and disadvantages associated with its use?

7. Discuss the advantages and disadvantages associated with the use of MBO as a performance appraisal technique.

8. Why is gaining user acceptance an important issue? Describe what can be done to help ensure that user acceptance is gained.

9. Why are peer ratings sometimes used to supplement supervisory ratings? What are some problems associated with their use?

10. What steps may an organization take to help ensure that its appraisal system is a fair one?

11. Describe how performance appraisal systems may be evaluated.

12. Compare and contrast the annual performance review conference with a periodic performance review session.

Experiential Exercises

Can This Appraisal System Be Legally Defended?

Overview

You will be examining the legality of the performance appraisal system used by your university to evaluate the performance of faculty. Half of you will be asked to attack the system legally; the other half, to defend it legally.

Steps

1. The instructor will explain the faculty performance appraisal system at your university, describing the five-step design described in this chapter (i.e., gaining support, choosing the instrument and rater, timing issues, and fairness procedures). Your instructor will also describe the role played by the appraisals in the promotion process. Feel free to ask questions. Make sure you understand how the process works.

2. Let's assume (hypothetically) that the promotion rate of female faculty is less than four-fifths the rate of male faculty. That is, the promotion system has a disparate impact against women. As you may recall from Chapter 2, when a selection (e.g., promotion) system produces a disparate impact, the employer must produce evidence of job-relatedness. Taking a Closer Look 8-1 presents the type of evidence needed to support the job-relatedness of a performance appraisal system.

3. The instructor will divide the class into teams of about four or five students each—half the teams will act as defendants (representatives of the university administration) and the other half as plaintiffs (a group of female faculty claiming sex discrimination in the promotion process).

4. Each team must now prepare its case for court. The defendants must assemble evidence that the system is job-related; the plaintiffs are to demonstrate the opposite (i.e., the system is not job-related).

5. A spokesperson for each group will present its case to the class; the plaintiff groups will present first.

6. After the final presentation, the instructor will act as judge and make a ruling. (There is no court of appeals!)

Developing a Performance Appraisal System

ABC University recently conducted a student survey to determine how students felt about their instructors. The university was surprised to learn that most professors were viewed in a negative light. Overall, the students did not enjoy their classes and felt the professors were uncaring. Some of the specific problems identified by the survey are as follows:

1. Many professors did not come to class prepared. They just seemed to "wing it."

2. Most professors were unwilling to help students with their course-related problems.

3. Professors were perceived as mean-spirited. When students questioned their grade, for instance, most professors would get mad and refuse to discuss the problem.

4. Classes were pretty boring, for the most part. Professors limited their teaching to lectures. There was very little class participation.

The president of the university believes that part of the problem might be the fact that there is no formal performance evaluation of faculty. She then hires a team of HR consultants (i.e., you) to study the problem and give her some recommendations. She is considering implementing a performance appraisal system and would use the results to make decisions regarding pay raises, promotions, and retention of faculty. She asks you to address the following questions:

1. Do you think the implementation of a formal appraisal system for faculty would help eliminate or minimize these problems? Explain.

2. If we do develop an appraisal system, how can we deal with the following questions?

3. How can we ensure that professors and department heads will support the system?

4. What kind of rating instrument should we use? Explain how the instrument will be relevant and contain clear performance standards. Give a sample of some of the rating scales so we can see what the instrument would look like.

5. What party or parties should actually conduct the ratings? Why?

6. How can we assure that the raters will provide accurate (error-free) ratings?

7. How often should the ratings be made?

8. How can we assure the ratings will be fair?

Divide into groups of 4 or 5 students and derive answers to each of these questions. Be prepared to present your answers and rationales to the rest of the class.

Case

Is a "Satisfactory" Rating Satisfactory?

Andrew Hilton, employed by Hamilton Chemicals as an electrical engineer for the past 26 years, has recently been promoted to management. His new position is engineering design services manager. He has 20 engineers from all disciplines reporting to him.

The unit has not been performing well. Morale and performance are at an all-time low. During the past two years, the unit's productivity has fallen by 25 percent, absenteeism has risen by 10 percent, and job-related injuries have risen by 12 percent.

Andrew suspects that the problem has been caused by the misuse of the performance appraisal system on the part of the previous manager, Ted Simpson. The workers are rated annually on a five-point graphic rating scale on the following job dimensions:

1. Safety
2. Ability to work with others
3. Contribution to the company's long-term growth
4. Contributions to productivity
5. Cost control
6. Attendance

During the past two years, Simpson gave each employee a "satisfactory" (3) rating on all six dimensions. Based on what he has observed during his first two months as manager, Andrew believes their ratings are erroneous. Six engineers have quickly surfaced as outstanding performers, and three are clearly unsatisfactory.

Questions

1. Why do you think Ted Simpson gave everyone a satisfactory rating?

2. Do you agree with Andrew that the performance appraisals may be contributing to the problem? Explain.

3. If Andrew chooses to give employees the ratings they deserve, do you think there will be a backlash, making many of the workers even more unhappy?

4. How should Andrew handle this situation?

References

1. Adapted from Johnson, G. (2004). Forced ranking: The good, the bad, and the ugly. *Training Magazine,* May, 1–6.
2. Larson, J.R., and Callahan, C. (1990). Performance monitoring: How it affects work productivity. *Journal of Applied Psychology, 75,* 530–38.
3. *U.S. v. City of Chicago.* 385 F. Supp. 543.
4. Lee, C. (1989). Poor performance appraisals do more harm than good. *Personnel Journal, 68,* 91–99.
5. Ibid.
6. Grenssing-Pophal, L. (2001). Motivate managers to review performance. *HRMagazine,* March, 44–48.
7. Robb, D. (2004). Building a better workforce. *HRMagazine, 49* (10), 86–93.
8. Lawler, E.E. (1976). Control systems in organizations. In M.D. Dunnette (ed.). *Handbook of Industrial and Organizational Psychology.* Chicago: Rand McNally.
9. Ibid.
10. Banks, C.G., and Murphy, K.R. (1985). Toward narrowing the research practice gap in performance appraisal. *Personnel Psychology, 38,* 335–346.
11. Longenecker, C.O., Sims, H.P., and Gioia, D.A. (1987). Behind the mask: The politics of employee appraisal. *The Academy of Management Executive, 1,* 183–193.
12. Cardy, R.L., and Dobbins, D.H. (1986). Affect and appraisal accuracy: Liking as an integral dimension in evaluating performance. *Journal of Applied Psychology, 71,* 672–678.
13. Dipboye, R.L. (1985). Some neglected variables in research on discrimination in appraisals. *Academy of Management Review, 10,* 116–127.
14. Krzystofiak, F., Cardy, R., and Newman, J. (1988). Implicit personality and performance appraisal: The influence of trait inferences on evaluations of behavior. *Journal of Applied Psychology, 73,* 515–521.
15. DeNisi, A.S., Robbins, T., and Cafferty, T.P. (1989). Organization of information used for performance appraisal: Role of diary-keeping. *Journal of Applied Psychology, 74,* 124–129.
16. Bretz, R.D., Milkovich, G.T., and Read, W. (1992). The current state of performance appraisal research and practice: Concerns, directions, and implications. *Journal of Management, 18* (2), 321–352.
17. Kleiman, L.S., and Durham, R.L. (1981). Performance appraisal, promotion, and the courts: A critical review. *Personnel Psychology, 34,* 103–121.
18. Johnson. Forced ranking.
19. Ibid.
20. Guido, M.J. (2004). Evaluating employee performance (Part 2). *Gallop Management Journal Online,* December 9, 1–5; http://gmj.gallup.com.
21. *Stallings v. Container Corp of America.* 75 FRD 511.
22. Jacobs, R., Kafry, D., and Zedeck, S. (1980). Expectations of behaviorally anchored rating scales. *Personnel Psychology, 33,* 595–640.
23. Kleiman, L.S., and Faley, R.H. (1986). Process-oriented variables and measurement of job performance: An examination of raters' weighting strategy. *Psychological Reports, 59,* 923–932.
24. Latham, G.P., and Wexley, K.N. (1981). *Increasing Productivity through Performance Appraisal.* Reading, MA: Addison-Wesley.
25. Wiersma, U., and Latham, G.P. (1986). The practicality of behavioral observation scales, behavioral expectation scales, and trait scales. *Personnel Psychology, 39,* 619–628.
26. Bernardin, H.J., and Beatty, R.W. (1984). *Performance Appraisal: Assessing Human Behavior at Work.* Boston: PWS-Kent.
27. Guido. Evaluating employee performance.
28. Carroll, S.J. (1986). Management by objectives: Three decades of research and experience. In S.L. Rynes and G.T. Milkovich (eds.). *Current Issues in Human Resource Management: Commentary and Readings.* Plano, TX: Business Publications.
29. Bernardin and Beatty. *Performance Appraisal.*
30. Ibid.
31. Schneier, C.E., Beatty, R.W., and Baird, L.S. (1986). How to construct a successful performance appraisal system. *Training and Development Journal,* April, 38–42.
32. Kleiman, L.S., Biderman, M.D., and Faley, R.H. (1987). An examination of employee perceptions of a subjective performance appraisal system. *Journal of Business and Psychology, 2,* 112–121.
33. Lee. Poor performance appraisals.
34. Grenssing-Pophal, L. (2001). Motivate managers to review performance. *HRMagazine,* March, 44–48.
35. Bernardin and Beatty. *Performance Appraisal.*
36. Ouchi, W. (1977). The relationship between organizational structure and organizational control. *Administrative Science Quarterly, 22,* 95–113.
37. Bretz, R.D., Milkovich, G.T., and Read, W. (1992). The current state of performance appraisal research and practice: Concerns, directions and implications. *Journal of Management, 18* (2), 321–352.
38. Miner, J.B. (1983). Management appraisal: A review of procedures and practices. In K. Pearlman, F.L. Schmidt, and W.C. Hammer (eds.). *Contemporary Problems in Personnel.* New York: John Wiley & Sons.
39. Thibadoux, G., Kleiman, L.S., and Greenberg, I.S. (1989). Coworker appraisals: An alternative method for evaluating job performance. *Today's CPA, 15,* 31–34.
40. Ibid.
41. Harris, M.M., and Schaubroeck, J. (1988). A meta-analysis of self-supervisor, self-peer, and peer-supervisor ratings. *Personnel Psychology, 41,* 43–62.
42. Thibadoux et al. Coworker appraisals.
43. Harris and Schaubroeck. A meta-analysis.
44. Williams, J.R., and Levy, P.E. (1992). The effects of perceived system knowledge on the agreement between self-ratings and supervisor ratings. *Personnel Psychology, 45* (4), 835–848.
45. Campbell, D.J., and Lee, C. (1988). Self-appraisal in performance evaluation: Development versus evaluation. *Academy of Management Review, 13,* 302–314.
46. Millman, J.F., Zawacki, R.A., Norman, C., Powell, L., and Kirksey, J. (1994). Companies evaluate employees from all perspectives. *Personnel Journal,* November, 99–103.
47. Becton, J.B., and Schraeder, M. (2004). Participant input in rater selection: Potential effects on the quality and acceptance of ratings in the context of 360-degree feedback. *Public Personnel Management, 33* (1), 23–30.
48. Pfau, B., and Kay, I. (2002). Does 360-degree feedback negatively affect company performance? *HRMagazine,* June, 55–59.

49. Waldman, D.A., Atwater, L.E., and Antonioni, D. (1998). Has 360-degree feedback gone amok? *Academy of Management Executive, 12* (2), 86-94.

50. Bernardin and Beatty. *Performance Appraisal.*

51. Stone, D.L., Gueutal, H.G., and McIntosh, B. (1984). The effects of feedback sequence and expertise of rater on perceived feedback accuracy. *Personnel Psychology, 37,* 487-506.

52. Ibid.

53. Baron, R.A. (1988). Negative effects of destructive criticism: Impact on conflict, self-efficacy, and task performance. *Journal of Applied Psychology, 73,* 199-207.

54. Bretz et al. The current state.

55. Kleiman et al. An examination of employee perceptions.

56. Ibid.

57. Bobko, P., and Colella, A. (1994). Employee reactions to performance standards: A review and research propositions. *Personnel Psychology, 47,* (1), 1-30.

58. Seijts, G.H., and Latham, G.P. (2005). Learning versus performance goals: When should each be used? *Academy of Management Executive, 19* (1), 124-131.

Determining Pay and Benefits

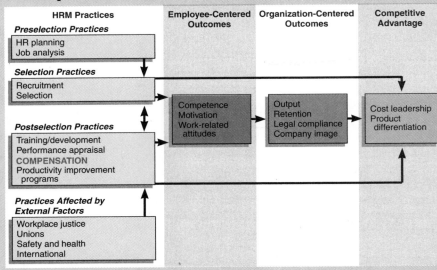

Chapter Nine

HRM Practices

Preselection Practices
- HR planning
- Job analysis

Selection Practices
- Recruitment
- Selection

Postselection Practices
- Training/development
- Performance appraisal
- **COMPENSATION**
- Productivity improvement programs

Practices Affected by External Factors
- Workplace justice
- Unions
- Safety and health
- International

Employee-Centered Outcomes
- Competence
- Motivation
- Work-related attitudes

Organization-Centered Outcomes
- Output
- Retention
- Legal compliance
- Company image

Competitive Advantage
- Cost leadership
- Product differentiation

Key Terms

comparable worth
compensable factors
Consolidated Omnibus Budget Reconciliation Act (COBRA)
defined benefit plan
defined contribution plan
employee contributions
Employee Retirement Income Security Act (ERISA)
Equal Pay Act (EPA)
equity
equity theory
exempt employees
external competitiveness
Fair Labor Standards Act (FLSA)
flexible benefit (cafeteria) plans
inputs

internal consistency
job evaluation
job evaluation committee
nonexempt employees
outcomes
pay grades
pay policy
pay policy line
pay range
point-factor method
salary survey
skill-based pay
Social Security Act
unemployment compensation
utilization review programs
workers' compensation

Chapter Objectives

Upon completion of this chapter, you will be able to:

- Explain how effective compensation systems enhance competitive advantage.
- Understand how people form perceptions about a pay system's equity.
- Describe how organizations can build an equitable pay system.

- Define the legal constraints imposed on organizational pay practices.
- Understand the various benefit options and their administration.

9-1 Gaining Competitive Advantage

9-1a Opening Case: Gaining Competitive Advantage at Old Country Buffet[1]

The Problem: A Turnover Problem among Frontline Service Employees

Old Country Buffet Restaurant was experiencing a turnover problem with its store managers, as the annual turnover rate hovered around 40 percent. When a good manager leaves the restaurant, the operation goes through turmoil and performance slips, typically costing the restaurant about $20,000 in sales. With approximately 160 managers leaving each year, the turnover problem was costing the restaurant over $3 million annually. David Goronkin, Vice President of Operations, noted that for the restaurant to grow, it had to improve its managers' retention rates.

The Solution: Implementing an Incentive Program for Managers

Old Country Buffet initiated an incentive program for its managers that was aimed at increasing sales and profits, while encouraging retention. The plan has two components. The first is the establishment of the Founder's Club. The restaurant rewards its Founder's Club members by providing them and their spouses with a weeklong, all expenses paid trip to the Bahamas. General managers earn their way into this club by meeting challenging sales and profit goals. The second component of the incentive program is paying its top managers (as determined by senior-level managers) a $20,000 bonus for signing a three-year commitment letter.

How the Incentive Plan Enhanced Competitive Advantage

Since implementing this program three years ago, the turnover rate for managers has dropped from 40 to 14 percent and restaurants' overall performance has improved, as managers have worked hard to meet their goals in order to qualify for membership in the Founder's Club. In its first year, only four managers qualified for membership; three years later, the number of grew to 272. Moreover, the restaurants managed by Founder's Club members have increased sales by 7 percent and guest counts by over 4 percent, resulting in a $43 million dollar increase in total profits for the restaurant.

9-1b Linking Pay and Benefits to Competitive Advantage

This chapter and the next focus on the issue of employee *compensation.* Employees receive compensation from a company in return for work performed. Most people think of compensation in terms of salary alone. However, it is more than that; it is "all forms of financial returns and tangible services and benefits employees receive as part of an employment relationship."[2] The phrase "financial returns" refers to pay, and "services and benefits" refer to such things as insurance, paid vacation and sick days, pension plans, and employee discounts.

This chapter focuses on the development of a firm's compensation system (i.e., the determination of pay levels and benefit plans). Chapter 10, "Implementing Productivity Improvement Programs," shows how compensation and other HRM interventions affect productivity.

An organization's compensation practices can have far-reaching effects on competitive advantage. As compensation expert Richard Henderson notes, "Probably no one cost of business is more controllable and has a greater influence on profits than labor costs."[3] If effective, a firm's compensation system can improve cost efficiency, ensure legal compliance, enhance recruitment efforts, and reduce morale and turnover problems. We now take a closer look at each of these issues.

Improving Cost Efficiency

Labor costs greatly affect competitive advantage because they represent a large portion of a company's operating budget. By *effectively* cutting these costs, a firm can achieve cost leadership. The impact of labor costs on competitive advantage is particularly strong in service and other labor-intensive organizations, where employers spend between 40 and 80 cents of each revenue dollar on such costs.[4] This means that for each dollar of revenue generated, as much as 80 cents may go to employee pay and benefits.

Compensation costs have risen sharply in recent years due primarily to the escalating costs of benefits:[5] During the past 25 years, the annual cost of benefits nationwide has risen from $250 billion to $740 billion.[6] According to management expert Shari Caudron, no other business expense during the next three years will affect the employer's bottom line as dramatically as the predicted 15 to 20 percent growth in health insurance premiums.[7] Organizations must contain these spiraling costs if they are to get a proper return on their human resource investments and thus gain competitive advantage.

When compensation-related costs escalate, the organization must find a way to offset them. In the past, companies passed higher compensation costs along to the customer in the form of higher prices. However, U.S. companies can no longer raise prices and remain competitive in light of fierce domestic and foreign competition, unfavorable exchange rates, and cheaper foreign labor costs.[8] Consequently, organizations unable to contain compensation costs may be forced to implement such adverse actions as pay freezes or massive layoffs.

Achieving Legal Compliance

A host of laws regulate corporate compensation practices. Some pertain to pay issues, such as discrimination, minimum wages, and overtime pay; others pertain to benefits, such as pensions, compensation for unemployment, and workers' compensation for work-related injuries. Organizations must understand and fully follow these laws or they could experience costly lawsuits or government fines.

Enhancing the Success of Recruitment Efforts and Reducing Morale and Turnover Problems

Pay and benefits are extremely important to both applicants and employees. The compensation received from work is a major reason for seeking employment for most people. Not only does compensation provide a means of sustenance and allow people to satisfy their materialistic and recreation needs, but it also serves to satisfy their ego or self-esteem needs.[9]

Consequently, if a firm's compensation system is viewed as inadequate, top applicants may reject that company's employment offers, and current employees may choose to leave the organization.[10] Moreover, disgruntled employees choosing to remain with the organization may begin to behave unproductively (e.g., become less motivated, helpful, or cooperative).[11]

9-2 HRM Issues and Practices

9-2a Influence of Compensation on Attitudes and Behavior

Because compensation practices heavily influence recruitment, morale, and turnover, it is important that applicants and employees view these practices in a favorable light. In the following section, we discuss how people form perceptions about a firm's compensation system and how these perceptions ultimately affect their behavior.

Pay Satisfaction: The Importance of Equity

One would expect that an individual's satisfaction with his or her compensation would simply be a function of the amount of compensation received: the higher the compensation rate, the greater the satisfaction. It may come as a surprise to learn that the amount of pay has been found to be less important that its perceived fairness or equity.[12]

To put this finding in perspective, consider the behavior of many professional athletes when negotiating a new contract. Ball players, for instance, offered as much as $9 or $10 million per year are often dissatisfied and demand larger salaries. In many instances, these demands stem from neither need nor greed. Rather, the demand for greater salaries often stems from perceptions of inequity. For instance, despite a $10 million salary, a player may feel that his pay is inequitable because a less capable player (or someone he perceives as being less capable) is earning an even higher salary.

Equity Theory

Because equity is such an important concern, individuals responsible for developing a firm's compensation system need to understand how perceptions of equity are formed. **Equity theory,** formulated by J. Stacy Adams, attempts to provide such an understanding.[13]

Adams' theory states that people form equity beliefs based on two factors: inputs and outcomes. **Inputs (I)** refer to the perceptions that people have concerning what they contribute to the job (e.g., skill and effort). **Outcomes (O)** refer to the perceptions that people have regarding the returns they get (e.g., pay) for the work they perform.

People judge the equity of their pay by comparing their outcome-to-input ratio (O/I) with another person's ratio. This comparison person is referred to as one's "referent other." People feel equity when the O/I ratios of the individual and his or her referent other are perceived as being equal. A feeling of inequity occurs when the two ratios are perceived as being unequal. For example, inequity occurs if a person feels that he or she contributes the same input as a referent other, but earns a lower salary.[14]

A person's referent other could be any one of several people. People may compare themselves to others

- Doing the same job within the same organization
- In the same organization, but performing different jobs
- Doing the same job in other organizations

For example, an assistant manager at Wal-Mart might compare her pay to other assistant managers at Wal-Mart, to Wal-Mart employees in other positions (both above and below her in the organizational hierarchy), or to assistant managers at Kmart.

equity Fairness.

equity theory A pay fairness theory that states that people form equity beliefs by comparing their outcome/input ratio to that of a referent other.

inputs The perceptions that people have concerning what they contribute to the job.

outcomes The perceptions that people have regarding the returns they get for the work they perform.

So how does one choose a referent other? Although the mechanism is largely unknown, one study found that people do not limit their comparisons to just one person—they have several referent others. When assessing the fairness of their pay, they compare themselves to *all* their referent others.[15] Perceived fairness is achieved only when *each* comparison is viewed as equitable. For example, the Wal-Mart assistant manager would consider herself underpaid when discovering that a Kmart assistant manager with the same experience was earning a higher salary, even if her two other comparisons (i.e., to Wal-Mart employees above and below her in the organizational hierarchy) were judged as being as equitable.

Impact of Equity Perceptions on Employee Behavior

When employees' O/I ratios are less than that of their referent others, they feel they are being underpaid; when greater, they feel they are being overpaid. According to equity theory, both conditions produce feelings of tension. When underpaid, they most often attempt to reduce tension in one of the following ways:[16]

- *Decrease their inputs* by reducing their effort or performance.
- *Escape the situation.* This response may be manifested by a variety of behaviors, such as absenteeism, tardiness, excessive work breaks, or quitting.

Research findings, for example, have linked underpayment to increases in absenteeism and turnover and to decreases in the amount of effort exerted on the job.[17] These links are especially strong among individuals earning low salaries.[18]

Contrary to equity theory predictions, tension-reducing responses occur only when employees believe they are underpaid.[19] Overpaid individuals do not respond because they feel little, if any, tension and thus have no need to reduce it. (The research findings on the issue of overpayment find overpayment to be just as satisfying as equity,[20] or somewhat dissatisfying, but not nearly as dissatisfying as underpayment.)[21]

When feeling underpaid, why do some people choose to decrease their inputs, while others choose to escape the situation? Researchers Sarah Rynes and George Milkovich shed some light on this issue when they found that employees' reactions to inequity depend on the source of the comparison: People react differently depending on whether the source of the inequity is internal or external. When perceptions of inequity are based on external comparisons, people are more likely to quit their jobs. For instance, a nurse working for Hospital A may move to Hospital B if the latter pays a higher salary. When based on internal comparisons, people are more likely to remain at work, but reduce their inputs (e.g., become less willing to help others with problems, meet deadlines, or take initiatives).[22]

9-2b Establishing Pay Rates within an Organization

We may conclude from our previous discussion that employees will believe their pay is equitable when they perceive these circumstances:

1. It is fair relative to the pay coworkers in the same organization receive (called *internal consistency*).
2. It is fair relative to the pay received by workers in other organizations who hold similar positions (called *external competitiveness*).
3. It fairly reflects their input to the organization (called *employee contributions*).

We now examine how a firm can achieve these aims when developing pay rates for each job.

Achieving Internal Consistency

To achieve **internal consistency,** a firm's employees must believe that all workers are being paid what they are "worth"; this is, company pay rates reflect the overall

internal consistency
Occurs when each employee's pay is fair relative to the pay coworkers in the same organization receive.

| Taking a Closer Look 9-1 | *Standards for Conducting Job Evaluations* |

Consistency

Job evaluation ratings should be consistent across both people and time. As we noted in Chapter 6, this standard is called *reliability;* it is achieved when two people evaluating the same jobs provide similar ratings, and when the ratings made by one person on two different occasions are similar.

Freedom from Bias

Self-interest must not enter the evaluation process. The process should be free of political considerations and personal biases. Those making the evaluations should be objective and refrain from trying to "take care of their own." For instance, department managers should not inflate evaluations for jobs in their own departments.

Correctability

Firms should provide mechanisms to modify inaccurate or out-of-date evaluations. Management should periodically review and update job evaluation results. Moreover, employees should be allowed to review the evaluations of their jobs and to appeal the ratings if dissatisfied.

Representativeness

All employees affected by the process should have their concerns represented.

Accuracy of Information

Job evaluation ratings must be based on accurate information. That is, those making the evaluations should be quite knowledgeable of the jobs being rated.

Source: Newman, J.M., and Milkovich, G.T. (1990). Procedural justice challenges in compensation: Eliminating the fairness gap. *Labor Law Journal,* August, 575–580.

contribution of each person's job to the organization. Because some jobs afford a greater opportunity than others to contribute, those holding such jobs should receive greater pay. Most would agree, for instance, that nurses should be paid more than orderlies because their work is more important; that is, it contributes more to patient care, which is a primary goal of hospitals.

For pay rates to be internally consistent, then, an organization must first determine the overall importance or worth of each job. A job's worth is typically evaluated based on "informed judgments" regarding such things as the amount of skill and effort required to perform the job, the difficulty of the job, and the amount of responsibility assumed by the jobholder. The systematic process for determining the worth of a job is called a **job evaluation.**

job evaluation A systematic process for determining the worth of a job.

Standards for Job Evaluation

Job evaluation judgments must be accurate and fair, given the fact that the pay each employee receives is so heavily influenced by them. Taking a Closer Look 9-1 displays the standards a firm must meet for ensuring the accuracy and fairness of job evaluations.

Most firms create a committee of individuals, called a **job evaluation committee,** for the purpose of making the evaluations. Those serving on the committee represent the various functional areas and thus, collectively, are familiar with all the jobs being evaluated. Such individuals typically include department managers, vice presidents, plant managers, and HR professionals (e.g., employee relations specialists, compensation managers). The committee chair is usually the HR professional or an outside consultant.

job evaluation committee A committee of individuals convened for the purpose of making job evaluations.

The major problem with job evaluation ratings is subjectivity, which can cause inaccurate and unreliable ratings. To minimize subjectivity, the rating scales used to evaluate jobs must be clearly defined, and evaluators should be thoroughly trained on how to use them. Moreover, the evaluators should be provided with complete, accurate, and up-to-date job descriptions.

EXHIBIT 9-1	Compensable Factors Used in the Point-Factor Method of Job Evaluation

Compensable Factor	Rating Criteria
Skill/know-how	Education
	Experience
Knowledge	
Effort	Physical effort
Mental effort	
Responsibility	Judgment/decision making
	Internal business contacts
	Consequence of error
	Degree of influence
	Supervisory responsibilities
	Responsibility for independent action
	Responsibility for machinery/equipment
	Fiscal responsibility
	Responsibility for confidential information
Working conditions	Risks
	Comfort
	Physical demands
	Personal demands

Source: De Cenzo, D.A., and Holviak, S.J. (1990). *Employee Benefits*. Englewood Cliffs, NJ: Prentice Hall.

How Job Evaluation Is Conducted

The job evaluation process is analogous to performance appraisal in that evaluators are asked to provide certain ratings on a form. Job evaluation ratings, however, focus on the requirements of the *job* rather than on the performance of the individual *jobholder.* Several methods may be used to evaluate jobs. We will limit our discussion to the point-factor method, which is the most commonly used approach.[23]

In the **point-factor method** of job evaluation, jobs are evaluated separately on several criteria, called **compensable factors.** These factors represent the most important determinants of a job's worth. A list of some commonly used factors and the criteria on which they are judged appears in Exhibit 9-1.

A point-factor rating instrument is illustrated in the appendix of this chapter. The rating scale used to evaluate the first factor (physical and mental effort) is shown in Figure 9-1 and explained in Exhibit 9-2. The development of a point-factor rating scale consists of the following steps:

1. Select and carefully define the compensable factors that will be used to determine job worth.

2. Determine the number of levels or degrees for each factor. The only rule for establishing the number of degrees is that some jobs should fall at each level.[24]

3. Carefully define each degree level. Each adjacent level must be clearly distinguishable.

point-factor method A job evaluation method in which each job is assigned points for compensable factors.

compensable factors Criteria representing the most important determinants of a job's worth.

Figure 9-1
Levels of Mental and Physical Effort

Sedentary

Some effort

Strenuous effort

> **EXHIBIT 9-2** | A Point-Factor Rating Scale for Judging Mental and Physical Effort

Factor 1: Physical and Mental Effort

Definition: This factor measures the physical, visual, and mental demands of the job. These demands should be assessed in terms of frequency, time, and severity. For instance, a job requiring occasional demands would not be evaluated as highly as one requiring almost continual demands.

Degrees and Definitions

1. Sedentary. Typically, the employee sits comfortably to do the work. The job requires normal expenditure of energy and little or no unusual physical effort or mental/visual concentration. (5 points)
2. The work requires some physical exertion, such as long periods of standing, recurring bending, stooping, reaching, and lifting of moderately heavy items. Or it requires some mental/visual concentration, such as that required in monitoring a process. (20 points)
3. The work requires strenuous physical effort, such as that needed for the continuous lifting, carrying, and moving of heavy objects. Or the work requires the continuous need for mental/visual concentration for long periods of time, which permits little or no interruptions, such as watching for defects on a fast-moving conveyor line. (50 points)

Source: Adapted from Swanke, J.A. (1992). Ways to tame workers' comp premiums. *HRMagazine,* February, 39–41.

4. Weigh each compensable factor in terms of its relative importance for determining job worth. *how can an employee raise revenue, lower cost?*
5. Assign point values to the degrees associated with each compensable factor. Factors assigned greater weights in step 4 would be allotted a greater number of possible points for each degree level.

When completing the job evaluation ratings, the evaluators rate each job, one factor at a time, until all jobs have been evaluated on all factors. They then calculate a total point value for a job by summing the points earned on each compensable factor.

This approach to job evaluation is difficult and time-consuming. However, most organizations believe that it is well worth the effort. If properly conducted, the overall score for each job should reflect its relative worth to the organization, thus enabling the firm to establish internal consistency.[25]

Assigning Jobs to Pay Grades

When job evaluations have been completed, jobs are grouped into **pay grades** based on the total number of points received. Jobs with the same or similar point values are placed in the same grade. An example of a point–pay grade conversion chart is illustrated in Exhibit 9-3. All jobs earning up to 150 points would be assigned to Pay Grade 1, jobs earning 151–300 points to Pay Grade 2, and so forth.

Administrators use pay grades because, without them, firms would need to establish separate pay rates for each job evaluation point score. Once jobs are classified into grades, all jobs within the same grade are treated alike for pay purposes; that is, the same range of pay applies to each job in a grade.

pay grades Job groupings in which all jobs assigned to the same group are subject to the same range of pay.

> **EXHIBIT 9-3** | Converting Job Evaluation Points into Pay Grades

Point Range	Grade
Up to 150	1
151–300	2
301–450	3
451–600	4
601–750	5
751–900	6
901–1,050	7

As they develop pay grade systems, companies must decide how many pay grades to establish. Most firms use 30 to 50 pay grades. However, some use as many as 100 of more; others use as few as five or six. The practice of limiting the number of pay grades eases the firm's administrative burdens. However, using a limited number of grades creates a situation in which jobs of significantly different worth fall into the same grade and receive the same pay. This outcome would lead to equity problems. For instance, consider an extreme example, in which a hospital chooses to use only three pay grades. All jobs earning 0–500 points are placed in Pay Grade 1; those earning 501–1,000 points are placed in Pay Grade 2; jobs earning more than 1,000 points are put in Pay Grade 3. Such a system could end up placing the jobs of nurse and nurse's aide in Pay Grade 1. If this outcome occurred, both sets of workers would receive the same salary. Understandably, the nurses would feel underpaid in this situation.

Achieving External Competitiveness

external competitiveness
Occurs when each employee's pay is fair relative to the pay received by workers in other organizations who hold similar positions.

A firm achieves **external competitiveness** when employees perceive that their pay is fair in relation to what their counterparts in other organizations earn. To become externally competitive, organizations must first learn what other employers are paying and then make a decision regarding just how competitive they want to be. They then establish pay rates consistent with this decision. For example, let's say that compared to its competitors, Wal-Mart wants to offer its managers the best salaries. It would thus try to learn what its competitors are paying and then offer its managers an even higher salary. We now examine how these steps are carried out.

Collecting Salary Survey Information

salary survey   A survey that seeks information on pay rates offered by a firm's competitors.

A **salary survey** provides information on pay rates offered by a firm's competitors for certain benchmark jobs (i.e., jobs that are performed in a similar manner in all companies and can thus serve as a basis for making meaningful comparisons).

Some firms gather this information from existing surveys already conducted by others, such as those produced by the Bureau of Labor Statistics. Trade associations also conduct surveys routinely for their members, or companies may hire consulting firms to gather such information. Salary information can also be found on a number of websites. Salary surveys conducted by others should be used when they reliably contain all the information needed by the company in question. When no such surveys exist, companies generally conduct their own by following the steps described in Taking a Closer Look 9-2.

Establishing a Pay Policy

pay policy   A company policy stipulating how well it will pay its employees relative to the market.

After the pay practices of other companies have been identified, the organization must determine how competitive it wants to be (or can afford to be). Specifically, it must set a **pay policy** stipulating how well it will pay its employees relative to the market (i.e., what competitors pay for similar jobs).[26]

The determination of a pay policy is a crucial step in the design of a pay system. If pay rates are set too low, the organization is likely to experience recruitment and turnover problems. If set too high, however, the organization is likely to experience budget problems that may ultimately lead to higher prices, pay freezes, layoffs, and so forth.[27]

The majority of firms pay at the market rate. Those paying above market are typically companies with the ability to pay who desire to attract and retain top-notch employees. Those paying below market generally do so because they are unable to pay higher salaries. Such companies often attempt to attract employees by linking pay to productivity or profits so that employees can earn more if the company does well.[28] Such practices are discussed further in Chapter 10.

When setting its pay policy, a company must consider its strategic plan. For example, if long-term employee commitment is a strategic goal, the organization should

Taking a Closer Look 9-2 — *Conducting a Salary Survey*

Determine What Information to Collect

The primary information sought in a salary survey is the amount of pay offered to incumbents in the jobs under study. This includes:

- The established salary range (minimum to maximum)
- The actual salary range (the lowest and highest salary currently being paid)
- The average starting salary
- The average salary level now being paid

Salary surveys also seek information regarding each company's total compensation plan, such as its forms of pay (e.g., merit pay, profit sharing, bonuses, commissions, shift differentials) and benefit options. This information is needed so that the entire compensation package offered by competitors can be assessed.

Select Benchmark Jobs

Organizations usually do not seek information about all their jobs when conducting a salary survey. Such a process is expensive and time-consuming. Rather, companies focus on several benchmark jobs. Benchmark jobs are jobs that are performed in a similar manner in all companies and can thus serve as a basis for making meaningful comparisons. Examples include such jobs as receptionist and floor nurse.

A minimum of 30 percent of the firm's jobs should be designated as benchmarks. When selecting benchmark jobs, the organization must ensure that:

- Each job is clearly defined so that the responding companies can identify which of their jobs match each of the benchmark jobs.

- The jobs represent all points along the pay hierarchy.
- The jobs encompass a sizable number of employees.

Select Which Companies to Survey

The next step in the process is to select specific companies to survey. To do so, a company must define its "relevant market"; that is, it must identify its competitors. Competitors are those firms with whom an organization competes for employees.

The relevant market varies for different types of jobs. For some jobs, such as clerical, the relevant market consists of all similarly sized companies in the local geographic area. The geographic area would be much broader for highly skilled occupations because a sufficient number of applicants is unlikely to be found in the local geographic area.

In some instances, the relevant market is also a function of the specific industry involved. For example, the relevant market for professors would be limited to colleges and universities; for tellers, it would be limited to banking institutions.

Because the relevant market varies according to the type of job under consideration, organizations must actually conduct several salary surveys—one for each relevant market.

- When the number of companies within a relevant market is small (say, less than 20), all of them are usually surveyed.
- When the market consists of a greater number of companies, organizations will usually select a representative sample to survey.

Source: De Cenzo, D.A., and Holoviak, S.J. (1990). *Employee Benefits.* Englewood Cliffs, NJ: Prentice Hall.

attempt to develop compensation strategies that will enhance retention, like establishing a generous retirement plan for long-service employees or adopting an incentive plan tied to tenure.[29] Recall the opening case: Old Country Buffet reduced its turnover rates by providing managers with incentives for remaining in their jobs for three more years. On the other hand, if hiring top-notch applicants is a strategic goal, as it might be in an R&D firm wanting to attract top engineers and scientists, then the firm should consider raising its starting salaries or offering better "perks," such as a generous relocation package or generous stock options.

Establishing Pay Rates

Once market rates for jobs are determined and a pay policy is established, an organization must price each of its jobs. Because market rates identified by a salary survey are usually restricted to benchmark jobs, how do organizations determine these rates for their nonbenchmark jobs?

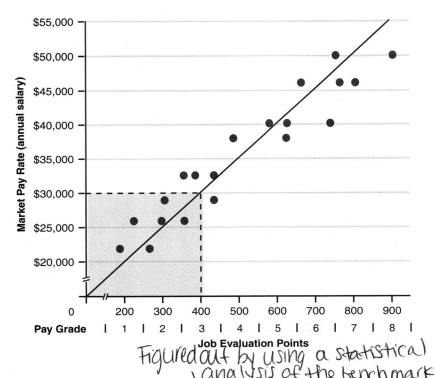

Figure 9-2
Scatterplot and Pay Policy Line Depicting the Relationship between Job Evaluation Points and Market Pay Rates

pay policy line
A regression line that shows the statistical relationship between job evaluation points and prevailing market rates.

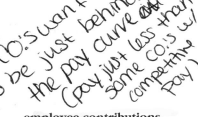

[handwritten: CO's want to be just behind the pay curve and (pay just less than some co's w/ competitive pay)]

employee contributions
Occurs when employees' pay fairly reflects their input to the organization.

pay range The minimum and maximum pay rates for all jobs within a pay grade.

[handwritten: Figured out by using a statistical analysis of the benchmark job data]

Using the data collected on the benchmark jobs, an organization would determine the statistical relationship (i.e., simple linear regression) between job evaluation points and prevailing market rates. (Recall our discussion of regression in Chapter 3, "Planning for Human Resources," when we described its use in forecasting.) This regression line is referred to as the **pay policy line.** The appropriate pay rates for nonbenchmark jobs are set based on this line.

Such a pay policy line appears in Figure 9-2. An HR professional could determine the market rate for Pay Grade 3 jobs, for example, by first finding the job evaluation point value falling at the midpoint of the pay grade (400 points). One then moves up vertically from that point until reaching the pay policy line. The market rate for that pay grade is the value on the y-axis ($30,000) that corresponds to that point on the pay policy line. The firm then adjusts it pay scale to reflect its pay policy. For instance, if it decides to pay 10 percent more than its average competitor, then Pay Grade 3 employees would earn $33,000 ($30,000 + 10%).

Recognizing Employee Contributions

Employee contributions equity is achieved when employees believe that their pay fairly reflects their level of contribution to the organization. To achieve this aim, an organization must first establish a pay range for each pay grade; it must then place each employee within that range based on his or her contribution to the organization.

Establishing a Pay Range

A **pay range** specifies the minimum and maximum pay rates for all jobs within a grade. When establishing pay ranges, most employers set the market rate at the midpoint of the range. The spread from the midpoint usually varies, becoming larger as one progresses to higher pay grades (see Figure 9-3). Most organizations establish a range spread of 10 to 25 percent for office and production work, 35 to 60 percent for professional and lower-level management positions, and 60 to 120 percent for top-level management positions.[30]

The mechanism for placing each employee within a pay range differs for new and existing employees. New employees are usually paid at the bottom of the pay range unless their qualifications exceed the minimum. For instance, say the pay range for an

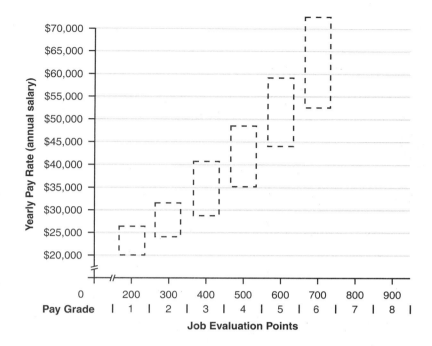

Figure 9-3
The Spread of Pay Ranges

entry-level HR position were $35,000–$50,000. A new hire without experience would start at $35,000. But one with experience, say three years, would start at a higher rate, perhaps $40,000.

Existing employees' contributions are usually recognized in the form of pay raises, typically granted on the basis of seniority and/or performance, as we shall see in Chapter 10. Some companies, however, have adopted a relatively new practice that ties pay raises to skill acquisition. We discuss this practice in the following paragraphs.

Skill-Based Pay

The use of **skill-based pay** is based on the assumption that workers who acquire additional skills can make a greater contribution to the organization and, consequently, should be paid more. Firms utilizing skill-based pay will thus grant employees pay increases for acquiring new, job-related skills. An example of the skill-based program used at General Mills appears in On the Road to Competitive Advantage 9-1.

A skill-based pay program is usually implemented as follows:[31]

1. Identify tasks that need to be performed.
2. Determine what skills are needed to perform the tasks.
3. Develop tests or measures to determine whether an individual has learned the skills.
4. Price each skill based on its value to the organization.
5. Communicate to employees the skills they can learn and how much they will be paid for learning them.

Skill-based pay systems have both strengths and weaknesses. Concerning strengths, such systems provide workers with a financial incentive to increase their skill levels. For instance, public school teachers often pursue a master's degree when provided with the incentive of a pay raise.

When workers acquire additional skills, the company also benefits. Earning a master's degree presumably makes one a better teacher. When used in production environments, like at General Mills, skill-based pay programs broaden workers' skills so that the company can gain greater flexibility in work scheduling. For example, when

skill-based pay
A compensation approach that grants employees pay increases for acquiring new, job-related skills.

Skill-Based Pay: Case Study at General Mills

I. Background
  A. Opening a new plant to manufacture Squeeze-it drink
  B. Stages of production process:
    1. *Materials handling:* Receive and stage raw materials and ship final product.
    2. *Mixing:* Combine raw materials for the fruit drink.
    3. *Filling:* Machines blow mold plastic bottles, fill them with juice, and seal the bottles.
    4. *Packaging:* Workers operate machines that successively package the bottles into six-packs, cases, and pallet loads; they also monitor the machines that perform quality checks.
  C. The traditional approach to jobs and pay
    1. Hire people to work at each stage in process.
    2. Use job evaluations and pay surveys to determine wages for each job.
  D. General Mills approach: Use of work teams
    1. Four self-regulating production teams of 15 employees and a small support staff
    2. Each team performs all the operations on its shift.
    3. One job title: Operator/mechanic. Perform all the routine maintenance work. The most important role of employees is to monitor and control the production process. Workers need to be able to detect production and quality problems as they arise and to communicate any problems to the appropriate employees, even if the problems are in work areas other than their own.
II. How the Skill-Based Pay Program Works
  A. Skill blocks
    1. Each production stage represents a block.
    2. There are three skill levels per block, representing increased degrees of knowledge and skill:
      • Level 1: Limited ability
      • Level 2: Partial proficiency
      • Level 3: Full competence (can analyze and solve production problems and conduct some major maintenance, such as rebuilding a machine)
  B. Pay progression
    1. A new employee is initially assigned to any block and is paid at the entry rate.
    2. After about three months on the job, the employee can become certified for Level 1 and receive a pay raise.

3. The employee then begins working at Level 2 within that skill block; the employee becomes certified and moves to Level 3 or to the entry level of a new block and begins the process over again.
4. An employee must stay within a block until reaching Level 2. Workers who are unable to become certified at that level are dismissed.
5. All levels are equal in value. Thus, each certification produces a pay raise of equal value.
  C. Training
    1. Training is available for each skill level.
    2. The production team manages the training. An employee who is certified for a given skill is responsible for training the next employee who rotates into the position.
    3. Employees must wait for openings in new areas before they can rotate and begin to train. Each skill block has a different number of positions. For instance, there are only two in material handling.
    4. A new employee usually can reach the top rate (Level 3 in all blocks) within four or five years.
  D. Certification
    1. Each skill block is broken down into a list of specific tasks, knowledge, and troubleshooting skills. These are organized into checklists.
    2. The employee acting as a trainer uses the checklists to determine whether the employee has acquired the skills and knowledge relevant to each level in the block.
    3. When the trainer feels the employee has attained the necessary skill, certification is recommended. At this point, the employee's entire team must approve the certification.
      • No time limit is set.
      • No test is given.
    4. If the employee cannot perform well at the next level (for which he or she has been certified), both the worker and trainer lose their previous pay raise.

Source: Ledford, G.E., and Bergel, G. (1994). *HRM Compensation.* Chicago: Commerce Clearing House.

several people know how to operate a particular piece of equipment, the organization can easily find a substitute when the usual equipment operator is absent from work.[32]

Other advantages associated with skill-based pay systems are as follows:

* The additional skills learned by the workers allow them to perform all portions of the production process. They can thus work together to end bottlenecks.

* Employees with broadened skills will no longer be limited to a perspective that comes from doing just one step in the process. Consequently, they

    * Can communicate more effectively with employees doing other parts of the production or service because they now understand what these people are doing

    * Can solve problems more effectively because they have a broader understanding of the organization

    * Would be more committed to see that the organization operates effectively because they have an overview of the entire operation

Many organizations such as Anheuser-Busch, Atlantic Richfield, DaimlerChrysler, Borg-Warner, Butler Manufacturing, and Westinghouse have begun to initiate skill-based programs during the past few years.[33] In fact, 51 percent of large companies are now using skill-based pay programs with at least some employees.[34]

Although the skill-based approach is becoming more prevalent, it can present several problems:

* Adds to labor costs because employees are paid more under such systems.

* May lead to inequity perceptions if two people are doing the same job, yet one is receiving greater pay for acquiring an additional skill.

* Is not cost-effective if the organization cannot make use of skilled employees in a way that adds significant value to its product or services. This would occur, for instance, if the system provided no incentive or opportunity for employees to use their newly acquired skills.[35]

* Creates a problem of determining when one employee has more skills than another. If such a determination is made on a subjective basis, it may lead to equity problems or even to claims of employment discrimination.

* The need to develop additional training programs and certification exams can become an administrative burden.

Thus, skill-based pay programs do not work equally well in all organizational settings. The ideal setting would probably be a company that has few hierarchical levels, engages in decentralized decision making, uses self-managed work teams, and emphasizes workforce flexibility and employee development.[36] Skill-based pay would probably be least effective in bureaucratic organizations that employ routine technologies under relatively stable conditions.[37]

9-2c Legal Constraints on Pay Practices

Several laws constrain pay and benefits practices. This section focuses on pay-related issues; benefits-related issues are addressed later when we discuss various benefit options.

The law imposes constraints on organizational pay practices in two major areas: (1) minimum wage and overtime and (2) pay discrimination.

Minimum Wage and Overtime

The primary law regulating minimum wage and overtime pay practices is the **Fair Labor Standards Act (FLSA)**. The FLSA is a 1938 federal statute covering all employers engaged in interstate commerce. Some small organizations, such as retail establishments, motion picture theaters, and taxicab companies, are exempt.[38] The act also

Fair Labor Standards Act (FLSA) A 1938 federal statute that regulates minimum wage and overtime pay.

Executive Employees

1. Primary duty must be managing the enterprise or managing a customarily recognized department or subdivision of the enterprise.
2. The employee must customarily and regularly direct the work of at least two or more other full-time employees or their equivalent.
3. The employee must have the authority to hire and fire other employees, or the employee's suggestions and recommendations as to the hiring, firing, advancement, promotion, or any other change of status of other employees must be given particular weight.
4. Salary must be at least $455 per week.

Administrative Employees

1. The employee's primary duty must be the performance of office or nonmanual work directly related to the management or general business operations of the employer or the employer's customers.
2. The employee's primary duty includes the exercise of discretion and independent judgment with respect to matters of significance.
3. Salary must be at least $455 per week.

Learned Professional Employees

1. The employee's primary duty must be the performance of work requiring advanced knowledge, defined as work that is predominantly intellectual in character and which includes work requiring consistent exercise of discretion and judgment.
2. The advanced knowledge must be in a field of science or learning.
3. The advanced knowledge must be customarily acquired by a prolonged course of specialized intellectual instruction.

4. Salary must be at least $455 per week.

Outside Sales Employees

1. The employee's primary duty must be making sales or obtaining contracts for services or for the use of facilities for which consideration will be paid by the client or customer.
2. The employee must be customarily and regularly engaged away from the employer's place or places of business.

There is no minimum salary requirement for this category.

Computer Employees

1. Primary duty of (an) application of systems analysis techniques and procedures, including consulting with users, to determine hardware, software, or system functional applications; or (b) design, development, documentation, analysis, creation, testing, or modification of computer systems or programs, including prototypes, based on and related to user or system design specifications; or (c) design, documentation, testing, creation, or modification of computer programs related to machine operating systems; or (d) a combination of duties described in (a), (b), and (c), the performance of which requires the same level of skills.
2. Employed as a computer systems analyst, computer programmer, software engineer, or other skilled worker in the computer field.
3. Must earn a salary of at least $455 per week or, on a fee basis, $26.63 an hour.

---

exempt employees
Employees whose pay and overtime are not regulated by the Fair Labor Standards Act.

nonexempt employees
Employees whose pay and overtime are regulated by the Fair Labor Standards Act.

exempts certain types of employees from its minimum wage and overtime requirements. Individuals holding such jobs are referred to as **exempt employees,** whereas all others are referred to as **nonexempt employees.** The criteria for determining whether a job is exempt were recently revised by Congress. The new criteria, which became effective in August 2004, are listed in Exhibit 9-4.[39]

Minimum Wage Provisions

In 1996, Congress amended the FLSA to raise the minimum wage to $5.15 an hour and to allow for a lower training wage ($4.25) for teenagers in the first 90 days of a job. Minimum wages are also specified in the wage and hour laws of most individual states. The FLSA specifies that when state minimum wage levels differ from that imposed by the FLSA, the employer must pay employees the *higher* of the two rates.

Overtime Provisions

The FLSA states that all nonexempt employees must be paid at a higher than usual rate for any overtime worked (i.e., all hours in excess of 40 in any given week). Specifically, the overtime pay rate must be no less than one and one-half times the employee's regular rate.

Legal Compliance with the FLSA

Each year about 75,000 claims are filed with the Department of Labor under the FLSA. Every year employers pay out over $100 million in wage-and-hour awards to employees. The average dollar amount has been steadily increasing each year due, in part, to a growing aggressiveness among claimants.[40]

Noncompliance with the overtime-pay provisions of the FLSA is the most frequent violation of the act. Such noncompliant acts are usually caused by employer ignorance of the law. Many employers, for instance, are not sufficiently familiar with the criteria for determining whether jobs are exempt or nonexempt. Such employers may unknowingly violate the FLSA overtime provisions by failing to pay overtime wages to nonexempt employees because they have been misclassified as exempt. For instance, many supervisory jobs are classified as exempt but, in reality, are nonexempt because the supervisor spends a great percentage of work time performing routine "line" duties.

Further, line managers sometimes misunderstand FLSA's definition of overtime work. This problem is discussed further in Section 9-3, "The Manager's Guide."

Pay and Discrimination

All of the various EEO laws covered in Chapter 2, "Understanding the Legal and Environmental Context of HRM," prohibit discrimination in pay based on protected group membership. The vast majority of cases litigated in this area have claimed sex discrimination. We now discuss the legal issues bearing on this topic.

The Equal Pay Act

The **Equal Pay Act (EPA),** passed as an amendment to the FLSA in 1963, prohibits sex discrimination in pay. Specifically, it bars employers from paying lower wages to one sex where the work of the two sexes is substantially equal (i.e., the jobs require an equal level of skill, effort, and responsibility and are performed under similar working conditions). This requirement is called the "equal pay for equal work" standard. Unequal pay for equal work is allowable, however, if the pay disparity between the sexes is based on differences in seniority, productivity, merit, or any factor other than sex.

Equal Pay Act (EPA)
An amendment to the FLSA that prohibits sex discrimination in pay.

The Gender Pay Gap

Despite the fact that the EPA has been in effect for more than 40 years, a significant pay gap still exists between the sexes. Women who worked full-time in 2003 earned only 80 cents for every dollar earned by their male counterparts.[41] The key question is "What causes this gap?" Has pay discrimination continued to run rampant, or is the pay gap merely a reflection of market factors?

Those espousing the "market factor" view attribute the pay gap to any or all of the following factors:

- Many more women than men work part-time.
- Women tend to stay in the workforce for shorter periods of time and thus have less seniority than men do.
- Women voluntarily choose to enter lower paying career fields.

Those holding the "discrimination" view believe that the disparity is largely due to the arbitrary undervaluing of jobs traditionally held by women; if women were paid based on their jobs' "true" worth, the pay gap would disappear. This "equal pay for equal *worth*" standard is called **comparable worth.**

Proponents of comparable worth believe that even if jobs are dissimilar, employees should receive equal wages if their overall worth to the employer is comparable. For example, if a hospital determined that the job of a nurse was as valuable as that of an HR professional, the two should be paid equivalent wages, despite the fact that the jobs are obviously different.

comparable worth
A standard for judging pay discrimination that calls for equal pay for equal worth.

Comparable Worth and the Law

Advocates of comparable worth initially tried to bring such lawsuits under the Equal Pay Act. This approach failed, however, because the EPA only applies when the work performed by the two sexes is substantially equal. Eventually, supporters of the comparable worth doctrine brought suit based on Title VII of the Civil Rights Act because this law is not bound by the "equal pay for equal work" standard.

The issue of comparable worth eventually came before the Supreme Court in 1981.[42] The case was filed by county prison matrons (i.e., female guards) who complained that they were being paid significantly less than the male guards despite the fact that the two jobs had a similar worth. Specifically, the difference in pay was 30 percent; the difference in worth was only 5 to 10 percent (as measured by job evaluations).

The Supreme Court had to resolve two issues: (1) Could pay discrimination lawsuits be brought under Title VII? (2) If so, could comparable worth be used as the basis for determining whether discrimination has occurred? Regarding the first issue, the Court ruled that Title VII did, indeed, apply to pay discrimination claims. However, the Court refused to rule on the second issue—comparable worth. Rather, the Court ruled in favor of the matrons because it concluded that the county intentionally discriminated against them, and intentional discrimination is clearly a violation of Title VII.

Although the legal status of comparable worth remains unclear, the following conclusions seem warranted: To win a comparable worth case, plaintiffs must prove disparate impact caused by intentional discrimination. Thus, when arguing a comparable worth case under Title VII, employees must demonstrate that significant salary differences exist between workers in male- and female-dominated jobs of comparable worth. If they prove this, the employer can still win the case if it convinces the court that the existing pay differences are not the result of intentional discrimination. It could argue, for instance, that the pay differences are merely a reflection of prevailing market factors.

For example, say a group of registered nurses (a job that is female-dominated) sues a hospital for sex discrimination because their pay is lower than that of the male-dominated HR professionals. The nurses could establish a *prima facie* case of discrimination by showing that the hospital's job evaluation study found the two jobs to be of equal worth. The hospital would win the case, however, if it could prove that the pay difference was not based on gender but, rather, on the fact that HR is the better paying profession.

9-2d Employee Benefit Options

Our discussion has thus far been restricted to the issue of pay. However, to compete for quality employees in today's marketplace, employers must do more than offer a "fair day's pay." Workers also want a good benefits package. In fact, employees have grown accustomed to generous benefits programs and have come to expect them.[43]

We now discuss the various benefit options that may be offered by employers.

Workers' Compensation

On average, an estimated 8.6 percent of the workforce, or about 9 million workers, are injured on the job each year.[44] Each state has **workers' compensation** laws that are designed to provide financial protection for such individuals. Specifically, these laws require the creation of a state-run, no-fault insurance system, paid for by employers. When workers suffer job-related injuries or illnesses, the insurance system provides compensation for

- Medical expenses
- Lost wages from the time of injury until their return to the job; employees are given a percentage of their income, the size of which varies from state to state
- Death (paid to family members), dismemberment, or permanent disability resulting from job-related injuries

Nationwide, payouts for workers' compensation have more than tripled in the past 20 years.[45] Much of this increase is due to fraud—workers falsely claiming injury in order to collect payments. The increase is also attributable to rising medical costs that

workers' compensation
A state-run, no-fault insurance system that provides income protection for workers experiencing job-related injuries or illnesses.

now account for as much as 60 percent of total workers' compensation costs in some states.[46]

The fastest growing category of workers' compensation claims is mental stress caused by things like job pressures, on-the-job harassment, time pressure, poor management, and job insecurity.[47] For example, a librarian was recently awarded workers' compensation by proving that she had become "emotionally disabled" because of stressful job conditions, supervisory criticism, and poorly defined areas of responsibility.[48] To successfully combat mental stress claims for workers' compensation, employers should:[49]

* Formulate a preventive strategy based on an analysis of the workplace to determine stress risks.
* Develop programs for stress reduction.
* Reduce levels of workplace stress.
* Teach workers how to handle stress.

Unemployment Compensation

The idea behind **unemployment compensation** is to provide income to unemployed individuals who have lost a job through no fault of their own.[50] Eligible workers receive weekly stipends for 26 weeks. The specific amount of the stipend, which varies from state to state, is determined by the wages the claimant was paid during the previous year.

Unemployment compensation laws in most states disqualify workers from receiving benefits under the following conditions:[51]

1. *Quitting one's job without good cause:* Workers who voluntarily quit their jobs are not eligible for unemployment compensation unless they can show good cause for quitting. Good cause exists only when the worker is faced with circumstances so compelling as to leave no reasonable alternative.

2. *Being discharged for misconduct connected with work:* If employees are discharged for misconduct, they are not eligible for unemployment, unless they can show that the discharge was unfair. To ensure fair discharges, employers should make employees aware of work rules through employee handbooks, posting of rules, and job descriptions, and must provide workers with adequate warnings prior to discharge (unless a serious violation, such as stealing, has occurred).

3. *Refusing suitable work while unemployed:* Eligibility for unemployment compensation is revoked if an employee refuses suitable work while unemployed. Individuals must actively seek work and make the required number of search contacts each week. Benefits are terminated if the claimant refuses a bona fide job offer or job referral.

Social Security

The **Social Security Act** of 1935, as amended, provides monthly benefits to retired workers who are at least 62 years of age, disabled workers, and their eligible spouses and dependents. Social Security is financed by contributions made by the employee and matched by the employer, computed as a percentage of the employee's earnings. Monthly benefits are based on the contributions made by the worker during the last three years of employment. The Social Security Act also provides Medicare coverage for anyone who is entitled to retirement benefits.

Continuation of Health Benefits

The **Consolidated Omnibus Budget Reconciliation Act (COBRA)** of 1984 provides for a continuation of health insurance coverage for a period of up to three years for employees who leave a company through no fault of their own. Such employees are required to pay the premiums themselves, but at the company's group rate.

unemployment compensation A system designed to provide income to individuals who have lost a job through no fault of their own.

Social Security Act A law that provides eligible workers with retirement and disability incomes and Medicare coverage.

Consolidated Omnibus Budget Reconciliation Act (COBRA) A law that provides a continuation of health insurance coverage for employees who leave a company through no fault of their own.

Taking a Closer Look 9-3   *Types of Health Insurance Programs*

Traditional

The employee gets coverage for visits to both doctors' offices and hospitals. Insurance covers expenses at a fixed rate, usually 80 percent. The employer pays all or most of the premiums for the employees and their dependents.

Health Maintenance Organizations (HMOs)

HMOs are organizations of physicians and other health care professionals who provide a wide range of services for a fixed fee. When participants need medical services, they pay a nominal per-visit charge of $5 or $10. Because members visit their health care facility more frequently, potential problems can be discovered and eliminated before they can become major health threats. Thus, HMOs can save money through preventative medicine. However, employees have a limited number of doctors from which to choose and must get approval from a "gatekeeper" physician for specialized treatment.

Preferred Provider Organizations (PPOs)

An employer has an agreement with doctors, hospitals, and other medical facilities to provide services at a discounted fee in return for the company's

participation, which creates increased business for the health facility. Employees may choose any "member" facility of their choice.

Point-of-Service Plans (POSs)

A hybrid of PPOs and HMOs, POSs are similar to PPOs in that the employer has an agreement with doctors, hospitals, and other medical facilities to provide services at a discounted fee in return for the company's participation. POSs are similar to HMOs in that employees have a limited number of doctors from which to choose and must get approval from a "gatekeeper" physician for specialized treatment. However, unlike HMOs, employees can go outside the network to receive services from noncontracted providers. However, employees must pay a higher deductible when using this option.

Self-Insured Medical Coverage

Many large employers have ventured into the insurance business and have established self-funded programs in which they assume all risks. By avoiding the "middleman" (i.e., the insurance companies), companies thus eliminate the overhead costs.

Insurance

Companies often offer employees three types of insurance programs as benefits.

Health Insurance

Basic health care plans cover hospitalization, physician care, and surgery. Several types of health insurance programs, described in Taking a Closer Look 9-3, are common.

According to the Bureau of Labor Statistics, up to 92 percent of full-time employees receive health care benefits.[52] At one time, employers paid virtually all insurance premiums. As health care costs escalate, most employers now require employees to pay at least part of the premiums.

Long-Term Disability (LTD) Insurance

LTD programs provide replacement income for an employee who cannot return to work for an extended period of time due to illness or injury. An LTD program may be temporary or permanent. The benefits paid to employees are customarily set between 50 and 67 percent of that person's income.[53]

Life Insurance

Life insurance plans cover 94 percent of all full-time employees.[54] The premiums are usually paid by the employer. Employee contributions, if required, are typically a set amount per $1,000 coverage based on age. Employees are often given the opportunity to expand their coverage by purchasing additional insurance.

Pensions

Pensions, or retirement incomes, may be the largest single benefit most employees receive. In most instances, employees become eligible to participate in company pension plans when they reach 21 years of age and have completed one year of service. After they have satisfied certain age and time requirements, employees become vested, meaning that the pension benefits they have earned are theirs and cannot be revoked. If they leave their jobs after vesting, but before retirement, employees may receive these benefits immediately or may have to wait until retirement age to collect them, depending on the provisions of their specific pension plan.

Types of Pension Plans

Employers may choose from two types of pension plans—**defined benefit plans** or **defined contribution plans.** Defined benefit plans specify the amount of pension a worker will receive on retirement. Defined contribution plans specify the rate of employer and employee contributions.

If a defined benefit plan is chosen, an employer is committing itself to an unknown cost that can be affected by rates of return on investments, changes in regulations, and future pay levels. Consequently, most employers in recent years have adopted defined contribution plans.[55]

Legal Constraints on Pension Plans

Companies establish pension plans voluntarily, but once established, the **Employee Retirement Income Security Act (ERISA)** of 1974 requires that employers follow certain rules. ERISA ensures that employees will receive the pension benefits due them, even if the company goes bankrupt or merges with another firm. Employers must pay annual insurance premiums to a government agency in order to provide funds from which guaranteed pensions can be paid. Additionally, ERISA requires that employers inform workers what their pension-related benefits include.[56]

Perquisites and Services

A host of possible perquisites and services may be offered to employees as benefits. Many of these are listed in Exhibit 9-5. As indicated in the exhibit, executives are frequently offered a variety of perquisites not offered to other employees. The logic is to attract and keep good managers and to motivate them to work hard in the organization's interest.[57]

---

defined benefit plan
A type of pension plan that specifies the amount of pension a worker will receive upon retirement.

defined contribution plan
A type of pension plan that specifies the rate of employer and employee monthly contributions.

Employee Retirement Income Security Act (ERISA) A law requiring employers to follow certain rules to ensure that employees will receive the pension benefits due them.

EXHIBIT 9-5	Perquisites and Services

Employee Perquisites
- Pay for time not worked (e.g., vacation, holidays, sick days, personal leave)
- Reimbursement for educational expenses
- Discount on company products or services
- Automobile and homeowner insurance
- Employee savings plans
- Tax-sheltered annuities

Employee Services
- Employer-sponsored child care and care for sick children
- Wellness programs
- Employee assistance programs

Executive Perquisites
- Club memberships
- Stock options
- Company cars
- Liberal expense accounts
- Reserved parking
- Personal finance assistance
- Relocation expenses
- Golden parachutes (general severance pay if job is lost because of merger or takeover)

The Cafeteria Plan at American Airlines

The cafeteria plan at American Airlines gives employees the opportunity to decide exactly where their company-paid benefit dollars will be spent and whether they want to purchase additional benefits at their own expense.

Employees may choose among several benefit options, such as dental, vision, and group life insurance, as well as such benefits as additional vacation time,

health and dependent care reimbursement, and cash. Should benefit costs increase, employees can decide whether to take less coverage or pay the additional amount to maintain the same coverage.

Source: Santora, J.E. (1990). America opts for flex. *Personnel Journal,* November, 32–34.

9-2e Benefits Administration

We now discuss two issues that must be addressed when an organization administers its benefit programs: flexible benefit plans and cost containment.

Flexible Benefit Plans

flexible benefit (cafeteria) plans Benefit programs that allow employees to choose among various benefits and levels of coverage.

Many employers now offer **flexible benefit plans,** also known as **cafeteria plans.** These plans allow employees to choose among various benefits and levels of coverage. Under a cafeteria plan, employees may choose to receive cash or purchase benefits from among the options provided under the plan. The cafeteria plan offered by American Airlines is described in On the Road to Competitive Advantage 9-2.

Flexible benefit plans present a number of advantages, as listed here:[58]

- Such plans enable employees to choose options that best fit their own needs. New workers, for example, may prefer cash; parents may prefer to invest their benefit dollars in employer-sponsored child-care programs; and older workers may decide to increase their pension and health care coverage.

- Deciding among the various options makes employees more aware of the cost of the benefits, giving them a real sense of the value of the benefits their employers provide.

- Flexible benefit plans can lower compensation costs because employers no longer have to pay for unwanted benefits.

- Employers and employees can save on taxes. Many of the premiums may be paid with pretax dollars, thus lowering the amount of taxes to be paid by both the employee and the employer.

Cost Containment

As we noted in the beginning of the chapter, benefit costs have been spiraling upward during the past several years. This trend has been caused by a number of factors, such as the following:[59]

- General increase in health costs

- Drastic escalation of prescription drug costs

- The continued development of expensive life-saving technology, such as MRIs

- The aging workforce. Older people require more health care, and the health care they receive is typically more expensive than that needed by younger workers.

- Increase in the usage of mental health professionals following the September 11, 2001, terrorist attacks

EXHIBIT 9-6	Strategies for Containing Workers' Compensation Costs

Accident Prevention
- Workplace inspections
- Safety training
- Safety committees
- Safety incentives

Claims Management
- Managed care
- Case management
- Early intervention

Audit Procedures
- Double-dipping with group medical
- Fraudulent workers' compensation claims
- Adherence to medical fee schedule

Medical Treatment
- Prearranged medical care
- Workplace physician house calls

According to figures collected by the C&B Consulting Group, the average annual cost per employee for medical coverage is now a staggering $5,266.[60] An employer can contain these costs while maintaining an attractive array of benefits by taking the following actions.

Contain Workers' Compensation Costs

Because an employer's workers' compensation premiums increase with each payout, firms can prevent unnecessary costs by scrutinizing the validity of each claim. Other cost containment strategies associated with workers' compensation are listed in Exhibit 9-6.[61]

Delete Benefits

Some employers cut costs by deleting or reducing some of the benefits they offer employees. This approach, however, can negatively affect both recruitment and retention.[62] A more viable approach is to offer benefits that are less costly, *but equally desirable.* Companies can continue to offer attractive benefits by implementing some of the cost containment strategies discussed next.

Implement Utilization Review Programs

Many companies implement **utilization review programs** in order to cut health care costs by (1) ensuring that each medical treatment is necessary before authorizing payment and (2) ensuring that the medical services have been rendered appropriately at a reasonable cost. These programs require hospital preadmission certification, continued stay review, hospital discharge planning, and comprehensive medical case management for catastrophic injuries or illnesses.[63]

utilization review programs Programs designed to minimize health care costs through the use of preauthorization and auditing procedures.

Choose the Right Health Insurance Carrier

Employers also closely examine their firm's health insurance carriers in order to address the following questions:[64]

- Is the program tailored to company needs?
- Are the prices competitive?
- Will there be a good provider/vendor relationship?
- Will payouts be accurate (e.g., will the correct amount be paid to the right person)?
- How good is the customer service?
- Is the insurance carrier financially secure?

Increase the Attractiveness of Benefits

Some employers have been able to increase the attractiveness of their benefit programs while holding costs constant, allowing an organization to get more of a "bang for its buck" from these programs.

Cafeteria benefit plans serve as an example of this approach.

9-3 The Manager's Guide

9-3a Compensation and the Manager's Job

What can line managers do to ensure that their company's compensation system has a positive impact on competitive advantage? We now discuss the line manager's role with regard to compensation matters.

A Manager's Responsibilities Regarding Pay

Evaluating the Worth of Jobs

Line managers help a company determine the worth of its jobs by ensuring that job evaluations are based on up-to-date and accurate job descriptions. In some instances, managers are called on to serve on job evaluation committees.

Negotiating Starting Salaries

In many firms, managers negotiate starting salaries when they hire new workers. Managers must bear in mind both equity issues and the legal requirements regarding equal pay for equal work/worth. For instance, offering a male applicant a higher starting salary than that offered to a female could be unlawful and would likely cause equity and morale problems.

Recommending Pay Raises and Promotions

Managers usually recommend pay raises and promotions. The importance of providing accurate performance appraisals for these purposes was addressed in Chapter 8, "Appraising Employee Job Performance." It is important to point out the connection between biased or otherwise inaccurate appraisals and inequitable pay decisions. Such an outcome could be damaging and lead to dissatisfaction, lowered performance, turnover, and discrimination lawsuits.

Compliance with the FLSA

Line managers must also ensure FLSA compliance. This responsibility entails keeping track of the hours worked by nonexempt personnel. It also means that managers must be sufficiently familiar with the overtime provisions of the FLSA to ensure that all overtime work is properly compensated. These provisions are spelled out in Section 9-3c, "HRM Skill-Building for Managers."

Notifying the HRM Department of Job Changes

Managers should notify the HRM department of any changes in the jobs they supervise with regard to job content or responsibility. Such jobs should be reevaluated and, if necessary, moved to appropriate pay grades.

A Manager's Responsibilities Regarding Benefits

Managers should become familiar with all benefits offered by their company and should be able to communicate this information clearly to applicants and employees. In addition, managers have certain responsibilities regarding workers' compensation and unemployment compensation as discussed next.

Dealing with Employees on Workers' Compensation Leave

Employees who file workers' compensation claims are often absent from their jobs for an extended period of time, and before long, they may begin to feel isolated from the workplace. To help overcome this feeling and to alleviate their fears, managers should regularly visit or call these employees. Such a practice helps maintain the workers' ties to their jobs and can also help reduce the suspicion that the workers may be faking their illness.[65]

Helping to Contain Unemployment Compensation Costs

Managers can also help the organization contain the cost of unemployment compensation claims. The funds for paying unemployment compensation come from a combined federal and state tax paid by employers. The state portion of the tax rises as the number of a company's claims increases.[66] Therefore, the employer's fiscal interest dictates that it challenge any invalid claims.

A frequently challenged claim for unemployment compensation arises when a worker has been discharged for misconduct and asserts that he or she is eligible for unemployment compensation because the discharge was unfair. To rebut such a claim, the manager must be able to provide necessary documentation to justify the appropriateness of the discharge. Documentation procedures are described in Chapter 11, "Complying with Workplace Justice Laws."

9-3b How the HRM Department Can Help

Although managers play an important role, the development and administration of a company's compensation system is primarily the responsibility of the HRM department.

Pay-Related Responsibilities

The HRM department is ultimately responsible for establishing rates of pay (e.g., overseeing the job evaluation process, conducting salary surveys, etc.). HR professionals also establish procedures for administering pay plans and for ensuring that they comply with antidiscrimination laws.

Benefits-Related Responsibilities

The HRM department takes the lead in selecting and administering the organization's benefit options. HR also communicates benefits-related information to employees.

Communicating Benefits-Related Information

An attractive benefits package cannot enhance competitive advantage unless employees recognize and appreciate its value. Unfortunately, employees often fail to appreciate their benefits because they are ignorant of the benefits' market value and cost.[67] A recent survey, for example, revealed that most employees think that their employer spends under 10 percent of its payroll costs on benefits, rather than the 30 to 40 percent they actually spend.[68] As the author of the study notes, "It's like buying an expensive gift and the recipient thinks you got it in the bargain basement."

To make employees aware of the value of their benefits, companies should inform them of the provisions of the benefits package and attempt to generate enthusiasm for it.[69] The information should be conveyed in several ways:[70]

1. Prepare an easy-to-understand handbook to describe the cost and coverage of each benefit option.
2. Draft periodic supplements to the handbook to keep it up to date.
3. Appoint an HR professional to be available for answering questions.

4. Conduct regularly scheduled training classes. Go over only one or two benefit areas per session to avoid information overload.

5. Use the company newsletter to get the word out on new benefits or for updates on existing programs.

9-3c HRM Skill-Building for Managers

Understanding the Overtime Provisions of the FLSA

As a manager, it would be your responsibility to assign overtime work. You must therefore understand the overtime provisions of the FLSA.

The act specifies that overtime must be calculated on a weekly basis. The work-week need not coincide with the calendar week, but may begin at any time. For instance, the workweek could begin on Tuesdays. Once this time is established, however, it must remain fixed. That is, once Tuesday is selected, the employer cannot change it to another day.

When calculating overtime, a worker's hours cannot be averaged over two or more weeks. Suppose, for instance, that a company uses a two-week pay period. If an employee works only 30 hours during the first week, but works 50 hours the second week, the firm cannot average these figures. The employee must be paid 10 hours of overtime for the second week.

Sometimes, managers allow workers to leave early, say for a doctor's appointment, with the promise that the worker will make up the hours on another day. If the time is made up during the following week, the worker may end up working in excess of 40 hours for that week and therefore be entitled to overtime. To avoid liability for overtime pay, you could schedule the make-up time for the same week in which the time off was granted.

You must also be aware of the fact that an employee may be entitled to overtime even if you have not specifically authorized it. This situation could occur under the following circumstances:

- The employee voluntarily works past quitting time in order to finish a task.
- The employee arrives at work early and begins working before the official start of the workday.
- The employee takes work home.

It does not matter that you never asked the employee to put in this extra time. What matters is that you knew or should have known this was occurring, and you did nothing to stop it.[71] To lessen the chance of having to pay for unauthorized overtime, you should take the following steps:[72]

1. Communicate the company's overtime policy to all nonexempt employees.

2. Do not pressure or even encourage employees to report for work early, stay late, or take work home.

3. Do not penalize employees simply because they work only scheduled hours and do not come in early or stay late without being told to do so.

4. Be aware of common employee practices. Are any employees arriving early or leaving late? If so, what are they doing? Are any employees taking work home?

5. Do not permit or require employees to put in extra, off-the-clock time.

Negotiating Starting Salaries

As a manager, you may be given discretion in negotiating starting salaries, usually within a fixed pay range, during the hiring process. The following approach to salary negotiations has been suggested:[73]

1. Understand that applicants will typically wait for you to make the first offer. About one-third of the applicants will try to negotiate a higher salary than origi-

nally offered. Remember that you have the greater bargaining power when the job market is tight—there are many applicants for a given position. If the applicant demands too high a salary, you can simply contact another applicant.

2. The initial salary offer you make should be based on two considerations: candidate qualifications and salary histories.

As a general rule, the initial salary offer should be commensurate with the applicant's skill level. If an applicant's qualifications do not exceed the minimum requirements of the job, the salary offer should be set at the minimum of the existing salary range. Applicants whose qualifications exceed the minimum should be offered more because their immediate contribution to the organization is expected to be greater. The maximum offer to such an applicant should generally be no higher than the midpoint of the salary range. To pay above that level could be a detriment to future motivation because it would severely limit the size and number of future pay raises.

When making a salary offer, you should also take the applicant's salary history into account. The offer should be about 10 to 30 percent greater than the applicant's previous salary to entice the candidate to accept the offer.

Chapter Objectives Revisited

1. Explain how effective compensation systems enhance competitive advantage.
   - Improve cost efficiency
   - Achieve legal compliance
   - Enhance the success of recruitment efforts and reduce morale and turnover problems

2. Understand how people form perceptions about a pay system's equity.
   - Outcome/input ratio: Employee perceptions concerning their organizational contribution/ Employee perceptions concerning the returns they get for the work performed
   - Referent others: People judge the equity of their pay by comparing their outcome-to-input ratio with another person's ratio. This comparison person is referred to as one's referent other.

3. Describe how organizations can build an equitable pay system.
   - Internal consistency
     - Job evaluation: A systematic process for determining the worth of a job
     - Pay grades: Job groupings in which all jobs assigned to the same group are subject to the same range of pay
   - External competitiveness
     - Salary survey: A survey that seeks information on pay rates offered by a firm's competitors
     - Pay policy: A company policy stipulating how well it will pay its employees relative to the market
     - Pay rates: The amounts of pay employees earn based on salary survey information and the company's pay policy

   - Employee contributions
     - Pay range: The minimum and maximum pay rates for all jobs within a pay grade
     - Skill-based pay: A compensation approach that grants employees pay increases for acquiring new, job-related skills

4. Define the legal constraints imposed on organizational pay practices.
   - Fair Labor Standards Act: A 1938 federal statute that regulates minimum wage and overtime pay
   - Pay discrimination
     - Equal Pay Act: An amendment to the FLSA that prohibits sex discrimination in pay by requiring equal pay for equal work
     - Comparable worth: A standard for judging pay discrimination that calls for equal pay for equal worth

5. Understand the various benefit options and their administration.
   - Benefit options
     - Workers' compensation: A state-run, no-fault insurance system that provides income protection for workers experiencing job-related injuries or illnesses
     - Unemployment compensation: A system designed to provide income to individuals who have lost a job through no fault of their own
     - Social Security: A law that provides eligible workers with retirement and disability incomes and Medicare coverage

- COBRA: A law that provides a continuation of health insurance coverage for employees who leave a company through no fault of their own
- Insurance: Popular options—health, life, and long-term disability insurance
- Pensions: Retirement incomes
- Perquisites and services: A host of possible perquisites and services may be offered to employees as benefits

- Administrative issues
  - Flexible benefit plans: Benefit programs that allow employees to choose among various benefits and levels of coverage
  - Cost containment: Various strategies, such as containing workers' compensation costs, deleting benefits, utilization review programs, choosing the right health insurance carrier, and increasing the attractiveness of benefits

Review Questions

Note: You can find the correct answers to these questions by taking the quiz and then submitting your answers in the Online Edition. The program will automatically score your submission. If you miss a question, the program will provide the correct answer, a rationale for the answer, and the section number in the chapter where the topic is discussed.

1. _____ is established by setting the organization's pay level in comparison with what the competition pays for similar work.
   a. Internal consistency
   b. External competitiveness
   c. Employee contributions
   d. Administration

2. According to the equity theory, which of the following conditions would produce the greatest feeling of equity for Person A? (Assume Person B is the "referent other.")
   a. Person A's O/I > Person B's O/I
   b. Person A's O/I < Person B's O/I
   c. Person A's O/I = Person B's O/I
   d. a.–c. would all produce the same feeling of equity.

3. The major problem associated with using only five or six pay grades is
   a. administrative difficulties.
   b. perceived inequity.
   c. going over budget.
   d. all of the above.

4. Pay rates for benchmark jobs are set on the basis of
   a. employee contributions.
   b. the overall worth of each job.
   c. the statistical relationship between job evaluation points and current pay rates.
   d. the statistical relationship between job evaluation points and prevailing market rates.

5. Which of the following categories is exempted from the FLSA?
   a. executive
   b. administrative
   c. professional
   d. all of the above

6. Pay differences between men and women performing the same job may be legally justified under certain circumstances, such as when the discrepancy is due to _____ differences.
   a. seniority
   b. productivity
   c. merit
   d. all of the above

7. In order to collect workers' compensation for an injury,
   a. the injury must be the worker's fault.
   b. the worker must have health insurance.
   c. the injury or illness must be job-related.
   d. all of the above

8. COBRA provides continued _____ coverage for employees who leave their jobs through no fault of their own.
   a. life insurance
   b. health insurance
   c. pension
   d. all of the above

9. Today, most organizations offer _____ pension plans.
   a. defined benefit
   b. defined contribution
   c. variable benefit
   d. variable contribution

10. The purpose of implementing a utilization review program is to
    a. improve the quality of medical treatment.
    b. cut the employer's health care costs.
    c. replace traditional health insurance programs.
    d. encourage the use of HMOs.

Discussion Questions

1. Define the term *compensation.*
2. Describe the impact of compensation practices on an organization's cost efficiency.
3. Describe the major principles of equity theory.
4. Define the terms *internal consistency, external competitiveness,* and *employee contributions.* Briefly describe how each of these states can be achieved through the pay-setting process.
5. Define *job evaluation.* Briefly describe the point-factor method of job evaluation.
6. What is pay policy? What factors must a firm consider when setting its pay policy?
7. What is a pay policy line? How is this line used when setting pay rates?
8. Describe the main provisions of the FLSA.
9. Compare and contrast the doctrines of "equal pay for equal work" and "equal pay for equal worth."
10. Under what conditions would a worker become disqualified from obtaining unemployment compensation?
11. Distinguish between a defined benefit and a defined contribution pension plan.
12. Describe three of the manager's roles with regard to pay and benefits.
13. Why is it so important for the HRM department to inform employees about all aspects of their benefit plans? How should this communication take place?
14. What provisions does the FLSA make for overtime work?

Experiential Exercises

Evaluating the Job of Instructor

Overview

You will be divided into teams for the purpose of evaluating the worth of a college instructor's job.

Steps

1. Divide into groups of five. Each group will serve as a job evaluation committee and work independently of other groups. Your task is to evaluate the worth of the job of college instructor of management using the point-factor method of job evaluation. The rating form is located in the appendix.
2. Read the following job description:

   This job entails teaching four undergraduate management courses per semester. The instructor must ensure the courses taught cover the essential subject matter areas specified by the Department of Management. How the courses are taught is entirely up to the instructor.
3. Begin the rating process by independently rating the job on Factor 1, Physical and Mental Effort.
4. Each group member must now disclose his or her rating to the other group members. If all Factor 1 ratings are the same, record that rating on a separate sheet of paper. If there is any disagreement, group members must discuss their ratings and arrive at a consensus. Record the consensus rating.
5. Now repeat the rating process, one factor at a time. Be sure to record your group's ratings for each factor.
6. Each group will now report its factor ratings to the instructor, who will record them on the chalkboard.
7. As a class, discuss the similarities and differences found in the ratings among the various groups. Where disagreements occurred, identify the possible reasons.
8. Discuss the advantages and pitfalls associated with the use of the point-factor method of job evaluation.

Evaluating General Mills' Skill-Based Pay System

1. Divide into groups of five and discuss the skill-based pay system used by General Mills (described in On the Road to Competitive Advantage 9-1).
2. Address the following questions:
   a. What are the advantages of using this approach to pay compared to using a traditional approach? What are the disadvantages?
   b. What practical difficulties do you think General Mills ran into when trying to implement this program?
3. The instructor will hold a class discussion for the purpose of discussing the answers given by each group.

Case

Resolving a Pay Inequity Dilemma

Ridgeway Hospital is a 296-bed medical and surgical center that, in addition to the full range of traditional medical services, provides cardiac care, cancer treatment, and emergency service. Located in a midsize metropolitan center, it maintains a payroll of 806 full-time employees.

Ridgeway makes every effort to ensure its pay system is internally consistent. Jobs are classified into 25 pay grades on the basis of job evaluation ratings, using the point-factor method. Each pay grade has a 25 percent spread from floor to ceiling. Employees with little or no experience are paid at the minimum of the range. As employees progress in their jobs, they are given pay raises commensurate with their level of job performance.

Employees appear to be satisfied with Ridgeway's pay system. There have been few formal complaints. However, after reviewing the hospital's turnover figures, Mary Craft, the compensation manager, noticed an unusually high turnover rate among the hospital's physical therapists. Mary decided to look into the matter to see if the hospital's pay practices were contributing to the problem.

Physical therapists are classified in Pay Grade 8. Ridgeway's pay range for this grade is $17,500 to $22,500. Mary did some checking and found that Langley Hospital, Ridgeway's chief competitor, pays its physical therapists $21,000 to $27,000. Obviously, Ridgeway's pay was not externally competitive.

Mary decided to call a meeting to discuss what should be done about this matter. Present at the meeting were Paul Peterson, vice president of human resources, and his assistant, Bill Johnson. Bill suggested that Ridgeway upgrade the job of physical therapist to Pay Grade 10 in order to bring the physical therapist pay scale in line with that of Langley's. Paul was skeptical of this idea, however. He felt that such a move would destroy the credibility of the hospital's job evaluation plan and cause a morale problem, especially among other employees classified in Pay Grade 8.

Questions

1. Do you agree with Paul that a reclassification of the job to Pay Grade 10 would cause a morale problem?
2. Can you think of a better solution to the problem? Explain.

References

1. Zuber, A. (1999). Buffets Inc. shows gratitude to managers through incentives. *Nation's Restaurant News, 33* (30), 59–62.
2. Milkovich, G.T., and Newman, J.M. (2002). *Compensation* (7th ed.). Homewood, IL: Irwin.
3. Henderson, R.I. (1994). *Compensation Management* (6th ed.). Englewood Cliffs, NJ: Prentice Hall.
4. Ibid.
5. De Cenzo, D.A., and Holoviak, S. J. (1990). *Employee Benefits*. Englewood Cliffs, NJ: Prentice Hall.
6. Kleber, L.C. (1989). Give your employees individual statements. *Personnel Administrator,* April, 64–68.
7. Caudron, S. (2002). Health-care costs: HR's crisis has real solutions. *Workforce,* February, 28–34.
8. Bowers, M.H., and Roderick, R.D. (1987). Two-tier pay systems: The good, the bad and the debatable. *Personnel Administrator,* June, 101–112.
9. Berkowitz, L., Fraser, C., Treasure, F.P., and Cochran, S. (1987). Pay, equity, job gratification, and comparisons in pay satisfaction. *Journal of Applied Psychology, 72* (4), 544–551.
10. De Cenzo and Holoviak. *Employee Benefits*.
11. Schiemann, W.A. (1987). The impact of corporate compensation and benefit policy on employee attitudes and behavior and corporate profitability. *Journal of Business and Psychology, 2* (1), 8–26.
12. Rice, R.W., Phillips, S.M., and McFarlin, D.B. (1990). Multiple discrepancies and pay satisfaction. *Journal of Applied Psychology, 75* (4), 386–393; Berkowitz et al. Pay, equity, job gratification.
13. Adams, J.S. (1965). Injustices in social exchange. In L. Berkowitz (ed.). *Advances in Experimental Social Psychology* (2nd ed.). New York: Academic Press.
14. Brockner, J., and Adsit, L. (1986). The moderating impact of sex on the equity-satisfaction relationship: A field study. *Journal of Applied Psychology, 71* (4), 585–590.
15. Rice et al. Multiple discrepancies.
16. Adapted from Adams, J.S. (1963). Toward an understanding of inequity. *Journal of Abnormal and Social Psychology, 67,* 422–436.
17. Sweeney, P.D. (1990). Distributed justice and pay satisfaction: A field test of an equity theory prediction. *Journal of Business and Psychology, 4* (3), 329–341.
18. Greenberg, J. (1987). Reactions to procedural justice in payment distributions: Do the means justify the ends? *Journal of Applied Psychology, 72* (1), 55–61.
19. Brockner and Adsit. The moderating impact.
20. For example, Brockner and Adsit. The moderating impact.
21. Ibid.
22. Rynes, S.L., and Milkovich, G.T. (1986). Wage surveys: Dispelling some myths about the "market wage." *Personnel Psychology, 39* (1), 71–90.
23. Cellar, D.F., Curtis, J.R., Kohlepp, K., Poczapski, P., and Mohiuddin, S. (1989). The effects of rater training, job analysis format and congruence of training on job evaluation ratings. *Journal of Business and Psychology, 3* (4), 387–401.

24. Brady, R.L., Person, L.N., and Thompson, S.E. (1982). *Comparable Worth Compliance Handbook.* Stamford, CT: Bureau of Law and Business.
25. Ibid.
26. Ibid.
27. Hester, T.M. (1992). Setting fair pay policy. *HRMagazine,* January, 75–78.
28. Ibid.
29. England, J.D. (1988). Developing a total compensation policy statement. *Personnel,* May, 71–73.
30. Ibid.
31. Lawler, E.E. (1992). Pay the person, not the job. *Industry Week,* December 7, 19–25.
32. Bunning, R.L. (1989). Skill-based pay. *Personnel Administrator,* June, 65–70.
33. Ingram, E. (1990). The advantages of knowledge-based pay. *Personnel Journal,* April, 138–140.
34. Murray, B., and Gerhart, B. (1998). An empirical analysis of a skill-based pay program and plant performance outcomes. *Academy of Management Journal, 41* (1), 68–78.
35. Lawler. Pay the person.
36. Bunning. Skill-based pay.
37. Mahoney, T.A. (1990). Multiple pay contingencies: Strategic design of compensation. *Human Resource Management, 28* (3), 337–347.
38. Kahn, S.C., Brown, B.B., Zepke, B.E., and Lanzarone, M. (1990). *Personnel Director's Legal Guide* (2nd ed.). Boston: Warren, Gorham, & Lamont.
39. Http://www.dol.gov.
40. Banning, K. (1991). Know the rules on pay and hours. *Nation's Business,* April, 50–51.
41. Http://www. bls.gov.
42. *Gunther v. County of Washington* (1981). 25 FEP Cases 1521.
43. Caudron. Health-care costs.
44. Roberts, K., and Gleason, S.E. (1991). What employees want from workers' comp. *HRMagazine,* December, 49–54.
45. Laabs, J.J. (1993). Steelcase slashes workers' comp costs. *Personnel Journal,* February, 72–87.
46. Resnick, R. (1992). Managed care comes to workers' compensation. *Business & Health,* September, 32–39.
47. LeVan, H., Katz, M., and Hochwarter, W. (1990). Employee stress swamps workers' comp. *Personnel Journal,* May, 61–64.
48. Ibid.
49. Ibid.
50. De Cenzo and Holoviak. *Employee Benefits.*
51. Wall, P.S. (1991). A survey of employment security law: Determining eligibility for unemployment compensation benefits. *Labor Law Journal, 42* (3), 179–185.
52. Stanton, M. (1990). Beyond your paycheck: An employee benefits primer. *Occupational Outlook Quarterly,* Fall, 2–9.
53. Ibid.
54. Ibid.
55. Ibid.
56. De Cenzo and Holoviak. *Employee Benefits.*
57. Ibid.
58. Masterson, J. (1990). Benefit plans that cut costs and increase satisfaction. *Management Review,* April, 22–24.
59. Caudron. Health-care costs.
60. Ibid.
61. Adapted from Swanke, J.A. (1992). Ways to tame workers' comp premiums. *HRMagazine,* February, 39–41.
62. Ibid.
63. Anderson, R.A. (1990). Handling health-care costs in the 90s. *HRMagazine,* June, 89–94.
64. Sturges, J.S. (1992). Examining your insurance carrier. *HRMagazine,* February, 43–46.
65. Roberts and Gleason. What employees want.
66. De Cenzo and Holoviak. *Employee Benefits.*
67. Wilson, M., Northcraft, G.B., and Neale, M.A. (1985). The perceived value of fringe benefits. *Personnel Psychology, 38* (2), 309–320.
68. Kleber. Give your employees individual statements.
69. Dudek, E.A. (1990). Flex plans: The future is now! *Pension World,* July, 10–12.
70. Davies, D.L. (1986). How to bridge the benefits communication gap. *Personnel Journal,* January, 83–85.
71. Kahn et al. *Personnel Director's Legal Guide.*
72. Ibid.
73. Extejt, M.M., and Russell, C.J. (1990). The role of individual bargaining behavior in the pay setting process: A pilot study. *Journal of Business and Psychology, 5* (1), 113–125.

Sample of a Point-Factor Method Evaluation Form

Factor 1: Physical and Mental Effort

Definition: This factor measures physical, visual, and mental demands of the job. These demands should be assessed in terms of frequency, time, and severity. For instance, a job requiring occasional demands would not be evaluated as highly as one requiring almost continual demands.

Degrees and Definitions

1. Sedentary. Typically, the employee sits comfortably to do the work. The job requires normal expenditure of energy and little or no unusual physical effort or mental/visual concentration. (5 points)
2. The work requires some physical exertion, such as long periods of standing, recurring bending, stooping, reaching, and lifting of moderately heavy items. Or it requires some mental/visual concentration, such as that required in monitoring a process. (20 points)
3. The work requires strenuous physical effort, such as that needed for the continuous lifting, carrying, and moving of heavy objects. Or the work requires the continuous need for mental/visual concentration for long periods of time, which permits little or no interruptions, such as watching for defects on a fast-moving conveyer line. (50 points)

Factor 2: Education and Experience

Definition: This factor refers to the amount of knowledge and understanding of the technical aspects of the job when one first enters the position. Some of this knowledge may be obtained through formal education and training programs; some may be obtained through experience.

Degrees and Definitions

1. The job requires no minimum education, previous experience, or training. (15 points)
2. The job requires some experience or training, but less than one year. (30 points)
3. The job requires technical vocational training or the experience equivalent (about one to three years). (60 points)
4. The job requires a college degree or the training and experience equivalent (about four to five years). (100 points)

5. The job requires a master's degree or the training and experience equivalent (about six to seven years). (150 points)

6. The job requires an advanced professional degree (e.g., law, medicine, doctorate). (210 points)

Factor 3: Judgment

Definition: This factor refers to the extent to which the individual is required to exercise independent judgment and the level of difficulty of these judgments. Consider the degree of initiative, ingenuity, and analytical abilities required.

Degrees and Definitions

1. When given an assignment, the individual is told what to do, when to do it, and how to do it. The job procedures are quite specific and readily understood. There is little or no choice in deciding what to do. (20 points)

2. Job activities are somewhat varied, yet procedures for doing the work have been established, and specific guidelines are available. The decision regarding what needs to be done involves various choices requiring the individual to know the difference among a few recognizable situations. (50 points)

3. The individual is told what do, but uses some judgment in determining how to do it. The chosen course of action must be selected from many alternatives. Existing guidelines are very general, and the employee must use some judgment in interpreting and adapting the guidelines when solving a specific problem. (90 points)

4. The individual is given general goals and must determine the specific methods for achieving these goals. Decisions regarding what needs to be done require the assessment of unusual circumstances and incomplete or conflicting information. Examples are interpreting data, planning work, and refining the techniques to be used. (140 points)

5. The individual has the responsibility of determining the appropriate goals. This requires extensive analysis to determine the nature and scope of the problem and to identify possible solutions. (200 points)

Factor 4: Contacts

Definition: This factor measures the job requirements for the frequency and level of contacts with others, and the persuasiveness required in the successful transaction of business.

Degrees and Definitions

1. All contacts are of a routine nature, normally not initiated by the employee. (20 points)

2. Contacts involve the exchange of information related to the normal flow of work. (50 points)

3. Contacts involve the need to explain and understand problems of average difficulty related to the normal flow of work. (90 points)

4. Contacts involve the selling of company services or products and the resolution of problems that are complex in nature. (140 points)

5. The purpose of the contacts is to justify, defend, negotiate, or settle matters involving significant or controversial issues. These contacts are necessary to secure concurrence or cooperation or to persuade others on the course of action. (200 points)

Factor 5: Consequence of Error

Definition: This factor measures the consequences of an error on internal company operations or on the company's customers, and what would be necessary to correct it. Consequence of error is measured in terms of loss of money, damage to machinery and equipment, and the impact of the error on the safety of others. Consider only typical types of errors.

Degrees and Definitions

1. The work involves little opportunity for error. All work is checked immediately. Cost of correction is negligible in terms of monetary loss. Presents no safety risk to others. (10 points)

2. Work involves an occasional opportunity to make errors of moderate size. Work is checked periodically. The error could affect the productivity and/or safety of others, resulting in minor accidents or equipment damage. The error could influence the satisfaction of an individual customer. (30 points)

3. There is a continuous opportunity for error that would be difficult to detect within a short period of time. The error could directly affect the company's total productivity or the satisfaction of a group of customers. (60 points)

4. The error would take a long time to detect and could lead to significant economic loss to the company or significantly hinder the reputation or public image of the company. (100 points)

Factor 6: Working Conditions

Definition: This factor considers the risks and discomforts surrounding the job and its environment.

Degrees and Definitions

1. The work environment involves everyday risks and discomforts that require normal safety precautions. The work area is adequately lighted, heated, and ventilated. (10 points)

2. The work environment involves moderate risk and/or discomforts that require safety precautions (e.g., working around moving parts, carts, or machines, or having to deal with irritant chemicals). Light, heat, or noise levels may be unsatisfactory. Employees may be required to wear earplugs, safety glasses, etc. (25 points)

3. The work environment involves high risks with exposure to potentially dangerous situations or unusual environmental stress. Examples are working under extreme weather conditions, working at great height, and being exposed to fumes, acid, dangerous chemicals, etc. (50 points)

Implementing Productivity Improvement Programs

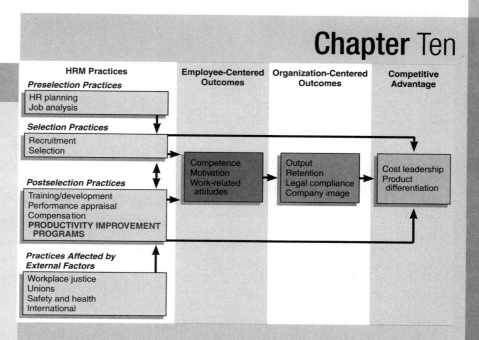

Key Terms

combination plans	McClelland's need-achievement theory
continuous quality improvement programs	merit pay guidechart
deferred plans	merit pay plan
distribution plans	pay-for-performance programs
employee empowerment programs	piece rate plans
expectancy theory	profit-sharing plans
extrinsic rewards	quality circles
gainsharing plans	reinforcement theory
informal participative decision-making program	Scanlon Plan
intrinsic rewards	self-managed work teams
job enrichment	straight piecework

Chapter Objectives

Upon completion of this chapter, you will be able to:

- Explain what productivity improvement programs are and how they contribute to competitive advantage.

- Define the standards for effective productivity programs developed within the framework of expectancy theory.

- Understand the rationale behind pay-for-performance programs.

- Describe the different types of pay-for-performance programs.

- Appreciate the rationale behind employee empowerment programs.

- Explain the various types of employee empowerment programs.

10-1 Gaining Competitive Advantage

10-1a Opening Case: Gaining Competitive Advantage at Lincoln Electric[1]

The Problem: Figuring Out How to Motivate Employees

The Lincoln Electric Company is a Cleveland-based manufacturer of welding machines and motors. When John C. Lincoln established the company in 1895, he was keenly aware of the importance of a highly motivated workforce and how the company's success, in fact, depended on it. Therefore, Mr. Lincoln had to ensure that each employee would work as diligently as possible for the good of the organization.

The Solution: Implementing an Employee Incentive System

Mr. Lincoln realized that the best way to motivate employees would be to link the company's reward and recognition system to its goals. To establish this connection, Lincoln developed and implemented a comprehensive incentive system. Its aim was to improve the company's overall performance by allowing contributing workers to share in the proceeds. The plan rewards employees for turning out high-quality products efficiently while controlling costs. The system includes the following components.

Paying by the Piece

Production workers are paid according to the number of "pieces" or product units they produce that are not defective. If a customer sends a defective part back to the company, the employee who produced it must repair it on his or her own time.

Providing Year-End Bonuses

To reward workers further for their efforts, Lincoln established a year-end bonus system that gives all workers the opportunity to nearly double their base wages. Workers get the bonus if the company's annual profits increase. The size of each employee's bonus check is a function of his or her job performance level. Job performance is evaluated twice a year. Supervisors rate employees twice a year on four criteria: output, quality, dependability (e.g., attendance and punctuality), and personal characteristics (e.g., attitude toward supervisors and coworkers, effort to share knowledge with others, and cooperation in adopting new methods).

Providing Stock Options

Lincoln also provides its employees with the option of buying company stock at a low cost. Employees are also given shares of company stock based on annual profits. Consequently, employees own more than 40 percent of total company stock. The intent of these plans is to give employees a sense of ownership in the company and provide them with incentives to produce more so that shared profits will be greater.

Because of the incentive system, workers at Lincoln make a lot of money. In 1992, for instance, production workers increased their base pay by an average of 75 percent, earning an average annual income of $45,000 (about twice as much as their counterparts in other companies).

Because the potential earnings at Lincoln are so great, the company receives nearly 1,000 unsolicited job applications per month! However, new employees quickly learn that Lincoln is not an easy place to work. There is no room for lazy or "laid-back" workers. There is a constant pressure to produce. Moreover, Lincoln provides no paid holidays or sick days, and overtime is mandatory. Workers get no credit for seniority, but must earn their bonuses and promotions entirely on the basis of merit. Not surprisingly, the turnover rate among new employees is quite high—20 percent resign within the first two months of employment.

How the Incentive System Enhanced Competitive Advantage

Has this incentive system helped to build a competitive advantage at Lincoln Electric? The answer is an unqualified "yes." The turnover rate among employees surviving the first two months is less than 3 percent. The company's productivity rate is two to three times greater than any of its competitors. Moreover, Lincoln Electric has maintained a stable price structure, despite the high salaries it pays workers. It has accomplished all this without implementing any layoffs, even in the period from 1981 to 1983 when sales declined by 40 percent. The company continues to excel. In 2004 sales hit an all-time high of $1.3 billion, representing a 28 percent increase over 2003.

10-1b Linking Productivity Improvement Programs to Competitive Advantage

As illustrated in the opening case, workers' job behavior can enormously impact competitive advantage. An organization cannot compete successfully unless workers help to achieve the organization's mission. This means that employees must attend work on a regular basis, come to work on time, work well with others, work "smart," and work hard.

According to one survey, more than 50 percent of U.S. workers believe they could increase their productivity if they tried, yet feel no motivation to do so.[2] The burden is thus on the shoulders of employers to find ways to motivate their workers to actively engage in "appropriate behaviors."

It is for this purpose that many firms have implemented *productivity improvement programs*. Although such programs approach motivation in various ways, all share the common goal of trying to improve productivity by increasing employee motivation.

Some programs attempt to motivate employees by offering **extrinsic rewards:** rewards given to employees by someone else (e.g., the employer), such as pay raises and bonuses. Other productivity improvement programs focus on **intrinsic rewards:** rewards that come from within, such as the good feeling one gets from successfully completing a challenging assignment. These programs attempt to motivate workers by making the work itself more rewarding.

extrinsic rewards Rewards that the employer gives to employees.

intrinsic rewards Rewards that come from within a person.

How can productivity improvement programs create or maintain a competitive advantage? As we saw at Lincoln Electric, a good program can motivate workers to increase productivity and can facilitate an employer's recruitment efforts.

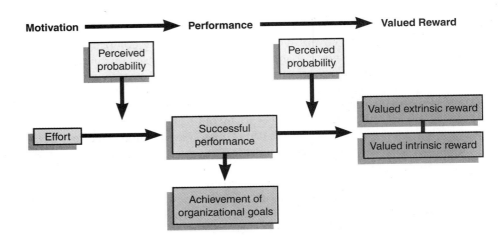

Figure 10-1
The Expectancy Theory Model

Improving Worker Productivity

As the name suggests, productivity improvement programs attempt to increase employee productivity. These programs can have rather dramatic effects on production quantity, quality, and efficiency—companies that use some type of productivity improvement program tend to be much more productive than those that do not.[3] For instance, when MetLife introduced its productivity improvement program in 1998, the companies return on equity was 7 percent. In two years, that figure jumped to 10.5 percent.[4]

These programs are successful because they motivate employees to engage in the appropriate job behaviors. To understand how they contribute to competitive advantage, one must first understand what motivates employees.

Many theories attempt to explain the motivational process. We focus our attention on just one, expectancy theory. We discuss the implications of some of the other motivational theories in Section 10-3, "The Manager's Guide."

Expectancy Theory

expecxtancy theory
A motivation theory that focuses on the effort-to-performance and performance-to-reward links.

Expectancy theory, illustrated graphically in Figure 10-1, states that workers make conscious decisions about how hard they are going to work to achieve organizational goals. Their decisions are based on perceptions of what they can gain from working hard.

Specifically, the theory states that employees will be highly motivated to the extent at which they perceive that (1) their efforts will lead to successful job performance and (2) their successful job performance will lead to outcomes or rewards they value. The greater the perceived probabilities that effort will lead to successful performance and that successful performance will lead to a valued reward, the greater the motivation.

Expectancy Theory and Productivity Improvement Programs

Successful productivity improvement programs are able to establish a clear connection between employee efforts and valued rewards; that is, employees must believe that they can gain valued rewards by working hard. Lincoln Electric's reward system has been successful because the company has clearly established this connection. The possible rewards are valued because they are so large (75 percent of base pay), and employees know how to earn them: Produce as many quality units as possible and engage in behaviors that lead to favorable performance appraisal ratings. When employees behave in this manner, a company's productivity increases and its competitive position improves.

Enhancing Recruitment Efforts and Retention Rates

Most people prefer to work in settings that allow them to earn rewards from their work. Organizations that offer rewards (either extrinsic or intrinsic) as part of productivity improvement programs thus usually attract more and better job applicants.[5] Remember that Lincoln Electric receives nearly 1,000 unsolicited job applications per month. Such companies also tend to experience higher retention rates. Lisa Weber, executive vice president for human resources at MetLife, attributes its low turnover rates to the new pay-for-performance program. The turnover rate among its top performers is only 6 percent, which is well below the industry average.[6]

10-2 HRM Issues and Practices

We now describe the various productivity improvement programs based on the allocation of extrinsic rewards. These programs, called **pay-for-performance programs,** link financial rewards to successful job performance. We then describe systems centering on intrinsic rewards. These systems, called **employee empowerment programs,** are designed to make work itself more rewarding by making the work more interesting and challenging and by giving employees a voice in important work decisions.

10-2a Pay-for-Performance Programs

Although the various pay-for-performance programs differ from one another in a number of ways, they have one important characteristic in common: Employees' financial rewards are linked directly to their performance.

Rationale for Pay-for-Performance Programs

Linking rewards directly to performance is intuitively appealing because most Americans believe that employees should be rewarded for good performance[7] and that exceptional performers should therefore earn greater rewards than mediocre ones.[8]

Linking rewards to performance also makes sense from an expectancy theory perspective. According to the theory, workers have little incentive for performing well if their efforts are unrewarded. On the other hand, when pay is linked to performance, overall performance should improve. Top performers should be motivated by large rewards to maintain high levels of performance, whereas low-level performers should be motivated to either increase their efforts or leave the company.[9] If the overall job performance improvement yields financial returns that exceed the cost of the rewards, a company's competitive advantage will improve. This is what happened at Fifth Third Bank, as illustrated in On the Road to Competitive Advantage 10-1.

One study found that the introduction of monetary incentives has a much greater impact on job performance than employee empowerment programs and concluded that "no other incentive or motivational technique comes even close to money with respect to its instrumental value."[10] Because pay-for-performance programs can so favorably impact competitive advantage, these programs have captured the attention of business owners and executives. In 1990, about 50 percent of all U.S. companies used some type of pay-for-performance system. By 2000, that figure rose to 80 percent.[11] The growing popularity of these programs rests on the belief that such programs can greatly increase employee motivation levels. For instance, Owens-Corning, an Ohio-based manufacturer, recently scrapped its "traditional" compensation program in favor of one that uses performance-related rewards given as stock options and profit sharing. This program decreases the employees' guaranteed annual base pay, but provides them with large bonuses if the firm performs at or above target levels. Owens-Corning employees are now more motivated to work hard so that the firm can meet its business goals.[12]

pay-for-performance programs Productivity improvement programs that link financial rewards to successful job performance.

employee empowerment programs Productivity improvement programs that make the work itself more rewarding.

The Pay-for-Performance Program at Fifth Third Bank

The incentive plan used by Fifth Third Bank, located in Cincinnati, was not working well. The plan offered very small performance incentives that were based on highly subjective and inconsistent performance ratings. The bank modified its incentive program in 2001 by taking the following actions:

- It developed cross-functional teams that were rewarded based on team performance.
- It established two different incentive programs—one for teams that acquired new business; the other, for teams that were responsible for creating and maintaining good customer relations.
- Objective performance measures were established for each team by the managers and the bank's vice president. Goals could be modified at mid-year, if necessary.

- New acquisition personnel could earn bonuses of up to 50 percent of their salaries for meeting acquisition goals, while customer relation teams could earn up to 20 percent of their salaries.

The bank's new incentive system was a complete success. By 2002, its second year of operation, net revenues had increased by 28 percent, fee income by 40 percent, and new customers by 35 percent. The profit generated by this plan was more than 10 times that of its cost. In 2002, *Forbes* magazine rated the bank as one of America's "Top Super Regional Banks."

Source: Anonymous (2003). Case study: How one company resurrected its incentive program. *IOMA's Pay for Performance Report, 3* (9), 4–7.

Potential Problems with Pay-for-Performance Programs

Although pay-for-performance programs can improve competitive positions, not all are as successful as those used at Lincoln Electric, MetLife, and Fifth Third Bank. In some cases, pay-for-performance programs create legal problems. When administered unfairly, a pay-for-performance system could violate Title VII of the Civil Rights Act. For example, if a bigoted employer were to deny a minority employee a well-earned pay raise, a costly discrimination charge could result.

Pay-for-performance programs also fail if they violate the standards listed in Exhibit 10-1. In the next section, we take a closer look at those standards and discuss how violations can be avoided or at least minimized.

Standards for Effective Pay-for-Performance Programs

In the following paragraphs, we describe pay-for-performance standards within the framework of expectancy theory. We then describe the various programs and examine how well each meets those standards.

EXHIBIT 10-1	Standards for Effective Pay-for-Performance Programs

Motivational Standards

- *Effort–performance links:* Employees must perceive that they can reach desired performance levels by engaging in appropriate behaviors.
- *Performance–reward links:* Rewards should be directly linked to successful job performance.
- *Value of reward:* The reward should be valued by employees.
- *Timeliness of rewards:* Rewards should follow shortly after the desired behaviors.

Cost–Benefit Standards

- *Performance–organizational mission links:* The performance being rewarded should be directly linked to the achievement of the organization's mission.
- *Cost efficiency:* Productivity gains from the program must more than offset the cost of the rewards.

Effort–Performance Links

According to expectancy theory, employees will be motivated to perform well to the extent they believe their own individual efforts can lead to successful performance. That is, they must believe that if they work diligently, they will perform well enough to qualify for the rewards. The pay-for-performance system must therefore make it clear to employees what behavior is expected of them and must set performance standards that are perceived as being achievable. If performance standards are set too high, employees may give up and decide not to attempt to reach them.

In addition to believing that their efforts will lead to successful performance, employees must also believe that those allocating the rewards will, in fact, recognize their performance as successful. The pay-for-performance program must therefore ensure that job performance is accurately measured; the ratings must reflect actual job performance levels. Moreover, the employees must believe this to be the case; that is, they must trust the system.

Performance–Reward Links

Expectancy theory states that rewards should be directly linked to performance. Employees will not be motivated to perform well if their successful performance goes unrewarded or if they can receive a reward for unsuccessful performance. A pay-for-performance system must thus be designed to ensure that a reward is received if and only if the desired level of performance is achieved. The rewards must be based on performance alone and not on some extraneous factor.

Value of Reward

According to expectancy theory, if employees do not value the reward, they will not be motivated to attain it. Thus, the reward offered by the pay-for-performance program must be great enough or important enough to act as an incentive.

Timeliness of Rewards

Research has demonstrated that the shorter the time interval between a behavior and its reward, the more likely it is that the reward will be motivating.[13] The most effective rewards are those given as soon as possible after the good behavior occurs.[14]

Performance–Organizational Mission Links

A pay-for-performance program cannot enhance competitive advantage unless rewarded performance contributes to the organization's overall mission. To be effective, the pay-for-performance program should encourage employees to engage in behaviors that help the company achieve its strategic goals. We noted earlier that the employees' performance standards should be achievable. To contribute to competitive advantage, they must also be challenging, encouraging employees to achieve their highest levels of performance.

Cost Efficiency

A pay-for-performance program would be of little value unless the financial gains resulting from increased productivity were greater than the corresponding increase in payroll costs. In other words, its ability to increase motivation and productivity is not enough; the pay-for-performance program must impact positively the organization's bottom line.

Merit Pay Plans

One type of pay-for-performance program is a **merit pay plan.** These plans grant employees annual pay raises based on their levels of job performance. Job performance is usually measured on an appraisal instrument completed by the supervisor.

merit pay plan A pay-for-performance program that grants employees annual pay raises based on their levels of job performance.

EXHIBIT 10-2	An Example of a Merit Pay Plan

Performance Rating	Merit Increase (Percent of Salary)
5	8–10%
4	5–7%
3	2–4%
2	No increase
1	No increase

(See Chapter 8, "Appraising Employee Job Performance," for a discussion of various appraisal instruments.)

In many companies, the size of the pay raise is directly linked to performance and is specified in advance in a **merit pay guidechart** (see Exhibit 10-2). The chart shows the size of the pay raise associated with each level of job performance.

Firms that do not use a merit pay guidechart give supervisors the discretion of determining the size of each subordinate's raise. For example, a company may provide supervisors with enough money to grant each employee a 4 percent raise and leave it to the supervisor to decide how this money is to be allocated. The absence of a guidechart makes the link between performance and rewards less clear.

How well do merit pay plans meet the standards listed in Exhibit 10-1? Let's take a look as we examine the strengths and weaknesses of these plans.

merit pay guidechart
A chart that shows the size of a merit pay raise associated with each level of job performance.

Strengths

Merit pay plans do establish effort-performance and performance-reward links; if an employee's effort leads to successful performance, the employee is rewarded by the organization. In theory, the ability to earn a reward is thus under the employee's control. If an individual performs well, the reward is granted regardless of how well others have performed their jobs or how well the company, as a whole, has done.

Publicized merit pay guidecharts serve to strengthen the performance-reward link. The guidechart represents the organization's promise that if employees perform at a given level, a specific reward will be granted. Employees therefore know exactly what reward their hard work can earn them.

Weaknesses

Unfortunately, merit pay plans often fail to successfully meet many, if not all, of the standards listed in Exhibit 10-1. It is not surprising then, that these plans often flounder. We discuss seven weaknesses, examples of which are presented in Exhibit 10-3.

First, as one might guess from our discussion in Chapter 8, a firm's performance appraisal system often impedes the effort-performance link. In some instances, it is difficult or impossible to isolate the contributions of each worker to a team effort. Moreover, supervisor ratings of job performances are often flawed and do not reflect employees' actual performance levels. If employees routinely receive ratings that are either lower or higher than deserved, motivation is hindered. Employees will say to themselves, "Why exert the effort? I won't (or will) get the reward regardless of how I actually perform my job."

Second, merit pay plans sometimes fail to establish a clear performance-reward link. When this occurs, trust between management and workers may be destroyed, and workers become skeptical and begin to doubt that their pay is really linked to performance.[15] This problem often surfaces in companies that do not publish merit pay guidecharts, but rather give supervisors the discretion to allot merit raises "as they see fit." Supervisors often base raises on factors other than job performance. For instance, one study found that managers frequently give pay raises to subordinates simply because their employees demand them, not because they have earned them.[16]

> **EXHIBIT 10-3**   An Employee's Complaints about Merit Pay

I hate my company's merit pay system because:

1. I do good work, but get a poor performance rating anyway because my supervisor doesn't like me. So there goes any chance for a raise!
2. I worked hard all year, expecting to get a nice raise. It turns out that Joe, whose performance was worse than mine, got a bigger raise simply because he threatened to quit his job if he didn't get one.
3. I know that the only way to get a raise is to work hard and perform well. But if I do get a raise, it won't be much, maybe 2 or 3 percent. It's just not worth the effort.
4. I clearly do the best work in my unit, so I deserve the biggest raise. But my wishy-washy supervisor rates my performance the same as everyone else's because she doesn't want anyone to be mad at her.
5. I know that if I work hard, I will get a raise. But I never think about the raise when I'm at work because it will be months before I ever get it. I'm just not that patient.
6. Last year I did great and got a wonderful raise. I'm happy with my salary now. I don't need any more raises, so I'm just going to take it easy this year.
7. I'll get a nice raise if I produce 20 widgets a day. So I'll work as fast as I can. I don't care if any of the widgets that I make are defective because it doesn't affect my raise.

Apparently, the squeaky wheel gets oiled. This phenomenon occurred under two conditions:

1. When the manager is dependent on a subordinate because of the subordinate's specialized expertise
2. When a subordinate threatens to appeal to an upper-level manager with whom he or she is well connected politically

Third, merit pay plans fail when employees do not value the rewards offered by the company. The merit pay pool is not unlimited; once raises are distributed to employees whose performance is adequate, there may not be enough money left to sufficiently recognize the outstanding ones.[17] Consequently, the raises received by outstanding workers are typically not much different from those received by acceptable workers—the difference is usually about 2 percent.[18] To most employees, the attainment of an outstanding rating is simply not worth the effort.

Some companies deal with this problem by placing restrictions on the number of pay raises supervisors may give. To contain costs, these firms institute quota systems that place a lid on the number of people who may receive the maximum pay raise. Thus, an outstanding performer may be denied this raise simply because the quota of top performers has already been filled.[19] Needless to say, such an individual would become quite dissatisfied and may become much less motivated in the future.

Fourth, the performance–reward link is hindered when supervisors are reluctant to make distinctions between members within their units. Fearing that such actions will destroy group cohesiveness, some supervisors believe it is better to distribute raises equally to all members of the group than to distribute them unequally according to job performance.[20] When supervisors take this approach, two negative consequences may occur:

1. Top performers will resent the fact that their reward is no higher than the low performers in the group.
2. Low performers will not be encouraged to improve their performance; after all, they will expect to receive a reward regardless of their individual performance levels.

A fifth problem with merit pay plans is the time lag that occurs between behavior and reward. In most merit pay systems, raises are granted once a year. Such an approach provides an employee with very little incentive to work hard throughout the entire year. An employee's behavior in January, for instance, is not likely to be influenced by the thought of a possible pay raise in December. To better motivate employee behavior, merit increases should be offered in a timelier manner. For instance, companies could grant raises quarterly, rather than yearly, and supervisors could give on-the-spot bonuses whenever exceptional work occurs.

Sixth, merit pay plans are not very cost-efficient. Merit raises are a lot more expensive than they first appear. Once a merit increase is earned, it becomes part of base pay and employees continue to receive it throughout their tenure with the company. The productivity gains generated by the merit pay plan must thus be quite substantial to offset these costs.

Seventh, to make matters worse, merit pay plans may actually hinder productivity if these plans fail to reward behaviors that contribute to organizational goals. In fact, some merit pay systems unintentionally reward behaviors that are counterproductive. Sears, for example, found this out the hard way in the late 1990s. Sears used a commission system based on gross revenues at its automotive repair stores. To Sears' surprise, this system motivated some employees to recommend unneeded repairs to unsuspecting customers in order to increase revenues. Sears was found guilty of consumer fraud and lost a ton of future business, as its reputation sunk to a new low.

The chief problem associated with this shortcoming is that merit plans often breed competitive behaviors, rather than cooperative ones.[21] For instance, an employee working under a merit system would be unlikely to help a coworker if doing so would jeopardize his or her own job performance.[22] When this problem surfaces, employees may:[23]

- Refuse to provide information on the status of a job as a way to gain an advantage over coworkers
- Grandstand; that is, develop and execute a major action designed to garner attention and recognition from supervisors
- Refuse to help others by sharing work experiences that would prevent others, for instance, from making the same mistakes

Recommendations

It would appear from this long list of possible weaknesses that organizations should scrap any ideas they may have about starting a merit pay plan. Some experts, in fact, have made this suggestion.[24] Most experts believe, however, that the use of these plans, even if flawed, beats any alternative (e.g., across-the-board raises or raises based solely on seniority). These experts take the view that merit pay plans, although not perfect, can be effective if properly designed and implemented. Management expert Janet Wiscombe offers the following recommendations:[25]

1. Ensure that managers are willing to make objective assessments of their employees' job performance.
2. Measure an employee's performance on the basis of job behaviors that have a proven impact on the success of the business.
3. Make payouts quarterly, not annually.
4. Frequently communicate performance expectations to employees.
5. Train managers to properly implement the system.

Another management expert, Edward Lawler, provides these recommendations to organizations interested in starting a merit pay plan:[26]

1. Think big; the program must pack a wallop. Reward should be large enough to make a real difference. The reward for top-performing employees should be 10 to 15 percent of their base salary; a 3 or 4 percent increase is simply not large enough to improve performance.
2. Make pay increases public. When given in public, the recipient not only enjoys the monetary value, but also the status and prestige it conveys.

3. Do not deliver rewards as a salary increase; use bonuses. Salary increases become annuities and are no longer available to use as rewards and incentives. With a bonus system, all variable pay is at risk so that the motivational incentive is always present. Bonuses should be awarded on a regular basis and should be tied directly to performance during a specified job cycle or time period.

4. Deliver rewards as soon as possible after the desired behavior takes place. Instant or spot rewards are a good example.

5. Make sure individual performance can be measured accurately; you cannot reward what you cannot measure. The most common reason merit pay plans fail is a poor performance appraisal system. The ideal measures are influential, objective, easily communicated, and inclusive of all the important behaviors the organization wishes to stimulate.

6. For the program to work, employees must believe management's claim that performance will be fairly rewarded. Employees will believe this only if they trust management. One of the best ways to establish the credibility of the system is to show employees openly how it works; show that the company's better performers are actually earning more money. Also, trust will be enhanced if employees take part in developing the system.

Piece Rate Plans

As the name suggests, **piece rate plans** base an individual's wages on the number of "pieces" or product units he or she produces. The organization first establishes performance standards to determine how many pieces a person can be expected to produce in a given period of time. Industrial engineers make these estimates based on time-and-motion studies. The firm sets wage rates based on how well workers perform relative to that standard. If they reach the standard, their pay typically equals the market rate for the job; if they exceed the standard, they receive higher than market wages.

Piece rate plans vary. Lincoln Electric used a **straight piecework** plan, paying workers a set amount for each unit produced. Here's how a piece rate would be established:

> Let's say the market pay for a widget producer is $6 per hour. The company's industrial engineers determine that a worker should be able to produce six widgets an hour. The piece rate would thus be set at $1. Workers can earn more or less than the market pay depending on how productive they are. If workers meet expectations and produce six widgets per hour, they will earn the market wage—$6 an hour. However, if they exceed the standard and produce seven widgets, for example, they will earn above-market wages—$7 an hour.

Alternatives to straight piecework pay different piece rates depending on whether the worker has met the standard. One variation, for instance, uses two piece rates: One rate is used when a worker meets or exceeds the standard; the other rate is used when a worker fails to meet it. For example, if the standard were six units per hour, a worker producing five or fewer units might be paid $1 per piece; one producing six or more units might be paid $1.25 per piece. Compared to straight piecework, this type of plan provides the workers with greater incentive for meeting and exceeding the standard.

Approximately 35 percent of U.S. companies currently use some form of piece rate plan,[27] mainly in production settings in which jobs are simple and highly structured and the achievement of performance goals is within employee control.[28] The question is "Can these plans enhance competitive advantage?" We now address this question as we examine some of their strengths and weaknesses.

piece rate plans Pay-for-performance programs that base an individual's wages on the number of "pieces" or product units he or she produces.

straight piecework A piece rate plan that pays workers a set amount for each unit produced.

Strengths

Piece rate plans clearly establish links between effort and performance and between performance and rewards:[29]

- Employees know exactly what they must do to earn the reward they desire.
- Unlike merit pay plans, the performance standards set in piece rate plans are objective and thus cannot be influenced by supervisory bias.
- Rewards are tied directly to performance—higher outputs result in higher pay.

Piece rate plans can also be cost-efficient. Workers do not receive above-market pay unless their production rates are high. An organization can thus ensure cost efficiency by establishing the appropriate rates. For instance, if each unit produced increases profits by $1, an organization can gain from this increase by paying the employees less than $1 for the production of that unit.

Weaknesses

Although piece rate plans often enhance competitive advantage by increasing productivity, they do have their shortcomings. Under piece rate systems, companies place a great deal of pressure on employees to produce, which can actually make them less productive. Many employees feel uncomfortable in that type of setting. Remember the turnover problem at Lincoln Electric; many new workers simply could not do the job and left the company. To consider this in the framework of expectancy theory, the value of the financial reward derived from high productivity may not be great enough to offset the stress some workers experience under this type of reward system. If employees are willing to relieve stress by accepting less pay for less effort, management has few options, short of dismissal or some other type of punishment.[30] In some instances, the majority of workers are unmotivated by the system and develop a norm that fosters a "slow-down" mentality. Coworkers who violate this norm are considered "rate-busters" and are pressured by others to slow down because their high productivity makes everyone else look bad.

Perhaps a more serious weakness associated with piece rate plans concerns the performance–organizational mission link. Not all of the behaviors encouraged by these programs contribute to the organization's mission. Consider the following problems:

- Workers paid by the piece may resist management's attempts to introduce new technology, innovative processes, or better management systems. These changes require adjustments to the piece rate system, and employees are very reluctant to accept such changes unless management can demonstrate that workers can earn more money by doing so.[31]
- Workers are not rewarded for suggesting new ideas that would improve production and quality or reduce scrap rates, and thus have no interest in doing so. Such workers view quality improvement efforts as being part of the manager's job.[32]
- Piece rate plans may cause employees to neglect aspects of their jobs not covered in the performance goals.[33] For instance, they may focus on quantity and neglect quality.
- Piece rate plans encourage competition rather than teamwork. If the job is relatively complex and requires teamwork for successful performance, the individual incentive plan should not be used.[34]

Gainsharing Plans

A major problem with both merit pay and piece rate plans is their emphasis on individual performance. Many organizations have begun to realize that total quality may be best achieved through effective teamwork. **Gainsharing plans** offer employees a cash award for meeting or exceeding goals based on the collaborative performance of a team of employees.[35]

gainsharing plans Pay-for-performance plans that offer employees a cash award for meeting or exceeding team-based goals.

The various gainsharing plans contain the common thread of motivating employees to increase production or reduce production costs.[36] The financial gains stemming from these activities are then shared with the employees. The unit whose performance is the basis of the gain may be the whole organization, a large subdivision, or a single unit. Most gainsharing plans feature the following:

- The organization has productivity goals that can be achieved through effective teamwork.
- Employees receive cash bonuses if those goals are met.
- Productivity is measured by an explicit formula with objective measures.
- Employees are encouraged to submit suggestions for cutting production costs or increasing productivity.

A number of gainsharing plans exist. For illustrative purposes, we limit our discussion to one—the **Scanlon Plan.** Developed more than 50 years ago, the Scanlon Plan aims to cut production costs, relative to output. When implementing the Scanlon Plan, a company must address the following questions: (1) What criteria should be used for determining whether production costs have been reduced? (2) What means can be employed to reduce these costs? (3) How shall the ensuing financial gains be allocated?

First, a firm must calculate the ratio of production cost/sales value of production (SVOP) that would be expected in a typical year. The ratio is usually determined by averaging the yearly production costs during a base period of three to five years. The types of production costs that would be examined are such things as raw materials, direct labor, indirect labor, depreciation utilities, supplies, and payroll (see Figure 10-2).

The following example illustrates how this ratio is used to determine bonuses:

> Let's say that in the base period, a firm's average annual SVOP is $1 million and the production costs are $250,000. As one can see, the ratio is 1:4 or 25 percent. The aim of the plan is to reduce the size of this ratio. Employees would receive bonuses during the next period if production costs were less than 25 percent of the SVOP. The size of the bonus pool is a function of the difference between the expected and actual production costs. For example, if during the next year, the company's SVOP were $1.5 million, the expected production costs would be 25 percent of that figure or $375,000. If the actual production costs were $300,000, the size of the bonus pool would be $75,000.

Second, firms must decide how production costs are to be cut. Formal suggestion systems elicit employee opinions because they know most about the production process. Employees should consider the questions in Exhibit 10-4 when trying to generate suggestions.

Scanlon plan A gainsharing plan in which workers share the gains produced by cutting production costs.

Raw Materials
Steel, hardware, cartons, casting, etc.

Salaried Personnel
Supervisors, clerks, managers, etc.

Direct Labor
The standard labor rate times allowed hours for each operation

Supplies
Tape, oil, maintenance parts, etc.

Indirect Labor
Maintenance, tool and die, material handling, setup, etc.

Utilities
Gas, electric, telephone

Depreciation
Wear and tear on machines, dies, buildings, etc.

Figure 10-2
Factors Affecting Production Costs

EXHIBIT 10-4	Questions for Employees to Consider When Generating a List of Suggestions for Cutting Production Costs

Methods

Can you
- Simplify current procedures?
- Group or combine jobs?
- Eliminate any unnecessary operations?
- Simplify own job?
- Suggest new methods?

Machinery or Equipment

Can you
- Simplify any machines or equipment?
- Improve machine output?
- Improve design or construction?
- Reduce machine setup time?
- Reduce machine downtime?
- Reduce maintenance costs?
- Change the machine, layout, or workplace to make it easier for you to produce more?

Paperwork

Can you
- Reduce or simplify filing?
- Combine or simplify forms?
- Eliminate unnecessary forms?
- Reduce chances for errors?
- Reduce phone, postage, or shipping costs?

Materials

Can you
- Simplify handling?
- Speed delivery?
- Find use for scrap?
- Reduce scrap, waste, and spoilage?
- Reduce material costs?
- Eliminate delays?

Source: (1979). *The Scanlon Way to Improved Productivity.* Athens, TN: Midland-Ross.

Here's how the typical suggestion system works. Employees submit ideas to a screening committee comprised of their elected peers within their operational unit. If the screening committee accepts the suggestion, it is passed to a second committee, which includes a steering committee member and management personnel. If accepted by this committee, the suggestion is implemented.

Third, the typical Scanlon Plan allocates bonuses in the following manner: 75 percent is paid out and 25 percent is held in reserve for lean periods in which there are no bonuses.[37] Of the money paid out, 25 percent goes to the company and 75 percent is distributed among employees. In some plans, each employee receives an equal share of the bonus; in other plans, the bonus is allocated as a percentage of an employee's gross income.

Strengths

Gainsharing programs have become very popular. Such programs are now being used by thousands of companies, involving millions of employees.[38] Gainsharing programs are most commonly found in manufacturing settings where productivity gains can be most easily measured. Recently, however, service organizations have also begun to implement these plans.[39]

Gainsharing plans have often been quite successful. Estimates of productivity improvement range from 15 to 20 percent in the first year alone.[40] If we view gainsharing in terms of the standards specified here, we can readily understand why these plans can be so successful.

First, the effort–performance and performance–reward links are strong, because employees know what needs to be done to trigger a payoff. The pay formula is stated in objective terms and is therefore protected from supervisory bias.

Second, programs also work because they link performance with the organization's mission. A well-designed gainsharing program rewards employees for activities that improve the company's overall productivity. For instance, gainsharing programs encourage employees to search for ways to eliminate unnecessary steps in production processes, make tools and equipment more accessible, and eliminate delays.[41]

Third, gainsharing programs also promote teamwork as employees realize that their own rewards will be greater when all employees work as effectively as possible. Employees are thus more likely to exchange ideas and share resources in order to help each other succeed,[42] as illustrated in On the Road to Competitive Advantage 10-2.

Use of Gainsharing at John Deere

John Deere, one of the largest equipment manufacturing and distribution organizations in the world, had become dissatisfied with its individual incentive plan. The plan, which rewarded individual productivity, discouraged employees from spending time to help one another. Moreover, the plan discouraged employees from sharing ideas to improve productivity for fear that the company would raise production output standards. In effect, the plan stifled creativity, penalized innovation, and discouraged cooperation. To encourage its employees to work together to find and implement better and more efficient ways to manufacture its products, John Deere developed a gainsharing plan that explicitly rewards cooperation and innovation. The plan has three major components. First, it measures and rewards team, rather than individual, performance. Second, it gives employees discretion to design their own production processes. And third, the cost savings resulting from having more efficient production processes are shared with the employees, as two-thirds of the savings are distributed to them. The new plan has benefited both the employees with increased compensation and the company with increased profits.

Source: Sprinkle, G.B., and Williamson, M.G. (2004). The evolution from Taylorism to employee gainsharing: A case study examining John Deere's continuing improvement plan. *Issues in Accounting Education, 19* (4), 487–503.

Fourth, gainsharing plans are cost-effective. Unlike merit increases, gainsharing payouts represent variable costs, so they create a win-win situation for employers. When productivity goals are met, everyone wins, because both the employer and employees share the gains. In a bad year, no payout is made.[43]

Weaknesses

Three main problems explain why nearly one-third of gainsharing programs fail.[44] First, employees may perceive that rewards are unfairly distributed. The problem is analogous to that which occurs when students work together on a group project and share the same reward (i.e., receive the same grade). Those contributing most to the group effort may feel cheated because their grades are no better than those who "skated by." In addition to feeling cheated, research findings suggest that such individuals may become less involved in their jobs and begin to lose interest.[45]

Second, employee suggestions for improving efficiency may dwindle over time. At first, ideas for cost cutting come rather easily. After a few years, however, the momentum often slows as employees run out of good ideas. Consequently, the plan begins to lose its effect on productivity improvement.[46]

Third, gainsharing plans may suffer if payout formulas are inflexible, especially in volatile environments where unexpected changes in the formula factors can make the formula obsolete. For example, the gainsharing plan of one company, an automobile parts manufacturer, became totally ineffective when the firm unexpectedly tripled the size of its workforce (increasing labor costs) and invested heavily in recapitalization. It never changed the formula to allow for increased labor costs. Consequently, the company unjustly denied employees their bonuses.[47]

Recommendations

Gainsharing programs are most likely to succeed under the following conditions:[48]

1. Management must orient the company culture to one of respect, cooperation, and open communication. Management must demonstrate its willingness to:
   - Listen to and support employee suggestions.
   - Go out and talk with employees.
   - Communicate honestly with employees.

2. The plan must be designed so that the payout is dependent on factors the employees can control, such as shipments, payroll costs, customer satisfaction, and quality.

3. Management must meet regularly with employees to share information and ideas and gather suggestions.
   - Management should share information about upcoming orders, customers' opinions about products received, quality efforts, shifts in product mix, and steps the company must take to remain competitive.
   - Management should elicit suggestions by holding gainsharing meetings, engaging in on-the-floor discussions, implementing a formal suggestion system, and forming problem-solving teams and task forces.

Profit-Sharing Plans

profit-sharing plans
Pay-for-performance plans in which a portion of the company's profits are contributed to individual employee accounts.

Profit-sharing plans are similar to gainsharing in the sense that they reward group, rather than individual, performance. The payout, however, is based on profits rather than gains. A portion of the company's profits is contributed to individual employee accounts.[49] There are three types of profit-sharing plans: **deferred, distribution,** and **combination.**[50]

deferred plans
An employee's profit-sharing earnings are distributed at retirement.

1. *Deferred plans:* An individual's profit-sharing earnings are distributed at retirement.

2. *Distribution plans:* The company fully distributes each period's earnings as soon as the profit-sharing pool is calculated.

distribution plans
An employee's profit-sharing earnings are distributed as soon as the profit-sharing pool is calculated.

3. *Combination plans:* Employees receive a portion of each period's earnings immediately; the remainder awaits future distribution.

The provisions included in most profit-sharing plans appear in Exhibit 10-5.

combination plans
Employees receive a portion of each period's profit-sharing earnings immediately; the remainder awaits future distribution.

Strengths

Profit-sharing plans have become quite popular.[51] The strengths of profit-sharing plans are similar to those of gainsharing. Both plans are designed to improve productivity by making employees' interests compatible with employers' goals. Therefore, if the employer does well, so do the employees. With profit sharing, however, the employees may gain a greater sense of ownership. This may help employees identify more closely with the organization, internalize its goals, and work harder to achieve them. As noted by one worker who was part of a profit-sharing program:[52]

> When the mill is your own, you really work hard to make a go of it. Everyone digs right in—and wants others to do the same. If they see anybody trying to get a free ride, they get on his back right quick. Group pressure here is more powerful than any foreman could be.

The potential benefits to be reaped by a profit-sharing plan are further illustrated by the example appearing in On the Road to Competitive Advantage 10-3 on page 288.

Weaknesses

Most profit-sharing plans share three main weaknesses. First, profit-sharing plans only marginally address effort-performance-rewards links. Payouts are based on performance measures (i.e., profits) that are influenced by a host of factors unrelated to employee effort. In other words, how well employees perform their jobs often has less impact on profits than such things as market conditions and foreign exchange rates.[53] Because employees may fail to see the connection between their individual efforts and profits, the payoff may seem too remote to serve as a motivational tool.[54]

Second, profit-sharing plans are not always cost-efficient. As noted, profit levels depend on many factors unrelated to employee behavior. One could argue that it is not cost-effective to share profits with employees if those profits were a result of something other than their performance.[55]

EXHIBIT 10-5 Provisions of Profit-Sharing Plans

Eligibility Requirements

An employee usually must complete an eligibility period prior to receiving an allocation of profits. For most companies, the period is one year. Some plans also have a minimum age requirement, usually 21.

Employer Contribution

In most cases, the company board of directors approves a percentage of profits to be set aside for the plan each year. Most use formulas for determining the amount of employee profit sharing. In 1989, the average employer contribution was 9.5 percent of profits.

Allocating Profits

Many companies base an individual's share of profits on their base pay. An employee earning $40,000 may receive twice the allotment of one earning $20,000. Other companies provide equal shares to all employees.

Investment Option

Once profits are allocated to employees, their accounts are typically invested into such things as company stock, a common stock fund, fixed-interest securities, and diversified investments.

Employee Contribution

Employees are not usually required to make contributions to profit-sharing accounts. However, some companies allow them to make voluntary contributions, which can be made on a pretax basis.

Vesting Schedule

Participants are usually required to be vested before gaining access to their funds. Vesting gives employees the right to receive benefits from the plan in the future. Most companies use gradual vesting in which a participant becomes vested in a percentage of the account each year, until fully vested. For example, an employee may become 20 percent vested each year, attaining full vesting after five years.

Withdrawal Provisions

Many plans allow employees access to their accounts. Recent Internal Revenue Service regulations, however, put constraints on employee withdrawals before retirement. There is a 10 percent penalty on funds withdrawn prior to the age of 59½ unless the employee can show a hardship.

Loan Provisions

Employees can gain access to their funds without tax penalty through loans. The loans must be repaid with interest, however.

Distribution

At retirement, most plans allocate a single lump-sum payment of the entire balance. Others spread the payments out over a fixed period of years.

Source: Florkowski, G.W. (1990). Analyzing group incentive plans. *HRMagazine,* January, 36–38.

A third problem concerns the use of deferred plans. Obviously, the rewards are not well timed from a motivation perspective; the thought of receiving money at a much later date may not motivate an employee right now. Although having limited motivational impact, such plans may still have a rather strong effect on employee retention rates. That is, employees may choose to remain with an employer to ensure a healthy retirement income.

10-2b Employee Empowerment Programs

As noted earlier, the goal of "employee empowerment" is to give employees greater voice in decisions about work-related matters. Their decision-making authority can range from giving suggestions, to exercising veto power over management decisions, to making the decisions themselves.[56] Employees can help decide a range of issues, from how their own jobs are to be performed, to working conditions (e.g., rest breaks, work hours), to company policy (e.g., how layoffs should be implemented).[57]

Many experts believe that organizations can improve productivity through the employee empowerment process. Empowerment can enhance productivity in two ways. First, it can strengthen motivation by providing employees with the opportunity to attain intrinsic rewards from their work, such as a greater sense of accomplishment and a feeling of importance. Intrinsic rewards can be more powerful than

Using Profit Sharing to Turn Around Productivity

Almost 10 years ago, Robert Frey and his partner bought a small, troubled company that made mailing tubes and composite cans. Profits were marginal, labor costs were out of control, and employee relations were poor. Today, the company makes a new mix of highly differentiated, specially protected, environmentally responsible composite cans; the workforce is flexible and deeply involved in the company's success; employee relations are excellent; and the company is making a lot of money because productivity has risen by 30 percent.

How was this startling turnaround accomplished? The introduction of a profit-sharing plan played a major role. The plan was formulated to pay out lots of money, enough to get everyone passionately involved in the effort to cut costs, increase sales, and make money. Frey reasoned that if employees got a part of the profits, then extra costs and expenses would come out of their pockets, too, and they would have a stake in cutting them. Frey pushed and prodded and required people to help solve problems related to their own jobs so that everyone could make more money. Although progress was painfully slow, the effects were eventually quite positive.

Full-time employees now routinely monitor the work of others to reduce waste and increase efficiency; absenteeism has virtually disappeared; and grievances are down to one or two a year.

Source: Frey, R. (1993). Empowerment or else. *Harvard Business Review*, September–October, 80–94.

extrinsic ones. They often have a greater value to the employee, and they are automatically linked to performance. That is, because they give these rewards to themselves, employees need not worry about whether management can be trusted to provide them. Workers thus become self-motivated. As motivation expert Frederick Herzberg notes:[58]

> I can charge a person's battery, and then recharge it, and recharge it again. But it is only when one has a generator of one's own that we can talk about motivation. One then needs no outside stimulation. One wants to do it.

Second, employee empowerment can improve productivity because the process leads to better decisions. Decisions are better because they are made by employees, and employees have a more complete knowledge of their work than do their managers.[59] Moreover, employees are more likely to accept (and thus implement) decisions when they have participated in the decision-making process.[60]

A number of different HRM programs are available that grant employee empowerment to some extent. We discuss the most common employee empowerment programs next.

Informal Participative Decision-Making Programs

informal participative decision-making program
An employee empowerment program in which managers decide just how much decision-making authority employees should have in each instance.

In **informal participative decision-making programs,** managers and subordinates make joint decisions on a day-to-day basis.[61] Employees do not enjoy blanket authority to make all work-related decisions; managers decide just how much decision-making authority employees should have in each instance. The amount of authority varies depending on such situational factors as the complexity of the decision and the importance of employee acceptance of the decision. Suggestions for determining what type of work situations would call for full employee participation are given in Taking a Closer Look 10-1.

Strengths

Several studies have examined the effects of informal participation decision-making programs. Although the results have been mixed, and thus cannot be considered

> **Taking a Closer Look 10-1** | *When to Engage in Employee Participative Decision Making*
>
> 1. ***When all possible solutions are equally effective.*** For example, consider employee vacation schedules. If one solution is as good as another, the group should be empowered to work the scheduling out.
> 2. ***When managers do not possess sufficient information or expertise to make a quality decision on their own.*** Managers should at least consult their employees before a decision is reached because employees can provide the needed information.
> 3. ***When managers do not know exactly what information is needed and/or where it is located.*** Again, managers should at least consult their employees before a decision is reached because employees can provide the needed information.
> 4. ***When the group's acceptance or commitment to effective implementation is crucial and the group is unlikely to accept a manager's unilateral decision.*** If employees' acceptance is crucial, participative decision making should be used because people accept decisions more willingly if
>
> they have had a voice in the decision-making process. The participation should be genuine; managers should not ask for employee input simply to give the appearance of participation. Employees can usually recognize this ploy and, if they do, feelings of distrust will develop.
> 5. ***When employees' goals are aligned with those of management.*** If employees do not share management's goals, participative decision making would be inappropriate because the two parties would be at cross-purposes.
> 6. ***When employees are likely to agree among themselves about preferred solutions.*** When disagreement among employees is anticipated, the use of participative decision making could cause serious rifts among employees. It is thus best if managers make the decision themselves, based on employee input.
>
> *Source:* Vroom, V.H. (1976). "Leadership." In M.D. Dunnette (ed.), *Handbook of Industrial and Organizational Psychology.* Chicago: Rand McNally.

definitive,[62] most studies have found that informal participative decision-making programs do, in fact, have a positive impact on productivity.[63] This type of program purportedly works well because it tailors the amount of employee empowerment to the specific situation. The key to using this approach successfully is choosing when to empower employees. Employees should be empowered in situations in which they can make decisions that are as good as or better than those that their managers make. Those using this method assume that in some cases the employees can make a better decision, but not in all cases. For instance, Taking a Closer Look 10-1 indicates that employees should not be empowered to make a decision when their interests are not aligned with those of the organization. The author has a personal example that attests to the accuracy of this principle. He was assigned to a committee of fellow professors, with the task of developing job performance standards for the entire faculty in the College of Business. The college's best interests would be served by performance standards that challenged the faculty to perform at the highest levels. But, their own best interests would be served by performance standards that did not place a whole lot of pressure on them. So what did the committee do? Shamefully, it developed standards that were rather easily attainable!

To further illustrate how this type of employee empowerment program tailors the level of empowerment to the situation, consider the following decisions:

1. Deciding which employees are to be given Christmas off and which are to be given New Years off
2. Deciding whether to purchase an expensive piece of technology to enhance productivity levels
3. Deciding which employee to lay off

> **EXHIBIT 10-6**   Job Characteristics That Enhance Intrinsic Motivation

Job Characteristics	Description and Rationale
Skill variety	The degree to which a job requires a variety of different activities to carry out the work. A job would have high skill variety if it requires a number of different skills and talents.
Task identity	The degree to which a job requires completion of the "whole" and identifiable piece of work. A job would have high task identity if the worker did the job from the beginning to end with a visible outcome.
Task significance	The degree to which the job has a substantial impact on the lives of other people, whether these people are in the immediate organization or in the world at large. A job would have high task significance if people benefited greatly from results of the job.
Autonomy	The degree to which the job provides the workers with autonomy. A job would have high autonomy if the workers were given substantial freedom, independence, and discretion in scheduling the work and determining the procedures to be used in carrying it out.
Job feedback	The degree to which the job provides the worker with knowledge of results. A job would have high job feedback if carrying out the work activities required by the job provided the individual with direct and clear information about the effectiveness of his or her performance.

Source: Hackman, J.R., and Oldham, G.R. (1980). *Work Redesign*. Reading, MA: Addison-Wesley.

In the first instance, employees would be given full empowerment because all possible solutions are equally effective and the group's acceptance is crucial. In the second, the manager would make the decision after asking for employee input because the manager may not possess sufficient information to make a decision on her own. In the third, the manager would make the decision without any employee input because employees would vehemently disagree among themselves about the preferred solution.

Weaknesses

The success of these programs also often hinges on whether employees want to participate in decision making. When desired, empowerment can be very motivating. Some employees, however, have no desire to make work-related decisions and view such programs with suspicion.[64]

Job Enrichment

Sometimes employees are not motivated because of the way their jobs are designed. Consider, for example, the job of an assembly-line worker who does nothing but place a screw in a hole as the product passes by on the production line. Such a job provides little opportunity for workers to gain intrinsic rewards.

job enrichment
An employee empowerment program in which jobs are redesigned to be more intrinsically rewarding.

Job enrichment aims to redesign jobs to be more intrinsically rewarding. Certain job characteristics (see Exhibit 10-6) have been identified as intrinsically rewarding or "enriching." When these characteristics are present in a job, employees will be motivated because they will have ample opportunity to gain intrinsic rewards. Jobs that lack these characteristics are good candidates for enrichment.

Once a job has been identified as needing enrichment, the organization must redesign it to incorporate these characteristics (skill, variety, autonomy, significance, and feedback). Some specific techniques for enriching a job are described in the following list:[65]

1. *Combine tasks:* This involves assigning tasks performed by different workers to a single individual. For example, in a furniture factory, rather than working on just one part of the production process, each person could assemble, sand, and stain an entire table or chair. This change would increase skill variety, as well as task identity, as each worker would be responsible for the job from start to finish.

2. *Establish client relationships:* Client relationships could be established by putting the worker in touch with the customers. For example, an auto dealership service department could allow its mechanics to discuss the service problems directly with the customer, rather than going through the service manager. By establishing client relationships, skill variety is increased because workers have a chance to develop new interpersonal skills. It also provides them with a chance to do a larger part of the job (task identity), to see how their work impacts customers (task significance), and to have more decision-making authority (autonomy).

3. *Reduce direct supervision:* Workers gain autonomy when they are given responsibility for doing things previously done by supervisors. For instance, clerks could be allowed to check for their own errors or be allowed to order supplies directly.

4. *Increase identification with product/service:* A company may accomplish this aim by linking employee names to final products. When people have to "sign" for their own work, they assume more responsibility for getting things done correctly. Assemblers could attach a tag to their output with names and work phone numbers. The firm could then invite buyers to call employees directly about any problems. Such increased identification would lead to an increase in task significance and job feedback.

Strengths

Many organizations have successfully enriched otherwise dull jobs. Because it makes jobs less automated, and thus more interesting and rewarding, enrichment often leads to improvements in productivity, quality, absenteeism rates, and retention.[66]

Weaknesses

As enriched jobs become less repetitive and routine, production may become less efficient. For example, allowing each person to assemble, sand, and stain an entire table or chair may be less efficient than an assembly-line approach. Job enrichment would be ill advised in situations where the loss in efficiency cannot be offset by productivity gains stemming from increased motivation. Moreover, employees preferring highly automated, easy jobs are likely to oppose job enrichment efforts. Although in the minority, some workers prefer jobs that are easy, yet boring.

Quality Circles

Employee empowerment can also be increased through the use of **quality circles.** A quality circle is a group of 6 to 12 employees who identify and resolve production problems within their unit. Circles usually meet once a week and are led by a coordinator who may be a supervisor within the work group or a member elected by the group.

quality circles
An employee empowerment program in which a team of six to twelve employees meets regularly to identify and resolve production problems within their unit.

To prepare circle members for their task, the organization usually provides training in problem identification, problem solving, statistical control procedures, and group dynamics.[67] Coordinators are typically trained in group dynamics, motivation, communication, and the operation of quality circles.[68]

Armed with this training, circle members work to identify and solve workplace problems regarding product quality and production efficiency using a five-step process, described in Taking a Closer Look 10-2.

Quality circles address varied problems. The following list of suggestions was generated by a quality circle at the Paul Revere Insurance Group:[69]

- Keep more money in the company's checking account. The funds in the company's checking account were often insufficient to pay claims. This problem was costing the company $5,000 a year in lost interest and other expenses.

- Ship certain material by truck, rather than air. This suggestion saved the company $27,000 annually.

Taking a Closer Look 10-2 | *Steps to Quality Circle Process*

Step 1: Problem Identification and Selection

The goal is to identify localized problems that may have gone unnoticed by upper management. In a typical first session, the group may produce a list of 10 to 30 problems by asking members to identify perceived problems. These problems are prioritized based on importance and the likelihood of finding a solution. Examples include the inability to obtain needed information about clients and delays in the production process.

Step 2: Problem Analysis

The circle gathers information needed to solve the problems at hand.

Step 3: Recommended Solutions

Possible solutions are usually compiled by brainstorming. Before agreeing to a solution, the group must consider the cost of the solution, the time and difficulty of imple-

mentation, the potential for success, and the potential impact of the solution on the business.

Step 4: Review by Management

When the group reaches consensus for a recommended solution, the circle presents it to management. Written recommendations are submitted first, followed by an oral presentation of the recommended solution.

Step 5: Management Response

Management gives an immediate response to the circle. If they reject the solution, management provides reasons and may then request alternative proposals. The acceptance rate for proposals submitted by quality circles typically ranges from 85 to 100 percent.

Source: Rafaeli, A. (1985). Quality circles and employee attitudes. *Personnel Psychology, 38* (3), 603-615.

- Send material to field claim representatives using reusable nylon bags instead of manila envelopes. This suggestion resulted in savings of $9,200 per year in postage and envelopes.

Strengths

Advocates claim that the use of quality circles improves productivity and efficiency by:

- *Getting valuable input from employees.* Employees are intimately involved in the work and are therefore in the best position to identify problems.
- *Improving communications* among workers and between workers and management.
- *Increasing motivation* through employee empowerment.

An illustration of a quality circle's possible impact on competitive advantage appears in On the Road to Competitive Advantage 10-4.

Weaknesses

continuous quality improvement programs
Programs that attempt to build quality into all phases of the design, production, and delivery of a product or service by empowering workers to trace product or service problems to their root causes and redesign production processes to eliminate them.

Quality circles do not always succeed. In fact, these programs have failed in more than 60 percent of the organizations in which they have been implemented because of the following problems.[70] First, quality circles are often used as a quick fix and do not address the real problems underlying poor productivity, quality, and employee morale. Second, the use of quality circles often creates an "insider-outsider culture," where non-circle members become jealous and hostile towards circle members.[71] Third, quality circles are sometimes operated improperly; companies do not pay enough attention to who is selected for circle membership, what projects they do, and who should act on their recommendations.[72]

Continuous Quality Improvement and Self-Managed Work Teams

Many companies have taken quality circles to the "next level" by implementing **continuous quality improvement programs.** Companies adopting this approach

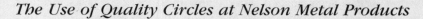

The Use of Quality Circles at Nelson Metal Products

The Nelson Metal Products Company, an automotive supplier in Gradville, Michigan, found itself floundering. It had a staggering rate of 2,500 defective parts per million produced. Ford and General Motors, its biggest customers, would not even let it bid for work.

In response to this problem, Nelson instituted a quality circle program to try to turn things around. The CEO met with employees at all levels to exchange views on why the company was losing money and customers and what improvements were needed. The company then hand-picked quality circle teams and trained them to identify "high priority, 'doable' projects."

One team figured out how to increase the production of a part from 80 to 140 an hour. Another team found ways to keep people outside the purchasing department from placing orders with vendors, thereby eliminating the tide of undocumented, and thus unpayable, invoices that had been flooding accounting.

As the result of this effort, Nelson's profits are now robust; defective parts are fewer than 10 per million; and Ford and General Motors are buying again.

Source: Duetsch, C.H. (1991). A revival of the quality circle. *The New York Times,* 23.

attempt to build quality into all phases of the design, production, and delivery of a product or service. These companies empower their workers to trace product or service problems to their root causes and redesign production processes to eliminate them by using various problem-solving and statistical techniques (e.g., statistical process control). Worker empowerment takes the form of **self-managed work teams.** Such teams consist of 6 to 18 employees from different departments who work together to produce a well-defined segment of finished work. The segment could be a final product, like a refrigerator, or a service, like a fully processed insurance claim.[73] Management gives team members authority to manage themselves. They plan, organize, and coordinate, and take corrective actions.[74] In short, they are given responsibilities usually held by supervisors. Not surprisingly, then, the supervisor's job disappears when self-managed work teams are used.

The use of continuous quality improvement programs has grown rapidly during the past decade, built on the successful experiences of numerous companies. Xerox, for example, was able to decrease the number of customer complaints by 38 percent; Motorola reduced the number of defects by 80 percent.[75] Proponents claim it succeeds because it is customer-focused and promotes sound management practices like teamwork, continuous learning, and continuous improvement.[76]

Continuous quality improvement programs are not always successful. The most difficult issue with which companies must deal is deciding how to effectively implement these programs. A number of obstacles must be overcome. Managers are often reluctant to give up their power, and the employees are often reluctant to accept their new responsibilities. To prepare team members for self-management, the organization must provide a considerable amount of training.[77] It takes a group of employees from two to five years to become a mature self-managed work team. Without proper training, virtually any team will bog down permanently in midprocess.[78] An organization must provide training in three areas:[79]

1. *Technical skills:* Cross-training, which allows team members to move from job to job within the team, is essential. Thus, team members should receive training in the specific skills that will broaden their personal contributions to the overall effort. Technical training is usually a mix of formal classroom instruction, on-the-job training, member tutoring, or mentoring.

2. *Interpersonal skills:* Team members must communicate effectively, both one on one and in groups with each other and with people outside the team. Cooperative decision making within and among teams demands the skills of group problem solving, influencing others, and resolving conflicts. Team members must

self-managed work teams
A form of employee empowerment in which teams of six to eighteen employees from different departments work together to produce a well-defined segment of finished work.

learn a basic approach to problem solving that helps them zero in on problem areas, gather facts, analyze causes, and select the best solutions.

3. *Administrative skills:* Self-managed work teams must perform tasks formerly handled by supervisors. The team must learn how to keep records, report procedures, budget, schedule, monitor, hire, and appraise the performance of team members. They must also learn how to deal with other parts of the organization, such as purchasing, payroll, engineering, and accounting.

Strengths

The research findings to date have been quite positive.[80] Proponents claim that self-managed work teams are effective because they empower employees to make decisions that affect their day-to-day business lives. Thus, these teams radically change the way employees value and think about their jobs.[81] As one writer notes:[82]

> The theory is simple: Create spirited teams of workers with different skills from different departments and give them the power to develop a product, manage a business, improve a system, or plan their own work schedules. When employees get control of their own destinies . . . they work faster, smarter and with an eye toward profitability.

Another advantage associated with the use of self-managed work teams is the greater flexibility they provide. Today's companies must be able to produce in small lots, customizing products to increasing demands. This calls for flexible work practices and workers who are able to move from job to job. Self-managed work teams make this flexibility possible because employees are cross-trained to perform all tasks. They can fill in for absent coworkers and respond quickly to changes in models and production runs.[83] A General Electric plant in Salisbury, North Carolina, for instance, can change product models a dozen times a day by using a self-managed work team. As a result, productivity has increased by 250 percent.[84]

Companies are using self-managed work teams throughout the United States, especially in the auto, aerospace, electrical equipment, electronics, food processing, paper, and steel industries.[85] These teams are particularly prevalent in manufacturing organizations, where newer manufacturing strategies, competitive pressures, and advanced production technologies place added responsibility on shop floor employees.[86] Among the companies that have adopted self-managed work teams are Xerox, Procter & Gamble, Federal Express, Boeing, Ford, General Motors, and General Electric. An example of how self-managed work teams are used at XEL Communications is provided in On the Road to Competitive Advantage 10-5.[87]

Weaknesses

Self-managed work teams present a number of potential weaknesses. One is the possible "turf battles" that may arise: Departmental rivalries often flare up when a team is formed. Consider the following example:[88]

> The Dow Chemical Plastics Plant in Michigan decided to use self-managed work teams to develop a plastic resin. The team was comprised of scientists and manufacturing managers. Interdepartmental problems arose quickly. The scientists wanted to spend several months examining new product options and building a prototype. The managers preferred producing a slight variation of an existing product. The two factions could not agree and eventually went their own way.

The absence of a supervisor may cause problems. For instance, without a supervisor, there is no one responsible for handling human relations problems. With no boss in sight, disputes can snowball.[89] Moreover, workers lack sufficient time to handle some of the traditional supervisory responsibilities, such as conducting employment interviews and training/orienting new employees.[90] Difficulties may also arise in the

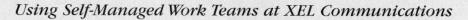
Using Self-Managed Work Teams at XEL Communications

XEL, a Denver-based telecommunications firm, has won a plethora of awards for product quality, including GTE's "Quality Award of Excellence" in 1997 and *Industry Week* magazine's "Ten Best Manufacturing Plants in the USA" in 1995. The company attributes much of its success to its use of self-managed work teams. In place for the past 10 years, these teams have been meeting daily, without a supervisor, to review what needs to be done. Longer meetings are conducted to discuss such topics as vacation planning and recurring production problems. Once per quarter, each team formally presents its accomplishments to management. During its first year, the use of self-managed work teams produced the following outcomes:

- Supervisory and support staff was cut by 30 percent.
- The cost of assembly dropped 25 percent.
- Inventory has been cut in half.
- Quality levels have risen by 30 percent.
- Cycle time (the period from start of production to finished goods) plummeted from eight weeks to four days.
- Sales have risen from $17 million to $25 million.

Source: Case, J. (1993). What experts forgot to mention. *INC.,* September, 66–77.

performance appraisal process. Self-managed work teams use peer, rather than supervisory, appraisals. The problems associated with peer evaluations were discussed in Chapter 8.

10-3 The Manager's Guide

10-3a Productivity Improvement Programs and the Manager's Job

The success of any productivity improvement program hinges on whether it can effectively motivate employees to behave in ways that contribute to the organization's goals. The day-to-day behavior of managers can have a crucial impact on whether that motivation takes place. In fact, motivating employees is considered to be the biggest challenge faced by managers today.[91] Let's examine the manager's role with respect to employee motivation.

Employee Motivation

Viewed from the perspective of expectancy theory, we see that managers can favorably impact employee motivation in three ways:[92]

1. *Strengthen the effort–performance link:* Managers should set goals that are challenging, yet achievable, establish clear performance expectations, and remove obstacles that impede employee performance.

2. *Strengthen the performance–reward link:* Managers should provide accurate performance appraisals, thus ensuring workers of the rewards they have earned.

3. *Provide rewards that are valued and perceived as being fair:* Managers should help select rewards that are valued by employees. In addition to recommending pay raises, a manager can bestow praise, recognition, added responsibility, greater autonomy, or simply an occasional pat on the back.

Informal Participative Decision-Making Programs[93]

Not all employees seek empowerment. Encouraging too much participation can alienate those employees who feel the manager is shirking his or her managerial responsibilities by passing the buck. The level of participation granted should therefore be commensurate with each employee's desire for challenge, responsibility, and opportunity to have a voice in work unit decisions.

Moreover, employees must believe they have the right to share work decisions with the manager. Managers must thus prove their commitment to participation. Supervisors can communicate this commitment by asking for (and implementing) employee input and feedback, and by providing employees with all the information needed to make good decisions.

Self-Managed Work Teams[94]

The obvious question here is "What role can a manager play in a work team that manages itself?" Managers must initially ensure that the transition to self-management runs smoothly. Effective managers provide these teams with strong encouragement and direction at the outset, and then gradually back off as team members develop their own leadership skills and team identity.

At this point, many managers will, unfortunately, lose their jobs. Those remaining with the company can perform the following functions:

1. *Serve as a technical consultant to teams:* The manager could be responsible for providing teams with product and process knowledge and assistance. For example, a production services team would need to realign formerly segmented tasks, such as vendor accounts, order entry, and machine scheduling, into interrelated team tasks. As a former supervisor, the manager would know each of these functions well enough to help team members coordinate the tasks involved. The manager could function as a troubleshooter, helping workers solve problems and remove bottlenecks.

2. *Serve as a facilitator:* The manager could help the team members work and communicate effectively with each other and with others in the organization. At first, the manager might run meetings. Later, he or she could sit in on meetings, helping the team find solutions. For example, the manager could ensure that all employees are following guidelines for participation in meetings.

3. *Serve as an area manager:* A manager may be asked to serve as a point of contact and to interpret management strategies for a group of four to six teams. Such a manager would focus on establishing interfaces between teams or between a team and the larger organization.

10-3b How the HRM Department Can Help

In addition to designing and evaluating the productivity improvement programs described in this chapter, the HRM department must see to it that the corporate culture is compatible with these programs. They must also train managers and employees to ensure the programs are implemented successfully.

Changing Corporate Culture[95]

The issue of corporate culture is especially important when implementing employee empowerment programs. Before implementing such a program, the HRM department must work with top management to establish the appropriate corporate culture—one that emphasizes the importance of employee participation and makes employees feel their input is desired.

In trying to establish a culture in which participation is valued, organizations must ensure that the process of establishing a participative environment is itself participatory. That is, such programs should not be imposed by decree. A more appropriate beginning would be to involve key managers and employees in initial decision making, giving them the opportunity to provide input on the feasibility, desirability, or operation of such programs.

Training

Any successful productivity improvement program requires some degree of training. We have already discussed the type of training needed to implement successfully self-managed work teams. Training is also needed to enhance the success of pay-for-performance programs. For instance, companies implementing a merit pay system should provide managers with performance appraisal training. Companies implementing gainsharing and profit-sharing plans should explain how rewards are determined and what they must do to earn them. For instance, workers must understand the gainsharing formula, how profits are computed, and so on.

10-3c HRM Skill-Building for Managers

The skills covered in this section deal with management activities that can lead to improved productivity. Specifically, we discuss how a manager can motivate employees by using intrinsic and/or extrinsic rewards.

Using Extrinsic Rewards to Motivate Employees

Reinforcement theory provides a useful guide to managers interested in using extrinsic rewards to motivate employees. Developed by psychologist B.F. Skinner, the theory stipulates that worker behavior can be shaped, modified, or changed by manipulating the system of rewards given or withheld for the relevant behavior.[96] The theory hinges on three basic assumptions:

1. Behavior that leads to positive consequences tends to be repeated.
2. Behavior that leads to negative consequences tends not to be repeated.
3. By manipulating consequences, you can shape a person's behavior.

reinforcement theory
A motivational theory that states that worker behavior can be shaped, modified, or changed by manipulating the system of rewards given or withheld for the relevant behavior.

The following six steps can be used to apply the principles of this theory to increase the motivational levels of your subordinates.

1. First, determine the specific behaviors in which you want your employees to engage. The behaviors you select should be observable and measurable. Do not select personality traits or attitudinal variables. Examples of behaviors that are both observable and measurable would be cutting rejects by 10 percent and cutting tardiness by 80 percent.

2. Establish a baseline measure for this behavior by measuring current performance levels. For example, determine how many times an employee was tardy during the last month. This step will provide a comparison to see if performance improves with the rewards you give.

3. The heart of the program: Analyze performance consequences. Ask "What occurs immediately following the targeted behavior?" and "What are the positive and negative consequences to the employee?" For instance, a tardy employee may experience the adulation of coworkers for "beating the system"—a positive consequence. The negative consequence may be the "dirty look" you give the employee when he or she enters the work site.

    Consider another example. Suppose an employee fails to wear a safety helmet. The positive consequence would probably be a feeling of comfort. A possible negative consequence would be an injury caused by an accident; if accidents were unlikely, this consequence would rarely occur.

4. Change the consequences. Employees will not be motivated to change their behaviors if consequences remain unchanged. You have three options: (1) You can eliminate the positive consequences associated with the behavior; (2) you can add positive consequences for improved behavior (praise, recognition, bonus); and/or (3) you can add negative consequences to the behavior. For example, to combat a tardiness problem, you could remove the positive consequence

by explaining to coworkers how the individual's tardiness hurts everyone. You could add positive consequences by praising the worker when he or she arrives at work on time. Or you could add negative consequences by disciplining the employee each time he or she is late. When choosing the appropriate option, you should consider these points:

- Not every employee finds the same consequences rewarding or punishing. Some prefer praise, some cash bonuses, and others may prefer to be given more work autonomy. Whenever possible, give subordinates some leeway in allowing them to develop their own reward system.
- Reinforce successively closer approximations to the desired work behavior. Continue to provide rewards as long as the employee's behavior is improving; one does not have to perform at the targeted level to earn a reward.
- Adding negative consequences is equivalent to punishing the employee. The problem with punishment is that its effects are temporary. Thus, this approach will be ineffective in the long run unless the punishment is continually applied. Moreover, the particular undesirable behaviors may be replaced with different, but equally negative ones. For instance, an employee who is punished for being tardy may stop that behavior, but may begin taking excessive work breaks. Additionally, punishment often undermines personal relationships.

5. Monitor and evaluate the effectiveness of the program by keeping records of the employee's behavior and comparing them with baseline figures. If the behavior does not improve, rethink the approach to step 3. You may need to change the consequence, for instance.

6. Once performance has improved, it will not be practical to reinforce it each time the behavior occurs. Continual reinforcement is ill advised because continually reinforced behavior ceases quickly when reinforcement stops. Therefore, in order to sustain the behavior, you should reinforce it periodically. For instance, in the tardiness example, you should initially praise the worker each time he or she is on time. When the problem abates, praise the worker occasionally, say, once a week.

Using Intrinsic Rewards to Motivate Employees[97]

One way to motivate employees with intrinsic rewards is to provide them with stimulating job assignments. Before you can effectively do this, you must be able to gauge the types of activities that each of your employees would find stimulating. A theory developed by D.C. McClelland can serve as a useful guide.

According to **McClelland's need-achievement theory,** all individuals are primarily motivated by one of three needs.

1. *Need for affiliation:* Individuals who are motivated by this need desire close interpersonal relationships.

2. *Need for achievement:* Individuals motivated by this need seek the opportunity to achieve in relation to a set of standards and have the desire to outperform others.

3. *Need for power:* An individual driven by this need seeks to direct and control others.

Knowing the type of need that drives an employee allows you to find intrinsically rewarding activities that will stimulate them. For instance, people with a high need for affiliation generally:

- Prefer team tasks
- Dislike projects with high conflict and/or poor communication
- Enjoy playing the role of coach or mentor
- Want friendship and close relations
- Focus on interpersonal skills

McClelland's need-achievement theory A motivational theory stating that all individuals are primarily motivated by one of three needs—affiliation, achievement, and power.

People with a high need for achievement generally:

- Prefer moderate risks
- Like to be held personally responsible for projects
- Enjoy playing the role of entrepreneur
- Want frequent feedback on their own performance
- Enjoy developing new skills and expertise

People with a high need for power generally:

- Prefer competitive tasks
- Like high-profile projects
- Enjoy serving as a leader
- Want key information
- Prefer using controlling skills

To motivate employees, then, you should try to assign work activities that help employees satisfy their most important need. For instance, if you were managing a person with a high need for power, you could:

- Place the person in a high-profile project involving a competitive activity—perhaps opening a new branch or plant in a competitor's locale.
- Place this person in a position of some authority (e.g., make that person a team leader or project manager) and charge him or her with developing new business contacts and gathering market data. This would give the person a chance to network and allow him or her to gain access to key information.

Chapter Objectives Revisited

1. Explain what productivity improvement programs are and how they contribute to competitive advantage.

   - Productivity improvement programs are incentive programs designed to improve organizational productivity/efficiency by increasing employee motivation and enhancing recruitment efforts.

2. Define the standards for effective productivity programs developed within the framework of expectancy theory.

   - Employees will be motivated to perform well to the extent they believe their own individual efforts can lead to successful performance.
   - Rewards should be directly linked to performance.
   - The shorter the time interval between a behavior and its reward, the more likely it is that the reward will be motivating.
   - Rewards offered by the pay-for-performance program must be great enough or important enough to make a difference.
   - Pay-for-performance programs should encourage employees to engage in behaviors that help the company achieve its strategic goals.

   - Pay-for-performance programs must significantly impact the organization's bottom line.

3. Understand the rationale behind pay-for-performance programs.

   - When pay is linked to performance, overall performance should improve—top performers should be motivated by large rewards to maintain high levels of performance; low-level performers should be motivated to either increase their efforts or leave the company.

4. Describe the different types of pay-for-performance programs.

   - Merit pay plans: Grant employees annual pay raises based on their levels of job performance. Job performance is usually measured on an appraisal instrument completed by the supervisor.
   - Piece rate plans: Base an individual's wages on the number of "pieces" or product units he or she produces.
   - Gainsharing plans: Offer employees a cash reward for meeting or exceeding goals based on the collaborative performance of a team of employees.

- Profit-sharing plans: Similar to gainsharing in the sense that they reward group, rather than individual, performance. The "payout," however, is based on profits rather than gains—companies make contributions to individual employee accounts based on profits.

5. Appreciate the rationale behind employee empowerment programs.
   - Empowerment can enhance productivity in two ways.
   - It can strengthen motivation by providing employees with the opportunity to attain intrinsic rewards from their work, such as a greater sense of accomplishment and a feeling of importance.
   - It can improve productivity because the process leads to better decisions.

6. Explain the various types of employee empowerment programs.
   - Informal participative decision-making programs: Managers decide just how much decision-making authority employees should have in each instance.
   - Job enrichment: Aims to redesign jobs to be more intrinsically rewarding
   - Quality circles: A group of six to twelve employees who identify and resolve production problems within their unit
   - Continuous improvement: Empowering work teams to trace product or service problems to their root causes and redesign production processes to eliminate them

Review Questions

Note: You can find the correct answers to these questions by taking the quiz and then submitting your answers in the Online Edition. The program will automatically score your submission. If you miss a question, the program will provide the correct answer, a rationale for the answer, and the section number in the chapter where the topic is discussed.

1. Which of the following criteria is *not* a standard for a successful pay-for-performance program?
   a. Effort must be tied to performance.
   b. Performance must be tied to rewards.
   c. The rewards offered must be valued by employees.
   d. To be most effective, rewards should be distributed once a year in a lump sum.

2. According to the expectancy theory, a merit pay guidechart is used to _____ the perceived performance-to-reward linkage.
   a. strengthen
   b. weaken
   c. keep constant
   d. none of the above. The effects of the guidechart vary according to the type of merit system used.

3. According to the research study reported in the text, supervisors are more likely to recommend an underserved pay raise for an employee if
   a. that employee demands a raise.
   b. the supervisor is dependent upon the worker because of the worker's specialized expertise.
   c. both a and b.
   d. neither a nor b.

4. Which of the following recommendations was made by expert Ed Lawler regarding how merit pay should be implemented?
   a. The best performers should receive a raise equal to 30 percent of their base pay.
   b. Pay raises should be used instead of bonuses.
   c. Instant or spot rewards should be given when exceptionally good behavior occurs.
   d. All of the above.

5. Which of the following statements about piece rate plans is true?
   a. Under a piece rate plan, employees know exactly what they must do to earn a reward.
   b. Performance standards are subjective and thus can be influenced by supervisory bias.
   c. Piece rate plans are not cost-effective in most cases—the costs often offset the gains.
   d. Piece rate plans encourage cooperative behavior among employees.

6. In most gainsharing plans, _____ percent of the "gains" are distributed to the workers.
   a. 100
   b. 75
   c. 35
   d. 9

7. Employee empowerment programs aim to strengthen employee motivation by
   a. making pay raises commensurate with job performance levels.
   b. enhancing job security.
   c. providing employees with the opportunity to attain intrinsic rewards from their work.
   d. all of the above.

8. Informal participative decision-making programs allow
   a. employees to make all job-related decisions.
   b. employees to make decisions concerning their working conditions, but not their job tasks.
   c. employees to provide input on important job decisions, but have no authority to actually make any decisions.
   d. managers to decide how much decision-making authority employees will have on a case-by-case basis.

9. A major weakness of job enrichment programs is that
   a. jobs often become less interesting.
   b. employee motivation frequently drops.
   c. quality is often reduced.
   d. production often becomes less efficient.

10. When assigned to a self-managed work team, workers need training in the following three areas:
    a. technical, interpersonal, and administrative.
    b. legal, cognitive, and motor.
    c. leadership, communications, and management.
    d. literacy, mathematics, and problem solving.

Discussion Questions

1. Using the framework of expectancy theory, explain the rationale behind productivity improvement programs.
2. How can effective productivity improvement programs enhance a firm's recruitment efforts?
3. Describe the standards to be met by pay-for-performance programs.
4. What is a merit pay plan and how well do such plans generally fare against the standards referred to in question 3? Be specific.
5. What is a piece rate plan? What are the main features distinguishing piece rate plans from merit pay plans?

6. Describe the formula used in the Scanlon Plan.
7. Describe the five characteristics present in an enriched job.
8. What is a self-managed work team? Discuss the strengths and weaknesses associated with this employee empowerment program.
9. Using an expectancy theory framework, describe the manager's role in employee motivation.
10. Describe an original example of a work situation where it would be appropriate for a manager to allow employees to participate fully in decision making.

Experiential Exercises

How Can This Job Be Enriched?

1. Break into groups of four or five students.
2. Allow about five minutes for each group member to describe briefly the job he or she currently holds (or one recently held).
3. Select the job that is least enriching according to the five characteristics mentioned in the text. If none of the students in the group has held a job, describe how your professor could enrich this course.
4. As a group, determine how this job could be enriched. Describe the interventions that could be implemented to enrich it, and explain what job characteristics (e.g., skill variety, autonomy) each would strengthen.
5. Select a group spokesperson to present your findings to the class.
6. The presentation of each spokesperson should adhere to the following format:

a. Describe the job as it is now performed.
b. Discuss your interventions and their rationale.
c. Discuss how successful you think the enrichment would be if it were actually implemented by the organization in question. For instance, do you think management would accept it? The workers? Would it be cost-efficient?

What Pay-for-Performance Program Would You Recommend?

Instructions: Described here are a number of scenarios involving different kinds of employees. Study each scenario carefully and answer the following questions:

1. What type of compensation program should be used?
   - Merit pay
   - Individual piecework
   - Group piecework
   - Gainsharing

- Profit-sharing plan
- Pay for performance should not be used.

2. For each pay-for-performance program you have chosen, indicate the primary obstacles to be faced when trying to implement the system. How would you deal with these obstacles?

Forklift Driver

Person drives a forklift for a small metals manufacturer. Worker picks up parts that have been boxed and loaded onto pallets and delivers them to warehouse for shipping. Worker then returns and waits for the next load to be readied.

Farm Laborer

Person works for the Jiffy Orange Juice Company in Orlando, Florida. The worker rises at 6:00 A.M. and is in the groves picking oranges by 7:00 A.M. Using century-old technology, the worker carefully places each ripe orange into the "picking bag" slung over the worker's shoulder.

The worker dumps the full bag into a box and starts all over again. This process is continued until quitting time.

Custodian

Person is a custodian for a large, nationwide hotel chain. The custodian's duties are to vacuum the hallways, clean the rest rooms, and carry refuse to the Dumpsters in the rear of the hotel.

Blackjack Dealer

Person is a blackjack dealer for an Atlantic City casino. The job consists of dealing blackjack at a blackjack table. The game is played according to rigid house rules (dealer must draw on 15 and stand pat on 16 or greater).

Chief Executive Officer

Person is a CEO for a small, independent furniture manufacturer. The CEO is responsible for the firm's performance in the areas of sales, new accounts, new products, profits, and return on assets.

Case

Does This Merit Pay Plan Have Any Merit?

Oglethorpe University uses a merit pay plan to determine annual pay raises for professors. Here is how the plan works: The performance of professors is evaluated by their department heads on an annual basis. The performance rating is based on three factors: teaching, scholarship, and service.

Teaching is evaluated primarily on the basis of student evaluations. At the conclusion of each course, the students are asked to fill out a 20-item questionnaire regarding the quality of the course and the effectiveness of the professor. The questionnaire was designed by a committee of professors and was approved by a majority of the faculty.

Scholarship is evaluated primarily on the basis of a professor's research publications. Department heads are instructed to consider both the quality and quantity of publications.

Service is measured on the basis of committee work within the university. Most department heads evaluate this factor by considering the number of committees a professor serves on and the importance of the committee. Some department heads give service credit to consulting work within the business community; others feel that such recognition is inappropriate because the sponsoring company is already reimbursing the professor for this work.

At the end of the academic year, professors submit a file to their department heads, documenting all their accomplishments in these areas. In addition, the department head receives a printout that summarizes the results of the student ratings for each course. After reviewing this information, he or she gives each professor an overall performance rating based on the following four-point scale. However, department heads may only give 20 percent of their faculty a rating of "4."

4: Outstanding; exceeds expectations
3: Good; meets all expectations
2: Adequate; meets most expectations
1: Inadequate; meets few, if any, expectations

The department heads are given a merit pool at the end of each year from which to distribute raises. They are told to grant raises on the basis of performance, but are given complete discretion on how this is to be done.

In an effort to evaluate its merit pay plan, OU conducted a survey. It sent all faculty members an open-ended questionnaire that asked them to state their opinion of the merit pay plan. None of the responses were favorable.

Questions

1. What do you think the major complaints were?
2. What, if anything, should the university do to improve its merit pay plan? If you suggest scrapping the plan, with what would you replace it?

References

1. Wiley, C. (1993). Incentive plan pushes production. *Personnel Journal,* August, 86–91.
2. Schneier, C.E. (1989). Capitalizing on performance management, recognition, and reward systems. *Compensation and Benefits Review, 21,* 20–30.
3. Guzzo, R.A., Jette, R.D., and Katzell, R.A. (1985). The effects of psychology-based intervention programs on worker productivity: A meta-analysis. *Personnel Psychology, 38* (2), 275–291.
4. Wiscombe, J. (2001). Can pay for performance really work? *Workforce,* August, 28–33.
5. McGinty, R.L., and Hanke, J. (1989). Merit pay plans: Are they truly tied to performance? *Compensation and Benefits Review,* September/October, 12–15; Lawler, E.E. (1988). Pay for performance: Making it work. *Personnel Journal,* October, 55–60.
6. Wiscombe. Can pay for performance.
7. McGinty and Hanke. Merit pay plans.
8. Markham, S.E. (1988). Pay-for-performance dilemma revisited: Empirical example of the importance of group effects. *Journal of Applied Psychology, 73* (2), 172–180.
9. McGinty and Hanke. Merit pay plans.
10. Rynes, S.L., Brown, K.G., and Colbert, A.E. (2002). Seven common misperceptions about human resource practices: Research findings versus practitioner beliefs. *Academy of Management Executive, 16* (3), 92–103.
11. Wiscombe. Can pay for performance.
12. Solomon, C.M. (1998). Using cash drives strategic change. *Workforce,* February, 78–81.
13. McCormick, E.J., and Ilgen, D. (1980). *Industrial Psychology* (7th ed.). Englewood Cliffs, NJ: Prentice Hall.
14. Schneier. Capitalizing on performance management.
15. Ibid.
16. Bartol, K.M., and Martin, D.C. (1990). When politics pays: Factors influencing managerial compensation issues. *Personnel Psychology, 43* (3), 599–614.
17. Baime, S.R. (1991). Incentives for the masses: A viable pay program? *Compensation and Benefit Review, 23,* 50–58.
18. Bialkowski, C. (1991). Where the raises are. *Working Woman,* September, 78–80, 116.
19. Brennan, E.J. (1985). The myth and the reality of pay for performance. *Personnel Journal,* March, 73–75.
20. Markham. Pay-for-performance dilemma.
21. Wisdom, B.L. (1989). Before implementing a merit system . . . . *Personnel Administrator, 34* (10), 46–49.
22. Baime. Incentives for the masses.
23. Wisdom. Before implementing a merit system.
24. Kohn, A. (1993). Why incentive plans cannot work. *Harvard Business Review,* September–October, 54–63.
25. Wiscombe. Can pay for performance.
26. Lawler. Pay for performance.
27. Bialkowski. Where the raises are.
28. *Appraisal and Merit Pay.* Washington, DC: National Academy Press.
29. Wilson, T.B. (1992). Is it time to eliminate the piece rate incentive system? *HRMagazine,* March/April, 43–49.
30. Ibid.
31. Ibid.
32. Ibid.
33. Milkovich, G.T., and Wigdor, A.K. (1991). *Pay for Performance: Evaluating Performance Appraisal and Merit Pay.* Washington, D.C.: National Academy Press.
34. Ibid.
35. Zingheim, P.K., and Schuster, J.R. (1992). Linking quality and pay. *HRMagazine, 37* (12), 55–59.

36. Swinehart, D.P. (1986). A guide to more productive team incentive programs. *Personnel Journal,* July, 112–117.
37. Ibid.
38. Kanter, R.M. (1987). From status to contribution: Some organizational implications of the changing basis for pay. *Personnel,* January, 12–37.
39. Bialkowski. Where the raises are.
40. Bullock, R.J., and Lawler, E.E. (1984). Gainsharing: A few questions and fewer answers. *Human Resource Management, 23* (1), 23–40; Petty, M.M., Singleton, B., and Connel, D.W. (1992). *Journal of Applied Psychology, 77* (4), 427–436; Paulsen, K.M. (1991). Lessons learned from gainsharing. *HRMagazine,* April, 70–74; and Rollins, T. (1989). Productivity-based group incentive plans: Powerful, but use with caution. *Compensation and Benefits Review, 21,* 39–50.
41. DeBettignies, C.W. (1991). Using gainsharing to improve financial performance. *Industrial Management,* May/June, 4–6.
42. Zingheim and Schuster. Linking quality and pay.
43. Baime. Incentives for the masses.
44. Bullock and Lawler. Gainsharing.
45. Mannheim, B., and Angel, O. (1986). Pay systems and work-role centrality of industrial workers. *Personnel Psychology, 39* (2), 359–377.
46. Swinehart, D.P. (1986). A guide to more productive team incentive programs. *Personnel Journal,* July, 112–117.
47. Ost, E. (1989). Gainsharing's potential. *Personnel Administrator,* July, 92–96.
48. Paulsen. Lessons learned from gainsharing.
49. Coates, E.M. (1991). Profit sharing today: Plans and provisions. *Monthly Labor Review,* April, 19–25.
50. Florkowski, G.W. (1990). Analyzing group incentive plans. *HRMagazine,* January, 36–38.
51. Ibid.
52. Pierce, J.L., Rubenfeld, S.A., and Morgan, S. (1991). Employee ownership: A conceptual model of process and effects. *Academy of Management Review, 16* (1), 121–144.
53. Panos, J.E. (1990). Managing group incentive systems. *Personnel Journal,* October, 123–124.
54. Ost. Gainsharing's potential.
55. Thornburg, L. (1992). Pay for performance: What you should know. *HRMagazine,* June, 58–61.
56. Pringle, C.D., and Dubose, P.B. (1989). Participative management: A reappraisal. *Journal of Management in Practice, 1* (1), 9–14.
57. Cotton, J.L., Vollrath, D.A., Froggatt, K.L., Lengnick-Hall, M.L., and Jennings, K.R. (1988). Employee participation: Diverse forms and different outcomes. *Academy of Management Review, 13* (1), 8–22.
58. Herzberg, F. (1990). One more time: How do you motivate employees? *Harvard Business Review,* January–February, 26–35.
59. Miller, K.I., and Monge, P.R. (1986). Participation, satisfaction, and productivity: A meta-analytic review. *Academy of Management Journal, 29* (4), 727–753.
60. Pringle and Dubose. Participative management.
61. Ibid.
62. Ibid.
63. Cotton et al. Employee participation.
64. Miller and Monge. Participation, satisfaction, and productivity.
65. Ibid.
66. Lawler, E.E. (1988). Choosing an involvement strategy. *The Academy of Management Executive, 2* (3), 197–204.
67. Barrick, M.R., and Alexander, R.A. (1987). A review of quality circle efficacy and the existence of positive-findings bias. *Personnel Psychology, 40* (3), 579–592.

68. Pasewark, W.R. (1991). A new approach to quality control for auditors: Quality circles. *The Practical Accountant,* March, 68–71.

69. Horn, J.C. (1986). Making quality circles work better. *Psychology Today,* August, 10.

70. Liverpool, P.R. (1990). Employee participation in decision making: An analysis of the perceptions of members and nonmembers of quality circles. *Journal of Business and Psychology, 4* (4), 411–422.

71. Ibid.

72. Duetsch, C.H. (1991, May 26). A revival of the quality circle. *The New York Times,* 23.

73. Orsburn, J.D., Moran, L., Musselwhite, E., and Zenger, J.H. (1990). *Self-Directed Work Teams: The New American Challenge.* Homewood, IL: Business One Irwin.

74. Ibid.

75. Stone, D.L., and Eddy, E.R. (1996). A model of individual and organizational factors affecting quality-related outcomes. *Journal of Quality Management, 1* (1), 21–48.

76. Church, A.H. (1995). Total quality management: Something old or something new? *The Industrial Psychologist, 32* (4), 55–63.

77. Case, J. (1993). What the experts forgot to mention. *INC,* September, 66–77.

78. Orsburn et al. *Self-Directed Work Teams.*

79. Ibid.

80. Lawler. Choosing an involvement strategy.

81. Norman, C.A., and Zawacki, R. (1991). Team appraisals-team approach. *Personnel Journal,* September, 101–104.

82. Stern, A.L. (1993, July 18). Managing by team is not always as easy as it looks. *The New York Times,* 14.

83. Hoerr, J. (1989, July 10). The payoff from teamwork. *Business Weekly,* 56–62.

84. Ibid.

85. Ibid.

86. Magjuka, R.J., and Baldwin, T.T. (1991). Team-based employee involvement programs: Effects of design and administration. *Personnel Psychology, 44* (4), 793–812.

87. Case. What the experts forgot.

88. Stern. Managing by team.

89. Case. What the experts forgot.

90. Ibid.

91. Buhler, P. (1988). Motivation: What is behind the motivation of employees? *Supervision, 49,* 18–20.

92. The source for much of the material in this section is Newsom, W.B. (1990). Motivation, now! *Personnel Journal,* February, 51–55.

93. Pringle and Dubose. Participative management; Harrison, T.M. (1985). Communication and participative decision making: An exploratory study. *Personnel Psychology, 38* (1), 93–116.

94. Orsburn, et al. *Self-Directed Work Teams.*

95. Pringle and Dubose. Participative management.

96. Steers, R.M., and Porter, L.W. (1979). *Motivation and Work Behavior.* New York: McGraw-Hill.

97. Hudy, J.J. (1992). The motivation trap. *HRMagazine, 37* (12), 63–67.

HRM Practices Affected by External Factors

Complying with Workplace Justice Laws

Chapter Eleven

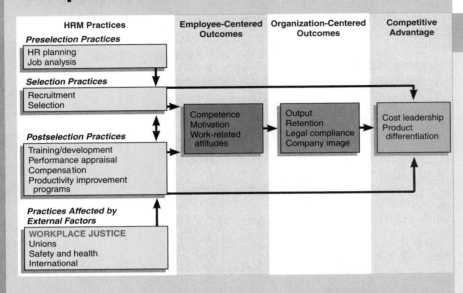

HRM Practices	Employee-Centered Outcomes	Organization-Centered Outcomes	Competitive Advantage

Preselection Practices
- HR planning
- Job analysis

Selection Practices
- Recruitment
- Selection

Postselection Practices
- Training/development
- Performance appraisal
- Compensation
- Productivity improvement programs

Practices Affected by External Factors
- WORKPLACE JUSTICE
- Unions
- Safety and health
- International

Competence
Motivation
Work-related attitudes

Output
Retention
Legal compliance
Company image

Cost leadership
Product differentiation

Key Terms

due process
employment-at-will
Family and Medical Leave Act (FMLA)
fetal protection policies (FPPs)
Freedom of Information Act
good faith and fair dealing
hostile environment
implied contract
intrusion upon seclusion
just cause

monitoring
Older Workers Benefit Protection Act (OWBPA)
Privacy Act
progressive discipline system
public policy
quid pro quo
sexual harassment
surveillance
workplace justice laws
wrongful termination

Chapter Objectives

Upon completion of this chapter, you will be able to:

- Understand how effective workplace justice policies enhance competitive advantage.
- Describe the antidiscrimination laws that dictate how employees should be treated on a day-to-day basis.
- Discuss the extent to which employee privacy rights are legally protected.
- Explain employee rights regarding unfair discharges.
- Discuss what management skills are needed to comply effectively with workplace justice laws.

11-1 Gaining Competitive Advantage

11-1a Opening Case: Gaining Competitive Advantage at the Marriott[1]

The Problem: Marriott's Open-Door Policy Fails to Resolve Employee Complaints

The Marriott Corporation used an open-door policy called "Guarantee of Fair Treatment" to handle employee complaints. To resolve a complaint, employees were to go through the chain of command. That is, if they had a complaint, such as discrimination or sexual harassment, they were to first bring the complaint to their immediate supervisor, next to the supervisor's boss, and finally to individuals further up the managerial ladder.

It soon became clear that the open-door policy was not working as evidenced by the large number of discrimination suits filed by employees. Some employees lodged suits because they were dissatisfied with the company's attempts to resolve their complaints; other employees, afraid to confront their bosses, chose to bypass the open-door system and took their complaints directly to court.

The Solution: Implementing a Peer Review Process

Marriott was determined to devise an effective complaint resolution process that would satisfy employee needs. To identify their needs, the company surveyed employees and conducted several focus groups that posed the question "What characteristics should the complaint resolution system include?" The results indicated that employees with complaints wanted a chance to air their concerns before impartial listeners who would promptly follow up. They also wanted assurances of no retribution.

Marriott initiated a peer review system. Here's how it works: Employees with a complaint are encouraged to first pursue the open-door policy. When the complaint reaches the senior executive in the business unit, the employee has the option of bringing the matter to the peer review panel. This panel, comprised of three peers and two managers (randomly chosen from among people specially trained to handle such disputes), makes final, binding decisions on all grievances brought before it. Although the panel may not change company policy, pay rates, benefits, or work rules, it has the authority to take actions to ensure that the company's policies and procedures are followed consistently. The panel meets and delivers a decision within 10 working days from the date of the employee appeal.

How the Peer Review Process Enhanced Competitive Advantage

According to Ron Brandrau, Marriott's director of EEO/affirmative action, feedback from both employees and managers has been overwhelmingly positive. The process is popular with employees because they feel panel members are fair and objective.

Management sees the panel as an opportunity to reinforce and clarify its corporate policy and work rules.

Has the program produced bottom-line results? The answer is a resounding yes. The number of EEO charges dropped by 50 percent in the first year and by 83 percent in the second. Given the high cost of litigation, these reductions yielded enormous savings. Because employees now had a complaint system they trusted, morale improved dramatically.

11-1b Linking Workplace Justice to Competitive Advantage

workplace justice laws
Laws that regulate the day-to-day treatment of employees.

Workers want to be treated fairly by their organizations. Most expect fairness; many demand it. The law also requires fair treatment. **Workplace justice laws** deal with the fairness of organizational practices that dictate the day-to-day treatment of employees. Organizations comply with these laws by instituting policies that recognize and protect individual rights and guarantee employee protection from any arbitrary treatment from management.[2]

A company can gain a competitive advantage by willingly complying with workplace justice laws. Competitive advantage can come from lower litigation costs, positive employee attitudes and behavior, and an excellent company image.

Reducing Litigation Costs

Workplace law infractions cost firms a lot of money. For example, nearly 70 percent of all employment claims result in monetary awards, the average of which is about $1.5 million. The cost is much greater when one considers court costs, legal fees, and time lost while managers and HR professionals collect documentation that will help defend the organization.[3] Indeed, legal actions have forced some otherwise financially healthy firms like the Manville Corporation into bankruptcy.[4]

Consider the following examples of workplace justice claims that have been filed and the size of the awards sought (or won) by plaintiffs:

- A California jury awarded an African-American employee of Brand Services more than $7.6 million in a race-based discharge suit.[5]

- A group of Texaco senior executives were in a meeting discussing a racial lawsuit lodged by 1,400 African-American professionals who claimed that Texaco refused to promote them because of their race. The secretly taped discussion revealed the use of racial slurs (including the "n" word) and a plot to destroy documents that were demanded in the discrimination suit. The firestorm of negative publicity was so intense that Texaco agreed to a $175 million settlement—the largest ever in a race discrimination suit.[6]

- An Iowa jury awarded $80.7 million to a former UPS employee who had sued for sexual harassment.[7]

Favorably Affecting Employee Attitudes and Behaviors

Employees who perceive unjust treatment usually respond by engaging in activities that ultimately harm a company's competitive advantage. For instance, they may respond actively by filing lawsuits or staging protests. They may respond passively by becoming less committed to their organizations, or by becoming poor organizational citizens (i.e., they may refuse to perform duties not included in their job descriptions, or become less cooperative).[8]

The link between workplace justice and organizational commitment has been documented by several empirical studies.[9] These studies indicate that organizational efforts to protect workers from arbitrary treatment and to ensure their basic rights enhance the employees' commitment to their organizations because workers view such efforts as an expression of the organization's concern for their well-being.[10]

Employees' decisions to behave as good organizational citizens bear directly on their perception of workplace justice. Employees who believe they are treated fairly will continue to be good organizational citizens to repay the organization for its fairness. On the other hand, employees who believe they have been treated unfairly may reduce citizenship behaviors.[11]

The topic of workplace justice is especially important today because of the growing diversity of the workforce, as we noted in Chapter 2, "Understanding the Legal and Environmental Context of HRM." Many organizations have failed to integrate minority groups successfully into their corporate cultures.[12] The level of job satisfaction for these individuals, for instance, is frequently much lower than it is for white males.[13] Certainly, the failure to comply with workplace justice laws, as evidenced by widespread harassment, prejudiced behavior, and the like, has contributed to this problem.

Promoting a Favorable Company Image

Justice in the workplace promotes a favorable image of the company within the community at large. A good corporate image can significantly boost a firm's recruiting efforts. One study, for example, found that companies that express a commitment to fair employment policies are more attractive to future job applicants than those lacking such a commitment.[14]

The presence of workplace justice within a company can also boost a company's image as a good place to work for women and minorities. Recently published accounts of "best companies" for women and for blacks have spotlighted some organizations (e.g., Merck, Xerox, Syntex, Hoffman-La Roche, and Hewlett-Packard) as leaders in effectively managing cultural diversity. Such recognition has provided a great boost to the recruiting efforts of these organizations.[15]

Moreover, having a good reputation for dealing with female and minority employees can favorably affect sales volume. Many customers prefer buying from companies that have a reputation for treating their employees well.[16]

11-2 HRM Issues and Practices

We first discuss workplace justice laws that address employment discrimination. We then turn our attention to workplace justice laws dealing with employee privacy rights and wrongful termination.

11-2a Workplace Justice and Employment Discrimination

We have already addressed employment discrimination in several chapters. We began in Chapter 2 by discussing discrimination law and how it is interpreted. We then discussed how this body of law applies to specific HRM practices such as selection, performance appraisal, and pay. We now discuss discrimination in the day-to-day treatment of employees. Specifically, we discuss sexual harassment, pregnancy discrimination, family and medical leave, discharge, layoffs, and early retirement.

Sexual Harassment

Sexual harassment at the workplace is a long-standing problem, affecting a large percentage of workers, especially women. Sexual harassment came to light during the mid-1970s and has since gained a great deal of national attention, especially in light of the Clarence Thomas Supreme Court justice confirmation hearings of the early 1990s and the charges of sexual harassment lodged against President Clinton by Paula Jones.

Sexual harassment is a form of sex discrimination and therefore violates Title VII of the Civil Rights Act (CRA). The number of sexual harassment complaints filed with the EEOC has increased at an alarming rate—it rose from 6,127 in 1990 to over 13,000 in 2004.[17] The number of actual incidents of sexual harassment could be as high as 130,00 per year, given the fact that only about 10 percent of sexual

sexual harassment
Unwelcome sexual advances, requests for sexual favors, and other verbal or physical contact of a sexual nature.

harassment victims ever file a formal complaint.[18] Some of the companies facing sexual harassment charges in the past few years are Mitsubishi, Philip Morris, Del Laboratories (cosmetics), and Astra USA (pharmaceutics).[19]

Sexual Harassment and Competitive Advantage

Acts of sexual harassment within a company can damage the firm's competitive position. Harassed employees may feel angry because they are being exploited as sex objects or because they think that their peers do not take their work seriously. Not only will they feel angry, but they may also fear being labeled as troublemakers if they complain.[20]

Sexual harassment causes numerous problems for employers. One is turnover; harassed employees may quit their jobs because they believe there is no way to remedy their situation. Other possible problems associated with the occurrence of sexual harassment include absenteeism, low morale, lack of effective teamwork, poor productivity, and employee stress and/or psychological problems.[21] Moreover, harassment lawsuits can be very costly. If a firm loses such a suit, it is liable for compensable damages (e.g., back pay) and, under the CRA of 1991, possible punitive damages. The Labor Department reports that these outcomes cost U.S. organizations approximately $1 billion annually.[22]

Who Is Protected by Sexual Harassment Law?

Sexual harassment law protects both men and women against sexual harassment. The most common occurrence (87 percent) is when a woman is harassed by a man.[23] Harassment committed by a member of the same sex is also prohibited, however. Moreover, the harasser can be the victim's supervisor, a coworker, or a nonemployee. The person filing the complaint does not have to be the one who was harassed; it can be anyone affected by the offensive conduct.

In 1980, the EEOC published a set of guidelines on sexual harassment that specified the behaviors that constitute sexual harassment and the circumstances under which such behaviors are illegal. The guidelines also stipulated employers' legal liabilities. These guidelines, endorsed by the U.S. Supreme Court,[24] are summarized in Taking a Closer Look 11-1.

Forms of Sexual Harassment

quid pro quo A form of sexual harassment in which victims are required to provide sexual favors in order to be hired, promoted, granted a pay raise, or allowed to keep their job.

hostile environment A form of sexual harassment in which victims are subjected to unwelcome, hostile, and intimidating working conditions.

Sexual harassment can fall into one of two categories: **quid pro quo** and **hostile environment.** The term *quid pro quo* is Latin for "this for that" (e.g., "If you do this for me, I'll do that for you."). In the context of sexual harassment, the term refers to a situation in which an employee or applicant must provide sexual favors in order to be hired, promoted, granted a pay raise, or allowed to keep a job.

Hostile environments are those in which employees are subjected to unwelcome, intimidating working conditions. A case involving the issue of hostile environment (*Harris v. Forklift Systems*) came before the Supreme Court in 1993. Ms. Harris claimed that her boss made her work environment hostile and intimidating by:

- Asking her to retrieve objects from his pocket
- Making derogatory statements, such as "You're a woman, what do you know?"
- Suggesting that she accompany him to a hotel to negotiate her raise
- Telling other employees that she promised sexual favors to secure an account

The lower courts ruled against Harris' claim of hostile environment because the boss' behavior did not seriously affect her psychological well-being. The Supreme Court reversed the lower courts' decision, however, stating the hostile behaviors need not cause the victim psychological harm. An environment is hostile if a *reasonable person* would judge it so:

> **Taking a Closer Look 11-1**   *Summary of EEOC Guidelines on Sexual Harassment*
>
> **Sexually Harassing Behavior**
>
> Unwelcome sexual advances, requests for sexual favors, and other verbal or physical contact of a sexual nature.
>
> **Sexually Harassing Behavior Is Unlawful When:**
>
> 1. Submission to such conduct is made either explicitly or implicitly a term or condition of an individual's employment.
> 2. Submission to or rejection of such conduct by an individual is used as the basis for employment decisions.
> 3. Such conduct has the purpose or effect of unreasonably interfering with an individual's work performance or creating an intimidating, hostile, or offensive working environment.
> 4. An employee is denied a job opportunity because it has been granted to someone who has submitted to the employer's advances.
>
> **When Is an Employer Held Responsible for Acts of Sexual Harassment Committed by Others?**
>
> 1. The employer is responsible for the acts of its agents and supervisory employees with respect to sexual harassment regardless of whether the employer knows or should have known of their occurrence.
> 2. The employer is responsible for the acts of sexual harassment committed by coworkers if the employer knows or should have known of the conduct, unless it can show that it took immediate and appropriate action.
> 3. An employer is responsible for the acts of nonemployees, with respect to sexual harassment of employees in the workplace, if (1) it knows or should have known of the conduct, (2) fails to take immediate and appropriate action, and (3) has the ability to control the conduct of nonemployees.

so long as the environment would reasonably be perceived, and is perceived, as hostile and abusive, there is no need to be psychologically injurious.

Another instance of hostile environment is illustrated in a court case in which an employer was found guilty of sexual harassment for these reasons:[25]

- Pictures of nude women appeared throughout the workplace.
- Male workers frequently made sexual comments.
- Coarse jokes, abusive graffiti, and offensive touching were commonplace.

Taking a Closer Look 11-1 depicts one other type of sexual harassment, called "reverse sexual harassment." This type occurs when a person is denied an employment opportunity that was given to someone who complied with requests for sexual favors. This form of harassment was found to occur in a court case in which a nurse was denied a promotion, even though she was more qualified than the employee who got the position. The nurse who was promoted was having a sexual relationship with the doctor who made the promotion decision. The action was ruled discriminatory because their relationship played a substantial role in the selection.[26]

How Does One Prove a Hostile Environment Case?

When a firm is charged with hostile environment, the court requires the employee to prove that the disputed behavior was unwelcome, based on gender, and abusive. Whether the employer knew of the behavior or should have known is also considered. To determine whether the behavior is unwelcome, the courts consider direct evidence (the employee told the harasser to stop) or indirect (the employee did not resist for fear of possible retribution).

To be considered sexual harassment, the challenged behavior must be gender-based; that is, the alleged victim must be chosen because of his or her sex. As noted by the Supreme Court in *Harris v. Forklift Systems,* "The critical issue is whether members of one sex are exposed to disadvantageous terms or conditions of employment to which members of the other sex are not exposed." Thus, even harassment that is lodged against someone of the same sex is illegal when only members of that sex have been harassed. The issue of same-sex harassment was addressed by the Supreme Court in its 1997 decision in *Oncale v. Sundowner Offshore Services.* The Court ruled that the firm was guilty of sexual harassment because it ignored the complaints of a male employee that three other male crewmembers forcibly and repeatedly subjected him to sex-related, humiliating actions.

The challenged behavior must also be severe or abusive. Abusiveness is a judgment call depending on the circumstances surrounding the behavior. Inappropriate sexual behavior would not be considered abusive unless it created a "hellish" environment that is "sufficiently severe or pervasive to alter the conditions of the victim's employment."[27] The courts look at a number of factors when making this judgment: the severity of the acts, their frequency, and the total number of days that they have been occurring. Judges use a sliding scale in jointly assessing the severity and frequency of the behavior. The more severe the behavior, the less frequent it needs to be in order to be classified as abusive.

The context of the situation is also important. For instance, in *Oncale,* the Supreme Court noted that patting an employee on the bottom would be considered abusive behavior in the context of an office; it would not be abusive, however, if a football coach smacked a player on the buttocks as he runs onto the playing field.

Can employers be held liable for sexual harassment when upper management is unaware of the behavior in question? This issue was addressed in two 1998 Supreme Court decisions (*Faragher v. City of Boca Raton* and *Burlington Industries Inc. v. Ellerth*). The court ruled that the employer is liable under such circumstances if the worker has suffered some tangible loss. For instance, if a woman was fired for refusal to sleep with her boss, the employer is liable even if it tried to prevent or correct the harassment. In cases of hostile environment where no tangible benefits have been lost, the employer is not liable if it can prove *both* the following:

- It exercised reasonable care to prevent and promptly correct the sexual harassment (i.e., had an effective sexual harassment policy).
- The employee unreasonably failed to take advantage of the corrective opportunities provided by the employer.

How Should an Employer Deal with Sexual Harassment?

An employer should take the following steps (see Figure 11-1):[28]

1. *Establish a written sexual harassment policy.* The policy should specify grievance procedures by which employees can bring claims of harassment to management's attention. These procedures should provide employees with opportunities to bypass their supervisor if the supervisor is the one being accused. Exhibit 11-1 shows EEOC guidelines for developing an effective sexual harassment policy.

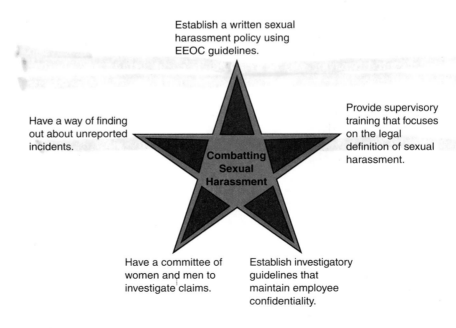

Figure 11-1
A 5-Point Method for Dealing with Sexual Harassment

> **EXHIBIT 11-1**   EEOC Guidelines for Developing a Policy on Sexual Harassment

1. Define sexual harassment and stress that such conduct will not be tolerated.
2. Establish a complaint procedure. The policy should designate an individual outside the direct line of supervision, such as an HR professional, to receive and investigate complaints.
3. Establish a time frame for investigations. Specify how long the investigation should take and when the firm expects a determination.
4. Establish appropriate penalties. State that anyone violating the sexual harassment policy will be subject to the appropriate penalty, which may range from a warning to a discharge.
5. Ensure confidentiality. Explain that the identity of both the complaining employee and the alleged harasser will be kept confidential—and keep that promise.
6. Provide protection against retaliation. Specify that no one who makes a complaint will meet with retaliation. Also, specify that witnesses will also be protected from retaliation.

2. *Provide supervisory training that focuses on the legal definition of sexual harassment.* In addition to holding formal training sessions, top management should also meet with employees to stress management's strong commitment to keep the workplace free of harassment.

3. *Establish investigative guidelines that maintain employee confidentiality* (see Section 11-3, "The Manager's Guide").

4. *Establish a committee composed of both men and women to investigate sexual harassment claims.* Committee members should receive training on how to investigate harassment claims.

5. *Establish a means of detecting unreported instances of sexual harassment within the company.* Attitude surveys and exit interviews may identify such instances.

Pregnancy Discrimination

Most women (approximately 80 percent) will become pregnant during their careers.[29] Firms should attempt to accommodate the special needs of these individuals. Competitive advantage can be enhanced by such accommodation, as illustrated by the findings of a two-year national study.[30] The study compared the work-related attitudes and behaviors of women working in "accommodating firms" to those working in "nonaccommodating firms." The findings indicated that women working in accommodating firms

- Were more productive
- Took fewer sick days
- Worked later into their pregnancies
- Were more likely to return to work after childbirth

Pregnancy Discrimination Act

The Pregnancy Discrimination Act (PDA) specifies that pregnancy discrimination is a form of sex discrimination and is therefore illegal.

According to the PDA, firms may not discriminate against employees on the basis of pregnancy, childbirth, or related medical conditions. EEOC guidelines on pregnancy discrimination state that employees who are temporarily unable to perform their jobs adequately because of a pregnancy-related condition must be treated in the same manner as employees who are temporarily disabled for other reasons. Some specific suggestions for complying with the PDA are presented in Taking a Closer Look 11-2.

Family and Medical Leave

The **Family and Medical Leave Act (FMLA)** of 1993 requires all employers of 50 or more employees to grant workers up to 12 weeks of unpaid leave per year for the

Family and Medical Leave Act (FMLA) A law stating that firms employing 50 or more workers must grant employees up to 12 weeks of unpaid leave per year for the care of a newborn child, an ill family member, or their own illness.

Taking a Closer Look 11-2 — *Suggestions for PDA Compliance*[31]

- Employers must apply all policies (e.g., absence, modified duty) consistently to both pregnant and nonpregnant employees. Inconsistent application can be taken as evidence of discriminatory intent.
- Employers may reject a pregnant applicant whose pregnancy is expected to make her unavailable during a critical business period, as long as it has strong evidence to support that expectation.
- Employers need to ensure that all supervisors, especially those that play a role in the discharge decision, refrain from making any negative comments regarding their employee's pregnancy. Such comments can be used as evidence of discrimination.

- The PDA does not guarantee that an employee will be reinstated to her old position following her maternity leave. When terminating such workers, the employer must present a legitimate, nondiscriminatory reason for its action.
- The PDA does not legally require employers to accommodate pregnant employees by offering them light duty assignments unless all other temporarily disabled workers are so accommodated.

---

care of a newborn child, an ill family member, or their own illness. Employees may take the leave all at once or in increments. Taking a Closer Look 11-3 describes the major provisions of the FMLA.

Although it helps employees, the FMLA can be quite costly to employers when they must replace workers on leave. Because women are more likely to use these leaves, companies that employ a majority of women will be especially hard hit.[32] Consider the case of Sibley Memorial Hospital of Washington, DC:[33]

> The hospital ran into difficulty when trying to replace one of its employees on leave. Because she worked in an extremely specialized position, the hospital could not find a replacement locally. In addition to paying the employee's medical benefits, Sibley thus had to pay for the replacement worker's round-trip airfare, pay her $400 a week for housing, rent her a car, and pay her a 12-week salary of about $13,000. To top things off, at the end of her leave, the employee informed the hospital that she would not be returning to work.

The FMLA protects employers from this type of problem in two ways: (1) It allows employers to exempt workers with the highest earnings and (2) it requires employees to reimburse the employer for insurance premiums paid during the leave if they

---

Taking a Closer Look 11-3 — *Provisions of the Family and Medical Leave Act of 1993*

Purpose of the Act

To allow most employees to take up to 12 weeks of unpaid leave each year for the following reasons:

- Childbirth or to care for a child in the first 12 months after childbirth
- Adoption or foster care, within the first 12 months of placement
- Care for a seriously ill spouse, child, or parent
- Care for the employee's own health problem if it renders the individual incapable of performing his or her job

Coverage

- All private, state, and federal employers who employ 50 or more people
- Employees who have worked for the employer a minimum of 12 months and at least 1,250 hours in the past year
- An employer can exempt an employee if that individual is one of their highest paid employees (upper 10 percent) and his or her absence will cause the employer serious financial loss.

Obligations

- Employers are obligated to maintain preexisting health insurance for employees and to restore returning employees to original or equivalent positions.
- Employees are obligated to provide 30 days' advance notice when possible. If not, notice should be given as soon as possible. The employee must certify the need for leave per a health care provider.
- If an employee is able to return to work, yet chooses not to, he or she must reimburse the employer for any insurance premiums paid during the leave.

Scheduling Leave

- The 12 weeks may be continuous or intermittent. When intermittent, the employer may transfer workers to positions that better lend themselves to intermittent leave. The transfer must be temporary, and the position must be equivalent to that held previously.
- Spouses working for the same company are both eligible for leave, but the total combined leave time is only 12 weeks unless the leave is due to personal health problems.

are able to return to work, yet choose not to do so. Although Sibley Memorial Hospital was not able to utilize the first protection (the employee's salary was not among the top 10 percent), it was reimbursed for its insurance payments.

Fetal Protection Policies

Fetal protection policies (FPPs) exclude women of childbearing age from jobs that could cause potential reproductive hazards, such as those involving toxins, and those that can cause sterility, infertility, sperm abnormality, stillbirth, miscarriage, birth defects, or damage to sexual organs. Such policies exclude all women regardless of their marital status, use of birth control, or childbearing intention. Women are exempted from an FPP only if they can show proof of surgical sterilization.[34] Employers issue FPPs because they want to:[35]

- Comply with OSHA (see Chapter 13, "Meeting Employee Safety and Health Needs"), which requires that employers provide a safe and healthy workplace, protecting workers from substances that could damage their reproductive health.

- Minimize potential legal liability arising from birth defects.

- Avoid publicity arising from lawsuits involving the birth of a deformed child— publicity that could be devastating to a company's image.

- Meet their moral obligation to prevent birth defects by keeping female employees away from workplace hazards.

Fetal protection policies can hinder job opportunities for many women. Some women are already being affected in that FPPs have been adopted by such companies as Cyanamid, Du Pont, Exxon, Firestone, General Motors, Monsanto, and Olin.[36] Many more could be affected in the future, because it has been estimated that as many as 20 million jobs could be closed to women if all companies with potentially hazardous environments adopted such policies.[37]

Because they adversely affect working women, FPPs, even if well-intentioned, may be discriminatory. The Supreme Court addressed this issue in a case in which a company's FPP barred all fertile women from jobs involving exposure to high amounts of lead. The Court ruled that the company's FPP was discriminatory because the dangers of lead exposure applied equally to men, and yet men were not barred from these jobs.[38]

What Is an Employer to Do?

If ever there was an issue that puts management squarely between "a rock and a hard place," fetal protection policies are it. On one hand, such a policy can be considered discriminatory. On the other, employers have both a moral and legal responsibility to protect workers from workplace hazards. Clearly, some sort of compromise solution is necessary. Some guidelines for dealing with this issue are offered in Exhibit 11-2.

Discharge and Discrimination

Employers discharge workers all the time in this country. In fact, more than three million people are fired each year.[39] Unfortunately, many individuals lose their jobs unfairly under situations that could lead to charges of employment discrimination.[40] A decision to discharge an employee is discriminatory if it is influenced by the employee's protected group membership (see Chapter 2).

An employer must thus prepare to defend itself against possible charges of discrimination each time a discharge decision is made. As noted in Chapter 2, if plaintiffs establish a *prima facie* case of discrimination, the employer must be able to demonstrate a legitimate, nondiscriminatory (or job-related) reason for its decision.

The evidence needed to justify the legal fairness of discharge decisions varies depending on the reason for the decision. We now explore the two most common reasons: employee misconduct and poor performance.

fetal protection policies (FPPs) Organizational policies that exclude women of childbearing age from jobs with potential reproductive hazards.

> **EXHIBIT 11-2**   Guidelines for Dealing with Fetal Protection Policies

Support Federal Research on Reproductive Risks

Management should cooperate with the federal government in its investigation of the effects of all known or suspected fetal hazards at the workplace.

Estimate the Extent of Health Risk for the Firm's Employees

Management should determine the extent of reproductive health risk for each known or suspected toxic substance employed.

Fully Inform Employees about Health Risks

Management should supply each worker with the most complete information available about potential workplace hazards.

Consider Technological Controls

Management should seek to control the impact of toxic substances on workers by using various engineering techniques such as improved ventilation systems and closed systems for chemical processing.

Reduce Employee Exposure to Toxic Substances

Companies should periodically remove employees from toxic environments through shift rotation or periodic transfers to safe environments.

Conduct Genetic Testing

Some people are more susceptible than others to certain diseases caused by toxic exposure. Genetic tests could be administered to screen out susceptible individuals from hazardous jobs.

Implement a Fetal Protection Policy

If they have no other feasible alternative, management should implement an FPP. The policy should apply to both sexes unless otherwise justified. If a woman can present evidence indicating that she is not likely to become pregnant, she should not be barred from the job in question.

Source: Randall, D.M. (1987). Protecting the unborn. *Personnel Administrator,* September, 88–97.

Employee Misconduct

Misconduct occurs when an employee commits an infraction of workplace rules. Although organizations may legally establish rules that serve their purposes, firms must also implement discipline and discharge policies for ensuring fair enforcement of those rules.

Discipline and discharge policies spell out the procedures the firm should follow if an employee violates the organization's code of conduct. In the absence of such a policy, managers may make discipline and discharge decisions unfairly or inconsistently, and thus leave the firm open to charges of discrimination or wrongful termination.

just cause   The reason for an employer's action is fair.

due process   Occurs when employees are informed of the charges against them and are given an opportunity to defend themselves.

progressive discipline system   A system in which discipline is enforced in increasingly severe steps.

Effective policies encompass the notions of just cause and due process. **Just cause** means that the cause of action should be a fair one (e.g., a violation of reasonable rules). **Due process** means that employees should be informed of the charges against them and be given an opportunity to defend themselves.

Most organizations adopt a **progressive discipline system,** one in which discipline is enforced in increasingly severe steps. The first step in a progressive discipline system is to give the employee an oral warning in which he or she is informed of the incorrect behavior and how to correct it (see Section 11-3c, "HRM Skill-Building for Managers").

If an oral warning fails to correct the behavior, discipline progresses to increasingly more severe levels: written warning, probation, suspension, and, ultimately, termination. Firms generally bypass the progressive discipline system when the violation in question is a major one, such as theft, drug use, or sabotage. In these instances, most companies recommend immediate discharge.

An effective discipline and discharge policy should incorporate the provisions listed in Exhibit 11-3.[41]

Poor Performance

Employers sometimes find it necessary to discharge workers because of poor performance, although discharge is usually considered a last resort. When such a dis-

EXHIBIT 11-3	Provisions to Include in a Discipline and Discharge Policy

- The employee should know the employer's expectations.
- The employee should be given notice of any failure to meet these expectations and the consequences of this failure.
- The employer's rules and regulations should be administered fairly.
- There should be an internal appeals procedure by which employees can challenge managerial decisions that affect job security.

Source: Adapted from Segal, A. (1992). Seven ways to reduce harassment claims. *HRMagazine,* January, 84–86.

charge is legally challenged, the employer must be able to convince a court that the discharge was performance-based and was thus not discriminatory. The more documentation of poor performance the employer can produce, the more convincing its argument.[42]

An effective performance appraisal system is crucial here. Clear performance standards should be set and communicated to employees; the appraisers should follow company guidelines when completing the ratings, and, when problems arise, employees should be told how they have failed to meet the standards.[43]

Other evidence that would buttress an employer's case includes the following:[44]

- Additional evidence of poor performance, such as notes, memos, records of customer complaints, or eyewitness testimony of poor performance
- Records that demonstrate that the discharged individual has been treated the same as others in the company who have had similar performance problems
- Evidence demonstrating that, prior to the discharge, the manager attempted to help the employee improve substandard performance by providing counseling

Layoffs and Discrimination

As noted in Chapter 2, massive layoffs have become common in today's business world. Unfortunately, layoff procedures are often wrought with legal perils.[45]

The most frequent legal challenge to layoff decisions is age discrimination, where management is charged with using layoffs as a convenient excuse for purging itself of older employees. Those guilty of this practice may be motivated by the (incorrect) belief that older workers are, as a rule, less productive than younger ones. Or they may simply want to save money by eliminating the highest paid workers.[46]

When defending itself, the employer must first demonstrate that the layoff was not simply a guise for discrimination.[47] Companies can justify layoff decisions by such evidence as lagging sales, growing inventory, or a depressed economy. Employers should also provide evidence that they considered all other options, such as transferring employees into vacant positions, placing them in newly created part-time positions, or allowing them to work a shorter workweek.

The employer must also be able to justify why it chose to lay off the complainant, rather than another employee; that is, it must demonstrate that its decision was based on genuine business concerns and was thus not a pretext for discrimination.[48]

Claims of discrimination can also be refuted by statistical evidence. Statistics can help an employer's case, for instance, if they could demonstrate that the workforce stayed the same with respect to age, sex, race, etc., after the layoff.

Early Retirement and Discrimination

Companies often encourage voluntary early retirement in conjunction with layoffs.[49] In the most common situation, the employer offers incentives to encourage older workers to take an early retirement. These efforts sometimes backfire, however, when retirees later file age discrimination charges, claiming they were coerced into retirement.[50]

Taking a Closer Look 11-4	*Provisions of the Older Workers Benefit Protection Act*

The waiver document signed by the employee must:

- Be clearly written (i.e., understood by an ordinary person)
- Inform employees of their rights under ADEA and OWBPA
- State that employees are not waiving their rights to claims occurring after the waiver is signed

- Provide the worker with something of value for taking early retirement beyond the employee's normal entitlement
- Give the employee 21 days to consider whether to sign the waiver (45 days in the case of layoff)
- Allow employees to revoke their decisions for up to seven days after they sign the waiver

Older Workers Benefit Protection Act (OWBPA)
A law that regulates written waivers of ADEA rights signed by early retirees.

A firm can avoid such charges by asking early retirees to sign written waivers of their right to sue under the Age Discrimination in Employment Act (ADEA). The waivers, however, must meet minimum standards stipulated by the **Older Workers Benefit Protection Act (OWBPA),** enacted in 1990. The major provisions of the OWBPA are explained in Taking a Closer Look 11-4.

11-2b Employee Privacy Rights

Most Americans will not tolerate intrusions into their private lives. They believe that certain activities in life should be closed to the scrutiny of others.[51] As U.S. Supreme Court Justice Louis Brandeis wrote in 1928, "the right to be let alone [is] the most prehensive of rights and the right most valued by civilized men."[52]

Privacy has become an extremely important workplace issue.[53] Privacy concerns surface at the workplace when organizations attempt to collect and/or disseminate information about employees in ways that intrude on their privacy. Privacy issues also surface when employee behavior is constrained by certain workplace rules and policies, denying employees the right to be left alone, or to do as they please.

Employee privacy concerns may arise during selection or during the term of employment. We discussed selection-related privacy concerns in Chapter 6 (e.g., drug and honesty testing, negligent hiring, background investigations, reference checking). This chapter focuses on organizational practices that impinge on the privacy of incumbent workers. First, however, we examine the possible effects of privacy invasion on competitive advantage.

Practices that employees view as intrusions on their privacy can have damaging effects on competitive advantage. For example, such practices may cause bitter resentment on the part of employees and foster a climate of fear and suspicion. Such a climate may seriously affect morale and lead to increased turnover, absenteeism, and reduced productivity.[54] Intrusive practices may also trigger expensive lawsuits.

We now examine four privacy-related practices that are legally regulated: (1) information collection and use, (2) search, (3) surveillance and monitoring, and (4) enactment of workplace rules.

Information Collection and Use

Employers have a right, indeed, a need to collect and maintain information about employees. As noted in Chapter 3, "Planning for Human Resources," most human resource information systems (HRISs) contain literally hundreds of facts on each employee. Much of this information also appears in each employee's personnel file.

Employees may justifiably lodge an invasion of privacy claim if the information collected by an employer is irrelevant to the employer's business needs.[55] A company needs a clear business reason for each piece of information collected and maintained on an individual. For example, a company should not collect information about an employee's spouse unless that information is needed for benefits administration or some other useful purpose. As a general rule, information pertaining to such personal issues as home ownership, previous marriages, sexual orientation, parents' occupations, and previous arrest records are usually of no concern to employers, and efforts to collect such information could pose legal threats to the company.[56]

Access to Employee Data

According to the **Privacy Act** of 1974, public-sector employees must be given access to any information in their files. Specifically, the act states that employees have the right to:

- Determine what information is being kept on them by their employers.
- Review that information.
- Correct erroneous information.
- Prevent the information from being used for a purpose other than that for which it was collected.

Although the Privacy Act does not cover private-sector employees, most companies do allow employees to access their own records as a good employee relations gesture. Prohibiting employees from seeing their own files may create doubts and suspicions regarding the company's good faith efforts to create strictly business-relevant personnel files.[57]

Who Has Access to Information?

The release of information maintained by government agencies is regulated by the **Freedom of Information Act** of 1966. The purpose of the act is to make most government records available to the public. Specifically, the act states that any individual may gain access to these records with proper authorization.[58] The act makes exceptions for personnel files and medical information. However, the public may still be given access to this information if its right to know outweighs the individual's right to privacy.[59]

In the private sector, legal constraints in this area stem from the common law of defamation (see Chapter 6). When releasing information about an employee, the employer must ensure that:

- The information is given in good faith.
- No malice is intended.
- The receiving party has a legitimate reason for wanting the information.

Searches

Employers may violate workers' privacy if they conduct an uninvited search of an employee's property or body.[60] Property searches include an employer's inspection of employees' personal belongings located on the employer's premises in lockers, desks, automobiles, or file cabinets. Body searches include pat-down frisks and strip searches.

Organizations typically conduct searches to prevent theft, detect the presence of alcohol or drugs, or recover stolen property.[61] The following circumstances, for example, triggered a body search at Kmart:

A female employee, working as a part-time cashier, was accused of stealing $20 from a customer. The manager asked the employee to accompany a female assistant manager and the customer to the women's public rest room. Upon entering the rest room, the employee was asked to disrobe in order to prove she did not have the money on her person.

Privacy Act   A law giving public sector employees access to any information in their files.

Freedom of Information Act   A law designed to make most government records available to the public.

Could this employee successfully sue her employer for invasion of privacy? To answer this question, one must first understand the legal principles underlying privacy suits. An employer's behavior in this area is regulated by the common law* of **intrusion upon seclusion.** This doctrine states that a person's privacy rights are violated when the intrusion upon his or her private concerns would be considered highly offensive to a reasonable person.[62] To be lawful, an employer's search must meet three criteria:

intrusion upon seclusion
A common law doctrine stating that a person's privacy rights are violated when the intrusion upon his or her private concerns would be considered highly offensive to a reasonable person.

1. A company must have a reasonable basis for conducting the search.
2. A set of written guidelines, issued by the company, should inform employees of its search policy.
3. The person conducting the search should take all reasonable precautions to ensure the search is not conducted offensively or abusively.

An employer could establish a reasonable basis for a search by showing that it had reason to believe that some wrongdoing has been committed. For example, a court ruled in favor of the Parks Sausage Company when employees challenged the company's right to search the lockers of all its second shift employees, a search that uncovered cocaine. The court ruled that because several employees had complained about drug use during that shift, the firm had a reasonable basis for conducting the search.

The courts are more likely to rule in favor of employers if searches are conducted in accordance with the company's written policy. The search policy should describe the circumstances under which searches will be conducted and specify the rights of employees in such instances. Exhibit 11-4 shows an example of a written search policy.

An organization conducting a search must do so in a manner that is not offensive or abusive. A court will rule that an employer's search is abusive if the "plaintiff alleges a set of facts which, if recited to an average member of the community, would arouse his [or her] resentment against the actor, and lead him [or her] to exclaim outrageous!"[63] In the Kmart case described earlier, the court ruled that the search was abusive because forcing the employee to disrobe in front of a customer was embarrassing and humiliating and caused the employee great emotional distress.

Surveillance and Monitoring

surveillance Tracking employee behavior outside the workplace.

monitoring Tracking employee behavior inside the workplace.

Many organizations engage in employee **surveillance** and **monitoring** activities, tracking the behavior of employees both on and off the job. Surveillance and monitoring methods include monitoring phone calls, email, and Internet use, watching employees through closed-circuit televisions, using private investigators to watch employees outside the workplace, and using global positioning systems to tract the employees' locations when using company vehicles and company-provided cell phones.[64]

Proponents of such practices claim that they serve a legitimate business purpose. For instance, monitoring the phone calls of employees who deal with the public helps organizations improve efficiency, provide employees with performance feedback, ensure customer satisfaction, and detect theft. For example, an organization can learn if employees respond politely to customers and whether they are giving customers correct information. Employers can then give employees corrective feedback, as necessary, to improve their performance. By monitoring computers, employers can measure computer-related worker productivity, such as speed of work, length of work breaks, number of keystrokes per hour, and so forth.[65]

Common law is defined as "a body of law that derives its authority from customs, rules of action, and decrees of the courts enforcing such customs and rules." It is the unwritten law of England, statutory, and case law of the American colonies before the American Revolution. [*Source:* Sovereign, K.L. [1994]. *Personnel Law* (3rd ed.). Englewood Cliffs, NJ: Prentice Hall.]

> **EXHIBIT 11-4** — A Written Company Policy on Searches: An Example
>
> 1. Searches will be conducted only when there is legitimate reason to believe that pilferage is taking place.
> 2. Employee consent to reasonable searches is a condition of continued employment.
> 3. Personal privacy will be respected during all searches. If possible, searches will be conducted away from other employees.
> 4. Searches may be unannounced. Random searches will be employed only when excessive pilferage occurs.

The majority of today's companies are monitoring employees' email and Internet usage for the following reasons: to protect themselves from computer viruses, harassment lawsuits, and leaks of confidential information, and to detect whether workers are wasting their work hours surfing the Internet.[66]

Surveillance and monitoring practices have their critics, however. Some people believe that such practices degrade employees, conjuring up the notion of "big brother." Monitoring employee behavior may also lead to stress and hinder employee morale.[67] One study, for example, found that the use of computer monitoring significantly reduced the job satisfaction of many employees and led to increased turnover.[68]

Legally, employer behavior must meet the standards of the common law doctrine of intrusion upon seclusion. Monitoring and surveillance are thus subject to the same restrictions as employee searches: The employer must have a legitimate business reason for engaging in these practices. Here is an example of a company's surveillance activity that was legally challenged on the grounds of privacy invasion:

> An employee missed work for several weeks because of an accident. The company was suspicious that the employee's claim of disability was false because he had not been able to produce a doctor's note. The employer thus hired a private investigator to monitor the employee's whereabouts. The investigator called the employee's home several times, watched the employee's home from a parked car, and walked past the house to see if the employee could be seen through a window.[69]

The employee claimed that these actions were highly intrusive and, therefore, violated his privacy rights. The presiding judge ruled for the company, stating that the surveillance activities served a legitimate business purpose: The failure to produce a doctor's note was a legitimate reason for suspecting that something was amiss.

In addition to common law restrictions, several states have enacted antisurveillance statutes. For example, Connecticut forbids employers from using any electronic surveillance system in areas designated for the health or personal comfort of employees (e.g., rest rooms, lounges, and locker rooms).[70]

Given that surveillance and monitoring activities can reduce employee morale and lead to possible legal problems, employers should proceed cautiously. If an employer decides to engage in surveillance and monitoring activities, it can minimize its legal liability by following the recommendations listed in Figure 11-2.

Workplace Rules

Organizations often impose rules to restrict certain types of employee behaviors such as theft, insubordination, drug use, or horseplay. Although such rules do, by their very nature, restrict workers' personal freedoms, most employees understand why companies need these rules and readily accept them.

Courts also recognize the need for workplace rules and usually allow companies to set any rules they feel are necessary, as long as those rules are enforced in a nondiscriminatory manner.

Employers' rule-making authority is not unlimited, however. Rules will likely be challenged if they restrict employee freedoms in areas that workers have traditionally viewed as highly private. In the following subsections, we discuss some of the more controversial rules set by employers.

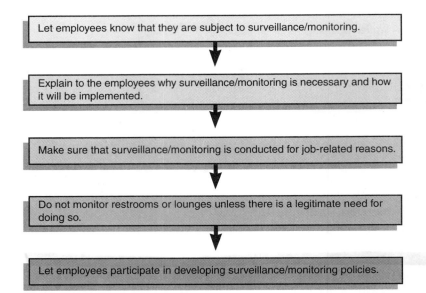

Figure 11-2
*Recommendations for
Implementing Surveillance
and Monitoring Practice*

Let employees know that they are subject to surveillance/monitoring.

Explain to the employees why surveillance/monitoring is necessary and how it will be implemented.

Make sure that surveillance/monitoring is conducted for job-related reasons.

Do not monitor restrooms or lounges unless there is a legitimate need for doing so.

Let employees participate in developing surveillance/monitoring policies.

No-Smoking Rules

Many companies have polices targeting smokers.[71] For instance:

- 27 percent limit the number of allowable smoking breaks.
- 17 percent terminate employees who are caught smoking in undesignated areas.
- 5 percent charge higher health care premiums for smokers.

Moreover, some companies refuse to employ smokers.[72] For example, Weyco Inc., a Michigan-based health benefits company, issued a policy in 2003 stating that all workers who were still smoking by January 1, 2005, would be terminated. In 2004 Union Pacific Railroad stopped hiring smokers in certain states. Alaska Airlines now requires applicants to pass a urine test for tobacco use in order to be considered for employment.[73]

Companies institute no-smoking rules for two reasons. One is the employer's concern for the well-being of its nonsmoking employees. Drawing on mounting evidence that passive smoke can cause throat cancer and other diseases, nonsmokers are demanding the right to work in a smoke-free environment. In fact, a growing number of states have passed antismoking legislation that legally bans smoking in public places, such as workplaces.

The second reason for banning smoking is a financial one. Because they pose health and safety risks, the employment of smokers may raise an employer's premiums for fire, health, disability, and life insurance.

What legal rights do smokers have? Very few. Smokers are not a protected group and therefore are not eligible for protection under federal antidiscrimination laws. Moreover, courts do not consider workplace smoking restrictions as violations of employees' privacy rights.[74] Smokers' greatest protection comes from state laws that make it illegal for companies to refuse to hire an applicant because he or she smokes. Twenty-nine states and the District of Columbia have recently passed such a law (see Figure 11-3).

Although the law does not require employers to consider smokers' rights when enacting nonsmoking policies, many companies try to help employees break the smoking habit. For instance, 32 percent of employers surveyed offer to pay for smoking cessation programs.

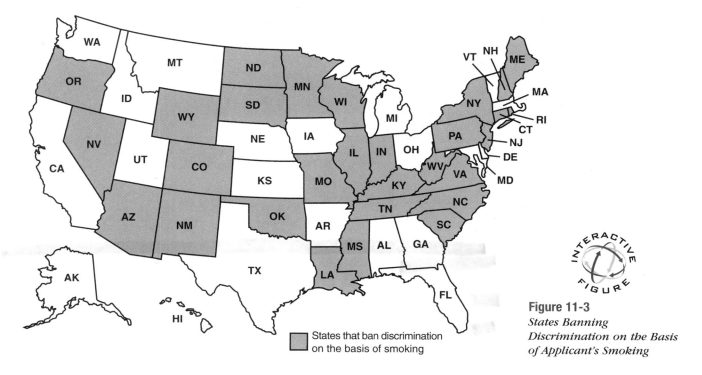

States that ban discrimination on the basis of smoking

Figure 11-3
States Banning Discrimination on the Basis of Applicant's Smoking

Rules Governing Romantic Relationships

Some employers have issued rules prohibiting employees from having romantic relationships with competitors in order to protect trade secrets.[75] Others prohibit managers from having romantic relationships with nonmanagement personnel. The concern here is that the "favored" employee may be more likely to be granted rewards, such as a promotion. There is also a concern that the "favored" employee may be denied rewards if the relationship were to end. In either instance, morale may suffer and claims of sexual harassment could be lodged.

The laws pertaining to this issue vary for public- and private-sector employers. In the public sector, rules regulating romantic relationships must comply with the *Fourth Amendment,* which guarantees public-sector employees a right to privacy. To justify legally a rule that restricts romantic relationships, a public-sector employer must have a compelling reason to enforce that rule. Fear that an employee would reveal state secrets if allowed to date certain individuals, like a foreign ambassador, would be considered a compelling need. So would a fear that an employee's job performance would be hindered if allowed to date the boss.[76] Most courts have rejected arguments that are centered on the issues of morality and company image.[77] For instance, rules prohibiting extramarital affairs or cohabitation could not be legally justified on moral grounds.

Private-sector employers have more leeway than public-sector ones in setting rules that restrict romantic relationships. The legal limits to an employer's rule-making authority are regulated by the common law of intrusion upon seclusion. Consequently, an employer may impose any rule it wants, as long as a reasonable person would not consider the rule outrageous.

Employee Misconduct outside the Workplace

Many employers impose rules that forbid employees from engaging in unlawful activities outside the workplace. For instance, some companies will suspend or discharge employees who have been arrested, jailed, and/or convicted of a crime.

EXHIBIT 11-5	Federal Statutes Prohibiting Wrongful Termination

Statute	Prohibitions
Antidiscrimination laws	Prohibit discharge based on protected group membership
Employee Retirement Income Security Act	Prohibits discharge designed to deprive employees of benefits
Fair Labor Standards Act	Prohibits discharge of employees who report a violation of this act
OSHA	Prohibits discharge for reporting violations of the act
National Labor Relations Act	Prohibits discharges that are intended to discourage union activity
Consumer Credit Protection Act	Prohibits discharge for garnishment or indebtedness
Whistle-Blower's Protection Act	Prohibits the federal government from discharging an individual for whistle-blowing
The Fifth and Fourteenth Amendments to the Constitution	Prohibit federal, state, and local governments from discharging workers without giving them due process

Does an employer have a legal right to regulate employee behavior outside the workplace? Yes, to some extent. If an employer discharges an employee for misconduct outside the workplace, it must be prepared to prove one of two things:

1. There is some relationship between the misconduct and the job (e.g., a bank teller is convicted of theft), *or*

2. The continued employment of the guilty individual would have a disruptive impact on the workforce (subordinates refuse to work for a manager who has been convicted of child molestation).[78]

11-2c Wrongful Termination and Employment-at-Will

An employer's legal right to discharge an employee is governed by a doctrine called **employment-at-will.** According to this doctrine, employers are free to discharge their employees for any reason, even an unfair one, unless the discharge is limited by contract or by federal or state statutes.

Statutes Prohibiting Wrongful Termination

Several statutes (see Exhibit 11-5) prohibit certain types of unfair or **wrongful termination.** In addition, union employees are protected from wrongful termination if their collective bargaining agreement specifies that discharges may be made only if there is just cause (see Chapter 12, "Understanding Unions and Their Impact on HRM").

The protections described earlier are not all-encompassing, however. Some apply only to certain employees: the Fifth and Fourteenth Amendments protect only government workers, and the collective bargaining agreements protect only those workers covered by the agreements. The remaining statutes listed in Exhibit 11-5 apply to the great majority of workers, but they cover only certain types of unfair discharges, such as those stemming from discrimination or retaliation.

In fact, the United States is the only industrialized nation in the world that does not fully protect all workers from wrongful termination! Consequently, it is *not* unlawful in this country for a nonunionized, private-sector firm to discharge someone for seemingly ridiculous or unfair reasons, such as putting too much cream in the boss's coffee! Although reprehensible, such discharges are often lawful.

Exceptions to the Employment-at-Will Doctrine

Employers' legal rights to fire employees at will has begun to diminish during the past decade or so as courts have noted some additional exceptions to the at-will doctrine. These exceptions draw on common law and vary from state to state. The common law violations that are most frequently lodged are those pertaining to public policy, implied contract, and good faith and fair dealing.

employment-at-will A legal doctrine stating that employers may discharge their employees for any reason, even an unfair one, unless the discharge is limited by contract or by federal or state statutes.

wrongful termination An unlawful discharge.

The Public Policy Exception

A **public policy** is any doctrine that serves the needs of society; if public policy is violated, society will suffer harm. Legislation, administrative rules, judicial decisions, or professional codes of ethics may generate such policies.[79]

public policy A doctrine that serves society and, if violated, will cause harm to society.

Today, 43 states prohibit employers from discharging an employee if that discharge violates a public policy.[80] A violation would occur if an employer fired someone for engaging in an activity encouraged by public policy, such as:

- Serving on jury duty
- Exercising his or her right to file a workers' compensation claim
- Whistle-blowing (filing a complaint that an employer is engaging in an illegal, immoral, or illegitimate practice)
- Participating in a legal proceeding contrary to employer's wishes

Employers would also violate public policy if they fire someone for *refusing* to perform an act condemned by public policy. Employees could litigate based on a public policy claim if they were discharged for:

- Refusing to commit perjury
- Refusing to commit an unlawful act, like fudging tax returns
- Refusing to steal secrets from a company's competitors

Parsons v. United Technologies, a 1997 case, illustrates the public policy exception. The plaintiff, a civilian, was fired for refusing the request of his Connecticut-based employer to travel to a war zone during Operation Desert Shield to make helicopter repairs. The employer's defense was employment-at-will; the discharge did not violate any existing laws. The court ruled for the plaintiff, stating that providing workers with a safe place to work was required by public policy.

The Implied Contract Exception

Most wrongful termination suits are brought under a legal theory known as **implied contract.**[81] In 38 states, statements written in an employee handbook or made during a job interview can imply contractual agreements. In such statements, employers may declare that an employee's job tenure is expected to be long term and that discharge will occur only with "good cause." Discharging someone unfairly could be considered a violation of this contract.

implied contract An unwritten contractual agreement.

The Good Faith and Fair Dealing Exception

When an employee feels that he or she has been discharged unfairly, but there is no implied contract between the employer and the employee, the employee may still be able to present a viable case of wrongful termination in some states. Such a case would depend on the argument that all contracts (even those with no promise of long-term employment) contain an implied promise of **good faith and fair dealing.** The 11 state courts that recognize this principle prohibit discharges that are particularly repugnant or unfair, such as:

good faith and fair dealing A common law prohibiting discharges that are particularly repugnant or unfair.

- Hiring an employee who must move his/her home from one city to another and then unfairly discharging that person within a short period of time
- Firing someone to prevent benefits from vesting or to prevent an employee from receiving earned commissions

Preventing Wrongful Termination

An employer may take one of two approaches to minimize the chances of losing a wrongful termination suit. One, the firm may avoid making any statements that promise long-term employment; i.e., statements that could be construed as creating an implied contract. An employer wishing to take this approach should do the following:

1. Include an at-will statement on the application form, such as the following one:

   I understand that my employment may be terminated, with or without cause, at any time, at the option of either the company or myself.

2. Place a disclaimer in the employee handbook, stating that the document is not to be interpreted as a contract—that it is provided as a matter of information only.

3. Train interviewers to avoid making comments to applicants that imply long-term job security.

Many companies take this approach mainly to maintain control over their discharge practices. These companies want to reserve their right to fire someone for any reason *they* feel is justifiable without having to provide detailed documentation to prove that they acted fairly. Other companies take this approach to buttress their position in case of wrongful termination complaints. Without an implied contract, employees filing a complaint will likely lack grounds for a suit.

Although legally wise, this approach tells employees, in effect, that they are subject to discharge at any time, for any reason. Many workers obviously feel uncomfortable working without any sense of job security.

As an alternative, companies can ensure that their discipline and discharge practices are fair in the first place and the fairness of any discharge can be proven through documentation. If discharge decisions are perceived as being fair and are well documented, terminated employees may be less angry and therefore less likely to sue. Moreover, fair procedures increase the likelihood that employers will prevail if a suit were lodged.[82] Section 11-3, "The Manager's Guide," suggests how fair discipline and discharge procedures can be implemented.

11-3 The Manager's Guide

11-3a Workplace Justice and the Manager's Job

As we noted earlier in the chapter, policies and procedures aimed at ensuring workplace justice are important because they let employees know that the organization values them and is interested in treating them fairly. Although line managers neither make policy nor establish procedures for ensuring workplace justice, their role is nevertheless vital. Managers (1) communicate workplace policies and procedures to their employees, (2) create work environments that foster adherence to policies and procedures, and (3) take appropriate action when possible policy violations arise.

Communicating Workplace Policies and Procedures
First, each employee must be fully aware of the company's code of conduct. Employees must understand policies and rules and be aware of the consequences for violating them. This information should be conveyed during orientation training and contained in employee handbooks.

Creating a Good Work Environment
Second, managers should try to create a work environment in which workers are motivated to voluntarily follow the rules. When employees adopt this attitude, disciplinary action is rarely needed. Managers can create the proper work climate by setting good examples, showing employees their concern for the workers' well-being, keeping them informed about problems, and dealing with employees in a firm, but fair manner.

Dealing Effectively with Possible Policy Violations

Third, managers must be able to deal effectively with "problem subordinates"—individuals who do not follow workplace rules. This role may be the most difficult for managers to play. As management expert John Veiga notes:[83]

1. One universal truth about managers is that all of them have problem subordinates.

2. Too many managers are unwilling to confront problem subordinates. Unfortunately, managers often bungle the job by exerting subtle pressure on the subordinate to leave the organization, rather than directly confronting him or her. Subtle pressure may take the form of giving undesirable assignments, holding back salary increases, denying certain "perks," and so forth.

3. Therefore, when problems persist, managers are as much at fault as subordinates.

4. Clearly, managers must examine their role in creating problem subordinates and figure out how to prevent such problem relationships.

5. Managers should *directly* deal with such subordinates. Problem individuals cannot be handled with kid gloves. The goal is to clarify the unwanted behaviors and their consequences. Establish clear-cut expectations; clarify what is wrong and what you expect to see changed.

Specific managerial skills for enacting workplace justice policies are covered in Section 11-3c, "HRM Skill-Building for Managers."

11-3b How the HRM Department Can Help

As we noted throughout the chapter, HR professionals help establish fair and just policies. Once such policies are designed, the HR professional plays three roles: (1) implementing fair policies, (2) developing a conflict resolution mechanism, and (3) assisting managers with workplace justice-related issues.

The Implementation of Discipline and Discharge Policies

In addition to helping an organization formulate its discipline and discharge policies, HR professionals can help implement the policy in at least two ways. First, they convey the organization's code of conduct to the employees during employee orientation and through training programs and employee handbooks.

Second, HRM departments maintain company-wide disciplinary records that can (and should) be reviewed before termination is proposed. HR professionals often review these records to determine whether the proposed disciplinary action is in line with past organizational actions.

Developing a Conflict Resolution Mechanism

Organizations can minimize negative affects of workplace justice-related disputes by implementing mechanisms to handle such disputes fairly. When handled in this way, disputes can often be resolved without having to go to court.

Most companies attempt to resolve disputes through an open-door policy. As we noted in the opening case, however, this procedure by itself is often insufficient. Descriptions of some alternative dispute resolution mechanisms follow:

- *Peer review panels:* We saw in the opening case how peer review panels operate.

- *Mediation:* Mediation is a "voluntary, nonbinding process in which disputing parties reach an agreement with the assistance of a neutral third party."[84]

- *Arbitration:* Arbitration is similar to mediation, except that, unlike the mediator's role, the arbitrator is granted the authority to make a binding decision.

- *Use of an ombudsman:* An ombudsman is granted the authority to investigate and resolve disputes. Such an individual is independent of management, usually reporting directly to the board of directors.[85]

Assisting Managers with Workplace Justice-Related Issues

HR professionals also serve as valuable resources to managers by helping them handle disciplinary problems. Assistance may take the form of day-to-day advice for dealing with difficult situations, or it may be given in the context of a formal training program designed to teach managers how to prevent/resolve disciplinary problems.

11-3c HRM Skill-Building for Managers

Managers need several skills to properly handle workplace justice-related responsibilities. They must be able to conduct disciplinary investigations, know how to investigate claims of sexual harassment, and be able to conduct disciplinary conferences with employees.

Conducting a Disciplinary Investigation

When discipline problems arise, managers must investigate. If you become aware of a possible violation of company rules, you should proceed as follows:

1. *Get the facts.* Gossip, rumors, and hearsay evidence often prove inaccurate. You want to be certain that the employee has engaged in the suspected behavior before taking any action. You should base corrective action on facts that you have personally verified.[86]

2. *Review applicable rules.* Ask yourself: "What workplace rule applies to this situation?" and "Did the employee know the rule and understand its application?" If not, the most appropriate action would be to talk to the employee, explain what the rule is, and why it exists.

3. *Meet with the employee.* Get the employee's side of the story. If the employee offers mitigating circumstances, check them out. Decide if these circumstances should influence your final decision.

4. *Decide what kind of discipline, if any, to recommend.* It is extremely important that a correct decision be made here. The decision will affect all members of the work group, not just the person in question. For instance, it may serve to make others in the work group aware of expected performance levels, which could result in improved group performance.[87] Moreover, management response to the problem sends other employees messages regarding:[88]

   - What constitutes a violation of this rule?
   - Does the rule really mean what it says?
   - What is the company's attitude toward violators of the rule?
   - Can our manager handle the problem?
   - What will happen to future violators of the rule?

   As you decide on the appropriate corrective action, consider the following factors:[89]

   - The circumstances surrounding the violation
   - The seriousness of the offense
   - The offender's past record
   - The offender's intent
   - The disciplinary action taken in similar situations in the past

5. *Provide proper documentation.* Proper documentation is vital to justify the fairness of your decision, in the event that the decision is later challenged. Document the incident as soon as possible. The courts frown on documentation that is "manufactured" after the fact. The documentation needed to support a disciplinary decision is listed in Taking a Closer Look 11-5.

Investigating Claims of Sexual Harassment

As noted in Taking a Closer Look 11-1, EEOC guidelines on sexual harassment hold an employer liable for the acts of its employees if a manager is aware (or should have

Taking a Closer Look 11-5 *Documentation Needed to Support Disciplinary Decisions*

Documentation

Proof that the behavior in question actually occurred

Proof that the employee was (or should have been) aware of the rule that was allegedly violated

Proof that the employee was notified of his/her violation and, where appropriate, was given sufficient warnings

Proof that other employees who have been found guilty of committing similar violations have been disciplined in a similar manner

What the Employer Must Do

Keep a written record of the chronology of events involved in the misconduct. This should be a factual account (avoid hearsay and do not make presumptions) that includes dates, times, places, witnesses, and the specific details of what happened.

Show evidence that the rule was communicated to the employee in posted notices, the employee handbook, or during orientation training.

Place written warnings in the employee's personnel file.

Show records of how other cases have been handled. Ask the following: Who else has committed similar transgressions in the past? How were they treated? Consider the employee's past work record and any other mitigating circumstances that would make this case different from others.

been aware) of the behavior, yet fails to take appropriate action. Therefore, as a manager, you should quickly and thoroughly investigate all claims of sexual harassment. The investigation should proceed as follows:[90]

1. Determine if the alleged behavior has actually occurred. During your first meeting with the employee voicing the complaint, you should be as sympathetic as possible. Ensure the employee that you take these charges seriously and will do everything possible to resolve the problem. Ask for a complete account of the incident(s) and for the names of any employees who can provide corroborating testimony.

   Interview the accused person, and inform him or her of the charges. Emphasize that retaliation against the claimant will not be tolerated. Ask the individual to give his or her version of the story. If the accused denies the allegations, try to corroborate facts from both sides.

   Check the personnel records of both parties. Be on the lookout for previous allegations of sexual harassment against the accused. Also check to see if the accuser has made the same complaint about others in the past.

2. If you conclude that the alleged behavior has occurred, determine if it could be legally construed as sexual harassment. Ask yourself:

   - Was the behavior unwelcome?
   - Was the employee denied an employment opportunity because he or she refused to comply with sexual requests?
   - Did the behavior affect the person's ability to perform the job or did it create a hostile/intimidating environment?

3. Determine the appropriate action to take. Discipline for sexual harassment should be based on the severity of the behavior. A serious offense, such as sexual assault, calls for harsh discipline—suspension, probation, or termination. Less serious offenses, such as off-color remarks or innuendoes, require less severe measures—a disciplinary meeting with the offender and a follow-up memo put in his or her personnel file. However, if the harassment persists, more severe forms of discipline are warranted.

Conducting a Disciplinary Conference

A disciplinary conference typically represents the first step in a progressive discipline system—the oral warning. The conference is supposed to correct, rather than punish, behavior. The conference should be conducted in a way that lessens the employee's tendency to become defensive. The key is to ensure that the employee understands (1) what he or she has done wrong, (2) why the behavior must be corrected, and (3) how the employee can correct the behavior. Furthermore, the offender must promise you that the inappropriate behavior will stop. To conduct a disciplinary conference, follow these steps:

1. *Get the facts*. Make sure you have conducted a proper investigation prior to this meeting.

2. *Arrange for the interview.* Select a private place and choose a time during which neither party will be interrupted.

3. *Put the employee at ease.* Inform the employee of your purpose and give assurances that you are willing to listen and will consider what the individual has to say.

4. *State the facts of the case.* Do not pass judgment or lecture the individual. Merely state the facts, as you understand them. For example:

"You have been 15 minutes late each of the past three days."

"Several people have informed me that you were smoking in a no-smoking area yesterday afternoon."

"Yesterday, I saw you leaving work with several of your work tools."

5. *Ask for reasons.* Ask the employee to explain why he or she engaged in such behavior. Remain objective; do not pass judgment.

6. *State the company policy that has been violated.* For example, "The company rule is that no employees are to take their work tools home without prior approval from their supervisor."

7. *State the reason for the policy and the possible harm caused by the employee's violation.* This step is designed to help the employee to understand the importance of the rule and why it should be followed. For example, you may state: "If workers take home tools without proper authorization, the company could be held liable if someone were to have an accident at home while using the tool. The company is also concerned about theft—without a record of loaned tools, there is no assurance that all tools will be returned."

8. *Get the worker to agree on the problem.* This is probably the most important step. Many workers will become defensive and argue that they had a good reason for doing what they did. For instance, a worker might argue that he sought to get the manager's permission to borrow the tools just before leaving work, but the manager was unavailable at the time. He may further argue that it's "no big deal, anyway"; he has worked for the company for 15 years and has had an exemplary record—he has certainly never stolen anything. He may also assure the manager that he knows how to use the tools, and the chances of an accident are nil.

   As a manager, you should not become embroiled in an argument at this point. Rather, your goal is to get the worker to agree that he or she has broken a rule that the company believes is fair, and that future instances of this behavior will not be tolerated.

9. *If disciplinary action is needed, state the action and the reasons for it.* State what action you will take now and what future action you will take if the problem goes unresolved.

10. *Involve the employee in a problem-solving discussion.* The purpose of this step is to find a solution to the problem. What must the employee do to prevent this problem from recurring? The employee should participate in seeking a solution, because people commit more to solutions that they have formulated. Managers should simply steer them in the proper direction.

11. *Have the employee summarize the problem and the agreed-on solution.* This step ensures a common understanding of the problem; it serves as a check to see whether both parties agree on what has transpired during this meeting.

12. *Agree on a follow-up date.* Arrange for a subsequent meeting (to be held after a reasonable length of time—say, two weeks) to discuss whether the worker has made satisfactory progress in resolving the problem.

13. *End the discussion on a positive note.* Ideally, employees should leave the conference with a positive attitude and not feel "browbeaten." Your goal is to demonstrate your confidence in them and to let them know that you are there to help. You should remind employees that their dependability and loyalty are highly regarded by the company and that you have every confidence in their ability to do the job correctly.

Chapter Objectives Revisited

1. Understand how effective workplace justice policies enhance competitive advantage.
   - Reduce litigation costs by preventing or winning suits.
   - Favorably influence employee attitudes and behavior.
   - Promote a good company image to boost recruitment and sales.

2. Describe the antidiscrimination laws that dictate how employees should be treated on a day-to-day basis.
   - The Civil Rights Act forbids the following types of sexual harassment:
     - Quid pro quo (including reverse sexual harassment)
     - Hostile environment
   - The Pregnancy Discrimination Act states that employees with a pregnancy-related condition must be treated in the same manner as employees who are temporarily disabled for other reasons.
   - The Family and Medical Leave Act states that employers of 50 or more employees must grant workers up to 12 weeks of unpaid leave per year for the care of a newborn child, an ill family member, or their own illness.
   - The Civil Rights Act mandates that fetal protection policies be administered in a nondiscriminatory manner.
   - The Civil Rights Act mandates that employers carefully document decisions when discharging employees for misconduct, poor performance, and layoffs.

3. Discuss the extent to which employee privacy rights are legally protected.
   - Employees may justifiably lodge an invasion of privacy claim if the information collected by an employer is irrelevant to the employer's business needs.
   - According to the Privacy Act of 1974, public-sector employees must be given access to any information in their files.
   - To be lawful, an employer's search should meet three criteria:
     - A company must have a reasonable basis for conducting the search.
     - A set of written guidelines, issued by the company, should inform employees of its search policy.
     - The person conducting the search should take all reasonable precautions to ensure the search is not conducted offensively or abusively.
   - Monitoring and surveillance are subject to the same legal standards as employee searches.
   - Controversial workplace rules that are carefully scrutinized by the courts include:
     - No-smoking rules
     - Rules governing romantic relationships
     - Rules governing employee misconduct outside the workplace

4. Explain employee rights regarding unfair discharges.
   - Employees are legally protected from unfair discharges if an employer's actions violate:
     - A statute
     - A collective bargaining agreement
     - A public policy
     - An implied contract
     - The covenant of good faith and fair dealing

5. Discuss what management skills are needed to comply effectively with workplace justice laws.
   - Ability to conduct a disciplinary investigation
   - Ability to investigate claims of sexual harassment
   - Ability to conduct a disciplinary conference

Review Questions

Note: You can find the correct answers to these questions by taking the quiz and then submitting your answers in the Online Edition. The program will automatically score your submission. If you miss a question, the program will provide the correct answer, a rationale for the answer, and the section number in the chapter where the topic is discussed.

1. When a person is denied an employment opportunity that was given to someone who complied with requests for sexual favors, it is called

    a. quid pro quo harassment.
    b. hostile environment harassment.
    c. reverse sexual harassment.
    d. none of the above; it is not a form of sexual harassment.

2. The Family and Medical Leave Act (FMLA) grants eligible workers

    a. up to 12 weeks of unpaid leave per year.
    b. up to 20 weeks of unpaid leave per year.
    c. up to 12 weeks of paid leave per year.
    d. up to 20 weeks of paid leave per year.

3. Which group of employees is exempted from FMLA coverage?

    a. men
    b. people over 55
    c. managers
    d. those with the highest earnings

4. Which of the following laws regulates the content of waivers signed by employees when taking an early retirement?

    a. Age Discrimination in Employment Act
    b. Waiver Rights Act
    c. Older Workers Benefit Protection Act
    d. Early Retirement Act

5. Which of the following provisions is included in the Privacy Act of 1974? Employees have the right to

    a. determine what information is in their personnel files.
    b. review the information in their personnel files.
    c. correct erroneous information in their personnel files.
    d. all of the above

6. In the Kmart case regarding the cashier who was accused of stealing $20, the court ruled in favor of

    a. Kmart because it had a reasonable basis for its search.
    b. Kmart because the search was conducted in private by a person of the same sex.
    c. the cashier because the search was embarrassing and humiliating.
    d. the cashier because she was wrongly accused of theft.

7. In the public sector, rules regulating romantic relationships must comply with the _____ Amendment.

    a. First
    b. Fourth
    c. Fifth
    d. Fourteenth

8. A worker is fired because she refused to steal important documents from a competitor. What common law would the worker use as a basis for a wrongful discharge suit?

    a. contract theory
    b. public policy
    c. good faith and fair dealing
    d. none of the above

9. A salesperson was unjustly fired in order to prevent the payment of an upcoming commission. What common law would the worker use as a basis for a wrongful discharge suit?

    a. contract theory
    b. public policy
    c. good faith and fair dealing
    d. none of the above

10. Which of the following statements regarding smokers in the workplace is *false?*

    a. Smokers are not a protected group under federal antidiscrimination law.
    b. Courts do not consider workplace smoking restrictions as violations of employee privacy rights.
    c. Federal law makes it illegal for companies to refuse to hire applicants who smoke.
    d. A number of states have passed legislation that legally bans smoking in the workplace.

Discussion Questions

1. Define workplace justice. Describe three ways in which the establishment of workplace justice contributes to an organization's competitive advantage.

2. What is sexual harassment? Under what conditions would an employer be liable for the sexual harassment of its employees?

3. Summarize the main provisions of the Pregnancy Discrimination Act and the associated EEOC guidelines.

4. The chapter explained that the decision to implement a fetal protection policy puts employers between a rock and hard place. Explain the employer's dilemma.

5. What type of evidence must an employer present, in court, to rebut claims of discrimination regarding discharge for poor performance? For layoff decisions that adversely affect older workers?

6. Summarize the three major laws designed to protect employee privacy rights.

7. Describe the three standards an employer's search must meet in order to ensure the searches are conducted legally.

8. Describe the pros and cons associated with employer surveillance and monitoring practices.

9. Define employment-at-will. Describe the three exceptions that have been recently applied to this doctrine.

10. How can a manager create a good work environment?

11. Summarize the steps a manager should take when dealing with a problem subordinate.

12. How should a manager handle a complaint of sexual harassment?

Experiential Exercise

Conducting a Disciplinary Conference

Overview

You will be given two disciplinary cases to role-play. The class will be divided into groups of four. Two people will role-play the first case; the other two will serve as observers. The two observers will be the role-players for the second case, and the other two will become the observers.

Instructions for Role-Players

1. Decide who will be the manager and who will be the subordinate.

2. Read the case.

3. Prepare for your task.
   - Manager: Review the steps for conducting a disciplinary conference and decide how you will follow them. Plan what you will say and how you will respond to the subordinate's possible comments.
   - Subordinate: Try to put yourself in the position of the subordinate depicted in the case. View this as an important issue to you and try to justify your behavior. Be prepared to present arguments in your defense. Do not make the manager's job easy!

4. Conduct the role-play. Take whatever time is necessary to complete the disciplinary conference. Manager, go through all 13 steps. You may refer to the

text during the conference to help you recall the steps.

Instructions for Observers

1. Read the case.

2. Review the steps to the disciplinary conference in the text.

3. Observe the role-play and take notes on how well the manager carried out each step. If the manager had a difficult time completing a step, note what he or she may have done wrong and how the step could have been more successfully carried out.

After the Role-Play

The purpose of the following activities is to give the manager feedback on his or her performance during the role-play. Emphasize what was done correctly, as well as what may have been done incorrectly. The post role-play session should proceed as follows:

1. The subordinate should discuss how he or she felt about the conference. Did the manager make him or her angry? Did the manager show concern for the employee? Did the employee leave the session with a positive attitude and a commitment to do better in the future? Are there any residual hard feelings?

2. The observers should discuss the manager's performance during each step of the conference. Were any steps not properly followed or not followed at

all? In what specific instances did the manager deal effectively with problems that arose? Give the manager suggestions on how to improve his or her performance in future disciplinary conferences.

Situation 1: The Manager's Side

You are Bill Smith, the head of the Economics Department at State Tech. You are having problems with one of your subordinates, Dr. Pat Jones. Pat is a moderately successful professor, a decent teacher, and a good researcher. However, most people view Pat as being quite arrogant and rude. As department head, you have had several talks with Pat about this problem. Yesterday, however, something happened that indicated that these talks were having no effect: During a department meeting, Pat got angry at some of the other professors over a disagreement about department policy. Pat verbally attacked one professor, Mary, in a vicious manner, making charges about her sexual preference that were clearly uncalled for. This scene created quite a disruption and caused the accused professor to break down in tears. After the meeting, Pat stormed into your office and accused you of not being supportive.

The Employee's Side

You are Dr. Pat Jones, an economics professor at State Tech. You know you have trouble getting along with people in your department, but you attribute that to the fact that you are superior to them. Your ideas are much better, and you are merely trying to show your colleagues the light. You have little respect for your department head, Bill; he is also inferior and refuses to back you in an argument, even when it is clearly evident that you are correct. You feel that others purposely try to aggravate you because they are jealous of you. The situation worsened yesterday when you became angry during a department meeting. There was a big disagreement about department policy. One of the professors, Mary, got you so angry that you verbally attacked her, making charges about her sexual preference. Although you're sorry that you lost your temper, what else could you do? Your boss gave you no support during the discussion, and that made you quite frustrated. After the meeting, you stormed into Bill's office to accuse him of not being supportive.

Situation 2: The Manager's Side

You are the manager of the Claims Department of the Prudent Insurance Company. Six months ago, you hired Chris Smith as a claims adjuster. Chris was told during orientation training that claims adjusters must always act professionally while on the job; they should dress and act appropriately at all times. Professional behavior was described as always being polite and cooperative, and never doing anything that would be considered in bad taste. Recently, you have noticed that during the past week or so, Chris has begun flirting with several coworkers of the opposite sex. You had not said anything to Chris about it, but decided you would keep a close eye on the situation. This morning, you walked into the supply room and found Chris engaging in intimate contact (i.e., passionate kissing) with another employee.

The Employee's Side

You are Chris Smith, a claims adjuster at the Prudent Insurance Company. In the beginning of your employment, you needed to concentrate on learning your job, and thus kept pretty much to yourself. Now that you feel more secure, you have become interested in establishing friendships with your coworkers. You get along best with members of the opposite sex and therefore have tried to strike up friendships with those individuals in particular. This morning, you were getting some forms out of the supply room, and before you knew it, Jan was all over you. Before you could do anything about it, your manager walked in.

Cases

Analyze the following two cases. Structure your analysis in the following manner:

1. What law(s) would form the basis for the plaintiff's charge?
2. What arguments should the plaintiff make?
3. What arguments should the employer make in its defense?
4. What would the court's decision be?
5. What rationale would the court give to support its decision?
6. Should the company have done anything differently in order to avoid the charges in the first place? If so, what?

Case 1: Sexual Harassment

Julie Jones was an assistant buyer for the ABC Company. Rod Burke, a salesperson for the company, had a crush on Julie. To show his affection for her, he constantly went through a set of courting gestures. Whenever she went by, he would do things like kiss the air, give her longing looks and make heavy sighs, pat her on the behind, and roll his eyes.

Not wanting to hurt her career by being labeled a troublemaker, Julie tried to ignore this behavior. She tried to keep it light and treated these passes with good humor. However, this approach was not working, so Julie decided to take action.

First, she checked the employee handbook that is given to all employees and found a clearly stated policy regarding sexual harassment that was in line with that recommended by the EEOC. She showed Rod a copy of this policy, but he merely laughed at her. She then told him she had no romantic interest in him and pleaded with him to stop. He refused, saying, "I know you really love it."

Feeling very frustrated, Julie quit her job and sued the company for sexual harassment.

Case 2: Privacy of Personal Records and Wrongful Termination

Howard Davis works for the DEF Company, a private-sector firm. In 1989, he began experiencing marital problems. His wife left him in 1990. As a result, he began having trouble sleeping, lost weight, and was constantly nervous.

At this point, Davis voluntarily made an appointment with DEF's contracted counseling service. He met with Jim Lewis, a professional counselor with a master's degree and 14 years of experience. After the first session, Lewis concluded that Davis was dangerous to the point of being suicidal to himself and homicidal to others. Lewis believed that Davis could easily be provoked into creating a life-threatening situation in the workplace. He felt the danger was imminent.

Without Davis' consent, Lewis contacted Bruce King, corporate manager of operations, and told him of his fears. Lewis recommended that Davis be discharged from his job and be urged to seek psychiatric treatment. King relayed this information to Susan Johnson, who is the HRM director at DEF. Johnson immediately discharged Davis, granting him two weeks' severance pay.

Davis filed suit against the company, stating that his privacy rights were violated and that his termination was wrongful.

References

1. Wilensky, R., and Jones, K.M. (1994). Quick response: Key to resolving complaints. *HRMagazine,* March, 42-47.

2. Schwoerer, C., and Rosen, B. (1989). Effects of employment-at-will policies and compensation policies on corporate image and job pursuit intentions. *Journal of Applied Psychology, 74* (4), 653-656.

3. Sunoo, B.P. (1998). After everything else—Buy insurance. *Workforce,* October, 45-50.

4. Barney, J.B., Edwards, F.L., and Ringleb, A.H. (1992). Organizational responses to legal liability: Employee exposure to hazardous materials, vertical integration, and small firm production. *Academy of Management Journal, 35* (2), 328-349.

5. Caudron, S. (1997). Don't make Texaco's $175 million mistake. *Workforce,* March, 1997.

6. Ibid.

7. Kunde, D. (1992, May 31). Former IDS division managers near trial in discrimination suit. *The Dallas Morning News,* 1H-2H. See also Sunoo, B.P. (1998). After everything else—Buy insurance.

8. Sheppard, B.H., Lewicki, R.J., and Minton, J.W. (1992). *Organizational Justice: The Search for Fairness in the Workplace.* New York: Lexington Books.

9. One study, for example, found organizational commitment to be enhanced by HRM activities that are perceived to be motivated by management's desire to show respect for the individual: Koys, D.J. (1988). Human resource management and a culture of respect: Effects on employees' organizational commitment. *Employee Responsibilities and Rights Journal, 1* (1), 57-68. Another study found that procedural justice is closely associated with organizational commitment and with trust in one's supervisor and in management: Folger, R., and Konovsky, M.A. (1989). Effects of procedural and distributive justice on reactions to pay raise decisions. *Academy of Management Journal, 32* (1), 115-130.

10. Rosen, B., and Schwoerer, C. (1990). Balanced protection policies. *HRMagazine,* February, 59-64.

11. Ibid.

12. Cox, T.H., and Blake, S. (1991). Managing cultural diversity: Implications for organizational competitiveness. *Academy of Management Executive, 5* (3), 45-56.

13. Ibid.

14. Schwoerer and Rosen. Effects of employment-at-will policies.

15. Cox and Blake. Managing cultural diversity.

16. Ibid.

17. Http://www.eeoc.gov/types/sexual_harassment.html.

18. Dubois, C., Faley, R., Kustis, G., and Knapp, D. (1999). Perceptions of organizational responses to formal sexual harassment complaints. *Journal of Managerial Issues, 11* (2), 202.

19. Reyolds, L. (1997, March 8). Sexual harassment claims surge. *HRfocus.*

20. Solomon, C.M. (1991). Sexual harassment after the Thomas hearings. *Personnel Journal,* December, 32-37.

21. Hoyman, M., and Robinson, R. (1980). Interpreting the new sexual harassment guidelines. *Personnel Journal,* December, 996-1000.

22. Moore, H.L., Cangelosi, Jr., J.D., and Gatlin-Watts, R.W. (1998). Seven spoonfuls of preventive medicine for sexual harassment in healthcare. *The Health Care Supervisor, 17* (2), 1-9.

23. Http://www.eeoc.gov.

24. *Meritor Savings Bank, FBS v. Michelle Vinson* (1986). United States Supreme Court, Docket N. 84-1979, June 19.

25. Ibid.

26. *King v. Palmer* (1985). 39 FEP Cases 877.

27. *Mast v. IMCO Recycling of Ohio* (2003). U.S. App 6th Cir. LEXIS 1940.

28. Adapted from Segal, A. (1992). Seven ways to reduce harassment claims. *HRMagazine,* January, 84-86.

29. (1989, May-June). Pregnancy: Nine to five. *Executive Female,* 13.

30. Ibid.

31. Kleiman, L.S., and Kass, D.S. (in press). Justifying pregnancy-related employment decisions under the Pregnancy Discrimination Act. *Journal of Individual Employment Rights.*

32. Gunsch, D. (1993). The Family Leave Act: A financial burden? *Personnel Journal,* September, 48-57.

33. Ibid.

34. Randall, D.M. (1988). Fetal protection policies: A threat to employee rights? *Employee Responsibility and Rights Journal, 1* (2), 121-128.

35. Ibid.

36. Randall, D.M. (1987). Protecting the unborn. *Personnel Administrator,* September, 88-97.

37. (1991). On the HRHorizon: Fetal protection policies. *HRMagazine,* January, 81-82.

38. *UAW v. Johnson Controls* (1991). 111 S.Ct. 1196.

39. Barrett, G.V., and Kernan, M.C. (1987). Performance appraisal and terminations: A review of court decisions since *Brito v. Zia* with implications for personnel practices. *Personnel Psychology, 40* (3), 489-503.

40. Schreiber, N.E. (1983). Wrongful termination of at-will employees. *Massachusetts Law Review, 68,* 22-35.

41. Adapted from Segal. Seven ways to reduce harassment claims.

42. Miller, C.S., Kaspin, J.A., and Schuster, M.H. (1990). The impact of performance appraisal methods on Age Discrimination in Employment Act cases. *Personnel Psychology, 43* (3), 555-578.

43. Ibid.

44. Ibid.

45. Hayes, A.S. (1990, November 2). Layoffs take careful planning to avoid losing the suits that are apt to follow. *The Wall Street Journal,* B1-B2.

46. Ibid.

47. Miller et al. The impact of performance appraisal methods.

48. Ibid.

49. Ibid.

50. (1991). Age discrimination. *Business and Legal Reports,* A19-A20.

51. Stambaugh, R. (1990). Protecting employee data privacy: *Computers in HR Management,* February, 12-20.

52. Cited in (1988, March 28). Privacy. *Business Week,* pp. 61-68.

53. Ibid.

54. Garland, H., Giacobbe, J., and French, J.L. (1989). Attitudes toward employee and employer's rights in the workplace. *Employee Responsibilities and Rights Journal, 2* (1), 49-59.

55. Ibid.

56. Ibid.

57. Ibid.

58. Sovereign, K.L. (1984). *Personnel Law.* Reston, VA: Reston Publishing.

59. Ledvinka, J.L., and Scarpello, V.G. (1991). *Federal Regulation of Personnel and Human Resource Management* (2nd ed.). Boston: PWS-Kent.

60. Kahn, S.C., Brown, B.B., Zapke, B.E., and Lanzarone, M. (1990). *Personnel Director's Guide* (2nd ed.). Boston: Warren, Gorham & Lamont.

61. Ibid.

62. Cited in Hames, D.S., and Dierson, N. (1991). The common law right to privacy: Another incursion into employer's rights to manage their employees? *Labor Law Journal,* 757-765.

63. *Gretencord v. Ford Motor Company* (1982). *Federal Supplement, 538,* Civil Act No. 81-228.

64. Canoni, J.D. (2004). Location awareness technology and employee privacy rights. *Employee Relations Law Journal, 30* (1), 26-31.

65. Carroll, A.B. (1989). *Business and Society.* Cincinnati: South-Western Publishing.

66. Zimmerman, E. (2002). When employee surveillance crosses the line. *Workforce,* February, 38-45.

67. Carroll. *Business and Society.*

68. Chalykoff, J., and Kochan, T.A. (1989). Computer-aided monitoring: Its influence on employee job satisfaction and turnover. *Personnel Psychology, 42,* 807-828.

69. *Seladan v. Kelsey-Hayes Company* (1989, January 24). *Northwest Reporter,* Court of Appeals, Michigan.

70. Kahn et al. *Personnel Director's Guide.*

71. Parekh, R. (2005). Companies fight tobacco use to lower health care costs. *Business Insurance, 39* (9), 4-5.

72. Parekh. Companies fight tobacco use.

73. Peterson, D.J., and Massengill, D. (1986). Smoking regulations in work place: An update. *Personnel,* May, 27-31.

74. Parekh, Companies fight tobacco use.

75. Libbin, A.E., and Stevens, J.C. (1988). The right to privacy at the workplace, Part 4: Employee personal privacy. *Personnel,* October, 86-89.

76. Ibid.

77. Ibid.

78. Bergsman, S. (1991). Employee conduct outside the workplace. *HRMagazine,* March, 62-68.

79. Arvanites, D.A., and Ward, B.T. (1989). Employment at will: A concept in transition. *Journal of Management Systems, 1* (2), 15-21.

80. Williamson, J.A., and Kleiner, B.H. (2003). New developments concerning the covenant of good faith and fair dealing. *Management Research News, 26* (2-4), 35-41.

81. Raisner, J. (1991). Relocate without making false moves. *HRMagazine,* February, 46-50.

82. Segal, J.A. (1990). Follow the yellow brick road. *HRMagazine,* February, 83-86.

83. Veiga, J.F. (1988). Face your problem subordinates now! *The Academy of Management Executive, 2* (2), 145-152.

84. Evans, S. (1994). Doing mediation to avoid litigation. *HRMagazine,* March, 48-51.

85. Fitzpatrick, R.B. (1994). Let's end legal war in the workplace. *HRMagazine,* March, 120, 118.

86. Boyd, B.B. (1968). *Management-Minded Supervision.* New York: McGraw-Hill.

87. Schnake, M.E. (1986). Vicarious punishment in a work setting. *Journal of Applied Psychology, 71* (2), 343-345.

88. Killiam, R.A. (1979). *Managers Must Lead!* New York: AMACOM.

89. Boyd. *Management-Minded Supervision.* Adapted from Webb, S.L. (1992). Investigating sexual harassment claims. *Executive Female,* May/June, 10-12.

90. Adapted from Webb, S.L. (1992). Investigating sexual harassment claims. *Executive Female,* May/June, 10-12.

Understanding Unions and Their Impact on HRM

Chapter Twelve

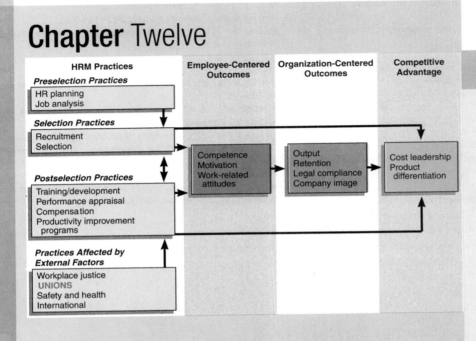

HRM Practices	Employee-Centered Outcomes	Organization-Centered Outcomes	Competitive Advantage
Preselection Practices HR planning Job analysis			
Selection Practices Recruitment Selection	Competence Motivation Work-related attitudes	Output Retention Legal compliance Company image	Cost leadership Product differentiation
Postselection Practices Training/development Performance appraisal Compensation Productivity improvement programs			
Practices Affected by External Factors Workplace justice UNIONS Safety and health International			

Key Terms

American Federation of Labor and Congress of Industrial Organizations (AFL-CIO)
arbitration
bargaining order
bargaining unit
certification election
closed shops
collective bargaining
collective bargaining agreement
decertification election
election phase
good faith bargaining
grievance
grievance system

Labor–Management Relations Act (Taft-Hartley Act)
Labor–Management Reporting and Disclosure Act (Landrum-Griffin Act)
local union
National Labor Relations Act (Wagner Act)
National Labor Relations Board (NLRB)
national unions
Norris-LaGuardia Act
open shops
petition phase
Railway Labor Act (RLA)
union instrumentality
yellow-dog contracts

Chapter Objectives

Upon completion of this chapter, you will be able to:

- Understand the impact of unions on a firm's competitive advantage.
- Explain the structure and membership patterns of unions.
- Describe the provisions of the major labor laws.
- Discuss how workers become unionized.
- Understand how collective bargaining agreements are negotiated and administered.

12-1 Gaining Competitive Advantage

12-1a Opening Case: Gaining Competitive Advantage at the Saturn Corporation[1]

Problem: Regaining Lost Market Share in the American Automotive Industry

The American automotive industry began losing market share to foreign imports in the early 1980s. The American public became convinced that Japanese cars were superior to American cars, providing better quality, dependability, and value. As their market share continued to shrink, inventory of finished American cars grew beyond acceptable limits. This problem led to an alarming number of layoffs in the U.S. automotive industry—300,000 in 1982 alone.

General Motors and the United Auto Workers (UAW) union were both hit hard by this "Japanese invasion." Declining profits caused GM to close many of its plants; UAW membership also declined during this period.

The Solution: Establishing a Cooperative Relationship between Management and Labor at the Saturn Corporation

In 1985, GM Chairman Roger Smith announced the creation of the Saturn Corporation. Saturn's goal was to produce high-quality, affordable automobiles in hopes of recapturing market share that had been seized by foreign competitors. To achieve this goal, Smith realized that Saturn's management strategies and practices needed to change from the traditional methods used at other GM plants. He also realized that Saturn's success would require a unique collaborative relationship between labor unions and management to replace their traditional adversarial relationship.

The first step was to form a feasibility study team comprised of GM management and their counterparts at the UAW. The team studied management practices worldwide to find those that would best fit the needs at Saturn. The entire spectrum of issues was examined. Neither party placed limits on topics for discussion; no idea was considered too far-fetched to be discussed.

The union–management team eventually formulated a management strategy that responds to both employee and company needs—one that promotes teamwork and encourages open communication. The strategy empowers team members to participate in decision making about matters that affect them. Specifically, the working agreement between Saturn and the UAW specifies that:

- The entire blue-collar workforce will be organized into self-directed work teams of about 100 employees. Each team has two "advisors," one being a union member; the other, a member of management.

- All decisions will be made through a consensus process, granting the union status as a full partner.
- All levels of the corporation will be governed by joint labor–management committees.

The team concept and the union–management partnership have allowed union team members an unparalleled voice in job design. Saturn's union leadership has access to far more information and decision-making opportunities than most progressive labor organizations, domestic or foreign.

How the Cooperative Relationship Enhanced Competitive Advantage

Has Saturn made strides toward regaining the competitive advantage earned by the Japanese? The answer is a resounding "yes." Researcher Saul Rubinstein collected data for 18 months on the success of this labor-management partnership. He concluded that Saturn's performance, particularly quality, was improved because of the enhanced interdepartmental coordination, more rapid response to problems, and better solutions through a greater flow of ideas. Because of the improved quality of its products, customers have overwhelmingly embraced Saturn cars as high-value and technologically advanced. J.D. Power and Associates, an independent automotive analyst, has rated Saturn's cars higher than all other brands with the exception of the more expensive Lexus and Infiniti. In 2000, Saturn won the following awards for excellence:

- J.D. Power rated it first in customer satisfaction.
- It won the *MotorWeek* Driver's Choice Award.
- IntelliChoice selected it as "The Best Overall Value of the Year."
- The SL and SW models were rated as "The Best Bets for 2000" by *The Car Book*.

In 2004 Saturn's Ion and Vue earned Strategic Vision's 2004 Total Quality Award for small and midsized SUVs.

12-1b Linking Unions to Competitive Advantage

Preceding chapters have emphasized that employment relationships are very important to workers. When employers are insensitive to worker needs, and when workers are powerless to redefine their working conditions to make their work more fulfilling, they seek some means to represent their interests more forcefully to their employer. Often they turn to a form of collective action, which may lead to formation of a union that will give workers a voice in shaping the employment relationship.

Unions are labor organizations "of any kind . . . in which employees participate and which exist for the purpose, in whole or in part, of dealing with employers concerning grievances, labor disputes, wages, rates of pay, hours of employment, or conditions of work."[2] Acting in concert, workers promote and protect what they perceive to be their collective interest by bargaining with representatives of the company.

We now discuss the role of labor and management relations in achieving a competitive advantage.

Containing HR-Related Costs

Employers can contain their HR-related costs by maintaining a union-free environment. The costs of operating in a unionized environment are much higher due to higher salaries and more generous benefit plans.[3] Consequently, most firms try to avoid unionization if they can. As we later discuss, companies can accomplish this feat by treating employees fairly and preventing them from becoming dissatisfied with their jobs.

Gaining Competitive Advantage at a Paper Mill

Industrial relations researcher Casey Ichniowski investigated the transformation in union–management relations at a paper mill between 1976 and 1990. During the first six years of the study, the mill's grievance rates and strike frequency were among the highest in the industry, and its productivity was among the lowest.

The 1983 contract between the company and the two United Paperworkers International Union locals changed HRM practices drastically. Most importantly, they implemented a "team concept," which brought about the following changes:

- Reclassified jobs into four broad categories
- Increased compensation
- Trained multiskilled workers capable of carrying out the broadened responsibilities in each of the new job categories

- Conducted employee attitude surveys to determine the workers' needs/wishes
- Held manager "listening" sessions with workers

As a consequence of these changes, the plant experienced dramatic gains in productivity and profitability. Further, grievance rates declined and strike activity ceased.

Source: Ichniowski, C. (1992). Human resource practices and productive labor-management relations. In D. Lewin, O.S. Mitchell, and P.D. Sherer (eds.). *Research Frontiers in Industrial Relations.* Madison, WI: IRRA.

Enhancing Productivity

Most managers believe that unions typically affect productivity in a negative way. They reason that the restrictive work rules and other union-imposed constraints on employers only hinder an organization's attempt to maximize productivity and profitability. However, much of the evidence points to just the opposite effect—unionized firms are often more productive than similar nonunion companies.[4]

The key issue here is the ability of the two parties, labor and management, to work well together. The opening case illustrates the progress that firms can make when management and unions work together effectively. The gain in competitive advantage experienced by the paper mill depicted in On the Road to Competitive Advantage 12-1 provides a further example. As a general rule, when relations between the parties are positive, unionization is associated with higher firm productivity. Conversely, when union–management relations are negative, unionization is associated with lower firm productivity.[5] Even when more productive, however, unionized firms are typically not as profitable as similar nonunion companies, as increases in productivity rarely offset the increased HR-related costs.

12-2 HRM Issues and Practices

12-2a Unions Today

The desire of working people for collective representation has a rich and vivid history. It is a story filled with charismatic figures and fierce (sometimes violent) struggle. The history of the labor movement in the United States is recounted in the appendix to this chapter. (Exhibit 12-6 following the appendix lists the important dates in the history of the labor movement.) In this section, we take a look at the current structure of unions and their membership patterns.

[Handwritten margin note: Unions: in which employees participate & exist for the purpose in whole or in part of dealing w/ employers concerning grievances, benefits, labor, safety.]

1900's-Unions were effective-safety regulations-for vast factories

The Structure of Unions

Local Unions

local union The union that directly represents the interests of its members.

The **local union** is where workers and their representatives interact most frequently and, consequently, it is the focus of everyday union–management relations. Members must pay dues to the local for the representation it provides.

Basically, local unions play two roles. First, they identify and negotiate plant (local) issues in national collective bargaining agreements. Local officials must be aware of members' views about all aspects of their working conditions in order to represent their constituents' interests effectively in the negotiations.

Second, local unions administer collective bargaining agreements or contracts, i.e., they ensure that the contract provisions are being followed. When members believe they have been denied an entitlement promised by the contract (e.g., the right to overtime work that is guaranteed by his or her seniority), the union will file a grievance to assure that terms of the contract are fulfilled.

National Unions

national unions Unions that represent workers throughout the country in a particular craft or in a specific industry.

National unions represent workers throughout the country in a particular craft or in a specific industry. Many national unions refer to themselves as international unions because they represent Canadian as well as American workers. National unions negotiate major labor contracts with large employers (e.g., those in the auto-motive and commercial aviation industries) and organize new local unions among unrepresented workers.

Most local unions must be chartered from parent national unions. Charters provide locals with professional services offered by the national union (e.g., assistance with collective bargaining and grievance administration). They also constrain the behavior of locals (e.g., preventing strikes or contract ratification without prior approval of the national). Locals pay dues to the national union for the staff and services it provides; the amount of dues locals pay is based on the size of their memberships.

The AFL-CIO

American Federation of Labor and Congress of Industrial Organizations (AFL-CIO) An organization that promotes cooperation among national unions in order to pursue organized labor's common objectives.

To amplify organized labor's voice, almost all large national unions join the **American Federation of Labor and Congress of Industrial Organizations (AFL-CIO).** Membership in the AFL-CIO is voluntary. Some important unions, like the United Electrical Workers and the National Education Association, are not affiliated with the AFL-CIO. Member unions lose none of their autonomy by joining the federation. The AFL-CIO has no power to intervene in the internal affairs of unions (e.g., it cannot interfere in union decisions about striking, bargaining, or assessing dues).

The AFL-CIO promotes cooperation among national unions in order to pursue organized labor's common objectives. Article XX of the federation's constitution establishes a dispute resolution procedure whereby complaints filed by one member union against another are settled by means of mediation and/or arbitration. The AFL-CIO also represents organized labor in political forums, providing lobbyists for legislative bodies and supporting pro-union candidates for elected public office.

Union Membership Patterns

U.S. union membership is difficult to estimate because of the absence of reliable reports on membership from the unions themselves.[6] Nonetheless, the Bureau of Labor Statistics estimates that approximately 15.4 million workers, or 12.5 percent of employed wage and salary workers, were represented by unions in 2004.[7] In 1960, this figure was 31.4 percent.[8]

Although the percentage of union workers has declined, unions continue to represent a large number of workers in the following industries: government, manufacturing, and transportation/public utilities.[9] Moreover, most large industrial corporations are unionized. For example, the United Automobile Workers (UAW) union represents employees at the Big Three American carmakers (General Motors, Ford, and DaimlerChrysler) and several joint ventures of Japanese and American automotive firms (e.g., New United Motor Manufacturing, Inc., the alliance between General Motors and Toyota formed to build Chevrolet Novas). The United Steelworkers represents employees in the major basic steel companies in the United States, and 12 industrial and craft unions coordinate bargaining with General Electric and Westinghouse Corporations.

Explaining the Decline in Union Membership

Opinion polls consistently reveal that union membership is desired by many more workers than are actually represented by unions, especially female employees.[10] What, then, accounts for union membership's consistent decline during the past 30 years?

Three explanations have been offered. The first emphasizes the shift in employment away from manufacturing, a traditional union stronghold, to service occupations, a sector in which unions have had little appeal. Although it is a popular explanation for the decline, research shows that structural changes in employment account for less than 25 percent of the decline.[11]

Second, and more important, employers generally oppose unions in this country and have always taken an aggressive stance against them. For example, in the 1920s and 1930s, they tried to discredit unions in the eyes of workers and provided them with several alternatives to unionism. For instance, employers advertised the "American plan," which stressed "rugged individualism" as a traditional American value in opposition to the "foreign" and "subversive" principles espoused by unions. Employers also established "company unions" that bore a superficial resemblance to unions in the sense that workforce representatives met with management to discuss working conditions. Because employers chose employee representatives and could veto any ideas presented in meetings with the representatives, company unions were merely a facade and were eventually outlawed by the Wagner Act.[12]

Today, employers continue to strongly oppose unions, but they use strategies that are more effective. These union prevention strategies are described in Section 12-3, "The Manager's Guide."

Third and perhaps most important, union membership has declined because employers often find permanent replacements for striking employees, diminishing the impact of the union's most powerful tool—the strike. According to a 1938 Supreme Court ruling, employers may hire permanent replacements for striking workers if striking because of economic issues such as pay, benefits, or better conditions of work.[13] Replaced strikers are guaranteed a preferential claim to the jobs they lost only if their replacements relinquished the work for some reason (e.g., retirement).

The use of replacement workers has been increasing since the 1981 replacement of striking air traffic controllers by President Reagan. For example, when 6,300 Greyhound drivers struck in March 1990, the company had 700 recruits ready and 900 in training.[14]

12-2b Labor Law

Key legislative actions pertaining to unions are described in the following sections.

Early Judicial Decisions

Because of its rulings in celebrated labor disputes in the nineteenth century (see the appendix at the end of this chapter), the judiciary quickly established a reputation as a strong ally of American business. In particular, courts had been quite willing to invoke antitrust legislation to prevent unions from taking "job actions" (e.g., strikes, boycotts). For example, when the American Railway Union struck against the Pullman Palace Car Company in 1894, employees were forced back to work by a federal judge who characterized the strike as a restraint of trade.[15] The United Hatters of North America's boycott against the Dietrich Loewe Company ended when the U.S. Supreme Court ruled it unlawful because the boycott limited the marketing of goods transported from one state to another.[16]

Finally, a Supreme Court ruling allowed employers to issue **yellow-dog contracts,** workers' promises that they would not organize, support, or join a union if the company hired them. The United Mine Workers (UMW) had tried to organize workers who had signed yellow-dog contracts. The Court enjoined the UMW, reasoning that by inducing workers to join the union, it was encouraging them to break valid (yellow-dog) contracts.[17]

yellow-dog contracts Now illegal, these contracts stipulate that workers will not organize, support, or join a union if hired by the company.

The Railway Labor Act

The 1926 passage of the **Railway Labor Act (RLA)** marked the beginning of a new era of government regulation of union–management relations, one that involved greater acceptance of unionism and collective bargaining. Although the railroad industry had long been subject to collective bargaining, the RLA provided a federal guarantee of railroad employees' rights to choose a bargaining agent. Further, the act compelled the railroads to bargain with the employees' representative and established federal machinery to resolve labor disputes.

Railway Labor Act (RLA) A law that compels railroads to bargain with employees' representatives and established mechanisms to resolve labor disputes.

The Norris-LaGuardia Act

In 1932, Congress passed the **Norris-LaGuardia Act,** which sharply curtailed the courts' involvement in labor disputes by limiting judges' powers to issue injunctions that restrained worker job actions. Although employers could still request injunctions, the court would grant them only if employers could show "substantial and irreparable injury" to their property. Further, injunctions had to identify the specific union conduct that was forbidden. The Norris-LaGuardia Act also declared yellow-dog contracts unlawful.

Norris-LaGuardia Act A law that limits judges' powers to issue injunctions that restrain worker job actions.

The National Labor Relations Act (Wagner Act)

The **National Labor Relations Act (Wagner Act),** passed in 1935, gave workers in most industries the right to form unions and bargain collectively without being subject to coercion by their employers. The act characterized the employer practices that would be considered as coercive or unfair, such as the following behaviors:

National Labor Relations Act (Wagner Act) Law giving workers the right to form unions and bargain collectively without being subject to coercion by their employers.

- Interfering with the workers' right of self-organization
- Discriminating against employees for engaging in union activities
- Refusing to bargain with employee representatives

A more complete listing of such behavior is shown in Exhibit 12-1.

The Wagner Act also established the **certification election** process to determine whether a majority of workers in a company wanted union representation, and it cre-

certification election An election to determine whether company workers want union representation.

EXHIBIT 12-1	Partial List of Unfair Labor Practices

• Threatening employees with loss of jobs or other reprisals	• Discriminating against union members in terms and conditions of employment:
• Questioning employees about their union sympathies in a coercive way	• Transferring a union activist to a worse shift
• Using industrial spies	• Providing nonunion employees with a higher salary than union members are paid
• Exhibiting violence against union activists	• Violating seniority rules
• Referring to union members as thugs, etc.	• Discharging a woman because of husband's union membership
• Discharging workers because they are union members or promote the formation of a union	• Closing a plant simply to send a message to workers in other plants that the firm "means business"
• Refusing employment to persons because of their former or current membership in a union	

ated the **National Labor Relations Board (NLRB)** to supervise certification elections and enforce the law. The board is comprised of five members appointed by the president to five-year terms.

Labor–Management Relations Act (Taft-Hartley Act)

In 1947, the NLRA was amended by the **Labor–Management Relations Act (Taft-Hartley Act).** At the time, the American public was somewhat disenchanted with unions, primarily because of an epidemic of strikes following World War II. Congress wanted to impose restraints on organized labor. The Taft-Hartley Act tried to restore a balance of power between employers and unions. The act made it possible for union members to rid themselves of their union by means of a **decertification election.** It also specified a set of unfair union labor practices, including:

- Coercing employees who are trying to exercise their collective bargaining rights
- Pressuring employers to discriminate against an employee or applicant because he or she is not a union member
- Refusing to bargain in good faith with an employer
- Forcing employers to pay for unneeded services, such as hiring more employees than are needed

The Taft-Hartley Act also gave the president of the United States the right to intervene in national emergency strikes (i.e., strikes that affect an entire industry in a way that imperils national health or safety). The president may prohibit workers from striking for 80 days, thereby giving the parties further opportunity to resolve any problems standing in the way of signing a collective bargaining agreement.

Last, the Taft-Hartley Act allowed states to pass legislation that would outlaw **closed shops,** companies that require union membership as a condition of employment. In "right-to-work states," **open shops** are the rule. Employees covered by the contract do not have to join the union nor may they be assessed a fee for the union representation from which they benefit. Union membership is thus purely voluntary. Twenty-two states, identified in Figure 12-1, have passed right-to-work legislation.

> **National Labor Relations Board (NLRB)** Created by the Wagner Act to supervise certification elections and enforce the law.
>
> **Labor–Management Relations Act (Taft-Hartley Act)** A law aiming to restore the balance of power between employers and unions.
>
> **decertification election** An election in which union members vote on whether they want their union to continue representing them.
>
> **closed shops** Companies that require union membership as a condition of employment.
>
> **open shops** Companies in which employees covered by the contract do not have to join the union or be assessed a fee for union representation.

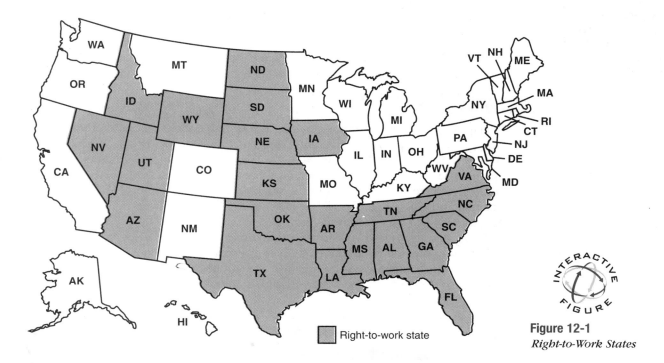

☐ Right-to-work state

Figure 12-1
Right-to-Work States

The Labor–Management Reporting and Disclosure Act (Landrum-Griffin Act)

Labor–Management Reporting and Disclosure Act (Landrum-Griffin Act)
Law designed to prevent corruption by regulating the internal affairs of unions.

The last major piece of federal legislation that focused on union activities was the **Labor–Management Reporting and Disclosure Act (Landrum-Griffin Act)** of 1959. Passed by Congress after a series of widely publicized hearings dealing with corruption in organized labor, this act regulated the internal affairs of unions. A bill of rights specified rules for nominating candidates for union office, holding elections, and disciplining members. The act also required unions to submit reports of all financial expenditures to discourage officers from using union funds for personal matters.

unions contributed to org. crime

12-2c Becoming Unionized

This section deals with the issues of why and how workers become unionized.

Why Do Workers Join Unions?

The major benefits accrued by joining a union are contained in the following list:

1. Higher salaries
2. Better benefits
3. Ability to speak one's mind without fear of reprisal
4. Better job security
5. Protection against unfair treatment
6. Gaining a sense of identity/unity

Although all workers value these things, why do only some workers choose to become unionized? Remember, only 14 percent of today's workforce is unionized. The reasons why workers join unions have been studied for years. The two found to be most important are job dissatisfaction and union instrumentality.

1. *Job Dissatisfaction*

Overall, this body of research indicates that worker job satisfaction is strongly associated with both the level of union organizing activity in a firm and the actual support of union representation among employees.[18] If workers are dissatisfied with bread-and-butter issues such as pay, job security, and supervisory practices, they are likely to unionize. Dissatisfaction with task characteristics, such as the sense of control over one's work and working conditions, also encourages individuals to join unions.[19]

2. *Union Instrumentality*

In general, job dissatisfaction is a necessary, but not sufficient, condition for an individual to become interested in union representation. Other, more specific job-related attitudes also play an important role. In particular, dissatisfied workers will seek union representation when they perceive that (1) acting as individuals, they are powerless to change the conditions in the workplace that are responsible for the dissatisfaction and (2) a large enough coalition of like-minded coworkers could improve conditions by taking collective action.[20]

union instrumentality The perceived ability of the union to provide important benefits to the worker.

This latter idea is known as **union instrumentality**, i.e., the perceived ability of the union to provide important benefits to the worker (e.g., eliminate sources of job dissatisfaction). The decision to organize a union is thus based on whether employees believe that they will be better off with a union than without one.[21]

How Do Workers Become Unionized? The Union Organizing Campaign

Establishing a union involves a complicated process consisting of three steps or phases: petition, election, and certification (see Figure 12-2). The process is not complete until the newly recognized union and the employer conclude negotiations on a collective bargaining agreement. We now discuss this process.

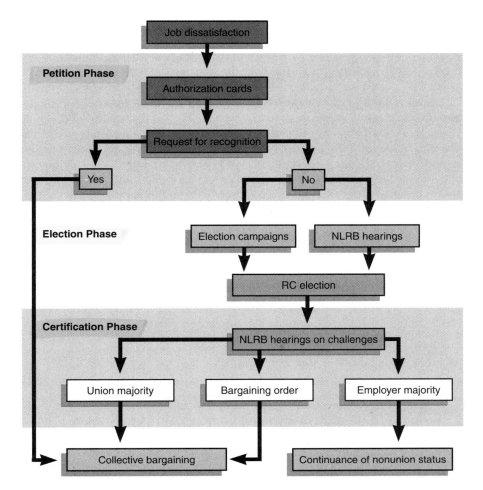

Figure 12-2
A Union Organizing Campaign

The Petition Phase — *hardest phase — where most $ is spent (to stop process)*

During the **petition phase,** workers express initial interest in union representation by signing authorization cards that empower a union to represent them in collective bargaining with the employer. The wording on these cards must state that the signer is authorizing bargaining rights to the union, and not simply expressing an interest in holding a certification election. Under current rules, at least 30 percent of eligible workers must sign authorization cards for there to be a sufficient "showing of interest" to trigger NLRB involvement in the certification process.[22] In practical terms, though, a union has little chance of winning an election if less than 50 percent of the workers sign these cards.[23]

The petition phase culminates when the union asks the employer for recognition as the bargaining representative of the workers. Such a request is often accompanied by some form of evidence (usually the signed authorization cards) that a majority of the employees want collective bargaining. Most employers deny such requests, forcing the union to petition the NLRB to hold a certification election.

The Election Phase

The **election phase** consists of three steps. First, the NLRB conducts representation hearings to determine the appropriate bargaining unit. The **bargaining unit** consists of those jobs or positions in which two or more employees share common employment interests and working conditions (e.g., similar duties, hours of work, compensation, production methods, and overall supervision). When such a community of interests exists, those workers may be reasonably grouped together to bargain collectively.

petition phase First phase of a certification election in which workers express initial interest in union representation.

election phase Second phase of a certification election, culminating in the actual election vote.

bargaining unit Positions covered by a bargaining agreement in which two or more employees share common employment interests and working conditions.

The NLRB's discretion to approve bargaining units is not unlimited. For example, professional employees cannot be included in the same bargaining unit with nonprofessional employees unless a majority of these professionals vote to be included in a mixed unit.[24] Also, given the potential threat to an employer's property in the event of a strike, plant guards cannot be included in bargaining units with nonguards.[25]

The second step of the election phase involves campaigning by both the union and the employer. Unions are at a disadvantage here because they have less access to workers in the bargaining unit than employers do. Therefore, employers must provide the union with the names, addresses, and telephone numbers of their employees within seven days after the parties consent to an election.[26] Most union organizing activity within firms takes place on the employees' own time and in nonwork areas. Union organizers make home visits to employees and distribute literature (handbills) at plant gates.

NLRB rules closely regulate employer conduct during anti-union campaigns. Employers may not give employees false or misleading information about the union. Although employers may certainly communicate their views about unionization (i.e., express clear preferences for staying nonunion), they may not threaten employees for pro-union activities. Nor may employers promise benefits to employees if they reject the union. Further, employers are forbidden to interrogate employees about their union sentiments. Exhibit 12-2 displays a more complete list of the NLRB's do's and don'ts for employers.

The third step is the election, itself, which is typically held on-site at the company. The NLRB requests that the union and the employer supply election observers to ensure that voters are members of the sanctioned bargaining unit. No one may be present in the polling area during the election except NLRB representatives and designated observers.

The Certification Phase

When the election process is completed, the NLRB certifies the results. As long as the NLRB does not find misconduct, they require a simple majority by either party to win the election. Should the employer receive a majority of the votes, the firm is not required to bargain and may continue to operate without a union. If the union wins, the employer must accept the union as the employees' collective bargaining agent.

> **EXHIBIT 12-2** | Employer Do's and Don't's for an Election Campaign

Employers May:

- Communicate to employees their preference for staying nonunion
- Hold "captive audience speeches" on company premises in an attempt to sway employees not to vote for the union
- Allow supervisors to campaign on behalf of management by holding union-related discussions with individual workers or small groups of workers
- Impose a "no solicitation" rule that forbids employees from discussing union matters on company time
- Ban a nonemployee union organizer from company property if the union has a reasonable alternative means of reaching individual employees with the union message, such as through home visits

Employers May Not:

- Give employees false or misleading information about the union
- Promise benefits to employees contingent upon their rejection of the union
- Hold a captive audience speech within 24 hours of the election
- Allow supervisors to discuss union-related matters with employees in an area where employees normally go to discuss management matters (e.g., plant manager's office)
- Threaten/coerce employees by engaging in any of the following actions:
  - Threaten to close or move plant
  - Deny wage increase or threaten wage reduction
  - Eliminate any existing benefits
  - Threaten to fire union supporters
  - Interrogate employees about their union sentiments (if coercive)

Either the employer or the union may file objections to the election within five days. These objections may be related to conduct by either party that affects the outcome of the elections.

After its deliberations, the NLRB may dismiss the charges and certify the election results, or it may order a rerun election. If the NLRB holds a rerun election, it may require the guilty party to publicly acknowledge misconduct during the initial campaign. If the NLRB finds evidence of gross misconduct on the part of the employer during the campaign, it may issue a **bargaining order.** A bargaining order directs an employer to accept collective bargaining with the union even if the employer won the election. The NLRB reasons that when an employer is guilty of outrageous and pervasive unfair labor practices, it not only undermines the union's authorization card majority but also intimidates workers to the point that a fair rerun election is not possible. The Supreme Court upheld the right of the NLRB to issue bargaining orders in a 1969 decision.[27]

bargaining order Issued by the NLRB, it directs an employer to accept collective bargaining with the union even if the employer won the election.

12-2d The Collective Bargaining Agreement

Collective bargaining is a system for governing relations between representatives of employers and employees through bilateral negotiations to reach mutual agreement about employment terms. This mutual agreement, called a **collective bargaining agreement,** covers all members of the bargaining unit, regardless of whether they are members of the union.

collective bargaining A system for governing relations between representatives of employers and employees through bilateral negotiations to reach mutual agreement about employment terms.

collective bargaining agreement The labor-management contract resulting from the collective bargaining process.

Negotiating a Collective Bargaining Agreement

Collective bargaining can take many forms. No one form is considered more effective; each was developed to deal with the particular characteristics of given industries and their unions. For instance, in some industries, such as coal mining, a single union negotiates a master contract with representatives of the various employers. In the automotive industry, "pattern bargaining" takes place: The agreement negotiated with one company is used as a prototype for other bargaining agreements. For example, the UAW selects one of the Big Three automakers as a target for negotiations. The other companies would typically ratify the agreement worked out in those negotiations, perhaps with a few minor changes. Yet, another form of bargaining takes place at major metropolitan newspapers, which traditionally bargain with as many as a dozen different unions such as the Pressman, Photoengravers, and American Newspaper Guild.

Preparation for Collective Bargaining

Both unions and management do a lot of preliminary work before actual negotiations ever start. For example, information must be gathered about contract settlements that are relevant to the bargaining, such as those in firms that produce similar goods and services. Both parties also must estimate the costs of their initial offers at the bargaining table. Finally, in the case of ongoing contractual relationships (as opposed to the negotiation of a first contract), both parties must examine their experience in attempting to administer the current contract. For example, if experience reveals that particular provisions of the contract were misunderstood and led to numerous grievances, the parties may wish to clarify the language in these sections of the agreement. Exhibit 12-3 lists the demands that unions typically make during negotiations.

Establishing a Bargaining Agenda

Both parties establish a bargaining agenda by identifying issues about which they want to bargain. NLRB rulings and various labor laws have defined three categories of bargaining items:

> **EXHIBIT 12-3** | Typical Union Demands

Compensation Issues

- Pay and benefits should be at or above that paid by the company's competitors.
- Workers should be given yearly cost-of-living adjustments (colas).
- Pay raises should be based on seniority.
- Shift differentials should be paid to 2nd and 3rd shift workers.
- Workers should be given paid time off for holidays, vacations, and sick leave.

Nonpay Issues

- Workers cannot be disciplined or discharged unless the employer can provide "just cause."

- Arbitration will be used to settle any grievance that cannot be settled to the satisfaction of both parties.
- The organization must take steps to ensure decent and safe working conditions for all workers.
- The following employment decisions will be based on seniority:
  - Shift choice
  - Overtime preference
  - Vacations
  - Promotions
  - Layoffs

[handwritten margin note: Cannot be bargained drinking, smoking on job]

Illegal bargaining items are matters about which bargaining is not permitted by law. For example, union security arrangements (e.g., closed and open shops) cannot be negotiated in right-to-work states.

[handwritten margin note: must be bargained]

2. Mandatory bargaining items are issues that must be negotiated if either party brings these matters to the table. Refusal to bargain about a mandatory item is considered an unfair labor practice. The NLRB has declared approximately 70 items to be mandatory items; some of these are presented in Exhibit 12-4.

3. Voluntary or permissive bargaining items (see examples in Exhibit 12-4) become part of the negotiations only if both parties agree to discuss them. Neither party can be compelled against its wishes to negotiate permissive items, and refusal to discuss these matters is not considered an unfair labor practice. Should the parties decide to negotiate a permissive item, failure to reach an accord on the matter cannot delay concluding a contract.

Choosing a Bargaining Strategy

Before actual negotiations take place, each party must decide on its priorities among bargaining items. Obviously, each party must attempt to conceal its priorities, although as the bargaining proceeds, the relative importance of each item will become apparent to experienced negotiators for the other side.

Priorities play a major role in determining bargaining strategy. For example, two items about which an employer may wish to bargain could be health benefits and

---

> **EXHIBIT 12-4** | Mandatory and Voluntary Bargaining Items

Mandatory Items

- Wages
- Hours of work
- Plant rules
- Work and production standards
- Pension and employee benefit plans
- Vacations and holidays
- Profit-sharing plans
- Reassignment of work from one group to another
- Successorship clause that would require a new owner of the business to assume the old employer's contractual obligation
- Grievance procedures
- In-plant food services and prices

- Management rights
- Polygraph testing of employees
- Decision to close a portion of a business and terminate workers

Voluntary Items

- Pensions and other benefits for persons previously retired
- Union participation in the establishment of company product prices
- Abandonment of company strike insurance plan
- Technological change in production methods
- Industry promotion plans

staffing rules that mandate work crew size. If the employer gives health benefits a greater priority than staffing, it may drop its demands for changes in staffing levels if the union agrees to make concessions on the health benefit issue.

Each party must also establish a range of bargaining objectives when preparing for negotiations. Using all of the information at its disposal about factors that influence settlement levels, each party estimates three bargaining objectives for each item to be negotiated:

1. The realistic bargaining objective is the expected value of the final settlement on a particular bargaining issue. Based on assessments of the climate for the negotiations (e.g., the degree of conflict apparent between the parties prior to the start of bargaining) and patterns or trends in other contracts in related companies, the realistic objective represents the settlement level perceived to be most likely for a particular bargaining item.

2. The optimistic bargaining objective indicates the most favorable settlement level perceived as possible by each party. Though not as likely to be achieved as the realistic objective, the optimistic objective is within the realm of possibility if negotiations unfold favorably.

3. The pessimistic bargaining objective represents the least favorable settlement that a party is willing to accept on a given negotiated issue. If the bargaining goes poorly for one of the parties, it will reluctantly settle at this pessimistic objective.

Figure 12-3 provides an example of union and management's optimistic and pessimistic bargaining objectives for staffing levels for production crews. Taken together, the bargaining ranges for the two parties jointly define the settlement range, which is the range acceptable to both parties.

Engaging in Good Faith Bargaining

Regardless of the bargaining strategy adopted, both parties must legally engage in **good faith bargaining;** the failure to do so is an unfair labor practice.[28] As defined by the Taft-Hartley Act, bargaining in good faith obliges both parties "to meet at reasonable times and confer in good faith with respect to wages, hours, and other terms and conditions of employment."[29]

good faith bargaining
Obliges both management and labor to meet at reasonable times and confer in good faith with respect to wages, hours, and other terms and conditions of employment.

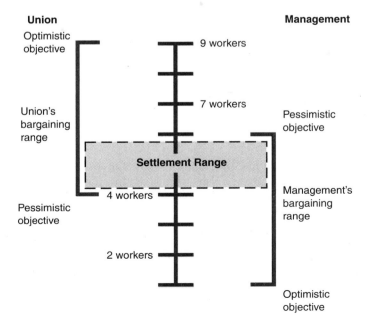

Figure 12-3
Bargaining Objectives for Staffing Requirements for Production Work Crews

A Case of Cooperative Bargaining at Xerox

The partnership between the management of Xerox's Webster plant and the Amalgamated Clothing and Textile Workers Union (which represents many of Xerox's production workers) is an example of how a company and a union can develop a shared business vision that involves workers in both operational and strategic issues. Employee representatives work side-by-side with management on two committees: the executive and policy committee and the joint planning committee. The executive and policy committees meet semiannually to establish strategic goals; the joint planning committee meets quarterly to determine how strategic plans will be implemented.

These joint committees are a significant expression of mutual respect between ACTWU and Xerox management. Consisting of approximately equal numbers of management and union representatives, these committees offer excellent opportunities for tapping knowledge, sharing information, and obtaining support for decisions from both sides. This type of cooperative activity has also spilled over into the collective bargaining process, which is expanded as joint decision making creates implicit contracts that are often made explicit in memos and company documents. In essence, negotiating becomes an ongoing process.

Source: For more information about this and other cooperative programs, see Applebaum, E., and Batt, R. (1993). American models of high-performance work systems. *Work Place Topics, 3* (1), 67–100.

The Taft-Hartley Act and its interpretation by the NLRB over the years have provided a number of guidelines for interpreting the meaning of the term "good faith." For instance, the act does not specifically compel either party to agree to a proposal or grant concessions in order to bargain in good faith. Further, the NLRB typically evaluates the totality of conduct by a party during the negotiations before determining whether it is bargaining in good or bad faith.

One type of bad faith bargaining is "surface bargaining"—presenting obviously unacceptable proposals or offering no alternative counterproposals. Bad faith bargaining may also include such tactics as complicating the scheduling of bargaining sessions or refusing to provide pertinent information. Finally, if the employer bypasses the official union bargaining representative and attempts to negotiate directly with its members, it would also be guilty of bargaining in bad faith.

Cooperative Bargaining

The relationship between management and a union need not be adversarial. As we saw in the opening case, the two parties can often work together for everyone's benefit. A partnership between management at Xerox's Webster plant and the Amalgamated Clothing and Textile Workers Union (ACTWU), illustrated in On the Road to Competitive Advantage 12-2, serves as another example of how a company and a union can develop a shared business vision that involves workers in both operational and strategic issues.

Administering a Collective Bargaining Agreement

After the union and the employer have negotiated a collective bargaining agreement, they are bound by its terms for the duration of the contract. Because the parties are likely to interpret contract provisions differently, disputes often arise. Therefore, both sides need some mechanism to fairly interpret the language of the agreement in specific situations.

grievance system A system that provides due process for claims of collective bargaining agreement violations.

Grievance Systems Defined

Contract disputes are resolved through a **grievance system.** Grievance systems are contractual provisions included in almost all collective bargaining agreements that provide due process for claims of contract violations. A **grievance,** which can be filed by either employees or employers, is an allegation that contract rights have been violated. Consider the following example:

> Suppose that a contract contains a provision that states that an employee will only be discharged for "just cause." A union member by the name of Mary Stevens insults her immediate supervisor in front of a number of other workers and managers. The company may believe that it has just cause for firing Mary; Mary may believe that such an extreme disciplinary action is unjust. This incident is likely to result in the union filing a grievance on behalf of Mary.

Common grievance issues include the following:

- Discipline and discharge
- Work assignments
- Employment decisions
- Production standards
- Working conditions
- Imposition of new rules

Role of Grievance Systems in Union–Management Relations

Grievance systems play at least two important roles in union–management relations. First, they provide a forum in which disagreements concerning violations of contract rights can be adjudicated. Thus, neither party must threaten or actually carry out some economic intimidation (e.g., a strike by the union or a lockout by the employer) in order to resolve the matter. Indeed, most contracts ban strikes and lockouts while the collective bargaining agreement is in force.

Second, grievance systems influence the way workers view organized labor. A survey of approximately 1,500 American workers revealed that grievance handling was considered the most important union activity.[30] The anticipation of assistance in resolving grievances has been found to differentiate workers who vote for union certification from those who vote against it.[31]

How Grievance Systems Operate

Typically, grievance systems incorporate three steps, although four-step procedures are not uncommon.[32] Figure 12-4 depicts these steps. The first step is the informal stage of the system during which the union steward (an employee who is elected to represent coworkers), the complainant, and the complainant's immediate supervisor try to resolve the matter before it is written up and becomes an official grievance. Succeeding steps in the system almost always involve higher level representatives of the union and employer.

→ Pg 354 fig.

The final step in virtually all grievance procedures is arbitration. **Arbitration** calls for a neutral third party to settle matters that cannot be resolved by bilateral discussions between union and management representatives. Support for the concept of grievance arbitration may be found in the Taft-Hartley Act:

> Final adjustment by a method agreed upon by the parties is hereby declared to be the desirable method for settlement of grievance disputes arising out of the application or interpretation of an existing collective bargaining agreement.[33]

What if the grieving employees believe that the union has not properly represented them? May they appeal an arbitrator's decision to the courts? The courts will generally refuse to hear such cases, unless employees can prove the union was grossly negligent in handling the grievance. Unions typically win 90 percent of such complaints.[34]

grievance An allegation that employer or employee contract rights have been violated.

arbitration A contract dispute mechanism in which a neutral third party settles matters that cannot be resolved by bilateral discussions between union and management representatives.

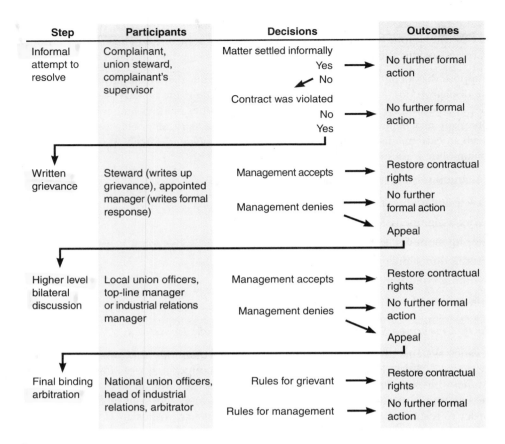

Figure 12-4
Steps in a Grievance System

12-3 The Manager's Guide

12-3a Unions and the Manager's Job

Line managers' roles differ in union and nonunion settings. In union settings, the focus is on adherence to the collective bargaining agreement; in nonunion settings, the focus is on union prevention.

Managing in a Union Setting

When managing in a union environment, managers must adhere to the provisions of collective bargaining agreements, which spell out procedures to be followed in such matters as work assignments, overtime, and employee discipline. Managers must be fully conversant with agreement provisions and must understand how grievance systems work. When conflicts arise, managers must try to resolve them before they mushroom into costly formal grievances. Conflict resolution skills are covered in Section 12-3c, "HRM Skill-Building for Managers."

Managing in a Nonunion Setting

As noted earlier, employees seek union representation when they believe the union can help eliminate sources of job dissatisfaction. Line managers' behavior can create job dissatisfaction among employees. According to one study, for instance, the basic underlying issue in approximately half of the union elections was arbitrary, tyrannical, and abusive supervisor behavior.[35]

Any management that gets a union deserves it—and they get the kind they deserve. No labor union has ever captured a group of employees without the full cooperation and encouragement of managers who create the need for unionization.[36]

Managers should manage in a way that keeps workers satisfied with their jobs or prevents them from becoming dissatisfied. In today's workplace, employees do not tolerate autocratic management tactics well. When managers use authority in abusive ways, workers often resist. As employees become more and more frustrated by this abuse, a "blow-up" often triggers union activity.[37]

To be effective, then, line managers must follow sound management principles: They must fairly allocate rewards and punishment and cultivate a climate that stresses open communication. Such management practices not only help a firm avoid unionization, but they also improve morale and productivity and thus enhance competitive advantage.

12-3b How the HRM Department Can Help

HRM departments in unionized firms help negotiate and administer collective bargaining agreements. In nonunionized firms, HR professionals often help devise union prevention strategies.

HRM Practices in a Union Setting

HR professionals must negotiate and consult with union officials about matters such as the assignment of workers to jobs, a range of compensation issues, and the administration of the collective bargaining agreement. Indeed, complying with the labor contract is the main focus of HRM practices in a unionized firm.

HRM Practices in a Nonunion Setting

HR professionals in nonunion settings often help devise strategies to prevent unionization. Various strategies have been used. Probably the best strategy is simply to utilize equitable HRM practices so that employees do not see any need for union representation.[38] For instance, many nonunion companies provide workers with a greater voice in determining work conditions and in installing their own formal grievance systems.[39]

Another union prevention strategy is the use of labor relations consultants. Typically, these consultants are either psychologists or attorneys who direct companies' efforts to prevent unions from gaining bargaining rights and guide efforts to decertify existing unions. They sometimes recommend employer resistance strategies that are unethical and/or illegal, such as:[40]

- Causing delays by means of legal challenges at every step of the organizing process
- Harassing or discharging workers who are leading the organizing campaign for the union
- Placing spies in the workplace

Although this form of consulting is reprehensible, it is nonetheless a growth industry because it helps achieve management's goal of remaining nonunion. For instance, research has found that consultant involvement has decreased the proportion of employees voting in favor of collective bargaining by 9 percent.[41] Further, for every month that certification elections can be delayed, the percentage of pro-union votes falls by approximately 0.5 percent, and the likelihood of the union prevailing drops by about 1 percent.[42] Even when a union wins the right to represent the workers in a company, consultants have prevented the negotiation of a first collective bargaining agreement in approximately 25 to 30 percent of their cases, thereby thwarting employees' desires for collective representation.[43]

An illustration of how such unethical behavior on the employer's part can thwart unionization attempts is presented On the Road to Competitive Advantage 12-3. After reviewing this and 129 other cases, industrial relations experts Richard Hurd and Joseph Uehlein argue that many employers have gone too far, disregarding the spirit and letter of labor law.[44] Such behavior can make it "virtually impossible for workers to achieve meaningful collective bargaining protections through the NLRB process."[45]

Has This Company Gone Too Far?

In February 1991, an organizing campaign was initiated by the International Association of Machinists (IAM) at Aero Metal Forms of Wichita, Kansas. This firm manufactures sheet-metal and fiberglass parts for the aircraft industry. A majority petition was signed within 10 days, and the president of the company was requested in writing to recognize the union. The president's response was to fire a union activist and an office employee who refused to perjure herself in connection with the dismissal of the activist.

After the IAM filed a petition for a representative election with the NLRB, the employer retained a law firm to advise and assist with the anti-union campaign. A series of captive audience speeches were held that warned employees that unionization would lead to strikes, and that the company was prepared to use its right to hire permanent replacements for strikers. The workers were further told that the company did not have to agree to union contract demands, and that negotiations could result in a loss of employee benefits because bargaining would start from scratch.

The campaign waged on the shop floor. Supervisors were trained to remain friendly and promise personal gains to workers who indicated that they would vote "no" to union representation. Union supporters were identified and harassed. One supporter received daily "in your face" harassment. One Friday morning, when he said, "I can't take it anymore," the owner suggested that he go home. The worker left and, upon returning on Monday, was informed that his action had been officially construed as quitting, and he was told he no longer had a job.

When the union election resulted in a tie vote (with three challenged ballots), the IAM filed several complaints about the campaign conduct of the company. The administrative law judge found the company guilty of unlawful interrogation, of threats of reprisal, and of illegal discharge of a union supporter. On appeal, the NLRB supported all of the previous rulings. It also reinstated the worker who was fired for failing to fabricate evidence against the union.

After considering the challenged ballots, the NLRB declared the IAM the winner of the election, seven votes to six. The union was certified about one year after the original election. However, by this time, all but one of the seven workers who voted for the union had been harassed into quitting, and union support was basically gone, making negotiation of a meaningful, collective bargaining agreement virtually impossible. The union can get none of the employees to participate in negotiations and expects to be decertified.

Source: Aero Metal Forms, Inc., and District 70, International Association of Machinists and Aerospace Workers, 310 NLRB No. 49, February 10, 1993.

12-3c HRM Skill-Building for Managers

As noted earlier, a manager's primary responsibility related to unionism is to engage in effective management practices. Perhaps the most important of these practices is managing interpersonal conflict. Conflicts invariably arise when dealing with subordinates. For instance, a head nurse may need to schedule half her staff to work on Christmas day. Conflict will almost surely arise when that choice is made as those selected begin asking "Why me?"

A manager's ability to handle conflict successfully is important in both union and nonunion settings. In union firms, failure to reach satisfactory resolutions could lead to formal grievances; in nonunion firms, it could create states of unrest that may eventually lead to union involvement.

Resolving Interpersonal Conflicts[46]

How should you respond when an interpersonal conflict arises? There are five possible approaches to handling such conflicts:

1. *Competition:* The manager sees this as a win-lose situation, and the aim is to win. The manager will thus try to impose his or her own will on the subordinate. For example, the head nurse referred to earlier could simply state that scheduling is her responsibility and that her decisions are final.

2. *Collaboration:* The manager attempts to resolve the conflict by searching for a solution that mutually benefits all parties concerned. For example, the head nurse could meet with the nurses and try to find an alternative solution to the scheduling problem that satisfies her and the other nurses.

find points of compromise

3. *Compromise:* This approach is similar to collaboration in that the parties search for an alternative to the original decision. With compromise, however, no solution is found that completely satisfies all parties; each must give up something. For example, the head nurse and her staff may agree that the Christmas schedule will stand as is, but may change the New Year's day schedule so that only those nurses off on Christmas will be assigned to work on New Year's.

4. *Avoidance:* In this approach, the manager is aware of the conflict, but chooses to ignore it. For example, the head nurse may hear the grumbling of those scheduled to work on Christmas, but refuse to discuss it openly.

5. *Accommodation:* Here, the manager simply gives in to the wishes of the employee. For example, if a particular nurse complains about working on Christmas, the head nurse would remove her from the schedule.

Although some conflict resolution strategies appear to be better than others, each has its place. The effectiveness of each strategy depends on the particular situation. The following listing identifies situations under which each strategy would be most appropriate:

Competition

1. When quick decisive action is vital
2. On important issues where unpopular actions need implementing
3. On issues vital to the organization's welfare, and when you know you are right
4. Against people who take advantage of noncompetitive behavior

Collaboration

1. To find an integrative solution when both sets of concerns are too important to be compromised
2. When your objective is to learn what your subordinates are thinking
3. To merge insights from people with different perspectives
4. To gain commitment by incorporating concerns into a consensus
5. To work through feelings that have interfered with a relationship

Compromise

1. When goals are important, but not worth the effort or potential disruption caused by using the competitive strategy
2. When opponents with equal power are committed to mutually exclusive goals
3. To achieve temporary settlements to complex issues
4. To arrive at expedient solutions under time pressure
5. To serve as a backup when collaboration is unsuccessful

Avoidance

1. When an issue is trivial, or more important issues are pressing
2. When you perceive no chance of satisfying your concerns
3. When potential disruption outweighs the benefits of resolution

4. To let people cool down and regain perspective

5. When gathering information supersedes immediate action

6. When others can resolve the conflict more successfully

7. When issues are merely symptomatic of a larger problem (the larger problem should be tackled)

Accommodation

1. When you find you are wrong—to allow a better decision to be made, to learn, and to show your reasonableness

2. When issues are more important to others than to you.

3. To build "social credits" for later, more important issues

4. To minimize loss when you are outmatched and losing

5. When harmony and stability are especially important

6. To allow subordinates to develop by learning from their mistakes.

Responding to an Employee Grievance[47]

Employees' grievances are often triggered by their managers' actions. The grievance may involve, for instance, an "unfair" performance appraisal, an unreasonable assignment, or perceived favoritism. These types of complaints can turn into formal grievances if the manager handles them improperly. When faced with this type of situation, you should follow these steps:

1. *Make an appointment to discuss the problem unless the problem is urgent and must be addressed immediately.* One reason for setting a time for another meeting is that you may be busy and thus unable to give the employee your full attention. This practice also gives the worker, who may be feeling very angry or upset, a chance to calm down.

2. *Do not become defensive, even if the complaint has no foundation.* When an employee complains to you about something you have done, do not attempt to "win" by successfully countering each argument with one of your own. Rather, view the situation as a problem that the two of you must work together to solve. Even when you feel the complaint has no foundation, you should respond empathetically. Show your interest through nonverbal behavior, such as posture (lean back with your arms uncrossed), facial expression, and eye contact.

3. *Let the person blow off some steam.* Give the worker an opportunity to "get it all out" without interruption. Employees will often calm down a bit after they have gotten their complaint off their chest. In some cases, just being able to express negative emotions to the boss will be enough to satisfy an employee.

4. *Set ground rules, if necessary.* If the worker begins verbally attacking you, it is probably a sign that he or she is more interested in hurting you than in solving a problem. When this happens, set some ground rules by calmly stating, "I'll be happy to discuss this problem with you, but we need to set some ground rules first. Let's stay away from any personal attacks."

5. *Redirect from accusations to specific behaviors.* To transform a personal complaint into a joint problem, you must redirect the conversation from general accusations to descriptions of specific behaviors. Ask for details about actions that form the basis for the complaints. For instance, if charged with favoritism, ask for specific examples. Check your level of understanding by summarizing the employee's main points and asking if your summary is correct.

6. *Agree with some aspect of the complaint without accepting all of its ramifications.* Demonstrate your concern for the employee by identifying aspects of the employee's complaint with which could can agree. This response demon-

strates your understanding of their point of view and your willingness to be reasonable: "You're right; I did give Tom an easier assignment than I gave you. Here's why . . ." If you cannot identify any areas of agreement, agree with the employee's perception of the problem: "I can understand why you thought I was playing favorites." Or "I can see why you would think that."

7. *Ask for suggestions of acceptable alternatives.* Change the tone of the conversation from negative to positive by asking the employee to suggest a specific solution rather than trying to determine who is right and wrong. For instance, ask: "What can I do in the future, so that this won't happen again?"

Chapter Objectives Revisited

1. Understand the impact of unions on a firm's competitive advantage.

   - Employers can contain their HR-related costs by maintaining a union-free environment. The costs of operating in a unionized environment are much higher due to higher salaries and more generous benefit plans.
   - In a union setting, employers can maximize productivity by establishing a harmonious relationship with the union.

2. Explain the structure and membership patterns of unions.

   - Locals: Identify and negotiate plant (local) issues in national collective bargaining agreements and administer collective bargaining agreements or contracts.
   - Nationals: Negotiate major labor contracts with large employers and organize new local unions among unrepresented workers.
   - The AFL-CIO: Promotes cooperation among national unions in order to pursue organized labors' common objectives.
   - Unions, mainly in government, manufacturing, and transportation/public utilities, represent about 14 percent of the U.S. workforce.

3. Describe the provisions of the major labor laws.

   - The Railway Labor Act: Provided a federal guarantee of railroad employees' rights to choose a bargaining agent
   - The Norris-LaGuardia Act: Sharply curtailed the courts' involvement in labor disputes by limiting judges' powers to issue injunctions that restrained workers' job actions
   - The National Labor Relations Act (Wagner Act): Gave workers in most industries the right to form unions and bargain collectively without being subject to coercion by their employers; established the certification election process to determine whether a majority of workers in a company wanted union representation; and created the National Labor Relations Board (NLRB) to supervise certification elections and enforce the law
   - The Labor–Management Relations Act (Taft-Hartley Act): Made it possible for union members to rid themselves of their union by means of a decertification election; specified a set of unfair union labor practices; gave the president of the United States the right to intervene in national emergency strikes; and allowed states to pass legislation that would outlaw closed shops
   - The Labor–Management Reporting and Disclosure Act (Landrum-Griffin Act): Regulated the internal affairs of unions

4. Discuss how workers become unionized.

   - Petition phase: Workers express initial interest in union representation by signing authorization cards that empower a union to represent them in collective bargaining with the employer.
   - Election phase: An election is held following union and management campaigns.
   - Certification phase: The NLRB certifies the union as the employees' collective bargaining agent if it receives a simple majority vote.

5. Understand how collective bargaining agreements are negotiated and administered.

   - Negotiation entails preparing, establishing a bargaining agenda, choosing a bargaining strategy, and bargaining in good faith.
   - Grievance systems are designed to resolve disputes between parties regarding contract interpretation.

Review Questions

Note: You can find the correct answers to these questions by taking the quiz and then submitting your answers in the Online Edition. The program will automatically score your submission. If you miss a question, the program will provide the correct answer, a rationale for the answer, and the section number in the chapter where the topic is discussed.

1. The AFL-CIO engages in all of the following activities on behalf of member unions *except*

   a. lobbying legislative bodies on issues of importance to organized labor.

   b. supporting pro-union candidates for public office.

   c. determining the fees that local unions may charge their members.

   d. providing a dispute resolution procedure to settle disputes by one union member against another.

2. Approximately what percent of the U.S. national labor force belongs to a union?

   a. less than 5 percent

   b. 15 percent

   c. 30 percent

   d. 50 percent

3. A yellow-dog contract is a contract

   a. in which workers promise not to organize, support, or join a union while working for their employer.

   b. that made workers members of the "company union."

   c. that protects a workers right to "blow the whistle" on health and safety violations.

   d. that punishes an employee for taking a job with a competitor of the firm with whom he/she currently works.

4. Which act gave workers in most industries the right to form unions and bargain collectively?

   a. Civil Rights Act of 1964

   b. Norris-LaGuardia Act

   c. National Labor Relations Act

   d. Railway Labor Act

5. Which of the following is *not* an unfair union labor practice as defined by the Labor–Management Relations Act?

   a. coercing employees who are trying to exercise their collective bargaining rights

   b. refusing to bargain in good faith with an employer

   c. pressuring employees to discriminate against nonunion employees

   d. striking for longer than 80 days

6. A bargaining unit consists of

   a. the union leadership that negotiates with management.

   b. both union and management negotiators.

   c. those jobs or positions in which common employment interests and working conditions are shared.

   d. the members of the National Labor Relations Board as well as union and management negotiators.

7. Which of the following items might represent an illegal bargaining item?

   a. pension benefits

   b. management rights

   c. grievance procedures

   d. closed-shop rules

8. The first step in resolving a labor contract dispute is to

   a. take the issue to arbitration.

   b. seek the help of the National Labor Relations Board.

   c. file a grievance.

   d. ask for a bargaining order.

9. During the election phase of union certification efforts

   a. unions have a distinct advantage over management because they have constant access to workers for organizing activities.

   b. management has the upper hand because unions are not permitted to communicate with workers within seven days of the election.

   c. the National Labor Relations Board is powerless to intervene.

   d. employers may not give employees false or misleading information about the union.

10. If the National Labor Relations Board finds evidence of gross misconduct during a union certification election, it will issue a

   a. restraining order.

   b. no-strike clause.

   c. bargaining order.

   d. injunction.

Discussion Questions

1. In what ways does the presence/absence of unions impact a firm's competitive advantage?

2. Why do employers typically resist unionization efforts?

3. Describe how the various labor laws have affected the balance of power between labor and management.

4. Describe the three phases of a union organizing campaign.

5. It was stated that employers must be careful during a union organizing campaign about what they say, when they say it, and where they say it. Explain.

6. Why do almost all collective bargaining agreements contain provisions that establish grievance systems?

7. Describe how a typical grievance system works.

8. What does it mean to be a committed union member? What is the basis for becoming a committed union member?

9. What is meant by the term *"right-to-work" state?*

10. Describe the various union prevention strategies used by employers.

Experiential Exercises

Assessing Local Labor–Management Relations

The class should be divided into two groups: one representing the union, the other management. Each group should proceed as follows:

1. The management group should make a list of three or four unionized employers in the vicinity. The union group should determine the identity of unions that represent the employees in these firms. If the employers will not supply this information, the state AFL-CIO organization can be contacted for this information, or there may be a local trade union council in the area that can furnish the information.

2. Check the local newspapers over the past three years for stories that report union–management issues at these employment sites (e.g., strikes, the settlement of a new collective bargaining agreement, a restructuring of the firm that may have necessitated the layoff of employees). This information should provide background for interviews with representatives of each party.

3. Conduct interviews. The management group should interview representatives of management. The union group should interview union representatives. During these interviews, collect information about each of the newsworthy events:

   • What was the basis for the event? For example, why did the strike occur? What necessitated the layoffs?

   • If the event was the negotiation of a contract, what major items did the union want to accomplish?

   • What did the employer want to accomplish? How does each of the parties feel about the eventual settlement?

   • Does the party perceive a need for a change in the labor legislation that regulates union-management relations in this country?

   • What do each of the parties believe are the workplace issues that lend themselves most to cooperation between the union and management?

4. When the members of the class return with this information, each union–management relationship should be discussed, one organization at a time. That is, those who interviewed a particular employer should present their findings. This presentation should be followed by that of the students who interviewed the union(s).

5. Compare the responses of the two parties after the presentation. Based on what has been reported (or not reported), can you estimate what the climate of union–management relations is like in the firm?

How Was That Conflict Resolved?

Break into groups of four or five students. Each group should identify a member who experienced a manager-subordinate conflict at work. The member should describe that conflict to the group and discuss how it was actually handled. The group members should then analyze the situation and determine whether the most appropriate conflict resolution strategy was used (see Section 12-3, "The Manager's Guide").

Each group should then make a presentation to the class. When presenting:

1. Describe the conflict situation.
2. Describe how it was actually handled.
3. Evaluate the handling of the conflict.
4. State whether there was a better way of handling the conflict and give your rationale. If you think it was handled properly, justify your conclusion.

Who Would Win This Grievance Case?

Divide into groups of four or five students. Review this case as an arbitrator would and determine whether the employer's actions should be upheld or overruled. Be prepared to discuss your group's rationale with the rest of the class.

Jan Golden, a forklift operator, was terminated from his job at the ABC Company.

What Jan Did

Jan was driving his forklift when another employee came by driving a box truck. Because the other employee was in Jan's way, Jan purposely ran into him and knocked the truck over. The employee was not hurt. When a witness confronted Jan about his behavior, Jan got belligerent and challenged him to a fight. The plant manager was told what happened. He then questioned other employees and learned the following: Jan continuously threatened to kill another employee who had once accidentally put a scratch in Jan's car. Jan once tried to run another employee down with his forklift and barely missed him. Another employee claimed that Jan threatened to kill him for being a perverted homosexual. Jan once got mad at a friend and falsely accused the friend of sexually assaulting

him. The plant manager fired Jan. Jan filed a grievance with his union steward.

Relevant Portion of the Collective Bargaining Agreement

Two types of violations will result in discipline:

- Type A: Rules that are so important that no violation will be permitted. One violation leads to a dismissal.
- Type B: Important rules that if violated do not necessarily lead to an immediate discharge. Employees may be put in a progressive discipline situation. Examples:
  - Intimidating fellow employees
  - Fighting on the premises

Past Practices of the Employer

During the life of the collective bargaining agreement, there had been seven cases of Type B violations. Progressive discipline was used in each case.

Jan's Argument

"I admit I was wrong to run my forklift into another employee. However, this is a Type B offense. It has been the employer's past practice to use progressive discipline in such cases. I should have been suspended for 3 days, not fired."

Company's Argument

"The collective bargaining agreement says that Type B infractions do not necessarily lead to discharge. In this case, it should because Jan is so dangerous to other employees."

Case

Supervisors Performing the Work of Members of the Bargaining Unit

Background of the Case

The Antarctic Air-Conditioning Company produces window air-conditioning units at a relatively modern plant in Tennessee. There are several assembly lines along which the air conditioners are built by incorporating subassemblies produced in other shops within the plant into the metal frames that house the completed units. Industrial engineering studies were performed to balance the various jobs along the line. On each of the three shifts, a supervisor is assigned to an assembly line. Further, the production department has established schedules for output on each of the lines.

On May 23, 1993, a supervisor, Larry, was observed working on the assembly line for an extended period of time. On this day, there were a number of regular employees absent, and a number of new replacement workers

were present in the area. The grievant, Sally, is the most experienced worker on the line. She asked the supervisor to explain why he was working on the job adjacent to hers on the line. She was told to get back to work because "there was too much work to do and not enough workers to do it!" At that point, Sally contacted her union steward, Mike. It was he who filed the grievance on behalf of Sally and the union for taking work away from members of the bargaining unit.

The Existing Collective Bargaining Agreement

The relevant provisions in the collective bargaining contract between Antarctic Air-Conditioning Company of Smithville, Tennessee, and the Allied Air-Conditioning Brotherhood of America, Local 69, are shown in Exhibit 12-5.

> ### EXHIBIT 12-5   Collective Bargaining Contract Excerpt
>
> **Article VII. Supervisors Working**
>
> Any supervisor at a plant shall not perform work on a job normally performed by an employee in the Bargaining Unit at such plant; provided, however, this provision shall not be construed to prohibit supervisors from performing the following types of work:
>
> a. Experimental, development, and other research work
> b. Demonstration work performed for the purpose of instructing and training employees
> c. Work required by emergency conditions
> d. Work which is negligible in amount and which also, under the circumstances then existing, it would be unreasonable to assign to a Bargaining Unit employee
>
> Work which is incidental to supervisory duties on a job normally performed by a supervisor, even though similar to duties found in jobs in the Bargaining Unit, shall not be affected by this provision.
>
> **Article XV. Grievances**
>
> **Scope**
>
> The grievance procedure may be applied to any differences, disputes, or complaints regarding the interpretation or application of this Agreement, or regarding matters of wages, hours, and working conditions excluded from or not covered by this Agreement.
>
> **Procedure**
>
> Grievances may be presented and discussed by an employee or his Union representative, or for a group of employees by the Union representative or representatives, in the following manner:
>
> - If an employee believes that he has a grievance, he may present and discuss such grievance with his immediate foreman, with or without his Union representative as the employee may elect, in an attempt to resolve the matter. The foreman shall be empowered to and shall attempt to resolve it.
> - The foreman, after discussion, shall promptly give his oral answer. If the employee is not satisfied with the foreman's answer, it may be brought to the Union representative, who shall be empowered to resolve, withdraw, or appeal the grievance.

The Union's Position

The union admitted that absenteeism was a problem on the assembly line in question. However, the union has contended for some time that absenteeism is the result of the arduous assembly line jobs that cause a number of workers to suffer injuries from the repetitive and strenuous nature of the work. Further, the union stated that the company had increased the speed of the line in order to meet the anticipated demand for air conditioners in the upcoming summer months and that the production schedule was the real reason for the supervisor's presence on the line.

The union suggested that the company could have recalled a number of former workers who were laid off during the winter months when the third shift was shut down. Although there had been no past precedents of settlements of grievances involving Article VII, the union demanded that the most senior worker be paid for half a day's work at double the normal hourly rate.

The Company's Position

First, the company produced records that showed that 8 of the normal crew of 37 assemblers were absent on May 23. The company argued that it is absolutely necessary on days when there is high absenteeism for supervisors to be able to work on the assembly line. Absenteeism is always a problem during the spring of the year because production schedules must meet the increased demand for air conditioners and because a great many of the employees "take time off" to tend to their commercial nurseries, which flourish in this particular area of the country. Because it is often necessary to use replacement workers for the absent workers, supervisors must be able to demonstrate the operations to the replacements.

On the day in question, Larry was trying to teach replacement workers taken from other departments in the plant to do the assembly jobs. Although most learned the jobs, a few just were not picking up the work and, consequently, Larry seemed to be spending a lot of time doing the assembly work. In the company's view, this is not a desirable situation given the fact that supervisors were forced to neglect their own responsibilities (e.g., seeing to it that maintenance on the equipment is performed and examining the output for a variety of defects). However, when a great many workers are absent, the line must be kept moving.

With regard to the union's request for a monetary award, the company, through its industrial relations manager, Arlene, said that the union had not demonstrated how Sally had been harmed by the fact that Larry was working on the line on May 23.

Questions

1. Acting as a union representative, prepare a statement of the grievance, pointing to contract language that was violated and the details of the incident that lead you to believe that it represented a contract violation.
2. Now put yourself in the position of a neutral third party such as an arbitrator. Render a decision as to which party would be likely to prevail. Justify your decision.

References

1. Charles, H., and Bennett, M.E. (1993). Union-management partnership in the application of technology: Saturn Corporation—UAW Local 1853. *Workplace Topics, 3* (1), 113–122; Rubinstein, S.A. (2000). The impact of co-management on quality performance: The case of the Saturn Corporation. *Industrial and Labor Relations, 53* (2), 197–218.
2. National Labor Relations Act, Section 2(5).
3. Freeman, R.B., and Medoff, J.L. (1984). *What Do Unions Do?* New York: Basic Books.
4. Ibid.
5. Ibid.
6. Chaison, G.N., and Rose, J.B. (1991). The macrodeterminants of union growth and decline. In G. Strauss, D.G. Gallagher, and J. Fiorito (eds.). *The State of the Unions.* Madison, WI: Industrial Relations Research Association.
7. Http://www.bls.gov.
8. Ballot, M. (1992). *Labor-Management Relations in a Changing Environment.* New York: John Wiley & Sons.
9. Bureau of Labor Statistics. Union members in 1992.
10. Shur, L.A., and Kruse, D.L. (1992). Gender differences in attitudes toward unions. *Industrial and Labor Relations Review, 46,* 89–102.
11. Mitchell, D.J.B. (1989). Will collective bargaining outcomes in the 1990s look like those in the 1980s? In B. Dennis (ed.). *Proceedings of the Spring Meeting of the Industrial Relations Research Association.* Madison, WI: IRRA.
12. National Labor Relations Act, Section 8(a)(2).
13. *NLRB v. Mackay Radio & Telegraph Company* (1938). 304 U.S. 333.
14. (1990, March 30). Replacement workers: Management's big gun. *The New York Times,* A24.
15. Lindsey, A. (1967). *The Pullman Strike.* Chicago: University of Chicago Press.
16. Beard, M. (1968). *A Short History of the American Labor Movement.* New York: Greenwood Press. Further, in *Duplex Printing Press Co. v. Deering* [254 U.S. 443 (1921)], the Court found that job actions by unions could be enjoined under the provisions of the Clayton Antitrust Act, a federal law that was presumed to exempt organized labor from antitrust injunctions.
17. *Hitchman Coal Co. v. Mitchell* (1917). 245 U.S. 229.
18. See Getman, J.G., Goldberg, S.B., and Herman, J.B. (1976). *Union Representation Elections: Law and Reality.* New York: Russell Sage Foundation; Hamner, W.C., and Smith, F.J. (1978). Work attitudes as predictors of unionization activities. *Journal of Applied Psychology, 63,* 415–421.
19. See Hammer, T.H., and Berman, M. (1981). The role of noneconomic factors in faculty union voting. *Journal of Applied Psychology, 66,* 415–421; Schriesheim, C.A. (1978). Job satisfaction, attitudes toward unions, and voting in a union representation election. *Journal of Applied Psychology, 63,* 548–552; Zalesney, M.D. (1985). Comparison of economic and noneconomic factors in predicting faculty vote preference in a union representation election. *Journal of Applied Psychology, 70,* 243–256.
20. Brett, J.M. (1980). Why employees want unions. *Organizational Dynamics, 8,* 47–59.
21. Ibid.
22. National Labor Relations Act, Section 9(c)(1)(A).
23. Sandver, M. (1977). The validity of union authorization cards as a predictor of success in NLRB certification elections. *Labor Law Journal, 28,* 696–702.
24. Labor-Management Relations Act, Section 9(b)(1).
25. Labor-Management Relations Act, Section 9(b)(3).
26. *Excelsior Underwear* (1966). 156 NLRB 1236.
27. *NLRB v. Gissel Packing Company* (1969). 395 U.S. 575.
28. Labor-Management Relations Act, Sections 8(a)(5) and 8(b)(3).
29. Labor-Management Relations Act, Section 8(d).
30. Kochan, T.A. (1979). How American workers view unions. *Monthly Labor Review, 102* (4), 23–41.
31. Montgomery, B.R. (1989). The influence of attitudes and normative pressures on voting decisions in a union certification election. *Industrial and Labor Relations Review, 42,* 262–279.
32. Bureau of National Affairs. (1989). *Basic Patterns in Union Contracts* (12th ed.). Washington, DC: Bureau of National Affairs.
33. Labor-Management Relations Act, Section 203(d).
34. McKelvey, J.T. (1985). *The Changing Law of Fair Representation.* Ithaca, NY: ILR Press.
35. Goodfellow, M. (1992). Avoiding unions in the insurance clerical field. *Best's Review, 10,* 114–121.
36. Hughs, C.L. (1976). *Making Unions Unnecessary.* New York: Executive Enterprises.
37. Goodfellow. Avoiding unions.
38. Porter, A.A., and Murman, K.F. (1983). A survey of employer union-avoidance practices. *Personnel Administrator,* November, 66–71.
39. A survey of 652 firms found that half of the companies had instituted a formal grievance procedure for their nonunion employees. See Berenbeim, R. (1980). *Non-Union Complaint Systems: A Corporate Appraisal.* New York: The Conference Board, Report No. 770.
40. Sloane, A.A., and Witney, F. (1994). *Labor Relations.* Englewood Cliffs, NJ: Prentice Hall.
41. Lawler, J.J., and West, R. (1985). Impact of union-avoidance strategy in representation elections. *Industrial Relations, 24,* 406–420.
42. Cooke, W.N. (1983). Determinants of the outcomes of union certification elections. *Industrial and Labor Relations Review, 36,* 402–414.
43. Cooke, W.N. (1985). *Union Organizing and Public Policy: Failure to Secure First Contracts.* Kalamazoo, MI: W. E. Upjohn Institute.
44. Hurd, R.W., and Uehlein, J. (eds.). (1994). *The Employer Assault on the Legal Right to Organize.* Washington, DC: Industrial Union Department, AFL-CIO.
45. Ibid.
46. Thomas, K.W. (1977). Toward multidimensional values in teaching: An example of conflict behaviors. *Academy of Management Review,* July, 487.
47. Whetten, D.A., and Cameron, K.S. (2001). *Developing Management Skills* (5th ed.). Reading, MA: Addison-Wesley.
48. Rees, A. (1962). *The Economics of Trade Unions.* Chicago: The University of Chicago Press.
49. Rayback, J.G. (1966). *A History of American Labor: Expanded and Updated.* New York: Free Press.

The Organized Labor Movement in the United States

Appendix

Compared to most institutions that affect commerce today, organized labor is more keenly aware of and influenced by its past. For example, labor history is an important component in almost all university labor studies programs (whereas the history of management is a less prominent part of formal management education) and is a frequent topic in the continuing education of labor officials. Consequently, a historical perspective is necessary to better understand current union behavior. A summary of these important events appears in the timeline in Exhibit 12-6.

Benevolent Societies

Although unions as we know them today did not exist in the United States prior to 1800, in the Colonial period there were numerous benevolent societies created by tradesmen to provide mutual aid, such as caring for members during times of illness or financial distress. These societies were formed with the stipulation that they were not to interfere with wages, hours of work, and other economic matters, but they did act as censors of the quality of work.

The Need for Unionization

The American labor movement began in the early 1800s. The predominantly agricultural society of the eighteenth century began to transform into an urban and industrial society, giving rise to wealthy merchant capitalists. These merchants were able to produce vast quantities of raw materials and supplies and store them in warehouses. "Manufactories" were begun that produced goods that competed with those of local shopkeepers, thereby placing pressure on these shopkeepers to reduce wages in order to rival the lower priced goods of the merchant capitalist. This led to an increased militancy among workers, who felt forced to form unions in order to maintain their wages.

The American labor movement thus has had a primary economic bent from the start. Its prevailing spirit has been characterized as "pure and simple business unionism."

The union is primarily, though not exclusively, engaged in advancing the interests of its members through seeking improvements in their wages, hours, and working conditions and is only secondarily concerned with broader programs of social reform.[48]

Employer Resistance to Early Unionization Efforts

Employers resisted these instances of worker militancy by forming associations of their own to hold down wages. The associations accomplished this aim by advertising

EXHIBIT 12-6	Important Dates in the History of Organized Labor

1786	Philadelphia printers conducted the first authenticated strike in the United States.
1806	Following a strike for higher wages, members of the Philadelphia Journeymen of Cordwainers were tried for criminal conspiracy in the first of a series of cases to determine whether unions were illegal combinations to raise wages and injure others.
1827	The first union of craftsmen from different trades was formed in Philadelphia. This city central was called the Mechanics' Union of Trade Associations.
1834	The National Trades' Union, the first attempt to create a national labor federation in the United States, was formed in New York City.
1852	The National Typographical Union, the first national union of workers from a single trade that endures to the present day, was organized.
1866	The National Labor Union, the first association of national unions, was formed.
1869	The Noble and Holy Order of the Knights of Labor was organized in Philadelphia.
1877	Federal troops were used for the first time in a labor dispute during a strike of railroad workers.
1886	At a convention in Columbus, Ohio, the American Federation of Labor was organized. The AFL was the first federation of national unions that still exists to the present day.
1908	Under the restraint of trade provision of the Sherman Anti-Trust Act, a boycott of D.E. Loewe and Co. by the United Hatters of Danbury was ruled illegal.
1914	The Clayton Act was passed to limit the use of injunctions against unions.
1917	In *Hitchman Coal & Coke v. Mitchell*, the U.S. Supreme Court upheld the legality of the "yellow-dog" contract.
1921	In *Duplex Printing Press v. Deering*, the U.S. Supreme Court ruled that nothing in the Clayton Act legalized secondary boycotts or protected unions from injunctions brought against them for restraint of trade.
1926	Passage of the Railway Labor Act prohibited employer interference in union organizing of railroad workers and required collective bargaining.
1932	Passage of the Norris-LaGuardia Act restricted employer use of federal injunctions in labor disputes and outlawed the "yellow-dog" contract.
1935	Passage of the National Labor Relations Act (Wagner Act) established the first national labor policy guaranteeing the rights of workers to organize unions and created the National Labor Relations Board to enforce these rights.
1937	After a three-month sit-down strike at its Flint, Michigan, plant, General Motors agreed to recognize the United Automobile Workers' union.
1938	Under the leadership of John L. Lewis, the Congress of Industrial Organizations (CIO) was formed.
1947	Passage of the Labor–Management Relations Act (Taft-Hartley Act) established procedures for handling strikes that created national emergencies and identified unfair union labor practices.
1955	The AFL and CIO merged.
1959	Passage of the Landrum-Griffin Act guaranteed union members a "Bill of Rights" and imposed a variety of reporting and disclosure requirements on unions.
1978	The Labor Law Reform Act, intended to facilitate the union organizing process, was filibustered to death in the U.S. Congress.
1981	President Reagan fires striking members of the Professional Air Traffic Controllers Organization.

for workers from out of town to replace striking employees and by using the courts to protect their interests.

The most noteworthy litigation took place between 1806 and 1810 in a series of six cases, known as the Cordwainer conspiracy cases. These cases tested the applicability of English common law to the concerted activities of labor organizations. Although the courts found that combinations of workers were legal and proper, they declared that almost any action taken by such combinations to further their economic interests (e.g., a strike, boycott, or demand for a closed shop) was illegal. These were the first of many unfavorable judicial verdicts that hampered the development of trade unions in the United States.

The Development of National Unions

The 1850s marked the beginning of the rapid development of national unions. The growth of unions at this time was related to the improvement in transportation and communication that widened product markets. Goods made in low-wage areas were sold in the same product markets as those made by local unions that had won higher wage scales and therefore charged more for their products. (Today, the flood of imports from low-wage, Third-World countries is creating the same problem for unionized American workers.) Thus, it became a goal of unions to remove labor costs as a factor affecting the price of competing products by organizing workers nationally.

The National Typographical Union was formed in 1850, followed by the formation of 10 more national unions prior to 1857, including the upholsterers, hat finishers, plumbers, railroad engineers, and stonecutters.[49] These national unions were loose associations of local unions in the same craft that represented craftsmen in different localities.

The Formation of Union Confederations

With the increase in the number of national unions, the time seemed ripe to create the first, grand consolidation of all of labor's forces. In 1866, William H. Sylvis, head of the Iron Moulders International, was the prime mover in the formation of the National Labor Union, which, prior to its demise in 1872, represented several hundred thousand workers. Another attempt to organize workers into a single big union was made by the Noble and Holy Order of the Knights of Labor in 1869. Importantly, both of these short-lived organizations did not represent strict craft unionism, and both tried unsuccessfully to promote industrial cooperatives that would lead to the abolition of the wage system by giving workers ownership of the means of production.

The American Federation of Labor (AFL) is the first confederation of labor unions that still exists today. Formed in 1886, with Samuel Gompers as its president, the AFL was a loose federation of national and international craft unions that represented skilled workers (e.g., carpenters, cigar makers, printers, and plumbers).

Unlike earlier attempts to form associations of labor organizations, the AFL did not impinge on the autonomy of the member unions and did not embrace radical economic or political ideologies. It favored the improvement of working conditions by means of collective bargaining and, prior to the 1930s, did not seek the interference of government or other agencies in helping to establish the conditions of work.

Because the member unions in the AFL were organized on a craft basis, they were not structured appropriately to represent the interests of the largely unskilled workers employed in many manufacturing industries such as automobiles, steel, and coal mining. Consequently, a new confederation was spawned to meet the needs of these workers—the Congress of Industrial Organizations (CIO), headed by John L. Lewis.

The CIO was thus established as a rival federation that engaged in organizing battles with AFL unions for the loyalty of industrial workers. This rivalry continued until the merger of the AFL and CIO in 1955. The agreement that created the AFL-CIO in no way changed the structure of the affiliated national unions, although it did provide the impetus for several union mergers. For example, the Barbers and Beauty Culturists of America (formerly CIO) reaffiliated with the Journeymen Barbers, Hairdressers, Cosmetologists, and Proprietors' International Union of America (formerly AFL).

Meeting Employee Safety and Health Needs

Chapter Thirteen

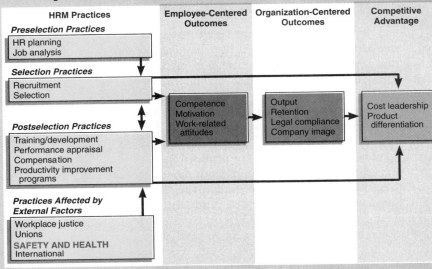

HRM Practices	Employee-Centered Outcomes	Organization-Centered Outcomes	Competitive Advantage
Preselection Practices HR planning Job analysis			
Selection Practices Recruitment Selection	Competence Motivation Work-related attitudes	Output Retention Legal compliance Company image	Cost leadership Product differentiation
Postselection Practices Training/development Performance appraisal Compensation Productivity improvement programs			
Practices Affected by External Factors Workplace justice Unions **SAFETY AND HEALTH** International			

Key Terms

carpal tunnel syndrome
Drug-Free Workplace Act
employee assistance programs (EAPs)
Employee Right-to-Know Law
employee wellness
employee wellness programs
ergonomics
National Institute for Occupational Safety and Health

Occupational Safety and Health Act
Occupational Safety and Health Administration (OSHA)
Occupational Safety and Health Review Commission
repetitive motion disorders
safety audits
safety committee
safety incentive program

Chapter Objectives

- Understand how effective safety and health practices can enhance an organization's competitive advantage.
- Describe safety and health requirements imposed by federal law.

- Explain the major causes of workplace accidents.
- Discuss how companies can prevent workplace accidents.
- Explain the major health issues at the workplace and how organizations can address them.

13-1 Gaining Competitive Advantage

13-1a Opening Case: Gaining Competitive Advantage at Appleton[1]

The Problem: Too Many Injuries

Appleton Manufacturing, headquartered in Wisconsin, is a manufacturer employing 3,400 people at locations throughout the United States and United Kingdom. The company's employees were plagued by the kinds of muscular and skeletal injuries typically found at heavy manufacturing sites. These injuries were costly, causing workers to miss work for extended periods of time and causing the company's insurance and other health care costs to escalate.

The Solution: Instituting a Wellness Center

The company dealt with this problem by establishing an on-site wellness center that offers physical rehabilitation, injury prevention, fitness training, and wellness education. The center is staffed by a licensed athletic trainer, a certified physical fitness specialist, and a nurse practitioner. The rehabilitation program is offered to help employees who have suffered both work- and non-work–related injuries. Its services include ultrasound, electric stimulation, paraffin baths, and hot and cold treatments. The injury prevention program focuses on ergonomic analysis. The center's staff examines each job, looking for such risk factors as awkward posture, excessive force, repetition, contact stress, and vibration. When risk factors are identified, the staff provides specific recommendations for risk reduction. For example, the staff recommended the use of a vacuum hoist to eliminate the need for employees to frequently lift boxes weighing between 35 and 80 pounds. The company's fitness center provides employees with a cardiovascular and weight training area that includes treadmills, stationary bikes, stair-climbers, rowing machines, weight machines, and free weights. In addition, the staff offers educational programs on injury prevention and holds periodic health fairs, at which employees are offered a number of free services, such as cholesterol testing, fitness assessments, body fat analysis, and blood pressure screening.

How the Wellness Center Enhanced Competitive Advantage

According to its director, Michele Stellrecht, the center has helped make Appleton a safer place to work. The program's benefits include the following list of outcomes:

- The company has saved $205,000 by reducing the number of rehabilitation treatments performed and the per session costs.
- The company has reduced by 28 percent the number of workdays missed due to injuries.

- There has been a significant reduction in workers' compensation costs, as the number of such claims has decreased each year since the program was implemented.
- The company's overall costs associated with soft tissue injuries have decreased by 22 percent over the past three years.

13-1b Linking Employee Safety and Health to Competitive Advantage

One of the biggest issues facing employers today is the safety and health of their employees. Workplace injuries are increasingly common. In 2003, for instance, the Bureau of Labor Statistics (BLS) reported a total of 4.4 million nonfatal and over 5,500 fatal work-related injuries.[2] The health of the workforce is also on the decline, as many workers' unhealthy lifestyles have placed them at high risk for heart attacks, strokes, cancer, and the like. Many suffer from emotional disorders such as drug dependency, stress, and depression that have physical consequences as well.

Organizations have a moral responsibility to ensure the safety and well-being of their members. Many are meeting this responsibility by helping society tackle some of today's serious health problems, such as substance abuse and AIDS. Such companies are establishing drug-free work environments and educating their employees about AIDS.

Organizational practices that promote safety and health can also help a company establish competitive advantage by reducing costs and complying with safety laws.

Reducing Costs

Workplace injuries and illnesses can be quite expensive. Accidents alone cost U.S. employers more than $60 billion per year[3] for medical and insurance costs, workers' compensation, survivor benefits, lost wages, damaged equipment and materials, production delays, other workers' time losses, selection and training costs for replacement workers, and accident reporting.[4]

An employer can minimize safety and health-related costs by instituting safety and wellness programs, as illustrated in the opening case. A similar program at DuPont netted an annual savings of $34 million or 3.6 percent of the company's net profits.[5]

Programs designed to minimize employee health problems can also create significant cost advantages by reducing absenteeism, turnover, and medical costs, and increasing productivity. The potential cost-effectiveness of an organizational health promotion program at Coors is illustrated in On the Road to Competitive Advantage 13-1.

Complying with the Law

State and federal governments strictly regulate organizational health and safety practices. Specific health and safety laws are discussed in Section 13-2, "HRM Issues and Practices." Note, however, that the government views safety and health violations very seriously, and the penalties for violating these laws can be quite severe. In addition to being issued large fines, employers who violate safety and health regulations can be held liable for criminal charges. The following examples illustrate the types of penalties associated with such violations:

- The government fined J&R Grading and Pipeline, Inc., $224,000 for the death of one of its employees. The victim was killed when the trench he was working in caved-in. According to government officials, the company "knowingly put employees in harm's way, and ultimately caused the death of a man by callously disregarding well-recognized safety practices."[6]
- HWM, Inc., of Hudson, New Hampshire, was fined $140,000 for the fatal accident of one of its employees. A forklift truck rolled down an incline, pinning and crushing the victim. The government found that the truck had been left unattended on the incline without its wheels having first been blocked to prevent its

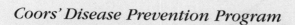
Coors' Disease Prevention Program

Coors initiated a disease prevention program that included health-risk assessments, nutritional counseling, stress management, and programs for smoking cessation, weight reduction, and aerobic exercise. A cost–benefit analysis revealed these activities will save the company at least $19 million during the next 10 years through decreased medical costs, reduced sick leave, and increased productivity. That translates into a $6.15 return on investment for every $1 spent.

Source: Caudron, S. (1991). Wellness works. *Industry Week,* February 4, 22–28.

rolling. The truck also had a defective parking brake and reel wheel, and the required daily inspection had not been conducted. HWM's neglect was judged to be willful, meaning that it knew what safeguards were necessary to protect workers but did not provide them.[7]

- Carolina Marine Handling was fined $169,447 for safety violations connected with a fatal accident in north Charleston. The fatality "was the direct result of management's disregard for the safety of employees engaged in longshore operations." Specifically, the investigation found that devices for handling cargo were used prior to proper certification, inspection, and testing.[8]

13-2 HRM Issues and Practices

13-2a Government Regulation of Safety and Health Practices at the Workplace

Federal laws regulate the safety and health practices of most organizations. We limit our discussion to laws that affect a majority of organizations, but note that several additional laws exist that cover particular segments of the workforce. For instance, numerous laws pertain to government contractors, to specific states, and to specific industries (e.g., transportation, nuclear power, food, and drug).

The Occupational Safety and Health Act
The **Occupational Safety and Health Act** of 1970 is probably the most comprehensive and wide-ranging legislation in this area. It applies to nearly all U.S. workplaces.[9] The act aims to ensure safe working conditions for every American worker by:[10]

1. Setting and enforcing workplace safety standards
2. Promoting employer-sponsored educational programs that foster safety and health
3. Requiring employers to keep records regarding job-related safety and health matters

Three separate agencies were created by the act:

1. The **Occupational Safety and Health Administration (OSHA)** develops and enforces health and safety standards.
2. The **Occupational Safety and Health Review Commission** hears appeals from employers who wish to contest OSHA rulings.
3. The **National Institute for Occupational Safety and Health** conducts health and safety research to suggest new standards and update previous ones.

Occupational Safety and Health Act A law designed to ensure safe working conditions for every American worker.

Occupational Safety and Health Administration (OSHA) The government agency responsible for developing and enforcing workplace health and safety standards.

Occupational Safety and Health Review Commission The government agency responsible for hearing appeals from employers who wish to contest OSHA rulings.

National Institute for Occupational Safety and Health The government agency responsible for conducting health and safety research to suggest new OSHA standards and to update previous ones.

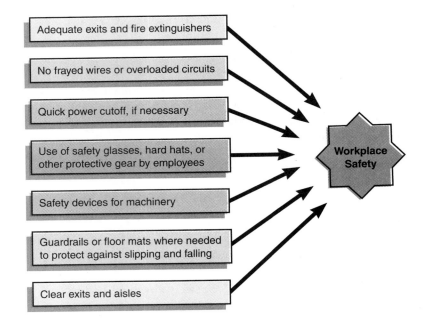

Figure 13-1
Fundamental Safety Issues Addressed by OSHA Safety and Health Standards

Source: Warner, D. (1991). Ways to make safety work. *Nation's Business,* December, 25–27.

The following discussion focuses on the safety standards imposed by OSHA and how they are enforced.

OSHA Standards

OSHA has issued literally thousands of safety and health standards. Areas of basic concern include fire safety, personal protection equipment, electrical safety, basic housekeeping, and machine guards. Each standard specifies such things as permissible exposure limit, monitoring requirements, methods of compliance, personal protective equipment, hygiene facilities, training, and record keeping.[11]

To comply with these standards, most mid- to large-sized organizations employ safety professionals to keep up with them and ensure that each is being met. These professionals face too many specific issues to mention here, but some of the most important issues they must address appear in Figure 13-1.

Enforcement of OSHA Standards

Companies with more than 10 employees are subject to routine OSHA inspections. Companies with fewer than 10 employees are exempt from such inspections but can be investigated if a safety-related problem is brought to the attention of OSHA. High-hazard industries, such as manufacturing firms, chemical companies, and construction companies, are subject to inspections regardless of the number of employees.[12]

OSHA conducts inspections based on the following priority classifications, which are listed in order of importance:[13]

1. *Imminent danger:* OSHA gives top priority to workplace situations that present an "imminent danger" of death or serious injury to employees. The company must take immediate corrective action.

2. *Fatality or catastrophe investigations:* The second highest priority is given to sites that have experienced an accident that has caused at least one employee to die or five or more to be hospitalized. The inspection aims to determine the cause of the accident and whether any violation of OSHA standards contributed to it.

3. *Employee complaint investigations:* OSHA responds third to employee complaints about unsafe working conditions. The speed with which OSHA responds depends on the seriousness of the complaint.

4. *Targeted industries:* OSHA targets high-risk industries, such as construction, ship-building, food processing, logging, and nursing homes.

In 2001, 50 percent of OSHA's inspections occurred at targeted industries and about 25 percent were responses to complaints or accidents.[14] When an OSHA inspection reveals that an employer has violated one of its standards, it issues a citation. The citation, posted near the site of the violation, lists the nature of the violation, the abatement period (i.e., the time frame within which the company must rectify the problem), and any penalty levied against the employer. Willful violations (i.e., those that an employer intentionally and knowingly commits) carry a penalty of up to $70,000 for each offense. If a death occurs because of a willful violation, the employer may be both fined and imprisoned.

Hazard Communication Standard (Employee Right-to-Know Law)

Congress enacted the Hazard Communication Standard (more commonly referred to as the **Employee Right-to-Know Law**) in 1984. This law gives workers the right to know what hazardous substances they are dealing with on the job. A substance is considered hazardous if exposure to it can lead to acute or chronic health problems. Federal and state agencies have compiled lists of more than 1,000 substances deemed hazardous under this law.[15]

Specific provisions of the Employee Right-to-Know Law are spelled out in Taking a Closer Look 13-1. In brief, the law requires all organizations to (1) develop a system for inventorying hazardous substances, (2) label the containers of these substances, and (3) provide employees with needed information and training to handle and store these substances safely.

Employers typically violate the OSHA Hazard Communication Standard more frequently than any other OSHA standard.[16] The majority of companies are cited for failing to have:[17]

- Written hazard communication programs
- Training programs for teaching employees about the chemicals they work with
- Material safety data sheets at the work site
- Properly labeled chemical containers

Government fines for right-to-know violations may be as high as $1,000 per chemical for first violations and $10,000 per chemical for second violations. Additional penalties for environmental crimes include fines up to $75,000 per day and imprisonment.[18]

The Americans with Disabilities Act (ADA)

Another law affecting organizational safety and health practices is the *Americans with Disabilities Act (ADA)*. As noted in Chapter 6, "Selecting Applicants," an individual is protected by the ADA if he or she is disabled, that is, if the individual has a physical or mental impairment that substantially limits one or more of the individual's major life activities. According to the ADA regulations, temporary, nonchronic impairments that are short in duration and have little or no long-term impact are usually not considered disabilities under the act. For example, broken limbs, sprains, concussions, appendicitis, or influenza are not disabilities. However, if a broken leg did not heal properly and resulted in permanent impairment that significantly restricted walking or other major life activities, it could then be considered a disability.

From July 1992 (when the law first took effect) through the end of September 2004, employees filed over 200,000 complaints with the EEOC.[19] About half of these charges were filed by employees who became disabled as the result of workplace conditions or injuries.[20] The greatest number of suits have been lodged by individuals with back impairments.[21] People also frequently claimed emotional, neurological and extremity impairments.[22]

Employee Right-to-Know Law A 1984 law that gives workers the right to know what hazardous substances they are dealing with on the job.

Taking a Closer Look 13-1

Provisions of the Employee Right-to-Know Law

1. Develop a written hazard communication policy describing how the organization is complying with the law. The policy should indicate:
   - What constitutes a hazardous substance
   - Who is responsible for administering the program
   - What hazardous materials are used by the organization
   - How information concerning hazardous materials is transmitted to employees
   - How, when, and by whom employees are to be trained in the right-to-know program
2. Provide material safety data sheets (MSDSs) for each substance in use at the workplace. The MSDS should specify:
   - The substance's hazardous components, chemical ID, common names, and worker exposure limits
   - The substance's physical and chemical characteristics, such as boiling point, melting point, and water solubility
   - The physical hazards stemming from the use of this substance, such as fire or explosion, and ways to handle these hazards
   - The substance's reactivity (i.e., whether the substance is stable) and situations to avoid so it will not react
   - The health hazards posed by the substance; the MSDS should specify how the chemical could enter the body and the possible health hazards upon exposure

   - Precautions for safety handling and use; i.e., what to do if it spills or leaks; how to dispose of the substance; how to handle the substance properly; how to store it
3. Clearly label each container housing a chemical. The container label should include:
   - The name of the chemical
   - The name of the manufacturer of the chemical
   - The physical hazards associated with the chemical (e.g., Will it explode? Will it catch fire? Is it radioactive?)
   - The health hazards associated with the chemical (e.g., Is it toxic? Could it cause cancer? Is it an irritant?)
   - The protective clothing, equipment, and procedures that are recommended when working with this chemical
4. Train all employees on how to deal safely with the chemical substance. The training should cover:
   - How to properly handle and store the chemical
   - The appropriate action to take when coming into contact with the substance
   - Safety precautions, protective equipment, and first aid
   - How to detect hazardous substance exposure (e.g., distinct odors) and how to read monitoring devices

---

Complying with the ADA

The key issue for employers trying to comply with ADA is how to handle situations such as job placement in which an applicant or employee is disabled. For instance, what should an employer do if it discovers that one of its employees has a chronic back ailment or has an infectious disease?

ADA regulations (summarized in the appendix of Chapter 6) provide guidance in this area. Briefly, the regulations specify that if a disability prevents someone from performing one or more of the essential job functions (i.e., fundamental job duties that must be performed by the jobholder), employers must try to accommodate that individual. The employer may not take an adverse action against the disabled employee unless it can prove an accommodation was impossible or infeasible (i.e., it would cause the employer an "undue hardship").

Penalties for ADA violations may be as high as $50,000 for initial violations and up to $100,000 for each subsequent violation. In addition, the Civil Rights Act of 1991 allows claimants to collect up to $300,000 in punitive damages for "willful" violations.

13-2b Employee Safety: Accidents and Accident Prevention

Despite laws designed to ensure safety at the workplace, U.S. companies' accident rates are alarmingly high. For instance, there were 1.3 million injuries at the workplace in the year 2003 that were serious enough to cause employees to miss at least one day of work.[23]

The Causes of Workplace Accidents

What causes all of these industrial injuries? These causes can be divided into three categories: employee error, equipment insufficiency, and procedure insufficiency. Examples of causes falling within each category are listed here:

- *Employee error:* Misjudged situations, distractions by others, neuromuscular malfunctions, inappropriate working positions, and knowingly using defective equipment

- *Equipment insufficiency:* Use of inappropriate equipment, safety devices being removed or inoperative, and the lack of such things as engineering controls, respiratory protection, and protective clothing

- *Procedure insufficiency:* Failure of procedure for eliciting warning of hazard, inappropriate procedure for handling materials, failure to lock out or tag out, and a lack of written work procedures

In 2003, these types of mistakes caused about 600,000 strains, sprains, and tears and about 100,000 bruises and contusions, cuts and lacerations, and fractures.[24]

Accident Prevention Strategies

Workplace accidents pose serious problems for employees and for a firm's competitive advantage, but employers can prevent most of them. As illustrated in the opening case, many preventive strategies work. Such strategies are described in the following paragraphs.

Employee Selection

Some people just seem to be accident-prone: "an accident waiting to happen." If some people do have inherent tendencies toward accidents, then organizations should be able to lower their accident rates by screening out accident-prone applicants.

Research studies have discovered that individuals with certain personality characteristics are more likely than others to be involved in industrial accidents. For instance, one study found that people with higher accident rates tend to be impulsive and rebellious, and they tend to blame outside forces, rather than themselves, for their mishaps.[25] Another study identified the following four "high-risk" personality characteristics (see Figure 13-2):[26]

- *Risk-taking:* High risk-takers actually seek out danger rather than try to minimize or avoid it.
- *Impulsiveness:* Impulsive individuals fail to think through the consequences of their actions.
- *Rebelliousness:* Rebellious individuals tend to break established rules, including safety rules.
- *Hostility:* Hostile individuals tend to lose their tempers easily and thus engage in aggressive acts, such as kicking a jammed machine.

Many organizations now use personality tests to screen out individuals with accident-prone tendencies. For example, some companies use a test (called the Personnel Selection Inventory—Form 3S) to assess applicants' safety consciousness. One part of the test measures the degree to which individuals perceive a connection between their own behavior and its consequences. As noted earlier, individuals unable to see this connection are at greater risk for accidents.[27]

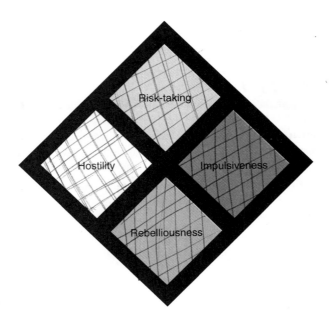

INTERACTIVE FIGURE

Figure 13-2
*The Four "High-Risk"
Personality Types*

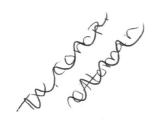

Employee Training

Employers who provide all new employees with training on safe and proper job procedures experience fewer accidents. Employees should learn how to perform each of their tasks as safely as possible. Training should be very specific, as illustrated in the example that follows. This example covers the procedures to be followed by employees working at a large food-manufacturing plant:[28]

- When picking up pans from the conveyor belt, pick up no more than two pans before you place them on the pan rack.
- Stack roll pans no higher than the rear rail of the pan rack.
- When you lift or lower the dough, keep both hands on the dump chain.
- When you pull the dough trough away from the dough mixer, hold both hands on the front rail and not on the rail sides.

Safety Incentive Programs

Although safety training is essential, employees do not always apply what they have learned. Just as many automobile drivers know it is wrong to exceed legal speed limits, but do it anyway, workers may choose to ignore instructions and carry out procedures in their own, unsafe way.

One way to mitigate this problem is to implement a **safety incentive program.** Such programs aim to motivate safe behavior by providing workers with incentives for avoiding accidents. The organization formulates safety goals (usually on a department-wide basis) and rewards employees if these goals are met. For example, a particular department may establish the goal of "reducing lost-time accidents by 50 percent over the next three months." If this goal were to be met, all employees within that department would receive an incentive reward, usually in the form of a cash bonus or merchandise.

Safety incentive programs often work quite well. For example, Willamette Industrial implemented a program because it was experiencing an average of 30 accidents per year that caused people to miss work. As a result of the program, the company went 450 days without a lost-time accident.[29]

Three problems often arise with safety incentive programs, however. In some cases, workers conceal their injuries and do not report them in order to keep their safety records intact.[30] There have even been cases where managers pressure

safety incentive program
An HRM program designed to motivate safe job behaviors by providing workers with incentives for avoiding accidents.

employees to conceal their accidents.[31] When injuries go unreported, injured workers relinquish their rights to workers' compensation (see Chapter 9, "Determining Pay and Benefits"), and firms remain unaware of safety problems, rendering them unable to take initiatives to prevent such problems from reoccurring. Second, workers may continue to perform in an unsafe manner (e.g., take risky shortcuts) because they remain unconvinced that such behavior is likely to result in accidents. Unfortunately, these employees are grievously mistaken; unsafe behaviors are a leading cause of accidents. According to one estimate, for every 100,000 unsafe behaviors there are 10,000 near-miss accidents, 1,000 recordable accidents, 100 lost-time accidents, and one fatality.[32] A third problem associated with safety incentive programs is that in some cases accidents are not caused by the employee's behavior, so why penalize the employee for such an incident?

Safety Audits

Because employees who "know better" often continue to engage in accident-causing behavior, many employers have redirected their focus from accident prevention to the prevention of unsafe acts that could lead to an accident. To do so, firms conduct **safety audits.** A safety committee or supervisors who observe employees on the job and correct unsafe behaviors generally conduct such audits. The procedure for conducting this type of audit is described in Section 13-3, "The Manager's Guide." At some companies the employees themselves are responsible for the observations. At Georgia-Pacific Color Box, for instance, the managers give their employees a checklist for making certain safety observations. Workers earn a $25 reward each quarter if they complete at least 80 percent of these observations. Since the program's inception, the company's OSHA-recordable incident rate dropped from 9.7 in 1997 to 1.6 in 2003.[33]

safety audits An audit of unsafe job behaviors aimed to prevent unsafe acts on the part of workers.

Accident Investigations

Accident investigations determine accident causes so that changes can be made to prevent the future occurrence of similar accidents. "Near misses" should also be investigated so that problems can be corrected before serious accidents occur.[34]

Supervisors always play a key role in accident investigations. For minor accidents, investigation may be limited to the supervisor meeting with the injured worker and filing a report. In large-scale investigations, the supervisor is usually part of a team of experts, which may also include an engineer, maintenance supervisor, upper-level manager, and/or safety professional.[35] Section 13-3, "The Manager's Guide," offers advice on how such investigations should be conducted.

Safety Committees

Safety committees often oversee organizations' safety functions. Comprised of both management and nonmanagement personnel, committees perform the following tasks:[36]

1. Assist with inspections and accident investigations.
2. Conduct safety meetings.
3. Answer workers' questions about safety programs.
4. Bring workers' safety concerns to management's attention.
5. Help develop safety incentive programs.
6. Develop ideas to improve workplace safety.
7. Prepare evacuation plans.
8. Prepare procedures for disasters such as tornadoes, hurricanes, etc., and contingency plans following the disaster.

safety committee A committee comprised of both management and nonmanagement personnel that is responsible for overseeing an organization's safety function.

Taking a Closer Look 13-2   *Types of Repetitive Motion Disorders*

- *Carpal tunnel syndrome:* A condition caused by pressure on the median nerve as it passes through the carpal canal, which is a passageway that sits between the wrist and the palm. The result is a combination of pain, numbness, or tingling radiating into the thumb, index finger, middle finger, part of the ring finger, and palm caused, for example, by constant typing.
- *Synovitis:* Inflammation of the tendon sheaths, or the synovial lining of the tendons

- *Tendinitis:* Inflammation of the tendons (i.e., the cables that attach muscles to bones)
- *Tenosynovitis:* Inflammation of both the tendon and the sheaths
- *Bursitis:* Inflammation of the bursa, a sacklike cavity that surrounds certain joints
- *Raynaud's phenomenon:* A vascular condition in which there are spasms or contractions of the blood vessels, leading to abnormal blanching, or whiteness, or what looks like a loss of circulation to the fingers

---

13-2c Employee Health Problems and Organizational Interventions

As we noted at the beginning of the chapter, employers' concern for employee well-being extends beyond the issue of workplace accidents; they are also concerned about employee health. In the following paragraphs, we identify the major health-related problems facing today's organizations and suggest alternatives for dealing with them.

Repetitive Motion Disorders

Nature and Extent of Problem

repetitive motion disorders
A set of physical disorders in which an individual's tendons become inflamed from the strains and stresses of repeated, forceful motions.

carpal tunnel syndrome
A repetitive motion disorder causing wrist pain that is caused by an overextension or twisting of the wrists, especially under force.

Repetitive motion disorders (sometimes referred to as repetitive stress injuries) affect tendons that become inflamed from the strains and stresses of repeated, forceful motions. People afflicted with these disorders often experience significant pain in various parts of the body, primarily in the neck, back, legs, arms, hands, wrists, or elbows. Taking a Closer Look 13-2 describes various repetitive motion disorders.

The most common repetitive motion disorder is **carpal tunnel syndrome,** so named because people experience pain in the eight wrist bones, or carpals, that form a tunnel. The disorder is caused by an overextension or twisting of the wrists, especially under force. Workers at greatest risk are those engaged in tasks requiring:

- Frequent, repetitive use of the same movements of the hand or wrist
- The generation of high force by the hand
- Sustained awkward hand positions
- The regular use of vibrating or handheld tools
- Frequent or prolonged pressure over the wrist at the base of the palm

Repetitive motion disorders are becoming epidemic: These disorders are now a leading cause of occupational injuries in the United States.[37] For instance, the BLS reports that the number of people inflicted each year with carpal tunnel syndrome ranged from 20,000 to over 40,000 during the 1992–1996 period.[38] A typical victim of carpal tunnel syndrome misses 25 days of work per year.[39] In all, more than half of the nation's workers, both blue and white collar, are subject to these disorders.[40]

Some 41 percent of white-collar workers have suffered significant symptoms of repetitive strain in their necks or arms.[41] Those at greatest risk include computer users in such fields as journalism, airline reservations, directory assistance, and data entry. For example, the Newspaper Guild reports that 4.5 percent of its membership (more than 1,500 people) have been afflicted.[42]

Among blue-collar workers, an estimated 13 percent suffer from repetitive motion disorders each year.[43] Auto assembly-line workers, chicken pluckers, meat cutters,

Ergonomic Approaches to Repetitive Motion Disorders

- *The Fresno Bee,* a California newspaper, has tried to minimize the onset of repetitive motion disorders among its video display terminal (VDT) operators by providing additional desk space, wrist rests, adjustable terminals, VDT document holders, new chairs, more knee space, and foot rests.
- The wrench used by workers in a manufacturing company for fastening lids onto steel drums required the same kind of pulling as a trigger on a gun. Workers thus had to flex their wrists fre-

quently—a high-risk activity for carpal tunnel syndrome. The company avoided possible problems by replacing the old wrench with a pneumatic air wrench that requires a less taxing motion. The new wrench is also counterweighted so workers do not have to support its weight.

Source: Heilbroner, D. (1993). Repetitive stress injury. *Working Woman,* February, 61–65; Moretz, S. (1990). Shaping a safer workplace. *Occupational Hazards,* October, 101–104.

---

postal employees, and bakers seem to be at greatest risk. For example, in meatpacking plants, where workers may make the same forceful cuts 20,000 to 30,000 times a day, nearly 8 percent of all full-time employees have been afflicted.[44]

Organizational Interventions

Clearly, repetitive motion disorders present both financial and legal risks to firms. Financially, repetitive motion disorders mean increased absenteeism and medical expenses, and decreased productivity.[45] Legally, the ADA mandates that employers accommodate individuals with repetitive motion disorders, if such accommodation poses no undue hardship.[46]

Companies have two main strategies for dealing with repetitive motion disorders. One is an ergonomic approach to the problem. **Ergonomics** is the science of designing and arranging workstations so that people and material interact safely and efficiently.[47] Examples of this approach are illustrated in On the Road to Competitive Advantage 13-2.

Employees can also receive training to deal with repetitive motion disorders. Employees should be trained to perform their jobs in ways that minimize the possibility of becoming afflicted. For example, VDT operators should be trained to perform their jobs according to the recommendations listed in Exhibit 13-1.

Physical fitness training can also effectively prevent repetitive motion disorders in some cases. Carpal tunnel syndrome, for instance, can be countered by strengthening hand and wrist muscles. A Subaru-Isuzu plant in Indiana has used these exercises (described in On the Road to Competitive Advantage 13-3) and has saved approximately 30 to 40 percent on rehabilitation costs.[48]

ergonomics The science of designing and arranging workstations so that people and material interact safely and efficiently.

EXHIBIT 13-1	Example of Training Material for VDT Operators Aimed at Preventing the Onset of Carpal Tunnel Syndrome

- Keep wrists relaxed and straight, using only finger movements to strike the keys.
- The typing table should be slightly higher than the elbows.
- Workers should rest their elbows at their sides or support them with special arm rests.
- Shoulders should be relaxed and remain level.
- Keys should be pressed using minimum pressure.

- The keyboard should be kept clean and in good working order to minimize resistance.
- When pressing hard-to-reach keys, workers should move their entire hand rather than overextending their fingers.
- Break up typing tasks with other activities, such as proofreading, filing, and telephone work, to rest fatigued muscles.

Source: Auerbach, J. (1991). Playing it safe at work. *FDA Consumer,* October, 16–19.

Exercise Program at Subaru-Isuzu to Prevent Repetitive Motion Disorders

The company provides a 45-hour program for all new workers to help them develop "key" muscles. During the first week, employees perform simple exercises, such as squeezing balls of putty to strengthen their arms and their grips while they receive other classroom instruction. Production workers engage in a more intense exercise program. They thread a clothesline through chains, twist ropes with bricks around broom handles, and screw nuts onto bolts buried in kitty litter to further improve their strength and flexibility.

Source: Gunch, D. (1993). Employees exercise to prevent injuries. *Personnel Journal*, July, 58–62.

Lower Back Disorders

Nature and Extent of Problem

As the following statistics demonstrate, lower back disorders (LBDs) rank right up there with repetitive motion disorders as a leading health problem at the workplace:

- LBDs account for approximately one-fourth of all workdays lost in the United States.[49]

- In 2003, 4,719 ADA complaints were lodged at the EEOC based on the claimants' lower back disorders.[50]

- Nationwide, back injuries cost employers between 15 and 20 billion dollars per year.[51]

Engaging in activities such as those listed in Exhibit 13-2 most frequently causes lower back disorders.[52] Occupations at greatest risk are trash collectors, nurses and

| **EXHIBIT 13-2** | High-Risk Activities for Sustaining Lower Back Disorders |

1. Lifting Objects
- Objects in the 25- to 35-pound range can be the most dangerous because they are often handled carelessly.
- Lifting and twisting simultaneously also poses higher risks.
- Lifting objects from the floor is much more hazardous than lifting them from a platform.
- Bulky objects that cause hands to be separated at a distance wider than the shoulders are more dangerous than objects that allow the hands to be held closer together.

2. Pushing and Pulling Objects
- Employees should use care and work with a partner when pushing or pulling heavy or awkward objects.

3. Carrying Objects
- Carrying has the same hazards as lifting. Certain "surprises" while carrying objects (e.g., shifts in weight as the object is being moved; slips of a hand or foot) lead to radical shifts in the stress being placed on various parts of the spine and can have deleterious effects.

4. Sitting
- Sitting for prolonged periods can create back problems.
- Working in cramped spaces or at chairs, desks, or workbenches that are not the correct height exacerbates problems caused by being in excessively sedentary jobs that force the employee to assume an improper posture.

5. Body Vibrations
- Many jobs, especially those involving heavy equipment (e.g., operating earth-moving equipment, off-road vehicles, and trucks), expose the worker to a great deal of vibration, which affects the resonance of the spine and creates muscle fatigue.

Source: Holenbeck, J.R., Ilgen, D.R., and Drampton, S.M. (1992). Lower back disability in occupational settings: A review of the literature from a human resource management view. *Personnel Psychology*, 45 (2), 247–278.

nurses' aids, truck drivers, heavy equipment operators, mechanics, maintenance workers, manual laborers, warehouse workers, protective services workers, and typists.

Organizational Interventions

Companies can take one of two approaches to mitigate this problem. First, an organization can attempt to prescreen individuals who either have existing back problems or are prone to develop such afflictions. The ADA restricts an employer from asking individuals if they have a history of back problems. Legally, firms may only inform applicants during employment interviews of the essential functions of the job and ask if there is anything that would prevent them from performing these duties.

Lower back problems may also be diagnosed in medical examinations. If a medical exam is administered, however, the ADA requires that it be given to all applicants, and only after an employment offer is made.

Even if a lower back disorder is detected, however, the employer may not automatically reject the applicant. The ADA dictates that the employer must first determine whether the condition would impede job performance and, if so, whether reasonable accommodation could be made, such as restructuring the job, modifying work schedules, or purchasing special equipment or other work devices.

Second, firms may try to prevent lower back disorders. These disorders can be prevented or minimized through job training (e.g., teaching employees proper lifting techniques) and fitness training to strengthen the lower back.

AIDS

Nature and Extent of Problem

As most people now realize, acquired immune deficiency syndrome (AIDS) has become a leading public health problem in the United States. In 1997, for instance, nearly 400,000 Americans died from AIDS, while another 633,000 were first diagnosed with it.[53]

Organizational Interventions

AIDS has become an extremely important employment issue. Although medical professionals assure us that AIDS cannot be transmitted through casual contact at the workplace, many employees are nevertheless fearful of "catching" the disease and vehemently oppose the idea of working with AIDS victims.[54]

This employee reaction places employers somewhere between a rock and a hard place because AIDS victims are clearly protected under the ADA. An employer cannot allow itself to be influenced by employee preferences and prejudices; it must hire and retain qualified HIV-infected victims unless the debilitating effects of the disease impede their job performance.

An employer's only legal option for dealing with this predicament is to educate employees about how the AIDS virus is transmitted (and how it is not transmitted). Education aimed at reducing worker anxiety about AIDS is most effective when it precedes, rather than follows, a crisis. Unfortunately, although training may minimize AIDS-related hysteria at the workplace, it will probably not eliminate it. Many workers are likely to cling to their misconceptions about the transmission of this disease.

Substance Abuse

Nature and Extent of Problem

Drugs and alcohol use pervades U.S. society. For instance, nearly 10 percent of all full-time employees use illicit drugs (primarily marijuana and cocaine),[55] and another 10 percent are alcoholics.[56] Substance abuse costs U.S. employers an estimated $1 billion a year in terms of lost productivity, accidents, workers' compensation, health insurance claims, and theft of company property.[57]

Drug-Free Workplace Act
A law stating that government contractors must take certain steps to ensure that their workplaces are kept drug-free.

Although most organizations are taking steps to keep their workplaces drug-free voluntarily, government contractors are required to take such steps. The 1988 **Drug-Free Workplace Act** states that government contractors must ensure a drug-free workplace by notifying employees about:

- The dangers of drug abuse in the workplace
- Its policy of maintaining a drug-free workplace
- Any available drug counseling, rehabilitation, and employee assistance programs
- The penalties that may be imposed upon employees for drug abuse violations occurring in the workplace

Organizational Interventions

Employers can combat substance abuse at the workplace by screening out applicants and discharging employees who have been identified as substance abusers. Substance abuse is most commonly detected through urine and blood tests. About 30 to 40 percent of *Fortune* 500 companies currently require drug testing of current or future employees, and more than 90 percent of those currently without drug testing programs are considering implementing them.[58] (As we noted in Chapter 6, these programs must comply with state and federal laws, primarily the Fourth Amendment to the U.S. Constitution.) Supervisors can also detect substance abuse by observing their employees' behavior. Some of the symptoms to look for are listed in Exhibit 13-3.

Detecting substance abuse early can be quite useful to a company, as illustrated by the findings of a U.S. Postal Service study, summarized here:[59]

In 1987, the postal service tested 5,465 applicants for drugs, but did not use these results in hiring decisions. About 4,000 of these applicants were eventually hired. In a three-year follow-up, those testing positive had a 66 percent higher absenteeism rate and a 77 percent greater termination rate than those testing negative. The postal service now estimates that had it not hired the drug-positive group, it could have saved $150 million in absenteeism, rehiring, retraining, and injury compensation costs.

> **EXHIBIT 13-3**   Signs of Substance Abuse

Physical Signs or Conditions
- Weariness, exhaustion
- Unusual untidiness
- Yawning excessively
- Blank stare
- Slurred speech
- Sleepiness
- Unsteady walk
- Sunglasses worn at inappropriate times
- Unusual effort to cover arms
- Changes in appearance after lunch or break
- Flushed cheeks

Mood
- Constant depression or extreme anxiety
- Irritability
- Suspiciousness
- Complaints about others
- Frequent emotional outbursts
- Mood change after lunch break

Work Attendance
- Frequent absences on Mondays and Fridays
- Frequent unreported absences, explained later as "emergencies"

- Unusually high incidence of colds, flu, upset stomach, headaches
- Frequent use of unscheduled vacation time
- Leaving work area more than necessary
- Unexplained disappearance from job site
- Frequent requests to leave work early

Job Performance
- Taking needless risks
- Frequent accidents
- Inconsistency in work quality
- General carelessness
- Lapses in concentration or memory
- Difficulty recalling instructions
- Misses deadlines repeatedly

Relationship to Others on the Job
- Argumentative
- Withdrawn or inappropriately talkative
- Violent behavior
- Overreacting to criticism
- Frequent borrowing of money from coworkers
- Refusal to talk to supervisor about work issues

Source: Kertesz, L. (1990). Limiting liability from drug abuse. *Business Insurance*, June 11, 15–16.

EXHIBIT 13-4 | Issues to Be Covered in a Company Substance Abuse Policy

The Rules Regarding Substance Abuse

- What types of drugs are forbidden?
- Is the recreational (off-the-job) use of drugs forbidden?
- Is alcohol allowed on the premises?
- May workers drink alcohol during lunch?

The Use of Drug Tests

- When and under what circumstances will drug tests be administered (e.g., randomly, as part of an annual physical, after an accident, when there is reasonable suspicion of substance abuse)?
- What type of test will be administered?

- Will those failing the test be given a second, confirmatory test?
- What type of "chain of custody" procedures will be used to ensure that the test specimen (e.g., urine sample) does not become contaminated?

The Handling of Policy Violations

- How will rule violations be handled?
- Will employees be treated more favorably if they voluntarily come forward with their substance abuse problem?
- Will an EAP be available? If so, will employee participation be confidential?

When dealing with current employees with drug problems, some employers take a rehabilitative approach: Help abusers overcome their problem through remedial counseling.[60] **Employee assistance programs (EAPs)** employ mental health professionals (usually on a contract basis) to provide services to workers who are experiencing substance abuse or other personal problems. For example, the EAP at the Chase Manhattan Bank helps employees resolve problems of drug or alcohol abuse, child care, elder care, marital or family relationship concerns, emotional distress, anxiety, depression, or financial difficulties.[61] Employees may seek help on a voluntary, confidential basis, or may be referred by a supervisor who suspects that the employee's declining job performance is being caused by personal problems.[62]

Many companies currently use EAPs.[63] The potential payoff of an EAP is evidenced by a study that found that every dollar spent on an EAP returned an estimated $3 to $5 in lower absenteeism and greater productivity.[64]

Employers must develop written substance abuse policies that specify their approach to handling these problems. The policy should address each of the issues presented in Exhibit 13-4, specifying the prohibited behaviors and the consequences employees will face if they break the rules. Such policies serve two purposes: (1) to act as a deterrent and (2) to establish a sound legal basis for taking punitive action (e.g., suspension or discharge).

employee assistance programs (EAPs) An HRM program that uses mental health professionals to help workers overcome substance abuse or other personal problems.

Employee Wellness

Nature and Extent of Problem

Employee wellness is a relatively new HRM focus that seeks to eliminate certain debilitating health problems (e.g., cancer, heart disease, respiratory problems, hypertension) that can be caused by a person's poor lifestyle choices (e.g., smoking, poor nutrition, lack of exercise, obesity). Such health problems have become quite prevalent: Cancer, heart, and respiratory illnesses alone account for 55.5 percent of all hospital claims.[65]

These ailments can cause workplace problems such as absenteeism, turnover, lost productivity, and increased medical costs. For instance, people who have high blood pressure are 68 percent more likely than others to have medical claims of more than $5,000 per year, and the cost of medical claims for smokers is 18 percent higher than it is for nonsmokers.[66]

employee wellness Freedom from certain debilitating health problems that can be caused by a person's poor lifestyle choices.

Organizational Intervention

Many organizations attempt to help employees improve or maintain their overall health by offering them **employee wellness programs.** Such programs provide employees with physical fitness facilities, on-site health screening, and programs to

employee wellness programs Programs that help employees improve or maintain their overall health.

help them quit smoking, manage stress, and improve nutritional habits. The employee wellness program at Apple Computer, for instance, offers fitness facilities, health education, and preventive medicine that includes:[67]

- A smoking cessation program
- Seminars on nutrition and weight management
- Health assessments that measure blood pressure and resting pulse rate
- Fitness evaluations that assess cardiopulmonary fitness level, strength, flexibility, body composition, and nutritional status
- Medical examinations that include physical exams and exercise strength tests to determine cardiovascular fitness

Employee wellness programs can be quite effective. Research indicates that participation in a wellness program reduces both absenteeism and turnover, and increases productivity.[68] A study conducted at Mesa Petroleum, for example, found that the productivity difference between participants and nonparticipants amounted to a yearly savings of $700,000.[69]

If they are to work, wellness programs must successfully enlist "high-risk" individuals—those in greatest need of the program.[70] Unfortunately, most employees who participate in wellness programs exhibit fewer risk factors to begin with—employees at high risk stay away in droves![71] Because at-risk individuals do not seek help, many employee wellness programs fail to meet their objectives.[72]

Employers must, then, find some way to motivate high-risk individuals to participate. Some companies offer positive inducements (e.g., cash bonuses) to individuals who participate; other companies focus their efforts on nonparticipants by imposing certain penalties. For example, they may increase insurance premium contributions of nonparticipants or raise their deductible levels.[73]

Workplace Stress

Nature and Extent of Problem

Stress runs rampant at most workplaces. According to one survey, for instance, 40 percent of Americans think their jobs are extremely stressful.[74] As we noted in Chapter 9, workers' compensation claims for stress-related workplace disabilities are rising rapidly. Accordingly, some experts are calling stress this country's fastest growing occupational disease.[75]

What stresses today's workers? A host of factors contribute. A fairly complete list of job stressors appears in Exhibit 13-5.[76] Given the pervasiveness of this list, it is easy to understand why workplace stress is so widespread. Indeed, it would be difficult to find anyone who is not currently facing at least one of these problems. Excessive amounts of stress can have debilitating health effects, such as ulcers, colitis, hypertension, headaches, lower back pain, and cardiac conditions. At the workplace, stress effects include irritability, fuzzy thinking, and a decline in creativity,[77] causing workers to perform poorly, quit their jobs, suffer low morale, generate conflicts with coworkers, miss work, or exhibit indifference toward coworkers and customers.[78] These stress-induced outcomes now cost U.S. businesses somewhere between $150 and $300 billion per year![79] It stands to reason then that organizational interventions that reduce employees' stress can yield a significant cost savings. This is what happened at Delnor Community Hospital in Chicago. After putting 500 employees through a stress-reduction program, turnover dropped from 28 to 6 percent, saving the hospital $1.4 million.[80]

Organizational Interventions

Companies can help eliminate, or at least minimize, job stress. Implementing the HRM practices described throughout this text can alleviate many sources of employee

---

EXHIBIT 13-5   Common Job Stress Factors

The Nature of One's Work
- Unclear supervisory directives
- Under- or overutilization of abilities
- Unrealistic deadlines for completing work
- Conflict between personal and organizational goals
- Work overload
- Unclear perceptions regarding one's role in the organization
- Having a great deal of responsibility, but little authority to make decisions

Interpersonal Relationships
- Conflicts between work groups

- Competition, rather than cooperation, among workers
- Poor relationships with coworkers
- Being a target of prejudice because of one's age, gender, race, etc.

Organizational and Management Practices
- Lack of support from management
- Lack of opportunity for growth and development
- Overly close supervision
- Not being allowed to express one's feelings
- Inadequate recognition/reward system
- Uncertainty regarding downsizing/layoffs

Source: Adapted from Overman, S., and Thornburg, L. (1992). Beating the odds. *HRMagazine,* March, 42–47; Evans, W.H. (1992). Managing the burnout factor. *Mortgage Banking,* October, 119–123.

---

stress. For instance, effective selection and training procedures can help ensure that workers are properly suited to the demands of their jobs; clearly written job descriptions can reduce worker uncertainty regarding job responsibilities; effective performance appraisal systems can relieve stress by clarifying performance expectations; and effective pay-for-performance programs can relieve stress by reducing worker uncertainty regarding rewards. Some of the specific actions a supervisor may take to reduce worker stress are discussed in Section 13-3, "The Manager's Guide."

Unfortunately, companies cannot always eliminate all sources of job stress; some stress may be inherent in the job. For instance, some jobs are dangerous (e.g., logging, police work, firefighting), and some place the worker in demanding interpersonal situations (e.g., customer relations specialists). When job stresses cannot be relieved, the worker must learn to cope with them. A firm can help by offering employees stress counseling or by providing them the opportunity to "work off" their stress through physical exercise. Some of the organizational interventions described earlier, such as the use of EAPs and wellness programs, can be helpful in this regard.

Workplace Violence

Nature and Extent of Problem

The following scenario is becoming increasingly typical:

> A woman warned her employer, the Equitable Life Assurance Society, that her estranged husband had threatened to come to the work site and kill her. Management, however, did not take her warning seriously and refused to tighten security. Her husband later burst into the office, opened fire, and killed two employees. A jury awarded the victims' families $5 million in their suit against Equitable Life.

Violence at the workplace is increasing rapidly, as indicated by the fact that number of violent acts rose by 61 percent from 2002 to 2003.[81] In total, about 2 million people per year are victimized by violent acts at the workplace, acts that include homicides, assaults, robberies, hostage-taking, hijackings, and rapes.[82] Because of their increasing frequency, violent acts are now considered a major workplace safety and health threat. Most violent acts are committed by employees against other employees, supervisors, or customers. But, as we saw in the Equitable Life example, nonemployees also commit violent acts at the workplace, most often at health care and social service settings.

Organizational Interventions

Organizational interventions aimed at preventing workplace violence satisfy employers' moral and ethical obligations to provide their employees with safe work environments. Moreover, as we discuss next, such interventions also help companies reduce their costs and comply with the law.

Workplace violence can cost employers a lot of money. Employers must pay for victims' medical and psychiatric care, repairs and clean-up, insurance rate hikes, and increased security measures. Additional costs are incurred as the result of absenteeism, because the average victim misses 3.5 days of work following an incident.[83]

Employers must also be concerned about workplace violence for legal reasons. The General Duty Clause of the Occupational Safety and Health Act states that employers can be cited for a violation if there is a recognized danger of workplace violence in their establishment, and they do nothing to prevent it.

In addition to being fined by OSHA, employers can also be sued by victims of violence. The average out-of-court settlement for this type of litigation is $500,000. The average jury award is $3 million.[84] The legal test for determining employer liability for violent acts committed by nonemployees is as follows. The employer is liable if:

- It knew or should have known that a criminal act was probable (e.g., it was warned about threats made to an employee).
- It could have reasonably protected the employee from criminal assault, but failed to do so.
- Its failure to protect the employee caused the subsequent injuries to occur (in other words, had the employer done its part, the injury would not have happened).

A similar legal test is used to determine employer liability for violent acts committed by employees. As we noted in Chapter 6, an employer is liable for negligent hiring if it knew or should have known of the applicant's violent tendencies, but decided to hire that person anyway. In a similar vein, successful negligent retention suits can be filed when an employer retains a current employee despite knowledge of violent tendencies. Employers are liable in these situations if they had (or should have had) information signaling the danger of future violent acts, but ignored this danger.

So what can a company do to minimize the occurrences of violent acts? In 1996, OSHA issued a set of guidelines listing some of the security measures that can be implemented to reduce the threat of violence. These measures include:

- Improved lighting
- Employee escort services to and from parking lots
- Reception areas that can be locked when no one is on duty
- A policy stipulating that there are always at least two people on duty
- Security systems, such as electronic access control systems, silent alarms, metal detectors, and video cameras
- Policies regarding visitor access (sign-in, identification badges)
- Curved mirrors at hallway intersections or concealed areas
- Bullet-proof glass

An employer should consider these measures in light of the level of risk at a particular work site. For example, metal detectors and bullet-proof glass would be appropriate for inner-city emergency departments, abortion clinics, and psychiatric facilities where violence is highest.

In addition to implementing OSHA recommendations, an employer can further minimize violent acts through the use of preemployment screening (discussed in Chapter 6), strict antiviolence and antidrug/alcohol policies, and training. All workers should be taught how to recognize early signs of a troubled or potentially violent person and how to respond to such persons. Managers should be further trained on how to properly handle terminations because such acts often trigger violence.

13-3 The Manager's Guide

13-3a Employee Safety and Health and the Manager's Job

Safety and health responsibilities represent very important parts of a manager's job. We first discuss the manager's safety-related responsibilities, and then direct our discussion to the issue of employee health.

The Manager's Role in Ensuring Employee Safety

Line managers are critical to the success of an employee safety system, playing three primary roles.[85] First, managers must help employees want to work safely. Managers should emphasize workplace safety during orientation training, and workers should be given constant reminders of its importance throughout their employment.

Second, managers must ensure that workers are doing their jobs safely. This role involves training, coaching, and monitoring. Managers must teach workers how to do their jobs safely by providing employees with information about the safety procedures to follow, warnings to heed, and precautions to take. Managers must also inspect work sites regularly to detect unsafe conditions and to ensure that workers are, in fact, following established work procedures.

Third, managers investigate accidents. As we noted earlier, thorough and prompt investigations of accidents or near-misses can prevent future accidents. The manager is often a central figure in these investigations.

The Manager's Role in Ensuring Employee Health

Managers play three roles in the area of employee health. One, they ensure legal compliance, primarily with regard to the ADA. The ADA mandates that employers be flexible when assigning work to employees that have either repetitive motion or lower back disorders. Managers must learn about these conditions and the ways they limit workers' abilities.[86]

Second, managers can alleviate worker stress. As noted earlier, employee stress can be caused by a wide variety of factors, many of which are under the manager's control. These are some of the specific actions managers can take:[87]

- Try to match job assignments to employee skills.
- Avoid placing unrealistic deadlines on employees.
- Encourage employees to voice their concerns.
- Provide appropriate training and orientation.
- Rotate assignments between high- and low-stress tasks as much as possible.
- Provide employees with clear explanations of assigned duties and the activities for which they will be held accountable.
- State specific criteria by which employee performance will be judged and exactly how their performance will be measured.
- Periodically, let employees know where they stand with regard to job performance, and discuss how they can improve their performance.

Third, managers must ensure the confidentiality of the information they possess concerning employee disabilities. As we noted in Chapter 11, "Complying with Workplace Justice Laws," personal information (e.g., AIDS, substance abuse) may be conveyed only to those people with a "need to know." Rarely, if ever, may coworkers be privy to this information.

13-3b How the HRM Department Can Help

HRM departments develop/select and evaluate the various safety and health programs described in this chapter (e.g., safety incentive, training, and employee wellness programs). HR professionals are also responsible for ensuring OSHA compliance and incorporating safety and health concerns in HRM practices.

Responsibilities Related to OSHA Compliance

We noted earlier that OSHA imposes many technical standards. Some organizations employ safety professionals to deal with them. Often "housed" within HRM departments, these individuals ensure that OSHA standards are met. Their other OSHA-related responsibilities include representing the firm during OSHA inspections, keeping records of accidents, and tracking hazardous substances.

Linking Safety and Health Concerns to HRM Practices

HR professionals must consider safety and health issues as they formulate HRM practices. Earlier in the chapter, we discussed the need to consider safety issues when developing selection, training, and ergonomic (i.e., job design) practices. Safety and health issues also arise when HR professionals conduct job analyses and help negotiate collective bargaining agreements. Job analysis documents must specify the physical and mental demands of the job, and collective bargaining agreements must specify employers' rights and responsibilities in ensuring employee safety and health.

13-3c HRM Skill-Building for Managers

Managers need a number of specific skills to successfully meet their safety and health responsibilities. Two skills, conducting safety audits and accident investigation, are addressed in the following paragraphs.

How to Conduct a Safety Audit[88]

In safety audits, managers seek to identify and eliminate unsafe job behaviors by systematically monitoring employees' work. Each employee should be monitored according to a planned schedule, generally on a weekly basis, as follows:

Step 1: Observation

Stop in the work area for a few moments and observe worker's activities, looking for both safe and unsafe practices. Use the following guide:

- Be alert to unsafe practices that the employee corrects immediately upon seeing you enter the area (putting on protective equipment, such as gloves or goggles).
- Note whether appropriate protective clothing is being worn.
- Observe how employees use tools.
- Scrutinize the safety of the work area. For instance, is the floor slippery?
- Determine whether rules, procedures, and operating instructions are being followed.

Step 2: Employee Discussion

These discussions should help employees recognize and correct their unsafe acts. When engaging in them, adhere to the following advice:

- If you spot an unsafe act, be nonconfrontational. Point out the violation and ask the worker to state what he or she was doing and what safety-related consequences may arise if such behavior continues. Your goal is to help, not blame. Audits should not result in disciplinary actions unless an individual consistently violates safety rules.

- As you observe your employees, encourage them to discuss any safety concerns they may have and ask them to offer any ideas for safety improvement.

- Commend any good performance that you observe.

Step 3: Recording and Follow-Up

Findings should be recorded in writing. Pursue any item discussed during the audit that requires follow-up.

How to Investigate Accidents[89]

When an accident occurs in your work area, your first responsibility is to ensure the safety of all employees:

- Make sure the injured are cared for and receive medical attention, if necessary.

- Guard against a more dangerous secondary event by removing danger sources and evacuating other personnel from the area, if necessary.

- Restrict access to the area so no one else will be harmed, and so the scene will not be disturbed.

You should then begin an investigation to identify both the immediate and underlying causes of the accident. The immediate cause is the event that directly led to the accident, such as a slippery floor, failure to wear safety gear, or failure to follow proper procedures.

Immediate causes, although easily found, are not always very helpful in suggesting how future incidents of this nature can be avoided. To accomplish this aim, you must discover the underlying cause of the accident. For example, suppose a worker slips and falls on spilled oil. The oil on the floor is the immediate cause of the accident, but you need to know why it was not cleaned up and why a machine was leaking oil in the first place. Poor training, lack of rule enforcement, low safety awareness, poor maintenance, or crowded work areas commonly underlie accidents.

Make sure the accident scene is kept intact until the investigation is finished. Remember that this will be the only chance you will have to view the scene exactly as it was at the time of the accident. If a camera is available, take photographs of the scene. Nothing related to the incident should be destroyed or discarded.

When conducting the investigation, you should inspect the location (e.g., check for chemicals, broken pieces of machinery) and interview injured or affected workers, eyewitnesses, and anyone else who may be familiar with the accident area. Interviews should be conducted immediately, while the incident is still fresh in everyone's mind. Ask individuals to give their own account of the incident; let them tell their stories without interruption, and then see if the various responses corroborate one another. Continue asking "Why?" until underlying causes surface. After these causes are identified, you should recommend any changes indicated by your findings.

How to Assign Dangerous Work[90]

Many jobs, such as police work and construction, involve significant risk of injury to employees. What should you do if one of your employees refuses to complete an assignment that is viewed as being too dangerous? The OSHA law gives workers the right to protect themselves from dangerous employment conditions. Under such conditions, a worker can legally refuse an assignment. A situation would qualify as being "too dangerous" if the following conditions apply:

- A reasonable person would conclude that there is a real danger of death or serious injury. Ask yourself, "Are the employee's apprehensions objectively reasonable?"

- There is insufficient time to eliminate the danger through regular channels.

- The employee sought from his employer, but was unable to obtain, a correction of the dangerous conditions.

Chapter Objectives Revisited

1. Understand how effective safety and health practices can enhance an organization's competitive advantage.

   - Reducing the following safety and health-related costs: Medical and insurance costs, workers' compensation, survivor benefits, lost wages, damaged equipment and materials, production delays, other workers' time losses, selection and training costs for replacement workers, and accident reporting
   - Legal compliance: Occupational Safety and Health Act, Employee Right-to-Know Law, Americans with Disabilities Act

2. Describe safety and health requirements imposed by federal law.

   - Occupational Safety and Health Act: Aims to ensure safe working conditions for every American worker
   - Employee Right-to-Know Law: Gives workers the right to know what hazardous substances they are dealing with on the job
   - Americans with Disabilities Act: Prohibits discrimination against disabled individuals

3. Explain the major causes of workplace accidents.

   - Employee error
   - Equipment insufficiency
   - Procedure insufficiency

4. Discuss how companies can prevent workplace accidents.

   - Employee selection: Prescreen "accident-prone" applicants.
   - Training: Train on safe and proper job procedures.
   - Safety incentive programs: Motivate safe behavior by providing workers with incentives for avoiding accidents.
   - Safety audits: Observe employees on the job and correct unsafe behaviors.
   - Safety committees: Oversee organizations' safety functions.

5. Explain the major health issues at the workplace and how organizations can address them.

   - Repetitive motion disorders: Affect tendons that become inflamed from the strains and stresses of repeated, forceful motions
     - Ergonomic approach
     - Employee training
   - Lower back disorders
     - Prescreen individuals who either have existing back problems or are prone to develop such afflictions.
     - Job training
     - Fitness training
   - AIDS
     - Educate employees about how AIDS is and is not transmitted.
     - Substance abuse
     - Screen out applicants and discharge employees who have been identified as substance abusers.
     - Rehabilitative approach: Help abusers overcome their problem through remedial counseling.
   - Employee wellness: The absence of certain debilitating health problems that can be caused by a person's poor lifestyle choices
     - Employee wellness programs: Provide employees with physical fitness facilities, on-site health screening, and programs to help them quit smoking, manage stress, and improve nutritional habits.
   - Workplace violence: Acts of assault, rape, and homicide committed by employees or nonemployees
     - Increased security measures
     - Employee selection, antiviolence and anti-drug/alcohol abuse policies, and employee training

Review Questions

Note: You can find the correct answers to these questions by taking the quiz and then submitting your answers in the Online Edition. The program will automatically score your submission. If you miss a question, the program will provide the correct answer, a rationale for the answer, and the section number in the chapter where the topic is discussed.

1. Which of the following items is not among the goals of the Occupational Safety and Health Act?

   a. requiring employers to keep records regarding job-related safety and health matters
   b. requiring employers to maintain an accident fund for distribution to employees as needed
   c. setting and enforcing workplace safety standards
   d. promoting employer-sponsored educational programs that foster safety and health

2. The Hazard Communication Standard requires that

   a. material safety data sheets (MSDSs) be written in a specific format for communication to employees.
   b. employees be notified about any threatening work situations in which they might be placed.
   c. pregnant women be kept away from work sites where hazardous material is stored.
   d. employees be told what hazardous substances they are dealing with on the job.

3. Which of the following four personality characteristics is not associated with having accidents at work?

   a. risk taking
   b. aggressiveness
   c. impulsiveness
   d. rebelliousness

4. Linking safe behavior with rewards is best accomplished using

   a. employee selection systems.
   b. safety incentive programs.
   c. training programs.
   d. hazard communication programs.

5. Safety audits focus primarily on

   a. analyzing safety documentation such as material safety data sheets.
   b. preventing accidents.
   c. unsafe acts or behavior.
   d. assessing compliance with labor–management agreements on safety.

6. The most common occupational injury is

   a. lower back pain.
   b. repetitive motion injury.
   c. substance abuse.
   d. AIDS.

7. According to the Americans with Disabilities Act, an examination to search for a history of lower back pain may be conducted

   a. after a review of the employment application has been completed.
   b. only after an employment offer has been made.
   c. at any time as long as all applicants undergo the examination.
   d. only after it has been determined that reasonable accommodation could be made for the applicant should lower back pain in fact be uncovered.

8. Approximately what percentage of the full-time labor force is plagued by substance abuse problem?

   a. less than 5 percent
   b. 10 percent
   c. 25 percent
   d. 50 percent

9. An employee is having difficulty controlling a weight problem. Which of the following programs is specifically designed to address this kind of problem?

   a. employee assistance program
   b. cafeteria benefits plan
   c. employee wellness program
   d. on-the-job training program

10. What is America's fastest growing occupational disease?

   a. AIDS
   b. workplace stress
   c. repetitive stress disorder
   d. lower back pain

Discussion Questions

1. Describe the safety program at Appleton. After reviewing the pertinent information in Section 13-3, "The Manager's Guide," which facet of the program do you think was most responsible for its success? Explain.

2. Briefly describe the two ways in which the use of effective safety and health practices can enhance competitive advantage.

3. Describe OSHA's priority classification for determining which organizations will be inspected.

4. What are the main provisions of the Employee Right-to-Know Law?

5. Describe three causes of workplace accidents.

6. Describe three strategies that may be used to prevent or minimize workplace accidents.

7. What are repetitive motion disorders? What steps can an organization take to prevent them?

8. Can an organization reject an applicant on the basis of having a lower back disorder? Explain.

9. Describe two approaches to handling substance abuse problems. In your opinion, which is the better approach? Why?

10. What is an employee wellness program? Why do such programs so often fail to meet their goals? How can they be improved?

11. It was stated that implementing the HRM practices described throughout this text could alleviate many sources of employee stress. Explain.

12. What steps can a manager take to minimize the occurrence of workplace accidents?

13. Summarize the steps involved in conducting an accident investigation.

Experiential Exercise

How Well Did Your Manager Manage Your Stress?

Overview

You will be asked to identify the stress factors in your current job and evaluate what, if anything, your manager did to alleviate this stress.

Steps

1. Break into groups of three to five students.

2. Identify a member of your group who is currently employed in a stressful job.

3. The jobholder should describe the stress factors to team members (use Exhibit 13-5 as a guide) and then describe what, if any, actions the manager took to try to alleviate these stresses.

4. Team members should discuss these actions. Were they appropriate? Were they the most appropriate? What alternative actions could have been taken?

5. Select a group spokesperson to present your findings to the class.

6. The presentation should include:

   a. A general description of the job

   b. A description of the most prominent stress factors

   c. A description and evaluation of what the manager did to help

   d. A description of what further actions, if any, should be taken by the manager

Cases

A Case of AIDS Hysteria

Ma and Pa's is a midsized restaurant located in Syracuse, New York. It employs 35 servers who are responsible for waiting tables. One server, George, has been a server there for three years and is considered one of the best. One morning, George comes in about an hour early to discuss a problem with his supervisor, Amy. Amy can see that George is very upset, actually on the verge of tears. He tells her that he has just seen his doctor and was informed that he is HIV positive. As yet, he has shown no overt symptoms of the disease. His doctor told him it could be years before the debilitating effects of the disease appear. Amy offers her sympathy and tells George not to worry as far as his job is concerned.

Fearful that horrible rumors about George's condition will quickly spread throughout the restaurant, Amy decides to inform all restaurant personnel of the truth of the matter. She holds a staff meeting later that evening and conveys the facts about George's condition, reminding the employees that there is really nothing to fear.

After the meeting, a group of six other servers, who work the same shift as George, tell Amy that they refuse to work with George. They state that no one really knows how AIDS is spread, and they're not willing to take any chances. Amy informs them that there is nothing she can do about this situation, that George's rights are protected under the law. They respond by asking, "What about our rights?" They then give Amy an ultimatum: Either George goes, or they will tell all the customers that one of the restaurant's servers has AIDS.

Questions

1. Was Amy correct in informing the other employees about George's condition? Explain.
2. Now that the "cat's out of the bag," what should the restaurant do to resolve this problem?
3. How should the problem have been handled in the first place?

I Won't Fly, Don't Ask Me

Simone Kelley is an executive for GreatIdeas, Inc., a Boston marketing firm. Her boss, Bob Collins, tells her that she must fly to San Francisco tomorrow to close out an important deal. Kelley, who has not flown since September 11, 2001, refuses the assignment. She tells Bob that she would be willing to take a train, but she is afraid to fly; she worries about another terrorist attack. Bob cannot send her by train because it would take too long. Furthermore, Simone is the only executive who could close this deal—the client likes her and refuses to deal with another executive.

Questions

1. Should Bob force Simone to fly to San Francisco? What other options does he have?
2. If Simone is forced to fly, but refuses, should she be disciplined? Does the company have a legal right to do so? (Review the pertinent information in Section 13-3, "The Manager's Guide.")

References

1. Halls, C., and Rhodes, J. (2004). *Employee wellness and beyond. Occupational Health and Safety,* 73 (9), 46-50.
2. Http://www.bls.gov/news.release/pdf/osh.pdf.
3. Warner, D. (1991). Ways to make safety work. *Nation's Business,* December, 25-27.
4. Peskin, M.I., and McGrath, F.J. (1992). Industrial safety: Who is responsible and who benefits? *Business Horizons,* May-June, 66-70.
5. Ibid.
6. Http://www.osha.gov/media/oshnews/oct98/reg4_98161.html.
7. Http://www.osha.gov/media/oshnews/oct98/reg1pres.html.
8. Http://www.osha.gov/media/oshnews/oct98/reg4_98175.html.
9. Kahn, S.C., Brown, B.B., Zepke, B.E., and Lanzarone, M. (1990). *Personnel Director's Legal Guide* (2nd ed.). Boston: Warren, Gorham & Lamont.
10. Ibid.
11. Ibid.
12. Ibid.
13. Ibid.
14. Http://www.osha.gov/as/opa/ashafacts.html.
15. May, B.D. (1986). Hazardous substances: OSHA mandates the right to know. *Personnel Journal,* August, 128-130.
16. Tompkins, N.C. (1993). At the top of OSHA's hit list. *HRMagazine,* July, 54-55.
17. Ibid.
18. Rhodes, D. (1989). Supervisors and tough environment laws. *Supervisory Management,* July, 29-34.
19. Http://www.eeoc.gov/stats/ada-charges/html.
20. Ibid.
21. Ibid.
22. Ibid.
23. Http://www.bls.gov/iif/home.htm.
24. Ibid.
25. Hanson, C.P. (1988). Personality characteristics of the accident involved employee. *Journal of Business and Psychology, 2,* 346-365.
26. Kamp, J. (1991). Preemployment personality testing for loss control. *American Society of Safety Engineers,* June, 123-125.
27. Jones, J.W., and Wuebker, L.J. (1988). Accident prevention through personnel selection. *Journal of Business and Psychology, 3,* (2), 187-198.
28. Komaki, J., Barwick, K.D., and Scott, L.R. (1978). A behavioral approach to occupational safety: Pinpointing and reinforcing safe performance in a food manufacturing plant. *Journal of Applied Psychology, 63* (4), 434-445.
29. Markus, T. (1990). How to set up a safety incentive program. *Supervision,* July, 14-16.
30. Rademaker, K. (1991). Insight into incentives. *Occupational Hazards,* November, 43-46.
31. Atkinson, W. (2004). Safety incentive programs: What works? *Occupational Safety and Health, 66* (8), 35-40.
32. Rademaker. Insights into incentives.
33. Atkinson. Safety incentive programs.
34. LaBar, G. (1990). How to improve your accident investigations. *Occupational Hazards,* March, 33-36.
35. Ibid.
36. Barenklau, K.E. (1989). Safety committee can be effective loss control tool. *Business Insurance,* November 20, 56.
37. Http://stats.bls.gov/news.release/osh2.nws.htm.
38. Ibid.
39. Ibid.
40. Ibid.
41. Heilbroner, D. (1993). Repetitive stress injury. *Working Woman,* February, 61-65.
42. Goldoftas, B. (1991). Hands that hurt. *Technology Review,* January, 43-50.
43. Ibid.
44. Ibid.
45. Benson, T.E. (1990). Poor design is truly a pain. *Industry Week,* July 16, 60-62.
46. Heilbroner. Repetitive stress injury.
47. Holland, T.H. (1991). Injury rates plummet with a behavior-management program. *Safety and Health,* November 50-53.
48. Gunch, D. (1993). Employees exercise to prevent injuries. *Personnel Journal,* July, 58-62.
49. Hollenbeck, J.R., Ilgen, D.R., and Crampton, S.M. (1992). Lower back disability in occupational settings: A review of the literature from a human resource management view. *Personnel Psychology, 45* (2), 247-278.
50. Http://www.eeoc.gov/stats.ada-merit.html.
51. Hollenbeck et al. Lower back disability.
52. Ibid.
53. Http://www.avert.org/suastaty.htm.
54. Dallier, T.J. (1989). Relieving the fear of contagion. *Personnel Administrator,* February, 52-58.
55. Rich, L.A. (1992). Drugs and drink: The safety connection. *Occupational Hazards,* May, 69-72.
56. Rumpel, D.A. (1989). Motivating alcoholic workers to seek help. *Management Review,* July, 37-39.
57. Kertesz, L. (1990). Limiting liability from drug abuse. *Business Insurance,* June 11, 15-16.
58. Faley, R.H., Kleiman, L.S., and Wall, P.S. (1988). Drug testing in the public and private-sector workplaces: Technical and legal issues. *Journal of Business and Psychology, 3,* (2), 154-186.
59. Rich. Drugs and drink.
60. Gerstein, L.H., and Bayer, G.A. (1990). Counseling psychology and employee assistance programs: Previous obstacles and potential contributions. *Journal of Business and Psychology, 5,* (1), 101-110.
61. Kirrane, D. (1990). EAPS: Dawning of a new age. *HRMagazine,* January, 30-34.
62. Soto, C. (1991). Employee assistance program liability and workplace privacy. *Journal of Business and Psychology, 5* (4), 537-541.
63. Kirrane. EAPS.
64. Ibid.
65. Overman, S., and Thornburg, L. (1992). Beating the odds. *HRMagazine,* March, 42-47.
66. Ibid.
67. Ibid.
68. Keaton, P.N., and Semb, M.J. (1990). Shaping up the bottom line. *HRMagazine,* September, 81-86.
69. Ibid.
70. Erfurt, J.C., Foote, A., and Heirich, M.A. (1992). The cost effectiveness of worksite wellness programs for hypertension control, weight loss, smoking cessation, and exercise. *Personnel Psychology, 45* (1), 5-27.
71. Cave, D.G. (1992). Employees are paying for poor health habits. *HRMagazine,* August, 52-58.
72. Caudron, S. (1990). The wellness payoff. *Personnel Journal,* July, 55-60.
73. Cave. Employees are paying.
74. Tyler, K. (2003). Cut the stress. *HR Magazine, 48* (5), 101-106.

75. Hendrickson, R.J. (1989). Proactive approach to minimize stress on the job. *Professional Safety,* November, 29–32.

76. Anderson, C.M. (1990). A departmental stress management plan. *Health Care Supervision, 8* (4), 1–8.

77. Tyler. Cut the stress.

78. Ibid.; Overman and Thornburg. Beating the odds.

79. Adapted from the following sources: Overman and Thornburg, Beating the odds; Evans, W.H. (1992). Managing the burnout factor. *Mortgage Banking,* October, 119–123.

80. Kaplan-Leiserson, E. (2000). Putting your Heartmath into it. *T&D,* February, 42–49.

81. Http://www/bls.gov/iif/oshwc/cfoi/cfch0002.pdf.

82. Wiscombe, J. (2002). Hot legal topics: Vigilance stops violence and lawsuits. *Workforce, 81* (10), 38–43.

83. Ibid.

84. Ibid.

85. Kalgaugh, M. (2004). 5 steps to a world-class safety system. *Occupational Health and Safety, 73* (9), 184–189.

86. Hollenbeck et al. Lower back disability.

87. Anderson. A departmental stress management plan; Evans. Managing the burnout factor; Hendrickson. Proactive approach.

88. Collinge, J.A. (1992). Auditing reduces accidents by eliminating unsafe practices. *Oil & Gas Journal,* August 24, 38–41.

89. LaBar. How to improve; Jacobs, H.C., and Nieburg, J.T. (1989). Accident investigations. *Occupational Health and Safety,* December, 13–16.

90. Pollard, C.T. (2002). Fear of flying. *HRMagazine,* January, 81–85.

Establishing HRM Practices in Foreign Countries

Chapter Fourteen

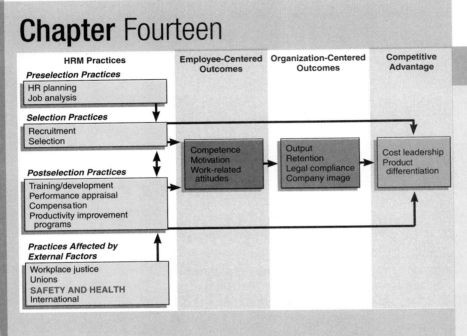

HRM Practices	Employee-Centered Outcomes	Organization-Centered Outcomes	Competitive Advantage
Preselection Practices HR planning Job analysis			
Selection Practices Recruitment Selection	Competence Motivation Work-related attitudes	Output Retention Legal compliance Company image	Cost leadership Product differentiation
Postselection Practices Training/development Performance appraisal Compensation Productivity improvement programs			
Practices Affected by External Factors Workplace justice Unions **SAFETY AND HEALTH** International			

Key Terms

artifacts
assumptions
conversational currency
cultue
expatriate

joint venture
reinforcement substation
repatriates
values
wholly owed subsidiaries

Chapter Objectives

Upon completion of this chapter, you will be able to:

- Understand why companies establish foreign operations and what must be done to maintain competitive advantage there.

- Understand why a company must account for cultural differences when establishing foreign operations.

- Explain why companies often choose expatriates to manage foreign operations.

- Describe the HRM issues regarding the use of expatriates.

- Describe the HRM issues regarding the management of host-country employees.

14-1 Gaining Competitive Advantage

In previous chapters, the opening case was used to illustrate how effective HRM practices can enhance competitive advantage. In this chapter, we take a different slant: We illustrate how a firm can lose competitive advantage as a result of ineffective HRM practices.

14-1a Opening Case: Losing Competitive Advantage at General Electric[1]

The Problem: Trying to "Americanize" a Newly Purchased French Firm

When General Electric (GE) restructured its corporate identity, it defined "medical technology" as one of its core business areas. To solidify its place in this industry, GE purchased a French medical equipment manufacturing firm, Cie Generale de Radiologie (CGR), a move that it predicted would generate $25 million in profits by the end of the first year.

To ensure that GE-CGR achieved the same success as its other endeavors, GE tried to "Americanize" the firm by establishing management systems based on the "American values" that worked so well for GE in the United States. GE believed that once American systems were in place and French managers were indoctrinated in the "American way," success would be guaranteed.

The Solution: "Americanizing" GE-CGR

GE executives planned seminars for the host-national managers to socialize their new French counterparts into "GE culture." The French managers were given T-shirts to wear at the seminar; the shirts bore GE's slogan, "Go for One," meaning "Our goal as GE managers is to be number one in the industry." The French managers wore the T-shirts to the training seminars, but they were highly insulted. One French manager stated, "It was like Hitler was back, forcing us to wear uniforms. It was humiliating." Needless to say, the seminar did not achieve its goal of building cohesion among the managers and their new employer, GE.

Americans also hung English-language posters that GE had used in the United States on the walls of the GE-CGR and flew GE flags from their flagpoles. To the Americans' surprise, French employees resented this practice. One aptly summed up the reaction by saying, "They came in here bragging—we are GE, we're the best and we've got the methods."

GE sent specialists in to rework GE-CGR's accounting system, making their procedures compatible with GE's. Unfortunately, these accounting system specialists were unfamiliar with French accounting and reporting systems, and GE's system was not congruent with French accounting standards. A compromise system took several months, during which time a lot of money and goodwill between the French and the Americans were lost.

How the Solution Hindered Competitive Advantage

GE-CGR lost $25 million in its first year, instead of making $25 million as projected. GE sent an executive to fix things by enacting a variety of cost-cutting measures familiar in the United States, but not in France: massive layoffs and closing of plants.

The reaction? Unhappy with the new environment, many French managers and engineers left and took jobs elsewhere. The total workforce shrank from 6,500 to 5,000. Imagine the subsequent recruiting problems GE-CGR had—after all, why would some young, hotshot engineer want to work for a company that was losing its best people? GE lost a portion of its competitive advantage in this industry due to cross-cultural misunderstandings and a poor human resource management strategy.

14-1b Linking HRM Practices to Foreign Competitive Advantage

After World War II, most American companies did not have to worry much about competition from overseas firms. The U.S. market was strong and large, and as long as a company had a good product, they did not need to go overseas with that product—they could make plenty of profit in the domestic market. During the past three decades, however, that situation has changed dramatically.

Staying Competitive: The Need to Compete in Foreign Markets

Increasing competition has forced many American firms to seek foreign markets in order to stay competitive. In the last two decades, U.S. exports have increased more than 10 times, and 700 out of 1,000 of the largest U.S. industrial firms expect that their growth in foreign markets will exceed their domestic growth within five years. U.S. companies own more than $350 billion in foreign assets. Foreign sales of U.S. companies increased at a rate of 10 percent a year during the last decade.[2] Coca-Cola, International Harvester, Gillette, Otis Elevator, and Dow Chemical are just a few U.S. firms that now make more than 50 percent of their profits from their foreign operations and sales.

International business operations appear in a variety of forms. The most common way medium to large companies "go international" is simply to set up foreign operations that they own; such operations are called **wholly owned subsidiaries.**

In some instances, American firms may join up with foreign firms and create new companies, called **joint ventures.** Joint ventures have mushroomed in recent years for two reasons. First, the local laws of some countries do not allow subsidiaries to be wholly owned by foreign companies. Often, such laws require that local operations have at least a 51 percent ownership. Second, joint ventures allow companies to draw on others' expertise: No one company can know everything it needs to know to sell or manufacture products across diverse worldwide business markets.[3] For instance, local firms may know how to best market and sell a product in a foreign country, but may lack production know-how. The American firm, on the other hand, may know how to best design and manufacture a product, but lack marketing experience in the foreign country.

wholly owned subsidiaries American-owned companies operating in a foreign country.

joint venture A company operating in a foreign country that is dually owned by an American and foreign firm.

The Impact of International HRM Practices on Employee Motivation, Satisfaction, and Performance

As businesses globalize their efforts further, they need to properly select, train, manage, compensate, and develop employees to work in cross-cultural environments. When companies cross borders and set up foreign subsidiaries, they can easily lose any competitive advantage if they try to superimpose American human resource practices onto the subsidiary. Yet, the failure to adjust to the foreign cultural environment is the key reason why expatriates often fail to succeed.[4] It never occurs to most executives to take any other course of action, because their practices have already been proven to be effective.

However, as GE-CGR's experience so vividly illustrates, inappropriate HRM practices can profoundly affect the motivation, satisfaction, and performance of foreign and expatriate employees. A company cannot effectively compete when it experiences internal conflict within its management ranks. When management teams are made up of people from different cultures who cannot get along, productivity suffers. For instance, researchers have concluded that most American–Japanese joint ventures do not fail because of poor planning, financial problems, or any of a host of business factors. Rather, American and Japanese managers seem to be unable to work together effectively.[5]

14-2 HRM Issues and Practices

In this chapter, we explore international human resource issues that arise in the context of subsidiaries and joint ventures. First, we discuss culture and cultural differences that must be considered as firms operate in foreign markets. Then, we discuss how firms must formulate and implement HRM practices within this international context. Then, our discussion centers on the issues of deploying U.S. managers and setting up HRM practices at foreign locations.

14-2a Understanding Cultural Differences

What Is "Culture"?

Many people think of culture as the aesthetic side of life; that a country's culture is reflected in tangible things like its dance, music, paintings, clothing fashions, and so on. Such tangible things do represent superficial aspects of culture, called **artifacts.** Although artifacts are the most visible signs of culture, like the tip of an iceberg, they rest on certain "invisible" underpinnings, lying beneath the surface—namely, values and assumptions. Artifacts are simply manifestations of the underlying values and assumptions shared by a group of people. To interpret a culture's artifacts, then, one must first understand the values and assumptions from which they flow.

artifacts Tangible things that represent the superficial aspects of a country's culture.

Values are the rules of societal propriety and impropriety that are shared by people within a culture.[6] In other words, they dictate which behaviors are appropriate and which are not. Cultural values are passed down from generation to generation.[7] People begin learning them from the time they are born. Over time, these values are continually reinforced by parents, teachers, peers, media, religion, and so forth.

values The rules of societal proprietary and impropriety that are shared by people within a culture.

Values evolve from society members' **assumptions** about life. Anthropologists believe that the assumptions held by a society evolve from that society's attempts to adjust to the world around it.[8] Societies have had to figure out how to best communicate, educate, feed, clothe, and govern the people within their boundaries. Over time, through experimentation with differing philosophies, methods, and ideas, these basic assumptions about life emerge.[9]

assumptions A society's beliefs that have evolved from its attempts to adjust to the world around it.

Culture and Behavior

Culture is a society's set of assumptions, values, and rules about social interaction. The culture in which one is raised programs the mind to react to the environment in certain ways. In essence, culture provides people with a mental road map and traffic signals.[10] The road map depicts the goals to be reached and the ways to get there; the traffic signals indicate who has the right of way, when to stop, and so on.

culture A society's set of assumptions, values, and rules about social interaction.

In other words, people have within their minds a kind of "cultural software."[11] They do not have to wake up in the morning and figure out how to greet people, how to behave in a classroom, how to dress, how to behave when invited to someone's house, or whether to eat with silverware or their hands. All of this is programmed in, and people are free to go about their day, pursuing goals within the confines of their culture's boundaries.

Cross-Cultural Differences in the Workplace

Part of one's cultural software involves rules and expectations about how people are to act in the workplace. These rules concern such work activities as the following:[12]

- How interviews should be conducted
- How managers should act with their subordinates
- How negotiations should be conducted
- How new information should be packaged for training purposes
- How people should be paid for their work

Different cultures' work behaviors appear in Exhibit 14-1. The exhibit contrasts some American cultural values with those of another country and illustrates how different values lead to different behavioral expectations.

Because of different behavioral expectations, cultures sometimes clash. For example, consider a situation in which a Japanese and an American manager, working for the same company, are trying to resolve a conflict. The Japanese abhor interpersonal confrontation and conflict, assuming that conflict is a negative part of human life that should be avoided at all costs. If conflict does occur, it should be resolved in a way that people will not lose the respect of their peers (i.e., not "lose face"). Problems in Japan are normally solved behind closed doors, and any potential for public embarrassment in business negotiations is carefully eliminated in advance.

On the other hand, U.S. culture dictates that conflicts should be brought out in the open and discussed in public, face to face. Imagine the potential problems that arise when American and Japanese managers try to resolve a conflict situation! Not much gets accomplished, and both parties can wind up frustrated and angry. However, this is the very problem many Americans face when working with the Japanese, because both sides bring different sets of values to each and every interaction.[13]

EXHIBIT 14-1	Work Behavior Associated with Different Cultural Values

Cultural Dimension: The Nature of People

- *American orientation/behavior:* People can change. Therefore, training is valuable because it gives people an opportunity to learn on the job.
- *Contrasting orientation/behavior:* People cannot change. The organization should emphasize selection over training. Select the right person for the job, and do not expect him or her to change.

Cultural Dimension: How People Relate to Others

- *American orientation/behavior:* People are individualistic. People should be hired on the basis of merit.
- *Contrasting culture/behavior:* Relationships dominate over individualistic concerns. The CEO's relative should be hired for the job.

Cultural Dimension: Primary Mode of Activity

- *American orientation/behavior:* Active. Employees should work hard to achieve goals.
- *Contrasting orientation/behavior:* Passive. Employees should work only as hard as needed to be able to live.

Cultural Dimension: Conception of Space

- *American orientation/behavior:* Private. Executives should hold important meetings behind closed doors and have the secretary screen all interruptions.
- *Contrasting orientation/behavior:* Public. Executives should hold important meetings in an open area, allowing for interruptions from employees and visitors.

Cultural Dimension: Time Orientation

- *American orientation/behavior:* Future/present. Policy statements refer to long-term goals, while keeping a focus on this year's bottom line and quarterly reports; innovation and flexibility to meet a dynamic and changing future are emphasized.
- *Contrasting culture/behavior:* Past. Policy statements this year reflect policy statements 10 years ago. The company intends to perform in the future as it has done in the past.

Source: Adapted from Adler, N.J. (1990). *International Dimensions of Organizational Behavior* (2nd ed.). Boston: PWS-Kent.

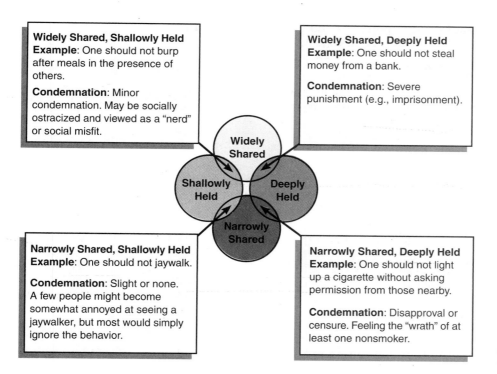

Widely Shared, Shallowly Held
Example: One should not burp after meals in the presence of others.

Condemnation: Minor condemnation. May be socially ostracized and viewed as a "nerd" or social misfit.

Widely Shared, Deeply Held
Example: One should not steal money from a bank.

Condemnation: Severe punishment (e.g., imprisonment).

Narrowly Shared, Shallowly Held
Example: One should not jaywalk.

Condemnation: Slight or none. A few people might become somewhat annoyed at seeing a jaywalker, but most would simply ignore the behavior.

Narrowly Shared, Deeply Held
Example: One should not light up a cigarette without asking permission from those nearby.

Condemnation: Disapproval or censure. Feeling the "wrath" of at least one nonsmoker.

Figure 14-1

The Degree of Condemnation Associated with Breaking Different Types of Cultural Rules

Source: Black, J.S., and Mendenhall, M. (1993). Resolving conflicts with the Japanese: Mission impossible? *Sloan Management Review,* 34 (3), 49–59.

How People React to Cultural Improprieties

Culture allows us to predict fairly accurately how others "should" behave in a variety of situations. Those who break cultural rules threaten that social predictability. When cultural rules are violated, people usually feel uneasy, anxious, and threatened, and the "guilty party" is often condemned or punished in some manner. The degree of condemnation depends on two factors: (1) the extent to which the broken rule is widely shared among a cultural group's members and (2) the extent to which the rule is deeply held and viewed as being important or sacred.[14] Figure 14-1 illustrates different types of cultural rules and the typical condemnation associated with each.

When working with people from other cultures, then, one must attempt to learn the rules of that culture and abide by them. Imagine the difficulty of trying to learn all of this in order to operate according to another culture's norms and values! But that is just what many Americans are now having to do. Section 14-3, "The Manager's Guide," offers some tips for managers who find themselves working in Japan.

14-2b The Use of Expatriates

International human resource management often focuses on the plight of **expatriate managers and employees**. An expatriate is "normally a professional/managerial employee moved from one country to, and for employment in, another country."[15]

Expatriates often find themselves transported, literally overnight, into new and alien social and business cultures. Despite these obstacles, such employees are almost always expected to perform well in their jobs immediately. Unfortunately, many people do not perform as effectively in foreign countries as they do in their home countries: An estimated 35 to 70 percent of American expatriates perform poorly in their foreign jobs.[16]

We now examine how the use of expatriates can enhance competitive advantage. We then discuss expatriates' legal rights regarding EEO and conclude by discussing specific expatriate-related HRM practices.

expatriate A professional/managerial employee moved from one country to, and for employment in, another country.

The Use of Expatriates and Competitive Advantage

As a company becomes involved in foreign subsidiaries or joint ventures, it must decide whether to fill its key management positions with expatriates or with managers from the host country. Most firms fill at least some of these positions with expatriates because, as noted later, expatriate managers can enhance competitive advantage in at least three areas: succession planning, coordination and control, and informational needs.

Succession Planning

Firms use assignments in foreign countries to "internationalize" future top managers. As we noted in Chapter 7, "Training and Developing Employees," effective succession planning involves the planned development of managerial talent for the future. To lead their firms to competitive advantage in the global marketplace of the twenty-first century, managers must understand many international aspects of business.[17] Increasingly, many companies find that managers cannot learn the needed international-related skills in corporate training classrooms; rather, managers must learn international aspects of their business through a real-world foreign experience.

Coordination and Control Systems

Expatriates do such things as open new markets, facilitate a merger or acquisitions, set up new technologies and systems, and strategically coordinate and control foreign operations, all of which can enhance a company's competitive advantage. By overseeing foreign operations, these managers can help ensure that such operations are congruent with corporate strategy and policy.

Informational Needs

Corporate headquarters need information about important foreign business functions to assess and update global strategic plans. Expatriate managers can become important sources of this information. Expatriates can communicate subsidiaries' needs and concerns back to corporate headquarters in a timely and effective manner.

Moreover, because foreign assignments generally last three to five years, expatriates can usually become thoroughly knowledgeable about their markets. Effective expatriate managers can communicate their useful market knowledge back to corporate managers, who may be ignorant about global markets. Expatriates can usually communicate such information more effectively than host-national managers because expatriates know the people back at headquarters and thus better understand their informational needs.

Expatriate Rights under the Civil Rights Act

What legal rights do expatriates have when working in foreign countries? For example, if a foreign culture excludes women from high-level managerial positions, is it legal for a U.S. company to discriminate against female managers when they choose candidates for an expatriate assignment in that culture? The issue is a thorny one and, over time, has been explored in a series of court cases. The courts have generally supported the idea that the Civil Rights Act affords EEO protection to expatriates. A few examples of these court cases are given in Exhibit 14-2.

On March 26, 1991, however, the Supreme Court reversed this trend by ruling that Title VII does not afford EEO protection to U.S. citizens working in foreign countries. The Court stated that the U.S. Congress had been silent on the geographical or transnational scope of Title VII protections and therefore argued against the application of Title VII statutes in the absence of a clear congressional expression of intent to the contrary.

In response to the Supreme Court's ruling, the U.S. Congress placed a provision in the Civil Rights Act of 1991 that provides[18]

EXHIBIT 14-2	Court Decisions Dealing with the EEO Rights of Expatriates

Love v. Pulliman (1976)

The court ruled that porters who were American citizens employed in Canada by an Illinois corporation were entitled to full protection of Title VII, and that aliens (i.e., Canadian citizens) employed by the same U.S. firm were protected under Title VII during that portion of the workweek when the alien was working in the United States.

Bryant v. International Schools Services, Inc. (1980)

U.S. citizens who were living in Iran and working for an American company were ruled to have full protection under Title VII against discriminatory practices.

Abrams v. Baylor College of Medicine (1986)

The Fifth Circuit Court of Appeals ruled that Jewish doctors who had been refused access to the College of Medicine's overseas program in Saudi Arabia were protected under Title VII.

Kern v. Dynalectron (1984)

A U.S. firm that offered helicopter service to Mecca, Saudi Arabia, required its pilots, who were U.S. citizens, to be Muslims. The reason for this policy was that local law punished non-Muslims who entered Mecca with death. Despite the fact that non-Muslim, American pilots were discriminated against, the court ruled in favor of the employer.

Source: Taylor, S., and Eder, R.W. (1995). U.S. expatriates and the Civil Rights Act of 1991: Dissolving boundaries. In M. Mendenhall and G. Oddou (eds.). *Readings and Cases in International Human Resources Management.* Cincinnati: South-Western.

. . . coverage [to] U.S. citizens employed in a foreign country, provided that compliance with this provision would not cause the employer to violate the law of the foreign country in which the workplace is located. To be covered under this provision, the U.S. citizen must be employed overseas by a firm controlled by an American employer. Control can be determined in several ways: interrelation of operations, common management, centralized control of labor relations, or common ownership or financial control of the corporation and the employer.

Thus, in many instances, American expatriates may sue their American employers, just as they do in the United States, for age discrimination, sex discrimination, race discrimination, and so forth.

Selecting Expatriates

Many companies err when selecting expatriates. A survey of 300 employers revealed that companies place too much emphasis on technical skills, and too little emphasis on personality.[19] That is, expatriates are selected based on their "track record" with the company—"If June did a good job in Chicago, then she'll probably do a good job in Tokyo." Although track record is important, personality traits often play a larger role in an employee's success at adapting to a new culture.[20] An individual's personality determines how well he or she adjusts to the living, working, and business conditions of host countries. When personality is ignored in the selection process, the expatriate is likely to be unproductive because of difficulty in adjusting to new cultural norms.

The personality traits that a successful expatriate should possess—ability to handle stress, reinforcement substitution, ability to develop relationships, and perceptual skills—are discussed next.

Ability to Handle Stress

Learning a whole new set of social, business, and day-to-day management norms can be highly stressful. Part of this learning process involves making mistakes and learning from those mistakes. Many of these mistakes amount to "cultural faux pas" that are vital to the learning process, but can be very embarrassing to the expatriate. Companies must thus choose expatriates who have a high stress tolerance. Stress-reduction training programs can also be helpful.[21]

Reinforcement Substitution

All of us have things in life that we find reinforcing or pleasurable, such as music, sports, or art. The nature of these pursuits varies across different cultures, however. When an expatriate finds that pleasurable aspects of life are not present in the host culture, he or she must be able to find other pleasurable pursuits that can serve as substitutes. This ability is called **reinforcement substitution.**

Consider sports, for example. An expatriate who enjoys NFL football is going to be out of luck if he or she is assigned to New Zealand, where the most popular sports are rugby, horse racing, cricket, and perhaps soccer. Our hypothetical expatriate is faced with two options:

1. Feel frustrated with the situation and mourn over losing this pleasurable aspect of life (perhaps he or she will ask friends back in the United States to mail video-tapes of NFL games)

   or

2. Attempt to adjust to the culture by, for instance, studying the rules of rugby, attending matches with coworkers, learning to appreciate the finesse and strategy of the sport, and thus become a fan.

The expatriate taking the latter approach has substituted his or her enjoyment of one form of sport with another. Research shows that those who respond in this way are more apt to adapt successfully to their new culture.[22]

Ability to Develop Relationships

Expatriates who seek out and develop relationships with host nationals are more effective than those who interact exclusively with fellow expatriates. Research substantiates that if expatriates develop relationships with host nationals, they gain mentors and guides—people who assist them in living happily and working productively in the host culture.[23] The closer expatriates feel to host nationals, the better they assimilate the new culture. Their management of host-national subordinates improves, as well.

Two skills associated with the ability to develop relationships are particularly important to the adjustment process. First, expatriates must be willing to communicate in the host language. Expatriates need not be fluent in the language; their level of fluency is less important than their willingness to attempt to communicate in that language.[24] Unfortunately, many, if not most, American expatriates make no attempt to learn new languages—they cope with their language deficiency by using interpreters at work and by shopping only at stores employing English-speaking clerks.

The second relationship skill is called **conversational currency:** collecting social and cultural tidbits and trivia, and then strategically inserting them into conversations with host nationals. Some research studies have shown that expatriates who engage in this behavior are happier and better adjusted than those who do not.[25] Expatriates who try to relate to fellow workers in this way also create stronger relationships with host nationals, as illustrated in On the Road to Competitive Advantage 14-1.

Perceptual Skills

A whole set of cognitive skills, termed *perceptual skills,* can also influence adjustment to a new culture. Included among them are these:

- Flexibility of one's belief systems
- Ability to avoid being judgmental about the belief and value systems of the host culture
- Ability to make flexible attributions about why host nationals behave the way they do
- High tolerance for uncertainty

reinforcement substitution
The ability to find substitutes for pleasurable pursuits that are unavailable in a new culture.

conversational currency
A relationship skill in which an expatriate inserts social and cultural tidbits and trivia into conversations with host-national employees.

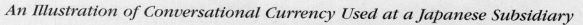

An Illustration of Conversational Currency Used at a Japanese Subsidiary

A U.S. expatriate in Japan manages a group of Japanese subordinates and has Japanese peer managers. The American memorizes Japanese proverbs, learns the names of popular Japanese entertainers, and follows the Japanese professional baseball league and sumo matches. At appropriate times in conversations with host nationals, the expatriate comments on the latest winning streak of a sumo wrestler, or quotes a Japanese proverb in order to illustrate a point.

Source: Mendenhall, M., and Oddou, G. (1985). The dimensions of expatriate acculturation: A review. *Academy of Management Review, 10* (1), 39–47.

Research has shown that expatriates with these skills adjust better to their experiences in foreign countries than those without them.[26]

Training Expatriates

Effective training programs can help people adjust to living and working conditions in new cross-cultural situations.[27] Such training should provide expatriates with a clear picture of the challenges they are about to face.[28] Specifically, expatriates should be taught:[29]

- How to understand and work effectively with people from different cultural, religious, and ethnic backgrounds
- How to manage multicultural teams
- How to understand global markets, global customers, global suppliers, and global competitors

Unfortunately, most companies fail to give expatriates the training they need. For instance, researchers have found that only 35 percent of U.S. firms offer any predeparture cross-cultural or language training for their expatriate managers. Thus, roughly 65 percent of American expatriates go overseas without any training whatsoever.[30]

Of the firms that do offer training, the training is often not very rigorous in nature. Training rigor is "the degree of mental involvement and effort that must be expended by the trainer and the trainee in order for the trainee to learn the required concepts."[31] Few existing expatriate training programs offer in-depth, skill-development training; instead, most of these courses involve watching films, listening to lectures, or talking with returned expatriates.

Firms should not be surprised, then, when expatriates struggle to succeed in foreign countries—expatriates get virtually no help when preparing to meet the varied challenges of their new assignments.

Appraising Expatriates' Job Performance

As we noted in Chapter 8, "Appraising Employee Job Performance," a firm's performance appraisal system can greatly impact the performance of its workers. Conducting valid performance appraisals, even stateside, is quite a difficult task. Conducting effective performance appraisals is even more challenging in the international human resource management arena.

Invalid Performance Criteria

Expatriates often receive inappropriate performance appraisals because the performance criteria common to the United States are often superimposed onto an expatriate manager even though those criteria might not make sense in the foreign culture. For instance, the job performance of American managers is often measured

Losing Competitive Advantage by Inappropriately Evaluating an Expatriate Manager's Job Performance in a Foreign Subsidiary

In Chile, he had almost single-handedly stopped a strike that would have shut down their factory completely for months. In a land where strikes are commonplace, such an accomplishment was quite a coup, especially for an American. However, because of exchange rate fluctuations with its primary trading partners in South America, the demand for their ore temporarily decreased by 30 percent during the expatriate manager's tenure. Rather than applauding this expatriate's efforts to avert a strike and recognizing the superb

negotiation skills he demonstrated, the home office saw the expatriate as being only somewhat better than a mediocre performer.

Source: Oddou, G., and Mendenhall, M. (1995). Expatriate performance appraisal: Problems and solutions. In M. Mendenhall and G. Oddou (eds.), *Readings and Cases in International Human Resource Management* (2nd ed.). Cincinnati: South-Western.

in terms of profits, rate of return on investment, cash flows, efficiency or input–output ratios, market share, and the like. However, these criteria may be less applicable in some other cultures. Expatriate managers may have less control over profit levels, for instance, because their profits are so heavily influenced by such extraneous factors as exchange rate fluctuations, price controls, depreciation allowances, general overhead charges, and availability of local debt financing. On the Road to Competitive Advantage 14-2 illustrates the appraisal-related difficulties experienced by an expatriate manager from the United States who was assigned to Chile.

Companies cannot simply use standard appraisal criteria in foreign countries and expect valid results. They must construct criteria according to each subsidiary's unique situation. More appropriate criteria for expatriate managers might include such dimensions as relationships with union leaders and individuals in local government, local market share, public image of the firm, negotiation skills, cross-cultural skills, community involvement, and employee morale.[32]

Rater Competence

When it comes to assessing expatriate managers' job performance, the key question is "Who should conduct the appraisals?"

Home office superiors who have never worked or lived in foreign countries often complete expatriates' appraisals. Lacking an understanding of the social and business contexts in which the work is performed, these appraisers have no feel for the unique challenges faced by expatriates. Under these circumstances, the chance of rater error increases dramatically. Consider, for example, the case of a high-potential manager who was assigned to the Tokyo office of his semiconductor company:

> Because of the difficulties of cracking a nearly impossible market, his stateside boss gave him a very low appraisal. On returning to the United States, he was physically and mentally exhausted from the battle. He sought a much less challenging position and got it because top management believed it had overestimated his potential. In fact, top management never did understand what the expatriate was up against in the foreign market.[33]

Rater Bias

Even if such an appraisal were made by a host-national manager who better understood the expatriate's challenges, its validity would not be assured. Individuals from different cultures consistently misinterpret each other's behavior, possibly biasing the appraisals.[34] Consider the following example:

> In France, women are allowed six months of maternity leave, and during that time, they are not legally allowed to do any work related to their jobs. An American expatriate manager in France had two secretaries taking maternity leave. The American asked them to work at home, unaware that such a request was illegal. Feeling sorry for her boss, one of the women complied with his request. When the American's French boss found out that the secretary was working at home, he became very angry and intolerant of the American's actions. As a result, the American was given a lower overall performance evaluation than he deserved.[35]

Overcoming Performance Appraisal Problems

It is very difficult to appraise performance accurately in cross-cultural work environments. The potential for misunderstanding is great. Unfortunately, there are no easy solutions. Companies should use multiple raters and make sure that some of those raters have lived and worked in the country in which the expatriate is working. However, expatriates must understand that their performance may be misunderstood and go unappreciated.

Compensating Expatriates

American expatriates usually receive very handsome compensation packages. In addition to base salary, expatriates receive a variety of financial incentives to accept overseas assignments, some of which appear in Exhibit 14-3. Although these lucrative packages may be necessary to entice expatriates, the packages themselves can become counterproductive in some ways. Company allowances often enable expatriates to live much better in foreign countries than they would back in the United States. In some instances, they are able to afford maids, chauffeurs, gardeners, nannies, and so forth. Expatriates can become used to their new lifestyle, making it difficult to go back to old ways of living and budgeting when they return home.

Moreover, these packages can hinder the internal consistency of the company's pay system, causing morale problems. For instance, host-national managers, who are the expatriates' peers and superiors, do not receive such extravagant compensation packages. As a result, these individuals may become quite jealous and resentful.

Repatriation

Eventually, expatriate managers must return home and find their place back in the home company. Returning expatriates are called **repatriates.** Companies often do not properly prepare for repatriation. Four problems have surfaced. First, research shows that between 60 to 70 percent of repatriates are not told what their job assignments will be prior to returning home.[36]

repatriates Expatriates who have returned home.

Second, repatriates often return to jobs that require much less autonomy and authority than the jobs they held in foreign countries. Moreover, their new job assignments often provide no opportunities to use the skills and knowledge they gained during their international assignment.

Third, expatriates may have difficulty readjusting to their native culture when returning home. For example, an American repatriate returning from a four-year stint in Switzerland may have become quite accustomed to certain aspects of that culture, such as low crime rate, clean streets, and nice-looking cars. The repatriate must now readjust to crime, trashy streets, beat-up and dirty cars.

The following example provides an additional illustration of this adjustment problem:

> I am Austrian by birth and lived in Germany until I was eighteen years old. Then I moved to the United States, and my ties to Austria and Germany have remained strong all these years. When I had the opportunity to work . . . in Germany for the

---

| **EXHIBIT 14-3** | Types of Allowances Given to Expatriates |

- **Foreign Service Premiums:** This is a sum of money that is simply a reward for being willing to move one's family to a new country. The sum is generally a percentage of one's base salary—usually between 10 and 25 percent.
- **Hardship allowance:** The hardship allowance is actually another foreign service premium added to the original one. It is based not only on having to go to a foreign country, but where you go. Hardship allowances are greatest when the expatriate is sent to places that have poor living conditions, a vastly different culture, less access to good health care, etc.
- **Cost of living allowances:** Cost of living allowances (COLAs) enable expatriates to maintain their standard of living. COLAs are given when the cost of living in the host country is greater than that in the United States.
- **Housing allowances:** The cost of housing in various parts of the world is much higher than it is in the United States. Large apartments in Tokyo or Hong Kong, for instance, can cost more than $10,000 a month. Housing allowances compensate expatriates for these higher costs.
- **Utility allowances:** Some companies give expatriates a fixed sum of money above their base salary to pay their utility bills. Other companies try to ascertain the difference in utility bills between the home and host countries, and give an allowance based on that difference.
- **Furnishing allowances:** Some companies offer to ship all of the expatriate's furnishings to the foreign assignment. A second approach is to pay for the local lease or purchase of furnishings by expatriates. A third approach is to give the

expatriate a fixed sum of money (usually between $8,000 and $10,000) to buy furnishings.
- **Education allowances:** Most expatriates send their children to private schools. Companies often pay the full cost of tuition, books, and supplies.
- **Home leave allowances:** Companies usually provide expatriates and their families with round-trip, business-class airfare to visit the home country at least once a year.
- **Relocation allowances:** This allowance makes up for any mistakes made in any of the other allowances for unforeseen complications. Expatriates receive about one month's salary.
- **Medical allowances:** Companies usually pay for all medical expenses. In hardship countries where medical facilities are inadequate, this includes emergency trips to other countries to receive medical care.
- **Car and driver allowances:** Most companies offer expatriate managers a car allowance. This enables the expatriate to lease, buy, or rent a car in the host country. In some cases, the expatriate is given funds to hire a chauffeur.
- **Club membership allowances:** In some countries, the only way an expatriate can gain access to recreational facilities (e.g., tennis courts, swimming pools, country clubs) is by joining clubs. Also, in many cultures, these facilities are important places in which to develop contacts and conduct business. This type of allowance is usually made on a case-by-case basis.
- **Taxes:** Many companies reimburse expatriates for taxes they pay in excess of what they would have paid had they remained in the United States.

---

last two years, I happily accepted . . . . Then came a Germany that I didn't recognize. I found the people very rigid and inflexible. I felt like a foreigner in a country where I had expected to feel very much at home. . . . The differences that caused me the most difficulties were the ones between the Germany that I had lived in years ago and the Germany I was returning to.[37]

Fourth, as mentioned earlier, expatriates may have become used to a higher quality of life in their host country. It can thus be quite a shock for them to discover that they are no longer seen as anyone special; there are no more elite private schools for their children, no company cars, no allowances for recreational activities, and so forth. Moreover, the repatriate's new salary may not go as far as the previous one did. All of these factors can be very frustrating.

HRM Interventions
Many experts have suggested that companies develop programs to deal with problems related to the deployment of expatriates, but to date very few companies have such programs in place.[38] Such programs should include mentoring, formalized career planning, and communication systems.[39]

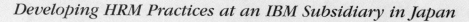

Developing HRM Practices at an IBM Subsidiary in Japan

When setting up its subsidiary in Japan, IBM decided to run the company just like a Japanese company. IBM-Japan's compensation, training, reward, selection, and career development systems parallel those in other large Japanese firms. Its employees consequently regard IBM-Japan as a Japanese, rather than an American, company. This approach has paid great dividends over the years to IBM in terms of its competitive strength in the Japanese marketplace and has allowed IBM-Japan to compete in hiring new college graduates and in retaining their best workers.

Mentoring

Companies should assign official mentors to expatriates taking overseas assignments. Mentors should then (1) keep track of the expatriate's performance in order to keep parent company executives appraised of the expatriate's successes and experiences, (2) keep expatriates updated regularly about what is going on in the parent company, and (3) assist the repatriate in finding a job in the parent company that would make use of his or her international expertise.

Formalized Career Planning

Companies need to integrate foreign assignments into their succession planning systems. If managers truly need international experience in order to be a top executive in the next century, then they must be properly selected and trained using the methods discussed in Chapter 7.

Communication Systems

Companies must encourage a flow of information back and forth between expatriate managers and parent company managers to ensure that expatriate managers are not forgotten. For example, both domestic and expatriate managers might attend periodic seminars or serve on committees or task forces made up of both domestic and expatriate managers. Expatriates can also keep abreast of company news via the Internet.

14-2c Developing HRM Practices in Host-National Countries

Companies must also consider cultural influences when devising HRM practices for host-national employees working within a foreign subsidiary. As GE learned, when a U.S. company's culture is not congruent with the artifacts, values, and assumptions of the host country's culture, all sorts of problems can arise.

Adjusting HRM Practices to the Norms and Culture of the Host Country

GE's experience in France demonstrates that firms must pay attention to how the HRM activities of its subsidiaries are traditionally carried out, and, for the most part, firms must adapt to host culture's norms and values that guide human resource practices in that country, as illustrated in On the Road to Competitive Advantage 14-3.

How, specifically, should a firm adjust its HRM practices with regard to the culture of its subsidiaries? There is no universal answer to this question; each culture is different. The principle firms should follow is simple, however:

> Ignorance of local custom invites disaster; knowledge of the laws, practices, and employer obligations in each country should form the basis for all international human resource practices.[40]

Training Malawian Managers

Originally a British colony, Malawi inherited a British administrative tradition, which is very Western and very bureaucratic. However, traditional Malawian cultural values, which emphasize membership and attention to status, also superimpose themselves onto business administrative systems.

The Malawian Culture

Workers in Malawi view employers as an extension of their families. They expect to be provided with a broad array of benefits from their employer, such as housing and transportation.

The Malawian society places great importance on status differences. The relationship between managers and subordinates is viewed as authoritative; workers give deference and expect managers to act paternally. Malawians view proper protocol as very important. Managers often resist accepting individual blame for their own mistakes and do not directly criticize their subordinates. Malawian managers rarely delegate authority because the culture believes that delegation strips managers of their authority and thus lowers their status in others' eyes.

An international organization setting up a local operation in Malawi must consider the following facts when developing training programs:

1. American models of innovation, motivation, leadership, etc., will not work well in Malawi. For example, most U.S. management experts believe that proper leader behavior depends on the situation: There is no one right way to lead. However, the Malawian culture believes that leaders should always be authoritative. Consequently, HR professionals must first learn how these issues apply in a Malawian culture and then train the Malawian workers accordingly.

2. Status-conscious Malawian managers will resent being ordered to attend a training program; they will interpret this gesture as an indication that they are considered "below average" performers. A company must thus carefully prepare a strategy to solicit trainee attendance in a way that will not cause managers to "lose face" with their peers or subordinates.

3. Training methods must be congruent with employee learning styles. Malawians learn best in "process-oriented" educational settings. Consequently, training methods that use small-group techniques and other "supportive learning" techniques should be used in lieu of those that focus on lecture and rote learning.

Source: Jones, M.L. (1989). Management development: An African focus. *International Studies of Management and Organization, 19* (1), 74–90.

In the following sections, we illustrate how a nation's culture can impact a firm's training and compensation practices.

Developing Training Programs

When American companies operate foreign subsidiaries, they must train their host-national workers. Many HR professionals simply try to apply successful U.S. training programs. This was the approach GE took in the opening case, and, as we saw, it failed. The problem was that GE managers did not consider French cultural values and norms associated with education in general, and with workplace education, in particular.

Before they set up a training program in a foreign subsidiary, HR professionals must understand how that culture views the educational process. For instance, in most Asian cultures, education is considered to be a very authoritarian phenomenon. The teacher is seen as the expert, as someone students should respect. Teachers impart knowledge through one-way conversation: The teacher tells, the student listens. Students do not ask questions, and teachers do not solicit students' opinions. The atmosphere is formal and respectful toward authority. U.S. educational techniques, which are less formal and encourage student participation, are ineffective in an Asian environment.

On the Road to Competitive Advantage 14-4 illustrates the cultural issues a company would face in setting up a training program in the African country of Malawi.

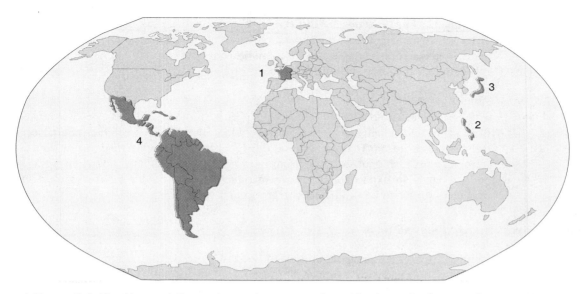

1. **France**: Subsidized transportation services and company restaurant lunches or luncheon vouchers are common.

2. **Philippines**: Workers receive a measure of rice, with better quality rice provided to skilled and professional workers. In many countries, flour, grain, or potatoes are provided as pay supplements.

3. **Japan**: Japanese companies tend to pay employees according to age and seniority as well as group or company performance, offering little or no pay differentials for individual performance or exceptional skills.

4. **Latin America**: Latin American firms often continue to pay aging, nonproductive workers as much as they do young, vigorous ones because they cannot force older workers to retire without making additional payments on top of termination indemnities.

Figure 14-2
*Compensation Strategies
of Various Countries*

Source: Dowling, P., and Schuler, R.S. (1990). *International Dimensions of Human Resource Management.* Boston: PWS-Kent.

Developing Compensation Systems

People around the world desire fair compensation for their work. However, cultural values and norms determine what people consider appropriate remuneration for their labor. Compensation strategies used in a number of countries are described in Figure 14-2.

The "trick" in designing compensation systems in international environments is to understand what motivates employees in each culture and to design the system around those motivators. Money, praise, or external symbols (a corner office, a personal parking space), although attractive to American employees, may not hold the same attraction for members of other cultures. Simply superimposing American compensation and reward systems onto a foreign subsidiary oftentimes will not only fail to work, but may actually damage the productivity of the workers in that subsidiary.

14-3 The Manager's Guide

14-3a International HRM Issues and the Manager's Job

Line managers' jobs can be significantly affected by international human resource management issues in two ways: (1) when a subordinate is sent to work in a foreign operation and (2) when managers themselves are selected as expatriates.

Managing Expatriate Subordinates

When one of the manager's subordinates goes to a foreign country as an expatriate, the manager often participates in the selection decision. Managers may also continue managing some aspects of the expatriate's job. For example, the manager may be responsible for performance appraisal and merit pay recommendations.

Human resource issues are difficult enough to manage in one's home culture. To successfully manage these functions cross-culturally, managers must successfully navigate "long-distance managing" as discussed throughout the chapter. As we have seen, this can be a complex and difficult task.

Expatriate Service

A line manager could also become an expatriate candidate. To successfully carry out this assignment, a manager must be able to adapt his or her management behavior to the culture of the host country. Some difficult problems could arise in this context. If, for example, the subsidiary's promotion system is based on individual performance, what is an expatriate American manager to do in Japan, where workers and managers prefer to be evaluated as a group or a team?

14-3b How the HRM Department Can Help

Helping expatriate managers understand how to work with, and for, people from different cultures is clearly a human resource problem and thus falls within the domain of the HR professional's responsibilities. To assure that a company's American employees can successfully work side by side with those from other cultures, HR professionals can advise management regarding the following HRM concerns:

- Who should be sent to a foreign country?
- What kind of training will they need, both before they leave and once they are abroad?
- What kind of compensation package will be needed to induce candidates to go to a foreign country?
- In what ways do the company's human resource policies and procedures need to be adjusted—country by country—due to different legal issues and cultural norms?
- How do performance appraisal systems need to be modified due to international differences?
- How may global management development programs be created that will successfully integrate career development, training programs, and succession planning?

14-3c HRM Skill-Building for Managers

Many companies send expatriates to work in cultures that are very different from their own. Those sent to Japan, for instance, often find the culture baffling. Here we cover a few of the "do's and don'ts" you would need to know about if assigned to Japan as an expatriate.

Understanding the Japanese Culture

Japanese business norms are very formal and well-defined. The informality of using first names and joking around that defines many American practices is not well regarded in Japan. Even exchanging business cards in Japan is formal: It is viewed as a ceremony. The business card is a symbol of the person, and the exchange of business cards symbolizes the new relationship between two parties doing business. Here are some guidelines on properly exchanging business cards:[41]

1. Keep your business card (meishi—pronounced "may-shee") handy at all times so you can hand it out immediately upon meeting someone, without fumbling around.

2. Stand when you give your meishi, and present your meishi by using one hand.

3. Hold out your meishi with the writing facing the recipient. Be sure to pronounce your name and your company name clearly.

4. The visiting party should be the first to give his or her meishi.

5. Receive your new acquaintance's meishi with both hands. Scan it immediately for vital information.

6. Try to use the name of your counterpart in the course of the conversation.

7. Do not play around with the meishi once received, but put it away safely in a cardholder.

8. Academic degrees (Ph.D., M.S., etc.) should not be printed on the card because the Japanese may consider them pretentious.

9. The standard meishi measures 9 cm × 5.5 cm.

10. Store your meishi in a file and follow up your initial contact with occasional calls and appropriate seasonal greetings.

Japanese business culture also demands that you conduct business at restaurants, clubs, bars, and other off-site locations. If you overlook cultural proprieties in these kinds of settings, you can destroy possible deals, because you will be seen as some-one who is not very intelligent or well-mannered. The following guidelines should be followed when you must meet clients or peers in seemingly social settings:

1. To create a good impression with your hosts, use chopsticks. If you absolutely cannot or do not want to do so, knives, forks, and spoons are available on request.

2. Japanese table manners are very different from those in the United States. For example, slurping soup, noodles, etc., is okay.

3. Japanese hold rice bowls up close to their mouths and shovel the rice into their mouths with their chopsticks.

4. Do not stick your chopsticks into the leftover rice in your bowl so that they stand up by themselves. This is not considered to be a polite thing to do—it is a sym-bol of death.

5. Do not be surprised if Japanese eat with their mouths somewhat open and make a variety of noises when they eat. They are not ill-mannered; they simply consider eating to be an enjoyable sensual experience.

6. Do not put soy sauce or any other kind of sauce on your rice. Doing this is akin to putting ketchup on mashed potatoes in the United States. The Japanese eat their rice steamed and put nothing on it, except an occasional garnish.

7. The Japanese drink a lot at meals. They will expect you to do the same. However, if you do not drink you may politely refuse, stating "sore wa nigate desu." Literally translated, this means something akin to "This is difficult or severe for me." Once you say this, they will not persist anymore but will assume that you cannot drink due to health reasons, religious beliefs, etc. If you simply say "no, thank you," they will interpret this as a signal that you do not like them and do not want to develop a business relationship with them.

8. When you are offered a toothpick after a meal, use it but cover the hand holding the toothpick with the other hand.

Understanding the Mexican Culture[42]
If assigned to a managerial position in Mexico, you must understand the culture and beliefs of the Mexican society and take management actions that are consistent with them. When facing such a situation, follow this advice:

- Most Mexican firms have a bureaucratic structure with power vested at the top. Employees below the senior management level have little authority. Supervisors are told what to do, then pass along these instructions to workers. Workers want managers to be paternalistic, but not dictatorial.

You should provide workers with close supervision. Deal with them in a respectful manner and show an interest in their personal well-being. Provide them with "perks" like food baskets and sponsor parties that celebrate a variety of events, such as holidays and birthdays. Praise them for being loyal and for following your directions.

- Mexican workers prefer that their managers keep a formal, somewhat distant relationship with them.

  You should wear business suits and avoid calling workers by their first names.

- Mexicans frown upon such practices as employee empowerment, open communication channels, and employee ownership.

  Do not involve workers in decision making. Do not explain why something is to be done, because workers perceive such behavior as a sign of weakness.

- Mexicans value harmony and have a low tolerance for adversarial relations. Obedience and respect are more important than independence and confrontation.

  Hold meetings to give orders and instructions. Do not ask workers to discuss or debate the issues at these meetings.

- It is much more important for Mexicans to have a congenial working environment than it is to make more money. Pay-for-performance programs should be avoided because they create social distance among employees.

  Motivate employees by giving emotionally charged speeches about the need to improve their group's performance.

Chapter Objectives Revisited

1. Understand why companies establish foreign operations and what must be done to maintain competitive advantage there.

   - Increasing foreign competition has forced many American firms to seek foreign markets in order to stay competitive.
   - When companies cross borders and set up subsidiaries, they can easily lose any competitive advantage if they try to superimpose American human resource practices onto the subsidiary.

2. Understand why a company must account for cultural differences when establishing foreign operations.

   - Culture is a society's set of assumptions, values, and rules about social interaction.
   - Because of different behavioral expectations, cultures sometimes clash.
   - When working with people from other cultures, one must attempt to learn the rules of that culture and abide by them.

3. Explain why companies often choose expatriates to manage foreign operations.

   - Succession planning: Firms use foreign assignments to "internationalize" future top managers.
   - Coordination and control systems: Expatriates can strategically coordinate and control foreign operations, which can give a company a competitive edge.
   - Informational needs: Expatriates can communicate subsidiaries' needs and concerns back to corporate headquarters in a timely and effective manner.

4. Describe the HRM issues regarding the use of expatriates.

   - Selection: Expatriates' needed skills:
     - Ability to handle stress
     - Reinforcement substitution
     - Ability to develop relationships
     - Perceptual skills
   - Training: Can help expatriates adjust to living and working conditions in new cross-cultural situations by providing them with a clear picture of the challenges they are about to face
   - Performance appraisal—Three expatriate-related problems:
     - Invalid performance criteria
     - Rater competence
     - Rater bias
   - Compensation: In addition to base salary, expatriates receive a variety of financial incentives to accept overseas assignments.

- Repatriation: Returning expatriates are called repatriates. Companies often do not properly prepare for repatriation.
- Repatriates are often not told what their job assignments will be prior to returning home.
- Repatriates return to jobs that require much less autonomy and authority than the jobs they held as expatriates.
- Repatriates may have difficulty readjusting to their native culture when returning home.
- Repatriates may have become used to a high quality of life in their host country and may have difficulty adjusting back home.

5. Describe the HRM issues regarding the management of host-country employees.
   - Firms should adapt to host culture norms and values that guide human resource practices in that country.
   - Training: Before they set up a training program in a foreign subsidiary, HR professionals must understand how that culture views the educational process.
   - Compensation: The "trick" in designing compensation systems in international environments is to understand what motivates employees in each culture and to design the system around those motivators.

Review Questions

Note: You can find the correct answers to these questions by taking the quiz and then submitting your answers in the Online Edition. The program will automatically score your submission. If you miss a question, the program will provide the correct answer, a rationale for the answer, and the section number in the chapter where the topic is discussed.

1. Which of the following terms is *not* included in the definition of culture?
   a. beliefs
   b. assumptions
   c. rules
   d. values

2. Knowledge of culture allows us to
   a. predict fairly accurately how individuals "should" behave in a variety of situations.
   b. predict exactly how individuals will behave in a variety of situations.
   c. predict the level of education of the workforce.
   d. predict the level of motivation of the workforce.

3. A professional/managerial employee who is moved from one country to, and for employment in, another country is called a
   a. host manager.
   b. foreign nationalist.
   c. expatriate.
   d. successor.

4. Regarding international assignments, the Civil Rights Act of 1991
   a. offers little protection to expatriates—the cultural values of the host country take precedence.
   b. is generally interpreted to afford EEO protection to expatriates.
   c. must be interpreted on a case-by-case basis to determine the rights of expatriates.
   d. protects expatriates only in certain countries.

5. Which of the following statements best describes the state of training for expatriates?
   a. Nearly all expatriates get extensive hands-on training in how to work with people with diverse backgrounds.
   b. Nearly all expatriates get low-level training that consists of watching films, listening to lectures, and talking with former expatriates.
   c. The majority of expatriates receive no training to help them succeed in their new assignment.
   d. Most expatriates receive training in business-related topics (e.g., global markets, global compensation) but little training in cultural matters related to their assignment.

6. Which of the following statements describes a significant problem when using host managers to evaluate expatriate performance?
   a. The host manager lacks commitment to the process of performance appraisal.
   b. The host manager has inadequate access to data for judging performance.
   c. The host manager consistently misinterprets the behavior of expatriates.
   d. The language barrier makes it impossible for host-managers to evaluate performance.

7. Individuals returning from international assignments are referred to as

    a. repatriates.
    b. expatriates.
    c. returned nationals.
    d. corporate aliens.

8. Which of the following is *not* one of the problems faced by individuals returning from an international assignment?

    a. Individuals are not told their job assignments upon return.
    b. Retirement savings accumulated while on assignment is subject to the repatriate tax.
    c. Individuals assume jobs with much less autonomy and authority than they had while on assignment.
    d. Individuals have trouble adjusting to the native culture.

9. When designing a compensation system for international operations, it is best to

    a. build the system around the worldwide interest in money, praise, and benefits.
    b. focus on salary, because the population in most foreign countries is not accustomed to receiving generous benefits packages.
    c. design the system around those factors that motivate the local workforce.
    d. make the system as similar to the stateside system as possible so that the transition from expatriate will be a smooth one.

10. Which of the following training techniques would be least successful in an Asian culture?

    a. lecture
    b. training video
    c. instructional manual
    d. role-playing

Discussion Questions

1. Describe the main organizational forms companies use when internationalizing their operations.

2. Define culture.

3. Why do companies use expatriate managers, rather than local managers, to oversee their foreign operations?

4. List and briefly describe the skills expatriates need in order to be successful.

5. What are the variables that cause performance appraisals of expatriates to often be invalid?

6. What problems are associated with the design of compensation packages for expatriates?

7. Describe the elements of an "ideal" program for managing expatriate managers.

8. What is the key principle to remember when adjusting headquarters HRM practices to foreign subsidiaries? Give an example of the principle from the text.

9. Describe the typical expatriate manager's compensation package.

10. Give three examples that illustrate how work-related behaviors are associated with cultural values.

11. Describe the responsibilities a manager must assume when one of his or her subordinates is selected as an expatriate.

12. Describe how one should exchange business cards in Japan.

Experiential Exercise

Understanding Culture's Influence

Overview

The purpose of this exercise is to help you develop a better understanding about the degree to which your own behaviors are influenced by our culture's values and assumptions about the world.

Steps

1. Review the following background information: Your group is a team of consultants that has been hired by a large Japanese subsidiary based in the United States. This subsidiary has had problems with their Japanese expatriates who have been assigned to work in the United States. Many of them find our business practices difficult to adjust to—they need to understand why we behave the way we do. The key part of the training program is to teach these Japanese expatriates the link between specific American business behaviors and the underlying values and assumptions that drive those behaviors. Particularly, the Japanese expatriates are having a difficult time understanding why Americans:

a. Change jobs so frequently

b. Are very informal with people in the office—even with their superiors

c. Do not take a long-range view in strategic planning

d. Are so direct in their speech with one another, and rarely apologize for mistakes

e. Make decisions so quickly without long, careful analysis

f. Prefer to be evaluated as individuals rather than as groups

2. Divide into small groups of five to seven people.

3. Your job is to link the values of the American culture with the behaviors in step 1. In other words, you must come up with reasons why Americans behave in these ways. Your group should develop a written list that specifies at least one reason for each of these behaviors.

4. Compare your findings with those of other groups. Upon what did you agree? Disagree? Could you reach a consensus among the groups?

Cases

XECORP's Decision to Enter Germany

Linda Grace was worried. As she entered the elevator, a number of thoughts went through her mind about what had just occurred in the strategic planning meeting. She had fought long and hard to be included in these meetings. When she first came to XECORP, human resource people were excluded from such meetings. Over time, she had been able to show that her department could offer significant value-added advice to top management. Now she was not so sure.

XECORP intended, she had just found out, to buy out a manufacturing facility in Germany. They wanted a report of the HRM issues associated with running a plant in Germany in two weeks. This was the first time XECORP had done anything beyond the United States besides exporting their product to foreign countries. Now, because much of their export market is in Europe, and in order to avoid possible future trade barriers, top management wanted to set up a subsidiary in Germany. The main reason seemed to be that they had found an ideal manufacturing facility that was for sale, at the right price, and with the right kind of equipment already installed and working.

Linda was an expert in U.S. HRM issues, but she knew nothing about Germany. As the elevator doors opened at her floor, and she walked to her office, she knew she needed to formulate a plan. "How can I go about finding everything I need to know about HRM in Germany to submit a comprehensive report in two weeks?"

Questions

1. This situation is not all that unusual in the world of international business: namely, having to confront a task about which you know little. How should Linda go about her task? Outline the steps she must take to come up with a good report.

2. Analyze the weaknesses in top management's decision to buy this factory in Germany. What have they not considered in this decision?

A Great Opportunity at Welingen Chemical

John Frankl was in a state of shock when he pulled into his driveway after his daily commute. What a difference one day can make! While at lunch with the president of Welingen, he was asked to head up the Taiwan office of Welingen. It was a start-up operation that had been in existence for only two years. The president stated that it was a great opportunity to gain executive-level experience, and when the compensation package was explained to him, he could hardly believe it.

John and his wife, Victoria, had never lived overseas. Except for their honeymoon in Europe and trips to the Caribbean, they had never left the Midwest. He was both excited and scared. He had never been to Asia, but how tough could it be? After all, they would live well and make a lot of money. Victoria could work as a consultant there, just as she was doing here, and the kids, Benjamin and April, were still young enough at six and nine to make a move like this with few problems.

He had already decided to take the position. After all, if he didn't, it would hurt his career. He couldn't wait to see the reaction on Victoria's face!

Victoria reacted with shock and concern when John told her of his "big news" over dinner. But she became interested when she heard about the compensation package, and she thought it would be an interesting challenge to begin a consulting business in Taiwan. She could even fly back and forth to work with her clients here, she thought. That night after the kids were in bed, they called both their parents to tell them the great news.

Questions

1. Are there factors that John and Victoria are not taking into consideration in making this decision to accept this offer? If so, what are they?

2. If you were John and Victoria's best friend, what advice would you give them based on your reading of this chapter? Be specific in your advice and defend your rationale.

References

1. (1990, July 31). GE culture turns sour at French unit. *The Wall Street Journal,* A11.

2. Adler, N.J. (1991). *International Dimensions of Organizational Behavior* (2nd ed.). Boston: PWS-Kent.

3. Daniels, J.D., and Radebaugh, L.H. (1992). *International Business: Environments and Operations* (6th ed.). Reading, MA: Addison-Wesley.

4. Toh, S.M., and NeNisi, A.S. (2005). A local perspective to expatriate success. *Academy of Management Executive, 19* (1), 132–146.

5. Black, J.S., and Mendenhall, M. (1993). Resolving conflicts with the Japanese: Mission impossible? *Sloan Management Review, 34* (3), 49–59.

6. Ibid.

7. Ibid.

8. Terpstra, V., and David, K. (1985). *The Cultural Environment of International Business.* Cincinnati: South-Western.

9. Ibid.

10. Black, J.S., Gregersen, H.B., and Mendenhall, M.E. (1992). *Global Assignments: Successfully Expatriating and Repatriating International Managers.* San Francisco: Jossey-Bass.

11. Hofstede, G. (1980). Motivation, leadership, and organizations: Do American theories apply abroad? *Organizational Dynamics,* Summer, 42–63.

12. Ibid.

13. Black and Mendenhall. Resolving conflicts.

14. Black, Gregersen, and Mendenhall. *Global Assignments.*

15. Dowling, P.J., and Schuler, R.S. (1990). *International Dimensions of Human Resource Management.* Boston: PWS-Kent.

16. Ibid.

17. Bowman, E.H. (1986). Concerns of CEOs. *Human Resource Management, 25,* 267–285.

18. Taylor, S., and Eder, R.W. (In press). U.S. expatriates and the Civil Rights Act of 1991: Dissolving boundaries. In M. Mendenhall and G. Oddou (eds.). *Readings and Cases in International Human Resources Management.* Cincinnati: South-Western.

19. Halcrow, A. (1999). Expats: The squandered resource. *Workforce, 78* (4), 42–47.

20. Ibid.

21. For a review of studies showing that stress reduction is important to expatriate adjustment, see Mendenhall, M., and Oddou G. (1985). The dimensions of expatriate acculturation: A review. *Academy of Management Review, 10,* (1), 39–47.

22. Ibid.

23. Ibid.

24. Ibid.

25. Ibid.

26. Ibid.

27. Black, J.S., and Mendenhall, M. (1990). Cross-cultural training effectiveness: A review and theoretical framework for future research. *Academy of Management Review, 15,* 113–136.

28. Oddou, G., and Mendenhall, M. (1991). Succession planning for the 21st century: How well are we grooming our future business leaders? *Business Horizons, 34,* (1), 26–34.

29. Black, Gregersen, and Mendenhall. *Global Assignments.*

30. Black, J.S. (1988). Work role transitions: A study of expatriate managers in Japan. *Journal of International Business Studies, 19,* 277–294; Oddou and Mendenhall. Succession planning; Tung, R.L. (1981). Selecting and training of personnel for overseas assignments. *Columbia Journal of World Business, 16* (1), 68–78; Baker, J.C., and Ivancevich, J.M. (1971). The assignment of American executives abroad: Systematic haphazard, or chaotic? *California Management Review, 13,* (3), 39–41.

31. Black, Gregersen, and Mendenhall. *Global Assignments.*

32. Robinson, R.D. (1983). *Internationalization of Business: An Introduction.* New York: Dryden Press.

33. Oddou and Mendenhall. Succession planning.

34. Mendenhall and Oddou. The dimensions of expatriate acculturation.

35. Ibid.

36. Black, Gregersen, and Mendenhall. *Global Assignments.*

37. Ibid.

38. Dowling and Schuler. *International Dimensions.*

39. Ibid.

40. Ibid.

41. International Division of Nissan Motor Company Limited. (1984). *Business Japanese: A Guide to Improved Communication.* Tokyo, Japan.

42. Schuler, R.S., Jackson, S.E., Jackofsky, E., and Slocum, J.W. (1996). Managing human resources in Mexico: A cultural understanding. *Business Horizons,* May–June, 55–61.

Conclusion

Working in the HRM Field

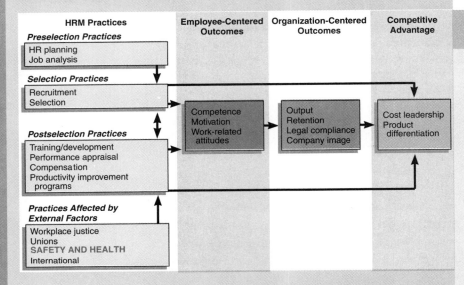

HRM Practices	Employee-Centered Outcomes	Organization-Centered Outcomes	Competitive Advantage
Preselection Practices			
HR planning Job analysis			
Selection Practices			
Recruitment Selection	Competence Motivation Work-related attitudes	Output Retention Legal compliance Company image	Cost leadership Product differentiation
Postselection Practices			
Training/development Performance appraisal Compensation Productivity improvement programs			
Practices Affected by External Factors			
Workplace justice Unions SAFETY AND HEALTH International			

Key Terms

certification

HRM generalists

HRM specialists

Chapter Objectives

Upon completion of this chapter, you will be able to:

- Explain the distinction between HRM generalists and specialists.

- Describe career patterns within the HRM field.

- Discuss the ethical responsibilities of HR professionals.

- Explain how HR professionals can increase their sphere of influence within organizations.

Throughout this text, we have described the various HRM practices and the roles played by HR professionals in developing and implementing them. We have yet to discuss the profession of human resource management, itself, however. We suspect (or at least hope) that by this point, many readers have become curious about the prospect of working in the HRM field. What kinds of jobs are out there? How well do they pay? How does one enter the profession? Are there good opportunities for career advancement and professional growth? We begin this chapter by addressing these questions. We then examine the major challenges facing today's HR professionals as they attempt to perform their jobs as effectively as possible

15-1 Employment in the HRM Field

Because firms are becoming increasingly aware of the impact of HRM practices on organizational effectiveness, career opportunities in the field are rapidly expanding. For instance, the Bureau of Labor Statistics estimates that the number of HR professionals in the United States is expected to increase by nearly 20 percent by 2006, compared to 1996.[1]

15-1a Career Options in HRM

Someone wishing to enter the HRM field may choose one of two routes. Just as a doctor may choose a career in general medicine (e.g., family practice) or specialized medicine (e.g., cardiology, pediatrics), an HR professional can become an HRM generalist or specialist.

HRM Generalists

HRM generalists perform virtually all facets of HRM. According to Mike Rogers, an HRM generalist at BankFirst in Oklahoma City, a "typical day" might consist of the following activities:[2]

- Conduct a reference check on an applicant.

- Arrange an employment interview.

- Work on a presentation explaining the company's new health care program.

- Bargain with a vendor over the cost of an HRIS.

- Clarify the wording of a section in the company's employee handbook.

- Answer an employee's question regarding the firm's pension plan.

HRM generalists
HR professionals whose jobs require them to perform virtually all facets of HRM work.

Entry-level HRM generalist positions are most often found in small to midsized organizations that employ few HR professionals—one or two people who must "do it all." Because of their many responsibilities, HRM generalists have neither time nor resources to conduct in-depth studies or projects. They usually hire outside consultants who specialize in these kinds of services. For example, consultants might help the organization revamp its compensation system, validate its selection practices, or analyze its training needs.

According to a 1998 survey sponsored by the Society for Human Resources Management, top corporate executive generalists earn an average salary of about $150,000.[3] HR managers who are one level below the top executive earn between $62,000 and $83,000, depending on the size of the company.[4] Entry-level generalists (i.e., HR assistants) average $27,000 annually.[5]

HRM Specialists

HRM specialists HR professionals whose jobs require them to perform specialized HRM tasks.

In larger organizations, each HR professional's area tends to be more focused, zeroing in on particular HRM tasks. Individuals holding these positions are called **HRM specialists.** Exhibit 15-1 describes some traditional and some newer HRM specialty areas. The average salaries for HR specialist positions in March of 2005 were:[6]

- Compensation manager: $98,758
- Benefits manager: $97,944
- Employee relations manager: $96,513
- Training manager: $96,764
- Organization development manager: $110,371
- Labor relations manager: $114,796

> **EXHIBIT 15-1** HRM Specialty Areas

Traditional Specialty Areas

- *Training/development:* Conducts training needs analysis; designs/conducts/evaluates training programs; develops/implements succession planning programs
- *Compensation/benefits:* Develops job descriptions; facilitates job evaluation processes; conducts/interprets salary surveys; develops pay structure; designs pay-for-performance and/or performance improvement programs; administers benefits program
- *Employee/industrial relations:* Helps resolve employee relations problems; develops union avoidance strategies; assists in collective bargaining negotiations; oversees grievance procedures
- *Employment/recruiting:* Assists in the HR planning process; develops/purchases HR information systems; develops/updates job descriptions; oversees recruiting function; develops and administers job posting system; conducts employment interviews, reference checks, and employment tests; validates selection procedures; approves employment decisions
- *Safety/health/wellness:* Develops accident prevention strategies; develops legal safety and health policies; implements/promotes EAP and wellness programs; develops AIDS and substance abuse policies
- *EEO/affirmative action:* Develops and administers affirmative action programs; helps resolve EEO disputes; monitors organizational practices with regard to EEO compliance; develops policies for ensuring EEO compliance, such as sexual harassment policies
- *HRM research:* Conducts research studies, such as cost–benefit analyses, test validation, program evaluation, and feasibility studies

New HRM Specialty Areas

- *Work and family programs:* Develops and administers work and family programs, including flextime, alternative work scheduling, dependent-care assistance, telecommuting, and other programs designed to accommodate employee needs; identifies and screens child- or elder-care providers; administers employer's private dependent care facility; promotes work and family programs to employees
- *Cross-cultural training:* Translates the manners, mores, and business practices of other nations and cultures for American businesspeople. Other cross-cultural trainers work with relocated employees' families, helping them adjust to their new environment.
- *Managed care:* As a company's health care costs continue to escalate, employers are embracing managed-care systems, which require employees to assume some of the costs. Employers hire managed-care managers to negotiate the best options for employees.
- *Managing diversity:* Develops policies and practices to recruit, promote, and appropriately treat workers of various ages, races, sexes, and physical abilities

Sources: (1993). The 25 hottest careers. *Working Woman,* July, 41–51; Beatty, L.K. (1993). Pay increases with changing HR landscape. *HRMagazine,* September, 78–80; Langer, S. (1990). Human resources: Who makes what? *Personnel Journal,* February, 102–106.

Entry-level salaries, of course, are much lower and vary by specialty area. Entry-level training positions, for example, pay an average salary of $36,200.

15-1b Career Entry and Growth

Career Entry

In most professions, a direct path leads to entry into the field. For instance, someone aspiring to be a lawyer, physician, accountant, or psychologist enrolls in appropriate educational programs and enters the field upon receiving a degree. HRM is atypical in this regard; people may enter the profession in a variety of ways. For instance, most of today's HR professionals enter the field through self-directed career changes.[7] Approximately one-third of these individuals entered HRM by transferring from another part of the company; the remainder entered from other fields such as education, social services, accounting, sales, and administrative secretarial positions.[8]

HR professionals entering the field directly out of college (about one-third of all HR professionals) traditionally come from a variety of academic backgrounds, such as business, psychology, and liberal arts.[9] More recently, however, HRM new hires have earned degrees in some area of business, such as HRM, management, or general business.[10] For instance, when they hire recent graduates for entry-level HRM positions, Bell Atlantic considers business school graduates with concentrations in business administration, finance and commerce, management, or industrial relations.[11] A recent survey of HR professionals revealed the following college majors: HRM (17 percent), business administration (23 percent), management (13 percent), psychology (12 percent), and labor/industrial relations (10 percent).[12]

What do companies look for in candidates for entry-level HRM jobs? According to management expert Bruce Kaufman, companies want candidates to possess:[13]

- Leadership and management skills
- Cross-functional HRM expertise (for generalist positions)
- Technological skills (e.g., computers, management information systems)
- Knowledge of international HRM issues
- Knowledge of business basics (i.e., accounting, finance, marketing, management, and economics)

Career Progression

As one might expect, large organizations provide the greatest opportunities for HRM career growth. Most senior-level HR professionals take one of two paths up the corporate ladder. Some begin their careers as specialists and eventually become managers of their specialty units. To advance beyond this level, they must broaden their skills and become HRM generalists. The other path to securing a senior-level HRM position is to begin as an assistant HRM generalist at a small plant or unit within the organization and advance into an HRM managerial role at successively larger plants or units. An HRM career in the manufacturing industry would typically progress as follows:[14]

1. The individual is hired as an HRM assistant at a manufacturing plant.

2. Within 5 or 6 years, the individual advances to the HRM manager's post at the plant.

3. Between 6 and 10 years, the HR professional becomes the HRM manager at a larger plant.

4. Between 11 and 15 years, the person reaches a senior-level HRM position at the divisional level and has several HRM generalists and/or specialists reporting to him or her.

5. Between 15 and 20 years, the person reaches a senior-level executive position, such as vice president of human resources.

Not everyone, however, can become VP of human resources. How do organizations determine who makes the successful climb? Although criteria vary from company to company, most firms consider the following:[15]

1. Job performance
2. Credibility with senior management
3. Interpersonal skills
4. Ability to manage people
5. Skill in specialty area
6. Ability to "play politics"

Professional Growth

A "profession" requires specialized knowledge and long, intensive academic preparation. Members of a profession are expected to conform to technical and ethical standards. The demand for professionalism within the HRM field has expanded rapidly in recent years as HR professionals' roles within organizations continue to escalate. As noted by management professor Carolyn Wiley, "As corporate recognition of the importance of HRM increases, so does the demand for professionalism in the field."[16] To grow professionally, HR managers must be prepared to continue their training and network with other HRM contacts, as we discuss next.

Professional Associations

The HRM field has quite a few professional organizations, the largest of which is the Society for Human Resource Management (SHRM). Primarily an HRM generalist organization, SHRM covers every aspect of HRM. With more than 100,000 members worldwide, SHRM's mission is to:[17]

- Provide its membership with ongoing government and media representation, education and information services, conferences and seminars, and publications that equip human resource practitioners to become leaders and decision makers within their organizations
- Strive to be the voice of the profession on human resource management issues
- Facilitate the development and guide the direction of the HRM profession
- Establish, monitor, and update the standards of the profession

Several other professional HRM associations focus on particular specialty areas within the field. Among them are the American Society for Training and Development, the International Personnel Management Association, the American Compensation Association, the Personnel Testing Council, the Society for Industrial and Organizational Psychology, and the Academy of Management.

Professional Certification

certification A designation indicating that an individual has demonstrated a mastery of a defined body of knowledge required for success in a field.

Individuals can enhance their professionalism by becoming certified. **Certification** represents a recognition that an individual has demonstrated a mastery of a defined body of knowledge required for success in a field.[18] Various HRM certification options are shown in Figure 15-1.

The primary certification designations are the professional in human resources (PHR) and the senior professional in human resources (SPHR), both of which are issued by the Human Resource Certification Institute. HR professionals can become certified as a PHR or SPHR by passing a comprehensive exam covering six areas: staffing, labor relations, compensation, training, safety, and management practice.[19] Since 1976, more than 29,000 HR professionals have become certified.[20]

Professional in human resources; senior professional in human resources (HR Certification Institute)

Certified compensation professional (American Compensation Association)

Certified employee benefit specialist (International Foundation of Employee Benefit Plans)

Associate safety professional; certified safety professional (Board of Certified Safety Professionals)

Occupational health and safety technologist (American Board of Industrial Hygiene/Board of Certified Safety Professionals)

Figure 15-1
Certification Options in HRM

Source: Wiley, C. (1992). The certified HR professional. *HRMagazine*, August, 77–84.

Continuing Education

To keep current in this rapidly changing field, HR professionals must continually update and expand their knowledge of HRM. They may need to attend conferences sponsored by professional associations, take courses within and outside the company, participate in degree programs, and read professional journals,[21] as outlined next.

1. *Conferences:* Most professional associations hold regional and national conferences annually. These meetings offer presentations made by HRM practitioners and academics, who discuss the results of their HRM experiences/research findings. Attendance at these conferences also provides HR professionals with the opportunity to "network" among their HRM colleagues.

2. *Seminars and training courses:* HR professionals can expand their knowledge base by attending seminars and training courses that provide information on recent developments within the HRM field. Topics include EEO updates, current trends in compensation and benefits, new methods for assessing applicant honesty, and the like. These programs are offered both externally (i.e., by consulting firms or at universities) and in-house. The most frequently offered in-house training programs address interviewing, performance appraisal, employee discipline, recruitment and selection, and grievance handling.[22] A list of HRM subjects offered by Digital Equipment Corporation is shown in Exhibit 15-2.

3. *Advanced academic degrees:* HR professionals increasingly earn advanced degrees. Approximately half of the certified PHR and SPHR professionals have had some postbaccalaureate study; 33 percent have master's degrees, and 4 percent have doctorates.[23]

   To decide what kind of graduate degree to pursue, HR professionals must choose whether to become generalists and seek MBAs, or specialists and seek specialized degrees in industrial and organizational psychology, industrial and labor relations, or human resource management.

   MBAs provide strong training in all major areas of business and thus give students the overall business perspective that most firms now desire (as we discuss later in the chapter). The downside of MBAs for HR professionals is that MBA

EXHIBIT 15-2   HRM-Related Courses Offered by the Digital Equipment Corporation

For Entry-Level HR Professionals

Knowledge of

- The organization and how it operates
- Compensation and benefits
- Employee relations
- Employment
- Training and development
- HR planning
- Personnel law/EEO/AA
- Cultural diversity
- Fundamentals of management
- Organizational and group dynamics
- Safety and health

Ability to

- Provide consulting
- Make presentations
- Provide public relations

For Mid-Level HR Professionals

Advanced knowledge of

- Leadership theory and practices
- One or more HRM disciplines

Ability to

- Manage change
- Create and maintain business partnerships
- Integrate HR plans with strategic plans
- Develop a management succession plan

For Senior-Level HR Professionals

Advanced knowledge of

- Two or more HRM disciplines
- Strategic organization consulting
- International business

Ability to

- Lead a culturally diverse workforce
- Provide strategic consulting
- Become a good business partner with senior-level executives
- Provide leadership and innovation at the corporate level

Source: Bailey, B. (1991). Ask what HR can do for itself. *Personnel Journal,* July, 35–39.

programs usually provide only a few courses in HRM. Specialized degrees, on the other hand, provide more in-depth HRM training, but often fail to cover adequately basic business topics, such as finance, accounting, marketing, and economics.

When deciding which program to enter, the best choice often depends on the HR professional's undergraduate major: Business majors, already schooled in the core business areas, usually seek specialized master's programs, whereas non-business majors usually seek MBAs.[24]

4. *Professional journals:* HR professionals can keep up with current HRM techniques and research findings by reading professional journals. HRM journals are generally either practitioner oriented or research oriented. Practitioner-oriented or trade journals contain articles dealing primarily with new ideas, practices, and solutions to specific problems in the field (e.g., "The five keys to effective employment interviewing" and "How to contain health insurance costs"). Articles presented in research-oriented or academic journals focus on applied HRM research and on theory development/testing (e.g., "Comparing the validity of personality and aptitude tests" and "Predicting employee motivation using expectancy theory"). Some of the leading practitioner- and research-oriented journals are listed in Exhibit 15-3.

15-2 Major Challenges Facing Today's HR Professional

As we have noted throughout this text, HR professionals are primarily responsible for developing HRM practices that enhance competitive advantage. HR professionals have two additional responsibilities: (1) to ensure that employees are treated ethically and (2) to ensure that their own talents are appropriately utilized by their companies. We now take a closer look at these responsibilities and discuss what HR professionals must do to meet them successfully.

EXHIBIT 15-3	Practitioner- and Research-Oriented HRM-Related Journals

Practitioner-Related Journals

- *Academy of Management Executive*
- *Accident and Analysis Prevention*
- *Business Week*
- *Compensation and Benefits Review*
- *Forbes*
- *HRMagazine* (formerly *Personnel Administrator*)
- *Human Resource Management*
- *Industry Week*
- *Nation's Business*
- *Personnel*
- *Personnel Journal*
- *Public Personnel Management*
- *Training*
- *Training and Development Journal*
- *Working Woman*

Research-Oriented Journals

- *Academy of Management Journal*
- *Academy of Management Review*
- *Administrative Science Quarterly*
- *Applied HRM Research*
- *Group and Organizational Studies*
- *Human Factors*
- *International Journal of Human Resource Management*
- *Journal of Applied Psychology*
- *Journal of Business and Psychology*
- *Journal of International Business Studies*
- *Journal of Management*
- *Journal of Safety Research*
- *Journal of Vocational Behavior*
- *Management International Review*
- *Personnel Psychology*
- *Personnel Review*

15-2a Organizational Ethics Related to HRM

Almost all HRM decisions have ethical consequences. Despite the abundance of laws designed to ensure fair treatment at the workplace, employees are often treated in an unethical manner.[25] In some instances, employers skirt the law; in others, the "letter of the law" is followed, but employees are nonetheless treated unfairly by management or by other employees.

Examples of Unethical Behavior

Examples of unethical workplace behavior are illustrated in Exhibit 15-4. According to a recent survey, the most serious ethical problems involve managerial decisions regarding employment, promotion, pay, and discipline that are based on favoritism, rather than ability or job performance.[26]

Workplace Ethics and the HR Professional's Job

HR professionals play three roles in the area of workplace ethics.[27] One is monitoring: They must observe the actions of organizational members to ensure that all

EXHIBIT 15-4	Unethical Situations Arising in the Workplace

- A man was hired into a predominantly female service department. Resenting his presence, the women in that department tried to disparage him at all turns and attempted to sabotage his credibility.
- A top executive requested raises for two of his department heads and denied raises to two others on the basis of favoritism.
- Several women complained about the behavior of a man in their department. His touching, comments, and inappropriate gestures were offensive and unwelcome.
- Many highly qualified job candidates were unfairly denied jobs because selection tests and other hiring techniques were not job related.
- A company bases its exempt/nonexempt status on salary level, rather than federal guidelines, in order to save money on overtime wages. Many employees were thus denied overtime pay because they were misclassified as exempt.
- Under pressure to meet affirmative actions goals, a manager refused to consider nonminority candidates and eventually hired an unqualified minority.
- The layoff list generated by a company was unethically (and illegally) constructed. Workers over age 40 were targeted, because use of this list would lower the average age of the company's workforce from 44 to 36.
- A manager's bad experience with a minority worker caused him to be overly cautious and very hesitant about hiring other minority workers, thus unfairly limiting job prospects for future minority applicants.

Source: Wiley, C. (1993). Employment manager's views on workplace ethics. *The EMA Journal*, Spring, 14–24.

individuals are treated fairly and legally. Second, HR professionals investigate complaints bearing on ethical issues, such as sexual harassment or violations of employees' privacy rights. Third, HR professionals serve as company spokespeople by defending the company's actions when confronted by a regulatory agency or the media.

Furthermore, HR professionals themselves should act ethically. When faced with ethical dilemmas, HR professionals must be willing to take a strong stand, even if it means putting their jobs at risk. If they choose to turn a blind eye, they become part of the problem and thus must assume some of the blame.[28] Examples of ethical dilemmas that could be faced by HR professionals include these:

- A male plant manager tries to fire a female employee because she would not sleep with him.
- The CEO orders the HR professional to get rid of the "deadwood" older employees under the guise of a layoff.
- A manager begins harassing an employee she dislikes to force him to quit.

HR professionals should be guided by the Society for Human Resource Management code of ethics, which dictates that HR professionals should:

- Maintain the highest standards of professional and personal conduct.
- Encourage employers to make fair and equitable treatment of all employees a primary concern.
- Maintain loyalty to employers and pursue company objectives in ways consistent with the public interest.
- Uphold all laws and regulations relating to employer activities.
- Maintain the confidentiality of privileged information.

15-2b Organizational Utilization of HR Professionals

HR professionals should also ensure that their organizations appropriately utilize their talents. As we have discussed throughout this text, HR professionals can contribute significantly to a firm's competitive advantage. Unfortunately, many firms set up roadblocks that prevent HR staffs from making such contributions.

The HRM function has traditionally been viewed as the Rodney Dangerfield of business: "They don't get no respect." The enormous benefits attached to better HRM practices are often ignored because many managers perceive that HRM cannot contribute to competitive advantage to the same extent that more innovative technologies and business strategies can. As an HR professional at Texas Instruments noted:[29]

> In the past, the HR function has been like a spare tire kept in the trunk. In an emergency, it's taken out, but as soon as the emergency is over, it's put away.

HR's failure to earn credibility with upper management has created two specific problems for HR professionals. First, upper-level managers often reject their advice and do not select HRM's best practices. Second, HR professionals are rarely asked for their advice on broader management issues. We now take a closer look at these two problems and how HR staffs can overcome them.

Gaining Support for HRM Best Practices

In describing the various HRM practices throughout this text, we have attempted to convey the notion that none is perfect; each has its good and bad points. Nevertheless, some practices, which we refer to as "best practices," have proven to be clearly better than others. For example, a recent study identified the following best practices.[30] A firm should

- Monitor the effectiveness of its various recruiting sources.

- Validate its selection practices.
- Conduct structured, rather than unstructured, employment interviews.
- Use cognitive ability tests and biographical inventories when selecting candidates for most jobs.

Surprisingly, these researchers found that most of the companies studied employed few, if any, of these practices. However, those that employed relatively more of these practices experienced higher levels of annual profit, profit growth, and overall performance.

Another study produced similar results, finding that best practices in training, performance appraisal, and employment interviewing are rarely used.[31] Specifically, relatively few companies have established procedures for assessing training needs and evaluating training effectiveness. Many organizations use graphic rating scales, and many continue to use unstructured employment interviews despite the superiority of structured ones.

Why Best Practices Are Not Chosen

These findings and many other studies highlight the value of engaging in best HRM practices. Our argument throughout this text has been that effective HRM practices can greatly enhance competitive advantage. Why then, do so many employers "shoot themselves in the foot" by ignoring this seemingly undeniable fact?

The failure to universally adopt many of HRM's best practices can be attributed to the following three factors:[32]

1. *Resistance to change:* Many companies recognize that some of their HRM practices are less than ideal, but hesitate to change them. Decision makers in these organizations often adopt the following attitude: "We've succeeded thus far with the old methods; it just isn't worth the effort to change them." Because they are satisfied with the status quo, these organizations remain stagnant unless forced to change by outside pressures, such as new EEO laws or intensified competition. For example, the current trends toward employee empowerment practices, gainsharing, skill-based pay, and self-managed work teams are not due to their recent discovery—these practices have been around for some time. Rather, use of these trends has come about because they help companies meet productivity pressures resulting from foreign competition and economic turbulence.

2. *Ignorance on the part of decision makers:* Senior-level managers who approve new HRM practices are often unfamiliar with the technical nuances of these practices and are thus unable to determine which ones are best. If these managers have many possible approaches, chances increase that they will choose an ineffective one. For instance, many companies use inadequate performance appraisal forms because, with all the choices available, senior managers cannot discern which is best. These decision makers often base their choice on "common sense," rather than on the practice's technical merits. They often rely on "quick fixes" suggested by management bestsellers (e.g., *The One Minute Manager*) or consultants with standard packages to sell—standard packages, even if sound, rarely apply to all situations. For example, a manager might engage a consulting firm to implement its "packaged" quality circle program to solve an employee motivation problem, when such a solution is inappropriate.

3. *Political considerations:* A variety of interest groups often object to new and potentially effective HRM practices because they have a vested interest in the old approaches.[33] For instance, a company may resist the need to revamp its compensation system because some politically powerful employees object, fearing the new system may classify them as being overpaid. Or a company may reject the idea of using an assessment center for managerial promotions because its managers prefer the current promotion system, despite its flaws.

How HR Professionals Can Gain Support for Best Practices

HR professionals can become very frustrated when they know that the organization is not taking full advantage of its HRM capabilities. In fact, this is probably the most frustrating aspect of the typical HR professional's job. So, what, if anything, can be done to overcome this problem?

Upper managers often allow this problem to surface because they do not understand the connection between HRM practices and competitive advantage; the benefits to be derived from effective HRM practices are difficult to translate into dollars and cents. That is, the bottom-line benefits to be gained from these practices are not as easily discernible as those produced by the introduction of new technology. Unlike the production manager who can often easily calculate the value of each piece produced, an HR professional cannot as easily measure the dollar-value benefit of an HRM practice, such as an innovative managerial training program that teaches administrative skills.

To overcome this problem, HR professionals must demonstrate the bottom-line implications of each HRM practice. This aim can be accomplished by linking traditional HRM practices, such as training, compensation, and selection, to tangible business goals.[34] The need for this type of analysis is illustrated in the following passage:[35]

> For some time now, I have had the uneasy feeling that a lot of what we do in the personnel or human resource field is largely misunderstood and underestimated by the organizations we serve. In part, we in the field are responsible for this state of affairs because much of what we do is evaluated only in statistical or behavioral terms. Like it or not, the language of business is dollars, not correlation coefficients.

Various methods are available for estimating the return of investment attributable to effective HRM practices. These methods are statistically complex and are thus beyond the scope of this book, but Wayne Cascio's book provides an excellent description of methods for determining the return on investment that can be attributed to various HRM practices.[36] For instance, the book describes how an organization can gauge the costs associated with employee turnover, absenteeism, and smoking, and the cost-related impact of employee attitudes and collective bargaining agreements.

15-2c Increasing the HR Professional's Sphere of Influence

A recent survey of over 200 HR professionals found that most (58 percent) do not consider themselves full-fledged participants at the firm's "executive table," often left in the dark when important executive decisions are made.[37] To ensure that companies use their skills more fully, HR professionals must dramatically increase their sphere of influence within their organizations. Their role should be one of full business partner.[38]

HR professionals must form a partnership with operating managers. Both parties recognize that one cannot build sustainable competitive advantage based solely on the type of products offered or the type of technology used. The only thing that will uphold a company's future competitive advantage is the caliber of people in the organization. HR professionals and line managers should both be concerned with how to effectively provide an environment in which people can do what they are capable of doing.

To be full business partners, HR professionals must shift from being the narrow specialists of the past to being members of general management teams. HR professionals must work side by side with managers as partners in handling all kinds of business activities, not just function-specific ones. The vice president of Scott Paper Company notes that the human resource executive must be "at the management table initiating ideas to make us more productive."[39] At L.L. Bean, for instance, "HR is no longer sitting on the sidelines. We're trying to figure out how to put together a catalogue and how to improve the turnaround time to our customers."[40]

Let's take a look at how an HR professional can increase his or her sphere of influence within an organization.

The Need to Acquire New Skills

To expand their role and become full business partners, HR professionals must branch out into management operations and other areas concerned with increasing productivity and reducing costs. Some specific issues that HR professionals can tackle to expand their organizational role include these:[41]

- *Organizational design:* Designing organizations in a way that best promotes productivity

- *International management:* Formulating approaches for successfully competing in an international marketplace

- *Organizational reengineering:* Facilitating transition/restructuring in the face of mergers, acquisitions, and reorganizations

To fulfill this new role, HR professionals must understand the business complexities of the company and operate within that mind-set.[42]

The only way HR professionals can overcome this negative image is by getting involved in business meetings and providing input on business decisions. The more we demonstrate that we have the capabilities and business acumen to be involved, the more receptive CEOs and board members will be.[43]

To provide input on important management decisions, HR professionals must thus become more knowledgeable of areas traditionally outside of the HRM realm. Knowledge of strategic planning, finance, and business management can help HR professionals better understand how their company operates (i.e., understand the business climate, the key issues, and what competitors are doing).[44] A more complete list of what HR professionals need to know and where they can acquire this background is presented in Exhibit 15-5.

HR professionals must also gain credibility with each of their constituents: employees, line managers, upper-level managers, and members of the board of directors. Let's take a look at how this aim can be accomplished.

Gaining Credibility with Line Managers and Employees

HR professionals should interact with line managers and employees. They should get out on the floor and find out what is really going on out there—what managers and workers think.[45] Moreover, they should solicit manager and employee input when they attempt to develop human resource programs. For example, to deal with productivity problems, HR professionals could form an interdisciplinary team that includes themselves, a quality expert, an experienced line manager, and one or more employees. Such a team could draw on both technical and political considerations when making its recommendations.[46]

Gaining Credibility with Upper Management and Board Members

HR professionals can gain credibility with these individuals by demonstrating how proposed HRM practices address the firm's strategic plan. Management expert Kevin Herring suggests that the way to accomplish this aim is to demonstrate how HRM practices can favorably impact business operations and the bottom line.[47] For instance, they could illustrate how certain HRM practices help reduce customer response time, meet marketplace demands, or improve product/service quality and production efficiency. A method for establishing an effective partnership with boards is described in Exhibit 15-6.

EXHIBIT 15-5   Competencies Needed by HR Professionals to Become Full Business Partners

Gain Knowledge of Your Organization

- Meet with managers to learn about the company's earnings/profits for the most recent fiscal year, the company's primary product/service lines and the revenue generated by each, and the company's chief competitors and relative market positions.

Gain Cross-Functional Experience

- "Shadow" another executive.
- Request temporary assignments to better understand another business function.

Gain International/Cross-Cultural Expertise

- Participate in a cross-cultural training program.
- Volunteer for membership on a task force addressing a global business issue.
- Volunteer for an overseas assignment.

Keep Current with Technology

- Use a computer as part of your job.
- Take courses to become conversant in current technological lingo.
- Volunteer to serve on a task force responsible for applying technology to solve HRM-related issues.

Develop HR Consulting Skills

- Gain knowledge in the following areas: management and organizational theory, organization change theory, job design, consulting approaches, strategic planning, systems theory, and project management.
- Develop the following skills: influencing others, diagnosis and analysis, feedback, applying research results to practical problems, and time management.
- Develop the ability to work with diverse populations, see the big picture, handle rejection or resistance, project a positive professional image.
- Be self-confident, sensitive to how your actions are perceived by others, determined, persistent, and objective.

Sources: Solomon, C.M. (1994). Managing the HR career of the '90s. *Personnel Journal,* June, 62–76; Green, M.E. (2002). Internal human resource consulting: Why doesn't your staff get it? *Public Personnel Management, 31* (1), 111–120.

EXHIBIT 15-6   How to Build a Partnership with the Board of Directors

1. Ask the CEO to advocate your direct interaction with the board. HRM departments can earn the respect and trust of the CEO by demonstrating their support of the company's business needs. HR professionals can build this trust through involvement in organization planning and management development.
2. Advocate only those proposals or programs that you believe are good solutions. HR professionals should not advocate all board proposals because they will lose credibility. Rather, they should discuss the pros and cons of each proposal.
3. Work with other departments and line managers to build ownership of programs. HR professionals should demonstrate knowledge of what is happening within the company and where the company is headed. They can do this by sharing information with other departments, such as marketing, operations, and finance, and by working directly with line management to identify organizational needs.
4. Use external resources (e.g., lawyers, consultants) for technical input. HR professionals should be aware of outside business forces, such as competitive practices in various industries or legislative developments, that will affect the company's future.

Source: Kuhns, J.A., and Amuso, L.E. (1993). Building a partnership with the board. *Personnel Journal,* November, 39–43.

Chapter Objectives Revisited

1. Explain the distinction between HRM generalists and specialists.

   - HRM generalists, who perform virtually all facets of HRM, are most often found in small to midsized organizations.
   - HRM specialists, found in larger organizations, have responsibilities that focus on particular HRM tasks.

2. Describe career patterns within the HRM field.

   - Two-thirds of HR professionals enter the field through self-directed career changes; one-third enter straight from college.
   - HRM specialists eventually become managers of their specialty units. To advance beyond this level, they must broaden their skills and become HRM generalists.
   - HRM generalists begin as HRM assistants at small plants or units and advance into HRM managerial positions at successively larger plants or units.

   - To grow professionally, HR professionals join professional associations, become certified, and continue their HRM education.

3. Discuss the ethical responsibilities of HR professionals.

   - HR professionals play three roles in the area of workplace ethics:
     - Monitor
     - Investigate complaints bearing on ethical issues
     - Serve as company spokespeople

4. Explain how HR professionals can increase their sphere of influence within organizations.

   - By demonstrating the bottom-line implications of each HRM practice
   - By working side by side with managers as partners in handling all kinds of business activities, not just function-specific ones

Review Questions

Note: You can find the correct answers to these questions by taking the quiz and then submitting your answers in the Online Edition. The program will automatically score your submission. If you miss a question, the program will provide the correct answer, a rationale for the answer, and the section number in the chapter where the topic is discussed.

1. Which of the following words would be most closely associated with the work of the HR generalist?

   a. management
   b. variety
   c. specialization
   d. redundancy

2. Most people enter the field of human resource management by

   a. completing an undergraduate degree in the field.
   b. completing an advanced degree in the field.
   c. entering an on-the-job training program.
   d. making a self-directed career change.

3. Which of the following professional organizations is best known for representing the interests of the HRM generalist?

   a. Society for Human Resource Management (SHRM)
   b. International Society for Performance Improvement (ISPI)
   c. Academy of Human Resource Development (AHRD)
   d. Society for Industrial and Organizational Psychology (SIOP)

4. If an HRM professional is certified, this means that

   a. the individual has registered with the relevant state board and has permission to practice human resource management.
   b. the individual has at least a master's degree in HRM or a related discipline.
   c. the individual belongs to the relevant professional associations.
   d. the individual has demonstrated a mastery of a defined body of knowledge.

5. Which of the following subjects is most often addressed in continuing education seminars for HR professionals?

    a. organizational development
    b. employee motivation
    c. job design
    d. interviewing

6. Which of the following roles is *not* one played by the HR professional regarding workplace ethics?

    a. monitoring behavior for ethical violations
    b. investigating complaints bearing on ethical issues
    c. serving as company spokesperson to defend company actions
    d. acting as final arbiter of ethical disputes

7. Upper management often resists the introduction of HRM "best practices" because

    a. they have been relatively successful using old practices and see little need to change.
    b. there is little evidence that the new practices can improve the organization's performance.
    c. they lack the in-house knowledge to implement such practices.
    d. the implementation of these practices requires the use of consultants, something most organizations cannot afford.

8. To increase their sphere of influence, HR professionals must

    a. increase their knowledge regarding the details of HRM "best practices."
    b. shift from being specialists to becoming members of general management teams.
    c. develop new ways of explaining the behavioral implications of HRM "best practices."
    d. insist on the same professional development opportunities as those provided to other functional areas.

9. One of the best ways for HR professionals to gain credibility with line managers and employees is to

    a. provide them with a statistical evaluation of the effectiveness of HRM programs.
    b. solicit their opinions during the development of HRM programs.
    c. invite them to a series of miniseminars that explains each of the firm's HRM programs.
    d. ensure that job openings in human resources are made known to them before being advertised to the general public.

10. To gain credibility with upper management and boards of directors, HR professionals should

    a. demonstrate how proposed HRM practices address the firm's strategic plan.
    b. involve upper management and the board in the development of HRM programs.
    c. increase their knowledge of HRM "best practices."
    d. take an antagonistic stance toward organized labor.

Discussion Questions

1. In what ways does the job of HRM generalist differ from that of HRM specialist?

2. Describe two ways of entering the HRM profession.

3. Describe the various ways in which HR personnel can enhance his or her professionalism.

4. What is the primary difference between practitioner-oriented and research-oriented journals?

5. Why do so many companies fail to utilize the best HRM practices? What can HR professionals do to rectify this problem?

6. What roles do HR professionals play in the area of organizational ethics?

7. The text states that HR professionals can no longer rely solely on their HRM expertise. Explain.

References

1. Http://stats.bls.gov/emptab21.htm.
2. Overman, S. (1993). A day in the life of an HR generalist. *HRMagazine,* March, 78–83.
3. Avery, M. (1998). HR pay growth accelerates. *HRMagazine,* November, 122–126.
4. Avery, M. (1997). Rising salaries reflect HR's new role. *HRMagazine,* November, 87–92.
5. Ibid.
6. Http://www.salary.com.
7. Louchheim, F., and Lord, V. (1988). Who is taking care of your career? *Personnel Administrator,* April, 46–51.
8. Harris, O.J., and Bethke, A.L. (1989). HR professionals two decades later. *Personnel Administrator,* February, 66–71.
9. (1989). 25 hottest careers. *Working Woman,* July, 67–79.
10. Harris and Bethke. HR professionals two decades later.
11. Louchheim and Lord. Who is taking care?
12. Wiley, C. (1992). The certified HR professional. *HRMagazine,* August, 77–84.
13. Kaufman, B.E. (1994). What companies want from HR graduates. *HRMagazine,* September, 84–86.
14. Williams, J.M. (1988). Planning your career climb. *Personnel Administrator,* April, 38–42.
15. Louchheim and Lord. Who is taking care?
16. Wiley. The certified HR professional.
17. Society for Human Resource Management. (1997). 1997 *Annual Report.*
18. Parry, J.F. (1985). Accredited professionals are better prepared. *Personnel Administrator,* December, 48–52.
19. Ibid.
20. Http://www.shrm.org/hrci.
21. Right Associates. (1987, August). *Career Concerns of Human Resource Professionals.*
22. Harris and Bethke. HR professionals two decades later.
23. Wiley. The certified HR professional.
24. Kaufman. What companies want.
25. Wiley, C. (1993). Employment manager's views on workplace ethics. *The EMA Journal,* Spring, 14–24.
26. Ibid.
27. Ibid.
28. DeLisle, P.A. (1993). Does HR deserve second-class status? *HRMagazine,* May, 60–61.
29. Caudron, S. (1994). HR leaders brainstorm the profession's future. *Personnel Journal,* August, 54–61.
30. Terpstra, D.E., and Rozell, E.J. (1993). The relationship of staffing practices to organizational level measures of performance. *Personnel Psychology, 46* (1), 27–48.
31. Johns, G. (1993). Constraints on the adoption of psychology-based personnel practices: Lessons from organizational innovation. *Personnel Psychology, 46* (3), 569–592.
32. Ibid.
33. Hambrick, D.C., and Cannella, A.A. (1989). Strategy implementation as substance and selling. *The Academy of Management Executive, 3* (4), 278–285.
34. Caudron. HR leaders brainstorm.
35. Cascio, W.F. (1987). *Costing Human Resources: The Financial Impact of Behavior in Organizations* (2nd ed.). Boston: PWS-Kent.
36. Ibid.
37. Wiscombe, J. (2001). Your wonderful, terrible HR life. *HRMagazine, 80* (6), 32–37.
38. Caudron. HR leaders brainstorm.
39. (1990, March 9). HR's newly emerging role. *The Wall Street Journal,* R33.
40. Ibid.
41. Bailey, B. (1991). Ask what HR can do for itself. *Personnel Journal,* July 35–39; Penezic, R.A. (1993). HR executives influence CEO strategies. *HRMagazine,* May, 58–59.
42. Solomon, C.M. (1994). Managing the HR career of the '90s. *Personnel Journal,* June, 62–76.
43. Caudron. HR leaders brainstorm.
44. Williams. Planning your career climb.
45. Fraze, J. (1989). The "H" stands for human. *Personnel Administrator,* January, 50–55.
46. Johns. Constraints on the adoption.
47. Herring, K. (2001). HR takes a hands-on approach to business and delivers results. *Workforce,* October, 44–50.

Glossary

360-degree feedback   An appraisal system for managers, who are rated by subordinates, peers, superiors, customers, and themselves.

A

ability inventory   A job analysis inventory that contains a listing of ability requirements.

Ability Requirements Approach (ARA)   A systematic method of recording job analysis information in which a job analyst specifies needed abilities from a list of all the possible abilities needed for any job.

action learning   A management development activity in which management gives candidates real problems to solve.

action plan   A plan developed by trainees at the end of a session that indicates the steps they will take on the job to apply the new skills.

affirmative action   An approach to eliminating employment discrimination by taking proactive initiatives to ensure proper minority group representation within an organization.

affirmative action plan (AAP)   A written statement that specifies how the organization plans to increase the utilization of targeted groups.

Age Discrimination in Employment Act (ADEA)   A law that protects "older workers" (i.e., ages 40 and over) from age discrimination in the workplace.

American Federation of Labor and Congress of Industrial Organizations (AFL-CIO)   An organization that promotes cooperation among national unions in order to pursue organized labor's common objectives.

Americans with Disabilities Act (ADA)   A 1990 law that prohibits employment discrimination based on a person's disability.

applicant-initiated recruitment   A method of external recruitment in which a company accepts unsolicited applications or resumes from individuals interested in working for the company.

arbitration   A contract dispute mechanism in which a neutral third party settles matters that cannot be resolved by bilateral discussions between union and management representatives.

artifacts   Tangible things that represent the superficial aspects of a country's culture.

assessment center   A selection technique that consists of work samples and other assessment techniques. It is primarily used to select managers.

assumptions   A society's beliefs that have evolved from its attempts to adjust to the world around it.

B

background investigation   An in-depth probe of an applicant's background usually conducted by an investigative agency.

bargaining order   Issued by the NLRB, it directs an employer to accept collective bargaining with the union even if the employer won the election.

bargaining unit   Positions covered by a bargaining agreement in which two or more employees share common employment interests and working conditions.

behavior consistency model   This model specifies that the best predictor of future job behavior is past behavior performed under similar circumstances.

behavior modeling   A training method in which trainees are shown how a task should be performed and then practice the task with feedback until they are competent.

behavior observation scale (BOS)   A rating instrument comprised of traits anchored by behaviors. Raters evaluate worker performance on each behavior.

behaviorally anchored rating scale (BARS)   A rating instrument comprised of traits anchored by job behaviors. Raters select the behavior that best describes the worker's performance level.

benefits   A form of compensation provided to employees in addition to their pay, such as health insurance or employee discounts.

BFOQ defense   When using a BFOQ defense, the employer argues that it purposely discriminated against all members of a protected group because they lack the bona fide occupational qualifications for the position in question.

biodata inventories   A selection technique in which an applicant's responses to background information questions are objectively scored.

biographical information blank   A biodata inventory consisting of a set of questions designed to cover a broad array of background information.

business factors   Attributes of a business, such as sales volume or market share, that closely relate to the size of the needed workforce.

C

campus recruiting   A recruiting method in which the firm's recruiters visit various college and university campuses to recruit individuals for positions requiring a college degree.

career development systems   A method of internal recruiting in which a firm places "fast-track" or high-potential employees on a career path where they are groomed for certain targeted jobs.

career resource centers   A location in which companies make learning opportunities available to interested managerial candidates.

carpal tunnel syndrome   A repetitive motion disorder causing wrist pain that is caused by an overextension or twisting of the wrists, especially under force.

case method   A training method in which trainees analyze realistic job situations.

central tendency error   Rating employees in the middle of the rating scale when more extreme ratings are warranted.

certification   A designation indicating that an individual has demonstrated a mastery of a defined body of knowledge required for success in a field.

certification election   An election to determine whether company workers want union representation.

change-related training   Training that enables employees to keep up-to-date with various types of changes dealing with technological advances, new laws or procedures, or a change in the organization's strategic plan.

Civil Rights Act (CRA) of 1964   A law that prohibits employment based on race, color, sex, religion, and national origin.

Civil Rights Act (CRA) of 1991   An amendment to the Civil Rights Act of 1964. Its passage made discrimination claims less difficult for employees to substantiate.

closed shops   Companies that require union membership as a condition of employment.

collective bargaining   A system for governing relations between representatives of employers and employees through bilateral negotiations to reach mutual agreement about employment terms.

collective bargaining agreement   The labor-management contract resulting from the collective bargaining process.

combination plans   Employees receive a portion of each period's profit-sharing earnings immediately; the remainder awaits future distribution.

comparable worth   A standard for judging pay discrimination that calls for equal pay for equal worth.

compensable factors   Criteria representing the most important determinants of a job's worth.

compensation   The pay and benefits that employees receive from the company.

competitive advantage   A status achieved by a company when gaining a superior marketplace position relative to its competition.

computer-based instruction (CBI)   A training method that uses a computer to instruct students through drills/tutorials, games, and simulations.

concurrent validation study   A criterion-related strategy in which current employees' selection scores are correlated with measures of their current job performance.

Consolidated Omnibus Budget Reconciliation Act (COBRA)   A law that provides a continuation of health insurance coverage for employees who leave a company through no fault of their own.

content-oriented strategy   A method of collecting validity evidence that focuses on expert judgment regarding the extent to which selection devices are properly designed and provide an accurate assessment of the needed worker requirements.

contingency personnel   Workers who are employed by a supplier agency and are "loaned" to the firm on a temporary basis for a fixed fee.

continuous quality improvement programs   Programs that attempt to build quality into all phases of the design, production, and delivery of a product or service by empowering workers to trace product or service problems to their root causes and redesign production processes to eliminate them.

conversational currency   A relationship skill in which an expatriate inserts social and cultural tidbits and trivia into conversations with host-national employees.

core personnel   Employees who are hired in the "traditional" manner; that is, they are placed on the organization's payroll and are considered "permanent employees."

corporate culture   The pattern of shared values, mores, and behaviors that separates one organization from others who are operating in the same industry.

cost leadership strategy   A strategy in which a company gains a competitive advantage by providing the same services or products as its competitors, but produces them at a lower cost.

criterion contamination   The inclusion of irrelevant performance criteria on a rating form.

criterion deficiency   The omission of pertinent performance criteria on a rating form.

criterion-related strategy   A method of collecting validity evidence that demonstrates statistically that someone who does well on a selection instrument is more likely to be a good job performer than someone who does poorly.

Critical Incident Technique (CIT) A systematic method of recording job analysis information that identifies specific work behavior that determines success or failure in executing an assigned task.

culture A society's set of assumptions, values, and rules about social interaction.

D

decertification election An election in which union members vote on whether they want their union to continue representing them.

defamation The unprivileged publication of a false oral or written statement that harms the reputation of another person.

deferred plans An employee's profit-sharing earnings are distributed at retirement.

defined benefit plan A type of pension plan that specifies the amount of pension a worker will receive upon retirement.

defined contribution plan A type of pension plan that specifies the rate of employer and employee monthly contributions.

demand forecasting A process used in HR planning that entails predicting the number and types of people the organization will need at some future point in time.

development Planned learning experiences that prepare workers to effectively perform possible future jobs.

disparate impact A form of employment discrimination in which an employment practice that is not job related has unequal consequences for people of different protected groups.

disparate treatment A form of employment discrimination in which employers treat people unfairly because of their membership in a protected group.

distributed practice A training procedure in which trainees practice a skill over several sessions.

distribution plans An employee's profit-sharing earnings are distributed as soon as the profit-sharing pool is calculated.

downsizing A management action taken to drastically reduce the size of a company's workforce.

drug tests Assessing individuals to detect possible drug use.

Drug-Free Workplace Act A law stating that government contractors must take certain steps to ensure that their workplaces are kept drug-free.

due process Occurs when employees are informed of the charges against them and are given an opportunity to defend themselves.

E

election phase Second phase of a certification election, culminating in the actual election vote.

employee assistance programs (EAPs) An HRM program that uses mental health professionals to help workers overcome substance abuse or other personal problems.

employee comparison systems Appraisal instruments that require raters to evaluate employees in relation to other employees.

employee contributions Occurs when employees' pay fairly reflects their input to the organization.

employee empowerment programs Productivity improvement programs that make the work itself more rewarding.

Employee Polygraph Protection Act (EPPA) A law that bans most private-sector (but not public-sector) employers from using polygraph tests in the selection of candidates.

employee referrals A method of external recruitment in which firms ask their employees to solicit applications from qualified friends and associates.

Employee Retirement Income Security Act (ERISA) A law requiring employers to follow certain rules to ensure that employees will receive the pension benefits due them.

Employee Right-to-Know Law A 1984 law that gives workers the right to know what hazardous substances they are dealing with on the job.

employee wellness Freedom from certain debilitating health problems that can be caused by a person's poor lifestyle choices.

employee wellness programs Programs that help employees improve or maintain their overall health.

employment-at-will A legal doctrine stating that employers may discharge their employees for any reason, even an unfair one, unless the discharge is limited by contract or by federal or state statutes.

equal employment opportunity (EEO) Providing equal treatment to all applicants and employees regardless of their race, color, sex, religion, national origin, age, or disability.

Equal Employment Opportunity Commission (EEOC) A government agency responsible for enforcing and interpreting federal antidiscrimination laws.

Equal Pay Act (EPA) An amendment to the FLSA that prohibits sex discrimination in pay.

equity Fairness.

equity theory A pay fairness theory that states that people form equity beliefs by comparing their outcome/input ratio to that of a referent other.

ergonomics The science of designing and arranging workstations so that people and material interact safely and efficiently.

executive search firms   Employment agencies used to recruit mid- and senior-level managers with salaries generally above $60,000.

exempt employees   Employees whose pay and overtime are not regulated by the Fair Labor Standards Act.

expatriate   A professional/managerial employee moved from one country to, and for employment in, another country.

expectancy theory   A motivation theory that focuses on the effort-to-performance and performance-to-reward links.

external competitiveness   Occurs when each employee's pay is fair relative to the pay received by workers in other organizations who hold similar positions.

extranet   Technology that links a company's intranet to outside organizations and vendors.

extrinsic rewards   Rewards that the employer gives to employees.

F

Fair Credit Reporting Act   A law designed to protect applicants' rights in the event of a background investigation conducted by an investigative agency.

Fair Labor Standards Act (FLSA)   A 1938 federal statute that regulates minimum wage and overtime pay.

Family and Medical Leave Act (FMLA)   A law stating that firms employing 50 or more workers must grant employees up to 12 weeks of unpaid leave per year for the care of a newborn child, an ill family member, or their own illness.

feedback   Information given to trainees that lets them know whether their behavior is correct.

fetal protection policies (FPPs)   Organizational policies that exclude women of childbearing age from jobs with potential reproductive hazards.

Fifth Amendment   An amendment to the U.S. Constitution that provides all federal employees with equal protection under the law.

flexible benefit (cafeteria) plans   Benefit programs that allow employees to choose among various benefits and levels of coverage.

flextime   A nontraditional work arrangement in which work hours are flexible in that workers must put in their eight hours, but can choose their starting and ending times.

forced distribution   Appraisal instrument that requires raters to assign a certain percentage of employees to each category of excellence.

four-fifths rule   A test used by the courts to assess the merits of a *prima facie* case of disparate impact. It is calculated by comparing the passing rate of the "disadvantaged" protected group with the rate of the "advantaged" group.

Fourteenth Amendment   An amendment to the U.S. Constitution that provides all state employees with equal protection under the law.

Fourth Amendment   Constitutional amendment granting privacy rights to public sector employees.

Freedom of Information Act   A law designed to make most government records available to the public.

G

gainsharing plans   Pay-for-performance plans that offer employees a cash award for meeting or exceeding team-based goals.

glass ceiling   An invisible, yet very real, barrier found in the structure of many organizations that has stymied the advancement of women and other protected groups.

good faith and fair dealing   A common law prohibiting discharges that are particularly repugnant or unfair.

good faith bargaining   Obliges both management and labor to meet at reasonable times and confer in good faith with respect to wages, hours, and other terms and conditions of employment.

graphic rating scale (GRS)   A rating instrument comprised of traits anchored by adjectives descriptive of job performance levels.

grievance   An allegation that employer or employee contract rights have been violated.

grievance system   A system that provides due process for claims of collective bargaining agreement violations.

group brainstorming   A technique of demand forecasting in which a panel of "experts" generates a forecast in collaboration.

H

halo effect   Ratings on each scale are influenced by the appraiser's overall impression of an employee.

help-wanted advertisements   A method of external recruitment in which a company places an advertisement of the position in the appropriate media (e.g., newspaper, magazine).

hostile environment   A form of sexual harassment in which victims are subjected to unwelcome, hostile, and intimidating working conditions.

HRM generalists   HR professionals whose jobs require them to perform virtually all facets of HRM work.

HRM specialists   HR professionals whose jobs require them to perform specialized HRM tasks.

human resource information system (HRIS)   A computerized information package that provides management with increasing capacity to record, store, manipulate, and communicate information to users.

human resource management   The organizational function that consists of practices that help the organization deal effectively with its people during the various phases of the employment cycle.

human resource planning A process that helps companies identify their future HRM needs and how those needs can be met.

I

Immigration Reform and Control Act (IRCA) of 1986 A law that prohibits discrimination based on national origin and citizenship.

implicit personality theory A rater's personal theory of how different types of people behave in certain situations.

implied contract An unwritten contractual agreement.

independent contractors Supplier agencies that provide companies with contingency workers to perform an entire work function.

informal participative decision-making program An employee empowerment program in which managers decide just how much decision-making authority employees should have in each instance.

inputs The perceptions that people have concerning what they contribute to the job.

interactive video training (IVT) A training method in which a TV screen and a videodisc (or videotape) player are hooked to a microcomputer, and trainees interact with the screen through a keyboard or voice command system.

internal consistency Occurs when each employee's pay is fair relative to the pay coworkers in the same organization receive.

intranet Internet networks that are accessible to people within a company.

intrinsic rewards Rewards that come from within a person.

intrusion upon seclusion A common law doctrine stating that a person's privacy rights are violated when the intrusion upon his or her private concerns would be considered highly offensive to a reasonable person.

J

job analysis A systematic procedure for gathering, analyzing, and documenting information about particular jobs.

job analysis inventory A job analysis questionnaire that contains only close-ended questions.

job content What workers actually do on their jobs.

job context The conditions under which a person's job is performed and the demands such jobs impose upon the individual.

job description A short (one- or two-page) written summary of job analysis findings.

job enrichment An employee empowerment program in which jobs are redesigned to be more intrinsically rewarding.

job evaluation A systematic process for determining the worth of a job.

job evaluation committee A committee of individuals convened for the purpose of making job evaluations.

job instruction training (JIT) A training method in which trainers demonstrate each step of a task, discuss its key points, and then provide the trainees with guided practice.

job posting A method of internal recruitment in which a job vacancy notice is posted and all qualified employees may bid.

job rotation A method of management development in which companies rotate trainees through a number of departments to serve managers.

job satisfaction The favorableness of employee attitudes toward their jobs.

job sharing A form of alternate work scheduling in which a full-time job is shared by two people.

joint venture A company operating in a foreign country that is dually owned by an American and foreign firm.

just cause The reason for an employer's action is fair.

L

labor leasors Supplier agencies that provide companies with contingency workers on a lease basis.

Labor-Management Relations Act (Taft-Hartley Act) A law aiming to restore the balance of power between employers and unions.

Labor-Management Reporting and Disclosure Act (Landrum-Griffin Act) Law designed to prevent corruption by regulating the internal affairs of unions.

lecture A training method in which the trainer teaches a topic by verbally communicating the information.

leniency error Ratings that are unduly favorable.

local union The union that directly represents the interests of its members.

M

management by objectives (MBO) A rating instrument comprised of objectives and performance standards for meeting them.

massed practice A training procedure in which trainees practice a skill in one session.

McClelland's need-achievement theory A motivational theory stating that all individuals are primarily motivated by one of three needs—affiliation, achievement, and power.

McDonnell-Douglas test A test used by the courts to assess the merits of a *prima facie* case of disparate treatment when "smoking gun" evidence is lacking.

mental ability tests Employment tests designed to measure an applicant's aptitude.

mentors   Experienced supervisors who are assigned to new managers to teach, guide, advise, counsel, and serve as role models.

merit pay guidechart   A chart that shows the size of a merit pay raise associated with each level of job performance.

merit pay plan   A pay-for-performance program that grants employees annual pay raises based on their levels of job performance.

mission statement   A declaration of the organization's overall purpose.

mixed-motive cases   A form of employment discrimination in which an employer bases an employment decision partly on a legitimate motive and partly on a discriminatory one.

monitoring   Tracking employee behavior inside the workplace.

multiphase training program   A training program administered in several sessions in which trainees are given "homework" that requires them to apply that lesson back on the job and to discuss this experience during the next training session.

N

National Institute for Occupational Safety and Health   The government agency responsible for conducting health and safety research to suggest new OSHA standards and to update previous ones.

National Labor Relations Act (Wagner Act)   Law giving workers the right to form unions and bargain collectively without being subject to coercion by their employers.

National Labor Relations Board (NLRB)   Created by the Wagner Act to supervise certification elections and enforce the law.

national unions   Unions that represent workers throughout the country in a particular craft or in a specific industry.

negligent hiring   Occurs when an employer negligently hires an applicant who is somehow unfit for the job and, because of this unfitness, commits an act that causes harm to another.

nonexempt employees   Employees whose pay and overtime are regulated by the Fair Labor Standards Act.

Norris-LaGuardia Act   A law that limits judges' powers to issue injunctions that restrain worker job actions.

O

Occupational Safety and Health Act   A law designed to ensure safe working conditions for every American worker.

Occupational Safety and Health Administration (OSHA)   The government agency responsible for developing and enforcing workplace health and safety standards.

Occupational Safety and Health Review Commission   The government agency responsible for hearing appeals from employers who wish to contest OSHA rulings.

Older Workers Benefit Protection Act (OWBPA)   A law that regulates written waivers of ADEA rights signed by early retirees.

online recruiting   Advertising job openings on the Internet.

on-the-job training (OJT)   A training method in which trainees are taught how to perform their jobs in the actual job setting.

open shops   Companies in which employees covered by the contract do not have to join the union or be assessed a fee for union representation.

organizational citizenship   The willingness of employees to engage in behaviors that help the organization to achieve its goals.

organizational commitment   The relative strength of an individual's identification and involvement in a particular organization.

organizational restructuring   When a firm modifies its structure to become less hierarchical by cutting out the "layer" of middle management.

orientation training   Training designed to inform new employees about their jobs, the company, and its policies and procedures.

outcomes   The perceptions that people have regarding the returns they get for the work they perform.

overlearning   Learning training material so well that it will be long remembered, even without frequent practice.

P

paired comparison   Appraisal instrument that requires raters to compare each possible pair of employees in terms of their job performance.

paper-and-pencil honesty tests   Written tests that employers use to estimate an applicant's propensity to steal from an employer.

pay   The wage or salary that employees earn.

pay grades   Job groupings in which all jobs assigned to the same group are subject to the same range of pay.

pay policy   A company policy stipulating how well it will pay its employees relative to the market.

pay policy line   A regression line that shows the statistical relationship between job evaluation points and prevailing market rates.

pay range   The minimum and maximum pay rates for all jobs within a pay grade.

pay-for-performance programs   Productivity improvement programs that link financial rewards to successful job performance.

performance aids   Devices given to trainees to help them remember training material when they return to their jobs.

performance analysis   A method of training needs analysis in which managers identify their employees' performance deficiencies and determine which of these deficiencies can be effectively remedied through training.

performance appraisal process   A process used by companies to measure the adequacy of their employees' job performances and communicate these evaluations to them.

performance appraisals   Assessments of employees' job performance levels.

performance standards   The level of performance that an employee is expected to achieve.

personality tests   Employment tests designed to assess a variety of personality characteristics that are important for applicants when hired for certain jobs.

petition phase   First phase of a certification election in which workers express initial interest in union representation.

piece rate plans   Pay-for-performance programs that base an individual's wages on the number of "pieces" or product units he or she produces.

point-factor method   A job evaluation method in which each job is assigned points for compensable factors.

polygraph tests   Physiological tests designed to ascertain truthfulness of the information given by the examinee.

Position Analysis Questionnaire (PAQ)   A systematic method of recording job analysis information in which the behavioral dimensions of a job are specified.

predictive validation study   A criterion-related strategy in which applicants' selection scores are correlated with measures of their subsequent job performance.

preferential treatment   Giving members of underutilized groups some advantage over others in the employment process.

Pregnancy Discrimination Act (PDA)   A law stating that firms may not discriminate against employees on the basis of pregnancy, childbirth, or related medical conditions.

***prima facie* case**   Established at trail when a complainant has been able to demonstrate the merits of his or her case sufficiently enough for the courts to agree to look into the matter further.

Privacy Act   A law giving public sector employees access to any information in their files.

private employment agencies   Privately run agencies that, for a fee, provide companies with clerical, blue-collar, technical, and lower-level managerial personnel.

product differentiation   Gaining competitive advantage by producing a product or service that buyers prefer.

productivity improvement programs   Organizational interventions designed to improve productivity by increasing employee motivation.

profit-sharing plans   Pay-for-performance plans in which a portion of the company's profits are contributed to individual employee accounts.

progressive discipline system   A system in which discipline is enforced in increasingly severe steps.

protected classifications   Categories of people (e.g., race, sex) who are legally protected from discrimination in the workplace.

protected groups   Subcategories of people within each protected classification (e.g., male, female).

public employment agencies   Run by each state under the auspices of the U.S. Employment Service, these agencies place workers in jobs that are primarily clerical and blue-collar positions.

public policy   A doctrine that serves society and, if violated, will cause harm to society.

Q

quality circles   An employee empowerment program in which a team of six to twelve employees meets regularly to identify and resolve production problems within their unit.

quid pro quo   A form of sexual harassment in which victims are required to provide sexual favors in order to be hired, promoted, granted a pay raise, or allowed to keep their job.

R

Railway Labor Act (RLA)   A law that compels railroads to bargain with employees' representatives and established mechanisms to resolve labor disputes.

ratio analysis   A process used in HR planning to determine future HR demand by computing an exact ratio between the specific business factor and the number of employees needed.

realistic job previews (RJPs)   Conveying to applicants what organizational life will actually be like on the job, warts and all.

reasonable accommodation   A legal concept that applies to situations where individuals are unable to successfully perform a job because of their religion or disability. The employer must consider viable strategies for helping these people overcome such inabilities.

recency error   An error that occurs when ratings are heavily influenced by recent events.

recruitment   An HRM practice designed to locate and attract job applicants for particular positions.

reference checking   Collecting selection information from an applicant's previous employers (or associates).

regression analysis   A statistical tool used in HR planning to determine the number of employees needed by a company at some future point in time.

reinforcement substitution   The ability to find substitutes for pleasurable pursuits that are unavailable in a new culture.

reinforcement theory   A motivational theory that states that worker behavior can be shaped, modified, or changed by manipulating the system of rewards given or withheld for the relevant behavior.

relevance   The degree to which the rating form includes necessary information.

reliability   An index reflecting the degree of self-consistency among the selection scores earned by an individual.

remedial training   Training designed to correct deficiencies in employee skill or knowledge levels or to improve employee attitudes.

repatriates   Expatriates who have returned home.

repetitive motion disorders   A set of physical disorders in which an individual's tendons become inflamed from the strains and stresses of repeated, forceful motions.

replacement charts   Charts indicating the availability of candidates and their readiness to step into the various management positions.

role-playing   A training method in which trainees spontaneously act out some problem involving human interaction.

S

safety audits   An audit of unsafe job behaviors aimed to prevent unsafe acts on the part of workers.

safety committee   A committee comprised of both management and nonmanagement personnel that is responsible for overseeing an organization's safety function.

safety incentive program   An HRM program designed to motivate safe job behaviors by providing workers with incentives for avoiding accidents.

salary survey   A survey that seeks information on pay rates offered by a firm's competitors.

sales force estimates   A technique of demand forecasting in which sales personnel are asked to estimate the demand for a new product based on their knowledge of customer needs and interests.

Scanlon plan   A gainsharing plan in which workers share the gains produced by cutting production costs.

selection   An HRM practice in which companies assess and choose from among job candidates.

self-managed work teams   A form of employee empowerment in which teams of six to eighteen employees from different departments work together to produce a well-defined segment of finished work.

severity error   Ratings that are unduly unfavorable.

sexual harassment   Unwelcome sexual advances, requests for sexual favors, and other verbal or physical contact of a sexual nature.

simple rankings   Appraisal instruments that require raters to rank-order their employees from best to worst, according to their job performance.

skill-based pay   A compensation approach that grants employees pay increases for acquiring new, job-related skills.

Social Security Act   A law that provides eligible workers with retirement and disability incomes and Medicare coverage.

straight piecework   A piece rate plan that pays workers a set amount for each unit produced.

strategic goals   The desired outcomes that must be reached for the firm to accomplish its mission.

strategic plan   A plan that specifies the courses of action a firm must take in order to meets its strategic goals.

strategic planning   A process in which a company specifies its overall purposes and objectives, and indicates how these are to be achieved.

succession planning   A systematic process of defining future management requirements and identifying candidates who best meet these requirements.

supply forecasting   A process used to estimate which organizational positions will be filled at some future point in time.

surveillance   Tracking employee behavior outside the workplace.

T

task force   A management development activity in which a team of trainees tries to resolve an actual organizational problem.

task inventory   A job analysis inventory that contains a listing of task statements.

telecommuting   A nontraditional work arrangement in which employees work at home.

temporary employment agencies   Supplier agencies that provide companies with contingency workers on a short-term, temporary basis.

tort law   Civil laws designed to discourage individuals from subjecting others to unreasonable risks and to compensate those who have been injured by unreasonably risky behavior.

training   Planned learning experiences that teach workers how to effectively perform their current jobs.

training evaluation   An assessment of the effectiveness of a company's training program.

training need   A problem, such as poor job performance or inadequate skill level, that can be rectified through training.

training objectives Statements describing what the trainees should be able to do as the result of training.

trend analysis A process used in HR planning in which the future demand for human resources is projected on the basis of past business trends regarding a business factor.

U

undue hardship A legal argument stating that an accommodation is not reasonable because it would unduly burden the employer.

unemployment compensation A system designed to provide income to individuals who have lost a job through no fault of their own.

union instrumentality The perceived ability of the union to provide important benefits to the worker.

unions Labor organizations in which employees, acting in concert, deal with employers on work issues.

utilization analysis A statistical procedure used for setting affirmative action goals. It compares the percentage of each protected group for each job category within the organization to that in the available labor market.

utilization review programs Programs designed to minimize health care costs through the use of preauthorization and auditing procedures.

V

validity An index of selection effectiveness, reflecting the extent to which applicants would perform the job as well as expected, based on the inferences made during the selection process.

validity coefficient An index of criterion-related validity reflecting the correlation between selection and criterion scores.

validity generalization strategy A method of documenting the validity of a selection device by demonstrating that the same (or similar) device has been consistently found to be valid in many other similar settings.

values The rules of societal proprietary and impropriety that are shared by people within a culture.

W

Web-based training A type of training for which students can download courses with a Web browser or run the courses interactively while connected to the Internet using computer software.

weighted application blank A biodata inventory containing the same questions as an application blank.

wholly owned subsidiaries American-owned companies operating in a foreign country.

work sample tests Employment tests that require applicants to perform some of the actual (or simulated) duties of the vacant position.

worker requirements The qualifications a worker needs to successfully perform a particular job.

workers' compensation A state-run, no-fault insurance system that provides income protection for workers experiencing job-related injuries or illnesses.

workplace justice A concept that addresses the issue of treating employees in a fair, nondiscriminatory manner.

workplace justice laws Laws that regulate the day-to-day treatment of employees.

wrongful termination An unlawful discharge.

Y

yellow-dog contracts Now illegal, these contracts stipulate that workers will not organize, support, or join a union if hired by the company.

Index

Note: Locators in *italics* indicate information outside the main text